CMT LEVEL II

CMT LEVEL II

Theory and Analysis

Readings Selected by

The CMT Association

iii

WILEY

CONTENTS

The CMT Association is a not-for-profit professional regulatory organization servicing over 4,500 market analysis professionals in over 85 countries around the globe. The CMT Association's main objectives involve the education of the public, the investment community, and its membership in the theory, practice, and application of technical analysis.

The CMT Association has the following stated mission:

- Attract and retain a membership of professionals devoting their efforts to using and expanding the field of technical analysis and sharing their body of knowledge with their fellow members.

- Establish, maintain, and encourage the highest standards of professional competence and ethics among technical analysts.

- Educate the public and the investment community of the value and universality of technical analysis.

The CMT Association's mission is to accomplish through the effective execution of a wide variety of professional services including, but not limited to, regional seminars, local chapter meetings, the maintenance of an extensive library of technical analysis material, and the regular publication of newsletters and journals.

CMT Association members and affiliates include technical analysts, portfolio managers, investment advisors, market letter writers, and others involved in the technical aspects of equities, futures, options, fixed income securities, currencies, international markets, derivatives, and so on.

Services provided to our members and affiliates are performed by a small NYC-based Headquarters staff, an active Board of Directors, Committee Chairs, and an extensive cadre of volunteers located in both U.S. and non-U.S. markets.

The Chartered Market Technician® (CMT) credential is the global standard for practitioners of technical analysis and technical risk management. It is a FINRA-recognized designation that sets apart CMT chartholders as specialists and value generators among active investment professionals.

The designation is awarded to those who demonstrate mastery of a core body of knowledge in risk management and portfolio management settings. The advanced technical expertise represented by the CMT charter immediately communicates to clients and employers the disciplined approach, academic rigor, and unique professional skill set that CMT chartholders possess.

The objectives of the CMT program are:

- To promote high ethical standards of education, integrity, and professional excellence.

- To guide candidates in mastering a professional body of knowledge.

- To professionalize the discipline of technical analysis.

Those candidates who successfully complete all three levels of the CMT examination and agree to abide by the CMT Association Code of Ethics are granted the right to use the CMT credential.

The curriculum for the CMT Association's CMT exam Level II is comprised of selected readings in the areas of technical analysis and other financial disciplines. The CMT Association curates each level of the three-volume curriculum, reviewing the available academic literature as well as practitioner scholarship. The process for selecting content for the curriculum and exams has three phases: (1) a job-analysis effort that reviews current practices among professionals who use technical analysis, (2) focus groups with subject matter experts, and (3) a review and deliberation by the CMT Test and Curriculum Committee to determine the best readings needed for exam quality.

From this effort the CMT Association is able to fashion these readings into a consolidated study curriculum for CMT candidates. The curriculum is designed to help candidates gain a broad understanding of the core body of knowledge and best practices for using technical analysis in forecasting and active money management. The CMT Association is indebted to the fine work of each author whose work is included in the curriculum as well as the volunteers who donate their time to the improvement of these publications.

■ About the Content Selections for Level II

Level II readings are designed to help candidates be prepared to apply technical analysis as a tool of forecasting and active money management. The chapters in this book are organized in such a way as to help candidates build on what they learned in Level I.

The book's readings are presented in four categories. These categories group 12 knowledge domains (those identified as part of the CMT Association's job analysis efforts) into more basic categories of usage that each Level II candidate should master: Price Study, Asset Relationships, System Development, and Active Money Management. One domain covered on the exam, Ethics, is not covered in this book, but rather by the *Standards of Practice Handbook* published by the CFA Institute.

An online index was created for these titles. Please go to
www.efficientlearning.com/cmt to gain access

Congratulations on qualifying yourself for the CMT Level II Exam. This exam will further extend your ability to produce uncommon insight in research and analysis. Completion of the Level II Exam allows you to apply for a FINRA Series 86 license, with which you can become a FINRA-licensed technical analyst. Being a technical analyst is not the only job function that makes use of the CMT designation. More and more Chartered Market Technicians are found in a variety of roles around the industry. The Level II Exam shows that you have sufficient depth of understanding about technical analysis to be among them. The exam is also a necessary stepping stone for the third and final level of exams.

The CMT Level II Exam measures the candidate's competency in the **application** of concepts, theory, and techniques covered by the required readings. CMT Level II candidates must demonstrate their ability to apply concepts identified in their Level I studies to relevant conditions or scenarios.

Exam time length: 4 hours, 15 minutes

Exam format: Multiple Choice

The curriculum is organized into four exam-specific categories of 12 knowledge domains that provide a framework for applying technical analysis concepts. The CMT Level II Exam tests the candidate's knowledge in the 12 domains mentioned previously. The four categories of these domains form a logical progression of building blocks in applying technical analysis.

1. Price Study
2. Asset Relationships
3. System Development
4. Active Money Management

Exam Topics and Question Weightings

Price Study				
1. Basic Charting	a. behavioral finance		5%	7
	b. Adaptive Market Hypothesis			
2. Market Indicators	a. breadth indicators		8%	13
	b. sentiment measures			
	c. volatility			
3. Construction	a. volume		3%	4
4. Trends	a. trendlines		15%	23
	b. multiple time frame analysis			
	c. breakouts			
	d. moving averages			
	e. trend strength indicators			
5. Price Patterns	a. gap analysis		15%	23
	b. support and resistance			
Asset Relationships				
6. Confirmation	a. oscillators and divergence		6%	9
	b. sector rotation			
	c. intermarket signals			
7. Cycles	a. seasonal cycles		3%	4
8. Selection and Decision	a. uncorrelated assets		10%	15
	b. relative strength			
	c. forecasting techniques			
System Development and Testing				
9. System Testing	a. algorithmic development		10%	15
	b. objective analysis of rules			
	c. performance measures			
10. Statistical Analysis	a. inferential statistics		7%	11
Active Money Management				
11. Risk Management	a. absolute and relative risk		15%	22
	b. risk modeling			
	c. value at risk			
	d. volatility risk			
	e. liquidity risk			
	f. diversification			
	g. leverage risk			
	h. portfolio risk management			
	i. risk-based performance measures			
Ethics				
12. Ethics	a. standards and practices		3%	4

CHART DEVELOPMENT AND ANALYSIS

Few possess the skill of effectively applying technical analysis in a professional setting. Mastering the knowledge and skills covered in the CMT Level II exam study curriculum will begin to separate candidates from the millions of casual chart readers throughout the world. Section I begins with a similar foundation to the classical tools of technical analysis, but adds more depth with a focus on application.

The section takes a closer look at the tools for identifying and capturing trends. These tools include both mathematical measuring devices such as momentum indicators, band studies, and oscillating indicators, as well as observed trend lines and support/resistance levels.

This section includes a chapter that delves into the implications of volume and open interest data, and explains how market breadth can indicate pending trend changes. This chapter also explains why volume can be a predictor of volatility.

The chapters on patterns add more details on how collections of bars or candles can signal subtle changes in the behavior of buyers and sellers. These changes may indicate a growing probability of change in a trend measured over a larger time frame.

■ What Candidates Need to Know

The biggest collection of questions on the exam comes from these chapters. Since the CMT Level II exam is focused on application, candidates must know more than just the names of patterns. Candidates should be able to identify entry points for trades and failure points for both trades or forecasts. Candidates should also have a clear understanding of gaps, confirmations, and divergences.

CHAPTER 1

Charting

From Perry J. Kaufman, *Trading Systems and Methods + Website,* 5th Edition (Hoboken, New Jersey: John Wiley & Sons, 2013), Chapter 3.

Learning Objective Statements

- Explain the six basic tenants of Dow Theory
- Interpret a chart data using various chart types (line, bar, candle, etc)
- Classify a given trend as primary, secondary, or minor fluctuations
- Analyze breakout signals for use in forecasting
- Recognize evidence for improving confidence in breakout signals
- Compare and explain trend signals over multiple time frames
- Draw valid trend lines
- Interpret the significance of trend line breaks

It is very likely that all trading systems began with a price chart, and we come back to a chart whenever we want a clear view of where the market is going. Nowhere can a picture be more valuable than in price forecasting. Elaborate theories and complex formulas may ultimately be successful, but the loss of perspective is easily corrected with a simple chart. We should remember the investor who, anxious after a long technical presentation by a research analyst, could only blurt out, "But is it going up or down?" Even with the most sophisticated market strategies, the past buy and sell signals should be seen on a chart. The appearance of an odd trade can save you a lot of aggravation and money.

Through the mid-1980s technical analysis was considered only as chart interpretation. In the equities industry, that perception is still strong. Most traders begin as chartists, and many return to it or use it even while using other methods. William L. Jiler, a great trader and founder of Commodity Research Bureau, wrote:

> One of the most significant and intriguing concepts derived from intensive chart studies by this writer is that of characterization, or habit. Generally speaking, charts of the same commodity tend to have similar pattern sequences which may be different from those of another commodity. In other words, charts of one particular commodity may appear to have an identity or a character peculiar to that commodity. For example, cotton charts display many round tops and bottoms, and even a series of these

constructions, which are seldom observed in soybeans and wheat. The examination of soybean charts over the years reveals that triangles are especially favored. Head and shoulders formations abound throughout the wheat charts. All commodities seem to favor certain behavior patterns.[1]

In addition to Jiler's observation, the cattle futures market is recognized as also having the unusual occurrence of "V" bottoms. Until recently, both the silver and pork belly markets have tendencies to look very similar, with long periods of sideways movement and short-lived but violent *price shocks,* where prices leap rather than trend to a new level. The financial markets have equally unique personalities. The S&P traditionally makes new highs, then immediately falls back; it has fast, short-lived drops and slower, steadier gains. Currencies show intermediate trends bounded by noticeable major stopping levels while interest rates and bonds have long-term trends.

Charting remains the most popular and practical form for evaluating price movement, and numerous works have been written on methods of interpretation. This chapter will summarize some of the accepted approaches to charting and the trading rules normally associated with these patterns. Some conclusions are drawn as to what is most likely to work and why.

■ Finding Consistent Patterns

A price chart is often considered a representation of human behavior. The goal of any chart analyst is to find consistent, reliable, and logical patterns that can be used to predict price movement. In the classic approaches to charting, there are consolidations, trend channels, top-and-bottom formations, and a multitude of other patterns that are created by the repeated action of large groups of people in similar circumstances or with similar objectives. The most important of all the chart patterns is the *trendline*.

Only recently have computer programs been able to interpret chart patterns; and only one book, Bulkowski's *Encyclopedia of Chart Patterns*[2] has managed to show a comprehensive analysis of chart formations. In all fairness, there can be numerous valid interpretations of the same chart. In order to identify a chart price formation, it is first necessary to select the data frequency (for example, daily or weekly), then the starting date and a time horizon (long-term or short-term), before a chart interpretation can begin. Given the wide range of choices, it should be surprising that any two analysts see the same patterns at the same time.

Chart analyses, frequently published in magazines, may themselves be the cause of the repeated patterns. Novice speculators approach the problem with great enthusiasm and often some rigidity in an effort to follow the rules. They will sell double and triple tops, buy breakouts, and generally do everything to propagate the survival of standard chart formations. Because of their following, it is wise to know the most popular techniques, if only as a defensive measure.

---

[1] William L. Jiler, "How Charts Are Used in Commodity Price Forecasting," *Commodity Research Publications* (New York, 1977).

[2] Thomas N. Bulkowski, *Encyclopedia of Chart Patterns* (New York: John Wiley & Sons, 2000).

What Causes Chart Patterns?

Speculators have many habits, which, taken in large numbers, cause recognizable chart patterns. The typical screen trader (not on the exchange floor), or an investor placing his or her own orders, will usually choose an even number—for example, buy Microsoft at $26.00, rather than at $26.15. If even dollar values are not used, then 50¢ and 25¢ are the next most likely increments, in that order. And, as the share prices get higher, the increments get farther apart. With Berkshire Hathaway (BKA) trading at $125,000 per share, placing an order at a $10 increment would seem very precise. In futures trading, the same is true. There are far more orders placed in the S&P Index at 1310.00 than at 1306.50, or 10-year Treasury notes at $115\frac{16}{32}$ instead of $115\frac{19}{32}$.

The public is also said to always enter into the bull markets at the wrong time. When the television financial news, syndicated newspapers, and radio carry stories of dangerously low oil supplies, a new cancer treatment drug, or the devastation of the nation's wheat crop, the infrequent speculator enters in what W. D. Gann calls the *grand rush,* causing the final runaway move before the collapse or the final sell-off before the rally; this behavior is easily identifiable on a chart. Gann also talks of *lost motion,* the effect of momentum that carries prices slightly past its goal. Professional traders recognize that a fast, volatile price may move as much as 10% farther than its objective. A downward swing in the U.S. dollar/Japanese yen from par at 1.0000 to a support level of 0.8000 could overshoot the bottom by 0.0100 without being considered significant.

The behavioral aspects of prices appear rational. In the great bull markets, the repeated price patterns and divergence from chance movement are indications of the effects of mass psychology. The classic source of information on this topic is Mackay's *Extraordinary Popular Delusions and the Madness of Crowds* originally published in 1841.[3] In the preface to the 1852 edition the author says:

> We find that whole communities suddenly fix their minds on one object, and go mad in its pursuit; that millions of people become simultaneously impressed with one delusion. . . .

In 1975, sugar was being rationed in supermarkets at the highest price ever known, 50¢ per pound. The public was so concerned that there would not be enough at any price that they bought and horded as much as possible. This extreme case of public demand coincided with the price peak, and shortly afterwards the public found itself with an abundant supply of high-priced sugar in a rapidly declining market. The world stock markets are often the target of acts of mass psychology. While U.S. traders watched at a distance the collapse of the Japanese stock market from its heights of 38,957 at the end of December 1989 to its lows of 7,750 in 2003, a drop of 80%, they were able to experience their own *South Sea Bubble* when the NASDAQ 100 fell 83.5% from its highs of 4,816 in March 2000 to 795 in October 2002. And, while the subprime crisis has taken years to play out, the

---

[3] Reprinted in 1995 by John Wiley & Sons.

unparalleled drop in value of nearly all investments at the same time, September 2008, was clearly an act of investor panic. Prices seem to drop suddenly at the time when buyers are most confident, then start the long climb up again. It should not be difficult to understand why contrary thinking has developed a strong following.

Charting is a broad topic to be studied in detail; the chart paper itself and its scaling are sources of controversy. A standard bar chart (or line chart) representing highs and lows can be plotted for daily, weekly, or monthly intervals in order to smooth out the price movement over time. Bar charts have been drawn on semilog and exponential scales,[4] where the significance of greater volatility at higher price levels is put into proportion with the quieter movement in the low ranges by using percentage changes. Each variation gives the chartist a unique representation of price action. The shape of the chart box and its ratio of height/width will alter interpretations that are based on angles. Standard charting techniques may draw trendlines at 45° or 30° angles across the chart; therefore, expanding or compressing a chart on a screen will change the angles. This chapter uses traditional daily price charts and square boxes.

It may be a concern to today's chartist that the principles and rules that govern chart interpretation were based on the early stock market, using averages instead of individual stocks or futures contracts. This is discussed in the next section. For now, refer to Edwards and Magee, who removed this problem by stating that "anything whose market value is determined solely by the free interplay of supply and demand" will form the same graphic representation. They continued to say that the aims and psychology of speculators in either a stock or commodity environment would be essentially the same, that the effect of postwar government regulations have caused a "more orderly" market in which these same charting techniques can be used.[5]

■ What Causes the Major Price Moves and Trends?

Prices can move higher for many months or even years, creating a *bull market*. They can also move down, creating a *bear market*. Although price moves can be as short as a few minutes or as long as decades (as happened with interest rates and gold), it is how each chartist defines a "trend" that is most important. Once recognized, the price trend forms a bias for trading decisions that can make the difference between success and failure. The long-term direction of prices is driven by four primary factors:

1. *Government policy.* When economic policy targets a growth rate of 4%, and the current growth rate is 1%, the Federal Reserve (the "Fed" or any central bank) lowers interest rates to encourage growth. Lowering rates stimulates business activity. The Fed raises interest rates and dampens economic activity to control inflation. Changing interest rates has a profound impact on the flow of investment money between countries, on international trade, on the value of currencies, and on business activity.

---

[4] R. W. Schabacker, *Stock Market Theory and Practice*, Forbes (New York, 1930), 595–600.
[5] Robert D. Edwards and John Magee, *Technical Analysis of Stock Trends* (Springfield, MA: John Magee, 1948), Chapter 16.

2. *International trade.* When the United States imports goods, it pays for it in dollars. That is the same as *selling* the dollar. It weakens the currency. A country that continually imports more than it exports increases its trade deficit and weakens its currency. A country that increases its exports strengthens its currency and its economy.

3. *Expectation.* If investors think that stock prices will rise, they buy, causing prices to rise. Expectations can lead an economic recovery although there is no statistical data to support a recovery. *Consumer confidence* is a good measure of how the public feels about spending. The economy is active when consumer confidence is high. A lack of public confidence following the subprime collapse dampened all economic activity and delayed the recovery for years.

4. *Supply and demand.* A shortage, or anticipated shortage, of any product causes its price to rise. An oversupply of a product results in declining prices. These trends develop as news makes the public aware of the situation. A shortage of a product that cannot be replaced causes a prolonged effect on its price, although the jump to a higher price may happen quickly.

▪ The Bar Chart and Its Interpretation by Charles Dow

The *bar chart*, also called the *line chart,* became known through the theories of Charles H. Dow, who expressed them in the editorials of the *Wall Street Journal.* Dow first formulated his ideas in 1897 when he created the stock averages in order to have a more consistent measure of price movement for stock groups. After Dow's death in 1902, William P. Hamilton succeeded him and continued the development of his work into the theory that is known today. Those who have used charts extensively and understand their weak and strong points might be interested in just how far our acceptance has come. In the 1920s, a New York newspaper was reported to have written:

> One leading banker deplores the growing use of charts by professional stock traders and customers' men, who, he says, are causing unwarranted market declines by purely mechanical interpretation of a meaningless set of lines. It is impossible, he contends, to figure values by plotting prices actually based on supply and demand; but, he adds, if too many persons play with the same set of charts, they tend to create the very unbalanced supply and demand which upsets market trends. In his opinion, all charts should be confiscated, piled at the intersection of Broad and Wall and burned with much shouting and rejoicing.[6]

This attitude seems remarkably similar to the comments about program trading that followed the stock market plunge in October 1987, where it was condemned as the cause of the crash. In 2011 we again had comments about high frequency trading "manipulating" the markets, and in Europe they have banned short sales to stem

---

[6] Richard D. Wyckoff, *Stock Market Technique, Number One* (New York: Wyckoff, 1933), 105.

volatility in the equity index markets. Of course, volatility continued to be high, but liquidity dropped. It's politics, not logic.

Charting has become an integral part of trading. The earliest authoritative works on chart analysis are long out of print, but the essential material has been recounted in newer publications. If, however, a copy should cross your path, read the original *Dow Theory* by Robert Rhea;[7] most of all, read Richard W. Schabacker's outstanding work *Stock Market Theory and Practice*, which is probably the basis for most subsequent texts on the use of the stock market for investment or speculation. The most available book that is both comprehensive and well written is *Technical Analysis of Stock Trends* by Edwards and Magee, now in its ninth edition.[8] It is focused on chart analysis with related management implications and a small section on commodities. For the reader who prefers concise information with few examples, the monograph by W. L. Jiler, *Forecasting Commodity Prices with Vertical Line Charts,* and a complementary piece, *Volume and Open Interest: A Key to Commodity Price Forecasting,* can still be found.[9] Two more recent publications that are widely read are John Murphy's *Technical Analysis of the Financial Markets* and Jack Schwager's *Schwager on Futures: Technical Analysis*, part of a two-volume set.

The Dow Theory

The Dow Theory[10] is still the foundation of chart interpretation and applies equally to stocks, financial markets, commodities, and the wide variety of investment vehicles used to trade them. It is part investor psychology supported by chart analysis. It is impressive that it has withstood the tests of more than 100 years. Charles Dow was the first to create an index of similar stocks—the Industrials and the Railroads, although today's components are very different from those in 1897. The purpose of the index was to smooth out erratic price movement and find consistency by combining less active stocks. Thin trading causes unreliable price patterns.

Dow's work can be viewed in two parts: his theory of price movement and his method of implementation. Both are inseparable to its success. Dow determined that the stock market moved as the ocean, in three waves, called *primary, secondary,* and *daily fluctuations.* The major advances and declines, lasting for extended periods, were compared to the tides. These tides were subject to secondary reactions called *waves,* and the waves were comprised of *ripples.* Readers familiar with other charting methods will recognize these patterns as the foundation of Elliott Wave analysis. In 1897,

---

[7] Arthur Sklarew, *Techniques of a Professional Chart Analyst* (Commodity Research Bureau, 1980).

[8] Robert D. Edwards and John Magee, *Technical Analysis of Stock Trends*, 9th ed. (Snowball Publishing, 2010).

[9] Two other works worth studying are Gerald Appel, *Winning Market Systems: 83 Ways to Beat the Market* (Great Neck, NY: Signalert, 1974); and Gerald Appel and Martin E. Zweig, *New Directions in Technical Analysis* (Great Neck, NY: Signalert, 1976).

[10] The rules of the Dow Theory in this section are based on a fine article by Ralph Acampora and Rosemarie Pavlick, "A Dow Theory Update," originally published in the *MTA Journal* (January 1978, reprinted in the *MTA Journal*, Fall–Winter 2001). Other parts of this section are drawn from Kaufman, *A Short Course in Technical Trading* (Hoboken, NJ: John Wiley & Sons, 2003).

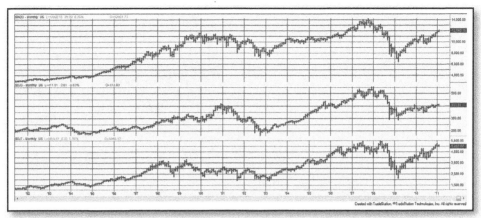

FIGURE 1.1 Dow Industrial, Utilities, and Transportation Indexes, 1991–2010. Dow originally created the industrial and railway averages to hide the large, erratic price moves caused by price manipulation and lack of liquidity. Dow Theory has been adapted to use the current versions of the major indexes, the Industrials (top panel), the Utilities (center panel), and the Transportation Index (bottom panel). Although these indexes represent different aspects of the economy, they have become highly correlated.

Dow published two sets of averages in the *Wall Street Journal*, the *Industrials* and the *Railroads,* in order to advance his ideas. These are now the *Dow Jones Industrial Average* and the *Transportation Index*. Figure 1.1 shows more than 20 years of history for the three most important averages the Industrials, the Transportation, and the Utilities.

The Basic Tenets of the Dow Theory

There are six fundamental principles of the Dow Theory that fully explain its operation.

1. The Averages Discount Everything (except "acts of God")   At the turn of the twentieth century there was considerably less liquidity and regulation in the market; therefore, manipulation was common. By creating averages, Dow could reduce the frequency of "unusual" moves in a single stock, that is, those moves that seemed unreasonably large or out of character with the rest of the market. Dow's Industrials average the share value of 30 companies (adjusted for splits); therefore, an odd move in one of those prices would only be $\frac{1}{30}$ of the total, reducing its importance so that it would not distort the results. The average also represented far greater combined liquidity than a single stock. The only large moves that would appear on a chart of the average price were price shocks, or "acts of God."

2. Classifications of Trends   There are three classifications of trends: primary trends, secondary swings, and minor day-to-day fluctuations. The primary trend, also called the *wave*, is the trend on a grand scale. When there is a wave of rising prices we have a *bull market*; when prices are declining there is a *bear market*. A wave is a major move over an extended period of time, generally measured in years. A clear bull market can be seen in the previous Dow charts (Figure 1.1) throughout all of the 1990s ending at the beginning of 2000, and again from 2003 through mid-2007.

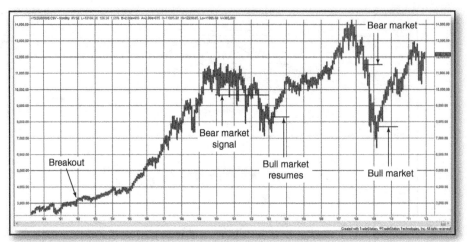

FIGURE 1.2   Bull and Bear Market Signals Are Traditional Breakout Signals, but on a Larger Scale.

Bull and Bear Market Formation (for Monthly or Weekly Prices)

The beginning of a bull or bear market is determined using a *breakout signal*, shown in Figure 1.2, based on large swings in the index value. The *bull market signal* occurs at the point where prices confirm the uptrend by moving above the high of the previous rally. The *bear market signal* occurs on a break below the low of the previous decline.

It is commonly accepted that a bull or bear market begins when prices reverse 20% from their lows or highs. In order to get an upwards breakout signal needed for a new bull market, we want to look at support and resistance levels (the previous intermediate high and low prices) separated by approximately a 10% price move based on the index value. This type of signal is called *swing trading*. At the top of Figure 1.2 the horizontal broken line should occur at about 20% below the absolute price highs, and the second peak should be approximately 10% higher than the previous swing low.

It is interesting to note that both bull and bear markets start with a price reversal of 20%. But 20% from the highs can be much greater than 20% from the lows. For example, in the sell-off in September 2008, the S&P was measured from its high of about 14,000 in late 2007. A decline to 11,200, or 2,800 points, triggered the bear market. In the first quarter of 2009, the S&P reached its lows of about 6,500. A new bull market began at 7,800, a rally of only 1,300 points. Thus the number of points needed to "officially" start a bull market was only 46% of the bear market trigger, showing a significant bias toward bull markets.

Bull and Bear Market Phases

In Dow Theory, the primary trends develop in three distinct phases, each characterized by investor action. These phases can be seen in the NASDAQ bull market of the late 1990s and the subsequent bear market (Figure 1.3).

The Bull Market

Phase 1: Accumulation. Cautious investors select only the safest and best-valued stocks to buy. They limit purchases to deeply discounted stocks at depressed

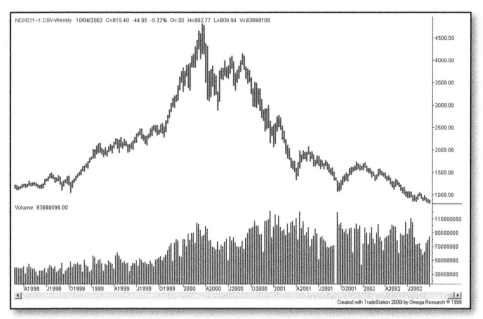

FIGURE 1.3 NASDAQ from April 1998 through June 2002. A clear example of a bull and bear market with a classic pattern of volume.

price levels and consider only primary services and industries, most often buying utilities and high yielding stocks.

Phase 2: Increasing volume. Greater investor participation causes increasing volume, rising prices, and an improving economic picture. A broader range of investors enters the market convinced that the market has seen its lowest prices. Secondary stocks become popular.

Phase 3: Final explosive move. Excessive speculation and an elated general population result in a final explosive move. Everyone is talking about the stock market; people who have never considered investing directly now enter the market. The public is convinced that profits will continue and buying becomes indiscriminate. Investors borrow to buy stocks. Value is unimportant because prices keep rising. Earnings and dividends are ignored.

The Bear Market

Phase 1: Distribution. Professionals begin selling while the public is in the final stages of buying. Stocks are distributed from stronger to weaker hands. The change of ownership is facilitated by less experienced investors who enter the bull market too late and pay what turn out to be unreasonably high prices.

Phase 2: Panic. Prices decline faster than at any time during the bull market and fail to rally. The news constantly talks about the end of the bull market. The public sees an urgency to liquidate. Investors who borrowed money to invest late in the bull market, trading on margin or leverage, now speed up the process. Some are forced to liquidate because their portfolio value has dropped below the critical point. The divesting of stocks takes on a sense of panic.

Phase 3: Lack of buying interest. The final phase in the sustained erosion of prices results from the lack of buying by the public. After taking losses, investors are not interested in buying even the strongest companies at extremely undervalued prices. All news is viewed as negative. Pessimism prevails. It is the summer of 2002.

Schabacker's Rules

Schabacker also had a simple guideline to identify the end of both a bull and a bear market.[11]

End of a Bull Market
1. Trading volume increases sharply.
2. Popular stocks advance significantly while some other companies collapse.
3. Interest rates are high.
4. Stocks become a popular topic of conversation.
5. Warnings about an overheated stock market appear on the news.

End of a Bear Market
1. Trading volume is low.
2. Commodity prices have declined.
3. Interest rates have declined.
4. Corporate earnings are low.
5. Stock prices have been steadily declining and bad news is everywhere.

Secondary Trends (Secondary Reactions Using Weekly or Daily Prices)

Secondary reactions are also called *corrections* or *recoveries* and can be identified using smaller swing values. Corrections in bull markets are attributed to the prudent investor taking profits. This profit phase can have an erratic start but is considered complete when prices rise above the previous secondary rally. The bull market is back in force when a new high occurs (see Figure 1.4), the point where a trader can enter a new long position. *Lines* may be substituted for secondary movements. In Dow Theory, a *line* is a sideways movement lasting from two to three weeks to months, trading in about a 5% range.

Characteristics of a Secondary Reaction

- There are a number of clear downswings.

- The movement is more rapid in the reversal (down during a bull market) than in the primary move.

- The reactions last from three weeks to three months.

- If the volume during the price drop is equal to or greater than the volume just prior to the decline, then a bear market is likely. If volume declines during the drop, then a reaction is confirmed.

---

[11] Adapted from James Maccaro, "The Early Chartists: Schabacker, Edwards, Magee," *Technical Analysis of Stocks & Commodities* (November 2002).

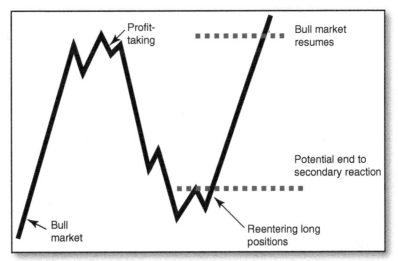

FIGURE 1.4 Secondary Trends and Reactions. A reaction is a smaller swing in prices that ends when a new high reinstates the bull market.

■ The atmosphere surrounding the decline is important. If there is a lot of speculation, then a bear market may develop.

Minor Trends (Using Daily Prices)
In Dow Theory, minor trends are the only trends that can be manipulated. They are usually under six days in duration. Because they are considered market noise, not affecting the major price direction, they are seen as frequent up and down movements.

3. The Principle of Confirmation For a bull or bear market to exist, two of the three major averages (the Industrials, the Transportation, and the Utilities) must confirm the direction. When first created, the Dow Theory required the confirmation on only the Utilities and the Railroads. Although much has changed since Dow devised this rule, the purpose is to assure that the bull or bear market is a widespread economic phenomenon and not a narrower industry-related event.

4. Volume Goes with the Trend Volume confirms the price move. Volume must increase as the trend develops, whether it is a bull or bear market. It is greatest at the peak of a bull market or during the panic phase of a bear market.

5. Only Closing Prices Are Used Dow had a strong belief that the closing price each day was the most important price. It was the point of evening-up. Not only do day traders liquidate all of their positions before the close of trading, reversing their earlier impact, but many investors and hedge funds execute at the close. Although liquidity was a problem during Dow's time, even actively traded stocks in today's market show increased price swings when a larger order is executed during a quiet period. There is always high volume at the close of trading, when investors with short and long time frames come together to decide the fair price.

Some traders believe that there is no closing price anymore, given the access to 24-hour trading; however, that is not yet true. Every market has a settlement price. This is usually at the end of the primary trading session (previously the *pit* or *open outcry session*). The settlement price is necessary to reconcile all accounts, post profits and losses, and trigger needed margin calls. Banks could not operate without an official closing time and settlement price.

6. The Trend Persists *A trend should be assumed to continue in effect until its reversal has been signaled.* This rule forms the basis of all trend-following principles. It considers the trend as a long-term price move, and positions are entered only in the trend direction. The Dow Theory does not express expectations of how long a trend will continue. It simply follows the trend until a signal occurs that indicates a change of direction.

Interpreting Today's S&P Using Dow Theory

After 110 years, can the Dow Theory correctly interpret the major market index, the S&P? Figure 1.5 shows the S&P 500, using continuous, back-adjusted futures prices, from 1994 through the middle of 2003. The sustained bull market that began in 1987, or possibly 1984, peaks near the end of the first quarter of 2002. There is a steady increase in volume, as Dow had foreseen, although volume does not peak at the top of the market—it starts to decline noticeably about three months before the top. We will see in the study of volume that volume spikes occur at extremes, but a longer-term volume confirmation is very important. Declining volume at the beginning of 2003 signals a divergence in sentiment that foretells the end of the bull market. Volatility increases as prices move towards the end of the uptrend, another predictable pattern. The price move from 1994 through the peak in 2002 shows both Phase 2 and Phase 3 of the bull market.

FIGURE 1.5 Dow Theory Applied to the S&P. Most of Dow's principles apply to the current marketplace, but some experience and interpretation is necessary.

The price decline in the third quarter of 1998 addresses the issue: Are there exceptions to the 20% rule that changes a bull market to a bear market? A 20% drop from a high of 1400 is 1120, very close to the point where prices stopped their decline and reversed. Dow never used the number 20%, and analysts would claim that, because of the speed of the decline and the quick recovery, this was not a bear market signal. Some of these decisions require judgment, some experience, and just a little bit of hindsight. Realistically, we cannot expect every Dow signal to always be correct, just as we cannot expect to be profitable on every trade. Long-term success is the real goal.

Transition from Bull to Bear in the S&P Looking again for a 20% reversal from the S&P highs of 1675, we target the price of 1340. This time, volume has declined into the highs and continues to decline quickly. From the second quarter of 2000 through the first quarter of 2001 prices fall sharply, giving back the gains from mid-1997, nearly three years. When prices break below 1300 they confirm the previous low at the end of 2000, making it clear that a bear market is underway.

During the subsequent decline, prices attempted to rally. There are four cases of a sharp "V" bottom followed by a significant move higher. After the low at 940 at the end of September 2001, prices move to about 1180, above the 20% reversal of 1128. However, after the first reversal to 1075 prices fail to move back above the highs, finally breaking below 1180 and continuing on to make new lows. Although the recovery exceeded 20%, the lack of a confirming breakout can be interpreted as a bull market failure. Not every pattern falls neatly into a rule.

We come to the last year of the S&P chart, where prices have resisted going below 850, and now appear to be moving above the level of 970 and about to confirm a bullish breakout. Is it the end of the bear market? Volume was the highest at the two lowest price spikes, and then declined. Many stocks are undervalued, according to experts, yet those same experts see no reason for the market to rally further because the recent rise has already reflected reasonable expectations for profits and growth in the next year. Who would be correct, Charles Dow or the talking heads of the financial news networks? It was Dow.

Dow Theory and Futures Markets

The principles of the Dow Theory are simple to understand. Major price moves are most important when they are confirmed by volume. They follow a pattern created by investor action that seems to be universal when seen from a distance. In order to implement his theory, Dow created an index that minimized the erratic moves in individual stocks due to lack of liquidity and price manipulation.

The primary features of the Dow Theory should hold for any highly liquid, actively traded market. This applies to index futures and most financial futures markets, as well as foreign exchange, which have enormous volume and reflect major economic trends. Because of the variety of products traded as futures and ETFs, an investor may be able to apply Dow's principle of confirmation using any two related financial markets, such as the S&P Index, 10-year Treasury notes, or the U.S. dollar index, in the same way that the Industrials, Utilities, and Transportation indexes were used for stocks. A strong economic trend often begins with interest rate policy and has a direct impact on the value of the currency, and a secondary effect on the stock market. Stock prices can be stimulated by lower rates or dampened by raising rates; therefore, confirmation from these three sectors is reasonable. When trading in futures, the nearby contract (the one closest to delivery) is most often used; however, the total volume of all futures contracts traded for each market must be used rather than volume for a single contract.

■ Chart Formations

While Dow Theory is a macro view of price movement, more often chart analysis deals with much shorter time periods. Most traders hold positions from a few days to a few weeks; however, they apply the same patterns to both shorter or longer intervals.

Chart analysis uses straight lines and geometric formations on price charts. It analyzes volume only in the most general terms of advancing and declining phases. Chart patterns can be classified into the broad groups of:

- Trendlines and channels

- One-day patterns

- Continuation patterns

- Accumulation and distribution (tops and bottoms)

- Retracements

- Other patterns

Of these, the most important is the *trendline*.

The Trend in Retrospect

It is easier to see the trend on a chart after it has occurred. Trying to identify the trend as it is developing is much more difficult. The monthly chart in Figure 1.6 shows a sustained upwards trend, but there is a slowing of that trend toward the end. Will the upward trend continue? Will prices begin a downward trend? Will they move sideways? The purpose of charting is to apply tools that provide the best chance of identifying the future direction of prices. If wrong, these tools also control the size of the loss.

The time interval is a key element when identifying a trend. Weekly and monthly charts show the major trends more clearly than daily charts. Longer-term charts remove much of the noise that interferes with seeing the bigger picture. Many chartists start by evaluating a weekly or monthly chart, then apply the lines and values developed on those charts to a daily chart. The weekly chart provides direction or biases the direction of trades while the daily chart, or even a 15-minute chart, is used for timing entries and exits.

FIGURE 1.6   The Trend Is Easier to See after It Has Occurred. While the upwards trend is clear, are prices going to continue higher, or is this the end of the trend?

■ Trendlines

The trendline determines the current direction of price movement, and often identifies the specific point at which that direction will change. The trendline is the most popular and recognized tool of chart analysis. Most analysts will agree that *the trend is your friend*; that is, it is always safer to take a position in the direction of the trend.

■ An *upwards trendline* is drawn across the lowest prices in a rising market.

■ A *downwards trendline* is drawn across the highest prices in a declining market.

Figure 1.7 shows a classic downwards trendline, *A*, drawn on a chart of Intel. It connects the highest price of $22 with price peaks at 18.00, 16.75, and 16.15 before ending at 15.50. When prices move through the trendline heading higher, the downtrend has been *penetrated*. This may end the downtrend or cause a new downtrend line to be drawn. In this case it was the end of the downtrend.

Redrawing Trendlines

Most trendlines are not as long-lived or clear as the downtrend in Intel, which was drawn after the fact. Instead, we will treat the uptrend as it develops. The first uptrend line, *B*, is drawn when the first reversal shows a second low point. The upwards trendline *B* is drawn across the lows of points 1 and 2. Although prices do not decline through trendline *B,* rising prices pull back to points 3 and 4, well above the trendline. At that point, we choose to redraw the upwards trendline connecting point 2 with 3 and 4, forming what appears to be a stronger trendline. Trendlines are considered more important when they touch more points. However, prices move up

FIGURE 1.7 Upwards and Downwards Trendlines Applied to Intel, November 2002 through May 2003.

quickly, and we decide to redraw the trendline connecting points 4 and 5. It is very common to redraw trendlines as price patterns develop. Care must be taken to draw the lines in a way that touches the most points, although some chart analysts would draw a line that connects points 1 and 5, crossing through points 2, 3, and 4, because the final picture seems to represent the dominant upwards price pattern. This can be seen as the broken line in Figure 1.7.

Support and Resistance Lines

Price movement creates patterns that reflect the combined perception that all investors have of the current economic situation. Trends result from confidence or concern about the health of business or the supply and demand of a product. When there is no dominant opinion, prices move sideways in a price range determined by current volatility levels—sometimes wide, sometimes narrow. Because there are always buyers and sellers, prices do not stand still. Investment funds continue to add and withdraw money from the market.

Periods of uncertainty form a sideways price pattern. The top of this pattern is called the *resistance level,* and the bottom is the *support level.* Once established, the support and resistance levels become key to identifying whether a trend is still in force.

A *horizontal support line* is drawn horizontally to the right of the lowest price in a sideways pattern. It is best when drawn through two or more points and may cross above the lowest price if it makes the pattern clear. It represents a firm price level that has withheld market penetration (or allowed minor penetration). It may be the most significant of all chart lines. In the chart of gold futures prices (Figure 1.8), the support line is drawn across the bottom of a sideways period, beginning at the first low price on the left but crossing slightly above the next lowest point. The support

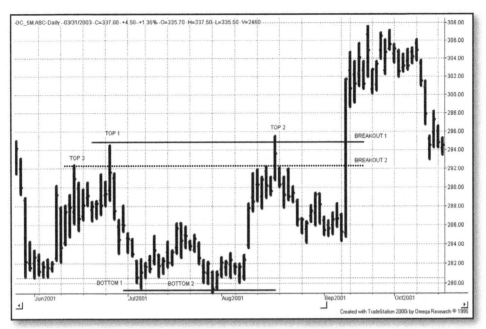

FIGURE 1.8 Horizontal Support and Resistance Lines Shown on Gold Futures Prices.

line could have been drawn at $280.50 to include the first cluster of low prices and crossing above the lows bars but representing a clear support level.

A *horizontal resistance line* serves the same purpose as the support line and is drawn across the highest highs of the sideways interval. It represents the price that has resisted upwards movement. Resistance lines are not normally as clear as support lines because they are associated with higher volatility and erratic price movement. In Figure 1.8 there are two choices for the horizontal resistance line. The most common selection would be the line that begins at top 1 and crosses below the high of top 2. In the same spirit as the support line, a resistance line could have been drawn much lower, beginning at top 3 and crossing above a cluster of highs while penetrating through the bars with tops 1 and 2.[12]

Note the Position of the Closing Price of the Bar A price bar that has the high price penetrating upwards through resistance but closes lower is considered a *failed breakout* and confirms the sideways pattern. The same is true for a failed penetration of the support level. You may choose to raise the resistance line to the high of that failed bar, but most chartists ignore it, keeping the resistance line at its original position. Then we can expect to see a number of high prices penetrate through the resistance lines as shown by the *breakout 2* line in Figure 1.8.

Resistance Becomes Support, and Support Becomes Resistance Horizontal support and resistance lines are strong indicators of change. If prices are moving

---

[12] In Carol Oster, "Support for Resistance: Technical Analysis and Intraday Exchange Rates," *FRBNY Economic Policy Review* (July 2000), the author shows that support and resistance levels specified by six trading firms over three years were successful in predicting intraday price interruptions. In addition, these levels were valid for about five days after they were noted.

sideways because investors are unsure of direction, then a move through either support or resistance is usually associated with new information that causes investors to act. Whatever the cause, the market interprets this as a new event. Having moved out of the sideways pattern, prices have a tendency to remain above resistance to confirm the change. If prices have moved higher, then the resistance line becomes a support line. If prices fall below the resistance line, the price move is considered a failed breakout. In the right part of Figure 1.8, prices break out above the resistance levels and then come back to test those levels. In this example, prices seem to confirm that the *breakout 2* line was the more realistic resistance line.

A Trendline Is a Support or Resistance Line   The angled trendlines in Figure 1.7 are also called support and resistance lines. An upwards trendline, drawn across the lows, is a *bullish support line* because it defines the lowest price allowed in order to maintain the upwards trend. The downward trendline, drawn across the highs, is a *bearish resistance line*. These angled trendlines are most reliable when used to identify major price trends. Horizontal lines work well for shorter time frames.

Back-Adjusted Data   All traders use online services to display charts. They can draw support and resistance lines using various tools supplied by the service and can convert daily data to weekly or monthly with a single click. When looking at prices that go back many years, the analyst must be sure that the older data is not *back-adjusted* in any way. For example, futures trade in contracts of limited maturity, and are most liquid during the last few months before expiration. Long-term charts put contracts together by back-adjusting the prices, so that the older data does not give the actual price at that time, but is altered by accumulated roll difference. Using those older prices as a guide for support or resistance doesn't make any sense.

This same problem exists for stocks that have split. The old price that you see on the chart may not be the actual price traded at that time. Floor traders are good at remembering the last major high or low and will trade against those prices, or buy and sell breakouts. When plotting the support and resistance lines, look for the data option that creates a history of prices without back-adjusting.

Rules for Trading Using Trendlines

The simplest formations to recognize are the most commonly used and most important: horizontal support and resistance lines, bullish and bearish support and resistance lines, and channels created using those lines. Proper use of these basic lines is essential for identifying the overall direction of the market and understanding the patterns formed as prices move from one level to another. Many traders will generate their buy and sell orders directly from their chart analysis. Other, more computer-oriented analysts have automated the more important trendlines, particularly horizontal support and resistance, which has become the basic breakout system. Major chart patterns create the underlying profitability of chart trading; the more complex formations, as we will discuss further, may enhance good performance but rarely compensate for losses resulting from being on the wrong side of the trend.

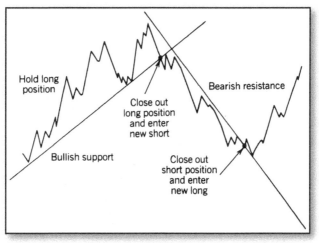

FIGURE 1.9 Basic Sell and Buy Signals using Trendlines.

Once the support and resistance lines have been drawn, a price penetration of those lines creates the basic trend signal (Figure 1.9). The bullish support line defines the upward trend, and the bearish resistance line denotes the downward one. For long-term charts and major trends, this is often sufficient. Some traders add the additional rule that once the price has penetrated a trendline, it must remain penetrated for some time period in order to confirm the new trend. Most false penetrations correct quickly.

Confirming the New Trend Direction   In actual trading, the price crossing the trendline is not as clean as in Figure 1.8. Most often prices that have been moving higher will cross below the trendline, then recross moving higher, then move lower again. The trendline is an important turning point, and there may be indecision that is reflected in a sideways price movement before prices reestablish a trend. To deal with this situation, traders may:

- *Wait a set time period* to confirm that prices remain on the new side of the trendline.

- *Wait for a reversal* after the penetration, then enter a trade in the new direction even if the reversal crosses the trendline again.

- *Create a small safety zone* (called a *band* or *channel*) around the trendline and enter the new trade if prices move through the trendline and through the safety zone.

Each of these techniques requires a delay before entering. A delay normally benefits the trader by giving a better entry price; however, if prices fall quickly through an upwards trendline and do not reverse or slow down, then any delay will result in a much worse entry price. Unfortunately, most of the biggest profits result from breakouts that never pull back. Catching only one of these breakouts can compensate for all the small losses due to false signals. Many professional traders wait for a better entry price. They may be steady winners, but they do not often profit from the biggest moves.

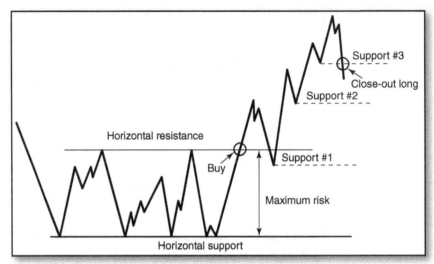

FIGURE 1.10 Trading Rules for Horizontal Support and Resistance Lines.

Trading Rules for Horizontal Support and Resistance Levels

As with angled trendlines, horizontal support and resistance lines show clear points for buying and selling. Also similar to angled trendlines, the horizontal lines become increasingly important when longer time intervals and more points are used to form the lines. The technique for entering trades using horizontal lines is similar to that using angled trendlines; however, the maximum risk of the trade is clearly defined.

- *Buy* when prices move above the horizontal resistance line
- *Sell* when prices move below the horizontal support line

Once a long position has been entered, it is not closed out until prices move below the support line. The maximum risk of the trade is the difference between the support and resistance lines. As prices move higher, each swing reversal forms a low from which a new horizontal support line is drawn. After the initial entry, single points are most often used to create the horizontal support and raise the level at which the trade will be closed out. Figure 1.10 shows the pattern of horizontal support and resistance lines as the trade develops. For a swing low to form, prices must reverse by more than some threshold number of points or percentage. Not every small reversal qualifies as a swing low.

Note that the first pullback in Figure 1.10 shows prices crossing below the original resistance line. This is a common occurrence, but the original line no longer holds the importance it had before it was broken. While it should provide support for the pullback (a resistance, once broken, becomes a support), it is more important to record the bottom of the new pullback as the support level. These new support levels need only one price point. After the third support level is drawn, prices rally but then fall back through the third level, at which point the long position is closed out. A short position, if any, is not entered until a new sideways price pattern is established and horizontal support and resistance lines can be drawn across more than one point.

Identifying Direction from Consolidation Patterns It is said that markets move sideways about 80% of the time, which means that sustained directional breakouts do not occur often, or that most breakouts are false and fail to identify a new market direction. Classic accumulation and distribution formations, which occur at long-term lows and highs, attempt to find evolving changes in market sentiment. Because these formations occur only at extremes, and may extend for a long time, they represent the most obvious consolidation of price movement. Even a rounded or saucer-shaped bottom may have a number of false starts; it may seem to turn up in a uniform pattern, then fall back and begin another slow move up. In the long run, the pattern looks as if it is a somewhat irregular, extended rounded bottom; however, using this pattern to enter a trade in a timely fashion can be disappointing. It is easier to average *in*, where smaller positions are entered at fixed intervals as long as the developing formation remains intact.

Most other consolidation formations are best viewed in the same way as a simple horizontal sideways pattern, bounded above by a resistance line and below by a support line. If this pattern occurs at reasonably low prices, we can eventually expect a breakout upwards when the fundamentals change. Occasionally, prices seem to become less volatile within the sideways pattern, and chartists take this opportunity to redefine the support and resistance levels so that they are narrower. Breakouts based on these more sensitive lines tend to be less reliable because they represent a temporary quiet period inside the larger, normal level of market noise; however, there are two distinct camps, one that believes that breakouts are more reliable after a period of low volatility and the other that prefers breakouts associated with high volatility.

Creating a Channel with Trendlines

A *channel* is formed by a trendline and another line drawn parallel to the trendline enclosing a sustained price move. The purpose of the channel is to define the volatility of the price move and establish reasonable entry and exit points. Up to now, the trendline has only been used to identify the major price direction. A long position is entered when the price crosses a downward trendline moving higher. The trade is held until the price moves below the upwards trendline. However, it is more common to have a series of shorter trades. While the biggest profits come from holding one position throughout a sustained trend, a series of shorter trades each has far less risk and is preferred by the active trader. Be aware that trendlines using very little data are essentially analyzing noise and have limited value.

Before a channel can be formed, the bullish or bearish trendline must be drawn. A clear uptrend line requires at least two, and preferably three or more major low points on the chart, as shown in Figure 1.11, where points 1, 2, and 3 are used. These points do not have to fall exactly on the line. Once the trendline is drawn, the highest high, point *B,* can be used to draw another line parallel to the upwards trendline. The area in between the two parallel lines is the *channel*.

In theory, trading a channel is a simple process. We buy as prices approach the support line (in this case the upwards trendline), and we sell as prices near the resistance line. These buy and sell zones should be approximately the bottom and top

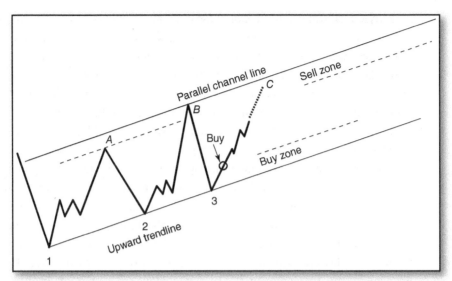

FIGURE 1.11 Trading a Price Channel. Once the channel has been drawn, buying is done near the support line and selling near the resistance line.

20% of the channel. Because the channel line is used to determine price targets, you might choose to draw the broken line across point *A*. The use of point *A* creates a channel that is narrower than the one formed using the higher point *B* and recognizes the variability of price movement. This allows you to take profits sooner.

If prices continue through the lower trendline after a long position has been set, the trade is exited. The trend direction has changed, and a new bearish resistance line, the downward trendline, needs to be drawn using points *B* and *C*, shown in Figure 1.12. Once the first pull-back occurs leaving a low at point 4, a parallel line is drawn crossing point 4, forming the downward channel. In a downward trending channel, it is best to sell short in the upper zone and cover the short in the lower zone. Buying in the lower zone is not recommended; trades are safest when they are entered in the direction of the trend.

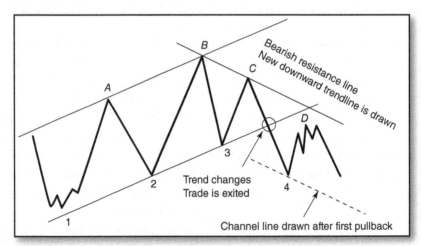

FIGURE 1.12 Turning from an Upward to a Downward Channel. Trades are always entered in the direction of the trend.

When the support and resistance lines are relatively horizontal, or sideways, the channel is called a *trading range*. There is no directional bias in a trading range; therefore, you can enter new long positions in the support zone and enter new shorts in the sell zone. In both cases, penetration of either the support or resistance lines forces liquidation of the trade and establishes a new trend direction.

■ One-Day Patterns

The easiest of all chart patterns to recognize occur in one day. They include gaps, spikes, island reversals, reversal days, inside days, outside days, wide-ranging days, and, to a lesser extent, thrust days. Some of these patterns are important at the moment they occur, and others must be confirmed by other factors.

Gaps

Price *gaps* occur when important news influences the market at a time when the exchange is closed. Orders accumulate to be executed on the next open. An *upwards gap* exists when the low of the current day is higher than the high of the previous day. If all trading were 24 hours, then we would see a fast, volatile move, but not a gap. For example, there are three popular ways to trade the S&P 500 index,

1. Futures, traded in the Chicago Mercantile Exchange pit from 8:30 a.m. to 3:15 p.m. (Central time)
2. Spyders (SPY) on the AMEX during the same hours
3. The electronic S&P mini-futures contract which trades nonstop from Sunday evening at 6 p.m. until Friday afternoon at 3:15 p.m. on the Globex platform

Gaps only exist when using the primary trading session (the *pit* session). Most afterhours trading is on light volume and may be ignored for charting purposes. An exception is in Europe where they have an extended session from the original 4 p.m. close (European time) to 10 p.m. or 10:30 p.m. to allow trading at the same time the U.S. markets are open. The markets then close and reopen when the normal European business day begins. For European markets it is best to use the combined sessions that start at about 9 a.m. and continue until about 10 p.m.

Economic reports are released by the U.S. government at 7:30 a.m. (Central time); therefore, they occur before the S&P pit trading and the SPDRs begin trading, but during the electronic emini S&P session. There is no gap in electronic trading, but the other markets will open sharply higher or lower to adjust to the current emini price. When the financial news shows give the expected open of the stock market, they are using the difference between the previous NYSE closing price and the current price of the electronic session. This creates frequent opening gaps in those markets.

Gaps can also occur because of a large cluster of orders placed at the point where the stock or futures market penetrates support or resistance. It is possible to have a gap during the trading session, immediately following bullish economic report, or

FIGURE 1.13 Price Gaps Shown on a Chart of Amazon.com.

concurrent with an anticipated news release of consequence, when there are a large number of buyers and few sellers. There is also the rarer case of an event shock such as September 11, 2001.

In charting, gaps are interpreted differently based on where they occur in the current price pattern. In some cases, a gap signals a continued move and in other situations it is expected to be the end of a price move. The four primary gap formations are shown on a chart of Amazon.com in Figure 1.13. They are:

1. The *common gap*, which appears as a space on a chart and has no particular attributes—that is, it does not occur at a point associated with any particular significance. A common gap appears in May 1999 during a downward move.

2. A *breakaway gap* occurs at a point of clear resistance or support. It occurs when there are a large number of buy orders just above a major resistance line, or sell orders below a support line. Most often this is seen after a prolonged period of sideways price movement when most chartists can draw the same horizontal support and resistance lines. The clearer the formation, and the longer the sideways period, the more likely there will be a large breakaway gap. The term *breakaway* requires some hindsight because it is applied only when the gap is followed by a sustained price move.

There are two breakaway gaps in Figure 1.13, the first shortly after prices make a new high, the second in the middle of the chart when prices break upwards through a steep downward trendline, and the last near the right of the chart when prices gap through a clear downwards trendline.

In order to trade a gap, a position must be entered in advance of the gap, as prices approach the support or resistance level. Once a long position is set and prices *gap up* you gain *free exposure,* which is the profit caused by the gap or by a fast market move in your favor. If prices do not gap up, they most often drift lower. The position can be exited with a small loss and reentered later.

3. An *exhaustion gap* occurs at the end of a sustained and volatile price move and confirms the reversal. Exhaustion gaps usually occur on the day after the highest price of the upwards move; however, in the Amazon chart, it is one day later. Because it signifies a clustering of orders anxious to exit the long side, it has all the signs associated with an exhaustion gap.

4. A *runaway gap* occurs at different points during a clear trend and confirms the trend. It does not appear to have any practical use because the trend can stop and reverse just after a runaway gap and it will be renamed an *island top,* or some other formation. When holding a long position, an upwards runaway gap quickly adds profits, but also signifies extreme risk.

Gaps can also be a hindrance to trading. A long position held when a downward breakaway gap occurs guarantees that any stop-loss order is executed far away from the order price. If the upwards breakaway gap occurs on light volume, it may be a false breakout. If a short is held, and if you are lucky, prices will fall back to the breakout level and then continue lower. If unlucky, you will be executed at the high of the move. In the final analysis, if the gap breakout represents a major change, a trade should be entered immediately *at the market.* The poor executions will be offset by the one time when prices move quickly and no pullback occurs. A breakaway gap on high volume is usually indicative of a strong move and a sustained change.

Filling the Gap   Tradition states that prices will retrace to *fill the gap* that occurred sometime earlier. Naturally, given enough time, prices will return to most levels; therefore, nearly all gaps will eventually be filled. The most important gaps are not filled for some time.

The gap represents an important point at which prices move out of their previous pattern and begin a new phase. The breakaway gap will often occur just above the previous normal, or established, price level. With commodities, once the short-term demand imbalance has passed, prices should return to near-normal (perhaps slightly above the old prices given inflation), but also slightly below the gap. When a stock price gaps higher based on earnings, a new product announcement, or a rumor of an acquisition, the price may not return to the previous level.

Trading Rules for Gaps

- A *common gap* is small and occurs with low volume and for no specific reason; that is, it is not the result of an obvious, surprising news release. Active traders will take a position counter to the direction of the gap, expecting the move to reverse and fill the gap, at which point they will take profits. If the gap is not filled within a few days, the trade is liquidated.

- A *breakaway gap* is the result of bunched orders at an obvious support or resistance area. When a clear sideways pattern has developed, place a buy order just under the resistance level in order to benefit from the jump in prices (free exposure) when the breakout occurs. If a gap occurs on the breakout, then prices should continue higher.

- A *runaway gap* is often found in the middle of a significant move. It is considered a good point to add to your position because the runaway gap confirms the move and offers additional potential profits.

- An *exhaustion gap* is best traded as it is being filled, and, even at that stage, it is highly risky. Sell during the move upwards, placing a stop above the previous high of the move. If this pattern fails, prices could move higher in an explosive pattern. If you are successive, profits could also be large.

Bulkowski on Gaps   Bulkowski includes an extensive study of breakaway, continuation, and exhaustion gaps. The statistics developed for these three cases all conform to the expected patterns, as shown in Table 1.1. Almost by definition, we expect a breakaway gap, one that occurs when prices move out of a sideways range, to mark the beginning of a new trend, and the exhaustion gap (which actually can't be seen until it reverses) to be the end of a trend. The continuation gap is somewhere in between and is only defined within the context of an existing trend.

The results of the breakaway gap, only 1% and 6% retracements, confirm that the breakouts often continue the trend direction. Strategies that take advantage of this are the *N*-day breakout, swing trading, and pivot point breakouts, providing that the observation period is greater than 40 days, the minimum considered to be a macrotrend.

Spikes

A *spike* is a single, highly volatile day where the price moves much higher or lower than it has in the recent past. A spike can only be recognized one day later because trading range of the following day must be much lower. It is easiest to show spikes in markets, such as U.S. 30-year Treasury bonds, that react to frequent economic reports. In Figure 1.14 there is a series of three spikes about four weeks apart.

An upward spike, as shown in Figure 1.14, is always a *local top* because a spike is a day with above-average volatility and must be bracketed by two lower days. In all three cases shown, the spike represented the high price for at least one week. Because the spike is a clear top, when prices begin to rise again, they usually meet resistance at the top of the spike. Chartists draw a horizontal resistance line using the high price of the spike,

TABLE 1.1	Percentage of Time Gaps Are Closed within One Week, Based on a Sample of 100 Stocks	
Gap Type	**Uptrends**	**Downtrends**
Breakaway	1	6
Continuation	11	10
Exhaustion	58	72

FIGURE 1.14 A Series of Spikes in Bonds. From June through October 2002, U.S. bonds show three spikes that represent local tops. The spikes represent clear resistance levels that cause a unique pattern in the upwards move.

which encourages selling at that level. After each spike the chart is marked with "failed test," showing the price level where resistance, based on the previous spike, slowed the advance. The spike did not stop the trend, but it did cause a unique pattern.

Quantifying Spikes A spike has only one dominant feature: a price high or low much higher or lower than recent prices. It must therefore also have high volatility. The easiest way to identify an upside spike is to compare the trading range on the day of the spike to previous ranges and to the subsequent day. This can be programmed in TradeStation by using the *true range* function and satisfying the conditions that the high on the day of the spike is greater than the previous and subsequent highs by the amount of $k \times$ *average true range* over n days,

```
Spike = high[1] - highest(high,n)[2] > k*average(truerange,n)[2]
                          and
             high[1] - high > k*average(truerange,n)[2]
```

In this code, *spike* is a logical variable (true-false). A spike that occurs yesterday (where [1] indicates yesterday and [2] two days ago) is tested to see that the high of the spike is greater than the high of the previous n days, greater than the average true range of the same n days by a factor of k, and also greater than the high of today by the same factor k. Note that the use of [2] ends the true range calculation on the day before the spike. The value of k should be greater than 0.75. Spikes satisfying $k > 1$ are more desirable but less frequent.

In Excel, the true range is

$$TRn = Max(Hn - Ln, Hn - Cm, Cm - Ln)$$

where *n* is the current row, *m* is the previous row $(n-1)$, and the high, low, and close $(H, L, \text{can } C)$ are in columns B, C, and D.

Island Reversals

An *island reversal* or an *island top* is a single price bar, or group of bars, sitting at the top of a price move and isolated by a gap on both sides, before and after the island formation. Combined with high volatility, this formation has the reputation of being a major turning point. The gap on the right side of the island top can be considered an exhaustion gap. In Figure 1.15, showing AMR during the first part of 2003, there is one island reversal in mid-April. This single, volatile day has a low that is higher than both the previous day and the following day. It remains the high for the next week but eventually gives way to another volatile price rise. *Island bottoms* also occur, but are less frequent.

Pivot Point Reversals and Swings A *pivot point* is a trading day, or price bar, that is higher or lower than the bars that come before and after. If the entire bar is above the previous day and the following day, the pivot point reversal is the same as the island reversal. If it is a very volatile upwards day but the low price is not above the high of the surrounding bars, then it is a spike. If it is not a volatile day, then it is a weaker form of a spike. If you were plotting swing highs and lows, the high of an upwards pivot point reversal day would often become the swing high. It is common to locate a *swing high* by comparing the high of any day with two or more days before and after. The patterns

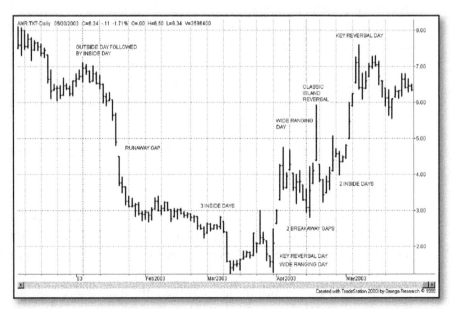

FIGURE 1.15 **AMR in Early 2003 Showing a Classic Island Reversal with Examples of Other One-Day Patterns.**

of the days on either side of the high bar are not important as long as the middle bar has the highest high. When more days are used to identify pivot points, these reversals are expected to be more significant; however, they take longer to identify.

According to tests by Colby and Meyers,[13] entries that occur based on a breakout of the highs or lows of the pivot points, called *pivot point channels,* are much more reliable than simply entering in the direction of the reversal based on the close of the last bar of the pivot point formation. For traders not interested in this very short-term strategy, a pivot point may help entry timing for any longer term method.

More recently, Colby[14] tested a *Pivot Point Reverse Trading System,* using the following rules:

- *Buy* (and close out short positions) when a pivot point bottom occurs and the close is higher than the previous close.

- *Sell* (and close out long positions) when a pivot point top occurs and the close is lower than the previous close.

Applying these rules to the Dow Jones Industrials (DJIA) for 101 years ending December 2000 showed nearly 7,000 trades (70 per year) with significant profits.

Cups and Caps   Another name given to the pivot point reversals are *cups* and *caps,* each determined by only three price bars, although another formation with the same name, *cup with handle,* is similar to a longer-term rounded bottom followed by a sideways or slight downward trend and a breakout to the upside. These two short-term formations are associated with trading rules that are identical to pivot point channels applied to the shortest time frame. Although some literature uses these formations backwards, a cap formation identifies a sell signal when the trend is up, while a cup is a setup for a buy signal in a downtrend. Once an uptrend is clear, a cap formation is found using either the daily closes or daily lows. For any three consecutive days, the middle day must have the highest close or the highest low. In a cup pattern, the middle day must have the lowest low or the lowest close of the three-day cluster. In both cases, the positioning of the highs and lows of the other two days are not important as long as the middle day is lower for the cup and higher for the cap.

The cup will generate a buy signal if:

- The cup formation is the lowest point of the downtrend

- The buy signal occurs within three days of the cup formation

- The current price closes above the highest high (middle bar) of the cup formation

The signal is false if prices reverse and close below the low of the cup formation, resuming the previous downtrend. This pattern is only expected to forecast a

---

[13] Tests of pivot point reversals and pivot point channels can be found in Robert W. Colby and Thomas A. Meyers, *The Encyclopedia of Technical Market Indicators* (Homewood, IL: Dow Jones-Irwin, 1988).

[14] Robert W. Colby, *The Encyclopedia of Technical Market Indicators* (New York: McGraw-Hill, 2003), 510–514.

downward price move of two days; however, every change of direction must start somewhere, and this formation could offer an edge. A cap formation is traded with the opposite rules.

Reversal Days and Key Reversal Days

A day in which there is a new high followed by a lower close is a *downwards reversal day*. An *upwards reversal day* is a new low followed by a higher close. A reversal day is a common formation, as seen in Figure 1.16, the Russell 2000 futures. Some of these days are identified; however, you can find many other examples in Figures 1.13 through 1.16. There have been many studies to determine the importance of reversal days for trading, but these are inconclusive. A reversal day by itself is not significant unless it can be put into context with a larger price pattern, such as a clear trend with sharply increasing volatility, or a reversal that occurs at the highest or lowest price of the past few weeks.

Key Reversals A *key reversal day* is a more selective pattern, and has been endowed with great forecasting power. It is also called an *outside reversal day,* and is a weaker form of an island reversal. A *bearish key reversal* is formed in one day by first making a new high in an upward trend, reversing to make a low that is lower than the previous low, and then closing below the previous close. It should be associated with higher volatility. Examples of key reversal days can be seen in Figures 1.14 and 1.15. It is considered more reliable when the trend is well-established.

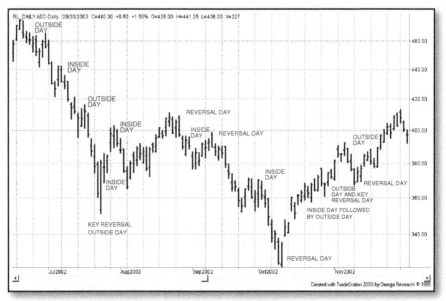

FIGURE 1.16   Russell 2000 during the Last Half of 2002 Showing Reversal Days, Key Reversal Days, Inside Days, and Outside Days.

As with reversal days, studies have shown mixed results using the key reversal as a sole trading indicator. The most complete analysis,[15] similar to others, concluded that the performance was "strikingly unimpressive." Even though tests have not proved its importance, traders still pay close attention to key reversals. Because this pattern has kept its importance, we can conclude that other factors unconsciously enter into the selection of key reversal days for trading. A successful trader's senses should not be underestimated; the extent and speed of the prior trend, a change in liquidity, a quieter market *tone,* or some external news may be essential in confirming the important reversals. The job of a system developer is to find those factors that will turn this pattern into a successful indicator. The best place to start is by assuming the attitude of those traders who see a reversal day as an important pattern.

Figure 1.16 shows a number of reversal days during the rapid drop of the Russell 2000 in January 2002. Three patterns of particular interest are the reversal days at the two extreme lows in July and October 2002, and the high in between, during August. Although there are many other reversal days embedded within other parts of the price move, the reversals off the lows are clearly at higher volatility than most other days, and follow very sharp, accelerating price drops. The reversal day that ends the intermediate high during August does not share these attributes; however, it tops a pattern that is not the dominant trend, but an upwards reaction within a previous sustained downtrend. If we focus on the characteristics of those reversal days that mark price extremes, rather than all reversal days, we should expect successful results.

Programming Key Reversal Days   A key reversal day can be recognized and tested using a computer program. In TradeStation's *EasyLanguage* the instructions for downward key reversal are

```
KeyReversalDown = 0;
if close[1] > average(close[1],n) and high >= highest(high[1],n) and
    low < low[1] and close < close[1] then KeyReversalDown = 1;
```

where the first term tests for an uptrend over *n*-days, the second term tests that the current day is the highest price of the same *n*-days, the third term verifies that a lower low has occurred, and the last term tests for a lower close. This can be done in Excel by using the *max* and *min* functions instead of *highest* and *lowest*. A TradeStation function to identify key reversals is *TSM Key Reversals* and can be found on the Companion Website along with an Excel spreadsheet of the same name.

Adding a volatility factor, so that the key reversal day has noticeably higher volatility than the previous days seems to select more significant patterns. In the spreadsheet, which uses heating oil from 2005 through 2011 as an example, the basic rules gave marginal gains, but a filter that took only trades where today's true range was greater than $1.5 \times$ *average prior 20-day true range* was much better.

---

[15] Eric Evans, "Why You Can't Rely on 'Key Reversal Days,'" *Futures* (March 1985).

2-Bar Reversal Patterns   Martin Pring[16] has called attention to a special 2-bar reversal pattern that frequently precedes a strong directional change. This pattern consists of two days that are essentially the mirror image of one another. Consider a market in which prices have been moving steadily higher. The first day of the pattern shows a volatile upwards move with prices opening near the lows and closing near the highs. On the following day, prices open where they had closed, trade slightly higher (nearly matching the previous day's highs), then fall sharply to close near the lows, giving back all of the previous day's move.

Following the 2-bar reversal to the downside, the next few days should not trade above the midpoint of the 2-bar reversal pattern. The smaller the retracement, the more likely there will be a good sell-off.

It is easy to explain the psychology of this pattern. The first bar represents the strong bullish feeling of the buyers, while the second bar is seen as complete discouragement at the inability to follow through to even higher levels. It will take some days before traders are willing to test the highs again. More traders may view this as a potential major reversal. High volume can confirm the reversal. The nature of the move to follow depends on the extent of the previous trend and the volatility. Four key factors in predicting a strong reversal are:

1. Stronger preceding trends
2. Wider, more volatile 2-bar patterns
3. Greater volume than in previous days
4. Smaller retracements following the 2-bar pattern

Wide-Ranging Days, Inside Days, and Outside Days

A *wide-ranging day* is a day of much higher volatility than recent days, but no requirement that it is higher or lower than other days. An *outside day* must have both a higher high and lower low than the previous day. *Inside days* are an example of *volatility compression*. All three patterns are very common but indicate that something special has happened. Examples of these patterns are shown in Figure 1.17, a one-year, active trading period for Tyco ending in July 2000, before any accounting scandal surfaced.

Wide-Ranging Days   A *wide-ranging day* is likely to be the result of a price shock, unexpected news, or a breakout in which many orders trigger one another, causing a large increase in volatility. A wide-ranging day could turn out to be a spike or an island reversal. Because very high volatility cannot be sustained, we can expect that a wide-ranging day will be followed by a reversal, or at least a pause. When a wide-ranging day occurs, the direction of the close (if the close is near the high or low) is a strong indication of the continued direction.

A wide-ranging day is easily seen on a chart because it has at least twice, or three times the volatility of the previous trading days. There is no requirement that it

---

[16] Martin Pring, "Twice as Nice: The Two-Bar Reversal Pattern," *Active Trader* (March 2003).

FIGURE 1.17   Wide-Ranging Days, Outside Days, and Inside Days for Tyco.

makes a new high or low relative to a recent move, or that it closes higher or lower. It is simply a very volatile day.

Outside Days   An *outside day* often precedes a reversal. An outside day can also be a wide-ranging day if the volatility is high, but when volatility is low and the size of the bar is slightly longer than the previous bar, it is a weak signal. As with so many other chart patterns, if one day has an unusually small trading range, followed by an outside day of normal volatility, there is very little information in the pattern. Selection is important.

Inside Days   An *inside day* is one where the high is lower than the previous high and the low is higher than the previous low. That is, an inside day is one where both the highs and lows are inside the previous day's trading range.

An inside day represents consolidation and lower volatility. In turn, lower volatility is most often associated with the end of a price move. After a burst of activity and a surge of upward direction, prices have reached a point where the buyers are already in and the price has moved too far to attract more buyers. Volume drops, volatility drops, and we get an inside day. An inside day is often followed by a change of direction, but that is not guaranteed. We only know that the event that drove prices up is now over. If more news surfaces to ignite prices, the next move could just as easily be up as down

In Figure 1.17 there are two inside days at the price peak on the top left of the Tyco chart. The first inside day is followed by a small move lower, then a small move higher, followed by another inside day. This last inside day precedes a major sell-off. On the right top of the chart there are two inside days immediately before another sharp drop.

Some analysts believe that a breakout from low volatility is more reliable than one following high volatility.

Some Notes about 1-Day Patterns   One-day patterns are very common; therefore, traders tend to be selective about when they are used. Taken as a group, patterns that are repeated frequently are less reliable and need to be combined with other patterns. Those that occur during periods of high or low volatility or volume may also be less dependable.

While a reversal day is clearly a 1-day formation and can be identified at the end of the trading day, and an opening gap is recognized instantly, most other 1-day patterns are not clear until the day after. An upwards spike and a downwards pivot point reversal both require the high of the next day to be much lower than the high of the spike or pivot day; and the island reversal must show a gap on the following day. Although they cannot be used at the end of the day on which they occur, these formations are reasonably timely for an active trader.

■ Continuation Patterns

Continuation patterns occur during a trend and help to explain the stage of development of that trend. A continuation pattern that occurs within a long-term trend is expected to be resolved by continuing in the direction of the trend. If prices fail to move in the direction of the trend following a major continuation pattern, then the trend is considered over. The primary continuation patterns are triangles, flags, pennants, and wedges. The larger formations of these patterns are more important than the smaller ones.

Symmetric, Descending, and Ascending Triangles

Triangles tend to be larger formations that occur throughout a trend. A *symmetric triangle* is most likely to occur at the beginning of a trend when there is greater uncertainty about direction. A symmetric triangle is formed by a price consolidation, where uncertainty of buyers and sellers results in decreasing volatility in such a way that prices narrow to the center of the previous trading range. In Figure 1.18 the symmetric triangle is formed at about the level of the previous support. The breakout from a symmetric triangle often marks the beginning of a longer-term trend.

Formation of a Descending Triangle

Even during a clear downward trend, prices will rally. Because the trend is clear, sellers are anxious to step in and sell these upwards moves, looking for the trend to continue. The top of this mid-trend rally is likely to be the last support point where prices broke out of a previous pattern. In Figure 1.18, the top of the first descending triangle comes very close to the breakout level of the symmetric triangle, and the larger descending triangle towards the lower right of the chart has its high point at the breakout of another descending triangle.

The recent lows of the new trend form a temporary support level, and prices may bounce off that level while short-term traders play for small profits. This action forms a *descending triangle*. As more traders are convinced that prices are still heading lower, rallies off the support level are sold sooner, causing a narrower pattern, until

FIGURE 1.18 Symmetric and Descending Triangles and a Developing Bear Market in Gold Futures.

prices finally break below support. The descending triangle is complete. In an upwards trend an *ascending triangle* would be formed.

Size of the Triangles   A triangle should take no less than two weeks to form; however, they can span a much longer period, occasionally up to three months. Larger formations represent periods of greater uncertainty. They may be followed by another symmetric triangle, again indicating that traders are undecided about direction. If the symmetric triangle is resolved in the current trend direction, the trend is in full force, and a large price move is expected.

Triangles can be consistent indicators of investor confidence. Because they reflect human behavior, they are not always perfect in appearance and not always consistent in pattern. It takes experience to identify the formation in a timely manner.

Flags

A *flag* is a smaller pattern than a triangle, generally less than three months for the long-term trader, and is formed by a correction in a bull market or a rally in a bear market. A flag is a congestion area that leans away from the direction of the trend and typically can be isolated by drawing parallel lines across the top and bottom of the formation. At the beginning of a trend, the flags may not lean away from the direction of the new trend as clearly as during a well-established trend. If the first flag after an upwards breakout leans down, it confirms the new upwards trend.

Figure 1.19 shows an assortment of triangles, flags, and pennants. There are two small flags, one in the middle of the chart and one in the lower right, each leaning upwards as expected in a downtrend. A larger flag slightly below center could also have been a symmetric triangle. Both patterns are resolved by a continuation of the trend.

TY_REV.CSV-Daily 02/20/2002 C=107.00 +.05 +0.05% O=107.00 H=107.33 L=106.70 V=282719

Symmetric triangle inside a
descending triangle

Flag

Pennant

Symmetric triangle
or a flag?

Flag

Triangle or
pennant?

Created with TradeStation 2000i by Omega Research © 1999

FIGURE 1.19 An Assortment of Continuation Patterns. These patterns are all
resolved by prices moving lower. A downward pennant can be found in the middle
of the chart.

Pennants

Pennants are irregular triangles normally leaning toward the trend, similar to a descending triangle in a downtrend but without a horizontal support line. A typical pennant can be seen in the middle of Figure 1.19. During a sustained trend, triangles are large, clear formations, with horizontal support or resistance lines, while pennants are consolidation formations requiring only that the lines converge. They usually lean in the direction of the trend, but that is not a requirement. A larger pennant should lean in the direction of the trend in a manner similar to a descending triangle; however, a small pennant may serve the same purpose as a flag and lean away from the trend.

Wedges

A pattern that looks as if it is a large pennant, with both sides angling in the same direction, but does not come to a point, is a *wedge*. In an upwards-trending market, the wedge should be rising as shown on the right side of the General Electric chart, Figure 1.20, near the end of 1999. The earlier wedge has nearly a horizontal upper line, bridging the pattern between a wedge and a rising triangle. A rising wedge is formed in the same way as an ascending triangle. Investors, convinced that the share price will rise, will buy smaller and smaller reversals even as prices make new highs. In the end, prices continue in the direction of the trend. In a typical rising wedge the lower line has a steeper angle than the upper line.

The angle of the wedge should be steeper as the trend becomes clear. The earlier wedge formation shown in Figure 1.20 is nearly symmetric. If we study the bigger

FIGURE 1.20 Wedge. A weaker wedge formation is followed by a strong rising wedge near the end of 1999 in this chart of General Electric.

picture, we can see that the uncertainty at the beginning of the trend is reflected in the symmetric formation, while the rising wedge occurs after the trend is well established and investors anticipate a continuation.

Run Days

Triangles, flags, pennants, and wedges represent the best of the continuation patterns. They can be identified clearly while they are still being formed and the direction of the breakout can be anticipated and traded. Other formations, such as *run days,* are not as timely. A run day occurs when the low of that day is higher than the previous *n* days, and the high of the day is lower than the subsequent *n* highs. When it occurs, this pattern confirms that a trend is in effect. The more days used to define the run day, the stronger the pattern. Therefore, a 5-day run day requires 11 days to identify, 5 before the run day and 5 after. Unlike the other continuation patterns, which have a breakout level that can be used as a trading signal, entering a long position after 11 days of a strong upwards move is not likely to be a good entry point. There are no trading rules or trading action associated with run days. They simply confirm what you have already seen on charts—that prices have been trending.

◼ Basic Concepts in Chart Trading

Having covered the fundamental chart patterns, there are some additional concepts that should be discussed in order to keep the proper perspective. Charting involves a great deal of subjective pattern identification; therefore, there may be a choice of patterns within the same time interval. There are also many cases where prices nearly form a pattern, but the shape does not fit perfectly into the classic definition.

Major and Minor Formations

In the study of charting, the same patterns will appear in short- as well as long-term charts. An upwards trendline can be drawn across the bottom of a price move that only began last week, or it can identify a sustained 3-year trend in the financial markets, or a 6-month move in Amazon.com. In general, formations that occur over longer time intervals are more significant. All-time highs and lows, well-defined trading ranges, trendlines based on weekly charts, and head-and-shoulder formations are carefully watched by traders. Obscure patterns and new formations are not of interest to most chartists, and cannot be resolved consistently unless traders buy and sell at the right points. Charting is most successful when formations are easy to see; therefore, the most obvious buy and sell points are likely to attract a large number of orders.

Market Noise

All markets have a normal level of noise. The stock index markets have the greatest amount of irregular movement due their extensive participation, the high level of anticipation built into the prices, the uncertain way in which economic reports and news will impact prices, and because it is an index. This is contrasted to short-term interest rates, such as Eurodollars, which have large participation but little anticipation because it has strong ties to the underlying cash market, governed by the central bank. The normal level of noise can be seen in the consistency of the daily or weekly trading range on a chart of the Dow or S&P. When volatility declines below the normal level of noise, the market is experiencing short-term inactivity. An increase in volatility back to normal levels of noise should not be confused with a breakout.

This same situation can be applied to a triangular formation, which has traditionally been interpreted as a consolidation, or a pause, within a trend. This pattern often follows a fast price change and represents a short period of declining volatility. If volatility declines in a consistent fashion, it appears as a triangle; however, if the point of the triangle is smaller than the normal level of market noise, then a breakout from this point is likely to restore price movement to a range typical of noise, resulting in a flag or pennant formation. Both of these latter patterns have uniform height that can include a normal level of noise, but they would not be reliable signals.

■ Accumulation and Distribution—Bottoms and Tops

Most of the effort in charting, and the largest payout in trading, goes into the identification of tops and bottoms. For long-term traders, those trying to take advantage of major bull and bear markets, these formations can unfold over fairly long periods. These prolonged phases, which represent the cyclic movement in the economy, are called *accumulation* when prices are low and investors slowly buy into their position, and *distribution* at the top, where the invested positions are sold off.

The same formations can occur over shorter periods and are very popular among all traders; however, they are not as reliable. There are many top and bottom formations that are popular and easily recognized. In order of increasing complexity, they are the *V*-top or *V*-bottom, the double or triple top or bottom, the common rounded top or bottom, the broadening top or bottom, the head-and-shoulders formation, and the complex top or bottom.

V-Tops and V-Bottoms

The *V-top* (actually an inverted "V"), which may also have a spike on the final day, is the easiest pattern to see afterwards, but the most difficult top formation to anticipate and trade. There have been times, such as in 1974, 1980, and 2000, when the frequency of *V*-tops were deceiving. *V*-tops are preceded by critical shortage and demand, and magnified by constant news coverage. In 1974, it was a combination of domestic crop shortage, severe pressure on the U.S. dollar abroad, and foreign purchases of U.S. grain that combined to draw public attention to a potential shortage in wheat. The news was so well publicized that novice commodity traders withdrew their funds from their declining stock portfolios and bought any commodity available as a hedge against inflation.

It could not continue for long. When the top came in soybeans, silver, and most other commodities, there was no trading for days in locked-limit markets; paper profits dwindled faster than they were made, and the latecomers found their investments unrecoverable. The public often seems to enter at the wrong time.

The most dramatic of all price moves was the technology bubble of the 1990s, ending with a peak in the NASDAQ index during March 2000. As you can see in Figure 1.21, prices rose faster near the end of the bull market, then collapsed just as quickly. It would have been reasonable to expect the move up to end any time after prices penetrated through 3,000, and difficult to expect them to reach 5,000.

FIGURE 1.21 A V-top in the NASDAQ Index, March 2000.

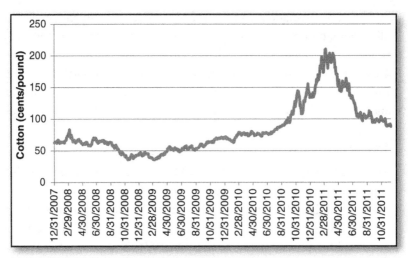

FIGURE 1.22   Cash Cotton Prices Showing V-Top in Early 2011.

Recently, there have been runs in many commodities, but cotton stands out as exceptional. Flooding in both Pakistan and Egypt has greatly reduced the supply causing prices to soar. Figure 1.22 shows prices in February 2011 at levels four times the normal price and a top has not yet formed. Normally, supply shortages in agricultural markets correct by the next season, but the current run has been so extensive that it may take more time to resolve. Inevitably, it will be solved in the same way, over one or two crop years.

The psychology of the runaway market is fascinating. In some ways, every *V*-top shares a similarity with the examples in Mackay's *Extraordinary Popular Delusions and the Madness of Crowds*. When beef is in short supply, the result of higher feed costs, the consumers do not tend to consider pork, fowl, or fish as an adequate substitute and will accept increased costs longer than expected. This is called *inelastic demand*. As prices near the top, the following changes occur:

- The cost becomes an increasing factor in the standard household budget.

- Rising prices receive more publicity.

- Movements for public beef boycotts begin.

- Grain prices decline due to the new harvest.

This becomes a matter explained by the *Theory of Elasticity*. It can be applied to the 1973 soybean, 1980 silver, and the recent cotton markets. The theory is based on the principle that when prices get high enough, four phenomena occur:

1. Previously higher-priced substitutes become practical (synthetics for cotton, reclaimed silver).
2. Competition becomes more feasible (corn sweetener as a sugar substitute, alternate energy).
3. Inactive operations start up (Southwest gold mines, marginal production of oil).
4. Consumers avoid the products (beef, bacon, silver, cotton).

Consequently, the demand suddenly disappears (the same conclusion arrived at by economists).

Announcements of additional production, more acreage, new products, boycotts, and a cancellation of orders all coming at once cause highly inflated prices to reverse sharply. These factors form a *V*-top that is impossible to anticipate with reasonable risk. There is a natural reluctance to cash in on profits while they are still increasing every day. The situation becomes even more perilous at the end of the move when more investors join the party. These latecomers who entered their most recent positions near the top will show a loss immediately and will need to get out of the trade first; they cannot afford a continued adverse move. Once a reversal day is recognized, there is a mad rush to liquidate. The large number of investors and speculators trying to exit at the same time causes the sharpness in the *V*-top and extends the drop in prices. There is a liquidity void at many points during the decline where there are no buyers and a long line of sellers. A *V*-top or *V*-bottom is always accompanied by high volatility and usually high volume. When the *V*-top is particularly extreme, it is commonly called a *blow-off*. A true *V*-top or *V*-bottom will become an important medium- or long-term high or low for that market.

Two V-Tops in Amazon.com   There is a classic *V*-top in Amazon.com during January 1999, shown in Figure 1.23, and another potential, smaller formation in April. This second one looked as though it was a *V*-top for two days, then quickly disappeared into a broader formation of no particular pattern. A *V*-top cannot be recognized after only a 1-day downturn. The final peak seen in Amazon in late April 1999 is broader than a classic *V*-top but could still be labeled the same.

FIGURE 1.23   Classic V-Top in Amazon, January 1999, and Two Other Tops.

When trading, you would expect rising prices to fail when they approach the level of a previous clear *V*-top, which forms significant resistance. In Figure 1.23, where prices began the second *V*-top, declined for two days, rallied for the next three days, then dropped sharply for two days, we would normally expect a further decline. In this case, prices made another attempt to break the highs, succeeded, then collapsed. After the last peak, it will be necessary to wait until the price falls below the support level at $75 in order to confirm the downward break, having been fooled on the previous move.

V-Bottoms   *V-bottoms* are much less common than their upside counterparts. They occur more often in commodity markets where supply and demand can change dramatically and leverage causes surges of buying and selling. Both *V*-tops and *V*-bottoms should be read as a sign that prices have gone too far, too fast. Both buyers and sellers need time to reevaluate the fundamentals to decide where prices should be. *V*-bottoms are usually followed by a rebound and then a period of sideways movement. Two good examples can be found in the crude oil chart, Figure 1.24, and in the stock market crash of October 1987.

Double and Triple Tops and Bottoms

The experienced trader is most successful when prices are testing a major support or resistance level, especially an all-time high in a stock or a contract or seasonal high or low in futures. The more often those levels are tested, the clearer they become and the less likely prices will break through to a new level without additional fuel. This fuel comes in the form of higher earnings or a change in the fundamental supply and demand factors.

A *double top* is a price peak followed, a few days or weeks later, by another peak, and stopping very close to the same level. A *double bottom*, more common than a double

FIGURE 1.24   Two V-Bottoms in Crude Oil.

top, occurs when two price valleys show lows at nearly the same level. Because prices are more likely to settle for awhile at a lower price than a high one, prices often test a previous support level causing a double bottom.

Tops and bottoms occur at the same level because traders believe that the same reason that caused prices to fail to go higher the first time will be the reason they fail the second time. The exceptionally high or low prices are the result of speculation rather than fundamentals. In the same way that some stocks will trade at price/earnings ratios far above any rational assessment of business prospects in the near future, commodity prices can be pushed to extremes by crowd psychology without regard to value. Traders, looking for a place to sell an unreasonably high price, target the previous point where prices failed. Although a classic double top is thought to peak at exactly the same price, selling in anticipation of the test of the top may cause the second peak to be lower than the first. Figure 1.25 shows one type of double top in crude oil. While some double tops are two sharp peaks, this one looks as though it was gathering energy. It penetrated slightly above the previous high, but could not sustain higher prices. Double tops are rarely perfect.

Double Bottoms   Bottoms are more orderly than tops. They should be quiet rather than volatile. They are caused by prices reaching a level that is low enough for the normal investor to recognize that there is little additional downside potential. Economists might call this the *point of equilibrium.* Neither buyers nor sellers are convinced that prices will continue to move lower. They wait for further news.

Double bottoms will often test the same price level because large-position traders and commercial users of commodities accumulate more physical inventory, or

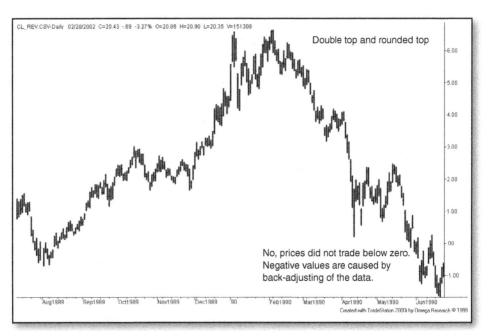

FIGURE 1.25   A Double Top in Crude Oil.

CSCO.TXT-Daily 12/21/2001 C=18.19 -.10 -0.55% O=.00 H=19.06 L=18.16 V=90588500

Double bottom confirmed

Double bottom

FIGURE 1.26   A Double Bottom in Cisco.

increase their futures position, each time the price falls to their target level. Once prices are low, there is less chance of absolute loss. Selling a double top can be very risky. The greatest risk when buying a double bottom is that your timing is wrong. If prices do not rally soon, you have used your capital poorly.

Cisco shows a double bottom in Figure 1.26, although it lacks the clear decline in volatility that we would like to see, and which accompanies commodities when they reach a price level near the cost of production. The small spikes down show four attempts to go lower, followed by a faster move up. When prices cross above the highs formed between the two bottom patterns, we have a completion, or *confirmation,* of the double bottom.

Traders will start to buy a double bottom when prices slow near previous low levels. They will also look for declining volume or confirmation in the stock price of another related company or a related sector ETF. Waiting for the breakout above the highs of the bottom formation is a safer signal for a conservative trader, but lost opportunity for a more active one.

Triple Tops and Bottoms   *Triple tops* and *triple bottoms* are considerably less common than double tops and bottoms; however, of the two, bottoms can be found more readily. Figure 1.27 shows a classic triple top in natural gas. A triple top can be formed from a *V*-top, but in this case, the first peak is an island reversal, the second is a spike, and the third an extended top that ends the move.

If we did not have the advantage of seeing the triple top afterwards, each of the individual tops would look as if it were the end of the move. After the first island reversal prices dropped $2; after the second peak there was another large gap down and a 1-day loss of more than $1. High volatility is normally associated with an extreme top. By waiting for a confirmation of a decline after the single or double top,

46

THEORY AND ANALYSIS

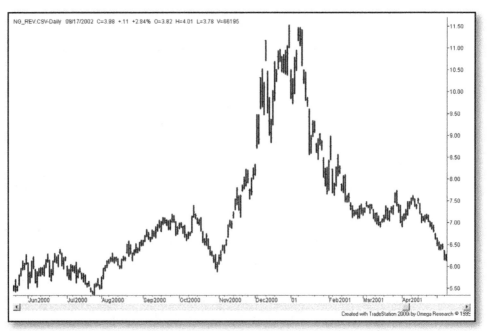

FIGURE 1.27   Natural Gas Shows a Classic Triple Top.

the trade would have been entered $1.50 to $2.50 below the top, and that position would be held while prices reversed to test the highs. Selling tops is risky business.

A triple bottom that can be traded is most likely to occur at low prices and low volatility, much the same as a double bottom. They show an inability to go lower because investors are willing to accumulate a position at a good value. For commodities, it is a good place for a processor to accumulate inventory.

The Danger of Trading Double and Triple Tops   There are many examples of double tops and a smaller number of triple tops. Ideally, there is a lot of money to be made by selling tops at the right place. However, the likelihood of this good fortune happening is less than it appears. Consider why a triple top is so rare. It is because prices continue higher and the potential triple top disappears into a strong bull market pattern.

This happens even more often with double tops. Every time a price pulls back from new highs, then starts moving up again, there is a potential double top. In a prolonged bull market, many double tops disappear in the move higher. Selection of the double top becomes important. This is done using volume, volatility, support, and resistance, and sometimes common sense. These confirming indicators are discussed throughout this book. Until then, it is important to recognize the difficulty of deciding whether the current pattern will be a single, double, or triple top, or simply a pause in a bull market. Although we would all like to be a seller at the highs, these tops are best sold after they are confirmed, that is, after a decline proves that the top has occurred. Even then, a new high should cause a fast exit from the trade.

As with other chart patterns, declining volume would be a welcome confirmation after the formation of the first top and would accompany each additional test of the top.

Extended Rectangle Bottom

Many of the important chart formations can be traded using a penetration of one of the support or resistance lines as a signal. Those with the most potential profitability occur on breakouts from major top or bottom formations. The simplest of all bottom formations, as well as one that offers great opportunities, is the *extended rectangle* at long-term low price levels. Fortunes have been made by applying patience, some available capital, and the following plan:

1. Find a market with a long consolidating base and low volatility. In July 2002 Amazon.com reaches a low with volatility declining. In futures, crude oil remained at low prices for 13 years, as seen in Figure 1.28. The bottom can be confirmed by a decrease in the open interest. When evaluating interest rates, consider using the yield rather than the price.
2. *Buy* whenever there is a test of its major support level, placing a stop-loss to liquidate all positions on a new low price. Increasing volume should confirm the buying, and with futures markets the upside breakout should be accompanied by increasing open interest. For crude oil, the resistance was between $21 and $22 because OPEC had set its OGSP (*Official Government Selling Price*) between $18 and $22.
3. After the initial breakout, buy again when prices pull back to the original resistance line (now a support level). Crude rallied from the lows to just under $40 before pulling back to the old resistance level at $19. Close out all positions if prices penetrate back into the consolidation area and start again at Step 2.
4. Buy whenever there is a major price correction in the bull move. These adjustments, or pullbacks, will become shorter and less frequent as the move

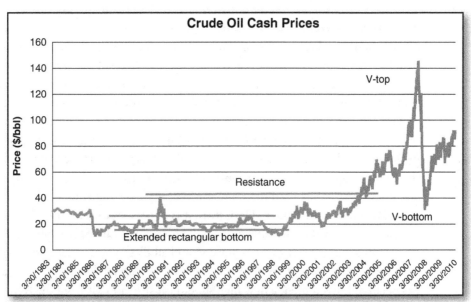

FIGURE 1.28 An Extended Rectangular Bottom in Crude Oil from 1986 through 1999.

develops. They will usually be proportional to current volatility or the extent of the price move as measured from the original breakout.

5. Liquidate all positions at a prior major resistance point, a top formation, or the breaking of a major bullish support line.

Building positions in this way can be done with a relatively small amount of capital and risk. The closer the price comes to major support, the shorter the distance from the stop-loss; however, fewer positions can be placed. In his book *The Professional Commodity Trader*, Stanley Kroll discussed "The Copper Caper—How We're Going to Make a Million," using a similar technique for building positions. It can be done, but it requires patience, planning, and capital. The opportunities continue to be there.

This example of patiently building a large position does not usually apply to bear markets. Although there is a great deal of money to be made on the short side of the market, prices move faster and may not permit the accumulation of a large position. There can also be exceptionally high risk caused by greater volatility. The only pattern that allows for the accumulation of a large short position is the rounded top, discussed in the next section. Within consolidation areas for commodities at low levels, there are a number of factors working in your favor: the underlying demand for a product, the cost of production, government price support (for agricultural products), and low volatility itself. There is also a clear support level that may have been tested many times. A careful position trader will not enter a large short-sale position at an anticipated top when volatility is high, but instead will join the buyers who contribute to the growing volume and open interest at a well-defined major support level.

Rounded Tops and Bottoms

When prices change direction over a longer time period they can create a rounded top or bottom pattern. A *rounded top* reflects a gradual change in market forces from buyers to sellers. In the stock market it is also called *distribution*. It is a clear sign that any attempt to move prices higher has been abandoned. Rounded tops often lead to faster and faster price drops as more investors liquidate their long positions or initiate shorts.

In Figure 1.29 we see two classic rounded tops in the German DAX stock index. The first is an example of gathering downside momentum as more investors become aware of the decline. Prices drop faster after a break of the double bottom. The rounded top offers a rare opportunity to accumulate a short position with relatively low volatility.

Rounded Bottom A rounded bottom, similar to a rounded top, is an extended formation where prices gradually turn from down to up. In Figure 1.30 we see a rounded bottom in the Japanese yen followed by a breakaway gap. Similar to the extended rectangle, the rounded bottom offers traders an opportunity to accumulate a large long position. In this case, the sharp rally as prices move through the high of the rounded bottom, followed by a runaway gap, clearly marks the end of

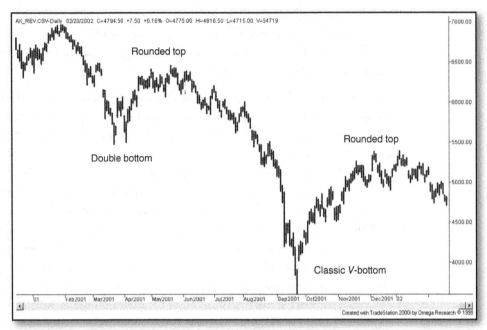

FIGURE 1.29 Two Rounded Tops in the German DAX Stock Index.

the rounded bottom. The breakout can be interpreted as a change in the supply and demand balance. A breakout, whether in stocks or futures, indicates that something new has entered the picture.

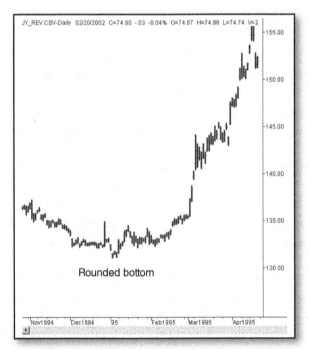

FIGURE 1.30 A Classic Rounded Bottom in the Japanese Yen.

Wedge Top and Bottom Patterns

We have seen a wedge formation as a continuation pattern in Figure 1.20, but a large ascending wedge can mark the top of a move and a large descending wedge the bottom. The dominant characteristic of the wedge is that volatility is declining towards the end. In Figure 1.31 there is a declining wedge in the Japanese yen. Volatility compresses until a breakout is inevitable. If the breakout had been to the downside, this wedge would have been interpreted as a continuation pattern. In this example, a breakout in the opposite direction is a strong indicator of a major reversal.

Head-and-Shoulders Formation

The classic top and bottom formation is the *head and shoulders,* accepted as a major reversal indicator. This pattern, well known to chartists, appears as a left shoulder, a head, and a right shoulder, seen in Figure 1.32. The head-and-shoulders top is developed with the following five characteristics:

1. A strong upward breakout reaching new highs on increasing volume. The pattern appears to be the continuation of a long-term bull move.
2. A consolidation area formed with declining volume. This can look much like a descending flag predicting an upwards breakout, or a descending triangle indicating a downwards breakout.
3. Another upwards breakout on continued reduced volume forms the head. This is the key point of the formation. The new high is not confirmed by increased volume, and prices drop quickly.

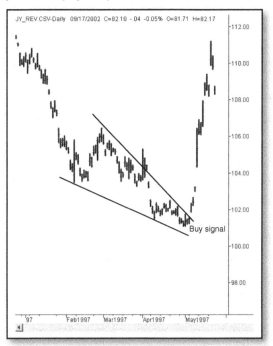

FIGURE 1.31   A Large Declining Wedge Followed by an Upside Breakout in the Japanese Yen.

FIGURE 1.32   Head-and-Shoulders Top Pattern in the Japanese Nikkei Index.

4. Another descending flag or triangle is formed on further reduced volume, followed by a minor breakout without increased volume. This last move forms the right shoulder and is the third attempt at new highs for the move.
5. The lowest points of the two flags, pennants, or triangles become the *neckline* of the formation. A short sale is indicated when this neckline is broken.

Trading Rules for Head and Shoulders   There are three approaches to trading a head-and-shoulders top formation involving increasing degrees of anticipation:

1. *Wait for a confirmation.*
   a. Sell when the final dip of the right shoulder penetrates the neckline. This represents the completion of the head-and-shoulders formation. Place a stop-loss just above the entry if the trade is to be held only for a fast profit, or place the stop-loss above the right shoulder or above the head in order to liquidate on new strength, allowing a longer holding period.
   b. Sell on the first rally after the neckline is broken. (Although more conservative, the lost opportunities may outweigh the improved entry prices.) Use the same stops as in Step la.
2. *Anticipation of the final shoulder.*
   a. Sell when the right shoulder is being formed. A likely place would be when prices have retraced their way half the distance to the head. A stop-loss can be placed above the top of the head.

b. Wait until the top of the right shoulder is formed and prices appear to be declining. Sell and place a stop either above the high of the right shoulder or above the high of the head.

Both steps 2a and 2b allow positions to be taken well in advance of the neckline penetration with logical stop-loss points. Using the high of the head for a protective stop is considered a conservative approach because it allows the integrity of the pattern to be tested before the position is exited.

3. *Early anticipation of the head.*

Sell when the right part of the head is forming, on the downwards price move, with a stop-loss at about the high of the move. Although this represents a small risk, it has less chance of success. This approach is for traders who prefer to anticipate tops and are willing to suffer frequent small losses to do it. Even if the current prices become the head of the formation, there may be numerous small corrections that will look like the market top to an anxious seller.

Volume was a recognized part of the classic definition of the head-and-shoulders formation and appeared in Robert D. Edwards and John Magee's *Technical Analysis of Stock Trends,* published in 1948. This is no longer considered as important. There are many examples of successful head-and-shoulders formations that do not satisfy the volume criterion. Nevertheless, declining volume on the head or the right shoulder of a top formation must be seen as a strong confirmation of a failing upwards move, and is consistent with the normal interpretation of volume.

▪ Episodic Patterns

There is little argument that all prices change quickly in response to unexpected news. The transition from one major level to another is termed an *episodic pattern*; when these transitions are violent, they are called *price shocks.* Until the late 1990s, there were very few price shocks in the stock market, the greatest being the one resulting from the terrorist attacks of September 11, 2001. Otherwise, price shocks can be caused by a surprising election result, the unexpected raising of interest rates by the Federal Reserve, the devaluation of a currency by an important Third World nation, sudden crop loss or natural disaster, or an assassination (or what we now call a *geopolitical event*). While price shocks are most common in futures markets, all markets are continually adjusting to new price levels, and all experience occasional surprises. Each news article, government economic release, or earnings report can be considered a mini-shock. A common price shock occurs when a pharmaceutical company's application for a new drug is unexpectedly rejected by the U.S. Department of Agriculture (USDA).

The pattern that results from episodic movement is exactly what one might expect. Following the sharp price movement, there is a period when volatility declines from its highs, narrowing until a normal volatility level is found and remaining at that level. In the Raytheon reaction to 9/11, the upwards price shock, shown in Figure 1.33 is followed by a volatile, unstable few days and then a steady decline in volatility as some level of equilibrium is found. The Raytheon price reacted opposite to most

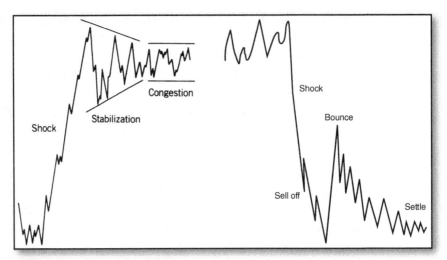

FIGURE 1.33 Episodic Pattern Shown in an Upward Price Shock in Raytheon Following 9/11/2001.

other stocks because it is a defense contractor, and a terrorist attack implies an increased amount of business from the government.

Unless the news that caused the price shock was an error, in which case prices immediately move back to levels prior to the news, prices will settle in a new trading range near the extreme highs or lows. It will take time for the market to absorb the consequences of the news, and many traders will find the risk too high to participate.

Price shocks have become the focus of much analytic work. Because a price shock is an unpredictable event, it cannot be forecast. This has a critical effect on the way in which systems are developed, especially with regard to the testing procedures. We understand at the time of the price shock that the event was entirely unexpected. However, years later, when the same prices are analyzed using a computer program, you might find that a trend or charting pattern *predicted* this move. The analysis records the profits as though they were predictable and you are now basing your conclusions on a false premise.

■ Price Objectives for Bar Charting

Most traders set price objectives and use them to assess the risk and reward of a potential trade. Objectives are most reasonable for short-term trading and successful objectives are based on straightforward concepts and not complex calculations. There is also a noticeable similarity between the price objectives for different chart patterns.

The simplest and most logical price objective is a major support or resistance level established by previous trading. When entering a long position, look at the most well-defined resistance levels above the entry point. These have been discussed in previous sections of this chapter. When those prior levels are tested, there is generally a technical adjustment or a reversal. The more well-established the support or resistance level, the more likely prices will stop. In the case of a strong upwards move, volatility often causes a small penetration before the setback occurs. A penetration of support or resistance, followed by a return to the previous trading range is considered a confirmation of the old range and a false breakout. Placing the price objective for a long position below the identifiable major resistance level will always be safe. The downside objective can be identified in a similar manner: Find the major support level and exit just above it.

When trading with chart patterns, it pays to be flexible. Regardless of which method you use to identify a profit target, be prepared to take profits sooner if the market changes. For example, you have entered a long in IBM at $160 and set your profit objective at $200. Prices move as predicted and reach $195 when volume starts to drop and the price pattern seems to move sideways. An experienced trader will say "close enough" and take the profit. Profit objectives are not perfect, only good guidelines. If you have set a single price target for a long position, and it falls slightly above a resistance level, then the lower resistance level should be used as the price objective.

Rather than rely on a single point, traders will fan out their target points around the most likely objective, dividing their goal into three or five levels. As each profit-target is reached the risk of the current trade is reduced as is the likelihood of turning a profit into a loss.

While waiting for prices to reach the objective, remember to watch for a violation of the current trend; trend changes take priority over profit objectives. If the trade is successful, and the goal is reached as expected, watch for a new pattern. If prices decline after the trade is closed out, then reverse and break through the previous highs or lows, the position may be reentered on the breakout and a new price objective calculated.

Common Elements of Profit Objectives

Most chart formations have a price objective associated with them. The common ground for all of them is volatility. Each chart pattern is larger or smaller because of the current price volatility; therefore, the price targets derived from these formations are also based on volatility. In general, the price objective reflects the same volatility as the chart formation and is measured from the point where prices break out of the pattern.

Profit Targets for Consolidation Areas and Channels

The most basic of all formations is the horizontal consolidation area, bounded on the top and bottom by a horizontal resistance and support lines. There are two possible profit targets, shown in Figure 1.34.

1. For any *horizontal consolidation pattern,* the target is above the breakout of the resistance line at a point equal to the height of the consolidation area (the resistance level minus the support level added to the resistance level). That makes the expected move equal to the extreme volatility of the consolidation area.
2. With *extended rectangular formations,* the upwards profit target is calculated as the width of the consolidation pattern added to the support level.

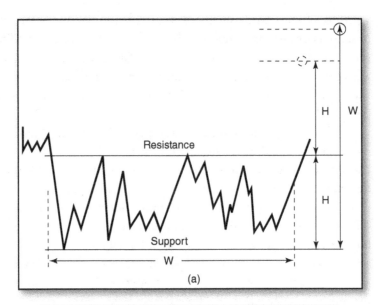

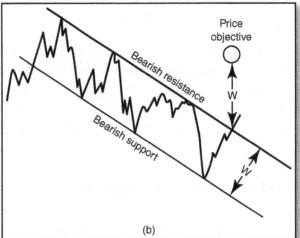

FIGURE 1.34 Price Objectives for Consolidation Patterns and Channels. (a) Two objectives for consolidation patterns. (b) Price objective for a channel.

Although price objective (2) is a well-known and popular calculation, it is unrealistic when the extended formation is very prolonged. The standard calculation, given in (1), is more reasonable. A third objective is more conservative but even more practical:

3. Use the average volatility of the consolidation formation, or reduce the target in (1) above by 20% to remove the extremes from influencing the objectives. A closer price target will be reached more often.

The price objective for a channel is the same as the traditional objective for a horizontal consolidation pattern. Because the channel is at an angle, it is necessary to measure the width of the channel as perpendicular to the angled support and resistance channel lines; then project that width upwards from the point of breakout. The length of the channel does not change the profit target. Again, you may want to make the target slightly smaller than the original channel.

Changing Price Objectives Using Channels Price objectives can be found as trends change and new channels are formed. Figure 1.35 shows the change from an upwards to a downwards trend. Once a breakout of an upwards channel has occurred (marked "First point of reversal"), we wait until the low is reached at *a*, followed by the reaction back up to *b*. A resistance line, 1*R*, can be drawn from the prior high *h* to the top of the latest move *b*. A line, 1*S*, can be constructed parallel to 1*R* passing through point *a*, forming the initial downward channel. Price objective 1 is on line 1*S* of the new channel and is used once the top at point *b* is determined. Price objective 1 cannot be expected to be too precise due to the early development of the channel. If prices continue to point *c* and then rally to *d*, a more reasonable channel can now be defined using trendlines 2*R* and 2*S*. The support line will again become the point where the new price objective is placed. The upper and lower trendlines can be further refined as the new high and low reactions occur. The primary trendline is always drawn first; then the new price objective becomes a point on the parallel trendline.

Targeting Profits after Tops and Bottoms

Because profit targets are based on the volatility of the underlying pattern, the profit targets for all top and bottom formations will seem very much the same. Looking back at Figure 1.27, natural gas, there is a triple top formation. Between each top is a reversal marking an important support level. The first pullback after the island reversal brought prices to 8.20, followed by a test of the top that formed the second peak. The second retracement stopped at 9.00 and was followed by the third peak. When prices finally drop through the highest support level at 9.00, we can treat it as a breakout and sell short.

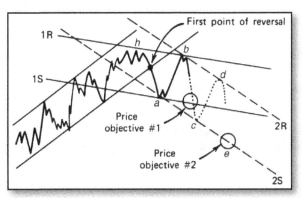

FIGURE 1.35 Forming New Channels to Determine Objectives.

If this chart showed a double top, then the point where prices fall below the support between two tops *confirms the top*. Breaking this support level indicates that the topping formation is completed. But this was not a double top; therefore, we can take the lower of the two support levels between the three tops as the major confirmation of the pattern. In the natural gas chart, the lower support was at 8.20. Using either support level gives a measurement of the triple top pattern based on the volatility of prices.

Calculating the Profit Target for a Top Formation

The profit target is found by measuring the height of the top formation and projecting it downwards from the point where the top is confirmed, that is, the break of the support level. For this example, profit targets will be calculated based on each of the support levels. The highest price of the move is 10.75. Let's examine two profit targets:

1. Using the support level of 9.00, the height of the top is 10.75 – 9.00, or 1.75. Projecting that downwards from the breakout point of 9.00 gives a profit objective of 7.25. The first major pause in the price drop stopped at about 7.00, still showing high volatility.
2. Based on the second support level of 8.20, the height of the top is 2.65, and the profit objective, measured from the break at 8.20, is 5.55. Prices reach 5.55, but only after stalling at about 6.50.

The first target is very achievable and realistic. Prices are very volatile, and a drop of 1.75 could occur very quickly. The second target is less realistic. When targeting a much larger decline, and beginning at a much lower point, it is unrealistic to expect volatility to continue at the same high level. In the decline of natural gas from January through March, volatility also declines, so that by March it appears as though the move is over. Although price targets can often be correct, those that are far away will be less reliable.

Profit Targets after a Bottom Formation   The same principle can be applied to calculate the profit target for bottom formations. The distance from the lowest price of the bottom to the confirmation point is projected upwards from the breakout. This method can be applied to any type of bottom formation. In Figure 1.26, the double bottom in Cisco spanned the price range from about 5.00 to 6.25. The volatility of the bottom pattern, 1.25, is projected upwards from the breakout at 6.25 to get the target of 7.50. Because volatility should expand as prices rise, the exact volatility calculation can be used as a conservative measure.

The Head-and-Shoulders Price Objective   In keeping with other price targets, the head-and-shoulders top has a downside objective, which is also based on its volatility. This objective is measured from the point where the right shoulder penetrates the neckline and is equal to the distance from the top of the head to the neckline (Figure 1.36). For a major top, this goal seems modest, but it will be a good measure of the initial reaction and is generally safe, even if a new high price is reached later.

A very similar example can be found in the Japanese yen (Figure 1.30). The neckline also angles up and to the right, and the price target finds the bottom of the first

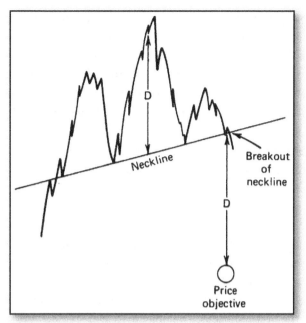

FIGURE 1.36 Head-and-Shoulders Top Price Objective.

major support level following the break of the right shoulder. The position of the price objective is so significant that the subsequent drop in prices creates a breakaway gap.

Triangles and Flags *Triangles* and *flags* have objectives based on volatility in a manner consistent with other patterns. The triangle objective is equal in size to the initial reaction, which formed the largest end of the triangle (Figure 1.37a). It may also be viewed as a developing channel rather than a triangle, with the ascending leg of the triangle forming the primary bullish trendline. The price objective then becomes the same as those used for channels.

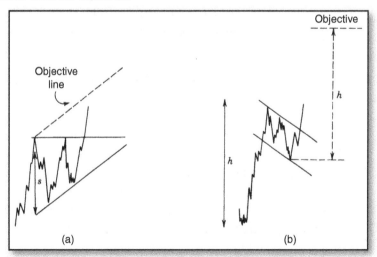

FIGURE 1.37 Triangle and Flag Objectives. (a) Triangle objective is based on the width of the initial sides. (b) Flag objective is equal to the move prior to the flag formation.

The flag is assumed to occur midway in a price move; therefore, the objective of a new breakout must be equal to the size of the move preceding the flag (Figure 1.37b). Recalling the comments on the problems associated with the decreasing volatility of the triangular formation, the use of the first reaction as a measure of volatility is a safe way to avoid problems. Using this technique with subsequent flags in a bull move will cause objectives to move farther away, becoming unrealistic.

The Rule of Seven   Another measurement of price objectives, the *Rule of Seven*, is credited to Arthur Sklarew.[17] It is based on the volatility of the prior consolidation formation and computes three successive price objectives in proportion to one another. The Rule of Seven is not symmetric for both uptrends and downtrends. Sklarew believes that, after the initial leg of a move, the downtrend reactions are closer together than the reactions in a rising market. Because the downside of a major bear market is limited, it is usually characterized by consolidation. Major bull markets tend to expand as they develop.

To calculate the objectives using the Rule of Seven, first measure the length L of the initial leg of a price move (from the previous high or low, the most extreme point before the first pullback). The objectives are:

1. In an *uptrend*:
   Upwards objective 1 = prior low + $(L \times 7/4)$
   Upwards objective 2 = prior low + $(L \times 7/3)$
   Upwards objective 3 = prior low + $(L \times 7/2)$
2. In a *downtrend*:
   Downwards objective 1 = prior high − $(L \times 7/5)$
   Downwards objective 2 = prior high − $(L \times 7/4)$
   Downwards objective 3 = prior high − $(L \times 7/3)$

The three objectives apply most clearly to major moves. During minor price swings, it is likely that the first two objectives will be bypassed. In Sklarew's experience, regardless of whether any one objective is missed, the others still remain intact.

■ Implied Strategies in Candlestick Charts

For a technique that is reported to have been used as early as the mid-1600s, Japanese candle charts were slow to find their way into the western method of analysis. Candle charts can be related to bar charts but offer additional visual interpretation. The *candles* are created simply by *shading* the piece of the bar between the opening and closing prices: white if the close is higher than the open and black if the close is lower than the open. The shaded area is called the *body* and the extended lines above and below the body are the *shadows*. With this simple change, we get an entirely new way of looking at and interpreting charts. The patterns become much clearer than the Western style of line chart.

---

[17] Arthur Sklarew, *Techniques of a Professional Chart Analyst* (Commodity Research Bureau, 1980).

Although many candlestick patterns have equivalent bar chart formations, there is an implied strategy in many of them. The following summary uses the traditional candlestick names representing the significance of the formation (see Figure 1.38):

■ *Doji,* in which the opening and closing prices are the same. This represents indecision, a temporary balancing point. It is neither bullish nor bearish. A *double doji,* where two dojis occur successively, implies that a significant breakout will follow.

■ *Engulfing patterns* seem at first to be the same as outside days in bar charting, but the pattern only refers to the part of the bar between the opening and closing prices. Engulfing patterns are considered exceptionally strong signals of price change. A *bullish engulfing pattern* has a black candle followed by a white, indicating a wide range with a higher close. The *bearish engulfing pattern* is white followed by black, showing a lower close on the engulfing day.

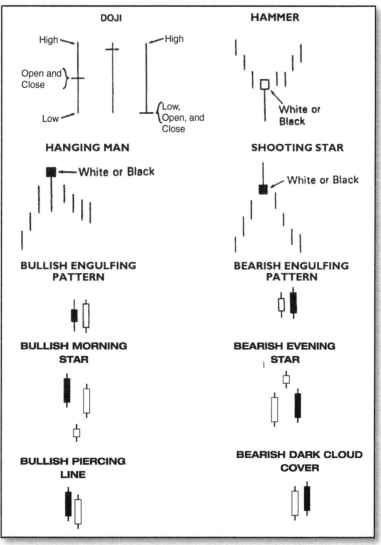

FIGURE 1.38 Popular Candle Formations.

- *Morning star* and *evening star* are 3-day patterns that show a similarity to an island reversal, but are more specific. In the morning star, a bullish reversal pattern, the first day has a lower close than the open, the second day (called the *star*, similar to the island bottom) has a higher close, and the final reversal day has an even higher close. The bearish reversal is just the opposite, with two higher closes followed by a reversal day with a lower close. If the star is also a doji, then the pattern has more significance.

- *Piercing line* and *dark cloud cover* are bullish and bearish reversals. The piercing line, a bullish reversal, begins with a black candle (a lower close) and is followed by a white candle in which the open is below the previous day's low and the close is above the midpoint of the previous day's body (the open-close range). The dark cloud cover is a bearish formation, the opposite of the piercing line.

- *Hammer*, a bullish reversal signal, showing the bottom of a swing, where the body is at the top of the candle, indicating an upwards change of direction, and the shadow is below the body. The body may be black or white.

- *Hanging man*, a bearish reversal pattern where the body of the candle represents the high of a swing, and the shadow lies below in the direction of the reversal. The body may be black or white.

- *Shooting star*, a bearish signal, also occurs at the top of a swing and has its body at the bottom of the candle with the shadow above. The body may be black or white.

Although these patterns are similar to Western bar chart formations, none of them are exactly the same. The hammer, hanging man, and shooting star are reversal patterns but can only be compared to the simple pivot point where the middle day is higher or lower than the bars on either side. None of these candle formations is exactly the same as a key reversal day or island reversal. The engulfing pattern is stronger than the typical outside day because the spanning of the prior day's range must be done only by the current day's open-close range.

The analysis of candle charts is a skill involving the understanding of many complex and interrelated patterns. For full coverage, Steve Nison's, *Japanese Candlestick Charting Techniques,* second edition, is recommended, as well as a selection of newer books, which can be found on Amazon.

Quantifying Candle Formations

The preciseness of the candle formations allow some patterns to be tested. The popular engulfing patterns can be defined exactly for a computer program as

> Bullish engulfing pattern = Previous open > previous close and today's
> open < previous close and today's close > previous open

> Bearish engulfing pattern = Previous close > previous open and today's
> open > previous close and today's close < previous open

Another technique uses the shadows as confirmation of direction. We can interpret an increase in the size of the upper shadows as strengthening resistance (prices are closing lower each day); an increase in the size of the lower shadows represents more support. One way to look at this is by defining

Upper shadow (white) = high − close   Lower shadow (white) = open − low
Upper shadow (black) = high − open   Lower shadow (black) = close − low

The sequences of upper and lower shadows can be smoothed separately using a moving average to find out whether they are rising or falling.[18]

A method for determining whether black or white candles dominate recent price movement is to use only the body of the candle, $B = close - open$, and apply a momentum calculation:

$$Body\ momentum = \frac{B_{up}}{B_{up} + B_{down}}$$

where B_{up} = the sum of the days where $B > 0$ (body is white)
B_{down} = the sum of the days where $B < 0$ (body is black)
14 = the recommended number of days

When the body momentum is greater than 70, the whites dominate; when the value is below 20 the blacks dominate. These thresholds indicate a built-in upwards bias.

Morning Star and Evening Star   Two formations that are easily programmed are the *morning star* (a bullish signal) and *evening star* (a bearish signal). Using the morning star as an example, the rules call for a long downward (black) candle followed by a lower (the open of the next bar less than the close of the previous long bar), less volatile white candle, and finally an upward thrust shown as a gap up body with the close higher than the open (another white candle).

When programmed (see *TSM Morning Star* and *TSM Evening Star* in the Companion Website), there are very few signals when we put restriction on the size of the bodies of the three days. Instead, we only required that the body of the first day be greater than the 20-day average, the second day less, and the third day greater. While there are still only a modest number of trades, the S&P performs well on the day following both patterns.

Qstick

As a way of quantifying the Candle formations, Tuschar Chande[19] created *Qstick*, a moving average of the body of the candle. It is intended to be an aid interpreting the charts but has simple trading rules as well.

$$If\ Body_t = Close_t - Open_t$$

and

$Q_t = average(period1, body)$, where *period1* is suggested as 8 days
$AvgQ_t = average(period2, Q)$, where *period2* is also 8 days

---

[18] Both "shadow trends" and "body momentum" are adapted from Tushar Chande and Stanley Kroll, *The New Technical Trader* (New York: John Wiley & Sons, 1994).

[19] Tushar Chande and Stanley Kroll, *The New Technical Trader* (New York: John Wiley & Sons, 1994).

Then the trading rules are

Buy when Q_t moves above $AvgQ_t$

Sell when Q_t moves below $AvgQ_t$

Pivot Points and Candle Charts

John L. Person suggests that the strategies inherent in candle formations can be combined with support and resistance levels derived from pivot points.[20] He uses the following calculations:

1. Pivot point, $P = (high + low + close)/3$
2. First resistance level, $R1 = (P \times 2) - low$
3. Second resistance level, $R2 = P + high - low$
4. First support level, $S1 = (P + 2) - high$
5. Second support level, $S2 = P - high + low$

Once a key formation for a top or bottom is recognized using candle charts, support and resistance levels calculated based on pivot points can be a strong indication of the extent of the following price move. Person used Dow futures to support his study.

The Best of the Candles

Bulkowski has summarized his own research in the success of various candles[21] as

- The best-performing candles had closing prices within $\frac{1}{3}$ of the bar low, followed by the middle and high, respectively.

- Candle patterns in a bear market outperform other markets, regardless of the breakout direction.

- Most candles perform best on days with higher volume.

- Candles with unusually long wicks outperform.

- Unusually tall candles outperform.

■ Practical Use of the Bar Chart

Trends Are Easier to See in Retrospect

As important as it is to identify the direction of price movement, it is much easier to see the trend afterward than at the moment it is needed. There is no doubt that all stocks and futures markets have short-term swings and longer-term bull and bear markets. Unfortunately, at the time you are ready to trade, it is not going to be clear

---

[20] John L. Person, "Pivot Points and Candles," *Futures* (February 2003).

[21] Thomas Bulkowski, "What You Don't Know About Candlesticks," *Technical Analysis of Stocks & Commodities* (March 2011).

whether the current price trend is a short-term pattern that is about to change or long-term persistent trend experiencing a temporary reversal.

The ease of seeing charts on a screen has made the past patterns clear. It seems natural to expect prices to trend in the future as clearly as they appear on a chart; however, it is not easy to do it in a timely fashion. The eye has a remarkable way of simplifying the chart patterns. The purpose of drawing a trendline is to recognize the direction even though prices can swing violently up and down during that trending interval. A new trend signal to buy or sell always occurs as the trend is changing; therefore, it is at the point of greatest uncertainty.

Success in systematic trading, whether using charts or mathematics, relies on consistency. In the long run, it comes down to probabilities. Success can be achieved by recognizing the trend in 60% of the cases. In a typical trend-following system, because individual profits are much larger than losses, it is only necessary to be correct 30% or 35% of the time.

Long-Term Trends Are More Reliable than Short-Term Trends

Charting is not precise, and the construction of the trendlines, other geometric formations, and their interpretation can be performed with some liberties. When using the simplest trendline analysis, it often happens that there is a small penetration of the channel or trendline followed by a movement back into the channel. Some think that this inaccuracy with respect to the rules makes charting useless; however, many experienced analysts interpret this action as confirmation of the trend. The trendline is not redrawn so that the penetration becomes the new high or low of the trend; it is left in its original position.

We must always step back and look for the underlying purpose in each method of analysis, whether interpretive or fully systematic. The trendline is an attempt to identify the direction of prices over some time period. Chartists can use a simple straight line to visualize the direction; they draw the uptrend by connecting the lowest prices in a rising market, even though each point used may represent varying levels of volatility and unique conditions. The chance of these points aligning perfectly, or forecasting the exact price support level, is small. A trendline is simply a guide; it may be too conservative at one time and too aggressive at another; and you won't know until after the trade is completed. Applied rigorously, charting rules should produce many incorrect signals but be profitable in the most important cases. The challenge of the chartist is to interpret the pattern of prices in context with the bigger picture.

Many price moves are called trends, but the most important and sustained trends are those resulting from government policy, in particular those that affect interest rates. Therefore, the most reliable trends are long-term phenomena because government policy develops slowly and is often long-term. During a period of recession, as we saw in 2001 and 2002, the Federal Reserve continued to lower interest rates incrementally, causing a major bull market in all fixed-income maturities. It is easiest to see this trend by looking at a weekly chart of the 10-year Treasury note, rather than an intraday, 1-hour chart. The more detail there is, the more difficult it is to see the long-term trend. Following the subprime collapse of 2008, the Fed and other central banks decided to lower rates to the absolute minimum and keep them there as long as necessary to stimulate the economy. Ultimately, this will result in a protracted bull market in both stocks and commodities.

The average daily impact of the long-term trend on prices is very small. For example, if yields were to drop a staggering 2% in one year, a rise of approximately 16 full points in price, the net effect each day would be a change of .064%, or $\frac{2}{32}$ in price. If prices move nearly one full point, $\frac{2}{32}$ or 1%, each day, that upwards bias would be overwhelmed by the daily market noise. It would be difficult to draw a trendline on a daily price chart until prices had drifted higher for a few months. Using a weekly chart removes much of this noise and makes the trend easier to see.

Multiple Signals

Some of the impreciseness of charting can be offset with confirming signals. A simultaneous breakout of a short-term trendline and a long-term trendline is a much stronger signal than either one occurring at different times. The break of a head-and-shoulders neckline that corresponds to a previous channel support line is likely to receive much attention. Whenever there are multiple signals converging at, or near, a single price, whether based on moving averages, Gann lines, cycles, or phases of the moon, that point gains significance. In chart analysis, the occurrence of multiple signals at one point can compensate for the quality of the interpretation.

Pattern Failures

The failure to adhere to a pattern is equally as important as the continuation of that pattern. Although a trader might anticipate a reversal as prices near a major support line, a break of that trendline is significant in continuing the downward move. A failure to stop at the support line should result in setting short positions and abandoning plans for higher prices.

A head-and-shoulders formation that breaks the neckline, declines for a day or two, then reverses and moves above the neckline is another pattern failure. *Postpattern activity* must confirm the pattern. Failure to do so means that the market refused to follow through; therefore, it should be traded in the opposite direction. This is not a case of identifying the wrong pattern; instead, price action actively opposed the completion of the pattern. Wyckoff calls this "effort and results," referring to the effort expended by the market to produce a pattern that explains the price direction. If this pattern is not followed by results that confirm the effort, the opposite position is the best option.

Change of Character Thompson[22] discusses the completion of a pattern or price trend by identifying a *change of character* in the movement. As a trend develops, the reactions, or pullbacks, tend to become smaller. Traders looking to enter the trend wait for reactions to place their orders; as the move becomes more obvious, these reactions get smaller, and the increments of trend movement become larger. When the reaction

---

[22] Jesse H. Thompson, "What Textbooks Never Tell You," *Technical Analysis of Stocks & Commodities* (November/December 1983).

suddenly is larger, the move is ending; the change in the character of the move signals a prudent exit, even if prices continue erratically in the direction of the trend.

A similar example occurs in the way that prices react to economic reports or government action. The first time the Federal Reserve acts to raise rates after a prolonged decline, the market is not prepared, and interest rate prices react sharply lower. Before the next meeting of the Fed, the market may be more apprehensive, but is likely to be neutral with regard to expectation of policy. However, once there is a pattern of increasing rates following signs of inflation, the market begins to anticipate the action of the Fed. A sharp move in the opposite direction occurs when the government fails to take the expected action.

Bull and Bear Traps   While it is not much of a consolation to those who have gotten caught, a failed downside breakout is called a *bear trap,* and a failed upwards breakout is a *bull trap.* A bear trap occurs when prices fall below a clear support line, generating sell signals. After a few days, prices move back above the support line, often accelerating upwards. A bull trap is a failed breakout of a resistance level. In both cases, prices appear to be continuing in the trend direction, but the final picture is a reversal. Although there is no advice on how to avoid bull and bear traps, the failed reversal should be recognized as soon as possible and the position should be reversed. Bull and bear traps often precede significant price reversals.

As with other top and bottom patterns, a confirmation of the bear trap is complete when prices move above the next higher resistance level. In the case of a failed flag formation in a downward trend, prices break lower, as expected, then reverse. The confirmation occurs when prices move above the top of the failed flag pattern. The same principle would be true of other failed chart formations; the failure is confirmed when prices retrace the entire pattern.[23]

Testing Your Skill

Recognizing a pattern is both an art and science. Not everyone has an eye for patterns; others see formations where no one else does. The first decision may be the most important: How much of the chart do you use? It is perfectly normal for different time intervals to show different trends. In some cases, arbitrarily cutting the chart at some previous date might cause a clear trend to disappear. The price scale (the vertical axis) of the chart is another variable not considered by some chartists. When applying methods requiring specific angles, the chart paper is expected to have square boxes. Because of the shape of the box, the formations may appear different from one piece of chart paper, or computer screen, to another.

The timeliness of the pattern identification is the most serious problem. Can the formation be interpreted in time to act on a breakout, or is the pattern only seen afterwards? At different stages of development, the lines may appear to form different

---

[23] See Christopher Narcouzi, "Winning with Failures," *Technical Analysis of Stocks & Commodities* (November 2001).

patterns. Before using your charting skills to trade, practice simulating the day-to-day development of prices using the following steps:

1. Hold a piece of the paper over the right side of the chart, covering the most recent months, or better still, have someone else give you the partial chart.
2. Analyze the formations.
3. Determine what action will be based on your interpretation. Be specific.
4. Move the paper one day to the right, or have someone else give you the next day's price.
5. Record any orders that would have been filled based on the prior day's analysis. Don't cheat.
6. Determine whether the new day's price would have altered your interpretation and trade.
7. Return to Step 3 until finished.

This simple exercise might save a lot of money but may be discouraging. With practice you will become better at finding and using formations and will learn to select the ones that work best. Very few traders base their trading decisions entirely on bar charts. Many refer to charts for confirmation of separate technical or fundamental analysis; others use only the most obvious major trendlines, looking for points at which multiple indicators converge. The general acceptance of bar charting analysis makes it a lasting tool.

■ Evolution in Price Patterns

A change has occurred in the stock market because of the S&P 500 index, SPDRs, and other index markets. If you think that stock prices are about to fall because of a pending interest rate announcement by the Fed, you can protect your portfolio by selling an equivalent amount of S&P futures. Afterwards, when you have decided that prices have stabilized, you can lift your hedge and profit from rising prices. It is an easy and inexpensive way to achieve portfolio insurance. You can also speculate in the S&P, NASDAQ, Dow, or sectors, rather than trade individual stocks.

When institutions and traders buy or sell large quantities of S&P futures, the futures price will drift away from the S&P cash index, which represents the weighted average of the actual component stock prices. *Program trading* is the process that keeps the price of futures and ETFs aligned with the cash price of the stocks that comprise those index markets. If you have enough capital, and the difference between the S&P futures price and the S&P cash index is sufficiently large, with the futures higher than the cash, you can sell the S&P futures and buy all of the stocks in the S&P 500 cash index. It is a classic arbitrage that brings prices back together. It is all done electronically in seconds.

But the ability to buy or sell all the stocks in the S&P at the same time has changed the patterns of individual stocks that are part of the S&P index. While at one time these stocks moved largely due to their own fundamentals, they now all move together. It no longer matters that IBM is fundamentally stronger than GE, or that Xerox is at a resistance level and Ford is at support, or even if a company is under investigation. When you buy the S&P futures, you buy all of the stocks at the same time.

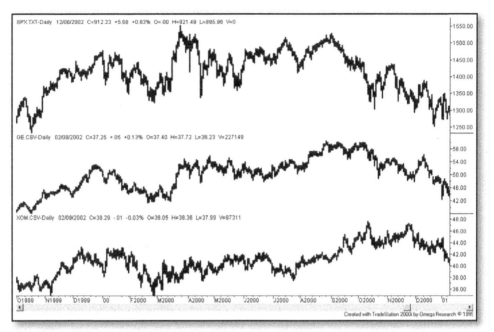

FIGURE 1.39 Similar Patterns in the S&P, GE, and Exxon.

Today's technical trader must keep one eye on the individual stock and the other eye on the index. Apple may have moved above its recent resistance level but stopped because the S&P Index is at its own resistance level, and there are more traders watching the S&P than even Apple. In today's market, you can anticipate when a stock will find support and resistance by looking at the S&P chart rather than at the individual stock chart.

Figure 1.39 shows the S&P 500 index, GE, and Exxon (prior to its collapse) over the same period from October 1999 through December 2000. Fundamentally, these three markets have little in common; however, the overall pattern of the three markets is remarkably similar, with most tops and bottoms occurring at nearly the same time. Because it is unlikely that the fundamentals of each company would result in such a similar price pattern, we can conclude that the S&P futures, combined with program trading, forces the patterns to be materially the same. This change in the way stocks are traded reduces the ability to get diversification by trading across sectors and increases risk.

Globalization: The Similarity of Asian Markets

There has been a noticeable and justifiable shift to Asian markets during the past five years. Their economies are booming while the United States and Europe are still trying to recover from the financial crisis. Although not all of the Asian stock markets are open to foreign investors, globalization has not passed them by. Figure 1.40 shows the equity index markets for Hong Kong (HSI), Singapore (SSG), Taiwan (STW), the Philippines (PHI), and Malaysia (KLI) as downloaded from Bloomberg. The patterns seem similar but the price levels are very different, making a comparison difficult.

By volatility-adjusting each price series and starting each at 100 on the first date (January 1, 2005), the five series look remarkably same, as shown in Figure 1.41.

FIGURE 1.40 Equity Index Prices for Five Asian Countries.
Data from Bloomberg.

It is understandable that, as trading partners, these countries are somewhat dependent upon one another, yet the similarity is surprisingly close. One possible explanation would be the traders. If traders believe that a poor economic sign in one country means that others will also share in bad times, then they sell the equity index markets, or individual stocks, in each country. That would be similar to Hewlett-Packard announcing worse than expected earnings and having traders sell Dell expecting the same. Often the closer relationships caused by traders show that the movement of money is more important than the fundamentals. This was clearly the case for the subprime collapse in September 2008, when all markets moved the same way as investors withdrew their funds as quickly as possible.

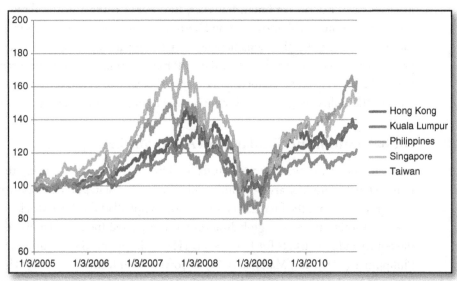

FIGURE 1.41 Asian Equity Index Markets Adjusted to the Same Volatility Level and Started at the Value 100.
Data from Bloomberg.

CHAPTER 2

Moving Averages

From Charles D. Kirkpatrick II and Julie R. Dahlquist, *Technical Analysis: The Complete Resource for Financial Market Technicians*, 3rd Edition (Old Tappan, New Jersey: Pearson Education, Inc., 2016), Chapter 14.

Learning Objective Statements

- Describe how moving averages are used to identify trends
- Describe the different ways to calculate various moving averages
- Explain the concept of directional movement
- Compare and contrast when to apply different styles of envelopes, bands, and price channels

One of the most successful methods of identifying and profiting from trends is the use of moving averages. A moving average is a constant period average, usually of prices, that is calculated for each successive chart period interval. The result, when plotted on a price chart, shows a smooth line representing the successive, average prices. Moving averages dampen the effects of short-term oscillations. Many of the most successful technical investment managers use moving averages to determine when trends are changing direction. Moving averages are especially useful in markets that have a tendency to trend.

Moving averages have been tested by academics and shown to have statistical significance. Brock, Lakonishok, and LeBaron (1992) were the first to demonstrate, using modern statistical bias-reducing methods, that moving average crossover signals have intrinsic value. As with most academic studies, the results of Brock, Lakonishok, and LeBaron's have been somewhat controversial. Even though some have since criticized their study, other researchers have validated their results. (Incidentally, the Brock, Lakonishok, and LeBaron study provides one of the more useful arguments against the Random Walk and Efficient Markets hypotheses.) Although the Brock, Lakonishok, and LeBaron study focused on the Dow Jones

Industrials, later studies have used moving average crossover systems for market data in other countries with generally the same positive results. Detry and Gregoire (2001) provided a summary of these studies.

There obviously is something to moving averages. Traders and trend investors, of course, have known all this for many years, but technical analysts now feel more comfort in what they have been doing. In this chapter, we discuss some of the moving average methods and strategies that technical analysts use, as well as introduce some variations on moving averages, such as Bollinger Bands, envelopes, and directional movement indicators.

◼ What Is a Moving Average?

The moving average is one of the oldest tools used by technical analysts. Daily fluctuations in stock prices, commodity prices, and foreign exchange rates can be large. Moving averages tone down these fluctuations—deemphasizing but sometimes distorting fluctuations. Technical analysts use moving averages to smooth erratic data, making it easier to view the true underlying trend.

The principal reason that moving averages are used is to smooth out shorter fluctuations and focus on the trend that fits with the investor's time horizon. A moving average by its nature is just one number that represents a net of certain past numbers. For example, a 20-day moving average is one number that represents all the prices for the past 20 days. As such, it filters out each one of the prices during the past 20 days and tells us how the group of 20 days, rather than its separate parts, is behaving.

◼ How Is a Simple Moving Average Calculated?

Table 2.1 contains the daily closing prices for WMT (Walmart) from November 18, 2014 through February 26, 2015. Most moving averages of prices are based on closing prices, but they can be calculated on highs, lows, daily means, or any other value as long as the price type is consistent throughout the calculations. We use closing prices.

TABLE 2.1	Price Data and Moving Average Calculations for WMT Daily Price Close Between November 18, 2014 and February 26, 2015							
Date	Open	High	Low	Close	10-Day SMA	26-Day SMA	10-Day EMA	10-Day LWMA
11/18/2014	83.50	83.92	83.34	83.79				
11/19/2014	83.96	85.64	83.92	84.99				
11/20/2014	84.80	85.29	84.04	84.58				
11/21/2014	85.34	85.44	84.58	84.65				
11/24/2014	84.85	85.61	84.77	85.40				
11/25/2014	85.42	85.51	84.39	84.95				

Date	Open	High	Low	Close	10-Day SMA	26-Day SMA	10-Day EMA	10-Day LWMA
11/26/2014	84.90	85.11	84.48	84.98				
11/28/2014	86.18	88.09	85.90	87.54				
12/1/2014	86.72	87.07	85.75	86.22				
12/2/2014	86.27	86.70	85.93	86.40	85.35		85.08	85.78
12/3/2014	85.96	86.00	84.68	84.94	85.47		85.05	85.71
12/4/2014	84.13	84.82	83.65	84.76	85.44		85.00	85.58
12/5/2014	84.90	84.90	83.51	84.12	85.40		84.84	85.34
12/8/2014	84.15	84.67	83.85	84.23	85.35		84.73	85.13
12/9/2014	83.65	84.21	82.65	83.56	85.17		84.52	84.80
12/10/2014	83.93	84.31	82.90	82.98	84.97		84.24	84.40
12/11/2014	83.18	84.50	83.16	83.83	84.86		84.16	84.19
12/12/2014	83.52	85.00	83.52	83.81	84.49		84.10	84.00
12/15/2014	84.26	84.70	83.05	83.94	84.26		84.07	83.90
12/16/2014	83.62	84.76	82.94	82.96	83.91		83.87	83.67
12/17/2014	83.28	84.26	82.95	84.23	83.84		83.93	83.73
12/18/2014	84.80	85.95	84.28	85.94	83.96		84.30	84.11
12/19/2014	86.26	86.34	85.16	85.16	84.06		84.46	84.33
12/22/2014	85.32	86.40	85.29	86.38	84.28		84.81	84.75
12/23/2014	86.69	87.08	86.36	86.66	84.59		85.14	85.18
12/24/2014	86.97	87.07	86.39	86.43	84.93	84.90	85.38	85.51
12/26/2014	86.18	87.14	86.01	86.91	85.24	85.02	85.66	85.87
12/29/2014	86.46	87.07	86.40	86.64	85.53	85.08	85.83	86.13
12/30/2014	86.52	87.13	86.48	86.79	85.81	85.17	86.01	86.36
12/31/2014	87.04	87.44	85.86	85.88	86.10	85.22	85.98	86.37
1/2/2015	86.27	86.72	85.55	85.90	86.27	85.24	85.97	86.33
1/5/2015	85.72	86.32	85.51	85.65	86.24	85.26	85.91	86.22
1/6/2015	85.98	86.75	85.79	86.31	86.36	85.31	85.98	86.23
1/7/2015	86.78	88.68	86.67	88.60	86.58	85.36	86.46	86.64
1/8/2015	89.21	90.67	89.07	90.47	86.96	85.52	87.19	87.35
1/9/2015	90.21	90.39	89.25	89.35	87.25	85.63	87.58	87.79
1/12/2015	89.36	90.31	89.22	90.02	87.56	85.83	88.02	88.29
1/13/2015	90.80	90.97	88.93	89.31	87.83	86.00	88.26	88.61
1/14/2015	87.65	88.52	86.50	86.61	87.81	86.10	87.96	88.39
1/15/2015	87.00	87.78	86.70	87.38	87.96	86.22	87.85	88.31
1/16/2015	87.20	87.46	86.23	86.77	88.05	86.34	87.66	88.09
1/20/2015	86.82	87.70	85.55	86.69	88.15	86.49	87.48	87.84
1/21/2015	86.10	86.91	85.71	86.64	88.18	86.59	87.33	87.57
1/22/2015	87.23	88.40	86.86	88.30	88.15	86.77	87.50	87.59
1/23/2015	88.42	89.26	87.89	88.51	87.96	86.94	87.69	87.66
1/26/2015	88.31	89.16	88.12	88.63	87.89	87.16	87.86	87.78

(continued)

TABLE 2.1 *(Continued)*

Date	Open	High	Low	Close	10-Day SMA	26-Day SMA	10-Day EMA	10-Day LWMA
1/27/2015	88.28	88.46	87.26	87.53	87.64	87.29	87.80	87.71
1/28/2015	88.02	88.23	86.77	86.82	87.39	87.32	87.62	87.56
1/29/2015	87.07	87.72	86.27	87.72	87.50	87.42	87.64	87.62
1/30/2015	86.66	87.36	84.90	84.98	87.26	87.37	87.16	87.17
2/2/2015	84.79	85.87	83.93	85.71	87.15	87.33	86.89	86.88
2/3/2015	85.83	86.53	85.66	86.19	87.10	87.32	86.76	86.71
2/4/2015	86.11	87.04	86.00	86.65	87.10	87.31	86.74	86.63
2/5/2015	87.11	87.36	86.56	87.28	87.00	87.33	86.84	86.66
2/6/2015	87.26	88.00	86.78	87.33	86.88	87.36	86.93	86.72
2/9/2015	86.97	87.19	85.64	85.91	86.61	87.36	86.74	86.54
2/10/2015	86.62	87.41	86.42	87.29	86.59	87.41	86.84	86.67
2/11/2015	86.63	87.12	85.92	86.34	86.54	87.44	86.75	86.62
2/12/2015	86.56	86.68	85.23	85.89	86.36	87.42	86.60	86.50
2/13/2015	85.84	86.16	85.32	85.81	86.44	87.31	86.45	86.40
2/17/2015	85.43	85.97	84.97	85.96	86.47	87.14	86.36	86.32
2/18/2015	86.00	86.30	85.52	86.29	86.48	87.02	86.35	86.28
2/19/2015	84.50	84.80	83.39	83.52	86.16	86.77	85.84	85.75
2/20/2015	82.73	84.38	82.55	84.30	85.86	86.58	85.56	85.41
2/23/2015	84.39	84.86	84.23	84.60	85.59	86.50	85.38	85.18
2/24/2015	84.52	84.82	83.92	84.57	85.46	86.39	85.23	84.99
2/25/2015	84.63	84.72	83.52	83.57	85.09	86.27	84.93	84.65
2/26/2015	83.85	83.86	83.27	83.80	84.83	86.16	84.73	84.42

Source: TradeStation

The most commonly used type of moving average is the simple moving average (SMA), sometimes referred to as an **arithmetic moving average.** An SMA is constructed by adding a set of data and then dividing by the number of observations in the period being examined. For example, look at the ten-day SMA in Table 2.1. We begin by summing the closing prices for the first ten days. We then divide this sum by 10 to give us the mean price for that ten-day period. Thus, on the tenth day, the ten-day simple moving average would be the mean closing price for WMT for Days 1 through 10, or $85.35.

On Day 11, the moving average changes. To calculate the moving average for Day 11, we calculate the mean price for Days 2 through 11. In other words, the closing price for Day 1 is dropped from the data set, whereas the price for Day 11 is added. The formula for calculating a ten-day simple moving average is as follows:

$$SMA_{10} = \sum_{i=1}^{10} data_i / 10$$

Of course, we can construct moving averages of different lengths. In Table 2.1, you can also see a 26-day moving average. This SMA is simply calculated by adding the 26 most recent closing prices and dividing by 26.

Although a moving average can smooth prices over any desired period, some of the more popular daily moving averages are for the periods 200, 60, 50, 30, 20, and 10 days. These periods are somewhat arbitrary and were chosen in the days before computers when the calculations had to be done by hand or on a crank adding machine. Gartley (1935), for example, used the 200-day moving average in his work. Simply, numbers divisible by 10 were easier to calculate. Also, the 10-day, 20-day, and 60-day moving averages summarize approximately two weeks, one month, and three months (one fiscal quarter) of trading data, respectively.

Once calculated, moving averages are plotted on a price chart. Figure 2.1 shows a plot of the 26-day simple moving average for WMT. From early November through late January, the moving average is an upward sloping curve, indicating an upward trend in Walmart's price. The daily fluctuations are smoothed by the moving average so that the analyst can see the underlying trend without being distracted by the small, daily movements.

FIGURE 2.1   SMA—26-day simple moving average (Walmart [WMT] daily: October 14, 2014–February 6, 2015)

A rising moving average indicates an upward trend, whereas a falling moving average indicates a downward trend. Although the moving average helps us discern a trend, it does so after the trend has begun. Thus, the moving average is a lagging indicator. By definition, the moving average is an indicator that is based on past prices. For example, Figure 2.1 shows an upward trend in WMT prices beginning in late October. However, an upward movement in the SMA does not occur until approximately early November. Remember that according to technical analysis principles, we want to be trading with the trend. Using a moving average will always give us some delay in signaling a change in trend.

Length of Moving Average

Because moving averages can be calculated for various lengths of time, which length is best to use? Of course, a longer time period includes more data observations, and, thus, more information. By including more data in the calculation of the moving average, each day's data becomes relatively less important in the calculation. Therefore, a large change in the value on one day does not have a large impact on the longer moving average. This can be an advantage if this large change is a one-day, irregular outlier in the data.

However, if this large move represents the beginning of a significant change in the trend, it takes longer for the underlying trend change to be discernable. Thus, the longer moving average is slower to pick up trend changes but less likely to falsely indicate a trend change due to a short-term blip in the data.

Figure 2.2, for example, shows both a 13-day and a 26-day SMA plotted for WMT. Notice how the shorter, 13-day moving average shows more variability than the longer, 26-day moving average. The 26-day moving average is said to be the "slower" moving average. Although it provides more smoothing, the 26-day smoothing average is also slower at signaling underlying trend changes. Notice the 13-day SMA troughs in late October/early November, signaling a change in trend; a week later, the slower, 26-day SMA is flat but and gradually turning upward. Thus, the 26-day SMA is slower to indicate a trend change.

Because spotting a trend reversal as soon as possible maximizes trading profits, the 13-day SMA may first appear to give superior information; however, remember that the faster SMA has a disadvantage of potentially giving a false signal of a changing trend direction. For example, look at early December in Figure 2.2. The 13-day SMA flattens out, suggesting an end to the upward price trend. After the fact, however, we can see that a trend reversal did not occur until mid-January. The 13-day SMA was overly sensitive to a temporary decrease in price. During this period, the slower 26-day SMA continued to signal correctly an upward trend.

Using Multiple Moving Averages

Analysis is not limited to the information provided by a single moving average. Considering various moving averages of various lengths simultaneously can increase the

FIGURE 2.2 Two moving averages—crossover as support and resistance zone (Walmart [WMT] daily: October 15, 2014–February 26, 2015)

analysts' information set. For example, as shown in Figure 2.2, a support or resistance level often occurs where two moving averages cross. Where the shorter moving average crosses above the longer is often taken as a mechanical buy signal, or at least a sign that the price trend is upward. Likewise, it is considered a sell signal when the shorter declines below the longer. Many successful moving average strategies use moving averages as the principal determinant of trend and then use shorter-term moving averages either as trailing stops or as signals. In some instances, moving averages are used to determine trend, and then chart patterns are used as entry and exit signals.

Using these types of dual moving average signals during a sideways trend in prices, however, can result in a number of whipsaws. This problem can be seen in Figure 2.3. This is essentially the same problem that occurs during the standard sideways trend in a congestion area. It is difficult to determine from such action in which way prices are going to break out. Meanwhile, they oscillate back and forth within the support and resistance levels. A moving average provides no additional information on which way the trend will eventually break. Indeed, a moving average requires a trend for a crossover to be profitable. This means that the analyst must be sure that

FIGURE 2.3 Moving average crossovers causing whipsaws in a flat trend (Walmart [WMT] daily: October 15, 2014–February 26, 2015)

a trend exists before using moving average crossovers for signals. Otherwise—and some traders are willing to take the risk of short-term whipsaws so they don't miss the major trend—a plurality of signals will be incorrect and produce small losses while waiting for the one signal that will produce the large profit. This can be a highly profitable method provided the analyst has the stomach and discipline to continue with the small losses, and it often is the basis for many long-term trend systems. It also demonstrates how, with proper discipline, one can profit while still losing on a majority of small trades.

■ What Other Types of Moving Averages Are Used?

Although we have discussed various lengths of moving averages, up to this point our discussion has centered on the most basic type of moving average calculation—the SMA. Remember that each day's calculation of the SMA represents adding the most recent day's price figure and dropping the earliest day's price figure. When calculating the simple moving average, equal weight is given to each daily observation. For a ten-day SMA, the information contained in the stock price for each of the ten days is given equal importance. However, in certain situations, the most recent stock price may have more bearing on the future direction of the stock than the ten-day old stock price does. If observations that are more recent contain more relevant information than earlier observations, we want to weight data in favor of the most recent observation. By calculating a weighted moving average, the most recent day's information is weighted more heavily. This weighting scheme gives the most recent observation more importance in the moving average calculation.

The Linearly Weighted Moving Average (LWMA)

Let us refer back to the example in Table 2.1 to calculate a linearly weighted moving average. A ten-day linearly weighted moving average multiplies the tenth day observation by 10, the ninth day by 9, the eighth day by 8, and so forth. The total of these numbers is added up and divided by the sum of all the multipliers. In this case, the total will be divided by the sum $10 + 9 + 8 + 7 + 6 + 5 + 4 + 3 + 2 + 1$, or 55. In Table 2.1, we find that the linearly weighted moving average for the first ten trading days is 85.78.

When using this ten-day moving average weighting scheme, the most recent trading data (Day 10) is given twice the importance of the price five days earlier (Day 5) and ten times the importance of the price ten days earlier (Day 1). As we go on to calculate the ten-day linearly weighted moving average for Day 11, the prices for trading Days 2–11 again will be weighted. Therefore, just as with the simple moving average, as the moving average is calculated for each successive day, the earliest trading day information is dropped from the data set being used in the calculation.

The Exponentially Smoothed Moving Average (EMA)

For some analysts, dropping off the earliest trading day's data that occurs with an SMA or linearly weighted moving average is problematic. If the most recent price reflects little change, but the earliest price, now being omitted, shows considerable change, the moving average can be unduly influenced by the discarding of the older data. A large change in the moving average that results from the deletion of early data potentially generates a false signal. This is called the "drop-off effect" (Kaufman, 1998) and is probably the most criticized aspect of a simple moving average.

Although it is easy to see how this early data is not necessarily as important in determining future price movement as the most recent prices, it is still information that may have value. With both the simple moving average and the linearly weighted moving average, this older information, which lies outside the length of the moving average, is being totally ignored. To address this issue and maintain this older information in the moving average calculation, analysts use the **exponential moving average (EMA)**.

To see how the exponential moving average is calculated, let us again refer to the example in Table 2.1. The simple ten-day moving average on Day 10 was 85.35. The closing price on Day 11 was 84.94, a lower value than the mean value for the previous ten days. To calculate the exponential moving average, we will use both the ten-day moving average (which represents the mean exchange rate for Days 1–10) and the closing price for Day 11. Thus, we are now using 11 days of price information. If we were going to calculate an SMA using these 11 days of information, each day's price would have a weight of 1/11, or 9.09% in the calculation. Remember, however, that we want to place a larger weight on information that is more recent. If we want the price information from Day 11 to have a weight twice as great as it would have in a simple moving average, it would have a weight of 2/11, or 18.18%. Of course, the total of all the weights in the calculation of the exponential moving average must sum to 100%. This leaves 100% minus 18.18%, or 81.82% weight to be placed on the ten-day moving average.

The general formula for determining the weight of the current day's data in the exponential moving average calculation is as follows:

$$\text{WEIGHT}_{current} = 2 \div (\text{number of days in moving average} + 1)$$

In our example, the calculation gives us $\text{WEIGHT}_{current} = 2 \div (10 + 1) = 18.18$ percent. If we were using a longer moving average, this weight would decrease in value. For a 19-day EMA, the calculation would be $2 \div (19 + 1)$ or 10%; a 39-day EMA would have a weight of $2 \div (39 + 1)$, or 5%.

The general formula for determining the weight given to the moving average in the calculation of the exponential moving average is the following:

$$\text{WEIGHT}_{ma} = 100\% - \text{WEIGHT}_{current}$$

In our example, we have $\text{WEIGHT}_{ma} = 100\% - 18.18\% = 81.82\%$.

Once we have the weights, the formula for calculating the exponential moving average is as follows:

$$\text{EMA}_{day\ i} = \text{WEIGHT}_{current} \times \text{DATA}_{day\ i} + \text{WEIGHT}_{ma} \\ \times \text{Moving Average}_{day\ i-1}$$

The exponential moving average for Day 11 in our example in Table 2.1 is calculated as the following:

$$\text{EMA}_{11} = .1818 \times 84.94 + .8182 \times 85.08 = 85.05$$

To calculate the exponential moving average for Day 12, we need only two pieces of information—the exponential moving average for Day 11 and the closing price for Day 12. The EMA_{12} would be calculated as follows:

$$EMA_{12} = .1818 \times 84.76 + .8182 \times 85.05 = 85.00$$

Figure 2.4 shows both a 26-day SMA and a 26-day EMA for WMT. Generally, the EMA will change direction more quickly because of the additional weighting that is placed on the most recent data. However, these two curves will usually track each other closely.

The EMA is used in a number of indicators and oscillators. In "Measuring Market Strength," for example, we looked at the McClellan Index. The McClellan Index uses a 19-day and a 39-day EMA. Because the 19-bar EMA has a smoothing factor of 0.10 and the 39-bar EMA has a smoothing factor of 0.05, these calculations are relatively easy. We will see later that a number of oscillators use an EMA, most prominently the MACD. The reason for the use of an EMA is that it is easily calculated and that it weighs more strongly the prices that are more recent. It is, thus, called an **exponential weighted moving average**.

FIGURE 2.4 Exponential versus simple moving average (Walmart [WMT] daily: October 15, 2014–February 26, 2015)

Wilder Method

Welles Wilder (1978) used another simple method to calculate a moving average that weights the most recent number more heavily. The formula for calculating Wilder's moving average is as follows:

$$MA_{day\ i} = ((n-1) \times MA_{i-1} + Price_{dayi}) \div n$$

For example, a 14-day Wilder moving average would be equal to the previous day's moving average figure times 13 (that is, $n-1$, where n is the number of items to be averaged) plus the current closing price, all divided by 14 (that is, n). Wilder's method of calculating a moving average should be used in the average true range (ATR), the relative strength index (RSI), and the directional movement indicator (DMI) calculations that he invented rather than the SMA or EMA. When using Wilder's indicators that are prepackaged in available trading and charting software, one must be sure that the calculations for moving averages are Wilder's. Some software programs use just an SMA or EMA and give results inconsistent with Wilder's methods.

Geometric Moving Average (GMA)

The geometric moving average (GMA) is used mostly in indexes. It is a simple moving average of the percent changes between the previous bar and the current bar over some past predetermined period. Using percentages rather than points does not change its range or dimensions like a price-based moving average. However, it still has all the other problems of equal weight and lag.

Triangular Moving Average

Taking a moving average of a moving average gives a doubly smoothed moving average. The triangular moving average (TMA) begins with a simple moving average of a predetermined number of bars and then, using those results, takes a moving average of a length of half the original number of bars. An example would be a 20-day SMA of daily closes smoothed in a ten-day SMA. The result is a smoothed line that emphasizes the weight of the middle of the price series. The benefit of this method is that it doubly smoothes the data and, thus, better represents the trend. However, the double smoothing also detracts from its sensitivity to trend changes.

Variable EMAs

The use of a variable moving average is suggested by Chande and Kroll (1994). This moving average is the same as an exponential moving average (EMA), but the weighting scheme is adjusted based on the volatility of the price data. This is done to make the EMA shorter during trading ranges when volatility is narrow and expand the EMA when price begins to trend. The desire was to reduce the number of adverse signals during a trading range.

There are a number of variations of this theme. For example, the Kaufman adaptive moving average (KAMA) involves an extremely complicated formula that adjusts an EMA for volatility and trend (Kaufman, 1998). The volume-adjusted moving average (Arms, 1989) is a somewhat complicated moving average, but its essence is that it emphasizes those bars with higher volume. In the September 2001 issue of *Stocks and Commodities Magazine*, John Ehlers presents MAMA and FAMA. MAMA, the MESA adaptive moving average, and FAMA, the following adaptive moving average, are EMAs that adapt to volatility using Hilbert's Transform based on the phase change of a cycle in the data. Needless to say, the calculation of these moving averages is complicated. A buy or sell signal is generated when the MAMA crosses the FAMA. In April 2004, *Active Trader Magazine* compared the effectiveness of using the MAMA-FAMA strategy to using an SMA for 18 stocks and found that the MAMA-FAMA strategy performed only slightly better than the simple method.

■ Strategies for Using Moving Averages

We have looked at a number of ways to calculate moving averages. Although each of these methods has its advantages and disadvantages, our main concern is not how to calculate a moving average but how to use moving averages to make money. Moving averages are widely used in the practice of technical analysis. They are a basic tool with a broad set of uses. Technical analysts use moving averages to determine trend, to determine levels of support and resistance, to spot price extremes, and for specific trading signals.

Determining Trend

Technical analysts use moving averages in four basic ways. First, moving averages are used as a measure of trend. The most common usage is comparing the current price with the moving average that represents the investor's time horizon. For example, many investors use a 200-day moving average. If the stock or market average is above its 200-day moving average, the trend is considered upward. Conversely, if the stock or market average is below the 200-day moving average, the trend is considered downward.

Figure 2.5 includes the same data with the moving average and the trend lines we used in "Trends—The Basics." You can see how the moving average tends to follow the trend line fairly well. The moving average then becomes a proxy for the trend line and can be used to determine when a trend is potentially changing direction, just as can a trend line. In the chart, for example, the later prices have held at both the trend line and the moving average.

FIGURE 2.5 Trend line versus simple moving average (Walmart [WMT] daily: October 15, 2014–February 26, 2015)

Determining Support and Resistance

Second, the moving average often acts as support or resistance. As we have seen from Figure 2.5, a moving average often duplicates the trend line; therefore, it can be an easy trailing stop mechanism for determining when a position should be liquidated or reduced. In addition, prices seem to halt at the vicinity of moving averages. In Figure 2.5, for example, WMT halted its rally in late November at the moving average and again halted its decline at the moving average in early December.

Determining Price Extremes

Third, the moving average is an indicator of price extreme. Because the moving average is a mean, any reversion to the mean will tend to approach the moving average. For trading purposes, this reversion is sometimes profitable when the current price has deviated substantially from that mean or moving average. Price has a tendency to return to the mean. Thus, a deviation from the moving average is a measure of how much prices have risen or fallen ahead of their usual central tendency, and being likely to return to that mean, this deviation then becomes an opportunity to trade with and against the trend. As always, trading against the trend is dangerous and requires close stops, but the reversion also provides an opportunity to position with the trend when it occurs. In addition, when prices continue substantially away from the trend, they are often signaling that the trend is changing direction.

An example of the deviation about a 10-day SMA is shown in Figure 2.6. This is a ratio of the close to its 10-day moving average. It is a stock with a strong upward trend (the dominant trend for our purposes). When prices are trending strongly, they naturally will deviate from the moving average in the direction of the trend more than they will against it. In Figure 2.6, you can see that the advances carry much higher above the equilibrium level of 1.00 than they do during a correction in the upward trend. Action signal lines can thus be established, by testing, at the levels that optimize counter-trend signals. In Figure 2.6, we have arbitrarily used 1.0450 as the ratio below which we would sell WMT even in its upward trend and 0.9750 as the buy level above which we go long. Following this method, we go long on October 21 at 76.02 and sell at 86.40 on December 2. Again, we go long on the upward break of the ratio buy level on December 15 at 83.94 and sell at 89.35 on January 9. We have made nice profits by trading along the trend. The last buy signal comes on February 3 at 86.19. Notice, however, that the trend line has been broken and that the trend may now be going sideways or downward. We sold at the high but hesitate to buy on the signal because of the potential trend change. What else can go wrong? Sometimes the trend is so strong that the ratio never reaches below the buy level. A buy entry stop should thus be placed above the bar where the sale took place. In the last example on the chart, where the trend may have changed, the buy may not work, but if it has a sell stop at its signal bar low, a breaking of that low would indicate a trend change downward and the buy and sell levels in the ratio would be the reciprocals of the upward trend levels. Before you try this system, you should be sure to test for the optimal ratio levels under all trend directions including a flat trend. In this example, we did not optimize the levels; thus, they should not be used until tested.

Giving Specific Signals

Fourth, some technical analysts use moving averages to give specific signals. These can occur when prices cross a moving average, when a shorter moving average crosses a longer moving average, and in some cases, when a third, even shorter, moving average crosses two longer ones. Generally, using two moving averages and their crossover as a signal has been successful, but with substantial drawdowns in capital in sideways markets because of the many unprofitable small trades that occur from the many false signals. Methods, such as using the ADX, described in the next section, have been developed to determine if prices are trending at a rate at which a moving-average crossover system will work. The MAMA-FAMA system described previously and other methods of adapting moving averages to changes in volatility are aimed at solving this drawdown problem. However, it will not go away, and thus, although the crossover methods are profitable over time, the investor must have patience and enough capital to withstand a series of small losses until a trend develops.

Of the four strategies, the most sensible use of moving averages is trend determination. The trend is where the technical analyst profits. If the moving average can help in determining the trend, it is a useful tool. Indeed, it is only during a trending market that moving average signals are profitable. A sideways market is costly in almost all cases, but it's especially so if the investor depends on moving average crossovers for signals. The deviation-from-trend method (see the section "Determining Price Extremes" above and Figure 2.6) is about the only moving average method that can profit in a flat trend. Once a directional trend has been established and identified, the next best method is to use price patterns and breakouts in the direction of the trend for timing of position entries. These methods will lag behind the major bottom and top of a price trend but will accrue profits and minimize losses while the trend is in effect. They are also the most popular method in professional trading systems, along with channel breakout systems such as Donchian's four-week rule

FIGURE 2.6 Ratio of current price to moving average (Walmart [WMT] daily: October 15, 2014–February 26, 2015)

that we discuss in the "Channel" section of this chapter. Finally, other configurations of moving average.

What Is Directional Movement?

One of the great contributions to the concept of trend and direction is the concept of directional movement that Welles Wilder (1978) developed in his book *New Concepts in Technical Trading Systems*. Wilder compared a stock's trading range for one day with the trading range on the previous day to measure trend. Positive directional movement occurred when the high for a day exceeded the high of the previous day. As shown in Figure 2.7, the amount of positive directional movement (+DM) is the day's high minus the previous day's high, or the vertical distance between the top of the two bars. If the low for the day is less than the previous day's low, negative directional movement occurs. The value of the negative directional movement (–DM) is the difference between the two lows.

Days on which the range is completely within the previous day's range are ignored, and a zero is given to the range excess. In addition, one day's trading range is sometimes much larger than the previous day's trading range. This can result in both a higher high and a lower low. When this happens, the greater difference wins. In other words, only a +DM or –DM may be recorded for a particular day.

Constructing Directional Movement Indicators

A moving average is calculated for both +DM and –DM, usually over 14 days, using the Wilder method of averaging. In addition, a 14-day average trading range (ATR) is calculated. Two indicators are calculated using this data. The positive directional movement indicator (DI+) is the ratio between the smoothed +DM and the TR; this calculation gives the percentage of the true range that was above equilibrium for those 14 days. The second indicator is the negative directional movement indicator (DI–), which is calculated as the ratio between the smoothed –DM and the ATR.

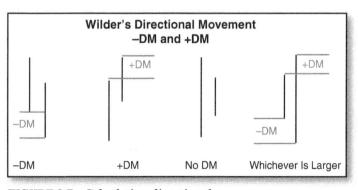

FIGURE 2.7 Calculating directional movement

Using Directional Movement Indicators

Figure 2.8 shows 14-day DIs for Walmart (WMT). Looking at this chart, an analyst sees a number of hints about trend. First, when one DI is higher than the other, the trend is in the direction of that DI. For example, from early November through late January, the DI+ was above the DI−, indicating that a majority of the 14-day ATR excess for WMT was on the upside during that period. The first major crossover occurred in early October when the DI+ crossed above the DI− (marked with "X1") indicating an upturn in the price trend, and the second occurred in late January when the DI− crossed above the DI+ (marked with "X2") and warned us that the trend had reversed downward. This confirmed the earlier downward break of the trend line. Thus, the DMI crossover is an important signal in analyzing trends.

Second, the minor crossover that occurred in early February (marked with a "mc") and lasted only a day is an important sign. It suggests that the direction of the trend is now sideways and, like a congestion area, it may break in either direction. Often, the two DIs come to equilibrium and then part in their original direction, as happened here, in which case the earlier trend resumes. At other times, the DIs

FIGURE 2.8 Directional movement indicator (Walmart [WMT] daily: October 15, 2014– February 26, 2015)

cross more dramatically and incisively, as they did in late January, and signal a trend reversal. When the two meet, therefore, is an important period. Wilder suggested placing a buy or sell stop at the price when the two first cross. In Figure 2.8, as the two DIs cross in early February, we do not know if this is a trend reversal. Thus, we place a buy stop at a price just above the price that occurred when the two initially crossed. If the trend is reversing, the price will hit our stop, and our position will be in line with the new upward trend. If the stop is not hit, the two lines will likely diverge again, and the old downward trend will continue without us.

Third, standard divergence techniques are valid in the DMI. In Figure 2.8, notice where the highest peak exceeded the earlier peak (price plot: dotted line from peak to peak) was not confirmed in the DI+, which failed to reach a new high at the same time (DMI plot: dotted line from peak to peak). This is a negative divergence that, although not an action signal, is a warning that the earlier upward trend is losing strength.

Fourth, the DIs can be used to create a directional index (DX). This DX then is used to create the average DX called the **ADX line** shown in Figure 2.9. The DX is calculated by taking the absolute difference between the values of the two DIs and dividing it by the sum of the two DIs. The DX is always positive and represents the tendency of the market to trend because it measures the DIs against each other. When one DI is very large compared to the other DI, the market is moving strongly in one direction and the value of the DX will be large.

The ADX is the smoothed value of the DX and is plotted on Figure 2.9. When the ADX is rising, the market is increasingly trending in either direction.

The ADX indicator is valuable in determining when to apply a moving average trend-following system. A rising ADX indicates an increasing tendency to trend in the corresponding prices. A low ADX or one that's declining indicates a flat or dull trend on one that is losing momentum. We know that the moving average cross-over systems have multiple whipsaws when the market is not in a directional trend but have profitable outcomes when the market is trending in either an upward or a downward direction. Many trend-following models use the ADX to determine when money should be committed to the markets.

Fifth, ADX peaks and troughs provide valuable information about the price trend. When the ADX peaks, it often signals a peak or trough in prices. In Figure 2.9, peaks in the ADX (marked with arrows) show how closely they coincide with up or down reversals in price. Because their pinpointing the end of trends is so accurate, ADX peaks are used as trading signals to close trend positions.

Troughs in the ADX are useful because they signify periods when the market has become dormant and trendless but is beginning to accelerate in a trend direction. When the ADX begins to rise, not necessarily from a low level, it signals a sudden increase in trending and is a time to look for entry into the trend. As we know from looking at congestion areas, a dormant period is usually followed by a dynamic period. This phenomenon can be seen in Figure 2.9 with the ADX troughs (marked with arrows within circles) associated with the dormant period turning into a trend with

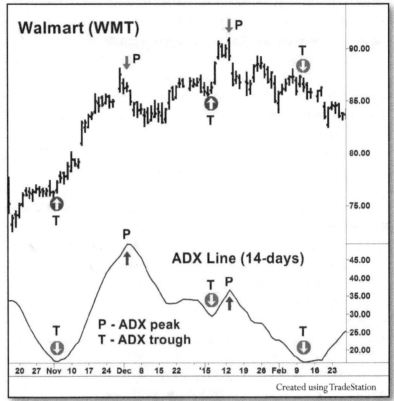

FIGURE 2.9 ADX line (Walmart [WMT] daily: October 15, 2014–February 26, 2015)

increasing momentum. When an ADX trough occurs, the trader or investor should be watching price closely for a breakout in either direction.

ADXs and DMIs can be used on weekly, monthly, and even shorter-term, intraday charts for clues as to trend strength and direction.

■ What Are Envelopes, Channels, and Bands?

The simple moving average represents the center of a stock's price trend. Actual prices tend to oscillate around that moving average. The price movement is centered on the moving average but falls within a band or envelope around the moving average. By determining the band within which prices tend to oscillate, the analyst is better able to determine the range in which price may be expected to fluctuate.

Percentage Envelopes

One way of creating this type of band is to use **percentage envelopes**. This method, also known as a percentage filter, was developed in an attempt to reduce the numerous unprofitable signals from crossing a moving average when the trend is sideways. This is a popular method used in most of the academic studies on moving average crossover systems. It is calculated by taking a percentage of the moving average and plotting it above and below the moving average (see Figure 2.10)—thus the term *envelope*. This plot creates two symmetrical lines: one above and one below the moving average.

This envelope then becomes the trigger for signals when it is crossed by the price rather than when the moving average is crossed. The percentage used in the calculation should be large enough that it encompasses most of the oscillations around the moving average during a sideways period and, thus, reduces the number of incorrect signals, yet it should be small enough to give signals early enough to be profitable once a trend has been established. This percentage must be determined through experiment because a slight difference in percentage can cause a considerable difference in performance.

One of the major problems with fixed-percentage envelopes is that they do not account for the changing volatility of the underlying price. During a sideways trend, when volatility usually declines, price action can be contained within a relatively

FIGURE 2.10 Percentage envelope about a moving average (Walmart [WMT] daily: October 15, 2014–February 26, 2015)

narrow band. When the trend begins, however, volatility often expands and will then create false signals using a fixed-percentage envelope. To combat this problem, the concept of bands that are adjusted for volatility developed.

Bands

Bands are also envelopes around a moving average but, rather than being fixed in size, are calculated to adjust for the price volatility around the moving average. They, thus, shrink when prices become calm and expand when prices become volatile. The most widely used band is the Bollinger Band, named after John Bollinger (2002).

Bollinger Band As we mentioned earlier, there are two principal ways to measure price volatility. One is the standard deviation about a mean or moving average, and the other is the ATR. Bollinger Bands use the standard deviation calculation.

To construct Bollinger Bands, first calculate a simple moving average of prices. Bollinger uses the SMA because most calculations using standard deviation use an SMA. Next, draw bands a certain number of standard deviations above and below the moving average. For example, Bollinger's standard calculation, and the one most often seen in the public chart services, begins with a 20-period simple moving average. Two standard deviations are added to the SMA to plot an upper band. The lower band is constructed by subtracting two standard deviations from the SMA. The bands are self-adjusting, automatically becoming wider during periods of extreme price changes.

Figure 2.11 shows the standard Bollinger Band around the 20-period moving average with bands at two standard deviations. Of course, both the length of the moving average and the number of standard deviations can be adjusted. Theoretically, the plus or minus two standard deviations should account for approximately 95% of all the price action about the moving average. In fact, this is not quite true because price action is nonstationary and nonrandom and, thus, does not follow the statistical properties of the standard deviation calculation precisely. However, it is a good estimate of the majority of price action. Indeed, as the chart shows, the price action seems to oscillate between the bands quite regularly. This action is similar to the action in a congestion area or rectangle pattern, except that prices also tend to oscillate within the band as the price trends upward and downward. This is because the moving average is replicating the trend of the prices and adjusting for them while the band is describing their normal upper and lower limits around the trend as price volatility changes.

Keltner Band Chester Keltner (1960) introduced Keltner Bands in his book *How to Make Money in Commodities*. To construct these bands, first calculate the "Typical Price" (Close + High + Low) ÷ 3, and calculate a ten-day SMA of the typical price. Next, calculate the band size by creating a ten-day SMA of High minus Low or bar

FIGURE 2.11 Bollinger Bands (Walmart [WMT] daily: October 15, 2014–February 26, 2015)

range. The upper band is then plotted as the ten-day SMA of the typical price plus the ten-day SMA of bar range. The lower band is plotted as the ten-day SMA to the typical price minus the ten-day SMA of bar range. (When the calculation is rearranged, it is similar to the use of an ATR. These bands are sometimes referred to as ATR bands.)

As with most methods, different analysts prefer to modify the basic model to meet their specific needs and investment strategies. Although Keltner's original calculation used ten-day moving averages, many analysts using this method have extended the moving averages to 20 periods. The 20-period calculation is more in line with the calculation for a Bollinger Band.

STARC Band   STARC is an acronym for Stoller Average Range Channel, invented by Manning Stoller. This system uses the ATR over five periods added to and subtracted from a five-period SMA of prices. It produces a band about prices that widens and shrinks with changes in the ATR or the volatility of the price. Just as with the Keltner Bands, the length of the SMA used with STARC can be adjusted to different trading or investing time horizons.

Trading Strategies Using Bands and Envelopes

In line with the basic concept of following the trend, bands and envelopes are used to signal when a trend change has occurred and to reduce the number of whipsaws that occur within a tight trading range. While looking at the envelopes or bands on a chart, one would think that the best use of them might be to trade within them from high extreme to low extreme and back, similar to strategies for rectangle patterns. However, the trading between bands is difficult. First, by definition, except for fixed envelopes, the bands contract during a sideways, dull trend and leave little room for maneuvering at a cost-effective manner and with profitable results. Second, when prices suddenly move on a new trend, they tend to remain close to the band in the direction of the trend and give many false exit signals. Third, when the bands expand, they show that volatility has increased, usually due to the beginning of a new trend, and any position entered in further anticipation of low volatility is quickly stopped out.

Bands, therefore, have become methods of determining the beginnings of trends and are not generally used for range trading between them. When the outer edge of a band is broken, empirical evidence suggests that the entry should be in the direction of the breakout, not unlike the breakout of a trend line or support or resistance level. A breakout from a band that contains roughly 90% of previous price action suggests that the general trend of the previous price action has changed in the direction of the breakout.

In Figure 2.11, a breakout buy signal occurs in early November, when the price breaks above the upper Bollinger Band, hinting that a strong upward trend is starting. The bands had become narrower during October. This band tightening, caused by shrinking volatility, is often followed by a sharp price move.

The only difference between a band breakout and a more conventional kind is that a band is generally more fluid. Because moving averages will often become support or resistance levels, the moving average in the Bollinger Band calculation should then become the trailing stop level for any entry that previously occurred from a breakout above or below the band. The ability of moving averages to be used as trailing stops is easily spliced into a system utilizing any kind of bands that adjust for volatility.

The other use for the moving average within a band is as a retracement level for additional entry in the trend established by the direction of the moving average and the bands. With a stop only slightly below the moving average using the rules we learned for establishing stop levels, when the price retraces back into the area of the moving average while in a strong upward trend, an additional entry can be made where the retracement within the band is expected to halt.

In testing band breakouts, the longer the period, it seems, the more profitable the system. Very short-term volatility, because it is proportionally more active, causes many false breakouts. Longer-term periods with less volatility per period appear to remain in trends for longer periods and are not whipsawed as much as short-term trends. The most profitable trend-following systems are long-term, and as short-term traders have learned, the ability of price to oscillate sharply is greater than when it is smoothed over longer periods. Thus, the inherent whipsaws in short-term data become reduced over longer periods, and trend-following systems tracking longer trends have fewer unprofitable signals. Bands are more successful in trending markets and are, therefore, more suitable for commodities markets than the stock market.

Another use for bands is to watch price volatility. Low volatility is generally associated with sideways to slightly slanted trends—ones where whipsaws are common and patterns fail. High volatility is generally associated with a strong trend, up or down. By watching volatility, especially for an increase in volatility, the analyst has a clue that a change in trend is forthcoming. To watch volatility, one should take a difference between the high band and low band and plot it as a line below the price action. Bollinger calls this line a **Bandwidth Indicator**. A rise in the bandwidth line, which results from increasing volatility, can be associated directly with price action. Any breakout from a pattern, support or resistance level, trend line, or moving average can be confirmed by the change in volatility. If volatility does not increase with a price breakout, the odds favor that the breakout is false. Volatility, therefore, can be used as confirmation for trend changes, or it can be used as a warning that things are about to change. This use of bands is more successful when combined with other methods of determining an actual trend change.

Channel

In discussing trend lines, we noted that a line can often be drawn parallel to a trend line that encompasses the price action in what was called a **channel**. For present purposes, that definition changes slightly by relaxing the requirement for a parallel line.

Channels have been described as something simpler than two parallel lines. For example, we mentioned the Donchian channel method that has been so successful even though it's been widely known for many years. Signals occur with the Donchian channel when the breaking above or below a high or low over some past period occurs (see Figure 2.12). This method does not require the construction of a trend line; the only requirement is a record of the highs and lows over some past period. In the case of the Donchian channel method, the period was four weeks (20 days), and the rule was to buy when the price exceeded the highest level over the past four weeks and sell short when the price declined below the lowest low over the past four weeks. Such systems are usually "stop and reverse" systems that are always in the market, either long or short. As is likely imagined, the channel systems are more commonly used in the commodities markets where long and short positions are effortless and prices tend to trend much longer.

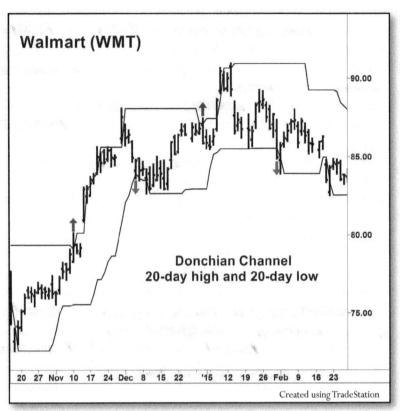

FIGURE 2.12 Donchian channel on daily closes (Walmart [WMT] daily: October 15, 2014–February 26, 2015)

■ Conclusion

The basic way the technical analyst makes profits is by identifying a trend in prices and riding that trend. At times, daily fluctuations in prices make it difficult for the analyst to view the basic underlying trend in prices. Moving averages are tools used to smooth this erratic data, making it easier to discern the genuine underlying trend.

Although there are various methods of calculating a moving average, the basic idea is to give a summary of the average or normal price history of a particular period. Because the moving averages are based on historical prices, by nature, they will be a lagging indicator of trends. The shorter the period covered by the moving average, the less of a lag there will be. However, using a shorter period also leads to more false signals. As usual, when choosing a moving average system, there is a trade-off between early trend reversal recognition and certainty of trend reversal. The use of envelopes, bands, and channels around the moving average can minimize the number of false signals by providing a larger range of price movement before a signal is triggered.

Box 2.1 gives a list of basic principles that the technical analyst should keep in mind.

BOX 2.1 TRADING RULES

We have covered a good deal of material regarding trends. Here are some of the key points to remember when investing:

- Riding the trend is the most profitable use of technical analysis.
- Trends can be identified with trend lines, moving averages, and relative highs and lows.
- Always pick a security that trends up and down. Flat or random trends are usually unprofitable.
- Be aware of the next longer period and shorter period trends from the one being traded.
- Always trade with the trend:
  - "Trend is your friend."
  - "Don't buck the trend."
- Breakouts from support or resistance levels, patterns, or bands usually signal a change in trend.
- A trend line breakout is at least a warning.
- The longer the trend, the more important the breakout.
- Confirm any breakout with other evidence, especially when entering a position. In exiting, confirmation is not as important.
- Always use stops—protective and trailing.
- Do not sell profitable positions too soon; just keep trailing with stops.

■ References

Arms, Richard W., Jr. *The Arms Index: An Introduction to the Volume Analysis of Stock and Bond Markets*. Homewood, IL: Dow Jones-Irwin, 1989.

Bollinger, John. *Bollinger on Bollinger Bands*. New York, NY: McGraw-Hill, 2002.

Brock, W., J. Lakonishok, and B. LeBaron. "Simple Technical Trading Rules and the Stochastic Properties of Stock Returns." *Journal of Finance* 47 (1992): 1731–1764.

Chande, Tushar S. and Stanley Kroll. *The New Technical Trader: Boost Your Profit by Plugging into the Latest Indicators*. New York, NY: John Wiley & Sons, Inc., 1994.

Detry, P.J. and Philippe Gregoire. "Other Evidences of the Predictive Power of Technical Analysis: The Moving Averages Rules on European Indexes." European Finance Management Association Meeting, Lugano, Switzerland, 2001, http://ssrn.com/abstract=269802.

Ehlers, John. "MESA Adaptive Moving Averages." *Technical Analysis of Stocks and Commodities* 19, no. 9 (September 2001): 30–35.

Gartley, H.M. *Profits in the Stock Market*. 3rd ed. (1981). Pomeroy, WA: Lambert-Gann Publishing Co., 1935.

Kaufman, Perry J. *Trading Systems and Methods*. 3rd ed. New York, NY: John Wiley & Sons, Inc., 1998.

Keltner, Chester W. *How to Make Money in Commodities*. Kansas City, MO: Keltner Statistical Service, 1960.

Wilder, J. Welles, Jr. *New Concepts in Technical Trading Systems*. Greensboro, SC: Trend Research, 1978.

CHAPTER 3

Time-Based Trend Calculations

From Perry J. Kaufman, *Trading Systems and Methods, +Website,* 5th Edition (Hoboken, New Jersey: John Wiley & Sons, 2013), Chapter 7.

Learning Objective Statements

- Correctly apply and explain the following tools: momentum, rate of change, moving average, accumulative average, reset accumulate average
- Contrast the use of various moving averages
- Explain the drop-off effect
- Determine the strength of a trend based on indicator data
- Select the correct definition of trend strength indicators

The purpose of all trend identification methods is to remove the underlying noise in the market, those erratic moves that seem to be meaningless, and find the current direction of prices. But trends are somewhat dependent upon your time horizon. There may be more than one trend at any one time, caused by short-term events and long-term policy, and it is likely that one trader will search for the strongest, or most dominant trend, while another will seek a series of shorter-term moves. There is no "right" or "wrong" trend but a choice of benefits and compromises.

The technique that is used to uncover a particular trend can depend upon whether any of the underlying trend characteristics are known. Does the stock or futures market have a clear seasonal or cyclic component, such as the travel industry or coffee prices; or does it respond to long-term monetary policy based on the cost of servicing debt or interest income? If you know more about the reasons why prices trend, you will be able to choose the best method of finding the trend and the calculation period.

Once you know that there is a fundamental relationship between data, a formula can be found that expresses one price movement in terms of the other prices and economic data. The predictive qualities of these methods are best when applied to data that have been seen before, that is, prices that are within the range of historic data. Forecasting reliability decreases when values are extrapolated outside the previous range of value. The most popular trend models, discussed in this chapter, ignore the reasons why trends exist and generalize the process of smoothing prices in order to find a trend's direction.

■ Forecasting and Following

There is a clear distinction between forecasting the trend and finding the current trend. Forecasting, predicting the future price, is much more desirable but very complex. It involves combining those data that are most important to price change and assigning a value to each one. The results are always expressed with a confidence level, the level of uncertainty in the forecast. There is always lower confidence as you try to forecast further into the future.

The techniques most commonly used for evaluating the direction or tendency of prices both within prior ranges or at new levels are called *autoregressive* functions. Unlike forecasting models, they are only concerned with evaluating the current price direction. This analysis concludes that prices are moving in an upward, downward, or sideways direction, with no indication of confidence. From this simple basis, it is possible to form rules of action and develop complex trading strategies.

All of these techniques make the assumptions that past data can be used to predict future price movement, and that the direction of prices today is the most likely forecast of the direction of prices tomorrow. For the most part, these assumptions have proved to be true. From a practical viewpoint, these trending methods are more flexible than the traditional regression models, but to achieve success they introduce a lag. A *lag* is a delay in the identification of the trend. Great effort has been spent trying to reduce this lag in an attempt to identify the trend sooner; however, the lag is the zone of uncertainty that allows the technique to ignore most of the market noise.

In an autoregressive model, one or more previous prices determine the next sequential price. If p_t represents today's price, p_{t-1} yesterday's price, and so on, then tomorrow's expected price will be

$$p_{t+1} = a_0 + a_1 p_t + a_2 p_{t-1} + \ldots + a_t p_1 + e$$

where each price is given a corresponding weight a_i and then combined to give the resultant price for tomorrow $p_{t+1} + e$ (where e represents an error factor, usually ignored). The simplest example is the use of yesterday's price alone to generate tomorrow's price:

$$p_{t+1} = a_0 + a_1 p_{t-1} + e$$

which you may also recognize as the formula for a straight line, $y = a + bx$, plus an error factor.

The autoregressive model does not have to be linear; each prior day can have a nonlinear predictive quality. Then each expected price p_{t+1}, could be represented by a curvilinear expression, $p_{t+1} = a_0 + a_1 p_t + a_2 p^2_{t-1} + e$, or by an exponential or logarithmic formula, $\ln p_{t+1} = a_0 + a_1 \ln p_t + a_2 \ln p_{t-1} + e$, which is commonly used in equity analysis. Any of these expressions could then be combined to form an autoregressive forecasting model for p_{t+1}. In going from the simple to the complex, it is natural to want to know which of these choices will perform best. Theoretically, the best method will be the one that, when used in a strategy, yields the highest return for the lowest risk; however, every investor has a personal risk preference. The answer can only be found by applying and comparing different methods, and experiencing how they perform when actually traded. It turns out that the best historic result often comes from *overfitting* the data, and is a poor choice for trading. Throughout the book there will be comparisons of systems and methods that are similar.

Least-Squares Model

The least-squares regression model is the same technique that is used to find the relationship between two markets—Barrick Gold and cash gold, corn and soybeans—or to find how price movement could be explained by the main factors influencing them, supply and demand. Most trading systems depend only on price; therefore, we will look again using the least-squares model with time as the independent variable and price as the dependent variable. The regression results will be used in an autoregressive way to forecast the price n-days ahead, and we will look at the accuracy of those predictions. The slope of the resulting straight line or curvilinear fit will determine the direction of the trend.

Error Analysis

A simple error analysis can be used to show how time works against the predictive qualities of regression, or any forecasting method. Using 10 years of General Electric (GE) prices, ending February 15, 2010, the slope and y-intercept are calculated for a rolling 20 days. The 1-, 2-, 3-, 5-, and 10-day ahead forecast is found by projecting the slope by that number of days. The forecast error is the difference between the projected price and the actual price. Figure 3.1 shows the price for GE from December 31, 2010, through February 15, 2011, along with the five forecast prices. Even though the price move seems to be increasing steadily, the forecasts get farther away as the days ahead become larger. This result is typical of forecasting error, regardless of the method, and argues that the smallest forecast interval is the best.

The method of finding the forecast error is shown in Table 3.1 (the full spreadsheet can be found on the Companion Website as *TSM General Electric regression error forecast*). Only the closing prices are needed, and they appear in column 3. The slope and intercept use the sequential numbers in column 1 for X, and the GE prices for Y. The n-day ahead forecast is

$$y_{t+n} = Intercept_t + Slope_t \times Price_t + n \times Slope_t$$

The standard deviations of the five forecast errors (Table 3.2), taken over the entire 10 years, shows the error increasing as the days-ahead increase. This confirms the

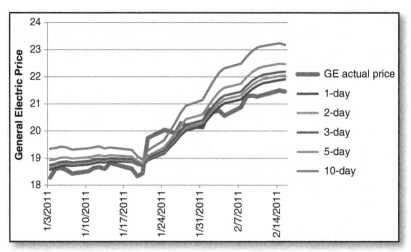

FIGURE 3.1 General Electric Price from December 31, 2010, through February 15, 2011. Forecast accuracy decreases as the forecast period increases.

expectation that forecasting accuracy decreases with time and that confidence bands will get wider with time. For this reason, any forecasts used in strategies will be 1-day ahead.

Limiting the Forecast to Direction

To be profitable trading a trending system, it is only necessary to be correct in one of the following two cases:

1. In more than 50% of the days you are correct in predicting whether prices will go up or down and the average up move is equal to the average down move.
2. Your forecast accuracy is less than 50% but the size of the correct moves is greater than the size of the incorrect moves.

Unfortunately, there is no way to prove that a particular method of forecasting, moving average, regression, or other techniques will be accurate over all calculation periods. The fact is that some calculation periods are profitable and others are not. Those that are profitable must satisfy one of the two conditions stated above. Therefore, the answer is *it's true when it works and not true when it doesn't work.*

Experience shows that the best choice of trending method will be the one that is profitable over most markets and most calculation periods. Even then, shorter calculation periods have no trend, so we need to restrict our statement to longer periods.

The methods discussed in the remainder of this chapter are all intended to identify the direction of prices based on past data. The trading systems that use them all assume that there is a better chance of prices continuing in that direction the next day. If the systems are profitable then the assumption was correct. There is sufficient performance history for macrotrend funds that justify this conclusion.

TABLE 3.1   General Electric Analysis of Regression Error Based on a 20-Day Rolling Calculation Period

Seq	Date	GE Close	Regression		Forecast					Forecast error				
			Slope	Intercept	1-day	2-day	3-day	5-day	10-day	1-day	2-day	3-day	5-day	10-day
n	2/1/2011	20.80	0.118	−351.689	20.438	20.556	20.675	20.911	21.502	−0.616	−0.669	−0.769	−1.128	−1.404
n + 1	2/2/2011	20.71	0.131	−390.484	20.673	20.804	20.934	21.195	21.848	−0.272	−0.420	−0.478	−0.791	−1.406
n + 2	2/3/2011	20.75	0.141	−422.673	20.886	21.027	21.168	21.449	22.154	−0.077	−0.194	−0.354	−0.535	−1.657
n + 3	2/4/2011	20.56	0.144	−432.439	21.019	21.162	21.306	21.594	22.314	0.326	0.244	0.115	−0.128	−1.616
n + 4	2/7/2011	20.87	0.146	−440.206	21.166	21.313	21.459	21.752	22.484	0.149	0.157	0.064	−0.262	−1.588
n + 5	2/8/2011	21.28	0.152	−458.803	21.367	21.519	21.672	21.976	22.738	−0.114	−0.118	−0.112	−0.369	−1.615
n + 6	2/9/2011	21.31	0.156	−471.628	21.544	21.700	21.857	22.169	22.952	0.057	0.003	−0.004	−0.115	−1.301
n + 7	2/10/2011	21.27	0.157	−471.985	21.675	21.831	21.988	22.301	23.084	0.274	0.249	0.189	0.179	−0.957
n + 8	2/11/2011	21.33	0.152	−459.262	21.769	21.921	22.074	22.379	23.141	0.345	0.370	0.342	0.264	−0.654
n + 9	2/14/2011	21.50	0.150	−452.185	21.879	22.029	22.180	22.480	23.231	0.269	0.331	0.357	0.252	−0.566
n + 10	2/15/2011	21.46	0.140	−419.686	21.914	22.054	22.193	22.473	23.173	0.419	0.461	0.528	0.516	−0.322

TABLE 3.2	The Standard Deviation of Errors for Different "Days Ahead" Forecasts				
Days Ahead	1	2	3	5	10
Stdev of Errors	1.137	1.336	1.519	1.860	2.672

■ Price Change over Time

The most basic of all trend indicators is the change of price over some period of time. This is written as

$$M_t = p_t - p_{t-n}$$

where M is called *momentum*, t is today, and n is the number of days. Sometimes this is called *rate of change*, but both momentum and rate of change are incorrect names. In mathematics, this is the *first difference*, and in physics it is *speed* (distance covered over time).

If the change in price is positive, we can say that the trend is up, and if negative, the trend is down. Of course, this decision is based only on two data points, but if those points are far enough away from each other, that is, if n is large, then the trend as determined by this method will be very similar to a simple moving average, discussed in the next section. The simplest method can often be the most robust; therefore, as you read about many other approaches to analyzing price, keep asking, "Is it better than the simple change in price?"

■ The Moving Average

The most well-known of all smoothing techniques, used to remove market noise and find the direction of prices, is the *moving average (MA)*. Using this method, the number of elements to be averaged remains the same, but the time interval advances. This is also referred to as a *rolling calculation period*. Using a series of prices, $p_0, p_1, p_2, \ldots, p_t$, a moving average measured over the most recent n of these prices, or data points, at time t would be

$$MA_t = \frac{p_{t-n+1} + p_{t-n+2} + \cdots + p_t}{n} = \frac{1}{n} \sum_{i=t-n+1}^{t} p_i \, , n \leq t$$

Then today's moving average value is the average (arithmetic mean) of the most recent n data points. For example, using three points $(n = 3)$ to generate a moving average starting at the beginning of the data:

$$MA_3 = (p_1 + p_2 + p_3)/3$$

$$MA_4 = (p_2 + p_3 + p_4)/3$$

$$\vdots$$

$$MA_t = (p_{t-2} + p_{t-1} + p_t)/3$$

If p_t represents a price at a specific time t, the moving average would smooth the price changes. When more prices, n, are used in the average, each price will be a smaller part of the average and have less effect on the final value. Using five successive prices is called a *5-day moving average*. When the next sequential price is added and the oldest is dropped off, the prior average is changed by $\frac{1}{5}$ of the difference between the old and the new values. If

$$MA_5 = (p_1 + p_2 + p_3 + p_4 + p_5)/5$$

and

$$MA_6 = (p_2 + p_3 + p_4 + p_5 + p_6)/5$$

then $c = p_2 + p_3 + p_4 + p_5$ can be substituted for the common part of the moving average. MA_6, the most recent value, can be solved in terms of MA_5, the previous value, to get

$$MA_6 = MA_5 + (p_t - p_{t-n})/5$$

This also gives a faster way to calculate a moving average. It can be seen that the more terms in the moving average, the less effect the addition of a new term will have:

$$MA_t = MA_{t-1} + (p_t - p_{t-n})/n$$

The selection of the number of terms, called the *calculation period*, is based on both the predictive quality of the choice (measured by the error but more often by the profitability) or the need to determine price trends over specific time periods, such as a season. For outright trading, the calculation period is chosen for its accuracy in identifying trend and the risk tolerance of the trader. Slower trends, using longer calculation periods, are usually better indicators of price direction, but involve larger risk. The stock market has adopted the 200-day moving average as its benchmark for direction; however, traders find this much too slow for timing buy and sell signals.

The length of a moving average can be tailored to specific needs. A 63-day moving average, ¼ of 252 business days in the year, would reflect quarterly changes in stock price, minimizing the significance of price fluctuations within a calendar quarter. A simple yearly calculation period, 252 days, would ignore all seasonality and emphasize the annual growth of the stock. Any periodic cycle that is the same length as the moving average length is lost; therefore, if a monthly cycle has been identified, then a moving average of less than 10 days (half the cycle length) would be best for letting the moving average show that cycle. At this point it is sufficient to remember that if there is a possibility of a cyclic or seasonal pattern within the data, care should be taken to select a moving average that is out of phase with that pattern (that is, not equal to the cycle period).

The length of the moving average may also relate to its commercial use. A jeweler may purchase silver each week to produce bracelets. Frequent purchases of small amounts keeps the company's cash outlay small. The purchaser can wait a few extra days during a week while prices continue to trend downward but will buy immediately when prices turn up. A 6-month trend cannot help him because it gives a long-term answer to a short-term problem; however, a 5-day moving average may give the trend direction within the jeweler's time frame.

User-Friendly Software

Fortunately, we have reached a time when it is not necessary to perform these calculations the long way. Spreadsheet programs and specialized testing software provide simple tools for performing trend calculations as well as many other more complex functions discussed in this book. The notation for many of the different spreadsheets and software is very similar and self-explanatory:

Function	Spreadsheet Notation	TradeStation Notation
Sum	=sum (list)	summation (value, period)
Moving average	=average (list)	average (value, period)
Standard deviation	=stdev (list)	stddev (value, period)
Maximum value	=max (list)	highest (value, period)
Minimum value	=min (list)	lowest (value, period)

In the spreadsheet notation, *list* is a series of rows. For example, (D11:D30) would be 20 rows in column D, and in *TradeStation* notation, *period* is the calculation period and *value* is the closing daily price series, *close* or C.

What Do You Average?

The closing or daily settlement is the most common price applied to a moving average. It is generally accepted as the "true" price of the day and is used by many analysts for calculation of trends. It is the price used to reconcile brokerage accounts at the end of the day, create the *Net Asset Value* (NAV) for funds, and for futures trading it is called *marked-to-market accounting*. A popular alternative is to use the average of the high, low, and closing prices, representing some sort of center of gravity. You may also try the average of the high and low prices, ignoring the closing price entirely.

Another valid component of a moving average can be other averages. For example, if p_1 through p_t are prices, and MA_t is a 3-day moving average on day t, then

$$MA_3 = (p_1 + p_2 + p_3)/3$$
$$MA_4 = (p_2 + p_3 + p_4)/3$$
$$MA_5 = (p_3 + p_4 + p_5)/3$$

and

$$MA'_5 = (MA_3 + MA_4 + MA_5)/3$$

where MA'_5 is a *double-smoothed* moving average, which gives added weight to the center points. Double smoothing can be very effective. Smoothing the highs and lows independently is another technique that creates a representation of the daily trading range, or volatility. This has been used to identify normal and extreme moves.

Types of Moving Averages

Besides varying the length of the moving average and the elements that are to be averaged, there are a great number of variations on the simple moving average. In the methods that follow, the notation assumes that the most recent day is t and the average is found over the past n days.

The Simple Moving Average   The simple moving average is the average (mean) of the most recent n days. It has also been called a *truncated moving average,* and it is the most well-known and commonly used of all the methods. Repeating the formula from earlier in this chapter,

$$MA_t = \frac{P_{t-n+1} + P_{t-n+2} + \cdots + P_t}{n} = \frac{1}{n} \sum_{i=t-n+1}^{t} P_i \ , \ n \leq t$$

The main objection to the simple moving average is its abrupt change in value when an important old piece of data is dropped off, especially if only a few days are used in the calculation. We also know that, if the new data, p_t, is greater than the oldest data item that will be dropped off, p_{t-n}, then the new average, MA_t will be greater than the previous average, MA_{t-1}.

Average-Modified or Average-Off Method   To avoid the end-off problem of the simple moving average, each time a new piece of data is added the previous average can be dropped off. This is called an *average-modified* or *average-off* method. It is computationally convenient because you only need to keep the old average value rather than all the data that was used to find the average. In general, the average-off method is

$$AvgOff_t = \frac{(n-1) \times AvgOff_{t-1} + P_t}{n}$$

The substitution of the moving average value for the oldest data item tends to smooth the results even more than a simple moving average and dampens the end-off impact.

Weighted Moving Average   The *weighted moving average* opens many possibilities. It allows the significance of individual or groups of data to be changed. It may restore perceived value to parts of a data sample, or it may incorrectly bias the data. A weighted moving average is expressed in its general form as

$$W_t = \frac{w_1 P_{t-n+1} + w_2 P_{t-n+2} + \cdots + w_{n-1} P_{t-1} + w_n P_t}{w_1 + w_2 + \cdots + w_n} = \frac{\sum_{i=1}^{n} w_i P_{t-i+1}}{\sum_{i=1}^{n} w_i}$$

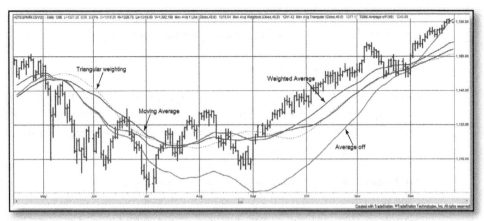

FIGURE 3.2 A Comparison of Moving Averages. The simple moving average, linearly weighted average, triangular weighted, and average off methods are applied to the S&P, April through December 2010.

The weighted moving average at time t is the average of the previous n prices, each price having its own weighting factor w_i. There is no restriction on the values used as weighting factors; that is, they do not have to be percentages that all total to 1. The most popular form of this technique is called *front-loaded* because it gives more weight to the most recent data (n) and reduces the significance of the older elements. For the frontloaded weighted moving average (see Figure 3.2).

$$w_1 \leq w_2 \leq \cdots \leq w_n$$

The weighting factors w_i may also be determined by regression analysis, but then they may not necessarily be front-loaded. A common modification to front-loading is called *step-weighting* in which each successive w_i differs from the previous weighting factor w_{i-1} by a fixed increment

$$c = w_i - w_{i-1}$$

The most common 5-day front-loaded, step-weighted average would have weighting factors increasing by $c = 1$ each day, $w_1 = 1$, $w_2 = 2$, $w_3 = 3$, $w_4 = 4$, and $w_5 = 5$. In general, for an n-day frontloaded step-weighted moving average:

$$w_{t-n+1} = 1$$

$$\vdots$$

$$w_{t-1} = n - 1$$

$$w_t = n$$

A TradeStation program for calculating an n-day, front-loaded, linearly weighted moving average is called *waverage*.

If simple linear step-weighting is not what you want, then a percentage relationship a between w_i elements can be used,

$$w_{i-1} = a \times w_i$$

If $a = 0.90$ and $w_5 = 5$, then $w_4 = 4.5$, $w_3 = 4.05$, $w_2 = 3.645$, and $w_1 = 3.2805$. Each older data item is given a weight of 90% of the more recent value. This is similar to *exponential smoothing* which will be discussed later in this chapter.

Weighting by Group Prices may also be weighted in groups. If every two consecutive data elements have the same weighting factor, and p_t is the most recent price, n is the calculation period (preferably an even number), and there are $n/2$ number of weights, then

$$W_t = \frac{w_1 P_{t-n+1} + w_1 P_{t-n+2} + w_2 P_{t-n+3} + w_2 P_{t-n+4} + \cdots + w_{n/2} P_{t-1} + w_{n/2} P_t}{2 \times (w_1 + w_2 + \cdots + w_{n/2})}$$

For two or more data points using the same weighting, this formula can be regrouped as

$$W_t = \frac{w_1 (P_{t-n+1} + P_{t-n+2}) + w_2 (P_{t-n+3} + P_{t-n+4}) + \cdots + w_{n/2} (P_{t-1} + P_t)}{2 \times (w_1 + w_2 + \cdots + w_{n/2})}$$

Any number of consecutive data elements can be grouped for a step-weighted moving average.

If the purpose of weighting is to reproduce a pattern that is intrinsic to price movement, then either the *geometric average*, $G = (p_1 \times p_2 \times p_3 \ldots p_n)^{1/n}$ or *exponential smoothing*, explained later in this chapter, may be a better tool.

Triangular Weighting

While the simple moving average or linear regression treats each price equally, exponential smoothing and linear step-weighting put greater emphasis on the most recent data. There is an entire area of study in which the period of the dominant cycle is the basis for determining the best trend period. *Triangular weighting* or *triangular filtering*[1] attempts to uncover the trend by reducing the noise in both the front and back of the calculation window, where it is expected to have the greatest interference. Therefore, if a 20-day triangular weighting is used, the 10th day will have the greatest weight, while days 1 and 20 will have the smallest.

To implement triangular weighting, begin with the standard formula for a weighted average, calculated for n days as of the current day t,

$$W_t = \frac{\sum_{i=1}^{n} w_i P_{t-n+1}}{\sum_{i=1}^{n} w_i}$$

where n is also called the size, or width, of the window. For triangular weighting, the weighting factors w_i will increase linearly from 1 to the middle of the window, at

---

[1] J. J. Payne, "A Better Way to Smooth Data," *Technical Analysis of Stocks & Commodities* (October 1989).

$n/2$, then decrease to the end at n. This has a slightly different form when the period is odd or even,

$$w_i = i, \quad \text{for } i = 1 \text{ to } int((n+2)/2)$$
$$n - i + 1, \quad \text{for } i = int((n+2)/2) + 1 \text{ to } n \text{ (even values of } n)$$
$$n - i, \quad \text{for } i = int((n+2)/2) + 1 \text{ to } n \text{ (odd values of } n)$$

where int is a function that returns the integer portion by truncation. For odd values of n, the weighting factor has the value i, where i ranges from 1 to $n/2$ (rounded up with the help of the function int) and the value of $n - i$ from $n/2$ to n. Instead of a triangular filter, which climbs in equal steps to a peak at the middle value, a *Gaussian filter* can be used, which weights the data in a form similar to a bell curve. Here, the weighting factors are more complex, but the shape of the curve may be more appealing,

$$w_i = 10^x \quad and \quad x = \frac{3}{2} \times \left(1 - \frac{2i}{n}\right)^2$$

Triangular weighting is often used for cycle analysis.

Pivot-Point Weighting

Too often we limit ourselves by our perception of the past. When a weighted moving average is used, it is normal to assume that all the weighting factors should be positive; however, that is not a requirement. The *pivot-point moving average* uses reverse linear weights (e.g., 5, 4, 3, . . .) that begin with a positive value and continue to decline even when they become negative.[2] In the following formula, the *pivot point*, where the weight is zero, is reached about ⅔ through the data interval. For a pivot-point moving average of 11 values, the eighth data point is given the weight of 0:

$$PPMA_t(11) = (-3p_{t-10} - 2p_{t-9} - 1p_{t-8} + 0p_{t-7} + 1p_{t-6} + 2p_{t-5}$$
$$+ 3p_{t-4} + 4p_{t-3} + 5p_{t-2} + 6p_{t-1} + 7p_t)/22$$

The intent of this pattern is to reduce the lag by front-loading the prices. The divisor is smaller than the usual linear weighted average (where the sum of 1 through 11 is 66) because it includes negative values. The general formula for an n-day pivot-point moving average is[3]

$$PPMA_t(n) = \frac{2}{n(n+1)} \sum_{i=1}^{n} (3i - n - 1) P_i$$

A computer program and indicator that calculates and displays the pivot-point moving average, both called *TSM Pivot Point Average*, are available on the Companion Website. The negative weighting factors actually reverse the impact of the price move for the oldest data

[2] Patrick E. Lafferty, "End-Point Moving Average," *Technical Analysis of Stocks & Commodities* (October 1995).
[3] Don Kraska, "Letters to S&C," *Technical Analysis of Stocks & Commodities* (February 1996), 12.

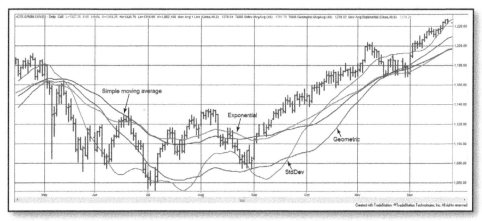

FIGURE 3.3 S&P Continuous Futures, April through December 2010, with Examples of the Simple Moving Average, Standard Deviation Average, Geometric Average, and Exponential Smoothing, All with Calculation Periods of 40 Days.

points rather than just give them less importance. For a short interval this can cause the trendline to be out of phase with prices. This method seems best when used for longer-term cyclic markets, where the inflection point, at which the weighting factor becomes zero, is aligned with the cyclic turn or can be fixed at the point of the last trend change.

Standard Deviation Moving Average

A unique trend calculation technique uses the standard deviation of prices.[4] This method creates a comparatively smooth trendline, *StdAvg*, by modifying the moving average value with a percentage of the standard deviation of prices. The following instructions are from the program *TSM Stdev Mvg Avg*, available on the Companion Website. It uses 5% of a 30-period standard deviation, and a 15-period moving average; however, each of these values can be changed. The result is shown for S&P futures in Figure 3.3.

```
SD = StdDev(close,30);
SDV = (SD - SD[1]) / SD;
StdAvg = Average(close,15) + .05*SDV;
```

■ Geometric Moving Average

The *geometric mean* is a growth function that is very applicable to long-term price movement. It is especially useful for calculating the components of an index. The geometric mean can also be applied to the most recent n points at time t to get a *geometric average* similar in function to a moving average

$$G_t = \left(p_{t-n+1} \times p_{t-n+2} \times \cdots \times p_{t-1} \times p_t \right)^{(1/n)} = \left(\prod_{i=1}^{n} p_{t-i+1} \right)^{(1/n)}$$

---

[4] Robert T. H. Lee, *Power Tools for Traders* (Hong Kong: MegaCapital Limited, 1997).

The daily calculation is more complicated but could be rewritten as

$$\ln G_t = \frac{\ln P_{t-n+1} + \ln P_{t-n+2} + \cdots + \ln P_{t-1} + \ln P_t}{n}$$

$$= \frac{1}{n}\left(\sum_{i=1}^{n} \ln P_{t-i+1}\right)$$

This is similar in form to the standard moving average based on the arithmetic mean and can be written in either spreadsheet or program code as

```
GA = average(log(price),n)
```

Note that some software will use the function *log* although the calculation is actually the *natural log*, ln. Other programs will allow the choice of *log(value)* or *ln(value)*. A weighted geometric moving average, for *n* days ending at the current day *t*, would have the form

$$\ln G_t = \frac{w_1 \ln P_{t-n+1} + w_2 \ln P_{t-n+2} + \cdots + w_{n-1} \ln P_{t-1} + w_n \ln P_t}{w_1 + w_2 + \cdots + w_n}$$

$$= \frac{\displaystyle\sum_{i=1}^{n} w_i \ln P_{t-i+1}}{\displaystyle\sum_{i=1}^{n} w_i}$$

The geometric moving average itself would give greater weight to lower values without the need for a discrete weighting function. This is most applicable to long data intervals where prices had a wide range of values. In applying the technique to recent index or stock prices, this distinction is not as apparent. For example, if the historical index values vary from 10 to 1000, the simple average of those two values is 505, and the geometric average is 100, but for the three sequential prices of 56.20, 58.30, and 57.15, the arithmetic mean is 57.2166, and the geometric is 57.1871. A 5-, 10-, or 20-day moving average of stock prices, compared to geometric averages of the same intervals, show negligible differences. The geometric moving average is best applied to long-term historic data with wide variance, using yearly or quarterly average prices.

■ Accumulative Average

An *accumulative average* is simply the long-term average of all data, but it is not practical for trend following. One drawback is that the final value is dependent upon the start date. If the data have varied around the same price for the entire data series, then the result would be good. It would also be useful if you are looking for the average of a ratio over a long period. Experience shows that price levels have changed because of inflation or a structural shift in supply and/or demand, and that progressive values fit the situation best.

Reset Accumulative Average

A *reset accumulative average* is a modification of the accumulative average and attempts to correct for the loss of sensitivity as the number of trading days becomes large. This alternative allows you to reset or restart the average whenever a new trend begins, a significant event occurs, or at some specified time interval, for example, at the time of quarterly earnings reports or at the end of the current crop year.

Drop-Off Effect

Many *rolling trend calculations* are distinguished by the *drop-off effect*, a common way of expressing the abrupt change in the current value when a significant older value is dropped from the calculation. Simple moving averages, linear regressions, and weighted averages all use a fixed period, or window, and are subject to this. For an n-period moving average, the importance of the oldest value being dropped off is measured by the difference between the new price being added to the calculation, t, and the one being removed, $t-n$, divided by the number of periods,

$$\text{Drop-off effect} = (p_t - p_{t-n})/n$$

A front-weighted average, in which the oldest values have less importance, reduces this effect because older, high volatility data slowly become a smaller part of the result before being dropped off. Exponential smoothing, discussed next, is by nature a front-loaded trend that minimizes the drop-off effect as does the average-off method.

CHAPTER 4

Trend Systems (Part 1)

From Perry J. Kaufman, *Trading Systems and Methods, + Website*, 5th Edition (Hoboken, New Jersey: John Wiley & Sons, 2013), Chapter 8.

Learning Objective Statements

- Explain three reasons why trend systems work
- Generalize how buy and sell signals are used with indicators and tools for measuring trend, such as: Moving Averages, Bollinger Bands, Keltner Channels, Percentage Bands, Volatility Bands, and combinations of bands and other indicators
- Describe how to apply the 10-day moving average rule in a trading system

The previous chapters developed the tools for calculating trends—a traditional moving average, various weighted averages, exponential smoothing, and regression. To profit from identifying the trend requires the use of trading rules and the selection of specific parameters that define the trend speed and an acceptable level of risk, among other factors. This chapter first discusses those rules that are necessary to all trading strategies and then gives examples of actual systems. The selection of trend speed is handled only briefly here but is continued with a detailed analysis of these and other systems throughout the book. It is most important to find trends that are robust, that is, that work across many markets and under varied economic conditions. At the same time they must satisfy an investor's risk tolerance. It is a difficult balance.

Trend systems are the preferred choice of Commodity Trading Advisors (CTAs). Some advisors are reported to be using the same systems devised in 1980. Barclay Hedge (BarclayHedge.com) reports that hedge funds had a total of $1,762.9 billion under management as of the first quarter of 2012, and managed futures totaling $328.9 billion. Investments from both institutions and individuals have been flowing into the industry at an increasing rate, up almost 500% since 2002.

■ Why Trend Systems Work

Trend analysis is the basis for many successful trading programs, some with audited performance published for more than 30 years. Being able to identify the trend is also important if you are a discretionary trader looking to increase your chances for success by trading on "the right side of the market." Trend systems work because

- *Long-term trends capture large price moves caused by fundamental factors.* Economic trends are most often based on government interest rate policy, which is both slow to develop and persistent. In turn, interest rates directly affect foreign exchange, the trade balance, mortgage rates, carrying charges, and the stock market.

- *Prices are not normally distributed but have a fat tail.* The fat tail means that there is an unusually large number of directional price moves that are longer than would be expected if prices were randomly distributed. The fat tail will generate exceptional trend profits, which are essential to a trend system's long-term success.

- *Money moves the markets.* Most trends are supported by the flow of investor funds. While this causes short-term noise, it also delivers the long-term trends. As trends become clearer to the general public, additional money flows in to continue the trend.

Trend trading works when the market is trending. It doesn't work in markets that are not trending. There is no magic solution that will generate profits for trending strategies when prices are moving sideways, and there is no one trending technique that is always best. You'll find that most trending methods have about the same returns over time but with different risk profiles. It is the risk profile and the trading frequency that distinguish one method from another, and those features will be discussed throughout this chapter.

How Often Do Markets Trend?

Is there a way to measure how often markets trend? One analyst defines a trend as 10 consecutive closes in the same direction, but that seems arbitrary and a small window. What if there were nine days up and one small down day?

A trend is a relative concept. It is relative to the trader's time horizon, and it is relative to the amount of noise and price swings that are acceptable within the trending period. Ultimately, a trend exists if you can profit from the price moves using a trending strategy.

The Fat Tail

The *fat tail* is a statistical phenomenon caused by a combination of market fundamentals and supported by human behavior. The net effect is that prices move in one direction much longer than can be explained by a random distribution. As a simple example, consider coin flipping as a classic way to produce a random distribution. In 100 coin tosses,

- 50 will be a head or a tail followed by the opposite head or tail.

- 25 will be two heads or two tails in a row.

- 12½ (if we could have halves tosses) will be three heads or three tails in a row.

- About 6 will be four heads or four tails in a row.

- About 3 will be five in a row.

- 1 or 2 will be six in a row of either heads or tails.

If price moves are substituted for coin flips, then heads would be a move up and tails a move down. If the pattern of up and down price moves follows a random distribution (and the up and down moves were of the same amount), then it would not be possible to profit from a trend system. But prices are not normally distributed. Price runs have a fat tail, which means that, instead of one run of 6 out of 100 days of trading, we may see a run of 12, or 3 runs of 6. That distribution is enough to make trend trading profitable.

Another factor is that these long runs translate into very large trading profits. It is not necessary to have every day go in the same direction in order to profit, only that the downward reversals during an uptrend not be large enough to change the direction of the trend and end the trade. The more tolerance for the size of the interim reversals, the more likely the fat tail can be captured.

If there are more runs of longer duration for every 100 daily price moves, what is the shape of the rest of the distribution? Figure 4.1 gives a theoretical representation of an actual price distribution compared to a random distribution. The extra movement that goes into creating the fat tail comes from the frequency of short runs. There are fewer runs of 1 and 2 and more runs greater than 6. The total remains the same.

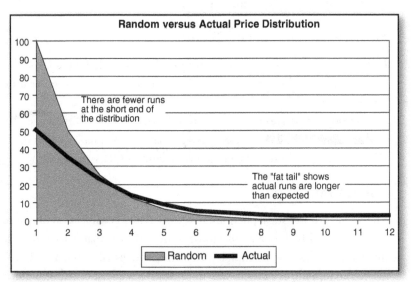

FIGURE 4.1 Distribution of Runs. The shaded area shows the normal distribution of random runs. The solid dark line represents the distribution when there is a fat tail. In the fat tail distribution, there are fewer short runs and an unusually large number of longer runs or a single exceptionally long run.

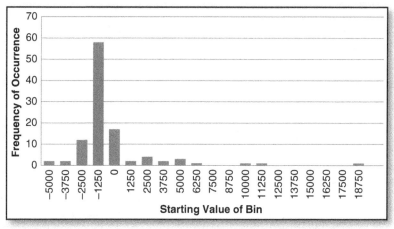

FIGURE 4.2 Frequency Distribution of Returns for S&P Futures Using a 40-Day Simple Moving Average Strategy. Results show a fat tail to the right.

Distribution of Profits and Losses

As a trader, you would want to know "How often is there a profit from a fat tail?" To find the answer, we'll apply the most basic trending system, a simple moving average that buys when the trendline turns up and sells short when it turns down. This will be discussed in more detail in the next sections. For now we need to know that results depend on both the market and the calculation period. Applying a simple 40-day moving average strategy to five diverse futures markets, 30-year bonds, the S&P, the euro currency, crude oil, and gold, the results of individual trades can be collected and displayed as a histogram (frequency distribution). The results of the S&P are shown in Figure 4.2.

In the frequency distribution, the bottom axis shows the starting value of the bins that hold the size of the profitable or losing trades, and the left scale shows the number of trades that fall into that bin. If the distribution was normal, then the shape would be a bell curve. This distribution is clearly extended far to the right, with one very large profit showing in the $18750 bin. That one profit offsets more than 30 losses in the largest bar marked −$1250. But the S&P is not the only market with this distribution; actually, the S&P has relatively smaller fat tails than other markets. Figure 4.1 shows the distribution sample. The tails to the right are very long and those to the left very short. It is important to remember that a pure trend strategy needs this distribution to be profitable.

Time Intervals, Market Maturity, and Trends

Trends are most easily seen using long-term charts, weekly rather than daily data, or daily rather than hourly data. The farther you step back from a chart, the clearer the trend. If you display a daily chart, there will be some obvious trending periods and some equally clear sideways moves. Change that to a weekly chart, and the trends will seem much clearer. Change that to an hourly chart, and you'll see mostly noise. Lower frequency data translate into better performance when using longer-term trends. While there are always fast trends that show profits in backtesting, they tend to be less stable and inconsistent in their returns. Trends using longer calculation periods are more likely to track

TABLE 4.1	Frequency Distribution for a Sample of Five Diverse Markets, Showing the Fat Tail to the Right and a Short Tail to the Left

Bin	1	2	3	4	5	6	7	8	9	10	11	12	13	14	15	16	17	18	19	20
Bonds	0	2	8	17	53	27	6	3	2	3	1	0	0	1	1	0	0	0	1	0
S&P	2	2	12	58	17	2	4	2	3	1	0	0	1	1	0	0	0	0	0	1
Euro	1	0	4	7	26	75	20	2	2	3	1	0	2	1	1	0	0	2	0	0
Crude	0	3	22	92	2	0	4	0	1	0	0	0	0	0	0	0	0	1	0	0
Gold	0	1	4	8	20	70	16	4	0	2	0	3	0	0	0	0	0	1	0	0

economic policy, such as the progressive lowering of interest rates by the central bank or a plan to allow the currency to weaken in order to stimulate exports and reduce debt.

Diverse markets may have very different trending qualities. Interest rate futures, money markets, and utility stocks are among the many investment vehicles closely tied to government rate policy and reflect the same long-term trend; this trend can persist for years. Foreign exchange is more complex and is constrained by monetary policy. Governments are more accepting of changes in the exchange rates if they occur slowly, but they will work hard to keep them within a target range. Most foreign exchange markets show clear but shorter trends compared to interest rates.

The stock market presents another level of difficulty. Individual stocks are driven by many factors, including earnings, competition, government regulation, management competence, and consumer confidence. Because the volume of trading in individual shares may vary considerably from day to day, these factors do not often net out as a clear trend. Stock prices may run up sharply on anticipation of better earnings or approval of a new drug, and reverse just as quickly within a few days. Liquidity, or volume, is an important element in the existence of a steady trend.

Individual stocks are also affected by concurrent trading in the index markets. When the S&P futures or the ETF SPY is bought and sold, all stocks within that index are bought and sold. If one company in the S&P 500 has just announced the loss of a major contract, but the overall market is strong, the share price of the suffering company may be dragged higher by arbitrage due to massive buying of the S&P index. This behavior makes for erratic price patterns in individual stocks.

Emerging markets are the exception. The introduction of a new market, such as the fictitious East European Stock Index, would be lightly traded but may be very trending. Initial activity would be dominated by commercials, such as banks, all of which would have a similar opinion on the economy of Eastern Europe. A small number of traders with the same opinion will cause very clear trends in the price. As the general public starts to participate, it adds liquidity while it also introduces noise, which in turn makes the trends less clear. Finding the trend then requires a longer time interval.

When using a trending strategy, select both the markets and the time frame that work with you. Longer calculation periods, lower frequency data, and markets that are more closely linked to their underlying fundamentals will all perform better.

■ Basic Buy and Sell Signals

Trends are based on the average always lagging price movement. It is the advantage and the disadvantage of the method. As the calculation period gets larger, the average

FIGURE 4.3   Amazon (AMZN) with a 40-Day Moving Average.

lags further. Figure 4.3 shows Amazon prices from April 2010 through February 2011 with a 40-day moving average. Clearly, the moving average smoothes prices. The basic idea behind using the moving average as a trend signal is to be long when prices are above the average and short when below. The rules are stated as

- *Buy* when prices cross above the trendline.
- *Sell short* when prices cross below the trendline.

Even with these simple rules, there are important choices to be made. Do you buy at the moment rising prices cross the trendline during the trading session, or do you wait for the price to close above the trendline? As seen in Figure 4.3, prices may cross back and forth through the trendline before settling on a final direction. If you subscribe to the belief that the closing price of the day is the most reliable price, then the number of trading signals can be reduced by using the rules:

- *Buy* when prices close above the trendline.
- *Sell short* when prices close below the trend line.

Another school of thought prefers the average of high and low prices, or the average of the high, low, and closing prices. A buy or short sale signal occurs when the (high + low)/2 or (high + low + *close*)/3 crosses above or below the current trendline value. In both of these cases, the averages could not be calculated until the end of the trading session because none of the three component values would be known until then.

Using the Trendline for Signals

The trendline represents the netting of all prices. Its purpose is to remove the price noise and show you the underlying price direction. Then it seems more reasonable to use the trendline to generate the trading signal. The change in the value of the trendline from the previous calculation to the current one is its direction—up, down, or unchanged. The direction of the trendline is a candidate for generating trading signals.

- *Buy* when the change in the trendline is up.
- *Sell short* when the change in the trendline is down.

The penalty for using the trendline as a trading signal is its lag. Figure 4.3 shows that, using a 40-day moving average, prices cross above the trendline during July a few days ahead of the point where the trendline turns up. The benefit using the trendline signal is that the trend turn is clear and more stable. During July and November, prices crossed back and forth through the trendline, but the trendline did not change direction; therefore, the trading signal remained the same.

Comparing Basic Trading Signals

The main differences between using a price penetration or the trendline to generate signals is that the trendline produces fewer trading signals, and those signals are delayed. If Amazon prices are used as an example, both methods of entry can be compared for a sample of calculation periods to see if one approach is consistently better than the other. Although this is a single example, it represents the general case.

As shown in Table 4.2, five calculation periods are used beginning with 5 days and doubling the period for each test. This maintains the percentage change in the calculation period and gives a better distribution sample. The two columns headed *Number of Trades* show that the trendline method has from 26% to 37% fewer trades and, for the most part, better performance. The *Profit Factor* is the performance ratio used by TradeStation equal to the gross profits divided by the gross losses. While not as good as the *information ratio* or *Sharpe ratio*, the results allow you to compare performance.

It appears that using the trendline signals is always better, but that is not necessarily the case. To be certain, you would need to compare a wide range of diverse markets rather than just Amazon. Even if these results seem compelling, it is always necessary to confirm the numbers to be confident of the answers and to be sure that you understand the process.

While it seems convincing that the trendline is best for the slower trends, it is not as clear for faster trading. For the case using a 5-day moving average, both methods netted a loss, but the price penetration shows a smaller loss. It is very possible that,

TABLE 4.2 Comparison of Entry Methods for 10 Years of Amazon (AMZN)

Signals using the trendline direction are shown on the left, and price penetration on the right.

Trend Calculation Period	Signal Using Trendline			Signal Using Price Cross			
	Total Profit/ Loss	Profit Factor	Number of Trades	Total Profit/ Loss	Profit Factor	Number of Trades	Increase in Trades
80	48.24	1.34	84	57.16	1.31	106	26%
40	94.42	1.46	120	32.21	1.12	164	37%
20	111.97	1.45	196	(7.31)	0.98	252	29%
10	(87.67)	0.81	292	(90.82)	0.82	370	27%
5	(90.31)	0.84	439	(49.15)	0.92	597	36%

for faster trading, the lag in the trendline is too much of a burden to overcome and the price penetration is better.

Anticipating the Trend Signal

Consistency is important. The system that is tested and the one that is traded should be the same. In this book, the closing price is used for most of the calculations; however, any combination of open, high, low, and close could be substituted. The normal process for generating a trading signal is to wait until prices close, then calculate the new moving average or trendline value, then see whether a crossing occurred or the direction of the trendline changed according to the basic buy and sell rules. But using the closing price for the calculation of the entry signal implies that you could enter on the close.

The process of waiting for the close price to perform the necessary calculations and generate a signal requires that orders be placed in the after-hours market or on the next open. While the trading system is indicating a new buy or sell signal as of the close of trading, you are entering the market significantly late. You are not following the system as it was tested. A practical solution to this dilemma is to record the prices shortly before the close, generate the trading signals, then enter the buy and sell orders for execution on the close. Occasionally, the order will be wrong because prices changed direction in the last few minutes of trading, but the cost of exiting the trade will usually be small compared to the improvement in overall execution.

The other alternative is to calculate, in advance, the closing price that will generate a signal using either the trendline method or the price crossing method. For an n day moving average the calculation is simple—the new moving average value will be greater than the previous value if today's price is greater than the price dropped off n-days ago. Because all of the other values in the average remain the same except for the first and last, the answer only needs those two values. If a 40-day average is used and the oldest price p_{t-0} was 30.25, then any price greater than 30.25 today would cause the trendline to move up, and any price greater than 30.25 would also cause an upwards price penetration. Then an order can be placed in advance to *buy at 30.26 stop*.

How important is this? A lot depends on the trending nature of the market. In other books, our discussion of market noise showed that the short-term interest rates had the lowest amount of noise, and the equity index markets had the most noise. Using the Eurodollar interest rates and the S&P 500 futures as the extremes, the method that enters using the trendline was compared when entries were taken on the current close, the next open, and the next close to assess the sensitivity of the total profits to entry delays. Table 4.3 shows the results.

All Eurodollar results show a profit for trades entered on the close of the day that a signal occurred. Longer trend periods were generally more profitable, confirming the premise that trends are more dominant in the long term due to government policy. When entries were delayed to the next open or next close, the results

TABLE 4.3 Comparison of Entries on the Close, Next Open, and Next Close

Results vary with the trending nature of the market. Analysis uses 10 years of S&P and Eurodollar interest rate futures, back-adjusted, ending in February 2011.

Calculation Period	Eurodollar Interest Rates						S&P 500					
	Today's Close		Next Open		Next Close		Today's Close		Next Open		Next Close	
	Total Profit or Loss	Profit Factor	Total Profit or Loss	Profit Factor	Total Profit or Loss	Profit Factor	Total Profit or Loss	Profit Factor	Total Profit or Loss	Profit Factor	Total Profit or Loss	Profit Factor
80	16150	2.87	16325	2.89	15630	2.75	(12325)	0.87	(10463)	0.89	16363	1.20
40	9603	1.61	9050	1.55	9383	1.61	(29138)	0.75	(26013)	0.78	5013	1.05
20	7745	1.37	6258	1.29	3850	1.16	13088	1.12	13900	1.13	22738	1.20
10	10773	1.40	8765	1.31	1165	1.04	(27925)	0.83	(22738)	0.86	(12550)	0.93
5	3368	1.09	(1715)	0.96	(870)	0.98	(21725)	0.90	(19588)	0.91	(56350)	−0.76

were worse. This is best seen in the profit factors, which measure reward to risk rather than only total profits.

The S&P is also clear but not as clean as Eurodollars. Equity index markets are noisy; that is, prices moving up are not expected to continue up for any sustained number of days. A new buy signal will usually happen on a day when prices are moving higher, but waiting until the next open or the next close could be better because of the noise. This was true for all calculation periods except 5 days. As for the calculation period, there was no particular pattern, although absolute losses were smaller as the trend period got longer, a modest confirmation that longer trends are better. We know from other tests and other markets that this limited example is generally true, but market characteristics always create exceptions.

Profile of a Simple Moving Average System

Using the moving average trendline as the basis for system signals, we chose a 40-day calculation period because it tends to be the fastest one that also identifies the major price trends. The profile of results is typical of any moving average system. Figure 4.4 shows the NASDAQ 100 for one year, ending February 2011. Buy and sell signals are generated from the direction of the trendline; there were no transaction fees.

The trading signals in Figure 4.4 show that the major upwards move is captured, but not before there are a number of false signals due to the trendline changes during sideways price periods. However, given enough tries, the trend surfaces, and the system gains a large profit, similar to the fat tail discussed at the beginning of this chapter. The profile of this NASDAQ example, shown in Table 4.4, is typical of longer-term trend-following systems. Of the 150 trades over 10 years, only 52 of them were profitable, about 35%. However, the average winning trade was much larger than the average losing trade, with a ratio of 2.22, and winning trades were held much longer than losing trades, supporting the adage "cut your losses and let your profits run." Finally, there were more

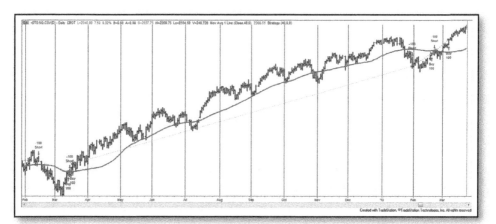

FIGURE 4.4 A Trend System for NASDAQ 100. Applying a 40-day moving average and taking the trading signals from the direction of trendline results gives a typical trend system profile.

TABLE 4.4	Performance Statistics for NASDAQ Futures, 10 Years Ending February 2011
Total profit	$11,880
Number of trades	150
Number of winning trades	52
Percentage of winning trades	34.7%
Average winning trade	1424.71
Average losing trade	−41.28
Win/loss ratio	2.22
Average bars in winners	31.65
Average bars in losers	6.64
Consecutive winner	6
Consecutive losses	10

consecutive losses than consecutive profits, but that follows because there are many more losses. The performance picture is that trend following gets in and out quickly when it has a loss but holds the trade whenever trends and profits develop. This category of strategy is called *conservation of capital*, referring to the feature that cuts losses quickly.

We can generalize the trend-following profile as:

- The percentage of profitable trades is low—often less than 30%.

- The average winning trade must be significantly larger than the average losing trade; actually, given only 30% profitable trades, the ratio must be greater than 100:30 to be profitable.

- The average winning trades are held much longer than losses.

- There is a high frequency of losing trades; therefore, there are also long sequences of losing trades.

There are many analysts that have a lifetime goal of improving these statistics, that is, capturing the long-term trend but improving the percentage of profitable trades. Some small amount of success is possible but not without changing the risk characteristics of trend-following systems. For example, if you add profit-taking (discussed throughout the book) or stop-losses, then you reduce or eliminate the chance of capturing the fat tail, which has been shown to be necessary for a long-term profit. Still, many traders do not like the idea of holding the trades for such a long time and giving back so much of the unrealized profits when the major trend changes direction. Different traders make different choices. A program to test the entry rules and execution options, including *long-only*, is *TSM Moving Average*, available on the Companion Website.

■ Bands and Channels

A good way to improve the reliability of signals without altering the overall trend profile is by constructing a *band*, or *channel*, around the trendline. It can be used to effectively slow down trading without sacrificing the biggest profits. If we accept the premise that the point of trend change is also the time of greatest indecision, then a simple way to avoid frequent false signals is by using a band.

Bands Formed by Highs and Lows

The most natural band is one formed from the daily high and low prices. Instead of applying the *n*-day moving average to the closing prices, it is applied separately to the highs and lows. Long positions are entered when today's high crosses the average of the highs and short sales when today's low crosses the average of the lows. To get a broad view of whether this is an improvement to entry points, the two most extreme markets (the Eurodollar considered the trendiest and the S&P the noisiest) are tested for 10 years with the five calculation periods used in an earlier example. Results are shown in Table 4.5.

For a highly trending market, such as the Eurodollar interest rates, entering later, on a penetration of either the highs or lows, is not as good as entering on a price penetration of the close. If this had not been determined from our study of noise in other works, these results would cause us to draw the same conclusion. Just the opposite is seen in the S&P results. Waiting longer to enter improves results noticeably, and, in the case of the 40-day trend, it turns a loss into a profit.

We can conclude that a band can be a profitable variation to a simple trend system, but not for all markets. The next question is "Are there other bands that work better?"

Keltner Channels

One of the original band calculations was by Keltner,[1] which goes as follows:

$$\text{(Average daily price)} \qquad AP_t = (H_t + L_t + C_t)/3$$

TABLE 4.5 Results of Using a Moving Average of the Highs and Lows, Compared to the Closes

	Eurodollar Interest Rates				S&P 500			
	Close Crossing		High-Low		Close Crossing		High-Low	
Calculation Period	Total Profit or Loss	Profit Factor	Total Profit or Loss	Profit Factor	Total Profit or Loss	Profit Factor	Total Profit or Loss	Profit Factor
80	16320	2.94	13842	2.18	30027	1.54	36443	1.74
40	16035	2.18	15000	2.02	(10337)	0.91	12402	1.14
20	10172	1.44	5167	1.20	5987	1.05	16512	1.15
10	2727	1.08	3667	1.11	(49000)	0.76	(33751)	0.82
5	7812	1.20	(337)	0.99	(106950)	0.64	(43760)	0.81

---

[1] Chester W. Keltner, *How to Make Money in Commodities* (Kansas City, MO: The Keltner Statistical Service, 1960).

(10-day moving average)	$MA_t = average(C_t, 10)$
(Upper band)	$UB_t = MA_t + AP_t$
(Lower band)	$LB_t = MA_t + AP_t$

These days we would tend to use true range, rather than the high-low range as a better representation of volatility.

Percentage Bands

Another simple construction is a percentage band, formed by adding and subtracting the same percentage of price from the trendline based on the closing prices. If c is the percentage to be used (where $c = 0.03$ means 3%), then

$$\text{(Upper band)} \quad B_U = (1 + c) \times MA_t$$
$$\text{(Lower band)} \quad B_L = (1 - c) \times MA_t$$

where MA_t = today's moving average value

Therefore, if the moving average value for Merck (MRK) is $33, and the band is 3%, then the upper band is 33.99 and the lower band is 32.01. Because the moving average is much smoother than the price series, the band will be uniform around the moving average, narrowing and widening slightly as prices decline and rise.

The band can be more sensitive to change if the current price p_t is used to calculate the band instead of the moving average trendline. The bands are then

$$\text{(Upper band)} \quad B_U = (1 + c) \times p_{t-1} + MA_t$$
$$\text{(Lower band)} \quad B_L = (1 - c) \times p_{t-1} + MA_t$$

The band is still oriented around the moving average trendline to prevent it from jumping up and down too often. Using the price to generate the band also requires that yesterday's price be used; otherwise the band would never be penetrated. Using a percentage band would work for stocks but not for futures. Most futures analysis uses back-adjusted data, and if the carry is mostly negative, then the oldest back-adjusted data could actually become negative. That doesn't affect a moving average trading signal, but it does make any percentage price calculation wrong. Back-adjusted historic prices are simply not correct.

If only a small buffer zone is needed, rather than one that adjusts over time, then a band based on absolute point value could be used. For example, stocks trading between $20 and $40 could have a $1 band. If your goal is to avoid a few very small variations around the time of trend change, then an absolute point value band may be a simple alternative solution.

Volatility Bands

To the degree that volatility increases as prices increase, the percentage band is a volatility band; however, that relationship is both long term and not as good as actually measuring the individual volatility for many stocks and futures markets. Regardless of the method, creating a band that is responsive to volatility may improve the reliability of trend signals. The independent smoothing of the high and low prices over any calculation period forms a natural volatility band. Although it may be practical to use the same smoothing technique or the same calculation period as the underlying trend (e.g., 10-day or 10% smoothing constant) for the high, low, and closing prices, it is not a requirement. If the same smoothing criterion is used, the band will be uniform with respect to the moving average of the closing price; if not, all three trendlines may weave around one another, which creates some practical problems.

There are many choices for measuring volatility and creating a band around the trendline. All of the methods of forming bands are subject to scaling. Scaling is accomplished by using a constant value as a multiplier or scaling factor; it increases or reduces the sensitivity of the band. If s is a scaling factor and c is a fixed percentage, then the following bands can be constructed:

$$B_t = MA_t \pm s \times c \times MA_t \qquad \text{(Percentage of trendline)}$$

$$B_t = MA_t \pm s \times c \times p_t \qquad \text{(Percentage of price)}$$

$$B_t = MA_t \pm s \times ATR_{t-1} \times MA_t \qquad \text{(Average true range)}$$

$$B_t = MA_t \pm s \times stdev_{t-1} \times MA_t \qquad \text{(Standard deviation)}$$

When $s = 1$, the scaling effect is nullified; for $s > 1$, the width of the band is increased; and for $s < 1$, the band width is reduced. In the choices above, MA was used to indicate a moving average, but any method of calculating the trend can be substituted, such as an exponential smoothing or a regression. Figure 4.5 shows the four types of bands applied to the S&P futures. All use a scaling factor of 2, which may be too close for some methods and too far for others. The purpose of the chart is to show the relative shape of the bands and distance from the prices.

In Figure 4.5 the center line is a 20-day moving average. The first two methods of calculating bands, the percentage of trendline and percentage of price, are almost

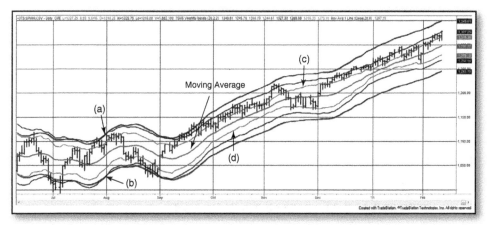

FIGURE 4.5 Four Volatility Bands around a 20-Day Moving Average, Based on (a) 2% of Trendline, (b) 2% of Price, (c) 2 × Average True Range, and (d) Annualized 20-Day Volatility.

identical, very smooth, and are the farthest from the center. The next band closer to the moving average is the average true range. It moves slightly farther apart when prices are more volatile. The band closest to the trendline is the annualized volatility, which is most sensitive to price changes.

Because the same scaling factor produces bands that are different for each method, it is difficult to compare them without finding the scaling factors that come closest to average band width for each technique. The bigger decision is whether it is more sensible to use a very smooth band or one that reacts to changes in price volatility. That decision is up to each trader.

It may be convenient to have separate exit and entry bands, the entries less sensitive than the exits so that the strategy exits quickly but enters slowly. Or, if the entry occurs on a penetration of the band, but the exit is based on the trendline, then trades are not reversed from long to short. That improves slippage because only half the number of shares or contracts are traded on each order, and may avoid some false signals.

Bollinger Bands

Perhaps the simplest and most robust measurement of price volatility is the standard deviation of the prices themselves, calculated over recent price history. This was the last method listed in the previous section. John Bollinger has popularized the combination of a 20-day moving average with bands formed using 2 standard deviations of the price changes over the same 20-day period. They are now frequently called *Bollinger bands*.[2] Because the standard deviation represents a confidence level, and prices are not normally distributed, the choice of two standard deviations equates to an 87% confidence band (if prices were normally distributed, two standard deviations would contain 95.4% of the data). In their normal use, Bollinger bands are combined with other techniques to identify extreme price levels. These are discussed later in this section.

Figure 4.6 shows Ford (F) plotted with a traditional Bollinger band. One of the characteristics of this band is that, once the price moves outside either

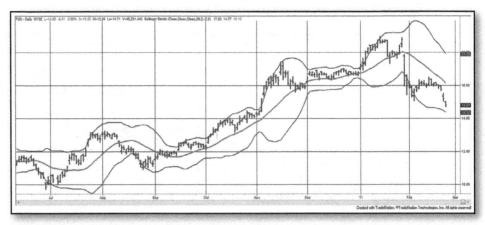

FIGURE 4.6 Bollinger Bands Applied to Ford.

[2] John A. Bollinger, Bollinger Capital Management, Inc. P.O. Box 3358, Manhattan Beach, CA 90266, www.bollingerbands.com. Also *Bollinger on Bollinger Bands* (New York: McGraw-Hill, 2001).

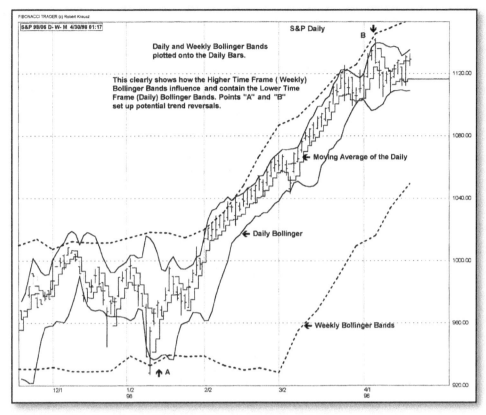

FIGURE 4.7 Combining Daily and Weekly Bollinger Bands.

Source: Chart created using The Fibonacci Trader by Robert Krausz. Used with permission from Fibonacci Trader Corporation, St. Augustine, FL. www.fibonaccitrader.com.

the upper or lower band, it remains outside for a number of days in a row. This type of pattern was typical of what used to be called *high momentum*. Note that the width of the band varies considerably with the volatility of prices and that a period of high volatility causes a "bubble," which extends past the period where volatility declines.

Figure 4.6 was created using the TradeStation indicator *Bollinger Bands*, which lets you vary both the calculation period for the trend and the number of standard deviations. But then, if it's not a 20-day average and 2 standard deviations, it's not a Bollinger band.

Bollinger bands can also be applied effectively to multiple time frames. An excellent example that uses a combination of weekly and daily data applied to the S&P 500 is seen in Figure 4.7. The price pattern follows the weekly Bollinger band higher, where the daily and weekly prices come together during the week of July 14.

Modified Bollinger Bands One of the significant problems with Bollinger bands, as well as any volatility measure based on historic data, is that the bands will expand after increasing volatility but are slow to narrow as volatility declines. An excellent correction[3] for this requires the following calculations for the center line, D,

$$M_t = \alpha \times C_t + (1 - \alpha) \times M_{t-1}$$
$$U_t = \alpha \times M_t + (1 - \alpha) \times U_{t-1}$$
$$D_t = \frac{(2 - \alpha) \times M_t - U_t}{1 - \alpha}$$

where C is the closing price and α is the smoothing constant, set to 0.15 to approximate a 20-day moving average. In order to correct the bulge in the bands following a volatile period, the upper and lower bands (BU and BL) are calculated as

$$m_t = \alpha \times |C_t - D_t| + (1 - \alpha) \times m_{t-1}$$
$$u_t = \alpha \times m_t + (1 - \alpha) \times u_{t-1}$$
$$d_t = \frac{(2 - \alpha) \times m_t - u_t}{1 - \alpha}$$
$$BU_t = D_t + f \times d_t$$
$$BL_t = D_t - f \times d_t$$

where f is the multiplier for the width of the band, suggested at 2.5 compared to Bollinger's 2.0. Figure 4.8 shows the modified Bollinger bands along with the original (lighter lines) for gold futures during the first part of 2009. While the new bands do not remove the bulge, they are faster to correct and more uniform in the way they envelop prices. Programs to calculate and display the original and modified bands are *TSM Bollinger bands* and *TSM Bollinger Modified*, available on the Companion Website.

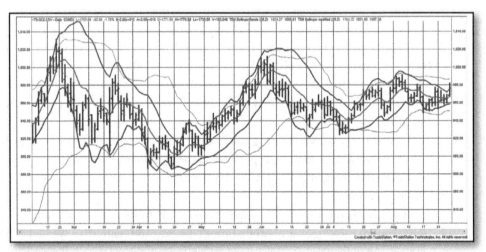

FIGURE 4.8 Modified Bollinger Bands Shown with Original Bands (Lighter Lines), Applied to Gold Futures, February–August 2009.

[3] Dennis McNicholl, "Better Bollinger Bands," *Futures* (October 1998).

THEORY AND ANALYSIS

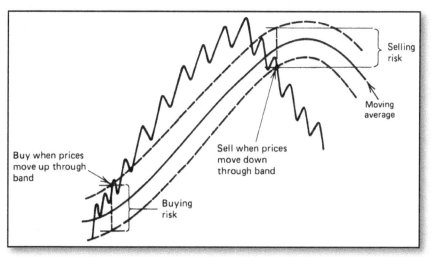

FIGURE 4.9 Simple Reversal Rules for Using Bands.

Rules for Using Bands

Regardless of the type of band that is constructed, rules for using bands to generate trading signals are limited. The first decision to be made is whether the trading strategy is one that is always in the market (a reversal strategy), changing from long to short and back again as the bands are penetrated. If so, the following rules apply:

- *Buy* (close out shorts and go long) when the prices close above the upper band.
- *Sell short* (close out longs and go short) when the prices close below the lower band.

This technique is always in the market with a maximum risk (without execution costs) equal to the width of the band, which changes each day (see Figure 4.9). Alternately, you may prefer to exit from each trade when prices move into the zone between the bands or when prices cross the original trendline.

- *Buy* (go long) when prices close above the upper band. Close out longs when prices reverse and close below the moving average value (the center of the band).
- *Sell short* when prices close below the lower band. Cover your shorts when prices close above the moving average value.

The band is then used to enter into new long or short trades, and the actual trendline at the center of the band is used for liquidation. If prices are not strong enough to penetrate the opposite band on the close of the same day, the trade is closed out but not reversed. The next day, penetration of either the upper or lower band will signal a new long or short trade, respectively.

This technique allows a trade to be reentered in the same direction in the event of a false trend change. If a pullback occurs after a close-out while no position is being held (as shown in Figure 4.10), an entry at a later date might be at a better price. It also reduces the order size by 50%, which is likely to improve the execution price

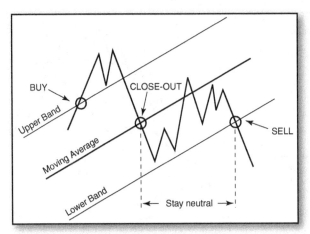

FIGURE 4.10 Basic Rules for Using Bands.

and add liquidity for large traders. The disadvantage is when the price changes direction and moves so fast that both the close-out and the new signal occur on the same day. Reversing the position immediately would be better in a fast market.

The high and low of the day may also be used as penetration criteria. Again using the outer bands for entry and the moving average for exit, apply the following rules:

- *Buy* when the high of the day penetrates the upper band, and close out longs when the low of the day penetrates the moving average.

- *Sell short* when the low of the day penetrates the lower band, and cover shorts when the high penetrates the moving average.

Using the trendline as an exit, risk is limited to half of the full band width. If the bands are narrow, there is a greater chance that an entry on an intraday high might also see an exit below the trendline on the close of the same day.

Timing the Order

The type of execution order placed when following a system will affect its results over the long term. The use of a moving average band identifies a change of trend when a breakout occurs. Buying at the point of the upside breakout or selling during a downside breakout often results in poor entry prices, and has been known to place the trader in a new trend at the point where prices are ready for a technical correction. In an attempt to overcome these problems, a number of rules can be used:

- *Buy* (or *sell*) on the close after an entry (intraday) signal has been indicated.

- *Buy* (or *sell*) on the next day's open following a signal.

- *Buy* (or *sell*) with a delay of 1, 2, or 3 days after the signal.

- *Buy* (or *sell*) after a price retracement of 50% (or some other value) following a signal.

- *Buy* (or *sell*) when prices move to within a specified risk level relative to a reversal or exit point.

The object is to enter a new position and see an immediate profit, or reduce risk. Some of these rules can be categorized as timing and others as risk management. If intraday prices are used to signal new entries and exits, a rule may be added that states:

> Only one order can be executed in one day; either the liquidation of a current position or an entry into a new position.

While better entry points will improve overall performance, an entry rule that is contingent on price action, such as a pullback, risks the possibility of not entering at all. A contingent order that is missed is guaranteed to be a profit. It might be better to combine the entry order, for example,

> Buy (or sell) after prices reverse by $0.50 \times$ ATR or enter on the next close.

Once you have decided on a timing rule, you must test it carefully. The perception of improvement does not always live up to expectations. In tests on trend-following systems conducted over many years, positions calculated on the close but delayed until the next open improved execution prices about 75% of the time but resulted in smaller overall total profits. Why? Fast breakouts that never retrace result in missed trades. Therefore, while three out of four executions returned a better price by a small amount, those improvements were often offset by the profitable breakouts that were never entered.

The Compromise between Reliability and Delay

As with most trading techniques, the benefits of one approach can also have negative factors. The use of a band around a trendline improves the reliability of the trading signal and reduces the total number of signals. The wider the band, the fewer signals. Both of these characteristics are significant benefits. But wider bands mean delayed entries; therefore, you cannot capture as much of the trend, and the average profits will be smaller. If the bands are too wide, then the average profits can decline to zero. The use of wider bands also means greater risk on each trade. It will be necessary to trade smaller positions or capitalize the account with a larger investment.

These are serious choices that must be made with every trading program. Although there are classic solutions to this problem, traders must choose the methods that complement their risk preference.

Bollinger on Bollinger Bands

While most trading strategies buy when there is an upwards penetration of the top band and sell when prices move below the lower band, the use of Bollinger bands is usually mean-reverting, or counter to the price direction. However, this can be unnecessarily risky, especially when prices are volatile. Bollinger recommends confirming a downside penetration using other indicators, primarily those based on volume and market breadth. If prices are moving lower but volume is not increasing and negative breadth is not confirming the downward move, then a buy signal is realistic.[4]

Bollinger uses the concept that volatility is cyclic, but without a regular period. He sees very low volatility as a forecast for high volatility and very high volatility forecasting low volatility, similar to the way traders use the CME Volatility Index (VIX). Based on this, a major price rally with dramatically higher volatility, that expands the bandwidth to extremes, should be sold when the bandwidth begins to narrow. This only applies to upwards price moves.

Combining Bollinger with Other Indicators

Williams[5] suggests that a number of indicators can be combined to capture volatile moves after a price contraction, using:

1. A standard 20-day, 2-standard deviation Bollinger band
2. A 20-day Keltner Channel
3. A 21-day Chaikin Oscillator to monitor the flow of funds

To enter a long position, the following conditions must be satisfied:

- The Bollinger bands constrict to inside the Keltner Channel while the Chaikin Oscillator is below zero.

- The Chaikin Oscillator crosses above the zero line.

For shorts,

- The Bollinger bands constrict to inside the Keltner Channel while the Chaikin Oscillator is above zero.

- The Chaikin Oscillator crosses below the zero line.

■ Applications of a Single Trend

For any trend technique, the selection of the calculation period—the interval over which you will define the trend—is the most important decision in the ultimate success of the trading system. Entry rules and timing improve performance but are considered refinements. The calculation period determines the frequency of trading and the nature of the underlying trend that will be targeted. Deciding the calculation period is more important than the method of identifying the trend. You can be profitable using a simple moving average, regression, breakout, or any other technique—if you can settle on the right time interval.

The previous sections have used examples of calculation periods without any claim that one time interval was better than another. We have discussed that the long-term

---

[4] John Bollinger, "John Bollinger of Bollinger Bands Fame," *Technical Analysis of Stocks & Commodities* (May 2002).

[5] Billy Williams, "Biting Off Profits with the Rattlesnake Breakout Method," *Futures* (October 2010).

trend mimics government policy of interest rates or economic growth; therefore, there is good reason to choose a longer calculation period. We also saw that the trends were clearer when looking at a weekly chart rather than at a daily, and it was not clear that an intraday chart had any persistent trends. But for most traders, the risk of using this long time frame is unacceptable; they prefer smaller profits and smaller losses associated with faster trading. There is now strategy development software that makes it easy to test a range of calculation periods to find the one that performed best in the past. This technique is called optimization. But the power of the computer is not always as good as simple human reasoning and common sense. The computer is best for validating an idea, not for discovering one.

Before the computer, analysts struggled with the same problem of finding the best calculation period. At first, the trend period was based on multiples of calendar periods, such as a week or a month, expressed as trading days. When these techniques were limited to a small group of analysts, these approaches were very successful. Many traders still subscribe to the idea that certain time intervals have value. The most popular calculation periods have been: 3 days, the expected duration of a short price move; 5 days, a trading week; 20 to 23 days, a trading month; 63 days, a calendar quarter; and of course, 252 days, a calendar year. Implied volatility calculations traditionally use 20 days. It is not clear where the 200-day moving average, used for stocks, came from.

More recently, a class of adaptive trends has appeared. These techniques attempt to change the speed of the trend based on a characteristic of price movement, such as volatility or noise.

The following sections include classic examples of well-known systems that use one trend, as well as a comparison of trading performance of the most popular single-trend techniques over a broad range of calculation periods.

A Simple Momentum System

The *n-day momentum* is defined as the change in price over n days. It's not actually "momentum" but that is the term commonly used by the industry. The simplest trend system is the one that buys when the n-day change is positive and sells when the n-day change is negative. For large values of n, the results will be surprisingly similar to a simple moving average system; therefore we will not give examples here. Keep in mind that momentum can be very effective even as it is very simple.

A Step-Weighted Moving Average

In 1972, Robert Joel Taylor published the "Major Price Trend Directional Indicator" (MPTDI), which was reprinted in summary form in the September 1973 *Commodities Magazine* (now *Futures*). The system was promoted and implemented through Enterex Commodities in Dallas and was tested in 1972 on historical data provided by Dunn and Hargitt Financial Services in West Lafayette, Indiana. It was one of the few well-defined published systems and served as the basis for much experimentation for current technicians and aspiring analysts.

TABLE 4.6	MPTDI Variables for Gold*			
Average Trading Range	Number of Days in Calculation	Weighting-Factors Progression	Entry Signal Penetration	Approximate Stop-Loss Point
50–150	2–5 days	TYPE A	100 pts	150 pts
150–250	20 days	TYPE B	200 pts	300 pts
250–350	15 days	TYPE C	250 pts	350 pts
350–450	10 days	TYPE D	350 pts	450 pts
450+	5 days	TYPE E	450 pts	550 pts

*100 points = $1 per ounce.

MPTDI is a moving average with a band. Its unique feature is that the calculation period and band width change based on price volatility, the current trading range. Because the method has distinct trading range thresholds (called steps), the method is called a *step-weighted moving average*. It is unique in its complete dependence on incremental values for all aspects of the system: the moving average, entry, and stop-loss points. For example, Table 4.6 shows what conditions might be assigned to gold.

If gold were trading in an average range of 250 to 350 points each day ($2.50 to $3.50 per ounce, but remember this was 1972), the weighting factor for the moving average would be TYPE C, indicating medium volatility (TYPE A is lowest). Using TYPE C with a 15-day moving average, the most recent 5 days are given the weight 3, the next 5 days 2, and the last 5 days are weighted by 1. The entry signals use the corresponding penetration of 250 points above the moving average for a buy and 250 below for a sell. The intraday highs or lows are used to trigger the entry based on values calculated after the close of trading on the prior day. A stop-loss is fixed at the time of entry equal to the value on the same line as the selected volatility. The penetration of the stop-loss will cause the liquidation of the current trade. A new signal in the reverse direction will serve as both the exit for the current trade and the entry for a new trade.

There is a lot to say in favor of the principles of MPTDI. It is individualized with respect to markets and self-adjusting to changing volatility. The stop-loss serves to limit the initial risk of the trade and allow the coordination of a money management approach. The fixed risk differs from moving averages using standard bands because a moving average and its band can back away from system entry points if there is a gradual reversal of the price trend. But there are some rough edges to the system. The incremental ranges for volatility, entry points, and stops seem to be a crude measure. Even if they are accurate in the center of the range, they must get less accurate at the extremes where volatility causes an abrupt change in parameter values when it moves from one range to another.

MPTDI sets the groundwork for a smoother, more adaptive process. Before such a process can be developed, however, it is necessary to study price movement at discrete levels, such as those shown in MPTDI. From discrete relationships it is possible to generalize a continuous relationship.

The Volatility System

Another method that includes volatility and is computationally simple is the *Volatility System*.[6] Signals are generated when a price change is accompanied by an unusually large move relative to average volatility. If the average volatility measured over *n* days is

$$V_t = \frac{1}{n} \sum_{i=t-n+1}^{t} TR_i$$

where TR_i is the *true range* on day *i* and V_t is the called the *average true range* on day *t*.

Trading rules are given as

- *Sell* if the close drops by more than $k \times V(n)_{t-1}$ from the previous close.

- *Buy* if the close rises by more than $k \times V(n)_{t-1}$ from the previous close.

The value of *k* is generally about 3.0. Note that the current price change is always compared to the previous volatility calculation.

The 10-Day Moving Average Rule

The most basic application of a moving average system was proposed by Keltner in his 1960 publication, *How to Make Money in Commodities*. Of three mechanical systems presented by Keltner, his choice of a moving average was based on performance and experience. The system itself is quite simple, a 10-day moving average using the average of the daily high, low, and closing prices, with a band on each side formed from the 10-day moving average of the high-low range (similar to a 10-day average true range). A buy signal occurs on penetration of the upper band and a sell signal when the lower band is broken; positions are always reversed.

The *10-Day Moving Average Rule* is basic, but it does apply the fundamental volatility principle by using the high-low range as a band, and serves as an early example of moving averages. Keltner expresses his preference for this particular technique because of its identification of minor rather than medium- or long-term trends, and there are some performance figures that substantiate his conclusion. As an experienced trader, he prefers the speed of the 10-day moving average, which follows the market prices with more reasonable risk than slower methods. A side benefit to the selection is that the usual division required by a moving average calculation can be substituted by a simple shift of the decimal place; in an era before the pocket calculator, who knows how much impact that convenience had on Keltner's choice.

The history of prices now shows us that price movement was much smoother up to the end of the 1970s and has been getting noisier ever since. A 10-day moving average, supplemented by a volatility band, was truly the state-of-the-art technology. While the shorter calculation periods are not generally successful for current price moves, the use of volatility to create bands has held up well over time.

[6] Richard Bookstaber, *The Complete Investment Book* (Glenview, IL: Scott, Foresman, 1984), 231.
[7] Jack K. Hutson, "Good TRIX," *Technical Analysis of Stocks & Commodities* (July 1983).

CHAPTER 5

Trend Systems (Part 2)

From Perry J. Kaufman, *Trading Systems and Methods, +Website*, 5th Edition (Hoboken, New Jersey: John Wiley & Sons, 2013), Chapter 8.

Learning Objective Statements

- Explain how a trader or investor would go about selecting the right moving average to use
- Explain the role of each moving average in a two-trend or three-trend method of trading
- Describe two general rules for generating an exit signal when using moving averages, and explain which one of the two is considered better than the other

■ Techniques Using Two Trendlines

There are many situations where two trends of different calculation periods can solve a problem better than one. It is often the case that there is a dominant, long-term trend driven by government interest rate policy. Trends based on fiscal policy can last for years and can be very successful. Most traders, however, are not likely to hold a single long-term trade for the full period of its move. Even if convinced of the ultimate outcome of the trade, there can be very large price swings along the way. Most traders would rather enter and exit the market many times, in the direction of the longer-term trend, each time taking a small profit but with much smaller risk. The final result may be lower total profits, but a much more comfortable risk level for each trade.

This problem can be solved with two simple moving averages or a combination of any two trendlines of different speeds. The slower trendline, using a longer calculation period, identifies the primary trend. The faster trendline is used for timing. The faster signal does not have to be a trend at all; it can be pattern recognition or any timing method. In this section, we will use the same trending techniques previously discussed to create a system. The longer calculation period will represent the major trend and the shorter period will be used for timing. Consider the idea that a good entry point is when there is a recent short-term surge of prices in the direction of the major trend. To

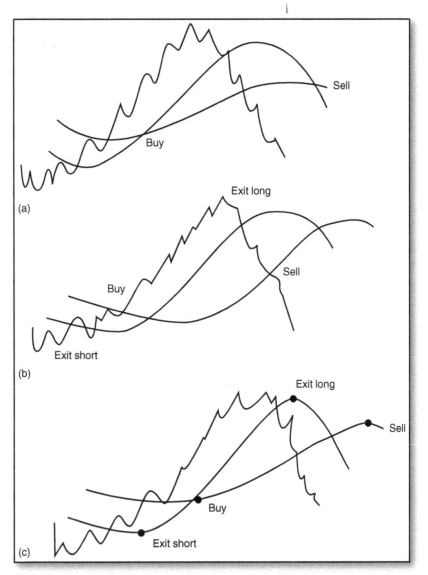

FIGURE 5.1 Three Ways to Trade Systems Using Two Moving Averages.
(a) Enter and exit when the trendlines cross. (b) Buy and sell when the
price crosses the trendlines, staying out of the market when prices are
between the trendlines. (c) Enter when both trendlines are moving in
the same direction; exit when they conflict.

implement this plan, select two moving averages, one noticeably faster than the other,
and apply one of the following sets of rules (also shown in Figure 5.1).

1. *Buy* when the faster moving average crosses the slower moving average going up. *Sell
   short* when the faster moving average crosses the slower moving average going down.
2. *Buy* when the current price crosses above *both* moving averages and close out
   long positions when prices cross below *either* moving average. *Sell short* when
   the current price crosses below *both* moving averages, and close out short positions when prices cross above *either* moving average.

3. *Buy* when the faster trendline turns up and the slower trendline is up. *Sell short* when the faster trendline turns down and the slower trendline is down. *Exit* the trade when the two trendlines are moving in opposite directions.

The first set of rules always has a position in the market, going from long to short and back again as the faster trend crosses the long-term trend. The second and third sets of rules create a neutral zone, where no position is held. Rule 2 attempts to extract the stronger part of the price move based on price, while Rule 3 looks for both trends to provide confirmation. Exiting a trade, rather than reversing, adds liquidity by reducing the order size and allows you to enter the next trade in the same direction as the previous one, instead of always reversing.

To further reduce the problem of whipsaws caused by erratic penetration of the trendlines in Rule 2, yet maintain a faster response to price change than Rule 3, a small band can be placed around each of the trendlines. Prices must move higher through the upper band before a buy signal occurs and then back through the lower band before that signal is reversed. It is a small safety zone that can eliminate the frequency of bad trades in proportion to the size of the band. With this technique you would want the band to be small; otherwise, you will interfere with the natural process that is the benefit of the two trendlines.

Donchian's 5- and 20-Day Moving Average System

The method claiming one of the longest recorded trading histories, beginning January 1, 1961, is *Donchian's 5- and 20-Day Moving Average.*[1] In 1961, when moving averages were considered state-of-the-art, there was less noise, and agricultural markets were the most liquid. The equivalent of a 1- and 4-week moving average would have worked well. Even now, the use of calendar periods—such as 21 and 63 days for a month and a quarter, respectively—may pick up trends driven by the action of major fund managers as they rebalance their portfolio each month, and also respond to price direction resulting from quarterly earnings reports.

Donchian's idea was to use a volatility-penetration criterion relative to the 20-day moving average, but with some added complication. The current price penetration must not only cross the 20-day moving average but also exceed any previous 1-day penetration of a closing price by at least one volatility measure. In this way Donchian places a flexible band around the 20-day trendline. One volatility measure can be calculated as the average true range over one or more days.

The 5-day moving average serves as a liquidation criterion (along with others) and is also modified by prior penetration and volatility. These features tend to make Donchian's approach an early rendition of self-adjusting rules. To maintain a human element, Donchian requires execution of certain orders to be delayed a day if the signals occurred on specific weekdays or before a holiday. The combination of different factors was the result of refinement over years of actual operation.

---

[1] Richard D. Donchian, "Donchian's 5- and 20-Day Moving Averages," *Commodities Magazine* (December 1974).

Rather than try to implement Donchian's idea exactly, the program *TSM Donchian Moving Average System*, available on the Companion Website, uses the calculations:

1. A 5-day moving average
2. A 20-day moving average
3. The average true range based on the longer moving average

These three calculations are then used with the rules

- If position is not long and $Close_t > MA5_{t-1} + 1ATR_{t-1}$ and $close_t > MA20_{t-1} + 1ATR_{t-1}$ then *buy*

- If position is not short and $Close_t < MA5_{t-1} - 1ATR_{t-1}$ and $close_t < MA20_{t-1} - 1ATR_{t-1}$ then *sell short*

- If position is long and ($Close_t < MA5_{t-1} - 1ATR_{t-1}$ or $close_t < MA20_{t-1} - 1ATR_{t-1}$) then exit long position

- If position is short and ($Close_t > MA5_{t-1} + 1ATR_{t-1}$ or $close_t > MA20_{t-1} + 1ATR_{t-1}$) then cover short position

Because the price level and volatility of the market have changed dramatically since 1960, new positions should be sized according their volatility

$$Position\ size = Investment/(ATR \times Big\ Point\ Value)$$

Where ATR is calculated over the longer moving average period and the *Big Point Value* is the conversion factor for a futures contract, for example $50 for corn and $1000 for U.S. bonds.

How did this strategy perform? Applying these rules to corn, which would have been the primary market during the 1960s, and without costs (which were much higher until the mid-1990s), the cumulative profits are shown in Figure 5.2. Although the rate of return has slowed, it seems remarkable that a simple method could have been consistently profitable for 50 years. For those analysts who are

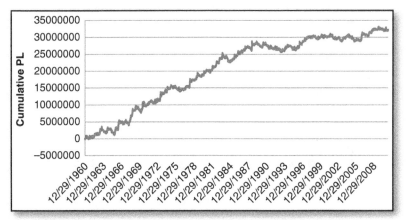

FIGURE 5.2 Donchian's 5- and 20-Day Moving Average System (somewhat modernized) Applied to Corn Futures from 1960.

interested, the program on the Companion Website allows the calculation periods to change as well as the penetration factor. Only corn was run for this example, and no parameters were tested or changed.

Donchian's 20- and 40-Day Breakout

One level slower than the 5- and 20-day average is Donchian's 20- and 40-Day Breakout. Instead of 1 week and 1 month, this looks at 1 month and 2 months. The method is far less complicated and only considers simple breakouts rather than using volatility bands. The rules are

> *Buy* when *today's high* > *high* of the past 40 days
>
> *Sell* short when *today's low* < *low* of the past 40 days
>
> *Exit* longs when *today's low* < *low* of the past 20 days
>
> *Exit* shorts when *today's high* > *high* of the past 20 days

Readers will recognize that this is the basis for the Turtle's trading method.

The Golden Cross and the Death Cross

The most popular stock market trending methods are the simplest, which does not mean they don't work. Of course, the 200-day moving average is shown as the key technical indicator on most financial networks, but 50, 100, and 200 days are equally popular. It is not clear how these began, but doubling the period is a simple way of keeping percentage changes the same and getting a good distribution of results over time.

The *Golden Cross* is the point at which the 50-day average crosses above the 200-day average indicating the beginning of a bullish move in the market. It has yielded very good results for the past 60 years and avoided the damaging declines of 2008. When the 50-day average crosses below the 200 day, it is ominously called the *Death Cross*.

In Figure 5.3, the results of Golden Cross are compared to the passive returns of the S&P index (SPX) and continuous futures, remembering that SPX cannot be

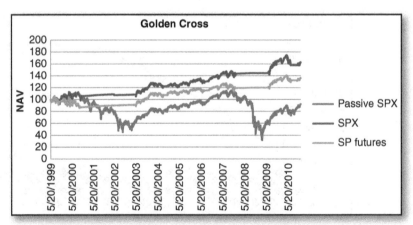

FIGURE 5.3 The Golden Cross Applied to the S&P Index (SPX) and Continuous Futures Compared to the Passive Returns of SPX.

traded. When the trend signal indicates a short sale, the 1-day returns of the 3-month T-bill rate are used for the daily returns. A spreadsheet named TSM Golden Cross can be found on the Companion Website.

For the 11 years beginning mid-1999, the passive return of the stock market was a loss of 7.8%. During the same period, the Golden Cross returned 66.7% using SPX and 36.7% using futures. While the cash index can be traded as the ETF SPY, the futures contract is reasonable alternative. In addition, futures can be leveraged considerably, increasing the returns (and the risk).

All the calculations are shown in the Golden Cross spreadsheet, but the way in which the returns of continuous futures are matched to SPX needs some explanation. While the daily returns of SPX are calculated as $\ln(p_t / p_{t-1})$, continuous futures are back adjusted and values can become negative. The annualized volatility of SPX was calculated in the classic way, but the annualized volatility of the futures was calculated based on the daily change in dollar value of the futures contract.

1. Begin with an arbitrary, but large, investment size
2. Calculate the daily returns based on the initial investment size
3. Calculate the rolling 20-day annualized volatility of the returns
4. Find the factor needed to make the annualized volatility 12%
5. Multiply the current returns by the previous volatility factor
6. Create the NAVs from the volatility-adjusted returns

In Figure 5.3 the annualized volatility of SPX is 11.5%, and the volatility of the futures returns is 10.9%.

ROC Method   Another classic method for trading the major index is *Woodshedder's long-term indicator.*[2] The rules are

- *Buy* when the 5-day ROC (rate-of-change) is below the 252-day ROC for two consecutive days.

- *Exit the long* when the 5-day ROC is above the 252-day ROC for two consecutive days.

- When there is no position, the system earns one-half of the cash 3-month T-bill rate.

In Figure 5.4, the results are compared to the Golden Cross, both using SPY as the basis for trading, from April 15, 1994 (the first available data for SPY plus the 252-day windup), through September 2011. No costs were charged although SPY has administrative cost included. The ROC method far outperformed the Golden Cross even with an annualized volatility of 14.1% compared to the Golden Cross volatility of 10.5%. Note that trading the SPY gave better returns than SP futures, shown in Figure 5.4.

---

[2] The *Woodshedder* blog can be found at www.ibankcoin.com/woodshedderblog and covers many other strategies. This method was reviewed by *MarketSci blog* on October 4, 2011, but used SPX (the cash index) rather than SPY.

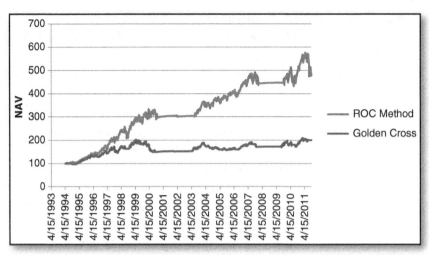

FIGURE 5.4 Comparison of Golden Cross and ROC Method Using SPY.

Staying Ahead of the Crowd

There is always an attempt to find out where others are placing their orders and get ahead of them. For example, if you know that most trend-followers are using a 30-day calculation period, then using a 28-day average might edge them out. During the 1980s and 1990s there was a trend system that used 8 and 18 days to beat the 10 and 20 days that was most popular. The following calculations would use *fastperiod* = 8 and *slowperiod* = 18. The *differenceperiod* = 9.

$$FasterAverage = Average(close, fastperiod)$$
$$SlowerAverage = Average(close, slowperiod)$$
$$TrendDifference = FasterAverage - SlowerAverage$$
$$DifferenceAverage = Average(TrendDifference, differenceperiod)$$

The trading rules were

Buy when *today's TrendDifference > yesterday's DifferenceAverage*
Sell short when *today's TrendDifference < yesterday's DifferenceAverage*

Although these calculation periods may not be profitable in today's markets, the idea of being slightly ahead of the crowd can give you *free exposure*, a small jump in profits caused by many orders following yours. If you can figure out where the crowd is buying and selling, then this concept will give you an edge.

■ Multiple Trends and Common Sense

If two trendlines can improve trading, it should follow that three or more are even better—but there may be more problems than benefits. Many analysts subscribe to the idea that *simpler is better*. A single moving average may not have a high percentage of profitable trades but the longer-term periods work because they capture the fat tail.

	Number	Days	Total		Avg Trade	%Prof
Trend	of Trades	Held	Profit	Ratio	Profit	Trades
60	164	31	16537	1.65	149	22.5
20	350	16	21737	1.44	62	31.0
Both	254	16	15310	1.50	92	34.6

TABLE 5.1 Comparison of 1 and 2 Trend Systems, Eurodollar Interest Rate Futures, 1990–2011

With the use of two trends, the number of combinations expands rapidly. Is there a *best* relationship between the slower speed and the faster one, that is, should the faster trend period be ¼ of the slower? Certainly, a 38- and 40-day combination will not offer much value, but is a 10-day and 40-day the right combination?

Consider something else. If a 10-day trend is not profitable, and a 20-day trend is not profitable, each taken on their own, but the combination is profitable, would you trade it? If, by computer testing, we were to "discover" that a combination of 2 or 3 trends was profitable, would you be convinced to trade it? Not likely, unless a very large percentage of the combinations were profitable or each trend served a particular purpose and had a calculation period that reflected that purpose.

For example, if longer-term trends are intended to track macro fundamental policy and were generally profitable, then that longer-term period would be a good candidate for one of the trends. But those trades can be held for months, and you don't like that profile, so you want a shorter trend to tell you when to get in and out of that trade, always holding a position in the direction of the long-term trend. Using Eurodollars with 60-day and 20-day trends over the past 20 years, with a $40 round-turn cost, Table 5.1 shows the change in performance. Both single trends do very well, but the 60-day holds trades for an average of 31 days, about 1½ months. The 20-day trend would be better, but the average profit per trade is only $62. By combining the two trends and trading only in the direction of the long-term trend, the profits per trade jump to $92, and the days held remain the same as the 20-day trend. Overall, you get slightly worse performance than the long-term trend but hold the trade for half the time. That makes sense because you are only trading the longs rather than both longs and shorts.

Another benefit of the two-trend method is that you are in the market only 50% of the time. That reduces your risk, especially the risk of a price shock. That is a benefit not to be taken lightly.

Three Trends

Is there a rationale for more than two trends? If the long-term trend is for market direction, and the shorter one is to reduce the length of the holding period, then the third could be using for entry timing. The third trend could be very fast, perhaps 3 days.

Gerald Appel[3] adds three rate-of-change (ROC) indicators together (actually momentum, the difference between the price today and the price n days ago), and applies the composite to the S&P index (SPX), all expressed in percent. He recommends buying when the composite crosses above 4% and exiting when it falls below 4%. If you consider the upwards bias in the S&P, the 4% threshold may not be arbitrary.

Modified 3-Crossover Model

The justification for using three trends is that one or more slower moving averages may result in a buy or sell signal at a time when the prices are actually moving opposite to the position that is about to be entered. This may happen if the trading signal is generated when the two moving average lines cross, rather than when price move through the averages. The slope of a third, faster moving average, $MA3_t - MA3_{t-1}$, can be used as a confirmation of direction to avoid entry into a trade that is going the wrong way. This filter can be added to any moving average or multiple moving average system with the following rule:

> Do not enter a new long (or short) position unless the slope of the confirming moving average (the change in the moving average value from the prior day to today) was up (or down).

The speed of this third, confirming moving average only makes sense if it is equal to or faster than the fastest of the trends used in the Crossover System. A program to test the three-trend model is TSM Modified 3MA Cross, available on the Companion Website.

In earlier tests of the 3-Crossover method compared to the 2-Crossover, results showed that the added timing in the 3-Crossover reduced the number of trades and increased the size of the returns per contract. Overall, the profitability remained about the same.

4-9-18 Crossover Model

During the late 1970s, the 4-9-18 Crossover model was very popular. It seems likely that the selection of 4, 9, and 18 days was a conscious effort to be slightly ahead of the 5, 10, and 20 days frequently used in moving average systems during that period. It is also likely to have been the outcome of the first computerized testing. Even now, high frequency traders continue to look for the smallest edge that keeps them ahead of the competition. In addition to the marginally faster calculation periods each moving average is (nearly) twice the speed of the prior, enhancing their uniqueness for recognizing different trends. Increasing the period in this way keeps a constant percentage difference.

To get an idea of how three trends compare to either one or two trends, a small test was run using Eurobund futures from 1990 to mid-2011. Granted this is a trending market, and one test does not reflect the big picture; nevertheless, the

---

[3] Gerald Appel, *Technical Analysis: Power Tool for Active Traders* (Upper Saddle River, NJ: FT Prentice Hall, 2005), 59.

TABLE 5.2	Comparison of Single Trend Results with a 2- and 3-Moving Average Crossover Strategies, Applied to Eurobunds, 1990 to Mid-2011			
Strategy	Net PL	Profit Factor	Trades	Profit/Contract
40-Day MA	13300	1.11	310	42
80-Day MA	55620	1.88	152	365
40-80 Crossover	35040	1.45	229	153
20-40-80 Crossover	61210	2.80	42	1457

results, shown in Table 5.2, were unexpected. Because we already know that faster trends are not performing as well in recent years as they did in the 1970s, the test of Eurobunds compared a 40-day and an 80-day calculation period with a 40-80-day crossover and a 20-40-80-day combination. The 3-crossover method outperformed all others but also reduced the number of trades by emphasizing the trend direction.

Comprehensive Studies

Because computerized testing platforms have made it easy for anyone to test any number of trends in combination, there have been very few comprehensive studies published since 1990. The exceptions are Colby's *The Encyclopedia of Technical Market Indicators* and Bulkowski's *Encyclopedia of Chart Patterns*, both of which show results in a standard form and make it easy to compare the differences between systems. But most traders seeking a strategy will need to test it themselves and add their own special features. Both Colby and Bulkowski will give you a good idea of which methods and patterns to avoid.

There is a great deal to learn from putting the results of various systems and markets side by side. Earlier in this chapter, there is an informative comparison of six major trending systems. In addition, a 2-trend crossover strategy is compared to the single trend methods. An objective of the testing process is to find parameters that succeed over time.

Selecting the Right Trend Method and Speed

Up to now, the selection of the right moving average, the one that will work in the future, has only been discussed in general terms. The success of a single calculation period for a single trend strategy does not mean that it is the right choice for trading. In addition, the best moving average speed for institutional or commercial participants may be very different from that of an active trader.[4] For example, a mutual fund receives new investments that must be moved into the market, collectively, once or twice each month. In the same way, a cattle feed lot will choose one time each month

[4] Perry J. Kaufman, "Moving Averages and Trends" in Todd Lofton, ed., *Trading Tactics: A Livestock Anthology* (Chicago: Chicago Mercantile Exchange, 1986).

to fix the price of new inventory. A 3-day moving average might generate 5 to 10 buy and sell signals in one month, each the result of a 2-day price move—an ineffective tool for either participant looking for just one place to enter the market. A calculation period of 10 days may come closer to generating the one buy signal needed for the fund or one sell signal that is best for the hedger. The noncommercial trader is not concerned about the frequency of trades, only the returns and risk.

For the trader or speculator, the right moving average speed is the one that produces the best performance profile. This profile could be simply maximum profits, or it could be a more complex combination of profits, risk, and time in the market.

Computer testing of a trend system or other trading strategies sometimes leads to solutions that are highly fitted. The computer may find that a 3-day moving average was slightly more profitable and had lower risk than a 20-day average. Our common sense tells us that the results of the 3-day system will be more difficult to attain in real trading because execution costs will have a larger impact. An occasional fast market may cause the execution price to be far off from the price indicated by the system signal. A slower trend selection with fewer trades is less affected by poor executions.

Dominant seasonal factors are an important influence on the calculation period of the trend. While some stocks, such as travel and leisure, can be highly seasonal, their seasonal price patterns can be overwhelmed by a strong trend in the overall market, as measured by the S&P 500. In fact, the arbitraging of the S&P 500 futures with the actual stocks has significantly changed the patterns of the many stocks, forcing many of them to have higher correlations. However, a grain trader knows that the price pattern has a clear cycle each year. At best, we can expect one long upwards move followed by a shorter, faster decline. Not all trend speeds can capture the profits in this pattern. For example, if the uptrend lasts for 6 months, a 6-month moving average will not see any of it; therefore, it is necessary to use a moving average with a period less than one quarter of the length of the trend. If computerized testing of a large range of moving average calculation periods results in a "best" moving average period of six months or more, that choice should be interpreted as a failure to capture the seasonal move.

We also discussed the "right" trend method earlier in this chapter. Tests over many years and many diverse markets will show that the differences in net returns using different trend strategies are small. Those differences will be larger when the trend speeds are faster. The most important differences are not in the profits but in the frequency of trades, the size of the individual returns, and the risk of each trade. Experience shows that the primary reason why trend-following systems work is because sustained price moves exist, driven mostly by government interest rate policy. Every trend-following system can capture these moves.

Selecting the Trend Speed

You can find a reasonable choice by simply looking at a price chart. The trends that two traders see are often different. Some traders immediately focus on long-term price

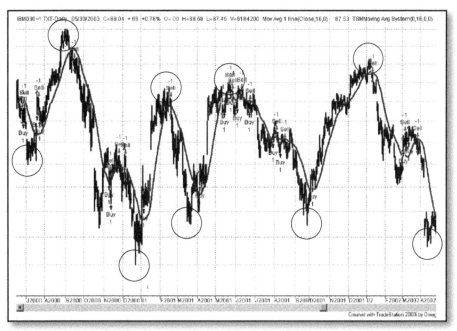

FIGURE 5.5 Finding the Moving Average Calculation Period from the Average Span of Peaks and Valleys.

trends; others see much shorter movements. To find your own best trend speed without the use of a computer, mark on a chart the beginning and end of each price move that you would like to capture. These trends may occur every few days, or only three or four times each year.

Using a daily price chart of IBM from July 2000 through May 2002 (Figure 5.5), the tops and bottoms of the major price swings that we would like to capture were circled. Noting that each gridline on the chart represents one month, there were eight tops and bottoms over a total period of 22 months. The average price swing was then 2¾ months, nearly one calendar quarter. Because it is so close to a quarterly value, which is the period of earnings reports, we will choose three months as the average swing period. Applying the rule of thumb that the trend can be isolated using a calculation period of one-quarter of the swing period, the moving average period becomes 16 days.

Applying a 16-day moving average system to the two years of IBM price data, buying and selling whenever the trendline changes direction, the trade results are shown in Table 5.3. There are a total of 36 trades, of which 20 were profitable (no transaction costs were used)—a very high percentage for a trend-following system. Total profits were better than $114 per share, on an average share price of about $100, showing that it is not necessary to optimize using a computer to create a successful trading program. Of course, there is no assurance that this pattern of swings will continue, but basing the decision on quarterly swings, which corresponds to earnings reports, is a hopeful sign.

| TABLE 5.3 | Performance of 16-Day Moving Average Applied to IBM from July 2000 through May 2002 |

Trade #	Entry Date	Entry Order	Entry Price	Exit Date	Exit Order	Exit Price	Profit/ Loss	Total P/L
1	6/29/2000	Sell	114.00	7/20/2000	SExit	117.25	−3.25	−3.25
2	7/20/2000	Buy	117.25	7/24/2000	LExit	112.50	−4.75	−8.00
3	7/24/2000	Sell	112.50	7/25/2000	SExit	112.00	0.50	−7.50
4	7/25/2000	Buy	112.00	9/18/2000	LExit	123.25	11.25	3.75
5	9/18/2000	Sell	123.25	11/9/2000	SExit	99.44	23.81	27.56
6	11/9/2000	Buy	99.44	11/10/2000	LExit	93.00	−6.44	21.12
7	11/10/2000	Sell	93.00	11/13/2000	SExit	97.44	−4.44	16.68
8	11/13/2000	Buy	97.44	11/27/2000	LExit	98.44	1.00	17.68
9	11/27/2000	Sell	98.44	12/5/2000	SExit	103.38	−4.94	12.74
10	12/5/2000	Buy	103.38	12/6/2000	LExit	96.75	−6.63	6.11
11	12/6/2000	Sell	96.75	1/5/2001	SExit	94.00	2.75	8.86
12	1/5/2001	Buy	94.00	2/20/2001	LExit	111.50	17.50	26.36
13	2/20/2001	Sell	111.50	4/5/2001	SExit	98.21	13.29	39.65
14	4/5/2001	Buy	98.21	5/11/2001	LExit	111.81	13.60	53.25
15	5/11/2001	Sell	111.81	5/15/2001	SExit	113.58	−1.77	51.48
16	5/15/2001	Buy	113.58	5/23/2001	LExit	117.40	3.82	55.30
17	5/23/2001	Sell	117.40	5/24/2001	SExit	119.60	−2.20	53.10
18	5/24/2001	Buy	119.60	5/29/2001	LExit	115.27	−4.33	48.77
19	5/29/2001	Sell	115.27	6/5/2001	SExit	116.97	−1.70	47.07
20	6/5/2001	Buy	116.97	6/12/2001	LExit	117.25	0.28	47.35
21	6/12/2001	Sell	117.25	6/22/2001	SExit	112.87	4.38	51.73
22	6/22/2001	Buy	112.87	6/25/2001	LExit	112.65	−0.22	51.51
23	6/25/2001	Sell	112.65	7/31/2001	SExit	105.21	7.44	58.95
24	7/31/2001	Buy	105.21	8/6/2001	LExit	106.51	1.30	60.25
25	8/6/2001	Sell	106.51	8/10/2001	SExit	104.95	1.56	61.81
26	8/10/2001	Buy	104.95	8/17/2001	LExit	104.59	−0.36	61.45
27	8/17/2001	Sell	104.59	10/5/2001	SExit	98.02	6.57	68.02
28	10/5/2001	Buy	98.02	1/11/2002	LExit	120.31	22.29	90.31
29	1/11/2002	Sell	120.31	3/4/2002	SExit	105.90	14.41	104.72
30	3/4/2002	Buy	105.90	3/6/2002	LExit	106.30	0.40	105.12
31	3/6/2002	Sell	106.30	3/12/2002	SExit	108.50	−2.20	102.92
32	3/12/2002	Buy	108.50	3/26/2002	LExit	102.90	−5.60	97.32
33	3/26/2002	Sell	102.90	5/22/2002	SExit	84.00	18.90	116.22
34	5/22/2002	Buy	84.00	5/24/2002	LExit	83.10	−0.90	115.32
35	5/24/2002	Sell	83.10	5/28/2002	SExit	82.08	1.02	116.34
36	5/28/2002	Buy	82.08	5/31/2002	LExit	80.45	−1.63	114.71

Another approach to finding the trend period is to consider the worst price retracement. In the IBM chart, the move from $87 to $105, beginning in November 2000 and lasting about two months, is the one to avoid. Remembering that a trend is neutralized with regard to a price move when the trend period is the same length as the total move, we apply a moving average of 42 days. This method successfully avoids the price correction and holds the downtrend, but the much slower trend nets a significant loss over the 2-year period. It is best to accept the frequent small losses that are natural in a trend-following system than attempt to remove them.

■ Moving Average Sequences: Signal Progression

Consider the case where you have selected a 20-day moving average to trade. You enter the day long Biotech, and you get a sell signal. However, you are unaware that the 19-day and 21-day moving averages did not get sell signals. This means that the day that was dropped off the calculation 20 days ago caused a slight shift not seen by the other neighboring trends. This can be an important piece of information when assessing the reliability of the trend signal.

A moving average is simply a consensus of direction. It is an approximation of values intended to steer a trader to the right side of the market at the right time. It is most fallible when prices are changing direction or going sideways. Any information that clears up the problem is helpful. For any trend system, it is best to see a steady progression of trend changes from the short term to the long term. This is seen in the following tables, where *u* is an uptrend and *d* is a downtrend associated with the calculation period above those letters.

In Table 5.4, prices have turned up in such a way that the trend calculation periods 1 through 19 show uptrends, while calculation periods from 20 and higher have not yet turned. Unfortunately, normal price movement is not often as uniform as this example. The shorter-term trends can be very erratic, and often appear in smaller, alternating groups of up and down trends (see Table 5.5). This is easily explained because adding and subtracting one day when only two, three, or four days are used in the moving average calculation can quickly change the direction of the trend. As you get to longer intervals, such as 20, 30, and 50 days, this is not the case, and in reality, it does not happen often. Yet when it does, the trend change is not to be trusted.

TABLE 5.4 Orderly Trend Change

Moving Average Period in Days																								
1	2	3	4	5	6	7	8	9	10	11	12	13	14	15	16	17	18	19	20	21	22	23	24	25
Trend u	u	u	u	u	u	u	u	u	u	u	u	u	u	u	u	u	u	u	d	d	d	d	d	d

TABLE 5.5 Erratic Trend Change for the Short Calculation Periods

Moving Average Period in Days																								
1	2	3	4	5	6	7	8	9	10	11	12	13	14	15	16	17	18	19	20	21	22	23	24	25
Trend u	u	d	d	u	d	u	u	u	u	u	u	u	u	u	u	u	u	u	d	d	d	d	d	d

TABLE 5.6 Progression of Trend Changes

	Moving Average Period in Days																								
	1	2	3	4	5	6	7	8	9	10	11	12	13	14	15	16	17	18	19	20	21	22	23	24	25
Trend	d	d	d	d	u	u	u	u	u	u	u	u	u	u	u	u	u	u	u	d	d	u	u	u	u	u
Trend	d	d	d	d	d	d	d	d	d	d	d	d	d	u	u	u	u	u	d	d	u	u	u	u	u

There are also cases where the longer trend begins to reassert itself and the results appear the same as in Table 5.4; however, the trend change occurs from the longer-term down (from right to left instead of left to right). The case we must watch for satisfies neither of these, but occurs in an erratic pattern, such as in Table 5.6. Here we see a dominant long-term uptrend with the very short end turning down. Because of another downturn a few days ago, which then disappeared, this most recent downturn also caused a shadow turn in the 20-day range. Is it a leading indicator or a false signal? All indications are that smooth changes in a trend are more reliable precursors of change. Another case is given in the second line of Table 5.6. Here, the smooth trend change from up to down is occurring from left to right; however, as it gets to 13 days, it also jumps ahead to 19 and 20 days, leaving days 14 through 18 still in an uptrend. For trends in this faster range, it appears best to wait for all fastest trends to change. As the calculation period becomes longer, it is unrealistic to expect all faster trends to be the same; therefore, you will need to settle for an orderly change in a group of trends faster than the target trend period.

An example of this process is shown in Figure 5.6. Moving average calculation periods of 5 to 50 days are shown in increments of five days for a total of 44 consecutive days. This illustration points out how the long-term uptrend (X) is breached by shorter-term, less consistent trends. Perhaps the best trend is the one with the majority of Xs or Os on the same line.

Averaging the Sequences

The idea of requiring consistency in a range of trends can be automated by selecting a range of calculation periods preceding a target period, finding the trend signal (an uptrend or downtrend), and then deciding according to one of two rules:

1. Average the final trend values to get the average trend result. Compare the previous average result with the current value to determine the direction of the trend.
2. Scan the trend directions for consistent progression.

When selecting the range of calculation periods, start from 1 if the target period is small (e.g., your intended trend is 15 days). If you are looking at an intermediate trend period, for example, 30 days, you may want to include the range from 20 to 30, or 20 to 32. A few up-and-down price moves that make the short-end erratic should not alter the medium-term trend direction. By extending the calculation periods slightly past the target period, you gain confirmation at the cost of a small lag.

The idea that trends are sensitive to small price changes and the drop-off effect is not a surprise. An alternative to examining sequences is simply to select a number

Moving Average Period										
Day	5	10	15	20	25	30	35	40	45	50
1	X	X	X	X	X	X	X	X	X	X
2	O	O	X	X	X	X	X	X	X	X
3	O	X	X	X	X	X	X	X	X	X
4	X	X	X	X	X	X	X	X	X	X
5	X	X	X	X	X	X	X	X	X	X
6	X	X	X	X	X	X	X	X	X	X
7	X	X	X	X	X	X	X	X	X	X
8	O	X	X	X	X	X	X	X	X	X
9	X	O	O	O	X	X	X	X	X	X
10	O	O	O	O	O	X	X	X	X	X
11	O	O	O	O	X	X	X	X	X	X
12	O	O	O	O	O	O	O	X	X	X
13	O	O	O	O	X	X	X	X	X	X
14	X	O	O	O	O	O	X	X	X	X
15	O	O	O	O	O	O	O	O	O	X
16	O	O	O	O	O	O	O	O	O	O
17	O	O	O	O	O	O	O	O	O	O
18	O	O	O	O	O	O	O	O	O	O
19	X	O	O	O	O	O	O	O	O	O
20	X	O	O	O	O	O	O	O	O	O
21	X	X	X	O	O	O	O	X	X	X
22	X	X	X	X	O	X	X	X	X	X
23	X	X	X	O	O	O	O	X	X	X
24	X	X	X	X	O	O	O	X	X	X
25	X	X	X	X	O	O	O	X	X	X
26	O	X	X	O	O	O	O	O	O	X
27	O	O	O	O	O	O	O	O	O	O
28	O	O	O	O	O	O	O	O	O	O
29	O	X	X	X	O	O	O	O	O	X
30	X	X	X	X	X	O	O	O	X	X
31	X	X	X	X	X	O	O	O	O	X
32	X	X	X	X	X	X	X	X	X	X
33	X	X	X	X	X	X	X	X	X	X
34	X	X	X	X	X	X	X	X	X	X
35	X	X	X	X	X	X	X	X	X	X
36	X	X	X	X	X	X	X	X	X	X
37	X	X	X	X	X	X	X	X	X	X
38	O	X	X	X	X	X	X	X	X	X
39	O	O	X	X	X	X	X	X	X	X
40	O	O	X	X	X	X	X	X	X	X
41	O	X	X	X	X	X	X	X	X	X
42	X	X	X	X	X	X	X	X	X	X
43	X	X	X	X	X	X	X	X	X	X
44	X	X	X	X	X	X	X	X	X	X

FIGURE 5.6 Sequences of Moving Averages.

of calculation periods and net out the trends looking for a consensus. That would remove any dependence on a single selection.

■ Early Exits from a Trend

By now we know that capturing the fat tail is necessary for the success of trend-following systems. However, there are always practical exceptions if you are allowed to add discretion to your trading decisions. One of the oldest truths for trend-following is "Take your losses and let your profits run." By imposing profit-taking, or even stop-losses, this can be changed to "Take your profits and let your losses run." There is a need to be very careful when making exceptions. But consider the following situation.

Interest rates have declined for nearly all of the 30 years from 1981 through 2011. For many traders, that's more than their entire professional career. To profit from this move, a slow trend system can track the 10-year Treasury note futures contract, a municipal or corporate bond index, or any number of varying maturity funds. If a 200-day trend were used, then there would be a lag of 100 days. That is, for a bond fund, the current value of the trendline would reflect the bond prices at the midpoint of the calculation period, 50 days. If the yield on interest rates had steadily dropped a total of 2% during the past year, then the trendline would be lagging about 1% behind current yields. That can translate into a large loss in unrealized gains.

One advantage of macrotrends is that they are based on a sustained economic policy. If that policy changes, then the trend is over, even if the trendline has not yet reversed direction. If the Fed were now to raise interest rates (or strongly hint that a rate hike is likely), it would signal a shift in policy. You can reasonably conclude that basis for the long-term uptrend in prices is over and that the trendline is due to turn down. A central bank rarely raises rates one month and lowers them the next. Because the very slow trend lags far behind the actual market price, it may be six months before the trendline actually signals a change of position. This will occur after a large part of your profits has been given back to the market. Exiting the trade when the fundamentals change would be a safe way of capturing more profits and being exposed to less market risk. Often, these decisions are clear only after the fact. In 2010 it seemed that Fed policy was going to change, yet 2011 was one of the strongest trend years in history, with yields reaching record lows.

■ Moving Average Projected Crossovers

If moving averages can successfully be used to identify the trend direction, it follows that a projection of the moving average will be valuable in anticipating when the trends will change. If a moving average trading strategy uses a single trend, the forecasted price ($CP1$) at which the standard n-day moving average line would cross is

$$CP1 = \frac{\text{Sum of last } N-1 \text{ prices}}{N-1} = \frac{\sum_{t-N+2}^{t} P_i}{(N-1)}$$

That is, an n-day moving average would cross the next price at the value equal to the $n-1$-day moving average.

The price ($CP2$) needed to cause two moving averages, of periods m and n, to cross is[5]

$$CP2 = m \times \left(\frac{\sum \text{most recent } m-1 \text{ prices}}{m} - \frac{\sum \text{most recent } n-1 \text{ prices}}{n} \right)$$

The projected crossover price is most useful when it is likely that a trend change will occur within a few days, that is, when the two moving averages begin converging and become close in value. Acting on the expected price would give the trader a great advantage in order execution. A chart of this, however, may not appear to be much different from a simple *relative strength* indicator. The difference between the price and the moving average line constitutes the relative strength.

The change in the projected crossover is considered a more valuable tool by Lambert.[6] He creates a *Market Direction Indicator* (MDI) with the following formula:

$$MDI = \frac{100 \times (\text{Crossover price}_{\text{previous}} - \text{Crossover price}_{\text{today}})}{\text{Average of past 2 day's prices}}$$

The point at which the MDI crosses the zero line moving higher is a buy signal, and the point where it crosses moving lower is a sell signal.

Forecasting When the Moving Average Will Turn   There are two basic rules for generating a moving average signal, when the price penetrates the moving average trendline and when the moving average trendline changes up or down. In the previous section, the forecast was based on when the price crosses the moving average, which is a very common way of generating a trading signal.

Tests often show that results are better when the trendline itself is used to generate the signal rather than the penetration. This was discussed earlier in the chapter, but the rationale goes that once prices have been included in the moving average, then it is the moving average that tells you the correct direction, and that the price penetration takes away from the value of the trendline. There are two reasons for this. The trendline is smoother than price movement, so the results are more uniform, and the price penetrations generate many more trades and additional costs.

Having decided to use the trendline, then how do you forecast when that line will change direction? It is simply whether today's price is greater or less than the price that is dropped off the end of the moving average period, n days ago. And, that being the case, using the moving average trendline is exactly the same as using the n-day momentum which states that you go long when today's price is greater than the price n days ago. It seems too simple, but in most cases the results are better than using the price penetration of a moving average.

[5] Calculation courtesy of Alexander Solodukhin, Mizuho Alternative Investments, New York.
[6] Donald R. Lambert, "The Market Directional Indicator," *Technical Analysis of Stocks & Commodities* (November/December 1983).

CHAPTER 6

Momentum and Oscillators

From Perry J. Kaufman, *Trading Systems and Methods, + Website*, 5th Edition (Hoboken, New Jersey: John Wiley & Sons, 2013), Chapter 9.

Learning Objective Statements

- Explain the purpose for using momentum and rate-of change studies in technical analysis
- Explain how to select and identify entry and exit signals of a trend following system using a momentum indicator
- Explain how to select and identify entry and exit signals of a mean reversion system using a momentum indicator
- Explain how to select and identify entry and exit signals of a trend following system using a MACD indicator
- Explain the differences that are observed when comparing simple momentum, RSI and Stochastic oscillators with similar calculation periods
- Identify entry and exit signals given by the standard forms of the following technical studies: Momentum, RSI, Stochastic, Williams %R, A/D Oscillator, Ultimate Oscillator, Relative Vigor Index, True Strength Index, TRIX, Money Flow Index, Herrick Payoff Index

The study of momentum and oscillators is the analysis of price changes rather than price levels. Among technicians, momentum establishes the speed of price movement and the rate of ascent or descent. Analysts use *momentum* interchangeably with *slope*, the angle of inclination of price movement usually found with a simple least squares regression (Figure 6.1). In mathematics it is also the *first difference*, the difference between today's price and the previous day. Momentum is often considered using terms of Newton's Law, which can be restated loosely as *once started, prices tend to remain in motion in more-or-less the same direction.*

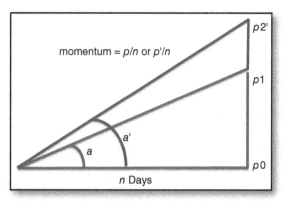

FIGURE 6.1 Geometric Representation of Momentum.

Indicators of change, such as momentum and oscillators, are used as leading indicators of price direction. They can identify when the current trend is no longer maintaining its same level of strength; that is, they show when an upwards move is decelerating. Prices are rising, but at a slower rate. This gives traders an opportunity to begin liquidating their open trend trades before prices actually reverse. As the time period for the momentum calculation shortens, this indicator becomes more sensitive to small changes in price. It is often used in a *countertrend*, or *mean reversion* strategy. The *change in momentum*, also called *rate of change, acceleration,* or *second difference,* is even more sensitive and anticipates change sooner.

Before beginning a discussion of various momentum calculations, a brief comment on terminology is necessary to understand how various techniques are grouped together. The use of a single price, such as Microsoft at $25.50 or gold at $1400, has no direction or movement implied. We are simply relating a price level and not indicating that prices are going up or down.

Next, we describe the speed at which prices are rising or falling. To know the speed, it is not enough to say that the S&P rose 3 points; you must specify the time interval over which this happened—"the S&P rose 3 points in 1 hour." When you say that you drove your car at 60, you really imply that you were going 60 miles per hour, or 60 kilometers per hour. This description of speed, or distance covered over time, is the same information that is given by a single momentum value. Then, if the *daily* momentum of the NASDAQ 100 is +10, it is rising at the rate of 10 points per day.

Having made a point of saying that momentum is change over time, which it is, the "industry" uses *momentum* to mean *price change* with the time implied (and often not even given) where *speed* is always the price change divided by the time interval. The same interpretation will be used here. The term *rate of change* (ROC) will also be used to describe *acceleration*, an increase or decrease in the speed; when the rate of change is zero, we are talking about speed and momentum.[1]

---

[1] Be careful about terminology. Many books and software use rate of change (ROC) interchangeably with momentum, the change in price over *n* days, rather than the change in momentum. Also, momentum indicators can also be used for mean reversion and may be called *oscillators* because their values swing from positive to negative.

You will see in this chapter that acceleration is more sensitive than speed. We will begin with the least sensitive indicator, momentum, increase to acceleration, and then address the variations and applications, including *divergence*, the most popular use of momentum indicators.

■ Momentum

Momentum is the difference between two prices taken over a fixed interval. It is another word for *speed*, the distance covered over time; however, everyone uses it to mean *change*. For example, today's 5-day momentum value *M* would be the difference between today's price p_t and the price five days ago:

$$5\text{-day momentum, } M = p_t - p_{t-5}$$

Using notation familiar to many programmers:

$$5\text{-day momentum} = \text{price} - \text{price}[5]$$

or

$$n\text{-day momentum} = \text{price} - \text{price}[n]$$

where the notation [n] refers to the price *n* days ago.

The momentum value M_t increases as the change in price increases over the same 5-day period. Figure 6.1 shows how the momentum changes as the price increases over the same time period. Over *n* days, the price moves from p_0 to p_1. It forms angle *a* and has a momentum of $p_1 - p_0$. If prices had increased to point p_2, then the momentum would have been greater, and the angle a′ would have been larger. For example, if the 5-day change in price is an increase of 100, then the momentum is simply 100, but the speed is $100/5 = 20$. If prices increase by 100 points over a 10-day time interval, the momentum would still be 100, but the speed, or slope, would be $100/10 = 10$. When calculating momentum, the interval of the calculation must always be stated. To avoid confusion, we state that the *5-day momentum is 20* and the *10-day momentum is 10*.

Today's 5-day momentum, which we will now show as $M(5)_t$ can range in value from the maximum upwards move to the maximum downwards move that the price can make in five days; the momentum is zero if prices are unchanged after five days. For stocks, there is no actual limit on the maximum price range over any time interval. In cases such as Enron, prices could collapse to zero in short order. From a practical view, most stocks and futures markets have a history of volatility that relates to their price level. The higher the price, the greater the price moves. As the price of gold rose to $1000 per ounce, the 5-day momentum could have been as high as $100 per ounce ($20 per day). When it was at $250 and investors lost interest, it may have shown a $1 per ounce change over five days.

Momentum is not volatility. Gold can move from $1200 to $1250 in two days then back to $1200 over the next three days and the momentum would be zero but the volatility would be high.

Figure 6.2 shows a typical pattern of momentum. Smooth prices are used to make the relationship between price change and momentum clear. During the first 15-day cycle, prices rise steadily, peaking on day 9. As prices rise at a slower rate

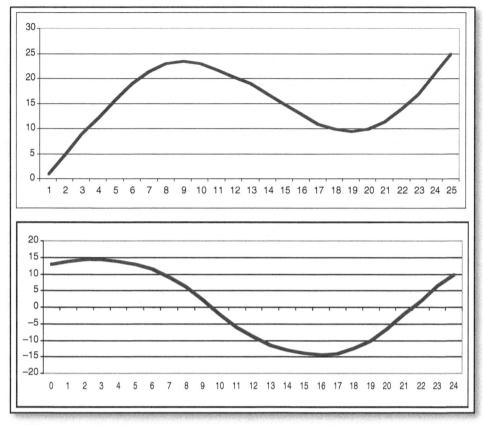

FIGURE 6.2   Price (top) and Corresponding Momentum (bottom).

during days 5 through 9 the momentum declines but remains above zero. As long as the 5-day momentum is greater than zero, prices are rising. The highest momentum value occurs on day 3 when prices have the largest positive price change.

On day 10 the momentum value is zero. Looking at the price chart, this occurs when the 5-day change in price is zero. The lowest momentum value occurs on day 16 when the prices have declined the most. After prices reach their lowest point and begin up, the momentum is negative but rising.

If prices always moved in the smooth pattern shown in Figure 6.2, then momentum would be a perfect leading indicator. You could buy when momentum turned up and sell when it turned down, and be ahead of the change in price direction. Unfortunately, prices movement is irregular; consequently, momentum values are irregular. Because momentum contains valuable information, we will look at a number of systematic ways to evaluate momentum and improve trading. These focus on extreme momentum values and momentum patterns, all of which have proved to be valuable additions to trading strategies, in particular to the timing of entries and exits.

Characteristics of Momentum

Momentum is a way of smoothing price movement and can serve the same purpose as a trend. Although the momentum values are not as smooth as a moving average, larger momentum periods reduce the extremes seen in the price chart. One key advantage of momentum is that it does not have the lag that exists in a moving average.

The AOL chart (Figure 6.3) compares 20- and 40-day moving averages at the top with 20- and 40-day momentum along the bottom. The 40-day momentum (dark line) is smoother and peaks at about the same place as the price. The faster 20-day momentum is not as smooth but peaks sooner than the 40-day momentum and actually leads the price movement. The peaks of the faster momentum represent the maximum price change over a 20-day period. Had prices continued higher at the same rate—that is, if prices had increased $1 per day—the 20-day momentum would have turned sideways and become a horizontal line.

The 20-day and 40-day momentum lines both peak significantly sooner than their moving average equivalents, showing that the speed represented by momentum is a more sensitive measure than the direction of a trendline. The cost of this leading indicator is the increased noise seen in the erratic pattern of momentum compared to the smoothness of the trendline.

Momentum can be used as a trend indicator by selling when the momentum value crosses downward through the horizontal line at zero and buying when it crosses above the zero line. Because there is more noise in momentum than in the equivalent moving average, you would want to draw a small band around the zero line about the width of the small variations in momentum. A sell signal would be given when the momentum falls below the lower band and a buy when it moves upward through the upper band. However, the momentum crossing zero is essentially the same as the moving average turning up or down. It means that the price today is the same as the price *n*-days ago.

FIGURE 6.3 20- and 40-Day Momentum (lower panel) Compared to a 20- and 40-Day Moving Average, Applied to AOL.

Momentum as a Percentage

It is always convenient to express all markets in the same notation. It makes comparisons much easier. For the stock market, momentum can be expressed as a percentage where a 1-day momentum is equivalent to the 1-day return,

$$\text{1-day momentum in percent} = \frac{(P_t - P_{t-1})}{P_{t-1}} = \frac{P_t}{P_{t-1}} - 1$$

or, because they are returns, the alternative can be used, $\ln \frac{P_{t-1}}{P_t}$. But momentum is most often calculated over more than one day; therefore, the n-day momentum as a percentage is

$$M(n) = \frac{P_t}{P_{t-n}} - 1$$

Using percentages does not work for futures markets because most data used for analysis are continuous, back-adjusted prices. Back-adjusting over many years and many contracts will cause the oldest data to be very different from the actual prices that occurred on those dates; therefore, percentages are incorrect. When using momentum with back-adjusted futures prices, it is best to use the price differences.

Momentum as the Difference between Price and Trend

The term *momentum* is very flexible. It is common for it to refer to the difference between today's price and a corresponding moving average value, in a manner similar to *beta*, which indicates the relative strength of a stock compared to an index. The properties of this new value are the same as standard momentum. As the momentum becomes larger, prices are moving away from the moving average. As it moves towards zero, the prices are converging with the moving average.

The upper panel of Figure 6.4 shows a 20-period moving average plotted on a daily chart of Intel during the 14 months ending May 2003. The center panel shows the standard 20-period momentum, the difference between prices that are 20 days apart. The bottom panel is the difference between the price and the 20-day moving average. The range of values for the center panel is approximately +6 to −11, and the scale on the lower panel is +3 to −7. Because a trendline lags behind price movement, the difference between the price and trendline is smaller at points where there are larger price swings and typically larger momentum values.

A comparison of the two lower panels of Figure 6.4 also shows that there are differences in the small movements but the overall pattern is the same. When a price moves to an extreme, it is generally farthest from the moving average and farthest from the price n-days ago; therefore, the most extreme points occur at exactly the same place. This momentum calculation has also been called *relative strength* because it is measured relative to a previous price or relative to a trendline.

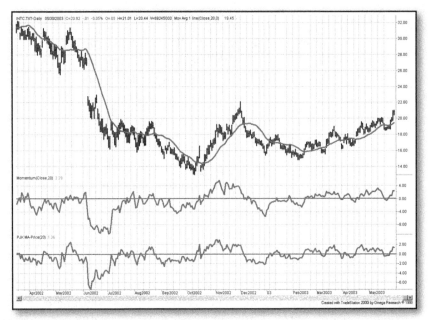

FIGURE 6.4 Momentum Is Also Called *Relative Strength*, the Difference between Two Prices or a Price and a Moving Average (lower panel). The traditional momentum calculation is shown in the center panel.

Momentum as a Trend Indicator

The momentum value is a smoothing of price changes and can serve the same purpose as a standard moving average. Many applications use momentum as a substitute for a price trend. By looking at the net change in price over the number of days designated by an *n*-day momentum indicator, intermediate fluctuations are ignored, and the pattern in price trend can be seen. The longer the span between the observed points, the momentum calculation period, the smoother the results. This is very similar to faster and slower moving averages.

To use momentum as a trend indicator, choose any calculation period. A *buy* signal occurs whenever the value of the momentum turns from negative to positive, and a *sell* signal is when the opposite occurs, as shown in Figure 6.5. If a band is used to establish

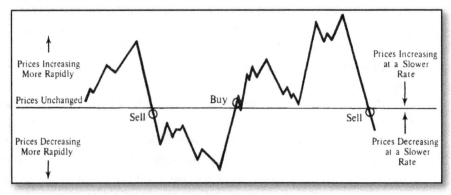

FIGURE 6.5 Trend Signals Using Momentum.

a neutral position or a commitment zone, it should be drawn around the horizontal line representing the zero momentum value.

In order to find the best choice of a momentum span, a sampling of different values could be tested for optimum performance, or a chart could be examined for some natural price cycle. Identify the significant tops and bottoms of any bar chart, and average the number of days between these cycles, or find the number of days that would closely approximate the occurrences of these peaks and valleys. Then use ½ or ¼ the number of days from peak to peak or valley to valley. These natural cycles will often be the best choice of momentum calculation interval (Figure 6.6). Momentum and oscillators, however, are more often used to identify abnormal price movements and for timing of entries and exits in conjunction with a longer-term trend.

Timing an Entry

Momentum is a convenient way of identifying good entry points based on small price reversals within a trend that are not large enough to change the direction of the trend. By choosing a much shorter time period for the momentum calculation (for example, 6 days) to work in combination with a longer trend of 30 to 50 days, the momentum indicator will show frequent opportunities within the trend. The short time period for the momentum calculation assures you that there will be an entry opportunity within about three days of the entry signal; therefore, it becomes

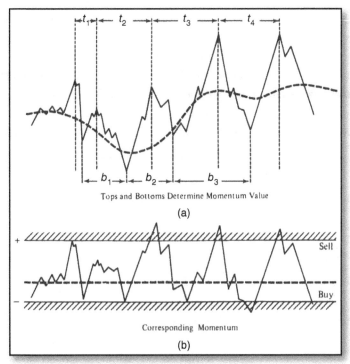

Tops and Bottoms Determine Momentum Value

(a)

Corresponding Momentum

(b)

FIGURE 6.6 **Relationship of Momentum to Prices. (a) Tops and bottoms determine momentum value. (b) Corresponding momentum.**

a practical timing tool. This is particularly useful when you view momentum as a countertrend signal, which will be discussed in the next section.

Identifying and Fading Price Extremes

An equally popular and more interesting use for momentum focuses on the analysis of relative tops and bottoms. All momentum values are bounded (although somewhat irregularly) in both directions by the maximum move possible during the time interval represented by the span of the momentum. The conditions at the points of high positive and negative momentum are called *overbought* and *oversold,* respectively.

A market is *overbought* when it can no longer sustain the strength of the current upwards trend and a downward price reaction is imminent; an *oversold* market is ready for an upward move. Faster momentum calculations (those using shorter calculation periods) will tend to fluctuate above and below the zero line based on small price changes. Longer calculation periods will take on the characteristics of a trend and stay above or below the zero line for the extent of the trend. In Figure 6.7, using S&P futures, the 20-day momentum in the center panel stays above zero for most of the period from September 2010 through February 2011. The very fast 3-day momentum in the bottom panel consistently penetrates the zero line, although the peaks on the upside are larger than those on the downside.

The values on the right scale of the two lower panels in Figure 6.7 show the range of price movement over the 20-day and 3-day periods. The 20-day scale goes from +100 to –60 while the 3-day scale is smaller, about +60 to –40. The 3-day momentum is not 3/20ths of the 20-day momentum because volatility does not increase linearly over time. That is, volatility can increase faster in a few days, but over longer periods it has up and down movement that limits the total move in one direction.

A system can take advantage of the momentum extremes by *fading the price movement* (selling rallies and buying declines). This is done by drawing two horizontal lines on the momentum chart (as shown in Figure 6.6b) above and below the zero line in such a way that the tops and bottoms of the major moves are isolated. These lines may be selected

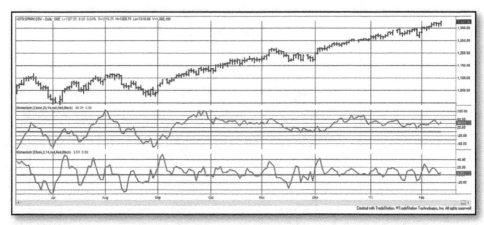

FIGURE 6.7 **20-Day Momentum (center panel) and 3-Day Momentum (bottom panel) Applied to the S&P, June 2010 through February 2011.**

- Visually, so that once the line is penetrated, prices reverse shortly afterwards.

- Based on a percentage of the maximum possible momentum value.

- A multiple of the standard deviation of momentum values. Using two standard deviations would position the lines so that only 5% of all momentum values penetrate above and below the two horizontal lines.

When positioning these bands, there is always a trade-off between finding more trading opportunities and entering the market too soon. Once these lines have been drawn, the entry options will be one of the following basic trading rules:

- *Aggressive.* Enter a new long position when the momentum value penetrates the lower bound; enter a new short position when the value penetrates the upper bound.

- *Minor confirmation.* Enter a new short position on the first day the momentum value turns down after penetrating the upper bound (the opposite for longs).

- *Major confirmation.* Enter a new short position when the momentum value penetrates the upper bound moving lower (the opposite for longs).

- *Timing.* Enter a new short position after the momentum value has remained above the upper bound for *n* days (the opposite for longs).

To close out a profitable short or long position, there are the following alternatives (the rules are symmetrical for longs and shorts):

- *Most demanding.* Close out long positions or cover shorts when the momentum value satisfies the entry condition for a reverse position.

- *Moderately demanding.* Cover a short position when the momentum penetrates the zero line, minus one standard deviation (or some other target point partway between the zero line and the lower bound).

- *Basic exit.* Cover a short position when the momentum value becomes zero.

- *Allowing an extended move.* Cover a short position if the momentum crosses the zero line moving up *after* penetrating that line moving down.

The *basic exit*, removing your trade when the momentum reaches the zero line, is the benchmark case. It is based on the conservative assumption that prices will return to the center of the recent movement (in other words, *mean reverting*). It is less reasonable to assume that prices will continually move from overbought to oversold and back again. Most statisticians would agree that the mean is the best forecast of future prices, and the zero momentum value represents the mean. You may try to increase the profits by assuming that the momentum value will penetrate the zero line by a small amount because there is always some amount of noise. However, if you require a larger penetration of zero to cause an exit, many of the exit opportunities will be lost. You can be more conservative by exiting somewhat before the zero line is reached, but then you also reduce your average profit.

The same momentum calculations, viewed over a longer time period, show one of the problems with using momentum for timing. Figure 6.8 covers a critical period,

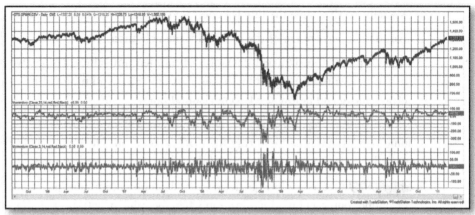

FIGURE 6.8 A Longer View of the 20- and 3-Day Momentum Applied to the S&P. The magnitude of the momentum values change over time.

from August 2005 through February 2011. Notice that the scale of the momentum values change dramatically from the beginning to the end of the chart. This is especially important for the 20-day momentum in the middle panel. For all of 2006, volatility was very low. Had we used momentum as an overbought/oversold indicator, the entry bands would have been at about ±30. For the 3-day momentum, it would have been closer to ±15. As we saw before, the faster momentum is more symmetric than the slower one. During 2006, there were more selling than buying opportunities.

Volatility increases in 2007. If buy entries were targeted as momentum values of −30 then traders would have held a 120 point loss as momentum dropped to −150. A similar pattern was repeated on the upside for sell signals. It would be necessary to increase the width of the buy and sell bands to ±75 and still hold larger losses waiting for a price reversal. But then comes 2008, and any countertrend entry, buying as prices fall, would have caused a complete loss of equity. However, let's say that we were able to avoid disaster and the entry-exit bands were at ±100 for the 20-day momentum and ±50 for the 3-day. Volatility finally declines and we get only the occasional entry signal. The bands need to be adjusted back down to a smaller range.

The problem with using momentum for timing is that the scale is unpredictable. Even if we waited for a reversal after penetrating the band there is no assurance that prices will not reverse and go to new extremes. Some risk protection is needed, a way of dynamically adjusting the bands or a different way of measuring momentum.

Risk Protection A protective *stop-loss order* can be used whenever you trade against the current price momentum. A stop-loss is a specific order to exit if the price goes the wrong way. This is most important with the *aggressive* entry, which advocates selling when the momentum value moves above the upper threshold line, regardless of how fast prices are rising. While the other entry options allow for a logic positioning of a stop-loss, the aggressive entry does not. You will simply need to decide, based on historic momentum values, where to limit your risk. With the other entry options, prices are no longer at their extremes, so that stops may be placed using one of the following techniques:

- Place a protective stop above or below the most extreme high or low momentum value.
- Follow a profitable move with a trailing, nonretreating stop based on fixed points or a percentage.
- Establish zones that act as levels of attainment (using horizontal lines of equal spacing), and do not permit reverse penetrations once a new zone is entered.

Risk protection must be flexible in the way it deals with volatility. As prices reach higher levels, increased volatility will cause momentum tops and bottoms to widen; with low volatility, prices may not be active enough to penetrate the upper or lower bounds. This is shown in Figure 6.8. Therefore, both the profits and risk of a trade entered at extremes must increase with volatility and higher prices. Stops could be based on a percentage of price or a multiple of volatility.

The aggressive entry option remains the greatest problem for controlling risk, where a short signal is given when prices are very strong. If an immediate reversal does not occur, large open losses may accrue. To determine the proper stop-loss amount, a computer test was performed using an immediate entry based on penetration of an extreme boundary and with a stop-loss at the close of the day for risk protection. The first results were thought to have outstanding profits and consistency until it was discovered that the computer had done exactly the opposite of what was intended—it *bought* when the momentum crossed the upper bound and placed a close stop-loss *below* the entry. It did prove, for a good sampling of futures markets, that *high momentum* periods continued for enough time to capture small but consistent profits. It also showed that the aggressive entry trading rule, anticipating an early reversal, would be a losing strategy. One should never forget that declining momentum does not mean that prices are falling.

The Trend Provides Protection   In these examples, momentum is not a strategy itself, but a way of entering a trend trade. When a trend signal first occurs, it is not entered. If the signal was long, then the strategy waits until the 3-day momentum penetrates the lower band. If prices continue lower, then the trend will change from up to down, and the position will be exited. It would not be necessary to have a stop-loss.

Profit Targets for Fading Extreme Moves   When using momentum as a mean-reversion strategy, the most reasonable exit for a short entered at an extreme momentum high, or a long position entered at a low, is when the momentum returns to near zero. Prices do not have an obligation to go from extreme lows to extreme highs; however, any extreme can be expected to return to normal, which is where momentum is zero. Returning to zero does not mean that all trades will be profitable. If there has been a strong upwards move that lasted longer than the calculation period of the momentum, then prices will be higher when momentum finally returns to zero. The trend is not your friend if it fights with your mean-reversion position.

The number of profitable trades can be increased by targeting a momentum level that is more conservative than zero. That is, if a long was entered at an extreme low, a sell would be placed 5% or 10% below the zero momentum line, based on the distance between the buying threshold line and zero. Trades that *almost* return to normal would then be closed out with profits, although the average size of the profit would be smaller. To increase the size of the profits per trade, you would target the opposite side of the zero momentum line; therefore, if you held a long position, you would wait until the momentum value was greater than zero by 5% or 10% of the range. The success of taking profits early or late depends on the amount of noise in the momentum values as it fluctuates near the zero value. In many cases where extreme prices are followed by a sideways pattern, momentum will fluctuate around zero so that there is ample opportunity to exit the trade at a better price.

High-Momentum Trading

Some professional traders have made a business of trading in the direction of the price move only when momentum exceeds the *high threshold level* rather than anticipating a change of direction. There is a small window of opportunity when prices are moving fast. They will usually continue at the same, or greater, momentum for a short time, measured usually in minutes or hours, but occasionally a few days. There is a lot of money to be made in a short time—but at great risk if prices reverse direction sooner than expected.

Price patterns have changed. There are many more day traders. When one stock breaks out above a previous high, everyone sees it as an opportunity for profit. Buy orders start to flow, and volume increases. Stocks that are normally ignored can attract large volume when prices make a new high. Traders ride the rising prices for as long as possible, watching to see when volume begins to drop, then they exit. Some may just target a modest profit and get out when that target is reached.

High-momentum trading is a fast game that requires tools that allow you to scan a wide range of stocks. You are looking for one that has made a new high after a long, quiet period. You may also continually sort stocks by the highest momentum values. You need to stay glued to your screen, enter fast and exit fast. It is a full-time commitment.

Moving Average Convergence/Divergence (MACD)

Many of the practical problems of fading prices using momentum are solved with the *Moving Average Convergence/Divergence* (MACD),[2] developed by Gerald Appel. The MACD uses momentum calculated as the difference between two trendlines, produced using exponential smoothing. This momentum value is further smoothed to give a *signal line*. The most common form of MACD uses the difference between a 12-day and 26-day exponential smoothing. The signal line, used to produce trading recommendations, is a 9-day smoothing of the MACD. The MACD can be created as follows:

Step 1: Choose the two calculation periods for the trend, for example, 20 and 40. Convert to smoothing constants using $2/(n + 1)$.

THEORY AND ANALYSIS

[2] From John D. Becker, "Value of Oscillators in Determining Price Action," *Futures* (May 1994).

FIGURE 6.9 MACD for AOL. The MACD line is the faster of the two trendlines in the bottom panel; the signal line is the slower. The histogram is created by subtracting the slower signal line from the MACD line.

Step 2: Calculate the slow trendline, *E*40, using the smoothing value 0.0243.

Step 3: Calculate the fast trendline, *E*20, using the smoothing value 0.0476.

Step 4: The *MACD line,* the slower-responding line in the bottom panel of Figure 6.9, is *E*20 − *E*40. When the market is moving up quickly, the fast smoothing will be above the slow, and the difference will be positive. This is done so that the MACD line goes up when prices go up.

Step 5: The *signal line* is the 9-day smoothing (using a constant of 0.10) of the MACD line. The signal line is slower than the MACD; therefore, it can be seen in the bottom panel of Figure 6.9 as the lower line when prices are moving higher.

The 20- and 40-day momentum lines, corresponding to the MACD line and the histogram, are shown in the center panel of Figure 6.9. It is clear that the MACD process smoothes these values significantly; therefore, it makes trading signals easier to see.

Reading the MACD Indicator The MACD is normally seen as it appears at the bottom of Figure 6.9. The MACD line is higher in an uptrend and lower in a downtrend. The histogram is created by subtracting the slower signal line from the MACD line. When the histogram is above zero, it confirms the uptrend.

The 40/20 MACD line is similar to the 40-day momentum line. We can compare the MACD in the lower panel with the 20- and 40-day momentum in the center panel and see that the peaks and valleys are in about the same place, but the MACD line is much smoother because it is the difference between two trendlines rather than prices.

You should note the point at which the MACD and signal lines turn down in May 2001, compared to the corresponding moving averages that are shown with prices in the top panel of the chart. The MACD leads the moving averages in showing the downturn and has only slightly more up-and-down variation in its values. The signal line also leads the moving averages in the downturn and is equally smooth.

Trading the MACD   The most common use of the MACD is as a trend indicator. For this purpose, only the MACD and signal lines are used in the following way:

> *Buy* when the MACD line (faster) crosses upwards through the signal line (slower). *Sell* when the MACD line crosses from above to below the signal line.

In the bottom panel of Figure 6.9, the buy signals that occur right after an extreme low in April and October of 2001 generated large gains. Unfortunately, there were many other crossings that generated losses; therefore, it is necessary to select which trades to enter. To accomplish that, the MACD uses thresholds similar to those shown for momentum, but in the opposite way. The MACD must first penetrate the lower band; then it must signal a new uptrend before a long position can be entered. In this way, it removes some of the whipsaws that might occur in a sideways market. Threshold levels were established by observing the historically high and low momentum values, shown as horizontal lines at the +2.00 and −2.00 levels in Figure 6.9. Sell signals would have been taken only after the MACD value had been above +2.00, and buy signals only when the MACD value had fallen below −2.00. The trading signals that satisfy these conditions are the *buy* signal in April, a *sell* in May, and a *buy* in October. However, fitting the threshold lines make them unreliable values for trading. One solution can be found in "An RSI Version of MACD" in the next section.

Appel has written extensively on the MACD, and many variations can be found in his book, *Technical Analysis.*[3] Many of the examples are interpretive, similar to the way we look at chart patterns. Appel also preferred using trends of 19 and 39 days for the NASDAQ composite. An equally important use of MACD is for divergence signals. *Bearish divergence* occurs when prices are rising but the MACD values are falling. Because this technique applies to many indicators in addition to the MACD, it is covered in detail in the section "Momentum Divergence" toward the end of this chapter.

■ Divergence Index

A method similar to MACD but one that uses an interesting combination of generalized techniques is the *divergence index*, the volatility-adjusted difference between two moving averages, for example, 10 and 40 days. Using general notation:

1. *Slow average$_t$ = 40-day average of the most recent prices*
2. *Fast average$_t$ = 10-day average of the most recent prices*
3. *Difference$_t$ = price$_t$ − price$_{t-1}$*

[3] Gerald Appel, *Technical Analysis, Power Tools for Active Investors* (Upper Saddle River, NJ: FT Prentice Hall, 2005).

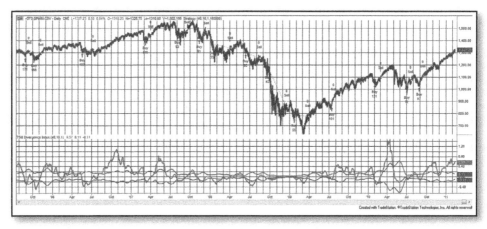

FIGURE 6.10 Divergence Index Applied to S&P Futures.

Then the divergence index (DI),

$$DI_t = \frac{Fast\ average_t - Slow\ average_t}{StDev\ (Difference_t, slow\ period)^2}$$

The standard deviation of the price differences, taken over the slow period of 40, volatility-adjusts the results. The trading rules require a band around zero to trigger entries.

$$Band_t = stdev(DI_t, slow\ period)$$
$$Upper\ band_t = factor \times Band_t$$
$$Lower\ band_t = -factor \times Band_t$$

where factor = 1.0. By using the standard deviation of DI, the band also adjusts to changes in volatility. In Figure 6.10 the index in the lower panel has high peaks followed by periods of low or varying volatility. The standard deviation allows the bands to widen or narrow according to the pattern of fluctuations. This example used the slow period for the standard deviation; however, the fast period would have caused more rapid changes to the band.

The trading rules are

Buy when the DI moves below the lower band while in an uptrend
Sell when the DI moves above the upper band while in a downtrend
Exit longs and shorts when the DI crosses zero

Figure 6.10 shows the DI and the upper and lower bands in the bottom panel. The top panel shows the trading signals for the S&P 500 futures contract.

▉ Oscillators

Because the representation of momentum is that of a line fluctuating above and below a zero value, it has often been termed an *oscillator*. Even though it does oscillate, the use of this word is confusing. In this presentation, the term *oscillator* will be restricted to a specific form of momentum that is *normalized* and expressed in terms of values that are limited to the ranges between +1 and −1 (or +100 to −100), +1 and 0, or +100 and 0 (as in a percent).

To transform a standard momentum calculation into the normalized form with a maximum value of +1 and a minimum value of −1, divide the momentum calculation by its maximum value over the same rolling time period. This allows the oscillator to self-adjust to changes in price or volatility. For example, in April 2006, Amazon was trading at about $34. During a 10-day period it had a high of $35.31 and a low of $31.52, a range of $3.79. During 10 days in February 2011, Amazon had a high of $191.40 and a low of $174.77, a range of $16.63. Therefore, a price move of $2 in 2006 would be the same as a move of $8.77 in 2011. By dividing $2 by $3.79 or $8.77 by $16.63 we get 0.52 in both cases. Hence, *normalization*, which is the basis for most momentum indicators, can be an excellent way to self-adjust to price changes.

The following sections show how a number of useful oscillators are calculated. In each case, the purpose is to have the indicator post high values when prices are at a peak and low values when they are in a valley. To be most useful, prices should reverse direction soon after the oscillator records values near its extremes.

Relative Strength Index

One of the most popular indicators for showing overbought and oversold conditions is the *Relative Strength Index* (RSI) developed by Welles Wilder.[4] It provides added value to the concept of momentum by scaling all values between 0 and 100. It is more stable than momentum because it uses all the values in the calculation period rather than just the first and last. It is a simple measurement that expresses the relative strength of the current price movement as increasing from 0 to 100. It is calculated as

$$RSI = 100 - \left(\frac{100}{1+RS} \right) = 100 \times \left(\frac{RS}{1+RS} \right)$$

where $RS = \dfrac{AU}{AD}$

AU = the total of the upwards price changes during the past 14 days
AD = the total of the downwards price changes (used as positive numbers) during the past 14 days

Once the first calculation has been made, both the AU and AD values can be calculated daily using an *average-off* method:

$$AU_t = AU_{t-1} + \frac{AU_{t-1}}{14} + \max(p_t - p_{t-1}, 0)$$

$$AD_t = AD_{t-1} + \frac{AD_{t-1}}{14} + \max(p_{t-1} - p_t, 0)$$

[4] J. Welles Wilder Jr., *New Concepts in Technical Trading Systems* (Greensboro, NC: Trend Research, 1978).

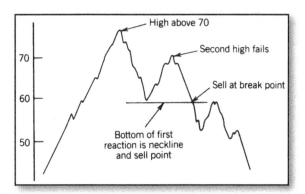

FIGURE 6.11 RSI Top Formation.

This method essentially subtracts an average value and adds the new value, if any. All price changes are treated as positive numbers. The daily calculation of the RSI becomes a matter of simple arithmetic. Wilder has favored the use of 14 days because it represents one-half of a natural cycle, in this case, 1 month. He has set the significant threshold levels for the RSI at 30 and 70. Penetration of the lower level is indicative of an imminent upturn and penetration of the upper level, a pending downturn. A chart of an RSI is shown along with a comparable momentum and stochastic indicator later in Figure 6.15.

Use of the RSI alone to generate trading signals often requires interpretation similar to standard chart analysis. Lines are drawn across the tops of the RSI values to indicate a downtrend. A head-and-shoulders formation can be used as the primary confirmation of a change in direction. Wilder himself used the RSI top and bottom formations shown in Figure 6.11. A break of the reaction bottom between the declining tops is a sell signal. In addition, the *failure swing,* or divergence (discussed later in this chapter), denotes an unsuccessful test of a recent high or low RSI value.

Wilder created other popular indicators. One of these is a momentum calculation called the *Average Directional Movement* (ADX). The ADX is a byproduct of the *Directional Movement*. Both of these indicators are actively used by traders.

Modifying the RSI An obvious objection to the RSI might be the selection of a 14-day *half-cycle.* Maximum divergence is achieved by using a moving average that is some fraction of the length of the dominant cycle, but 14 days may not be that value. If a 14-day calculation period is too short, then the RSI would remain outside the 70-30 zones for extended periods rather than signaling an immediate turn. In practical terms, a 14-day RSI means that a sustained move in one direction that lasts for more than 14 days will produce a very high RSI value. If prices continue higher for more than 14 days, then the RSI, as with other oscillators, will go sideways. The idea is to pick the calculation period for which there are very few larger sustained moves, and 14 may be that value. If more frequent overbought and oversold conditions are needed, then the period could be lowered to 10. At the same time, the zones could be increased to 80-20. Some combination of calculation period and zone will usually give the frequency of trades that is needed.

A study by Aan[5] on the distribution of the 14-day RSI showed that the average RSI top and bottom value consistently grouped near 72 and 32, respectively. Therefore, 50% of all RSI values fall between 72 and 32, which can be interpreted as *normally distributed*, and equivalent to about 0.675 standard deviations. This would suggest that the 70-30 levels proposed by Wilder are too close together to act as selective overbought/oversold values, but should be moved farther apart. The equivalent of 1.5 standard deviations is a comfortable trade-off between frequency of trades and risk. It is generally safer to err on the side of less risk. If there are too many trades being generated by the RSI, a combination of a longer interval and higher confidence bands will be an improvement.[6]

Further Smoothing with N-Day Ups and Downs   Instead of increasing the number of days in the RSI calculation period, a smoother indicator can be found by increasing the period over which each of the *up* and *down* values are determined. The original RSI method uses 14 individual days, where an *up day* is a day in which the price change was positive. Instead, we can replace each 1-day change with a 2-day change, or an *n*-day change. If we use 2-day changes, then a total of 28 days will be needed, so that each 2-day period does not overlap another; there will be 14 sets of two days each. Using 14 sets of 2 will give a smoother indicator than using 28 single-day changes.

RSI Countertrend Trading   Momentum indicators are used for timing and counter-trend trading. Normally, it is the absolute overbought or oversold level that is the trigger for a trade. However, either a very fast move in price or an extreme value for a momentum indicator could be a criterion for a reversal. When $RSI_t - RSI_{t-k} > a$, or when $RSI_t - RSI_{t-k} < -a$, where a is a threshold value, we could sell and buy, respectively. This also increases the number of trades because it does not require that $RSI_t > 0$, only that it has moved quickly. Exits can be taken when momentum returns to near zero, or after *n* days. A program to test this is *TSM RSI Countertrend*, available on the Companion Website.

Net Momentum Oscillator   Another variation on the RSI is the use of the difference between the sum of the up days and the sum of the down days, called a *net momentum oscillator*.[7] If you consider the unsmoothed RSI = $100 \times (S_u/(S_u + S_d))$ then the net momentum oscillator would be

$$CMO = 100 \times (S_u - S_d)/(S_u + S_d)$$

This method replaces some of the indicator movement lost to smoothing in the normal RSI, and shows more extremes. This may also be done by shortening the number of periods in the RSI calculation.

The 2-Day RSI   Among the interesting information published on MarketSci Blog[8] is Michael Stokes's "favorite" indicator, the 2-day RSI, which replaces each 1-day

---

[5] Peter W. Aan, "How RSI Behaves," *Futures* (January 1985).

[6] For another interesting approach to RSI optimization, see John F. Ehlers, "Optimizing RSI with Cycles," *Technical Analysis of Stocks & Commodities* (February 1986).

[7] Tushar S. Chande and Stanley Kroll, *The New Technical Trader* (New York: John Wiley & Sons, 1994).

[8] Free subscriptions are available at MarketSci Blog email@marketsci.com. The author, Michael Stokes, presents his own ideas and analysis of various systematic approaches.

closing price change with a 2-day change; otherwise, the calculations and the number of data points are the same. If you already have a program to calculate the RSI, you only need to change the statement $p_t - p_{t-1}$ with $p_t - p_{t-2}$ to get overlapping 2-day data. Or, to try an n-day RSI, replace the "2" with your choice of days. The effect of using combined 2 days instead of 1 is some smoothing and a general increase in volatility.

Stokes uses threshold levels of 10 and 90 for the S&P and the rules

Buy on the next close when the 2-day RSI penetrates the threshold of 10 moving lower

Sell short on the next close when the 2-day RSI penetrates the threshold of 90 moving higher

Exit one day later on the close

Figures 6.12a and b are from the MarketSci Blog on December 9, 2008. Figure 6.12a shows that the profitability of the RSI reversed in about 1998. From 1970 to 1998 it was a good trend indicator; that is, when the RSI moved above 90 the S&P continued up. After 1998 it has been a much better mean-reverting indicator. Figure 6.12b is the result of applying a method of scaling in to trades according to the following rules:

If the RSI < then *buy* this %		If the RSI > then *sell short* this %	
< 5	100%	> 95	100%
< 10	75%	> 90	75%
< 15	50%	> 85	50%
< 20	25%	> 80	25%

On day t the RSI was 14, and we entered 50%, but then on day $t + 1$ the RSI dropped to 8; it was not clear whether we added an extra 25%, but we assume that is the case. Then the trade is exited if we do not add on the next day. Because the RSI

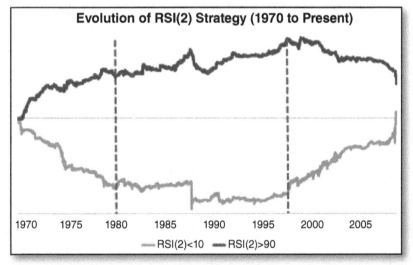

FIGURE 6.12a Performance of the 2-Day RSI, MarketSci Blog's Favorite Oscillator, from the December 9, 2008, Posting, Simple Entries <10 and >90 Applied to the S&P, 1970 through 2008.

FIGURE 6.12b **A Breakdown of Longs and Short Sales Using the Scaling-in Method, S&P 2000 through 2008.**

can stay above or below 50 for long periods of time, an exit rule that waits for the RSI to cross 50 is not likely to be successful. Stokes's approach of exiting after one day seems much safer. Figure 6.12b separates the longs and short sales from 2000 through 2008, showing that both sides performed well, a very desirable outcome. Having good performance for longs and shorts is not common because many markets have an upwards bias (especially the stock market). However, 1-day trades are sensitive to costs. Traders will need to see if the returns per share, or per contract, are sufficient to cover commissions and slippage.

A Standard 2-Period RSI In Figure 6.13 a standard 2-period RSI is shown in the middle panel and the traditional 14-day RSI in the lower panel. Both are applied to NASDAQ futures, from August 2005 through September 2008, which appears at the top. The classic RSI penetrates the extremes of 30 and 70 but does not reach

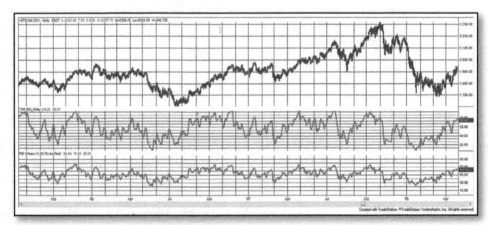

FIGURE 6.13 **2-Period RSI (center panel) Compared with the Traditional 14–Day RSI (bottom panel), Applied to NASDAQ Futures, August 2005 through September 2008.**

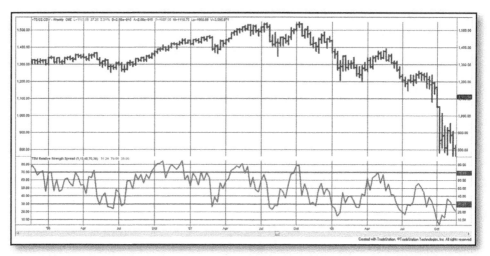

FIGURE 6.14 RSI Applied to the Spread between a 10-Week and 40-Week Moving Average of S&P Futures.

20 or 80, while the 2-period RSI touches near 15 and 85 a number of times. We might expect a 2-period oscillator to jump between 0 and 100 every day that prices changed direction, but the average-off calculation slows down the process and makes the 2-period chart a somewhat more volatile version of the standard RSI.

An RSI Version of MACD While the MACD creates a histogram of the difference between two moving averages, we can make that pattern easier to interpret by applying the RSI to the spread of the moving averages. In Figure 6.14 a 5-day RSI is applied to the difference between the 10- and 40-week moving average for the emini-S&P futures. Using the standard 30-70 thresholds, this seems to find credible points where prices are overbought and oversold.

Stochastics

The *stochastic* indicator, created by George Lane, is an oscillator that measures the relative position of the closing price within a past high-low range. It is based on the commonly accepted observation that closing prices tend to resist penetrating the high prices of the past few days, the place where a horizontal resistance line would be drawn on a chart. Similarly, in a downtrend prices must be able to close below the lows of the past few days for the move to continue. When the market is about to turn from up to down, for instance, it is often the case that the highs are higher than previous days, but the closing price settles nearer the low of the day, failing to indicate a continuation of the uptrend. This makes the stochastic oscillator different from the MACD, which uses the difference between two trends, and the RSI which uses only the closing prices. The stochastic uses the high, low, and close and unlike the other oscillators, there does not have to be any smoothing to introduce a lag.

The three indicators that result from the stochastic measurement are called %K, %D, and %D-slow. These indicators show increasingly slower interpretation of price movement, with %D being the most popular as a single indicator; however, %D and %D-slow are often used together to produce a trading signal. Calculation of these indicators for today's value t over the past 5 days, are

$$\text{Initial (raw) } \%K_t = 100 \times \frac{C_t - L_t(5)}{R_t(5)}$$

$$\%D = \text{``}\%K\text{-slow''} = \frac{\%K_t + \%K_{t-1} + \%K_{t-2}}{3} = \left(\frac{\sum\limits_{i=t-2}^{t} \%K_i}{3} \right)$$

$$\%D_t\text{-slow} = \frac{\left(\sum\limits_{i=t-2}^{t} \%D_i \right)}{3}$$

Where C_t = today's closing price
$L_t(5)$ = the low price of the last 5 days
$R_t(5)$ = the range of the last 5 days (highest high minus lowest low) as of today.[9]

Calculating the 10-Day Stochastic for Hewlett-Packard (HPQ)   Using an Excel spreadsheet, each of the stochastic components can be calculated in only a few columns. In Table 6.1, the historic prices for Hewlett-Packard are imported into columns A–D. The 10-day stochastic calculations, columns E–J, are:

1. Column E, the 10-day high using the function *Max.*
2. Column F, the 10-day low using the function *Min.*
3. Column G, calculate the high-low range by subtracting F from E.
4. Column H, row n, calculate the raw stochastic %K as (Dn-Fn)*100/Gn.
5. Column I, the *%Kslow* is the 3-day average of %K, column H.
6. Column J, *%Dslow* is the 3-day average of %K-slow, column I.

The raw stochastic in column H of the spreadsheet shows that values start above 90% and drop to 6% in a few days. This happens when prices close near the highest or lowest prices of the past 10 days. When calculating the stochastic, today's close is always included in the *max, min,* and *range* calculations. If today's price is the highest or lowest of the calculation period, then the raw stochastic will have a value of 100 or 0. The full spreadsheet *TSM Stochastic calculation for HPQ,* can be found on the Companion Website.

Comparing the Stochastic to Momentum and the RSI   The calculations for momentum, RSI, and the stochastic are very different; therefore, we would expect a

---

[9] Harry Schirding, "Stochastic Oscillator," *Technical Analysis of Stocks & Commodities* (May/June 1984).

TABLE 6.1 Excel Example of 10-Day Stochastic for Hewlett-Packard (HPQ)

	A	B	C	D	E	F	G	H	I	J
Row	Date	High	Low	Close	10-Day High	10-Day Low	10-Day Range	%K	%K-Slow	%D-Slow
1	1/3/2011	43.49	42.22	42.74						
2	1/4/2011	43.77	43.01	43.63						
3	1/5/2011	44.22	43.40	44.20						
4	1/6/2011	44.96	44.18	44.88						
5	1/7/2011	45.39	44.71	45.09						
6	1/10/2011	45.05	44.57	44.86						
7	1/11/2011	46.06	45.20	45.43						
8	1/12/2011	45.71	45.27	45.64						
9	1/13/2011	45.84	45.31	45.65						
10	1/14/2011	46.40	45.61	46.25	46.40	42.22	4.18	96.41		
11	1/18/2011	46.42	46.08	46.34	46.42	43.01	3.41	97.65		
12	1/19/2011	46.48	46.08	46.32	46.48	43.40	3.08	94.81	96.29	
13	1/20/2011	46.79	45.76	46.78	46.79	44.18	2.61	99.62	97.36	
14	1/21/2011	47.64	46.83	47.23	47.64	44.57	3.07	86.64	93.69	95.78
15	1/24/2011	47.59	46.66	47.55	47.64	44.57	3.07	97.07	94.44	95.16
16	1/25/2011	47.83	46.88	47.08	47.83	45.20	2.63	71.48	85.07	91.07
17	1/26/2011	47.28	46.57	46.88	47.83	45.27	2.56	62.89	77.15	85.55
18	1/27/2011	46.98	46.58	46.74	47.83	45.31	2.52	56.75	63.71	75.31
19	1/28/2011	46.69	45.36	45.51	47.83	45.36	2.47	6.07	41.90	60.92

chart of these indicators to vary considerably from one another. However, there are surprising similarities among the three, even calculated over the same 14-day period, as shown in Figure 6.15. The momentum and stochastic both show how today's price relates to the prices over the calculation interval; therefore, we would expect them

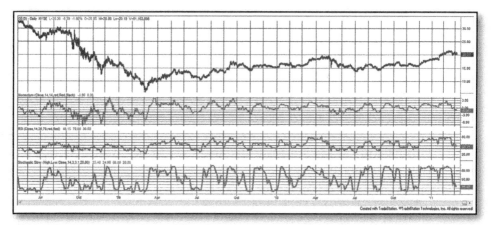

FIGURE 6.15 Comparison of Simple Momentum, RSI, and Stochastic, All for 14-Day Calculation Periods, General Electric, May 2008 through February 2011.

to be most similar, and that appears to be true. Both have peaks at the same place, although the *%D-Slow* stochastic has a smoother overall line due to the two successive 3-day averages.

The RSI chart does not seem to be lagged, instead it is dampened, appearing to have less volatility. In fact, the highs and lows rarely touch 70 and 30, while the stochastic highs and lows often go above 90 and below 10, even though it is smoothed. The overall impression of the stochastic is that it moves faster and exaggerates the swings.

Trading the Stochastic   Traditionally, the stochastic can be traded by using a combination of a slower and faster calculation to give signals, or by combining extreme stochastic values for entry or exit timing with a trend. To use the stochastic by itself, *%D* and *%D-slow* can take on the role of the faster indicator and the slower signal line in the same way as the MACD and its signal line were used. The fastest calculation, *%K*, is not often used due to its instability.[10] Figure 6.16 shows the two 20-day calculations, *%D* and *%D-slow*, along the bottom of an S&P futures continuation chart from December 2001 through September 2002. A 60-day moving average is in the top panel.

The downtrend in the S&P during 2002 produces two good sell signals using the stochastics. In March and August, the slower *%D* penetrates above the 80% threshold and crosses the signal line moving down. A third peak in May touches near 70% and would produce an additional sell signal if the upper threshold were set lower. During a sustained

FIGURE 6.16   20-Day Stochastic (bottom) and a 60-Day Moving Average for the S&P Futures Continuation Series.

---

[10] It is common practice to use the notation *%K* and *%D* to mean *%K-slow* and *%D-slow*, respectively. All writings on the stochastic use the smoothed values, rather than the initial *%K* calculation, regardless of the omission of "-slow." Any use of *%K* in this text also refers to *%K-slow* unless specifically stated.

downtrend, it is common for the indicator values to fall below the lower threshold and remain there for extended periods. Although the rolling calculation is intended to self-adjust, the most practical solution is to combine the stochastic signals with a trend.

The 60-day moving average, shown along with prices in the upper part of Figure 6.16, indicates a downtrend for the entire period of the chart. Using the relatively slow 20-day stochastic, the penetration of the upper 80% threshold gives very good timing for short sale entries, and avoids the problems of an unfavorable distribution of stochastic values. The 20-day stochastic does not indicate where to exit the downtrend. A faster stochastic can be used to produce more frequent sell signals that can be applied as follows

> *Enter a short sale* after the trend has turned down on the first stochastic sell signal (the stochastic crosses the signal line going down).
> *Enter a long* after the trend has turned up on the first stochastic buy signal.

The problem with all timing rules is that, if prices move higher and do not retrace, then there will not be a stochastic signal, or it will occur well after there would have been profits in the trade. Many of the lost opportunities can be eliminated by using a faster stochastic calculation period. It is particularly dangerous to use a timing rule for exiting a position. Delays in entering are lost opportunities, but delays exiting are real trading losses.

Left and Right Crossovers

The faster *%K-slow* will usually change direction sooner than the *%D-slow*, crossing the *%D-slow* line while it is still moving in the prior trend direction. The opposite case, when the *%D-slow* turns first, indicates a slow, stable change of direction and is a more favorable pattern (Figure 6.17a). Using the fast *%K-Slow* and the slower *%D-Slow*, the following patterns have been identified:

> *Hinge.* A reduction in the speed of either the *%K-slow* or *%D-slow* lines, shown as a flattening out, indicates a reversal on the next day (Figure 6.17b).
> *Warning.* An extreme turn in the faster *%K-slow* (from 2 to 12%) indicates at most two days remaining in the old trend.
> *Extremes.* Reaching the extreme *%K-slow* values of 0 and 100 requires seven consecutive days of closes at the highs (or lows). The test of these extremes, following a pullback, is an excellent entry point.
> *Set-up.* Although the line chart shows higher highs and lows, if the *%D-slow* line has lower lows, a *bear market set-up* has occurred. Look for a selling opportunity on the next rally (Figure 6.17c).
> *Failure.* An excellent confirmation of a change in direction occurs when *%K-slow* crosses *%D-slow* (after penetrating the extreme level), then pulls back to the *%D-slow* line, but fails to cross it again (Figure 6.17d).

Creating a Stochastic from the RSI

Any series or indicator value can be converted to a raw stochastic, *%K*, without adding lag by replacing the closing price with the indicator value. This creates a measure

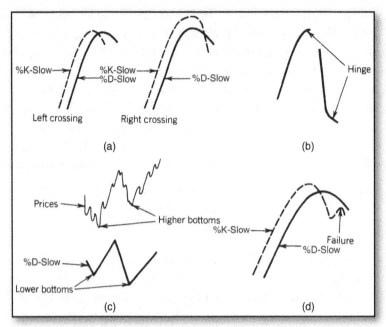

FIGURE 6.17 Lane's Patterns. (a) Left and right crossings. (b) Hinge. (c) Bear market set-up. (d) *%K-slow* failure.

of where that indicator lies in its high-low range over the calculation period and may simplify the generation of buy and sell signals. A stochastic created from an RSI would be[11]

$$n\text{-}day\ StochRSI = \frac{RSI_{today} - RSI_{n\text{-}day\ low}}{RSI_{n\text{-}day\ high} - RSI_{n\text{-}day\ low}}$$

Williams's Oscillators

Larry Williams has been known for his development of trading methods based on oscillators since his publication of the *A/D Oscillator* in 1972. The three techniques described below have some similarities, even though the last one, the *Ultimate Oscillator*, was published 13 years later.

A/D Oscillator In 1972, Jim Waters and Larry Williams published a description of their *A/D Oscillator*. For their method, *A/D* means *accumulation/distribution* rather than the popular notation of advance/decline, a well-known indicator for stocks. They used a unique form of relative strength, defining *buying power* (BP) and *selling power* (SP) as

$$BP = high - open$$

$$SP = close - low$$

---

[11] Tushar Chande and Stanley Kroll, *The New Technical Trader* (New York: John Wiley & Sons, 1994).

where the values used were today's open, high, low, and closing prices. The two values, BP and SP, show the additional buying strength (relative to the open) and selling strength (compared to the close) in an effort to measure the implied direction of the day's trading. This definition of buying and selling power is still used today. The combined measurement, called the *Daily Raw Figure* (DRF) is calculated as

$$\frac{(H-O)+(C-L)}{(H-L)+(H-L)} \qquad DRF_t = \frac{BP_t + SP_t}{2 \times (H_t - L_t)} \qquad \frac{2}{n+1} = \frac{3}{10} \qquad 20 = 3n+3 \qquad 17 = 3n$$

The maximum value of 1 is reached when a market opens trading at the low and then closes at the high: $BP_t - SP_t = H_t - L_t$. When the opposite occurs and the market opens at the high and closes on the lows, the $DRF = 0$. Each price series develops its own patterns, which can be smoothed or traded in many ways similar to a momentum index. The Waters-Williams A/D Oscillator solves problems of volatility and limit moves (although there are very few markets with trading limits any more) in futures markets. *DRF* completely adjusts to higher or lower trading ranges because the divisor itself is a multiple of the day's range; because each day is treated independently, the cumulative values of the momentum index are not part of the results.

This day-to-day evaluation has no memory and causes DRF to be very volatile, yet it still takes on the pattern of the underlying market. If fewer trades are preferred, the DRF can be smoothed. In the example in Table 6.2, a 0.30 exponential smoothing was used (selected arbitrarily) and the entry bands narrowed from 80-20 to 70-30 to reflect fewer extreme prices. Because the 1973 examples used soybeans, this example will do the same, but for 2011 data. Table 6.2 shows the calculations for the DRF and the smoothed DRF. The DRF is plotted as bars on a scale of 0 to 1.00 in Figure 6.18 and is extremely erratic. The solid line is the smoothed DRF. Once plotted, two horizontal lines can be drawn to isolate the peaks and bottoms of DRF; the top part becomes a zone representing an overbought condition, and the bottom zone represents oversold. For this chart, the 80-20 levels were used, although we expect this to be consistent over time because the range used in the denominator normalizes volatility. Even though we do not claim that these thresholds are predictive, the original article by Waters and Williams had lines drawn in a similar place. The thresholds for the smoothed DRF were set at 70-30.

| TABLE 6.2 | A/D Oscillator and Trading Signals, Soybeans, January 1, 2011 through March 4, 2011 |

					Raw DRF			30% DRF Smoothing		
Date	Open	High	Low	Close	DRF	80-20 Signal	Entry (Lagged)	DRF	70-30 Signal	Entry (Lagged)
1/3/2011	1409.00	1422.00	1388.00	1392.00	0.250			0.250		
1/4/2011	1391.25	1403.50	1370.50	1382.50	0.367			0.285		
1/5/2011	1385.00	1408.00	1375.00	1406.50	0.826	Sell ↘		0.447		
1/6/2011	1405.50	1411.75	1389.00	1391.00	0.181	Buy ↘	1405.50	0.368		
1/7/2011	1389.75	1395.50	1373.25	1378.00	0.236	Buy	1389.75	0.328		

(continued)

TABLE 6.2 *Continued*

					Raw DRF			30% DRF Smoothing		
Date	Open	High	Low	Close	DRF	80-20 Signal	Entry (Lagged)	DRF	70-30 Signal	Entry (Lagged)
1/10/2011	1381.00	1407.50	1379.00	1393.50	0.719	Buy		0.445		
1/11/2011	1395.00	1401.50	1368.25	1370.00	0.124	Buy		0.349		
1/12/2011	1372.50	1440.00	1372.00	1428.00	0.908	Sell ↘		0.517		
1/13/2011	1431.75	1445.50	1426.00	1429.00	0.429	Sell	1431.75	0.491		
1/14/2011	1431.50	1442.50	1418.00	1435.50	0.582	Sell		0.518		
1/18/2011	1425.25	1443.00	1421.25	1426.25	0.523	Sell		0.519		
1/19/2011	1429.50	1444.75	1415.25	1424.50	0.415	Sell		0.488		
1/20/2011	1426.00	1434.00	1396.50	1427.25	0.517	Sell		0.497		
1/21/2011	1428.75	1440.00	1418.00	1425.25	0.420	Sell		0.474		
1/24/2011	1425.50	1439.50	1409.75	1417.50	0.366	Sell		0.441		
1/25/2011	1417.25	1421.00	1383.25	1387.50	0.106	Buy ↘		0.341		
1/26/2011	1388.50	1404.00	1377.25	1398.50	0.687	Buy	1388.50	0.445		
1/27/2011	1402.25	1414.00	1391.00	1412.50	0.723	Buy		0.528		
1/28/2011	1414.50	1436.25	1405.50	1411.00	0.443	Buy		0.503		
1/31/2011	1408.25	1426.50	1407.50	1426.00	0.967	Sell ↘		0.642		
2/1/2011	1426.50	1453.50	1421.25	1451.00	0.880	Sell	1426.50	0.713	Sell ↘	
2/2/2011	1452.50	1465.00	1446.50	1457.00	0.622	Sell		0.686	Sell	1452.50
2/3/2011	1459.00	1465.50	1447.00	1448.50	0.216	Sell		0.545	Sell	
2/4/2011	1451.50	1455.75	1435.25	1446.50	0.378	Sell		0.495	Sell	
2/7/2011	1451.00	1456.75	1434.25	1437.50	0.200	Sell		0.406	Sell	
2/8/2011	1438.00	1450.00	1427.00	1447.25	0.701	Sell		0.495	Sell	
2/9/2011	1450.00	1468.75	1448.00	1464.00	0.837	Sell		0.598	Sell	
2/10/2011	1464.25	1468.00	1443.00	1446.00	0.135	Buy ↘		0.459	Sell	
2/11/2011	1444.75	1454.50	1423.00	1429.00	0.250	Buy	1444.75	0.396	Sell	
2/14/2011	1431.75	1438.00	1413.25	1416.00	0.182	Buy		0.332	Sell	
2/15/2011	1416.00	1422.00	1378.00	1381.25	0.105	Buy		0.264	Buy ↘	
2/16/2011	1382.25	1389.00	1370.00	1378.50	0.401	Buy		0.305	Buy	1382.25
2/17/2011	1378.50	1418.75	1378.50	1416.50	0.972	Sell ↘		0.505	Buy	
2/18/2011	1417.50	1421.25	1373.00	1381.00	0.122	Buy ↘	1417.50	0.390	Buy	
2/22/2011	1391.00	1397.50	1311.00	1311.00	0.038	Buy	1391.00	0.284	Buy	
2/23/2011	1310.00	1335.00	1296.25	1331.50	0.777	Buy		0.432	Buy	
2/24/2011	1332.25	1336.75	1310.25	1329.25	0.443	Buy		0.436	Buy	
2/25/2011	1328.75	1399.25	1322.00	1375.00	0.799	Buy		0.545	Buy	
2/28/2011	1378.00	1380.25	1357.75	1364.75	0.206	Buy		0.443	Buy	
3/1/2011	1368.00	1376.50	1353.75	1375.25	0.659	Buy		0.508	Buy	
3/2/2011	1374.50	1399.00	1372.00	1394.25	0.866	Sell ↘		0.615	Buy	
3/3/2011	1390.50	1414.50	1384.50	1412.00	0.858	Sell	1390.50	0.688	Buy	
3/4/2011	1410.25	1424.50	1395.75	1414.00	0.565	Sell		0.651	Buy	

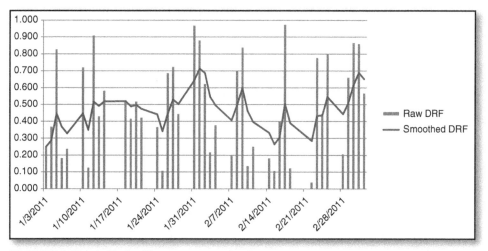

FIGURE 6.18 A/D Oscillator.

The rules for using the A/D Oscillator were not defined in the original article, but some simple rules could be:

- *Sell* when the DRF (or smoothed DRF) penetrates into the overbought zone. Close out all accumulated long positions (if any) and go short on the open of the next trading day.

- *Buy* and exit the short position when the opposite conditions occur.

- All positions are entered on the next open after a signal.

For risk control, positions could be exited if the DRF does not post a lower value (for shorts) within one or two days, and the opposite for longs. In Table 6.2 no stops were used. Long positions were held until a short signal occurred, and shorts until a long was signaled. If the DRF (or smoothed DRF) enters an overbought or oversold zone more than once without the opposite zone being entered, an additional position can be added, although that was not done in the example. Following these rules, the A/D Oscillator showed nine trades, six of them profitable. For the smoothed DRF there were only two trades, both profitable. The amount of smoothing can easily be changed. For more signals, increase the smoothing constant so that it's greater than 0.30. An Excel spreadsheet and a TradeStation program, both named *TSM AD Oscillator*, can be found on the Companion Website.

Although this example was very good, there are potential problems in the A/D Oscillator. The first happens on locked-limit days (where the market opens at the allowable limit and does not trade). In that case the open, high, low, and close are all the same and the DRF cannot be calculated because the divisor is zero. Fortunately, there are few markets in which that can happen, but it did recently in cotton. A more basic problem concerns gap openings. A much higher opening

MOMENTUM AND OSCILLATORS

with a stronger close would also upset the resulting DRF value. Consider the following example:

	Open	High	Low	Close	DRF	ΔRFs	ΣΔDRF
Monday	43.00	44.00	40.00	41.00	0.25		
Tuesday	42.00	42.00	39.00	40.00	0.17	−0.17	−0.17
Wednesday	38.50	38.50	38.00	38.00	0.00	+0.17	0.00
Thursday	42.00	42.00	39.00	40.00	0.17	−0.33	−0.33
Friday	40.00	43.00	40.00	42.00	0.83	+0.50	+0.17

Note that on Wednesday, the DRF indicates that the momentum has reversed, but in fact the price is falling rapidly and gives no indication of recovering; it may actually be gaining momentum. On Thursday the price soars up and closes in the midrange, but the DRF shows a new downward momentum. The problem seems to be related to lack of association with the prior closing price. The daily movement can take on different appearances if the entire range was above or below the closing price. To form this link, replace the current high or low with the prior closing price, in the manner of the *true range* calculation, if that price was outside the current trading range. The following example shows that the results smoothed out and leaves the trend intact.

	Open	High	Low	Close	DRF	ΔDRF	ΣΔDRF
Monday	43.00	44.00	40.00	41.00	.25		
Tuesday	42.00	42.00	39.00	40.00	.17	−.17	−.17
Wednesday	38.50	(40.00)	38.00	38.00	.37	+.04	.13
Thursday	42.00	42.00	(38.00)	40.00	.25	−.12	−.25
Friday	40.00	43.00	40.00	42.00	.83	+.58	+.33

Linking the Current Day with the Prior Day Another oscillator can be constructed using the highs and lows relative to the prior close:

$$O_t = \frac{H_t - C_{t-1}}{H_t - L_t}$$

The two days are linked together, and the ratio of the high price relative to the prior close is measured against the total range for the day. For the normal case, $H_t \geq C_{t-1} \geq L_t$; but if C_{t-1} replaces either H_t or L_t to extend the range, the value of O_t will be either 1 or 0 for these extreme cases. As with the A/D Oscillator, the values derived from this method may also be smoothed.

Oscillators are not the only tools for measuring momentum or for determining overbought or oversold conditions. Because momentum is very different from either a charting technique or a moving average, it is valuable either on its own or as a confirmation of another method.

A word of caution: Trading against the trend can be exciting and profitable, but at considerably greater risk than a trend-following system. The problem with selling an overbought condition is that it is much more difficult to hold losses to a minimum. A long position may be entered while prices are falling fast, and they may continue to fall at the same speed after you are long. Even a quick exit may sustain substantial losses.

%R Method   After the publication of Williams's *How I Made One Million Dollars . . . Last Year . . . Trading Commodities*, the %R oscillator became well known. It is a simple way of calculating where today's closing price fits into the recent trading range. Using the last 10 days, define

$$\%R = \frac{Buying\ power}{Range} = \frac{High_{10} - Close_{today}}{High_{10} - Low_{10}}$$

Williams's 10-day %R is different from a *10-day stochastic,* because it measures how strong the market closed today compared to the high of the past 10 days. It is also conceptually upside down; that is, as the close gets stronger the value of %R gets smaller. It may be intuitively easier to work with if you use $1.0 - \%R$. Williams viewed this as a timing device to add positions within a major technical or fundamental trend. This same approach was discussed with regard to the stochastic, and is shown in Figure 6.16. Trades were not entered if they contradicted the major market direction.

The Ultimate Oscillator   In the *Ultimate Oscillator,* Williams seems to combine his original idea of the A/D Oscillator with a great deal of Wilder's RSI.[12] He adds the unique feature of three concurrent time periods in order to offset the negative qualities of the short time period used for the %R, without slowing the system too much. The Ultimate Oscillator uses the following steps:

1. Calculate today's *buying pressure BP$_t$* by subtracting the *true low* from the closing price, $BP_t = C_t - TL_t$. The true low TLt $= \min(Lt, Ct{-}1)$.
2. Calculate today's *true range,* $TR_t = \max(H_t - L_t, H_t - C_{t-1}, C_{t-1} - L_t)$.
3. Total the buying pressure BP_t separately over the three intervals 7, 14, and 28 days, designated as SB_7, SB_{14}, and SB_{28}.
4. Total the true range TR_t over the same three periods, SR_7, SR_{14}, and SR_{28}.
5. Divide the sum of the buying pressures by the corresponding true range, that is, SB_7/SR_7 and scale by multiplying the 7-day value by 4 and the 14-day value by 2. All three calculations are now in the same scale.

Notice that the nearest seven values for the buying pressure and the true range are each used seven times, that is, they are multiplied by both the scaling factors

---

[12] Larry Williams, "The Ultimate Oscillator," *Technical Analysis of Stocks & Commodities* (August 1985).

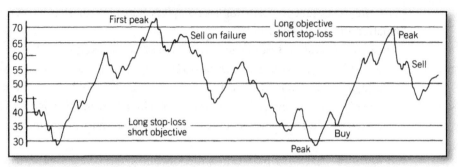

FIGURE 6.19 Williams' Ultimate Oscillator.

of 4 and 2, and used once more in the 28-day calculation. Williams has created a step-weighted momentum, assigning values of 7, 3, and 1 to the first 7 days, second 7 days, and last 14 days, respectively. The last 14 days account for only 10% of the total.

The rules for using this oscillator (Figure 6.19) are:

1. A *sell set-up* occurs when the oscillator moves above the 50% line, peaks at a high value, declines, and then moves higher. If the oscillator fails to move above the peak on the next rally, a *short sale* order can be placed when the oscillator fails on the right shoulder. This is a traditional top confirmation signal.
2. Short positions are closed out when a long signal occurs, when the 30% level is reached, or if the oscillator rises above 65% (the *stop-loss* point) after being below 50%.
3. A *buy* signal is given using the opposite formation as the short signal (rule 1).
4. Close out longs when a short signal occurs, when the 70% level is reached, or if the oscillator falls below 30% (after being above 50%).

Relative Vigor Index

John Ehlers, who has contributed extensively in the mathematical analysis of prices, in particular using cycles, has created the *Relative Vigor Index* (RVI), a very smoothed momentum indicator.[13] The basic form of RVI is

$$RVI = (Close - Open)/(High - Low)$$

However, the final RVI uses a 4-day symmetric weighting (similar to a triangular weighting) of the *close − open* in the numerator, and a similar symmetric weighting of the *high − low* in the denominator.

RVI is conceptually similar to the A/D Oscillator; however, the RVI is smoothed in a special way that targets a particular price cycle and eliminates the 2-bar cycle and its associated unwanted frequencies. While it is preferable that the price series

---

[13] John F. Ehlers, "Relative Vigor Index," *Technical Analysis of Stocks & Commodities* (January 2002).

be analyzed for its cycle period, Ehlers suggests using 10 as the nominal value. The RVI is calculated as

$$N_t = [(C_t - O_t) + 2 \times (C_{t-1} - O_{t-1}) + 2 \times (C_{t-2} - O_{t-2}) + (C_{t-3} - O_{t-3})]/6$$

$$D_t = [(H_t - L_t) + 2 \times (H_{t-1} - L_{t-1}) + 2 \times (H_{t-2} - L_{t-2}) + (H_{t-3} - L_{t-3})]/6$$

$$Numerator_t = \Sigma\, N_i,\ i = t - n + 1,\, t$$

$$Denominator_t = \Sigma\, D_i,\ i = t - n + 1,\, t$$

$$RVI = Numerator_t / Denominator_t, \text{ while } Denominator_t \neq 0$$

$$RVI\ signal\ line_t = (RVI + 2 \times RVI_{t-1} + 2 \times RVI_{t-2} + RVI_{t-3})/6$$

where O_t, H_t, L_t, and C_t are today's open, high, low, and closing prices and n is the calculation period, nominally 10.

The RVI signal line is used in the same manner as the MACD signal line. After a peak in the RVI value, showing an overbought situation, the sell signal occurs the first time that the RVI crosses the RVI signal line moving lower.

■ Double-Smoothed Momentum

Important contributions to the study of momentum have been made by William Blau.[14] In addition to creating new momentum indicators, he has added substantial value to the old ones.

True Strength Index

Much of Blau's work combines double smoothing of momentum values (1-period price differences) which has surprisingly little calculation *lag* given the amount of smoothing. By using the first differences, he has based the calculations on values more sensitive than price and then slowed them down by smoothing. In effect, he speeds up the price movement before slowing it down. The net result is that the final index value has less lag than we would normally expect, and the index line is much smoother than a standard moving average. Blau refers to this as *using momentum as a proxy for price*. One of Blau's most popular indicators is the *True Strength Index* (TSI) which combines these features:

$$TSI(close, r, s) = \frac{100 \times XAverage(XAverage(close - close[1], r)s)}{XAverage(XAverage(absvalue(close - close[1], r)s)}$$

Where r = the calculation period of the first momentum smoothing
s = the calculation period of the second momentum smoothing
$close - close[1]$ = the 1-day momentum

---

[14] William Blau, *Momentum, Direction and Divergence* (New York: John Wiley & Sons, 1995).

$XAverage(close, period)$ = the TradeStation function for exponential smoothing

$AbsValue$ = the TradeStation function for absolute value

A spreadsheet to calculate the True Strength Index for crude oil, *TSM True Strength Index*, and a program indicator, *TMS True Strength*, are available on the Companion Website. The spreadsheet code, which is easily entered, is set up as follows:

1. Column *B* is the closing prices
2. Column *C* is the 1-day difference in prices
3. Column *D* is the first smoothing, where D3 = C3 and D4 = D3 + H2*(C3-D3)
4. Column *E* is the second smoothing, E4 = D4, and E5 = E4 + H3*(D5-E4)

The smoothing constants in *H* are derived from the days in *G* using $2/(n+1)$. A sample of the spreadsheet appears in Table 6.3.

The numerator and denominator of the TSI differ only in that the denominator takes the absolute value of the price changes (the 1-day momentum). This guarantees that the denominator will be at least as large as the numerator. The 1-day differences are first smoothed over the period *r*, and then the result is smoothed over the period *s*. The relationship between the standard momentum (the difference in prices over *r* days) and the TSI can be seen in Figure 6.20 for Intel (INTC). The standard 20-day momentum indicator (second panel) has the typical erratic pattern of prices, and a slight lead identifying the peaks. The TSI is much smoother with peaks and valleys lagging prices slightly (third panel). If more smoothing is necessary to avoid false signals, a *signal line* can be created by smoothing the TSI using a 3-period moving average, then buying when the TSI crosses the signal line after a high or low value was reached. This can be a basic trend signal, or it can be applied in the manner of MACD. The slight lag in the TSI seems a small problem compared to the extreme noise of the momentum calculation.

TABLE 6.3   TSI Calculations Using Two 20-Day Smoothing Periods

	A	B	C	D	E	F	G	H
Column	Date	Crude	Diff	Smooth 1	Smooth 2			
2	1/3/2011	96.35				Smooth 1	20	0.0952
3	1/4/2011	94.18	−2.17	−2.170		Smooth 2	20	0.0952
4	1/5/2011	95.1	0.92	−1.876	−1.876			
5	1/6/2011	93.18	−1.92	−1.880	−1.876			
6	1/7/2011	92.83	−0.35	−1.734	−1.863			
7	1/10/2011	94.05	1.22	−1.453	−1.824			
8	1/11/2011	95.91	1.86	−1.137	−1.758			
9	1/12/2011	96.42	0.51	−0.980	−1.684			
10	1/13/2011	95.85	−0.57	−0.941	−1.613			

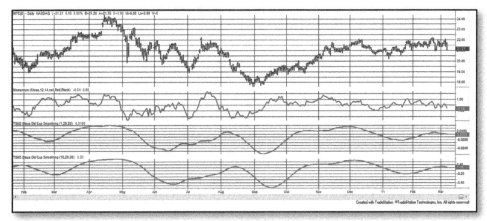

FIGURE 6.20 Comparing the TSI with 10-20-20 Smoothing (bottom) to a Standard 20-Period Momentum (center) Using INTC from January 2001 through March 2002.

Additional Smoothing without Adding Lag In creating the TSI, Blau missed an opportunity to improve the smoothing with only a minor increase in the lag. Instead of taking the 1-day differences, substitute the *n*-day differences in the first step. This smoothes the trendline even more at the cost of a slight additional lag. Figure 6.20 shows the TSI with a 10-day difference followed by two 20-day exponential smoothings in the bottom panel.

Anticipating the Turn When working with trendlines that are very smooth, such as the 10-20-20 TSI, you can anticipate the change in the trend direction most of the time. Instead of waiting for the smoothed trendline to change from up to down, you can sell when it gets to a "near-zero slope" and is continuing to flatten. This anticipation can greatly reduce the lag and improve performance even at the cost of a few false signals.

Double-Smoothed Stochastics

Because of Blau's great interest in double smoothing, he defines the general form of a *double-smoothed stochastic* as:

$$DS(q,r,s) = \frac{100 \times XAverage(XAverage(close - Lowest(low,q),r),s)}{XAverage(XAverage(Highest(high,q) - Lowest(low,q),r),s)}$$

Where *Close − Lowest(low,q)* = the numerator of Lane's raw stochastic, the lowest low over the past *q* periods

Highest(high,q) − Lowest(low,q) = the denominator of Lane's stochastic, the greatest high-low range over the past *q* periods

XAverage((...,r),s) = an exponential smoothing of the numerator, first calculated over *r* periods, then over *s* periods

TRIX

Similar to Blau's double smoothing is *TRIX,* a triple-smoothed exponential that is most often used as an oscillator. Introduced by Jack Hutson,[15] it is created using steps similar to Blau except that there are three exponential smoothings and the differencing is done at the end. Typically, the same smoothing constants (calculation periods) are used for each smoothing. This method has been applied to daily, hourly, or even 1-minute price data.

1. Calculate the natural log (ln) of the closing prices (daily or intraday bars). This implicitly corrects for price volatility; however, it is commonly omitted from the calculation because back-adjusted data in futures will cause errors.
2. Calculate the *p*-period exponential smoothing of the closing prices, or the ln of the closing prices, to get *trend* 1.
3. Calculate the *q*-period exponential smoothing of *trend* 1 to get *trend* 2.
4. Calculate the *r*-period exponential smoothing of *trend* 2 to get *trend* 3.
5. Get the 1-period differences of *trend* 3 by subtracting each value from the previous value. As with the added smoothing of the TSI, the 1-period differences can be replaced with the *s*-period differences.
6. Scale the results by multiplying by 10,000. This is an attempt to get TRIX scaled to a positive integer value for charting and may also be omitted.

The resulting TRIX indicator acts as an oscillator due to Step 5. It can be very smooth when the calculation periods are larger; it also reduces the lag because of the differencing step. TRIX can be used as a trend indicator by buying when the value of TRIX crosses above zero and selling when it crosses below zero. It can produce buy and sell signals sooner by buying when the TRIX value is rising for two or three consecutive periods, and selling when TRIX is falling for two or three consecutive periods. Because the triple smoothing results in a very smooth TRIX value, trading signals can safely use the change in TRIX as an advance indicator of trend.

Figure 6.21 compares TRIX (center panel) with the TSI (lower panel), both based on first differences, but using the smoothing constant of 1.0 to negate one of the steps. The point is to show that TRIX is actually smoother because the differences are taken at the end rather than the beginning. The lag in TRIX is slightly more than the TSI, but it would be unnecessary to use *n*-day differences for TRIX to get further smoothing; therefore, TRIX may have less lag in its final form.

Changing the Divisor

All return calculations divide the price change from yesterday to today by the starting value, yesterday's price. There is no rule that says that you cannot divide the change by the current price,

$$r_t = \frac{Close_t - Close_{t-1}}{Close_t} - 1$$

---

[15] Referenced in Robert W. Colby, *The Encyclopedia of Technical Market Indicators* (New York: McGraw-Hill, 2003) as "Good Trix" by Jack K. Hutson, *Technical Analysis of Stocks & Commodities* 1, no. 5.

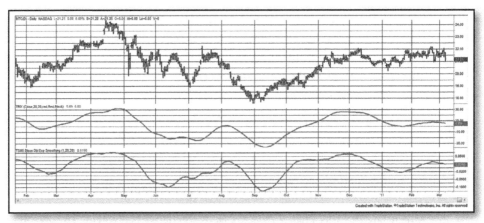

FIGURE 6.21 Comparison of TRIX (center panel) and TSI (lower panel) Using Two 20-Day Exponential Smoothings Applied to INTC.

While this would result in only small changes, the cumulative effect is said to add stability to an indicator that is based on returns.

An Oscillator to Distinguish between Trending and Sideways Markets

The lack of predictability of trending markets is the greatest problem for the analyst. Based on the idea that the trend component is stronger when price is further from fair value, and the noise (sideways movement) is greater when price is near value, an oscillator can be created to show the strength of the trend component based on this concept,

$$Strength\ Oscillator_t = \frac{Average(Close_t - Close_{t-1}, n)}{Average(High_t - Low_t, n)}$$

As the trend increases, the average change in closing prices becomes larger relative to the high-low range for the day. During an unusual period, when the market gaps open, it would be possible for the differences in the closing prices to become larger than the daily range. In a sideways market, both the change in the closes and daily range will get smaller, but the net price change over period n should be close to zero. This oscillator can be smoothed by taking the change in price over two or three days (for example, $close_t - close_{t-3}$), rather the most recent day, as well as taking the high-low range over the same number of days. The indicator and function, *TSM Strength Oscillator*, can be found on the Companion Website.

Adding Volume to Momentum

A momentum indicator can also incorporate volume by multiplying the price change over n periods by the total volume over that same period. The use of the cumulative volume over the period, or even better, the average volume, will help to stabilize the volume, which is often erratic when seen as only one day's activity. The *average volume* will appear to be the same magnitude as the volume and can be plotted along with it on a chart. That gives the *momentum-volume indicator (MV)*, shown mathematically and in programming notation:

$$MV_t = (P_t - P_{t-n}) \times \frac{\sum_{i=t-n+1}^{t} volume_i}{n}$$

```
MV = (close-close[n])*average(volume,n)
```

Alternately, the price change over *n* periods could have been divided by *n* to give a per unit value. The following sections will include those techniques that combine price change and volume or open interest.

Scaling by a Percentage or Volatility

The same conversions can be applied to momentum with and without volume. Using a percentage rather than price will add some robustness over long test periods. Because volatility often increases faster than a fixed percentage of the price when prices rise, momentum can be scaled according to a shorter measure of true range. If the true range is averaged over 20 to 65 days, approximately one month to one quarter, then the 1-day change in price will become a relative momentum value. By using a much longer period for averaging the true range, you can create a stable profile of the volatility changes in the underlying market.

Percentage momentum with volume
```
%MV = (close - close[n]) / close[n] * average(volume,n)
```
Momentum with volume scaled by true range
```
TRMV = (close - close[n]) / average(truerange,p) * average(volume,n)
```
where *truerange* is always calculated for the most recent period (e.g., 1 day), and the average of the 1-day true ranges for the past *p* days is *average(truerange,p)*.

Volume-Weighted RSI

In the same way that the RSI accumulates the price changes for positive days and divides by the sum of the negative changes, it is possible to weight each day by its volume to add another factor, called *money flow*,[16] to the calculation. A positive or upwards day is when the average of today's high, low, and close is greater than the previous average. Each average is then multiplied by the volume, giving the daily

---

[16] Gene Quong and Avrum Soudack, "Volume-Weighted RSI: Money Flow," *Technical Analysis of Stocks & Commodities* (March 1989).

THEORY AND ANALYSIS

money flow, and a ratio of the past 14 days is used to create a *money ratio* and finally a *money flow index,* both steps similar to Wilder's RSI.

$$Moneyflow_t = Volume_t \times \frac{High_t + Low_t + Close_t}{3}$$

$$Moneyratio_t = \frac{\sum_{i=t-13}^{t} Moneyflow_i \, if > 0}{\sum_{i=t-13}^{t} Moneyflow_i \, if < 0}$$

$$Moneyflowindex_t = 100 - \frac{100}{1 + Moneyratio_t}$$

Herrick Payoff Index

Using the change in the underlying value of the futures contract, rather than only the change in price, the *Herrick Payoff Index*[17] (HPI) combines volume and open interest to generate an indicator that is not bounded as is the basic momentum calculation. The daily value is:

$$HP_t = cf \times V_t \times (M_t - M_{t-1}) \times \left[1 + \left(\frac{M_t - M_{t-1}}{|M_t - M_{t-1}|} \right) \left(\frac{2 \times |OI_t - OI_{t-1}|}{\min(OI_t, OI_{t-1})} \right) \right]$$

Where $t =$ today
$t - 1 =$ the previous day
$cf =$ the conversion factor (value of a one big point move)
$V_t =$ today's volume
$(M_t - M_{t-1}) =$ the difference in the mean values, $M = (high + low)/2$, where vertical bars denote absolute value
$|OI_t - OI_{t-1}| =$ the absolute value of the change in open interest (for futures)
$\min(OI_t, OI_{t-1}) =$ the smaller of the open interest for today or the previous day

The expression that divides the change in mean prices by the absolute value of the same change is used to create a value of $+1$ or -1. The index HP_t is then scaled down to a manageable value and smoothed using a 0.10 smoothing factor, s (about 19 days). This complex formula for HPI can also be written in programming code as

```
HP = BigPointValue*volume*((high-low)/2 - (high[1]-low[1])/2)*
        (1+(((high-low)/2 - (high[1]-low[1])/2) /
      absvalue((high-low)/2 - (high[1]-low[1])/2))*2*
       (absvalue(opint - opint[1])/lowest(opint,2))))

HPI = smoothedaverage(HP,19)
```

---

[17] From the original *CompuTrac* manual, which became the Dow Jones Telerate division, and finally just Dow Jones.

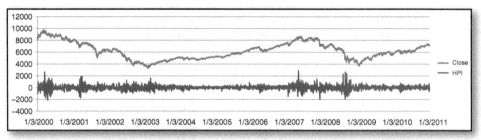

FIGURE 6.22 The Herrick Payoff Index Applied to the DAX, 2000 through February 2011.

Most analysts who use the Herrick Payoff Index divide the HPI by 100,000 to scale the value to a more usable level (in the example below it is scaled by 1,000,000). The final series, when seen along with prices, may appear volatile and require interpretation, often using trendlines. This is due to the fluctuations in volume and open interest, which are smoothed over 20 days, rather than a longer period. The Herrick Payoff Index may be helpful, despite its volatility, because it is a combination of factors not included in most other indexes. It has patterns that appear to lead price change to compensate for its noisy behavior. A spreadsheet, *TSM Herrick Payoff Index for DAX*, and a program, *TSM Herrick Payoff*, can be found on the Companion Website.

Figure 6.22 gives an idea of how the HPI reacts to prices, in this case using the German DAX from 2000 through February 2011. It shows higher volatility at the turning points and very low volatility during the upwards trends from 2004 to 2006 and again in 2010. It turns out that volume is a good surrogate for volatility and might actually be a good forecaster of volatility.

Comments on the Use of Volume

Volume is an important piece of information, but it can be difficult to interpret. It fluctuates in a much larger range than price, and may be 50% higher or lower from day to day. While it indicates market interest and potential volatility, there are many days for which a high or low volume does not have a consistent reaction.

In general, adding volume to an indicator results in a more volatile, erratic series. Therefore, the first steps in using volume are:

1. Create a long-term, smoothed volume series.
2. Locate days with extremely high volatility to identify only those exceptional days where continued high volatility should follow.
3. Low volume should not be determined by a single day, but by either a few unusually low days clustered together or by a decay in the smoothed volume over a modest time period.

CHAPTER 7

Volume, Open Interest, and Breadth

From Perry J. Kaufman, *Trading Systems and Methods, + Website*, 5th Edition (Hoboken, New Jersey: John Wiley & Sons, 2013), Chapter 12.

Learning Objective Statements

- Explain how to interpret information from the following data: daily volume, total volume, futures open interest, tick volume, Equivolume, Herrick Payoff Index (as it relates to volume)
- Distinguish features of intraday volume patterns from volume patterns on daily charts
- Explain why volume is a predictor of volatility
- Identify the key information provided by each of the following technical studies: Average Volume, Normalized Volume, Volume Momentum and Percentage change, Force Index, Volume Oscillator, On-Balance Volume, Money Flow Index, Volume Count Indicator, Volume Accumulator, Intraday Intensity, Price and Volume Indicator, VWMACD, Elastic Volume Weighted Moving Average (eVWMA), and VWAP
- Evaluate how each of the following breadth indicators might be used for confirmation: Advancers vs. Decliners, up volume and down volume, Sibbett's Demand Index, Bolton-Tremblay, Shultz, McClellan Oscillator, Upside/Downside Ratio, Arms Index, Thrust Oscillator, New Highs and Lows

Patterns in volume have always been tied closely to chart analysis of both the stock and futures markets. Volume is a valuable piece of information that is not often used, and one of the few items, other than price, that is traditionally considered valid data for the technician. Nevertheless, there has been little research published that relates volume to futures markets; its popular use has assumed the same conclusions as in stock market analysis.

The stock and futures markets have two other measures of participation that are related. In equities, the large number shares being traded allow for measurements of *breadth*. In the same way that the stock index has become a popular measure of overall market trend, the *breadth of the market* is the total number of stocks that have risen or fallen during a specific period. When you have the ability to view the bigger picture of market movement, breadth seems to be a natural adjunct to the index. In addition, tallies of *new highs* and *new lows* may add value to a trading decision. This chapter will look at different way these statistics can complement other indicators.

In futures, *open interest* is the measurement of those participants with outstanding positions; it is the netting out of all open positions (longs and short sales) in any one market or delivery month, and gives an understanding of the depth of participation and anticipated volume. A market that trades only 10,000 contracts per day but has an open interest of 250,000 is telling the trader that there are many participants who will enter the market when the price is right. These are most likely to be commercial traders, using the futures markets for hedging. Unlike the stock market, which can only trade a fixed number of outstanding shares, the futures market can add net contracts for every new buyer and short seller and reduce the *interest* in the market when both buyers and sellers liquidate.

■ A Special Case for Futures Volume

In futures markets, where you trade contracts for delivery in specific months, the volume of each contract is available, along with the total volume of all contracts traded for that market. Spread transactions within that market, for example, buying the March delivery and selling June, are not included in the reported volume, a point that is inconsistent with stocks, which report both sides of a high frequency trade. In futures, volume data and open interest are officially posted one day late, but estimates are available for many markets during the day on services such as Bloomberg. Total volume of crude oil is estimated every hour; it is released to news services and is available on the Internet.

Individual contract volume is important to determine which delivery month is most active. Traders find that the best executions are where there is greatest liquidity. Analysts, however, have a difficult time assessing trends in volume because there is a natural increase in volume as a contract moves from deferred to delivery, from second month out to the nearby, and traders most often roll their positions to the closest delivery month. There is a corresponding decline in volume as a contract approaches its delivery date. Because spread volume is not posted, movement between delivery months does not affect the volume patterns.

Each futures market has its unique pattern of volume for individual contracts. Some, such as the interest rates, shift abruptly on the last day of the month prior to delivery, because the exchange raises margins dramatically for all traders holding positions in the delivery month. Currencies are very different and tend to trade actively in the nearest month up to one or two days before that contract goes *off the board*. While volume increases slightly in the next deferred contract, anyone trading sizable positions will need to stay with the nearby contract to just before the end.

Other than for determining which contract to trade, and perhaps the size of an order that the market can absorb, an analysis of volume as discussed in this chapter will use total volume (the aggregate of all contracts) in order to have a series that does not suffer the patterns of increasing and decreasing participation based on the coming and going of individual delivery months. When traders roll from the nearby to the next deferred contract, the transactions are usually executed as a spread, and those trades are not included in the volume figures. Because positions are closed out in one contract and opened in another there is no change in the open interest.

The stock market equivalent to using total volume would be to add the volume for all stocks in the same sector or industrial group. This would help to smooth over those periods when the volume is concentrated in a few stocks following a news or earnings release, only to switch the next week when other stocks in the same sector are noticed.

Tick Volume

The popularity of quote machines and fast trading requires a measurement of volume that can be used immediately to make decisions. Lacking a service such as Bloomberg with continually updated volume, *tick volume* can be substituted. Tick volume is the number of recorded price changes, regardless of volume or the size of the price change that occurs during any time interval. Tick volume relates directly to actual volume because, as the market becomes more active, prices move back and forth from bid to asked more often. If only two trades occur in a 5-minute period, then the market is not liquid. From an analytic view, tick volume gives a reasonable approximation of true volume and can be used as a substitute. From a practical view, it is the only choice. Higher-than-normal tick volume at the beginning of the day implies higher volume throughout the day. Tick volume patterns are discussed later in this chapter.

■ Variations from the Normal Patterns

The *W* Intraday Pattern

One note of warning when using intraday volume or volume indicators to confirm price direction: The patterns in volume have a dominant *W* pattern throughout the day. They begin high, drop quickly, increase modestly near midday, fall again, then increase significantly toward the close of trading. To decide that a buy signal is more important near the end of the trading day because volume was rising is not correct; volume is always higher at the beginning and end of the day. You may conclude, in general, that the beginning and end of the day, or higher-than-average volume produces more reliable trading signals; however, an intraday volume confirmation must be compared against the normal volume for that time of day.

Open interest and market breadth have seasonal patterns. In agricultural markets, farmers hedge in larger numbers during the growing season than in the winter, raising the open interest. In stocks, there is a lot of activity associated with the end-of-year positioning for tax purposes and traditional rallies during holiday seasons. Volume is low during the summer when many investors take their vacations. None

TABLE 7.1	Microsoft Daily Volume by Year from June 1998 through May 2003	
Period	Average	StDev
Jun98–May99	62,861,035	21,511,856
Jun99–May00	64,512,077	34,741,178
Jun00–May01	83,915,101	35,621,716
Jun01–May02	64,638,359	21,125,063
Jun02–May03	79,584,139	22,129,923
Jun98–May03	*71,105,478*	*27,832,841*

of these changes indicate that something special is occurring. These variations are discussed in detail later in this chapter.

Variance in Volume

Nearly all volume analysis uses smoothed or averaged data because volume can vary substantially from one day to the next. As an example, Table 7.1 shows the breakdown of Microsoft (MSFT) volume for the five years from June 1998 through May 2003. While the volume was higher during the price peak of January 2000, the overall numbers show consistency at an average of 71 million shares per day.

Table 7.1 also shows the standard deviation of the daily volume changes, which is about 38% of the average volume. One standard deviation of this magnitude says that 68% of the days will show *changes* in daily volume ranging from 41 million to 101 million shares. Looking at it in reverse, 32% of the days will show changes in volume less than or greater than 41 million and 101 million shares. Compare that to the price of Microsoft during the same period, which ranged from $20 to $60 but had 1 standard deviation of $0.957—that is, the daily change in price was less than $1, or about 2.9% of the $33.38 average price. Keep in mind that this variation is the basis for most of the volume indicators and strategies.

Volume Spikes

Madness is the exception in individuals but the rule in groups.

—*Nietzsche*

A *volume spike* is a single day on which the volume was much higher than the previous day—at least twice as high, perhaps three or four times. A volume spike is a warning that something happened, most likely the result of a surprising news release or new economic data. It could be the crescendo of a few days of rising volume associated with sharply rising or falling prices.

A volume spike is a clear, positive action by investors. It implies that a very large number of investors, perhaps even the general public, all hold the same opinion on the direction of the market and feel compelled to act on that opinion at the same time. It is the result of mass behavior discussed by Mackay in his famous book,

FIGURE 7.1 AOL Price and Volume Showing Three Major Volume Spikes and Declining Volume while Prices Rise at the End of 1999.

Extraordinary Popular Delusions and the Madness of Crowds. A volume spike means that everyone has jumped into the boat at the same time. Traditional interpretation of a volume spike is that it indicates the end of a price move, that is, the boat sinks.

AOL shows three good examples of volume spikes in Figure 7.1. The highest volume days in April, August, and September 1999, and in January 2000 all occur at the bottom of a price move. Prices reverse direction immediately after the spike, and usually that reversal is substantial. A volume spike does not indicate the strength of the price reversal, it simply tells you that the current move is exhausted. It may turn out to be a major top or bottom, or simply a local turning point.

Volume spikes are a good example of extremes and the clearest cases for trading. The theory of a spike is that, when everyone has entered the market, there is no one left to buy (or sell) and prices must reverse. The crowd is always wrong—at least their timing is always wrong.

Drop in Volume

Although a drop in volume is less impressive than a volume spike, it can be equally important. Volume can decline because there is little interest in a stock or futures market, which often happens when prices are very low. Volume can also drop when a price reaches *equilibrium*, the price at which buyers and sellers agree is *fair value*. Volume may also drop on the day before a holiday, or just by chance.

While there can be seasonal and other predictable patterns associated with a decline in volume, they all represent a lack of conviction, or a perceived lack of potential price movement, on the part of the traders. In Figure 7.1 there is a steady decline in the average volume from October 1999 through the end of 1999 while prices moved steadily higher. This period had only one-half the volume traded earlier in the year and is interpreted as a lack of investor support for higher prices. Having been hurt earlier in the year, more investors stood aside on the second rally and, while AOL prices did top the previous highs, another sell-off followed. This declining pattern fits the standard interpretation of volume.

■ Standard Interpretation

The interpretation of volume has been part of the trading culture from its beginning. Volume is always considered in combination with price movement:

Volume	Price	Interpretation
Rising	Rising	Volume confirms price rise
Rising	Falling	Volume confirms price drop
Falling	Rising	Volume indicates weak rally
Falling	Falling	Volume indicates weak pullback

This interpretation implies that *volume confirms direction*. When volume declines, it indicates that a change of direction should follow because there is no general support for the price move. Therefore, *volume normally leads price*. It has also been said that 1-week returns accompanied by declining volume tend to reverse the next week. Using weekly data would smooth the volume and may well add consistency.

The classic interpretation of volume was published in the monograph by W. L. Jiler, *Volume and Open Interest: A Key to Commodity Price Forecasting*, a companion piece to his most popular *Forecasting Commodity Prices with Vertical Line Charts*.

In both the futures and stock markets, volume has the same interpretation: When volume increases, it is said to confirm the direction of prices. Price changes that occur on very light volume are less dependable for indicating future direction than those changes associated with relatively heavy volume. An additional uncertainty exists for stocks that are not actively traded, and for low-priced shares where the total dollar volume can be small. In these cases, it might be best to look at the accumulated volume of similar companies or its sector.

Volume and Open Interest

Open interest is a concept unique to futures markets, but helps to explain the depth of the market as well as trader expectations. New *interest* in a market is the result of new buyers and sellers meeting, which increases the open interest, the net of all outstanding contracts being traded. The following table explains the combinations of buyers and sellers that changes open interest:

Buyer	Meets	Seller	Change in Open Interest
New		New	Increase in open interest
New		Old	No change in open interest
Old		New	No change in open interest
Old		Old	Decrease in open interest
Where	"New" buyer (seller) is a trader with no market position seeking to be long (short). "Old" buyer (seller) is a trader who had previously entered a short (long) position and seeks to exit.		

When the open interest increases while prices rise quickly, it is commonly interpreted as more traders entering long positions. This may seem strange because for every new buyer of a futures contract there must be a new seller; however, the seller is likely to be someone looking to hold a position for a few hours or days, looking to profit from the normal ups and downs of price movement. The position trader, who is willing to sit for much more time holding a long position, is the one who is attributed with the open interest. In reality, no one knows. However, if prices keep rising, the shorts are more likely to be forced out while the longs have staying power.

The traditional interpretation of changes in volume and open interest (for futures markets) can be summarized as:

Volume	Open Interest	Interpretation
Rising	Rising	Confirmation of trend
Rising	Falling	Position liquidation (at extremes)
Falling	Rising	Slow accumulation
Failing	Falling	Congestion phase

Three generally accepted notions for the use of volume and open interest are:

1. Open interest increases during a trending period.
2. Volume may decline but open interest builds during an accumulation phase. Volume occasionally spikes.
3. Rising prices and declining volume/open interest indicate a pending change of direction.

There is a traditional interpretation for the combined movement of price direction, volume, and open interest.

Prices	Volume	Open Interest	Interpretation
Rising	Rising	Rising	New buyers are entering the market.
Falling	Falling	Falling	Longs are being forced out; the downtrend will end when all sellers have liquidated their positions.
Rising	Falling	Falling	Short sellers are covering their positions causing a rally. Money is leaving the market.
Falling	Rising	Rising	New short selling. Bearish money is entering the market.

Exceptions

No method is without exceptions, including volume patterns in the stock market. There are days or periods when volume is expected to change, and must be considered in the analysis. For example, volume is expected to decline:

On the first day of the week.
On the day before a holiday.
During the summer.

The most important exception to rising prices and rising volume is the volume spike, which signals a change of direction rather than a confirmation.

Volume is also higher on *triple witching day* (or *quadruple witching day*, if you include futures on stocks), when S&P futures, options on futures, and options on the individual stocks all expire at the same time.

In the futures markets, there are similar patterns. Lighter volume exists during holiday periods and summer months, but may be heavier on Fridays and Mondays during a trending market or a weather market for agricultural products (uncertainty over rain, drought, or frost over the weekend). Liquidation often occurs before the weekend and positions are reentered on the first day of the next week.

Richard Arms' Equivolume

Most of the techniques for using volume discussed in this chapter will multiply or accumulate volume, creating an index that rises faster as volume increases. *Equivolume*, a charting method introduced by Richard Arms,[1] takes the unique approach of substituting volume for time along the bottom scale of a chart. When volume increases, the price bar is elongated to the right; therefore, an upwards move on high volume will appear as a higher box that is also wider.

There are no systematic methods for using Equivolume included here and its applications parallel standard chart interpretations; however, analysts can represent this type of chart by creating a new price series in which the daily closing price is repeated based on the relative volume. For example, if the normal volume day causes a closing price to be repeated 10 times, then a day with twice the volume will repeat that price 20 times, and a day with half the volume will show 5 prices. This approach may cause a short-term moving average trend to look strange; however, a linear regression or long-term trend should reflect the importance of varying time.

Herrick Payoff Index

The *Herrick Payoff Index* (HPI) is the most popular calculation that combines price, volume, and open interest. It is designed to gauge the strength of the current trend, and has been applied primarily to futures prices.

---

[1] See www.armsinsider.com/education/armsonthemarket/equiv_chart.asp for examples.

Volume Is a Predictor of Volatility

Most often high volume and high volatility occur at the same time. It is easy to see on a chart that one confirms the other. However, not all days that have high volume also have high volatility. Even on days with high volume, the price can close nearly unchanged from the previous day. We need to look at those days as a sign of *potential volatility*—a large number of traders all with their own objectives somehow managed to offset each other. Tomorrow, if there is an imbalance in the buyers and sellers, and volume is still high, prices could break out in either direction. Therefore, *high volume means high risk*, even on those days when the risk does not materialize.

■ Volume Indicators

Both the stock and futures markets have numerous indicators that use only volume, or those that add volume, intending to make other calculations more robust. The following section gives the most popular of these indicators, most of which originate in the stock market; many use the number of advancing and declining stocks. Readers should note the way in which the data is used from one technique to another and consider the significance of these changes. They are discussed at the end of this section.

Average Volume

The most basic of all volume indicators is the *average*, and the calculation most commonly used for the equity markets is 50 days, although it may be reasonable to use the same period as the price average that is being used. Then, if you are tracking the 200-day moving average, a 200-day average of the volume would make sense. Anything less than 50 days is not likely to be smooth.

Normalizing the Volume

It is always convenient to normalize prices to view them compared to the recent average. This can also be done for volume. Letting the calculation period, N, be either 50 or 200 days, we can normalize the volume and represent the result as a percent,

$$NormVol_t = 100 \times \frac{V_t}{\left(\sum_{i=t-P+1}^{t} V_t\right)/N}$$

The normalized volume lets us say that "today's volume is 20% higher than the volume over the past 200 days." This can be seen in the third panel of Figure 7.2, showing Microsoft prices and volume.

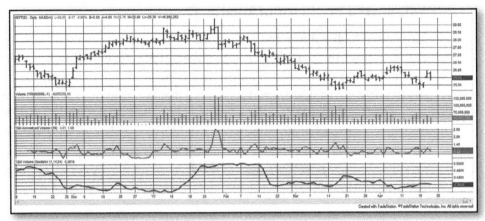

FIGURE 7.2 Microsoft Prices (Top), Volume (Second Panel), Normalized 50-Day Volume (Third Panel), and Volume Oscillator from Ratio (Bottom), Based on 14- and 34-Day Periods.

Volume Momentum and Percentage Change

Two other basic volume indicators are *momentum* and *rate of change*. These techniques treat volume as they would price. For momentum, this means finding the change in volume over a specific time interval; percentage change measures the size of the volume change relative to the starting value. If t is today and n is the number of days back (the observation period), then

$$Volume\ momentum_t = Volume_t - Volume_{t-n}$$

$$Volume\%_t = \frac{Volume_t - Volume_{t-n}}{Volume_{t-n}}$$

Because of the high variance in volume from day to day, volume momentum tends to increase the erratic pattern. It will be necessary to smooth the volume momentum in order to have a useful indicator.

Force Index

Devised by Alex Elder, the *Force Index* is the change in price multiplied by the daily volume,

$$Force\ Index_t = (Close_t - Close_{t-1}) \times Volume_t$$

The Force Index will be positive or negative if the price change was higher or lower. It is also not limited to daily charts, but can be applied to weekly or monthly data, as can many of the other methods in this chapter. Once the daily Force Index is calculated, it should be smoothed. For timing entries and exits, it is suggested that a 2-day exponential moving average (EMA) with a smoothing constant 0.667 be used to avoid unnecessary noise in the indicator. For longer-term analysis, a 13-day EMA (smoothing constant 0.1428) should be used. Consistent with the idea of noise, the 2-day smoothed Force Index *buys* when the value is low and *sells short* when it's high;

however, the 13-day value is treated as a trend, giving a buy signal when it crosses above zero and a sell when it crosses below zero. Signals remain in effect until the smoothed Force Index crosses the zero line in the other direction.

Volume Oscillator

Visualizing the pattern of volume can be very helpful, and the simplest way to do this is with a *volume oscillator*, which addresses the issue of erratic data by using two smoothed values. A volume oscillator is a two-step process and may use trends of any calculation period. Here, 14- and 34-day periods are used.

Method 1

Calculate the difference between a short-term and long-term average of volume. Using 14 and 34 days gives

$$VO(Diff)_t = \frac{\sum_{i=t-14+1}^{t} V_i}{14} - \frac{\sum_{i=t-34+1}^{t} V_i}{34}$$

Method 2

Calculate the ratio of a short-term and long-term sum of volume. Again, using 14 and 34 days,

$$VO(Ratio)_t = \frac{\sum_{i=t-14+1}^{t} V_i}{\sum_{i=t-34+1}^{t} V_i}$$

Once calculated, the oscillator values can be displayed as a histogram or a line chart. Figure 7.2 shows Microsoft from November 2010 through April 2011 in the top panel, volume in the second panel, the normalized 50-day volume in the third panel, and the volume oscillator using the ratio at the bottom. In this example, the volume oscillator does not confirm the upwards or downwards trends. Perhaps that is the correct interpretation because these trends were short lived.

On-Balance Volume

Made famous by Joseph Granville, *On-Balance Volume*[2] is now a byword in stock analyst circles. On days when prices close higher, it is assumed that all volume represents the buyers; on lower days, the volume is controlled by the sellers. The volume is then added or subtracted from a cumulative value, *OBV*, to get today's value.

IF *Today's price change* $(p_t > p_{t-1})$ then $OBV_t = OBV_{t-1} + Volume_t$

---

[2] Robert W. Colby and Thomas A. Meyers, *The Encyclopedia of Technical Market Indicators* (New York: McGraw-Hill, 2003), is a comprehensive study of most market indicators, including On-Balance Volume and some other techniques in this section.

$$\text{IF } \textit{Today's price change } (p_t < p_{t-1}) \text{ then } OBV_t = OBV_{t-1} - \textit{Volume}_t$$

The result is a volume-weighted series, which serves to smooth out the erratic nature of the data. In the following formula, the expression in parentheses simply uses the closing prices to produce a value of $+1$, 0, or -1, which then determines whether today's volume will be added or subtracted from the volume series:

$$OBV_t = OBV_{t-1} + \frac{Close_t - Close_{t-1}}{|Close_t - Close_{t-1}|} \times Volume_t$$

Determining the OBV manually is a simple accumulation process as shown in Table 7.2. On day 2 prices closed higher; therefore, the volume of 30 (assume thousands) is added to the starting volume of zero. On the next day, the price was again higher, and the volume is added to the total. On day 4 the price drops so that day's volume is subtracted from the total. In this example, volume was higher when price closed up and lower when prices closed down. This is the ideal pattern in a market with a clear uptrend. Traditionally, the advantage of recording the OBV is in observing when the trend of the prices diverges from the OBV values. The general interpretation of OBV is given in Table 7.3.

TABLE 7.2 Calculating On-Balance Volume

Day	Closing Price	Daily Volume (in 1000s)	On-Balance Volume
1	310	25	0
2	315	30	30
3	318	27	57
4	316	15	42
5	314	12	30
6	320	28	58

TABLE 7.3 Interpreting On-Balance Volume

Price Direction	OBV Direction	Interpretation
Up	Up	Clear uptrend
	Sideways	Moderate uptrend
	Down	Weak uptrend near reversal
Sideways	Up	Accumulation period (bottom)
	Sideways	No determination
	Down	Distribution period (top)
Down	Up	Weak downtrend near reversal
	Sideways	Moderate downtrend
	Down	Clear downtrend

Because a volume series has many erratic qualities caused by large variations in volume from day to day, it is most often used with a moving average trend of up to 100 weeks, then identifying a simple volume direction when the OBV value crosses the trend. An upward trend in volume is interpreted as a confirmation of the current price direction, while a downturn in volume can be liquidation or uncertainty. It is intended that the OBV values be used instead of price for making trading decisions.

In Figure 7.3, the OBV is plotted along with the volume at the bottom of the GE chart, covering from December 2010 through April 2011. The pattern of the OBV is similar to the pattern of prices in the top panel even though it is created from volume. The primary difference between the price chart and the OBV line is that the peak in the center is flattening and the OBV does not decline as far. This divergence in the center of the chart, prices moving higher than the OBV, would be interpreted as a divergence in which prices will stop rising.

The spreadsheet code, *TSM OBV*, is available on the Companion Website.

Substituting the OBV for Price in a Moving Average   If the OBV systematically improves, then we can use the OBV instead of price to find trend signals. In Figure 7.4, the S&P emini prices are shown in the top panel with a 40-day moving average, and the volume, OBV, and a 40-day moving average of the OBV are in the bottom panel. The corresponding moving average trendlines are equally smooth, but slightly different on the far right where prices rise sooner than the OBV.

It would be necessary to do a comprehensive test on many markets to find out if the OBV produced better trend results than simply using the price. We already know that the S&P and stocks in general are not the best choice for trending; therefore, tests of interest rates would be more interesting. Volume indicators that combine the price move with volume are additional possibilities. An example of a strategy, *TSM OBV Trend*, that applies a trend to a volume indicator can be found on the Companion Website.

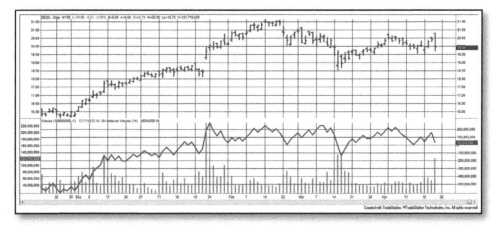

FIGURE 7.3   On-Balance Volume Applied to GE from December 2010 through April 2011. Volume is shown on the left lower scale and the OBV on the right lower scale.

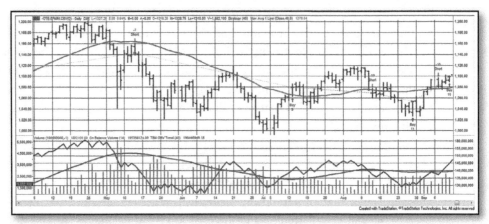

FIGURE 7.4 S&P prices are shown with the volume, OBV, and a 40-day trend of the OBV in the bottom panel. Trading signals are derived from the OBV trendline. A corresponding 40-day moving average is shown in the top panel.

Money Flow Index   A simple variation of On-Balance Volume uses the average of the high, low, and closing prices instead of only the close. It is called the *Money Flow Index*, and has been compared to the RSI.

$$TP_t = (H_t + L_t + C_t)/3$$

$$\text{If } TP_t > TP_{t-1} \text{ then } MFP_t = MFP_{t-1} + TP_t \times V_t$$

$$\text{If } TP_t < TP_{t-1} \text{ then } MFN_t = MFN_{t-1} + TP_t \times V_t$$

$$MFI_t = 100 - \frac{100}{\left(\dfrac{1 + MFP_t}{MFN_t}\right)}$$

Volume Count Indicator   An indicator that closely resembles On-Balance Volume is a running total of the days when volume increases minus the days when volume declines. That is, add 1 to the cumulative value on a day when today's volume is greater than the previous day; otherwise, subtract 1. This *Volume Count Indicator* (VCI) can be written as:

$$VCI_t = VCI_{t-1} + \frac{V_t - V_{t-1}}{|V_t - V_{t-1}|}$$

Volume Accumulator

A variation on Granville's OBV system is Mark Chaiken's *Volume Accumulator* (VA). Instead of assigning all the volume to either the buyers or the sellers, the Volume Accumulator uses a proportional amount of volume corresponding to the relationship of the closing price to the intraday mean price. If prices close at the high or low of the day, all volume is given to the buyers or sellers as in the OBV calculation.[3] If the close is at the midrange, no volume is added. This can be accomplished with the following calculation:

$$VA_t = VA_{t-1} + \left(\frac{Close_t - Low_t}{High_t - Low_t} - 0.50 \right) \times 2 \times V_t$$

Accumulation Distribution

Similar to the Volume Accumulator, and also developed by Mark Chaiken, the *Accumulation Distribution* indicator as well as the Intraday Intensity, the Price and Volume Trend, and the Positive and Negative Volume Indexes use a concept that relates to buying and selling pressure. This compares the strength of the close compared to the open divided by the trading range. It is also called *money flow* in some references. In the following formula, the previous close can be substituted for the open if the opening price is not available.

$$AD_t = AD_{t-1} + \frac{C_t - O_t}{H_t - L_t} \times V_t$$

Intraday Intensity

Intraday Intensity uses the distribution of daily trading range to create a new indicator. If the intraday low is further from the close than the intraday high, in other words, prices close nearer to the high, then the indicator increases in value.

$$II_t = II_{t-1} + \left(\frac{(C_t - L_t) - (H_t - C_t)}{H_t - L_t} \right) \times V_t$$

Price and Volume Trend, the Positive Volume Index, and the Negative Volume Index

The *Price and Volume Trend* (PVT)[4] applies volume to the daily percentage price change, which can be positive or negative. Note that this cannot be used for back-adjusted futures prices, only for cash markets, stock prices, and indexes.

$$VPT_t = VPT_{t-1} + \left(\frac{C_t}{C_{t-1}} - 1 \right) \times V_t$$

There are two variations on the *Positive Volume Index* (PVI) and *Negative Volume Index* (NVI). Both take the approach that a single indicator that adds and subtracts volume based on market direction is not as informative as two separate series that can be viewed at the same time. In the first variation, the direction of the closing price

---

[3] Both OBV and the Volume Accumulator are characterized as "momentum" systems.
[4] Dennis D. Peterson, "Positive Volume Index," *Technical Analysis of Stocks & Commodities* (April 2003). Also see Norman G. Fosback, *Stock Market Logic* (The Institute for Economic Research, 1985).

determines whether volume is added to the positive or negative index. In the second variation, higher or lower volume, compared to the previous day, is the basis for adding to the positive or negative index.

Variation 1, the close as the determining factor:

$$\text{If } C_t > C_{t-1} \text{ then } PVI_t = PVI_{t-1} + V_t$$

$$\text{If } C_t < C_{t-1} \text{ then } NVI_t = NVI_{t-1} + V_t$$

Variation 2, the volume as the determining factor:

$$\text{If } V_t > V_{t-1} \text{ then } PVI_t = PVI_{t-1} + \frac{C_t}{C_{t-1}} \times V_t$$

$$\text{If } V_t < V_{t-1} \text{ then } NVI_t = NVI_{t-1} + \frac{C_t}{C_{t-1}} \times V_t$$

In Norman Fosback's *Stock Market Logic*, the author studied stock trends from 1941 through 1975 based on variation 1 and concluded that:

- If the *PVI* trend is *up* there is a 79% chance that a bull market exists.

- If the *PVI* trend is *down* there is a 67% chance that a bear market exists.

- If the *NVI* trend is *up* there is a 96% chance that a bull market exists.

- If the *NVI* trend is *down* there is a 50% chance that a bear market exists.

In order to find the trend of either the *PVI* or *NVI*, a 6-month (127-day) or 1-year (255-day) moving average was applied to the individual index values.

Aspray's Demand Oscillator

Using direction to separate volume into two series of *Buying Pressure* and *Selling Pressure*, Aspray then nets them into his own *Demand Oscillator*.[5] Note that during a rising market the Selling Pressure has been *divided* by a percentage of the volume, which has been scaled to be greater than 1. The following calculations show the separate steps needed to create Aspray's *Demand Oscillator*:

For rising prices:

$$\left(\textit{Buying Pressure} \right) BP_t = V_t$$

$$\left(\textit{Selling Pressure} \right) SP_t = \frac{V_t}{K \times \dfrac{C_t - C_{t-1}}{C_{t-1}}}$$

[5]Thomas Aspray, "Fine-Tuning the Demand Index," *Technical Analysis of Stocks & Commodities* (June 1986), and "Demand Oscillator Momentum," *Technical Analysis of Stocks & Commodities* (September 1989).

For declining prices:

$$BP_t = \frac{V_t}{K \times \dfrac{C_t - C_{t-1}}{C_{t-1}}}$$

$$SP_t = V_t$$

and where

$$K = \frac{3 \times C_t}{\left[\displaystyle\sum_{i=t-9}^{t} \left(\max\left(H_t, H_{t-1}\right) - \min\left(L_t, L_{t-1}\right)\right) \right] / 10}$$

and

$$Demand\ Oscillator_t = BP_t - SP_t$$

K is a volatility scaling factor that is 3 times the closing price divided by the 10-day moving average of the maximum 2-day high-low combined range, and has a value likely to be well over 100. For example, if the S&P is trading at 1,000 and the average volatility is 15 full points (which is very high for a 10-day average), then $K = 3000/15 = 200$.

Tick Volume Indicator

In a manner similar to Wilder's RSI, Blau double-smoothes the tick volume as a way of confirming price direction. The *Tick Volume Indicator*, seen in Figure 7.5, is calculated as

$$TVI(r,s) = \frac{100 \times DEMA(upticks, r, s) - DEMA(downsticks, r, s)}{DEMA(upticks, r, s) + DEMA(downsticks, r, s)}$$

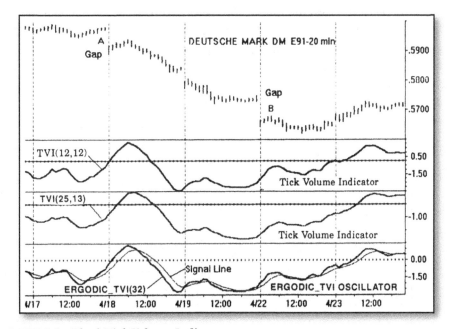

FIGURE 7.5 Blau's Tick Volume Indicator.

Source: William Blau, *Momentum, Direction, and Divergence* (New York: John Wiley & Sons, 1995), 45.

TVI ranges from −100 to +100 and *DEMA* (Double Exponential Moving Average) is the double smoothing of the downticks or upticks. The exponential smoothing is first calculated over *r* bars, and the result of that smoothing is again smoothed over the past *s* bars. This technique differs from Blau's price smoothing because it does not first create a momentum series; therefore, the *TVI* will be lagged slightly less than half the sum of the two calculation periods.

Volume-Weighted MACD

The MACD is based on the difference between two moving averages. To add volume, the closing prices for each day are multiplied by the corresponding volume, and each moving average is normalized by the average volume over the same period. The recommended calculation periods are 12 and 26 days, the standard MACD values. A signal line, also the same as MACD, is the exponentially smoothed VWMACD line using a 0.20 smoothing constant, the equivalent of about 9 days.

$$VWMACD_t = \left(\frac{\sum_{t=t-12+1}^{t} C_i \times V_i}{\sum_{i=t-12+1}^{t} V_i} \right) - \left(\frac{\sum_{t=t-26+1}^{t} C_i \times V_i}{\sum_{i=t-26+1}^{t} V_i} \right)$$

Figure 7.6 uses a program *TSM Volume Weighted MACD*, available on the Companion Website, to plot the VWMACD for euro currency futures, which appears in the bottom panel. The heavier line is the VWMACD, and the thinner, smoother line is the signal. As with the MACD, the rules are to enter a new long position when the VWMACD crosses above the signal line, and the opposite for shorts. When compared to the MACD, this variation appears to make only small changes, yet a slight improvement in timing can be a great advantage in trading.

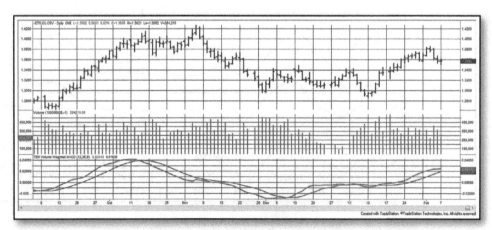

FIGURE 7.6 Volume-Weighted MACD Applied to Euro Currency Futures.

Variably Weighted Moving Average Using Volume

A unique approach taken by Christian Fries[6] uses the relationship between the number of outstanding shares, the current price, and the volume of the next period or the next trade, to create an *Elastic Volume-Weighted Moving Average (eVWMA)*. Using the difference between the number of outstanding shares and the number of shares being traded he creates a weighting factor. That weighting factor causes the previous trend value to have more importance when fewer shares are traded and less weight when relatively more shares are traded. The net effect is that the weighted average is more responsive to change when relatively more shares are traded.

$$eVWMA_t = \frac{(OS - V_t) \times eVWMA_{t-1} + V_t \times C_t}{OS}$$

where OS = the number of outstanding shares.

Using Merck (MRK) as an example, the total outstanding shares was set to 200 million, based on an observed maximum daily volume of approximately 150 million. By keeping the outstanding shares slightly bigger than the maximum volume, the indicator will vary across a wider range and show more of its characteristics. Figure 7.7 compares the eVWMA to a standard exponential smoothing of 0.10. The results are very similar although the eVWMA tracks closer to the price in the center of the chart.

Substituting Open Interest for Volume Using Futures

Futures volume can create very different results from volume for stocks. The markets themselves—energy, gold, and even interest rates—have been in an uptrend for years. This causes many of the indicators, especially OBV, to move steadily higher, while it appears to oscillate when applied to stocks over the past 10 years.

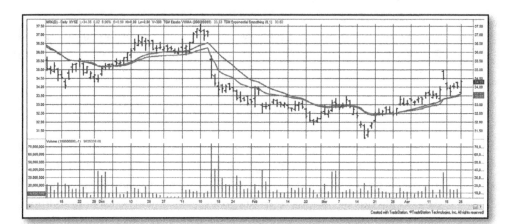

FIGURE 7.7   Elastic Volume-Weighted Moving Average Applied to Merck (MRK) Compared with a 0.10 Exponential Smoothing.

---

[6] Christian P. Fries, "Elastic Moving Averages," *Technical Analysis of Stocks & Commodities* (June 2001).

It has already been mentioned that futures volume comes in two parts, contract volume and total volume. Contract volume begins at zero, increases as the contract moves from deferred (many months away from delivery) to the nearby delivery, then back to zero as the contract expires. Open interest follows a similar pattern. To avoid this pattern, total volume is used instead of contract volume. In the same way, futures data shows contract open interest and total open interest. That data varies in the same pattern as volume; however, open interest is much more stable than volume. Similar to volume, open interest increases as market activity increases; therefore, it reflects the same fundamentals.

Total open interest can be a preferable substitute for volume in many of the indicators covered in the previous sections. It should be remembered that open interest, as well as volume, is usually available on downloaded data one day late. These numbers could be manually downloaded from Bloomberg, but it is safer to use them as a longer-term indicator, which best suits their purpose.

A spreadsheet example of applying OBV to S&P futures, using both total volume and total open interest, is available on the Companion Website as *TSM OBV*.

VWAP

As a note, order executions can be placed as a *VWAP*, a *volume-weighted average price*. For larger positions, this would return an average price representing how actively the market traded at different levels throughout the day. It is most convenient for hedge funds that do not want to force prices higher by placing an excessively large buy order at one point during the day, or even on the close. Equally spaced orders that ignore liquidity use *TWAP*, a *time-weighted average price*.

■ Breadth Indicators

Market breadth measures the imbalance between the number of advancing and declining stocks on a given day. It is the percentage of rising stocks to the total number of stocks traded. In general, more advancing issues should add confidence to an upwards price move in the same way that volume confirms price. A net increase in the S&P 500 while more issues are declining should generate concern that the upwards move is poorly supported.

The information for advances and declines is published along with stock prices each day. You may also want the volume of advancing issues and the volume of declining issues. Both of these values can be found in the *Wall Street Journal* under "Trading Activity." In this section, the CSI data series, UVDV, will be used. In addition, we will look at the new highs and new lows using CSI data MKST, to see if those numbers add value to price analysis.

To interpret the CSI data files, use the following guide. The normal field designation is in the heading and the actual content is below.

Series	Date	Open	High	Low	Close	Volume	OpInt
UVDV	Date	Total traded	Advanced	Declined	Unchanged	Up Volume	Down Volume
MKST	Date	Total traded	Advanced	Declined	Unchanged	52-Week Highs	52-Week Lows

Market breadth indicators are typically used as a confirmation of price direction. The table below shows that the interpretation of market breadth is the same as the relationship between volume and price.

Market Breadth	Price	Interpretation
Rising	Rising	Breadth confirms price rise
Falling	Falling	Breadth confirms price drop
Falling	Rising	Breadth does not confirm price rise
Rising	Falling	Breadth does not confirm price drop

The measurement of breadth must relate to what you are trading. If 75% of the stocks in the Dow rise, the S&P Small Cap Index can still be lackluster or declining. Investors shift from small-cap stocks to the S&P 500 and then to the Dow when they are looking for safety. The breadth of the overall market, or the breadth of large caps, is not enough to confirm an upwards trend in the small caps.

It is worth noting that Gerald Appel, a well-known market analyst and technician, points out that, when using market breadth, it is best if it is equally weighted (i.e., a simple count).

Separating Advancing from Declining Volume

The most basic of all techniques for determining market breadth is the *Advance-Decline Index*, which creates a new series by adding the net of the number of advancing and declining stocks each day. Unchanged issues are ignored.

$$Advance\text{-}Decline\ Oscillator_t = Advances_t - Declines_t$$

$$Advance\text{-}Decline\ Index_t = Advance\text{-}Decline\ Index_{t-1} + Advances_t - Declines_t$$

In some of the techniques that follow, only the oscillator, or single-period calculation, may be shown. An index can be created by accumulating these values.

Sibbett's Demand Index

One method that smoothes volume by using the total activity of the past 10 days is James Sibbett's *Demand Index*. The technique bears a resemblance to the approach used in Wilder's RSI. It can be used as an oscillator with individual daily values or accumulated into an index. Where $n = 10$, the individual days are calculated as the sum of the upside volume divided by the sum of the downside volume:

$$Demand\ Index_t = \frac{\sum_{i=t-n+1}^{t} upside\ volume_i}{\sum_{i=t-n+1}^{t} downside\ volume_t}$$

The values for upside and downside volume can also be found in the *Wall Street Journal* under the heading "Trading Activity." Arthur Merrill, another well-known stock analyst, has suggested using $n = 5$.

Bolton-Tremblay

Introducing the net advancing stocks compared to the number of stocks that were unchanged, the Bolton-Tremblay approach also includes a form of geometric weighting of the results. In the following calculation, BT is the daily Bolton-Tremblay value, and BTI is the index resulting from accumulating the individual daily values.

$$BT_t = \frac{Advancing_t - Declining_t}{Unchanged_t}$$

$$\text{If } BT_t > 0 \text{ then } BTI_t = BTI_{t-1} + \sqrt{BT_t}$$

$$\text{If } BT_t < 0 \text{ then } BTI_t = BTI_{t-1} - \sqrt{BT_t}$$

The Bolton-Tremblay calculation will have large spikes on days when the advancing or declining breadth is very strong, which make the unchanged number of stocks in the denominator very small.

Schultz

Schultz chose to look at the advancing stocks only as a percentage of the total stocks, which puts the results in the convenient range of 0 to 100:

$$Schultz \; A/T_t = \frac{Advancing_t}{Total \; stocks_t}$$

McClellan Oscillator

The *McClellan Oscillator* starts with the net advances (NA) and then creates an oscillator by subtracting two smoothed trends, 19 and 39 days, based on the net advances, in a manner similar to the MACD. Converting the 19- and 39-day calculation periods to smoothing constants using $2/(n+1)$ we (conveniently) get $s_1 = 0.10$ and $s_2 = 0.05$.

$$NA_t = Advances_t - Declines_t$$

$$E1_t = E1_{t-1} + s_1 \times (NA_t - E1_{t-1})$$

$$E2_t = E2_{t-1} + s_2 \times (NA_t - E2_{t-1})$$

$$McClellan \; Oscillator_t = E1_t - E2_t$$

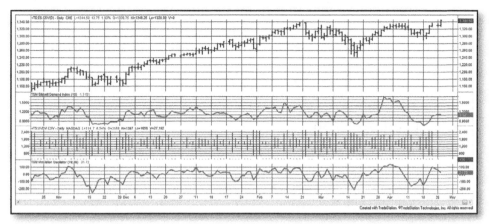

FIGURE 7.8 S&P Futures (Top Panel), Sibbett's Demand Index (Second Panel), the Up/Down Volume (Third Panel), and the McClellan Oscillator (Bottom Panel).

Figure 7.8 compares Sibbett's Demand Index with the more complicated McClellan Oscillator. S&P futures prices are in the top panel, the Demand Index in the second panel, the up and down volume in the third panel, and the McClellan Oscillator at the bottom. The scales of the two indicators are very different. The Demand Index is a ratio; therefore, it varies above and below 1.0, and reflects the upside/downside volume over a rolling 10-day period. The McClellan Oscillator uses a longer calculation period and smoothes even further using exponential smoothing.

Both indicators stay slightly above neutral during the long upward move, but the most interesting feature would be the extreme highs and lows, which are clearer in the McClellan Oscillator, corresponding nicely to two price lows and one peak. The high point that ended the long upwards move shows as divergence in the two indicators, a pattern that is not as easy to identify at the time, but can be very useful.

Upside/Downside Ratio

A simple *Upside/Downside Ratio* (UDR) is similar to Sibbett's Demand Index but is not smoothed. With this ratio, it is easier to see the asymmetry of the calculation. When the declining volume is very low, for example only 20% of the total volume, the UDR will have a value of 4.0. In contrast, if the advancing volume is low (20% of the declining volume), the ratio is 0.20. There is no upside limit when stocks are advancing but the downside ratio is limited to the range between 0 and 1. This is a familiar pattern for advancing and declining prices expressed as a percentage. High values of the UDR are expected to precede a bull market period.

$$UDR_t = \frac{Advancing\,Volume_t}{Declining\,Volume_t}$$

Arms Index (TRIN)

Richard Arms explains the relationship between the number of advancing and declining stocks, and the up and down volume, in the *Arms Index*, more popularly known as

TRIN, the *Trader's Index*. It divides the ratio of the number of advancing and declining stocks by the ratio of the volume of the advancing and declining stocks.

$$TRIN_t = \frac{Advancing\ stocks_t\ /\ Declining\ stocks_t}{Advancing\ volume_t\ /\ Declining\ volume_t}$$

Thrust Oscillator

Tushar Chande's *Thrust Oscillator* (TO) uses the same values as *TRIN* but creates a bullish oscillator by multiplying the number of advancing stocks by the volume of the advancing stocks and subtracting the comparable declining values, then dividing by the sum of the two.

$$TO_t = 100 \times \frac{Adv\ stocks_t \times Vol\ of\ adv\ stocks_t - Decl\ stocks_t \times Vol\ of\ decl\ stocks_t}{Adv\ stocks_t \times Vol\ of\ adv\ stocks_t + Decl\ stocks_t \times Vol\ of\ decl\ stocks_t}$$

The Thrust Oscillator is used as an overbought/oversold indicator to complement another strategy that would decide on the major direction of the market. Values of ±30 may be used to identify overbought and oversold levels, respectively. Whenever an indicator is not smoothed, the extremes become the most interest points of action.

Figure 7.9 shows the Thrust Oscillator (second panel) along with S&P futures (top panel). The bands of ±30 give short-term indications of overbought and oversold days and occur more frequently during a sideways price move. For the 3-month period when the S&P was steadily rising, the indicator gave many more buy signals (penetration of the bottom band) than sell signals, a good outcome.

When studying both the Arms Index (TRIN) and the Thrust Oscillator (TO) it would seem sensible to express all the component values as percentages of the whole. That is, the number of advancing and declining stocks should each be divided by the total number of stocks, and the volume of the advancing and declining stocks should each be divided by the total volume of all shares traded. This would make

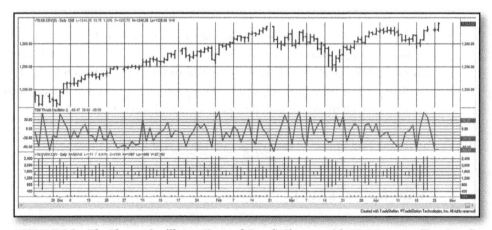

FIGURE 7.9 The Thrust Oscillator (Second Panel) Shown with S&P Futures (Top Panel).

those days with low relative volume less important. In the current calculations, inactive days might produce highly distorted values.

New Highs and Lows

There is very little literature on the use of the number of new highs and lows that occur daily, yet the data are available and can be used in ways similar to market breadth. The most obvious way to represent this data is by creating a *High-Low Index* (HLX),

$$HLX_t = HLX_{t-1} + NH_t - NL_t$$

where *NH* are new 52-week highs and *NL* are new 52-week lows. Another approach would be a simple ratio of the new highs compared to the combined new highs and lows, over the past *n* days,

$$HLR_t = \frac{\sum_{i=t-n+1}^{t} NH_i}{\sum_{i=t-n+1}^{t} (NH_i + NL_i)}$$

Gerry Appel[7] uses this *High-Low Ratio*, smoothed over 10 days, and generates a buy signal when the ratio crosses above a threshold of, for example, 0.80 or 0.90, and a sell signal when it crosses back below that level. In Figure 7.10, the S&P futures are shown with the HLR in the middle panel, and the high-low data in the bottom panel. The top line of the middle panel is 0.90 and might serve as a threshold to extract high-momentum trades during the steady uptrend. It may also be useful to create a fast smoothing of the HLR to use as a signal line, in the same manner as MACD, which would avoid the need for a strict threshold entry and exit value.

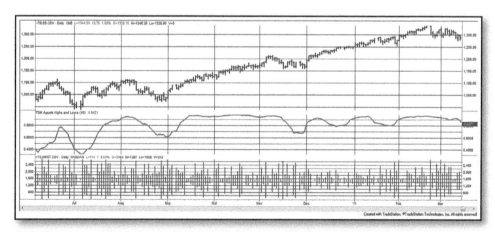

FIGURE 7.10 S&P Futures (Top Panel) Shown with the High-Low Ratio (HLR) in the Second Panel, and the High-Low Data at the Bottom.

[7] Gerald Appel, *Power Tools for Active Traders* (Upper Saddle River, NJ: Financial Times Prentice Hall, 2005), 126.

Baskets of New Highs and Lows

Another method includes buying a basket of stocks making new highs and selling a basket of stocks making new lows. Naturally, this assumes that each stock making a new high will sustain that direction because there has been some fundamental change in its earnings or structure that the market sees as positive. Similarly, those stocks making new 52-week lows have negative fundamental changes. To avoid unnecessary risk, the long basket and short basket must have the same volatility.

Is One Volume or Breadth Indicator Better than Another?

The final test of a successful indicator is whether it adds value to your trading decisions. This can be determined by programming the indicator into a strategy and testing the rules over a reasonable historic time period. Before doing that, we should decide what an increase or decrease in volume or breadth is telling us, and how we will use that information for trading. Volume and breadth indicators are more difficult than those that use price because the values have greater variance. That makes translating a sound concept into a profitable strategy more difficult. If performance testing does not confirm our expectations, then the indicator needs to be applied differently. There seems no doubt that volume and breadth data are telling us something, and uncovering those messages would improve our trading performance.

Looking at the previous selection of indicators, we see that small net changes in price can result in all volume being designated to one market direction. This is the case with Granville's On-Balance Volume and in the Bolton-Tremblay method. Is it reasonable to add all volume to the accumulated index if the S&P gained only a fraction of one point? On a single day this may seem to be arbitrary, but just as in many basic systems, over a long period of time the net effect of this decision is sound.

The changes made by Mark Chaiken, which take a percentage of volume based on the relative close of prices within the daily range, seem very sensible and avoid the all-or-nothing technique used in On-Balance Volume. Sibbett's Demand Index, by using the sum of 10 days' volume, avoids this problem completely and smoothes out results, a situation often needed when using the highly variable values of volume and breadth.

By seeing these indicators close together, they appear to be a collection of minor manipulation of data. Traditional technicians still advocate interpretation using trend lines, divergence, or new highs and lows. Instead of having to interpret only the difficult movements of prices, they have added an equally difficult series of volume or breadth. While it is clear that volume and breadth contribute to the understanding of a price move, you must first be able to test whether you can use that information profitably. To do that, some fully systematic method is needed to insure that any approach can be implemented and validated.

Breadth as a Countertrend Indicator

All the literature favors using breadth to confirm direction, but Connors argues the opposite.[8] He trades the advance/decline (*AD*) ratio as follows:

> *Sell* the index when *AD* > 2.0
> *Buy* the index when *AD* < 0.50
> *Exit* the trade after 5 days unless a reverse signal occurs

Using the series UVDV-I or MKST-I defined earlier in this section, we added the SPX in column 2, then created the advance/decline ratio. The buy and sell rules were applied, but because there were very frequent signals, all trades were held until an opposite signal occurred, rather than for 5 days. The total PL (in percent) is shown in Figure 7.11. Complete calculations can be found in the Excel spreadsheet, *TSM MKST-I Market Breadth*, on the Companion Website.

■ Interpreting Volume and Breadth Systematically

Most systematic approaches to volume apply a long-term smoothing method to the data and then identify trend changes to confirm price direction. This can be implemented with any of the accumulation indexes, but not with single-day momentum or oscillator values. For the oscillators, most analysts have taken the approach that high volume confirms a new price direction; extreme volume, on the other hand, is more likely to be a reversal signal. If volume and price peaks do not occur at the same time, a volume peak should precede a trend change. A decline in volume has also been used to confirm direction, but it is more likely to indicate that prices have reached equilibrium, and that a further advance or decline requires additional confirmation.

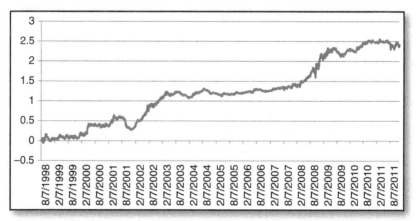

FIGURE 7.11   Total PL Using the AD Ratio as a Countertrend Signal.

[8] Larry Connors, "Fade the Breadth," *Futures* (January 2005).

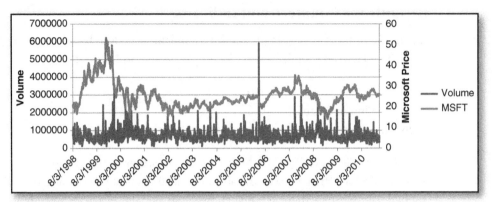

FIGURE 7.12 Microsoft Prices with Volume Along the Bottom.

Identifying a Volume Spike

A *volume spike* is one of the clearest and best examples of useful volume information. In its most obvious form, a volume spike is a day when the volume is at least twice that of other days over a period generally longer than one month, most likely longer than three months. Volume spikes may come in clusters due to an unstable political or economic situation; however, it is normally associated with the end of a significant price move.

Figure 7.12 shows 12 years of Microsoft prices with volume along the bottom. There are a few dozen times when volume spikes. Just after 2000 there is a cluster of spikes that are associated with the end of the tech bubble, a price drop of 50% in just a few weeks. Most of the spikes on the chart fall on days with large price moves and precede reversals. While the reversals are not always large, the volatility spike marks the end of the current move.

A simple spike can be measured as exceeding a threshold, *T*, where *T* is a multiple of the average volume, *AV* = *average (volume, n)*, over the recent *n* days. Then a volume spike exists if today's volume is greater than the average volume on the previous day times its multiplier, $V_t > T \times AV_{t-1}$.

Most cases are not as clear as a 1-day spike following much lower volume. More likely, volume has increased significantly over the past two or three days, culminating in a spike that is much higher than the average volume, but may only be 25% higher than the previous day. The solution to this is to lag the average volume so that it does not reflect the increasing volume of the recent few days.

We will make the assumption that volume resulting in a spike takes no longer than three days to develop. We can safely say that the average volume, lagged five days, should not reflect the recent rise in volume. Then a volume spike would be identified when

$$V_t > \frac{\sum\limits_{i=t-n-5}^{t-5} V_i}{n}$$

The right part of this formula is the average volume over n days beginning $t - n - 5$ days ago and ending $t - 5$ days ago. If t is today, then the average volume stops five days ago; therefore, it is not influenced by recent volume data.

Volume spikes are not as extreme when dealing with futures markets and indexes. In Figure 7.13 NASDAQ futures are shown with total (all contracts) volume for a period in May 2010. Higher volume days correspond to two cases where prices reversed from lows, and the peak in the center of the chart is associated with low volume. Both situations offer an opportunity to improve trading.

In the crude oil chart, Figure 7.14, the spikes in volume can be seen as frequently occurring at price reversal points, while lower volume may be indicative of the continued price direction. Although there are no comprehensive tests available to confirm these observations, high volume seems to precede a price reversal, even if it lasts only one day.

Moving Average Approaches

Not all analysts agree that higher volume is a reversal signal. A straightforward way of using higher volume to confirm a trend is to calculate a 10-day moving average

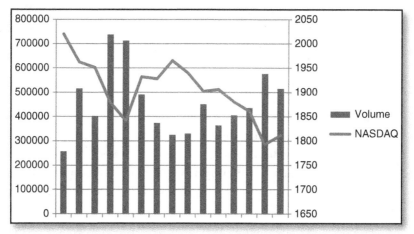

FIGURE 7.13 NASDAQ Prices and Volume Show Both High and Low Volume Associated with Price Reversals.

FIGURE 7.14 Crude Oil Futures (Back-Adjusted), with Total Volume Shown as a Line.

of the volume as a complement to a 20-day trend position.[9] By simply requiring the current volume to be greater than the average volume over those past 10 days, you introduce the idea of greater participation associated with the new trend. An additional important benefit is that this volume condition acts as a filter, eliminating a substantial number of trades. If the net returns are the same, the volume-filtered approach is far better because you are out of the market more, reducing your risk and not reversing your position every time there is a new signal. That improves liquidity.

A similar method was proposed by Waxenberg.[10] A 10-day moving average of the volume is calculated as the normal level, and a change in trend must be confirmed by a 20% increase in volume above this norm. (The 20% threshold acts as an additional smoothing filter, but may be replaced by a longer trend and smaller threshold.) Extremes in a price move can be found at points that exceed approximately a 40% volume increase. Applied to the stock market, Waxenberg used the extreme volumes to indicate the end of a sell-off. To add more flexibility over longer test periods, and to adapt more quickly to volatility changes, Bollinger bands (based on 2 standard deviations, or 95% probability) can be substituted for the fixed percentage thresholds.

Alternately, using 13 days of volume, subtract the total down volume from the total up volume. A plot of the results will serve as a momentum indicator from which overbought and oversold levels can be identified. If these values are unstable due to lack of liquidity, they may be smoothed using a short-term moving average.

Advance-Decline System

Advance and decline values, as with most volume figures, can be more useful if they are smoothed. By combining peak values of the net of smoothed advancing and declining shares with a directional move in price, Connors and Hayward have created a basic system structure that they named CHADTP[11] (*Connors-Hayward Advance-Decline Trading Patterns*). This system tries to identify reversal patterns by applying the following steps:

1. Add the past 5 days of advancing issues on the New York Stock Exchange.
2. Add the past 5 days of declining issues on the New York Stock Exchange.
3. Subtract the 5-day sum of declining issues (Step 2) from the advancing issues (Step 1).
4. Divide by 5 to get the average daily value.

$$CHADTP = (Sum(AdvancingNYSE,5) - Sum(DecliningNYSE,5)) / 5$$

[9] Alex Saitta, "A Price and Volume-Based System," *Technical Analysis of Stocks & Commodities* (March 1996).

[10] Howard K. Waxenberg, "Technical Analysis of Volume," *Technical Analysis of Stocks & Commodities* (March 1986).

[11] Laurence A. Connors and Blake E. Hayward, *Investment Secrets of a Hedge Fund Manager* (Chicago: Probus, 1995).

To trade using this oscillator, Connors and Hayward have determined that ±400 are the extreme levels where the values have been overbought and oversold. Based on this, we can apply the following rules to the S&P futures:

1. *Sell short* when CHADTP > + 400 and the S&P futures trade 10 basis points below the low of the previous day; *buy* when CHADTP < − 400 and the S&P futures trade 10 basis points above the high of the previous day.
2. Note that the oscillator does not have to exceed its recent extremes on the day of the buy or sell signal.
3. Timing is best if the signal occurs at the same time as a newspaper commentary indicating "depressed volume," or volume significantly below the 3-month average, which is seen as an excess of cash waiting to enter the market.

This system targets returns over a 5- to 7-day period. A drop in the oscillator, which results in values in the midrange, is an opportunity to exit. A standard price oscillator can be constructed to generate overbought and oversold signals within this time frame. An opposite entry signal would reverse the position.

We should be aware that this method was developed in 1995 when the S&P was lower and less volatile. As of 2011, the DJIA is about four times its 1995 value, while the S&P is only about one-third higher. However, the markets are more volatile now. A change of 10 basis points (0.10%) in the S&P is about 1.30 points, which is likely to happen every day. Raising the threshold to 50 or 100 basis points may make it easier to assess the value of this method.

Breadth as a Countertrend Indicator

Equities have a tendency to be mean reverting because they have more noise than most other sectors. That seems to hold true for market breadth. Larry Connors has shown that more declining stocks is an excellent leading indicator of a stock market advance.[12]

- If declining NYSE stocks are greater than advancing NYSE stocks for at least three days in a row, then the S&P averaged a gain of 0.50% the following week.

- If declining NASDAQ stocks are greater than advancing NASDAQ stocks for at least two days in a row, then the NASDAQ 100 index gained an average of 0.80% the next week.

- If declining NYSE stocks were at least twice the NYSE advancing stocks, then the S&P gained an average of 0.60% the following week.

In addition, when the opposite occurred, all three situations showed essentially no gain in the respective index during the following week. The observation period was 1996–2003, which contained extreme bull and bear markets.

---

[12] Larry Connors, "Fade the Breadth," *Futures* (January 2005).

■ An Integrated Probability Model

If there is a noticeable relationship between price, volume, and open interest (or market breadth), then a probability model can be constructed to test its importance.[13] To do this it is necessary to construct a 1-day-ahead forecast using a simple linear regression model and then backtest weighting factors for each element. Because of powerful software products, this has become a very manageable process. Using TradeStation's *EasyLanguage*, each 1-day-ahead forecast is determined using the previous *n* days:

Price forecast:	$Pf = Price + LinearRegSlope(close, n)$
Volume forecast:	$Vf = Volume + LinearRegSlope(volume, n)$
Open interest forecast:	$Of = Opint + LinearRegSlope(opint, n)$
On-Balance Volume forecast:	$OBVf = OBV + LinearRegSlope(OBV, n)$

The function *LinearRegSlope* returns the 1-period increase or decrease in the input value based on a straight-line fit of the past *n* days. That value can be added to the current price, volume, open interest, or On-Balance Volume to get the 1-day-ahead forecast. The calculation period *n* can be selected by subtracting the actual next-day value from the forecast and creating an error series that can be measured using a standard deviation. The number of days, *n*, that generates the smallest standard deviation is the best forecast period. It is possible that the optimal forecast period will differ for each of the four items above but a robust solution would seem to be the one period that minimized the errors across all the components.

Having found the four 1-day-ahead forecasts, an index can be created that gives one weight w_1 to the price forecast and the remaining weights, $1 - w_1$, to a combination of the other three factors. This assumes that price is the most important predictor of price. Then

$$Forecast\ index = w_1 Pf + (1 - w_1) \times (w_2 Vf + w_3 Of + w_4 OBVf)$$

This formula can be backtested for values of w_1, w_2, w_3, and w_4 where $\sum w = 1$. The final index can be used instead of price for determining the trend. It will still require a moving average, or some smoothed line, to signal new uptrends and downtrends; however, the results, if successful, should be more reliable than using only price.

One advantage of testing the weighting factors is that, if one of the four elements is not helpful in predicting a trend, the weighting factor should be near zero. Another approach, that does not cluster the nonprice data together, would be to treat each item separately in the classic form:

$$Forecast\ index = w_1 Pf + w_2 Vf + w_3 Of + w_4 OBVf$$

---

[13] Based on the May 1995 "CSI Technical Journal," Commodity Systems Inc., Boca Raton, Florida.

■ Intraday Volume Patterns

Identifying increases and decreases in volume during the trading day must consider the patterns caused by the flow of orders during the day and the way traders enter orders. During the past five years, there has been a great improvement in timely reporting of intraday volume for both stocks and futures markets. Services such as Bloomberg have continually updated volume for nearly all markets. Prior to this, only tick volume was the practical alternative. Tick volume represents the number of price changes that occurred during any time interval. It turns out that the frequency of price changes is directly related to the actual volume traded. If you purchase intraday data from CQG, it will have tick volume in each price bar.

Time Stamps

One point to note is that CQG time stamps each bar at the beginning of the interval. It is because they accumulate the data as it occurs, so that 5-minute bars that are stamped 10:00, 10:05, and 10:10 have the data from 10:00:00 through 10:04:59, 10:05 through 10:09:59, and 10:10:00 through 10:14:59, respectively. For many applications, users may want to shift those times to show the end of the bar rather than the beginning. That way, if you are matching the time of the bar with the closing time of the session, those times will match. Otherwise, if the closing time is 4 p.m., or 16:00, the last 5-minute bar will be stamped 15:55. Also note that because these bars are time stamped at the beginning, the last bar of the day will have only the trading that occurred in the last 1 minute of the session. For example, the U.S. bond chart has the last interval posted at 14:00, the Chicago closing time. All trading starting at 14:00 will be captured, which is only the last minute, yet it shows very high volume. You may want to combine the last bar with the previous bar.

Intraday Patterns

Figure 7.15 shows the intraday tick volume patterns for four futures markets, crude oil, the German DAX, NASDAQ, and U.S. 30-year bonds. The charts represent the average number of price changes in each 15-minute interval for the years 1995 through 2005, for the nearest contract to delivery. Each market has a somewhat different pattern.

Before Europe became a viable, accessible market, intraday volume patterns tended to have a very symmetric U-shaped pattern, with the highest volume at the open and close. The bottom of the U always came at midday when traders took their lunch break. This can still be seen in the NASDAQ chart, Figure 7.15c. As European markets increased in volume the patterns changed so that volume was greatest while both the United States and Europe were open, then declined as European traders ended their business day. In Figure 7.15b, the DAX shows a sharp drop from 17:30, then one strong bar on the close at 18:00 (6 pm). Soon after 2005, the Eurex extended hours to match the U.S. trading sessions, so the DAX now trades until 20:00, the close of the U.S. equity index markets. We should expect the U-shaped pattern in the late session to be extended to 20:00.

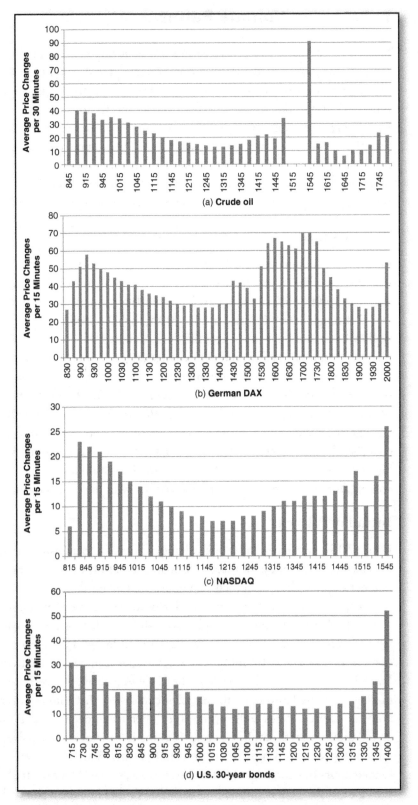

FIGURE 7.15 Intraday, 15–Minute Tick Volume Patterns, 1995 to 2005.

Crude oil shows two *U*-shaped patterns, the first for the primary session, originally called the *pit session*, and the second for the evening session. Now crude trades 24 hours, although we should always expect this same volume pattern bounded by normal daily business hours in the country where the product is traded. Then the CME Nikkei contract will have very low volume and an unclear pattern because we trade it during our business hours, while Japanese business sleeps.

It should not be surprising to see the extreme clustering at both ends of the trading day. Orders enter the market early in reaction to news and events that occurred after the close of the previous day's trading. Many analysts based trading decisions on the previous day's data but perform their calculations and analyses after the close. The end of day is active due to liquidation of the positions of day traders who do not want overnight risk. Orders that allow you to specify that you want to be filled at the settlement have reduced the slippage and increased the benefit of trading on the close.

Relative Changes in Volume

Whether using actual or tick volume, decisions made using, for example, 15-minute volume patterns should compare each 15 minutes of the current day with the same 15 minutes of the prior day or with the average of that 15-minute interval over some range of days. While it may be sensible to use increasing intraday volume as a condition for entering a new trade, if the trade signal is in the second half of the day, then each interval generally increases in volume; therefore, the condition is always true. If the trading signals were in the morning, the condition would always be false.

In order to use intraday volume correctly, you must consider different cases:

1. The volume of the opening bar must be compared to the volume of the same bar on the previous day, or the average volume of that bar on the past *n* days.
2. The second bar can then show volume as a percentage of the first bar. By keeping a history of this percentage value, we then will know if today's second bar is relatively stronger or weaker than the average.
3. We can track the relative strength or weakness of every bar compared to the opening bar and compared to the average bar of the same time.

Using this information, it is possible to anticipate a stronger or weaker close for the day. It is also generally true that an open on higher volume will indicate higher volume throughout the day. We could then also expect higher volatility. Days with significantly lower volume would be associated with less volatility and less directional movement.

■ Filtering Low Volume

Minutes, hours, or even days that have little market activity are likely to be associated with uncertain price direction. If the British pound moves $0.50 in the mid afternoon of the U.S. market, we know that volume is normally light because the London and European markets are closed. The intention of a volume indicator is to identify positive moves in volume that can be used as a confirmation of price direction. Eliminating those days with low volume, or with marginal price moves, may increase the dependability of the volume indicator.

Removing Low-Volume Periods

Including low-volume periods in a volume index may make the index movements unreliable. There is a similar situation in statistics, where a number of statistical values are slightly skewed to one side. Each value on its own is not noticeably important, but collectively they cause a bias. Some analysts believe that the collective weight creates significance, while others favor ignoring values that are so small they are insignificant and perhaps confusing.

The decision to remove low volume days, or intervals, means that a series of low volume days that results in a collective change will be ignored. If you have decided that removing those days makes sense, then measure the daily or intraday volume against a threshold created using the average volume minus one or two standard deviations of the volume. Using a 1 standard deviation filter will remove the lowest 16% of the days; a 2 standard deviation filter removes 32% of the days.

This type of filter is best applied to a volume index, such as On-Balance Volume. For example, we find that the average volume on the New York Stock Exchange is 1.5 billion shares, and 1 standard deviation of the volume is 0.25 billion shares. We decide that the volume filter is 2 standard deviations; therefore, any day with volume below 1.0 billion shares will be ignored. Applying this to On-Balance Volume, using TradeStation code:

```
Volumethreshold = average(volume, n) - volumefilter*stddev(volume, n)
  If volume < volumethreshold then VFOBV = VFOBV[1]
    else VFOBV = VFOBV + (close - close[1])/
        absvalue(close - close[1])) + volume;
```

we would effectively ignore all days, leaving the OBV unchanged, when the volume was below the threshold.

Removing Volume Associated with Small Price Moves

If you agree with the concept of removing days with low volume, then there is the similar case of very small price moves. Indicators such as On-Balance Volume post all volume as either a positive or negative contribution to the index, based on the direction of prices on that day. It is fair to question the validity of posting all volume to the upside when the S&P 500 closed up a minimum move of 25 basis points (+0.25) or the Dow closed up 1 point. It could just as easily have closed down that amount. In a manner similar to filtering low-volume, periods in which prices moved very little may be eliminated by using a standard deviation of the price changes as a filter. Days that are within ±0.10 or ±0.25 standard deviations of the average would be ignored. The *Price-Filtered On-Balance Volume, PFOBV*, would then be found using the code:

```
pricethreshold = average(price - price[1], n) +
    f*stddev(price - price[1], n)
if absvalue(price - price[1]) < price threshold then PFOBV = PFOBV[1]
    else PFOBV = PFOBV[1] + ((close - close[1])/
        (absvalue(close - close[1])) * volume
```

where n = the number of periods in both the average and standard deviation
         f = the number of standard deviations used to filter minimum volume

Note that, in the case of a minimum price threshold, the rules look at price change, which can be positive or negative. For a volume threshold, there is only a one-sided test using the value of volume.

■ Market Facilitation Index

In weighing the likelihood that prices are indicating a direction, rather than a false start, the tick volume compared to the price range for the same period, called the *Market Facilitation Index*,[14] can measure the willingness of the market to move the price. This concept is interesting because it is not clear that high volume results in a large price move, although high volume appears to set up the conditions for high volatility. If the Market Facilitation Index increases, then the market is willing to move the price; therefore trading that benefits from higher volatility should improve.

$$\text{Market Facilitation Index}_t = \frac{\text{Trading range}_t}{\text{Volume}_t} = \frac{H_t - L_t}{V_t}$$

The results of combining the change in tick volume and the Market Facilitation Index are interpreted as:

Tick Volume	Market Facilitation Index	Interpretation
Up	Up	Confirmation of direction
Down	Down	False direction, do not take trade
Down	Up	Poor entry timing, approach with caution
Up	Down	Potential new trend, end of old trend

[14] Bill Williams, *Trading Chaos* (New York: John Wiley & Sons, 1995).

CHAPTER 8

Bar Chart Patterns

From Charles D. Kirkpatrick II and Julie R. Dahlquist, *Technical Analysis: The Complete Resource for Financial Market Technicians*, 3rd Edition (Old Tappan, New Jersey: Pearson Education, Inc., 2016), Chapter 15.

Learning Objective Statements

- Explain the controversy over whether tradeable patterns exist in technical analysis
- Describe the influence that computer technology has had on the study of patterns
- Explain the proper application and use of classic bar chart patterns such as triangles, flags, pennants, double/triple tops or bottoms, broadening formations, diamond tops and bottoms, rounding tops and bottoms, and head-and-shoulders patterns
- Compare the historical performance measures of major bar chart patterns

Traditionally, technical analysis has been closely associated with price patterns, perhaps even more than it should be. Prior to the advent of the computer, hand-drawn charts of prices were the only technical resources available. Trend lines and patterns were the principal means of analyzing price behavior. The computer has diversified technical analysis because it has made other mathematical relationships easier to calculate.

After discussing some of the basic characteristics of patterns, we look at classic bar chart patterns—those used by the majority of technical analysts and having the longest history of use. In "Short-Term Patterns," we consider short-term patterns, candlesticks, one-and two-day patterns, and other patterns that are not so widely used. There are as many different patterns as the combinations of price open, high, low, and close can accommodate. Generally, shorter patterns are more common and less reliable, and longer patterns are more complex and less frequent. In addition, as a rule, the more complicated the pattern, the less likely it will be profitable, and the more frequent a pattern, the less likely it will be profitable. The best patterns seem to be in the middle of frequency and complexity. We address these. There are many reference books on other patterns that you can investigate, but most fail to give any special advantage over the classic patterns. However, the books by Thomas N. Bulkowski, used as a primary source here, are by far the most researched and detailed.

■ What Is a Pattern?

In the literature and usage of technical analysis, the terms **pattern** and **formation** are used interchangeably. We will do the same. A *pattern* is simply a configuration of price action that is bounded, above and below, by some form of either a line or a curve.

The lines that bind price movement in a pattern can be trend lines or support/resistance lines. In this chapter, we apply the concepts and terminology that we studied in "Trends—The Basics," regarding these lines. When studying patterns, we add a new concept—prices being bound by a curve instead of a straight line. A *curve* is a less definite arc drawn with either a "smiley face" for a bottom curve or a "frown" for the top curve. The lowest level in a bottom curve is a support level, and the highest level in a top curve is a resistance level. Curves simply define a support or resistance level with curved rather than straight lines. A pattern can be bounded by any combination of curves or lines as long as the upper and lower bounds are defined well enough for a breakout level to be established.

Common Pattern Characteristics

The focus of this chapter is bar chart price configurations. Thomas N. Bulkowski has accomplished the most comprehensive modern study of bar chart patterns in his twin books *Encyclopedia of Chart Patterns*, 2nd edition (2005) and *Trading Classic Chart Patterns* (2002). Bulkowski observed more than 700 stocks over ten years on a daily basis and cataloged their results under varying conditions. In total, over two market periods he found and analyzed 12,385 chart patterns. Although his analysis of patterns was, of course, subject to his potential bias, it was consistent and included a significantly large number of examples. Much of the material—specifically the statistics—in this chapter relies on Bulkowski's work. Bulkowski has a Web site (www.thepatternsite.com) that explains in significant detail all the patterns we discuss and more. Before we begin discussing some of the particular patterns, however, we need to explain some vocabulary related to the general characteristics of bar chart patterns.

Entry and Exit   All patterns have a combination of an entry and an exit. The entry describes the trend preceding the formation, and the exit is usually the signal for action. A pattern can occur after a decline, in which case, the entry is from above,

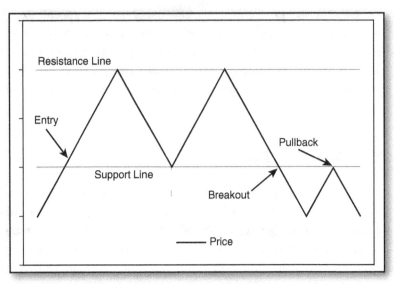

FIGURE 8.1 Double top with breakout down

or after an advance, in which case, the entry is from below. The exit, of course, can also be downward or upward. Figure 8.1, a double bottom, shows an entry from above and an upward breakout. On the other hand, a top formation has an entry from below and an exit downward. A consolidation in a larger uptrend has an entry from below and an exit upward. Thus, all patterns are described with these four variables: entry from above, entry from below, downward exit, and upward exit. These variables are important because statistically, in each pattern type, some of these characteristics are more reliable, occur more frequently, or are more profitable than others.

Fractal   The bars in a bar chart can be any period: weekly, daily, minute, and so on. Bar chart patterns are fractal. This means they can occur in any bar chart, regardless of the bar period. A triangle formation, for example, can occur in hourly bars or weekly bars. The pattern is always the same type and will always have the same general characteristics. This is odd but true. Indeed, looking at a bar chart pattern without a specified time horizon, a technical analyst who is experienced in pattern recognition cannot tell the periods of the bars.

Pullbacks and Throwbacks   Pullbacks occur when prices break out downward and then "pull back" to their breakout level. Throwbacks occur when prices break out upward and then "throw back" to their breakout level (Edwards and Magee, revised 2007). Figure 8.1 shows an example of a pullback. Neither a pullback nor a throwback is easily or precisely defined, but you know one when you see it. The interesting aspect of this price behavior is that invariably a pullback or throwback will decrease the extent of the eventual move in the direction of the breakout. Thus, although each may provide a second opportunity for action at the breakout level, the subsequent rise or fall generally will be less than if there were no pullback or throwback. Tactically, this implies that a breakout should be acted upon immediately; waiting for the retracement will diminish profitability, and you may very likely miss the entire price move.

Pullbacks seem to occur more frequently on downward breakouts with less-than-average volume, and throwbacks occur more frequently with upward breakouts on above-average volume. Because pullbacks and throwbacks seem to undermine performance, the ideal situation, as a rule, is that on an upward breakout, less volume is preferred, and on a downward breakout, more volume is preferred.

Failures   All breakouts can fail in any of the formations—some more than others. Remember that a breakout is a signal that prices are beginning to trend, either upward or downward. This is particularly frustrating to the beginner who desires perfection. As we have seen, however, perfection is not in the lexicon of technical analysis. It is favorable odds, or an "edge," for which we are looking. Bulkowski's definition of a failure, which we use, is when a breakout occurs and the price fails to move at least 5% in the direction of the breakout.

■ Do Patterns Exist?

Some academics and investors believe that patterns do not exist. They believe either that price action is completely random or, at least, is indecipherable. However, even if order does exist in market prices, it is possible that it cannot be recognized with present mathematical models because it is so complex. The methods used in chaos theory, neural networks, and other esoteric mathematical models may prove useful sometime in the future, but not now. Thus, there is still the realistic question of whether patterns do exist in prices. Technical analysts swear they do, but in many cases, analysts are not mathematically sophisticated enough to demonstrate their validity.

As mentioned in "History and Construction of Charts," the unpublished article by Hasanhodzic et al. (2010) on a study of online video game players (http://arora.ccs.neu.edu) attempting to distinguish between financial market price statistics in moving chart form from random permutations of the same data with immediate feedback found that these people could "consistently distinguish between the two types of time series" (p. 1). This experiment seemed to give evidence that humans can learn to distinguish patterns and real data from random series whereas computers, so far, cannot.

If prices do have patterns, what causes them? This has been a debate for at least a century and has coalesced into a belief that patterns are the result of human behavior, which, conveniently, is indecipherable. It is, however, why technical analysts are very much interested in the new behavioral finance and neurological studies. They hope that the biases and tendencies in human behavior now being measured and gradually understood by behavioral finance students will eventually explain why price patterns seem to exist.

Behavioral Finance and Pattern Recognition

The first fact to acknowledge about chart patterns is that they have not been proven to exist or to be profitable. Although many investors and traders swear by certain formations, their evidence is largely anecdotal. Added to this is the tendency to see patterns in random data.

Humans have a tendency to want patterns in data and other information and to see them when they do not exist. Superstitions are derived from the erroneous and coincidental observations of patterns that do not exist but are created because of the desire to have a pattern. B. F. Skinner, a famous Harvard psychology professor, studied pigeon behavior in a number of stimulus-response situations to see if the pigeons would react to various stimuli and thus "learn" responses. The reward for the correct response was usually food. In one experiment, he decided to give pigeons just food without a stimulus to see what they would do. Invariably, in trying to make sense out of stimulus-response, the pigeons responded in different manners by creating their own stimulus, some bobbing, some developing strange head motions, thus creating their own superstition, when a real stimulus did not exist (Skinner, 1947).

Humans are similar in their desire to have some kind of stimulus, even if it is a black cat crossing the road, and develop supposedly predictive relationships when none actually exists. This is a special danger in price analysis because the desire to see a pattern can occur when no pattern actually exists.

Humans are also poor statisticians and tend to put more weight on recent history than what is statistically warranted. An experiment by Kahneman and Tversky (1982) showed that in flipping coins, which have a statistical probability of landing on their heads 50% of the time regardless of what side they landed on earlier, observers began to expect more heads in the future when the sequence of heads turned up more frequently, and they were surprised when that did not occur. Their subconscious brains expected more heads because that was the most recent history of flips, even though the odds had not changed. In the technical analysis of patterns, the analyst must guard against superstition or what is often called "market lore." Frequently these statements contradict other statements or are just plain wrong. An example is that "a descending triangle always breaks downward." You will see how this is not borne out by fact when we discuss triangles. Pattern and trend analysis must be based on evidence alone.

Humans also tend to see the future as the past and look backward rather than forward. This bias is likely the reason that trends in prices exist in the first place and why prices rise or fall until they reach some exhaustion limit rather than adjusting immediately as the EMH would suggest. For this reason, humans have difficulty in recognizing when past signs or patterns are no longer valid. Studies have shown that the human brain releases dopamine (a pleasure sensation chemical and, thus, a reward) when a human takes action that has worked before. Thus, the pleasurable action is desirable and overcomes any cognitive reasoning that might suspect the action is wrong. This problem is especially prevalent and potentially very dangerous in the financial markets where change is constant.

"In a world without change, the best way to find cheese is to return to the location where it was found previously. In a world with change, however, the best way to find cheese is to look somewhere new" Burnham (2005, p. 284), paraphrasing from Johnson (1998). In other words, the chart pattern and trend reader should look for failure rather than believe in the constancy of previous patterns. Schwager (1996) suggests that profitability from failed patterns is often greater than from correct patterns.

■ Computers and Pattern Recognition

Analysts began recognizing chart patterns in the days when prices were plotted daily by hand. Aside from trend lines, patterns were the beginning of technical analysis, and for this reason, many nontechnicians mistakenly believe that patterns are all that technicians study. Floor traders and market makers still plot intra-day charts of prices for their use in trading short periods, but the computer has changed technical analysis considerably. On a computer screen, charts of minute-to-minute, even tick-to-tick prices can now be displayed, and from them, various patterns can be recognized. This has led to impersonal contact with prices, different from the days when each bar was plotted individually and the "feel" for price action was more easily learned. In addition, the time horizon for traders off the floor has become shorter. The ability to see almost instantly a change in price behavior combined with lower commission costs and less slippage, all due to the introduction of computers, has led traders to speculate on shorter-term trends and patterns.

The computer did not make the study of patterns any easier, however. Patterns change and adjust to new markets. Some of the old patterns do not seem to work very well anymore, and others have taken their place. Patterns are also subjectively determined, and in many cases they are perhaps invalid. Tests are being made currently on their validity—a difficult enterprise because patterns are more visually based than mathematically based. They are peculiar to humans in that, like recognizing a friend's face out of a collage of faces, a particular chart pattern must be recognized out of a series of patterns in prices. Like quantifying your friend's face, quantifying a chart pattern is not easily accomplished. Only through practice, many mistakes, and many correct interpretations that go wrong is the technical analyst consistently able to recognize patterns. This is how the art of technical analysis developed before the computer, and although the computer is now taking over both in plotting and in analyzing, the chart patterns still exist and are used by many practitioners. Recent authors of books on technical chart methods will attest to the longevity of certain patterns and their fractal nature. The analysis of price patterns remains, although less emphasis is placed on it.

The analyst using a computer is able to compute more quickly various ratios, averages, spreads, and so on. Computer usage also has the advantage of giving the technician the ability to test these new calculations as well as the old ones for accuracy and statistical significance. The old-time technical analyst had to rely on many years of experience to determine the reliability of formations and indicators and often, for example, stayed up late at night with a hand-crank adding machine calculating indicators and oscillators. As we know from studies of behavior, anecdotal experience can be deceiving, but with the advent of the computer, we can now objectively study many oscillators, averages, and other methods that before were impractical to study. The computer has "cleaned" up a lot of the folklore about patterns and trends and eliminated those that have little or no validity. It has made technical analysis more of a science than an art. Remarkably, although understandable from the previous discussion of human behavior, many of these old inaccurate methods are still used.

■ Market Structure and Pattern Recognition

The markets, of course, have also changed since the beginning of technical analysis and the first recognition of patterns, and with this change, patterns have changed and become less accurate. First, the proliferation of technical knowledge has led to the recognition of specific patterns when they occur. Of course, once a pattern is widely recognized and acted upon, its effectiveness diminishes. Thus, patterns in widely traded securities tend to be less accurate than in those quiet trading securities that few traders watch.

In the stock market, ownership has become concentrated in relatively few hands that tend to act in concert. These "hands" are the institutional holders of securities. They tend to act together when news is announced; thus, by their large positions and anxiousness to get in or get out, they cause patterns to self-destruct. Although it is difficult to prove, when a large institution is the dominant owner of a stock and has knowledge of technical principles, there is a temptation to "manipulate" a chart formation and cause false breakouts. This can cause havoc with the short-term trader who is watching the same patterns develop.

Finally, the advent of derivatives in large quantities has influenced the price and volume action in individual securities for reasons other than the prospects for the underlying company. Addition or deletion from a market index or basket can suddenly introduce buying or selling unrelated to the pattern developing.

BOX 8.1   FOR FURTHER READING

There are many good reference books devoted to the study of patterns in market prices. Some of these are listed here.

Bar Chart Patterns

Encyclopedia of Chart Patterns by Thomas N. Bulkowski
How Charts Can Help You in the Stock Market by William Jiler
How Technical Analysis Works by Bruce Kamich
Profits in the Stock Market by H. M. Gartley
Technical Analysis by Jack Schwager
Technical Analysis Explained by Martin Pring
Technical Analysis of Stock Trends by Robert Edwards, John Magee, and W. Bassetti
Technical Analysis of the Financial Markets by John Murphy

Point-and-Figure Patterns

Point and Figure Charting by Thomas J. Dorsey
Study Helps in Point & Figure Technique by Alexander Wheelan
The Chartcraft Method of Point and Figure Trading by Abe Cohen, Earl Blumenthal, and Michael Burke
The Definitive Guide to Point and Figure by Jeremy du Plessis

Trading—Short-Term Patterns

Connors on Advanced Trading Strategies by Laurence Connors
Dave Landry's 10 Best Swing Trading Patterns and Strategies by David Landry
Encyclopedia of Candlestick Charts by Thomas N. Bulkowski
Japanese Candlestick Charting Techniques by Steve Nison
Long-Term Secrets to Short-Term Trading by Larry Williams
Market Wizards by Jack Schwager
New Concepts in Technical Trading Systems by J. Welles Wilder, Jr.
Street Smarts by Laurence Connors and Linda Bradford Rashke
Trading Systems and Methods by Perry J. Kaufman
Trade Chart Patterns Like the Pros by Suri Duddella

■ Bar Charts and Patterns

You know how to plot a bar chart. It is the most common chart of price behavior and has been used ever since continuous trading data became available. You learned how to determine support and resistance zones and trend lines using bar charts. Bar chart patterns form by combining support and resistance zones and trend lines. In all cases, a pattern finalizes when a breakout occurs from the pattern. In some instances, a pattern will just dribble into inactivity, in which case it should be ignored, but most patterns result in a legitimate breakout in one direction or the other. The breakout may be false, of course, and we look at how to handle that occurrence. Patterns are, thus, never exactly the same from example to example and are fit into generic categories with common characteristics based principally on the direction of internal trends and their intersections.

Traditionally, we divide patterns into two categories: continuation and reversal. This is a holdover from Schabacker (1930), and used by Edwards and Magee (revised, 2007), who needed to break patterns into easily understood and recognizable divisions. Unfortunately, as Edwards and Magee recognized, patterns cannot always easily be relegated to a specific reversal or continuation category, and such a description can often be misleading. Instead, patterns can occur in both modes. For this reason, we prefer to abandon the standard method of differentiating patterns into "continuation" and "reversal," and although we still use the terms when appropriate, we instead describe the simplest patterns first and progress to the more complex.

■ How Profitable Are Patterns?

Studies of chart performance and reliability are scarce. The problem, of course, is the difficulty in defining a chart pattern on a computer. In 1970, one of the authors of this book and Robert Levy (1971) devised a method to identify patterns by recording the sequence of reversal points relative to their immediate past reversal points. This sounds complex, perhaps, but using only five reversal points, almost all simple chart patterns can be identified and their results recorded. Arthur Merrill (1997) took this study method and with some variation tested it on the Dow Jones Industrial Average. In both studies, the results showed that chart patterns as defined had little predictive ability. Several patterns showed some statistical reliability, but not enough to prove the case for technical price patterns in general.

In a 1988 study by Lo and MacKinlay, more sophisticated statistical methods were used to see if patterns existed in individual prices. The study had mixed results. Although it did not negate the possibility of patterns, neither did it prove that patterns existed.

The most comprehensive study to date is that of Bulkowski (2005). Many of the statistics mentioned in each pattern section later in the chapter are taken from his more recent work on trading classic patterns (2002). The intriguing nature of Bulkowski's studies is that many of the old observations seen in the classic literature are turning out to be questionable, especially for maximum performance. As examples, volume trend within a pattern, slope of trends, and breakout volume may not be as relevant as others had originally thought.

Remember also that Bulkowski's observations are in retrospect. We can easily identify many chart patterns after they have occurred and when we have observed the results. The real talent comes in identifying a chart pattern while it is evolving in real time and profiting from its completion. For this ability, only study, practice, and experience will suffice.

Finally, the results from Bulkowski's observations are relative only. They cannot be assumed to be profitable in the future, as they appeared to be during the trial period. The value of his study is not in determining the value of chart pattern analysis itself but in determining which of the classic patterns are more profitable with less risk. From Bulkowski's studies, it appears that pattern analysis outperforms the market (S&P 500) on average in every instance. This might or might not be true, but for our purposes, we are more interested in which patterns to study as being the most likely to profit over others.

BOX 8.2   USING BREAKOUT PRICE TO SET PRICE TARGETS

Bar charts can project price targets once a formation completes with the breakout. Most targets are measured from the breakout price. Targets are infrequently used because most technicians are satisfied with just being on the right side of the trend, want only to ride that trend, and believe that targets are generally inaccurate. In many patterns, however, this is not so. Generally, the target is calculated by taking the height of the pattern and adding it to the breakout price. In each of the following trading boxes, we describe the target peculiarities for each pattern and the success percentages.

◼ Classic Bar Chart Patterns

We begin by looking at classic chart patterns. These patterns generally have been recognized and used for more than a hundred years. Only recently have there been tests of their reliability and profitability.

Double Top and Double Bottom

A double formation is about the simplest of the classic formations. A double top consists of only three reversal points: two peaks separated by a trough. For it to be a true double top, the initial price must enter the pattern from below the trough price, and the exit signal must occur on the breakout below the trough low price. The best performing of the double tops is the "Eve and Eve" double top patterns. The tops are rounded and wide with some irregularity. According to Bukowski, the two peaks must be at or within 5% of each other's price level, and the middle valley should be around 10% or more from the lowest peak. The double top, thus, resembles the rectangle formation (described next) with less detail. The pattern forms over 2 to 6 weeks: the longer, the less reliable. A projection from the break below the trough is under the **Measured Rule** that hypothesizes a decline equal to 73% of the distance in points from the highest peak to the trough. The double bottom is the mirror image of the double top.

Newspaper and media commentators who want to sound like technical analysts frequently use the term *double* formation often when it is not a true double pattern. A true formation is only valid when the intervening reaction reversal point has been penetrated. The danger of acting prematurely is great; roughly 64% of these patterns fail to penetrate the breakout level and instead continue on their original trend. When the pattern is completed with a breakout, however, it is very accurate.

The failure rates are 11%. This means that the odds of making a profit from a double top downward breakout are minimally risky. Bulkowski ranks the overall performance rank at 2 out of 21, a very high ranking. This ranking is a composition of the pattern's failure rate, average profit, pullback/throwback rate, and percent of trades reaching a price target.

BOX 8.3 TRADING DOUBLE FORMATIONS

If one observes a double pattern, several important observations must be made before acting to improve the chances of profit. First, never buy until the breakout has occurred. Second, look for flat bases either at the same level as the twin bottoms or slightly higher and earlier. Third, look for an absence of a consolidation area above the formation. Fourth, look for what is called an "Eve & Eve" variety. Volume doesn't seem to be important, although it is usually higher on the first "hump."

Rectangle (Also "Trading Range" or "Box")

In the earlier discussion on trading ranges and sideways trends, we effectively described a rectangle pattern. It is one of the simplest of patterns, consisting of a resistance line above and a support line below (see Figure 8.2). Each resistance or support line must also be a trend line, which means that it must touch roughly the same price reversal at least twice. This added requirement is what separates it from a double top or bottom formation, which only requires that three price reversals occur. Prices are bounded by and oscillate between the two lines, and they eventually exit, or break out, in one direction or the other. The pattern can have a slight tilt upward or downward, but the trend lines defining the support and resistance zones are always parallel. It appears similar to a horizontal channel. It often has false or premature breakouts, neither of which is predictive of the eventual breakout direction.

BOX 8.4 FALSE AND PREMATURE BREAKOUTS

These breakouts are not exits from a formation but instead are minor breakouts above or below breakout levels that quickly return into the formation. They can occur at support and resistance levels as well as at trend lines. A "false" breakout is one that breaks out in the direction opposite from the direction of the final breakout, and a "premature" breakout is one that breaks in the same direction as the eventual exit breakout. In retrospect, these breakouts can have predictive value, but at the time either occurs, it is almost impossible to tell what type it is. When they occur frequently, they warn that a strict breakout discipline must be used to avoid triggering action before the actual exit breakout.

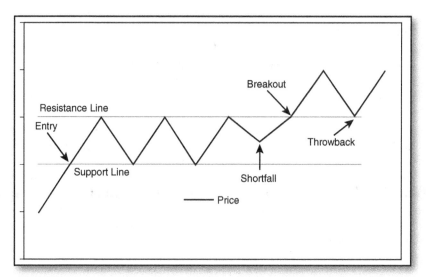

FIGURE 8.2 Rectangle with entry up and breakout up

Within the rectangle formation, prices do not necessarily always reach the two zones but may fall short (a "shortfall" or "partial"). Sometimes this is a warning as to the direction of the eventual breakout. As an example, when well along the way of the formation of a rectangle, prices begin to reverse before declining all the way to the underlying support zone; buyers are getting a little more anxious and the odds increase for a breakout upward. Bulkowski reported that such a shortfall within the latter stages of the pattern is accurate 60% to 90% of the time in predicting the direction of eventual breakout depending on the breakout direction. More than half the time, prices throw back or pull back to the breakout zone, providing another action point but one with less profit potential. Edwards and Magee estimated that about 40% of the time, a pullback or throwback would occur. When the breakout occurs on a gap, the odds decrease that a retracement will occur.

Volume is often an important factor in any formation. In the rectangle pattern, however, a rising or declining volume trend within the pattern has little or no effect on the results after the breakout, although declining volume is more common. Results increase, however, when volume increases on the breakout itself.

Depending on the rectangle entry and exit (that is, whether it is a reversal or continuation pattern), the failure to reach 5% was between 9% and 16%. The worst was the declining coninuation pattern (entry from above, exit down). Bulkowski ranked the overall performance of rectangles in the middle of the classical pattern pack.

> **BOX 8.5 TRADING RECTANGLES**
>
> Edwards and Magee claimed that rectangles are more often continuation patterns, but as a reversal pattern, they occur more frequently at bottoms. This is likely why Bulkowski mostly found upward breakout rectangle patterns. An upward breakout, however, should never be assumed. Indeed, two out of three rectangles are continuation patterns, and the initial expected direction of the breakout should be in line with the previous trend.
>
> Rectangles have the bad habit of producing false breakouts. Indeed, more than 75% of early breakouts are false. This is a large enough figure to hint as to the eventual final breakout direction, but it requires close breakout and stop discipline. Once the final breakout has occurred, the failure rate is very low. These failures are called **busted rectangles** and occur if the breakout fails to gain at least 10% before returning to the rectangle and breaking out in the opposite direction. Upward initial breakouts bust 22% of the time, and downward initial breakouts bust 42% of the time. Thus, it pays to be sure that the breakout is real. Another hint is the existence of shortfalls. Shortfalls occur later in the formation and can anticipate the breakout. The volume trend during the formation of the pattern gives no hint as to the breakout direction and has only a minor effect on performance.
>
> Some traders will trade within a rectangle, buying at the support level and selling at the resistance level. This is not recommended, however, unless the rectangle is particularly wide from top to bottom. Trading has many costs inherent in acting on the buys and sells. The obvious costs are commissions, slippage, and width of the spread. Additionally, when trading within two bounds, the bounds are not exact, nor will a trade be executed exactly at the bound. Thus, sell orders must be placed a certain distance, a specified filter, below a resistance zone, and buy orders a certain distance above a support zone. To be able to absorb these costs and price filters, the trader is limited to rectangles that are sufficiently high, from support to resistance. One who attempts this kind of trading must be watching the price action incessantly and be ready to scalp the few points in between the bounds and filters in an instant. Most traders and investors are unable to do this.
>
> A target can be calculated by adding the height of the rectangle formation to the breakout price. According to Bulkowski, in rectangles, the upward target is reached or exceeded 91%–93% of the time, and in downward breakouts, the target is reached or exceeded 65%–77% of the time. The difference in percentages is based on the entry, whether upward or downward, but in all cases, the target is a relatively accurate figure and can be used for risk/reward calculations.

Triple Top and Triple Bottom

The triple top and bottom formation is just a rectangle with the number of touches to the support or resistance line being three. It is, thus, more specific than the rectangle and is less common. Each peak in the top should be at the same level and have roughly the same shape. The middle peak can be slightly lower than the other two. As in the double formations, confirmation only comes with a price breakout below the two bottoms. Pullbacks are common (63% of the time) and diminish the breakout performance. Tops only project 40% of the formation width below the breakout

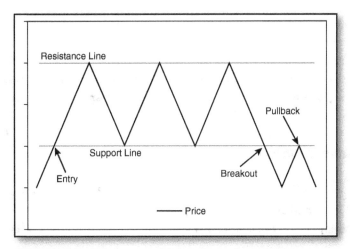

FIGURE 8.3 Triple top with breakout down

level but reach the projection within the first two weeks. Figure 8.3 shows a triple top with a breakout down, and Figure 8.4 shows a triple bottom with a breakout up. As you can see, they are the mirror image of each other. Sometimes in a triple bottom, the second peak is slightly higher than the first. This is favorable, and the breakout is the line between the two peaks. The patterns are rare and usually depend on the underlying market trend. They rank in the top third of classic patterns. Their failure rates very low (10% for bottoms, 4% for tops).

Standard Triangles

The rectangle pattern is bounded by parallel lines. If the same general pattern has non-parallel boundary lines such that when extended into the future they cross each other, the formation is a *triangle* pattern. Triangles can be the result of an upward-sloping

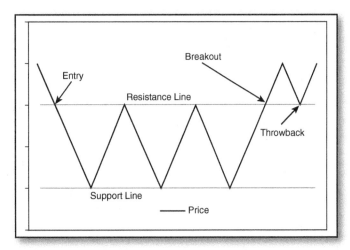

FIGURE 8.4 Triple bottom with breakout up

lower bound or a downward-sloping upward bound. Thus, there are a number of possible combinations of the two lines.

In this section, we look only at the standard triangle patterns. In these triangles, the point at which the two lines extend and cross over each other is called the **apex** or the **cradle**, and the distance between the first high reversal point and the first low reversal point within the triangle is called the **base**.

When the lower bound is a horizontal support zone and the upper is a downward slanting trend line, it is called a **descending triangle**. When the lower trend line is rising and the upper bound is a horizontal resistance zone, it is called an **ascending triangle**. When the upper bound is declining and the lower bound is rising, it is called a **symmetrical triangle**. When both the upper bound and lower bound are slanting in the same direction and converging, it is called a **wedge**, and when the two lines are diverging regardless of slope, a reverse triangle, it is called a **broadening pattern**. When we combine a broadening pattern with a triangle, usually a symmetrical triangle, we get what is called a **diamond pattern**.

Descending Triangle

Figure 8.5 shows a descending triangle with a breakout down. Its bounds are a lower horizontal support line and a declining upper trend line; price should touch each line at least twice and should generally "fill" the triangle's space. It can be entered from any direction. The breakout is more common to the downside (64%), but the upward breakout is more reliable and profitable (47% to 16% average gain). This formation can be stretched high and wide and is sometimes difficult to recognize. The trend lines defining its boundaries are almost never exact and are loaded with

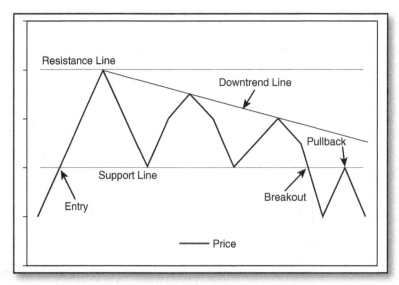

FIGURE 8.5 Descending triangle with breakout down

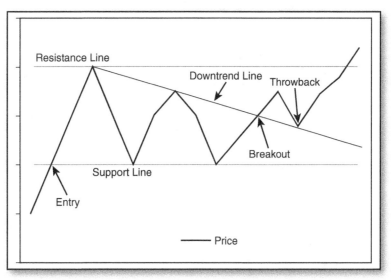

FIGURE 8.6 Descending triangle with breakout up

false intrabar breakouts; therefore, strict breakout strategy is required. However, prices often explode out of it and produce sizable gains. It can also be wild and guarantee an exciting ride. It will break out and run, break out and pull back to its trend line, break out and pull back to its cradle, or break back through the cradle, create a sizable trap, and then reverse back in its original breakout direction and run. In other words, when you enter on a breakout from a descending triangle, the subsequent action must be watched carefully.

Upward breakouts on gaps add considerably to performance and are definitely something to look for. On downward breaks, gaps seem to have little effect. Average breakout distance from the base to the cradle is 64%, most powerful at 80%. Entering from below and upward sloping volume equals better performance.

Figure 8.6 pictures a descending triangle with a breakout up. The typical pattern shows declining volume throughout its formation. However, increasing volume during the formation of an upward breaking descending triangle, although less frequent, is more favorable than declining volume. This contradicts the conventional opinion that advancing volume negates the pattern and represents a reason for screening it out for consideration. In the downward breakouts, declining volume during the pattern formation helps postbreakout performance only slightly. The amount of volume traded on the actual upward breakouts has little effect on the postperformance, but in downward breakouts, an increase on the breakout helps performance slightly. In many ways, the upward breaking descending triangle is similar to a failed head-and-shoulders top.

Ascending Triangle

A horizontal upper bound of resistance combined with an upward sloping lower bound of support defines an ascending triangle (shown in Figure 8.7 with a breakout

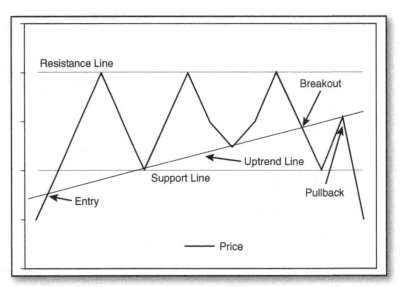

FIGURE 8.7   Ascending triangle with breakout down

down). The characteristics in this pattern are just as erratic as in descending triangles—lots of action up and down. Breakout points must be chosen carefully because of the pattern's nature to have many small false breakouts, and declining volume is common but not necessary. Upward breakouts occur 77% of the time, and breakouts happen roughly 61% of the distance (time) from the base to the cradle. The overall performance rank is roughly in the middle of all patterns, with a little more favorable for downward breakouts. Failure rates are between 11% and 13% depending on breakout direction. This is about average.

Symmetrical Triangle (Also "Coil" or "Isosceles Triangle")

When the upper bound is downward sloping and the lower bound is upward sloping, a symmetrical triangle is formed (see Figure 8.8). The term **symmetrical** gives the impression that both lines should have the same angle but in different directions. However, the slope of the two boundaries being formed at congruent angles is not a requirement. Thus, "symmetrical" is not an accurate description but is the term most commonly in use for this pattern. The less commonly used term **coil** is often a more accurate description.

Like the other standard triangles, the prices must touch each border trend line at least twice and meanwhile cover the area of the triangle with price action. Volume usually trends downward during the pattern formation (86% of the time), and the breakout is usually upward (54% of the time). Symmetrical triangles have many false breakouts and must be watched carefully. A strict breakout system must be used that allows for such false moves. The breakout commonly occurs between 73% and 75% of the length of the triangle from base to cradle. This formation does not

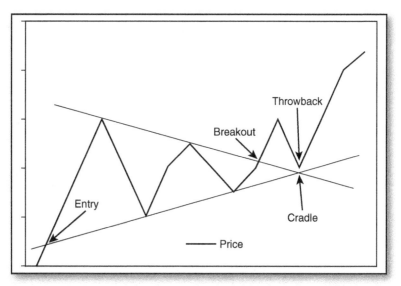

FIGURE 8.8 Symmetrical triangle with breakout up

occur as frequently as the descending or ascending triangle, but it is still common relative to other chart patterns. Throwbacks and pullbacks occur 37% and 59% of the time, respectively, and, as in most patterns, when they occur, they detract from eventual performance. This implies that for actual investment or trading, the initial breakout should be acted upon, and if a pullback or throwback occurs, the protective stop should be tightened. It does not imply that a pullback or throwback should be ignored, but that instead, performance expectations should be less than if no pullback or throwback had occurred. Gap breakouts do not seem to affect the performance on the upside but do give a few extra percentage points on the downside. Increasing volume trend seems to be associated with better results once the breakout occurs. High volume on breakouts, both upward and downward, adds considerably to the performance of the formation and is something to look for. Overall performance is slightly below the mean for classic patterns.

BOX 8.6 TRADING TRIANGLES

The ideal situation for trading triangles is a definite breakout, a high trading range within the triangle, an upward-sloping volume trend during the formation of the triangle, and especially a gap on the breakout. These patterns seem to work better with small-cap stocks in a rising market.

Triangles are plentiful. For example, the upward failure of a head-and-shoulders top before any break through the neckline is a form of an upward-breaking descending triangle. This is one likely reason that such head-and-shoulder top pattern failures are so profitable.

Although triangles are plentiful, their patterns suffer from many false and premature breakouts. This requires that a very strict breakout rule be used—either a wide filter or a number of closes outside the breakout zone. It also requires a close protective stop at the breakout level in case the breakout is false. Once these defensive levels have been exceeded and price is on its way, the trader can relax for a little while because the failure rate after a legitimate breakout is relatively low. Trailing stops should then be placed at each preceding minor reversal.

There are many old rules about when a breakout should occur within a triangle. Some, such as Murphy, say that one-half to two-thirds the distance from the base to the apex is appropriate. Others, such as Edwards and Magee, use the one-half to three-quarters rule. In fact, the breakout can occur at any time once the triangle has been defined by legitimate upper and lower converging trend lines. Edwards and Magee do point out that the longer the distance, the more likely the performance will be less, but this also is not necessarily true. The highest percentage performance does come from breakouts generally around 60%–70% of the distance from the base to the cradle. However, in symmetrical triangles, the best performance comes from late breakouts in the 73%–75% distance. Thus, the old rules are partially correct but not strictly so.

Generally, the volume trend during the formation of a triangle declines, but in the case of an upward breaking descending triangle, an ascending triangle, and a downward breaking symmetrical triangle, an upward-sloping volume trend gives better results. Declining volume is not a reason to disregard the pattern, however. Volume on the breakout seems more desirable in symmetrical triangles, but it cannot hurt in others. Gaps are better predictors of performance in the upward-breaking descending triangle and the downward-breaking symmetrical triangle, but they are not necessary.

An initial target for these patterns is calculated by adding the base distance—the vertical distance between the initial upper and lower reversal point prices—to the price where the breakout occurred. In an upward-breaking descending triangle, for example, this target is reached better than 67% of the time. Other triangles have relatively the same success rate—higher in upward trends than in downward trends. This is why a wide trading range is preferred within the triangle—it suggests a higher target price on the breakout.

Broadening Patterns

A broadening pattern exists when we take the standard rectangle pattern and draw the bound lines diverging from each other into the future rather than converging as in a standard triangle. As pictured in Figure 8.9, the price range is increasing during the broadening pattern, as opposed to the narrowing price range that is associated with the standard triangle patterns. The terms **megaphone**, **funnel**, **reverse triangle**, and **inverted triangle** all refer to broadening patterns. The broadening pattern also comes in many variations. One is similar to ascending and descending triangles in that one of the bounds is horizontal. The other bound then slopes away from the horizontal line either above or below. A final variation is the broadening wedge. This pattern is similar to a wedge pattern (see Figure 8.9) except the bounds trend in the same direction but diverge instead of converge as in a wedge. None of these variations seems to have any above-average performance statistics except the

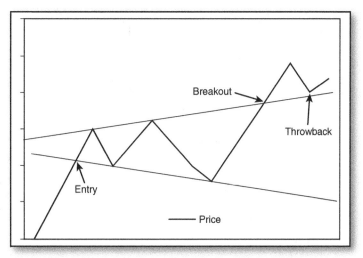

FIGURE 8.9 Broadening formation with breakout up

ascending broadening wedge, which has both bounds rising and diverging. Upward breakouts in this pattern rank 6 out of 23 in Bulkowski's scale and have failure rates at 2%, which is almost negligible.

Broadening formations are the least-useful patterns for a number of reasons. First, they are relatively rare in occurrence and are often difficult to identify. Second, and more important, they are difficult to profit from. Because the boundary trend lines are separating over time, the breakout lines are constantly moving away from each other. In an upward breaking broadening pattern, this means the upper breakout level is getting higher and higher along the upper trend line (refer to Figure 8.9). By getting higher and higher, not only is it using up much of any potential gain after a breakout, but it is moving farther from any realistic protective stop level, thus increasing the risk. Finally, the raw performance statistics show that performance of a broadening pattern is average at best, and its failure rate is above average. One of the most profitable patterns utilizing a broadening pattern, however, is when it is combined with a symmetrical triangle into a diamond top, which we discuss next.

Diamond Top One of the less frequent but profitable patterns is the diamond (see Figure 8.10). It consists of a combination of a broadening pattern and a symmetrical triangle and usually occurs at the top of a sharp upward rise in prices. It is rare at price bottoms.

Because it combines two types of triangles, the diamond is the most difficult to observe. Remember that to establish a trend line, two extreme points that a line can be drawn between must be identified. In a standard broadening formation, the upper trend line slopes upward and must, therefore, have two peaks—the latter higher than the former. Likewise, the lower trend line must have two troughs—the latter lower than the former—and each line must be formed at the same time as

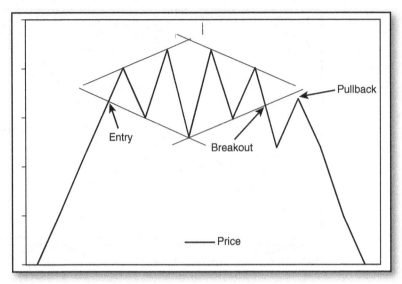

FIGURE 8.10 Diamond pattern with breakout down

the other. The first reversal point depends on the entry direction, of course, and because diamonds are mostly top formations, the entry direction is generally from below. This means that the first reversal point will be a peak. After that, the first trough will appear, then the next higher peak, and then the next lower trough. When trend lines have been drawn to connect these reversal points, we have a broadening formation. Now we must observe a symmetrical triangle immediately after the broadening formation to establish a diamond pattern. The trend lines in a symmetrical triangle converge, as in all standard triangles, and must have at least two peaks and troughs to establish each trend line. The first reversal peak and trough may be the last reversal points in the broadening formation or the next reversal points following the broadening formation. Often the trend lines in the symmetrical triangle will be parallel to the trend lines in the broadening pattern, but this is not a requirement.

Bulkowski's figures show that around 58% of the time, the preceding price action in a diamond top was a steeply rising trend. When this occurs, the odds increase that the breakout from the diamond will be downward and will be equally as steep, and 82% of the time, it will retrace the entire prior rise. These figures are only valid for downward breakouts from a top, which occur 67% of the time. Upward breakouts from a diamond top have a poor performance history and should be avoided. Thus, action should only be taken once the pattern has been identified and the downward breakout has occurred.

Diamond bottoms have the same configuration as diamond tops and are the best patterns that Bulkowski ranks. They are number 1 in performance when they fail and break down (about 31% of the time). Even when they break upward, their ranking is 8 out of 23.

As in most patterns, volume usually declines (67% of the time) during its formation, but declining volume is not necessary. Indeed, rising volume is a plus for performance after the breakout.

Pullbacks are common in diamond patterns, occurring more than 53% of the time. These pullbacks tend to detract from performance when they occur but are not that significant. The best combination is when downward breakout occurs on below-average breakout volume and no pullback. The failure rate is relatively low at 4%–10%. These low numbers equate, to some extent, with risk. Combined with the above-average median return, these numbers suggest that, although rare, when a diamond top is identified, it has an above-average chance of being profitable with minimum risk.

BOX 8.7 TRADING DIAMONDS

The diamond formation, once properly defined, tends to have a fast-moving price run on the breakout. Indeed, if the postbreakout price behavior is sluggish, the position should likely be closed or a close trailing stop placed near the current price. The price objective is usually the distance that the entry price traveled to reach the diamond. A steep entry is usually followed by a steep exit.

Wedge and Climax

A wedge pattern is a triangle pattern with both trend lines heading in the same direction. A rising wedge has both lines headed upward, with the lower bound rising more quickly than the upper bound, as pictured in Figure 8.11. The declining wedge has both lines headed downward, with the upward bound falling more quickly than the lower bound. The lines cross in the future, just as in a standard triangle, and the nomenclature for the crossover and height is the same.

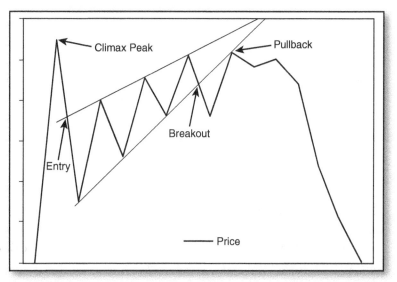

FIGURE 8.11   Rising wedge with breakout down from a climax peak

Rather than the rectangle as the basis for this formation as it is with standard triangles, consider a channel. A **channel** is two parallel trend lines either rising or declining. In the earlier discussion of channels, we noted that when the channel line, drawn parallel to the trend line through the opposite set of reversal points, begins to slope toward the trend line, it suggests that players are becoming less enthusiastic with the trend line direction. For example, in an upward-sloping channel, the channel line above the trend line connecting the downward reversal points begins as a line parallel to the upward trend line. If a later rally within the channel fails to reach the channel line, the new channel line through the new downward reversal and the last downward reversal will have a lesser slope than the underlying trend line, and if projected into the future, it will eventually meet the trend line. This new configuration of channel and trend line is a **rising wedge**. It suggests in the example that sellers have become a little more anxious than before, and by implication, that the trend line will soon be broken. Indeed, the statistics bear this out. Almost all declining wedges (92%) break out upward, and most rising wedges (69%) break out to the downside (Bulkowski, 2010).

Wedges are one of a few patterns that can be consolidation patterns against the prevailing trend, consolidation patterns with the trend, or topping patterns, especially when accompanying a climax. They occur more often during consolidations but are more dramatic after a climax.

Let us look at rising wedges first. Rising wedges occur either during a long downward price trend or after an upward climax. The ones that occur during a downtrend appear as weak rallies against the trend. As mentioned previously, they invariably break again to the downside and continue the downtrend. Declining wedges are almost the same pattern and occur under similar circumstances, only in the opposite direction.

A market climax occurs when prices accelerate. At these times, the underlying trend line is gradually adjusted at a steeper slope in line with the direction of prices. In an upward accelerated trend, the support reversal points occur at levels higher than the projected trend line and cause that trend line to be adjusted to a steeper slope. This can occur several times as prices accelerate upward. The climax itself usually comes on extremely high volume and a sharp reversal. After a climax has occurred and prices have settled down, invariably a "test" occurs that attempts to rally back through climax extreme peak. The pattern most often associated with the failure of that test—in other words, when the test fails to exceed the climax extreme or only exceeds by a small amount—is a rising wedge (refer to Figure 8.11). In the case of a climax low after a panic, the test wedge is the declining variety (see Figure 8.12).

At a climax peak, when the test is a rising wedge pattern, the odds are extremely high that the breakout will be downward. Because the emotion and commitment

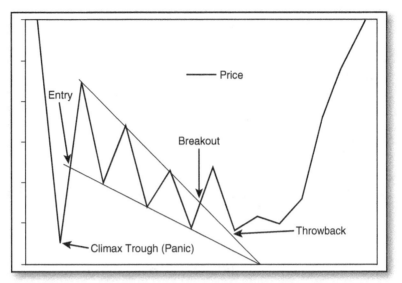

FIGURE 8.12 Declining wedge with breakout up from climax trough

have been exhausted at the climax peak and are unable to return during the test, the downward break in the wedge pattern is the sign of a longer-term downward reversal. Thus, the wedge is a reversal pattern, even though it may not occur at the actual climax peak high.

Other rising wedges can occur as a consolidation during a sustained downward trend and occasionally will end at the top of a weakening upward trend.

Because trend lines often converge in the same direction when a wedge is not present, Bulkowski requires that at least five reversal points be touched to qualify the pattern as a wedge. This means three points on one trend line and at least two on the other. Otherwise, the pattern is not accurately identified and may fail to show the results seen in actual wedge patterns.

Another characteristic of wedges, in both the consolidation and the reversal varieties, is declining volume during the formation of the wedge. Declining volume occurs in three-quarters of the formations, and when it does, the postperformance improves over those wedges with increasing volume. Breakout volume seems to be irrelevant to postperformance. Pullbacks and throwbacks have high odds of occurring and when present detract from subsequent performance.

The performance rank for wedges is in the lower quartile of all the other classic patterns, and its failure rate is considerably lower for upward breakouts (8%–11%) than for downward breakouts (15%–24%). The rising wedge with a downward breakout is the least reliable.

■ Patterns with Rounded Edges—Rounding and Head-and-Shoulders

The patterns we have considered up to this point have been defined by straight lines. When we begin to define patterns with curved lines, we become more indefinite than with using straight lines such as trend lines. This does not make the patterns any less useful, but it does make them more difficult to describe specifically.

Rounding Top, Rounding Bottom (Also "Saucer," "Bowl," or "Cup")

Rounding tops and bottoms are formed by price action that reverses slowly and gradually, rather differently from the spike with definite and sharp reversal characteristics. Volume in the bottoms seems to follow the same trend of lessening as prices gradually approach the bottom and increasing as they gradually turn upward again. In a rounding top, volume tends to follow the same pattern of lessening as prices decelerate and increasing as prices gradually turn down. Rounding usually takes time, and within its process, it has many minor up and down, short-term trends. Rounding is, thus, more conceptual than specific.

However, many formations depend on rounding for their description. The most famous is the "cup-and-handle" formation described in detail by O'Neil (1988) but referred to in many earlier publications. This formation, as shown in Figure 8.13, is a variation of the rounding bottom that shows a **lip** after the rise from the bottom and a small congestion area that reverses downward for a short while called a **handle**. The high of the lip establishes, in this type of rounding bottom, the resistance level to watch for an upward breakout. Sometimes the breakout never occurs, and prices keep declining in the handle, continuing to new lows. Traditionally, the cup-and-handle is considered to be a bottoming reversal pattern. However, Bulkowski has found that when it is a continuation pattern from an earlier low, it is much more reliable and profitable. It still only ranks 13 out of 23, despite its popularity.

Rounded bottoms are more common than rounded tops, but neither materializes often. They tend to be longer-term patterns, more easily identified in weekly or even monthly charts. They are reversal patterns, but they can also appear in long price consolidations. Shorter-term rounded formations, often called **scallops**, are usually

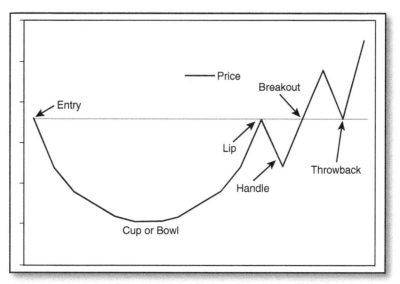

FIGURE 8.13 Cup or bowl and handle variety of a rounding bottom with breakout up

continuation patterns that are equally difficult to define. Rounded bottoms rank 5 out 23 in performance and have a low 5% failure rate. Tops have the same performance rank, when breaking downward, but a slightly higher failure rate of 9%–12%. They are difficult to recognize and often require weekly or monthly charts to identify. They are also difficult to trade. First, the breakout level is not easily defined, except in cup-and-handle patterns. Second, they are slow to develop and often fail to break out.

Head-and-Shoulders

The head-and-shoulders pattern is probably the most famous technical pattern. Its name is often used when ridiculing technical analysis, yet its profitability is high, relative to other patterns, and it is one of the few that the Lo, Mamaysky, and Wang (2000) study showed had statistical significance.

Head-and-shoulders is a complex pattern because it combines all three potential characteristics of a pattern: trend lines, support or resistance lines, and rounding. It is most often seen at a top or bottom, but it can occur in its normal state or as a failed formation in a consolidation. Mostly, it should be traded only after it has formed completely. Its complexity causes many impatient analysts to anticipate its formation and to act prematurely. Its performance and success rate are high, but only after it has formed completely and satisfied all its requirements. We describe the traits of a head-and-shoulders top. The bottom formation (see Figure 8.15) is the reverse in every way except where noted.

An uptrend, but not necessarily a long-term trend, precedes a head-and-shoulders top. Thus, as shown in Figure 8.14, the head-and-shoulders top pattern is entered from below. (The head-and-shoulders pattern can also occur within a consolidation

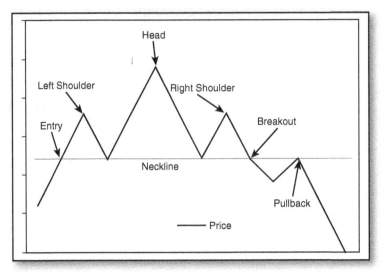

FIGURE 8.14 Head-and-shoulders top with breakout down

rather than at the end of a trend, but such occurrences are rare and more likely a series of triangles or a rectangle with a false downward breakout at the "head.")

The head-and-shoulders top pattern is a series of three well-defined peaks, either sharp or rounded. The second peak is higher than the first and third peak. This middle, higher peak is called the **head**. The first peak is called the **left shoulder**, and the third peak is called the **right shoulder**. Both the left and right shoulders must be lower than the head, but the two shoulders do not have to be the same height. In fact, a left shoulder peak slightly higher than the right shoulder peak adds a little to the postbreakout performance of a top formation. (A head-and-shoulders bottom is pictured in Figure 8.15. In the bottom pattern, a right shoulder low that is slightly lower than the left shoulder low adds to performance.)

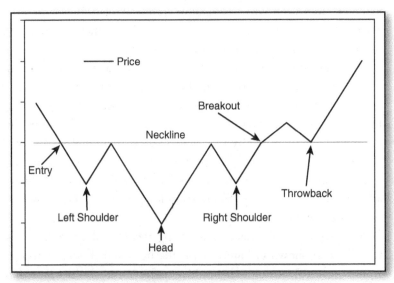

FIGURE 8.15 Head-and-shoulders bottom with breakout up

The peaks in the head-and-shoulders top formation are roughly equidistant from each other. The shoulders should appear roughly symmetrical about the head and should peak at roughly the same level. Symmetry is important and makes the formation more identifiable. Occasionally, more than two shoulders appear. These formations are called "complex head-and-shoulders" and have roughly the same performance and failure rates as the standard two-shoulder variety. As in the standard, the multiple shoulders appear symmetrically on both sides of the head. Rarely, a "two-headed" variety appears, and it, too, shows the same performance and failure rates as the standard. There is also the "unbalanced" version, as described by Edwards and Magee, but it is difficult to describe accurately and seems to fit only those formations that might be head-and-shoulders but cannot be formally categorized as such. The standard is the most common and the one to look for.

The bottoms between the peaks form a recognizable trend line. Technicians call this line the **neckline**. Although the neckline is often horizontal, as in a support line, it also can be down-ward or upward sloping. Indeed, there is some evidence that an upward-sloping neckline in a top formation produces better performance than the standard horizontal neckline. (In a bottom formation, the same rules hold except the neckline is now resistance rather than support. In a bottom formation, a downward-sloping neckline increases postbreakout performance over an upward-sloping neckline but not over the horizontal one.) Tilting the slope of the neckline to an extreme, however, destroys the head-and-shoulders pattern and its likely consequences.

Volume is usually highest on the rise into and at the peak of the left shoulder and decreases throughout the formation. This is not a requirement, however, because those formations with decreasing volume, although slightly less frequent, have a slight performance edge at tops. (Increasing volume has a slight edge in head-and-shoulders bottoms.) Higher volume on either shoulder does not affect performance at a top, but a bottom, higher volume on the right shoulder than on the left shoulder adds considerably to postbreakout performance.

Breakout and action signals occur when prices, after completing the right shoulder, break below the neckline. The breakout is a requirement for the formation. Second-guessing before completion of the pattern can be dangerous. Sometimes the right shoulder does not form completely, and prices fall short of breaking the neckline and rise to penetrate above the right shoulder peak. Not only is this a failure, but it also is an opportunity, provided the analyst had not anticipated a breakdown and acted prematurely. The head-and-shoulders failure of this type is profitable, according to Schwager (1996). The standard failure, however, is when prices break below the neckline and then reverse back upward through the right shoulder. This kind of failure is relatively rare.

The breakout often occurs on increased volume, but decreased volume is not a sign of an impending failure. It just occurs less frequently. Increasing volume on a bottom formation improves performance, whereas decreasing volume on the breakout from a top pattern increases performance.

Pullbacks or throwbacks are frequent—roughly 45%–63% for bottoms and 60%–67% for tops. In summary, the head-and-shoulders pattern—aside from being the best known, even among nontechnicians—is the most reliable and profitable of the classic formations.

The performance rank for the standard head-and-shoulders top is 1, the highest ranking possible. Complex tops have a rank of 3, standard bottoms a rank of 7, and complex bottoms a rank of 9. Both top and bottom patterns, therefore, are high on the list of performance.

We have seen in most other patterns that when a pullback or throwback occurs, the comparative performance suffers. This is also true in head-and-shoulders patterns. The failure rates for both top and bottom formations are low. Only 3%–4% failed a 5% gain or more from tops and bottoms. In short, the head-and-shoulders formation has a high rate of reliability as well as profitability.

BOX 8.9 TRADING HEAD-AND-SHOULDERS PATTERNS

Once a pattern has been observed using the preceding descriptive features, the neckline becomes the most important factor. The neckline is where the breakout level resides. Never should one act in anticipation of a break through the neckline. The risk of failure is too great, and as we have seen with the upward break of a descending triangle, the strongest upward formation, the rise from descending peaks and a flat neckline, can be substantial. This is equally true with head-and-shoulders bottom formations. The ascending triangle with a breakout down is also a powerful formation. Thus, breakout stops should be placed outside the right shoulder reversal point. Once the breakout is triggered, the risk of failure declines substantially. If the breakout is through the neckline, use the standard statistics as a guide, but if the breakout is a failed head-and-shoulders through the right shoulder extreme, use the appropriate triangle statistics as a guide.

The price target for a head-and-shoulders pattern is relatively accurate. It is calculated like the others by taking the height of the formation and projecting it up or down from the breakout price. The height is measured by drawing a vertical line from the peak of the head to where it intersects the neckline and measuring the number of points between the two. This holds for flat as well as sloping necklines.

Shorter Continuation Trading Patterns—Flags and Pennants (Also "Half-Mast Formation")

For efficient use of trading capital, consider trading with flags and pennants. They are frequent formations with extremely rapid and relatively reliable outcomes. After a breakout in either direction or either pattern, prices usually run immediately, having few pullbacks or throwbacks and low rates of failure. Some successful traders use only flags and pennants because of these advantages. Flags and pennants are really variations of the same formation. The flag is a short channel that usually slopes in the opposite direction from the trend. The pennant is a short triangle that does the same. Both of these patterns are pictured in Figure 8.16.

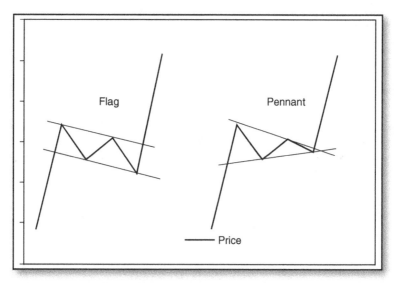

FIGURE 8.16 Flag and pennant in upward trend

Both flags and pennants are preceded by a steep, sharp price trend, best at 45 degrees rather than straight up. Flags preceded by a rise of 90% or more have almost a zero failure rate and an average return of 69%. This variety is the best of all chart patterns. Two parallel trend lines in a small channel that resembles a flag form the pattern, and the slope of the channel can be in any direction, but most commonly the best performance comes when it slopes away from the preceding trend. Flag formations occur over a short period—usually a few days to a few weeks; the best flag is less than 15 days. Volume usually declines throughout the formation of the flag. In fact, this downward trend in volume is found in almost four out of every five flags that occur.

The pennant pattern is the same as the flag except that the trend lines converge, forming a miniature triangle, instead of being parallel. The direction of the formation is usually opposite from that of the immediately preceding price trend, but in stronger moves, it can be horizontal or even trending in the same direction as the underlying trend. Pennants differ from wedges in that they are shorter in time and require a sharp move preceding them. Wedges tend to be longer-term patterns. Falling volume throughout the formation is even more common with pennants; 90% of pennants are characterized by a downward trend in volume.

Two types of failures can occur. First, a breakout in the opposite direction from the previous trend can occur. Second, a failure can occur after breakout. Because a flag or a pennant is usually a continuation formation, the breakout should be expected in the direction of the preceding trend, provided it is steep and sharp. When the breakout goes opposite to that trend, the failure invariably returns to the earlier trend, but only after a few heart palpitations have occurred first and a few protective stops have been triggered.

FIGURE 8.17 The measured rule (X—U.S. Steel, daily: June 4–December 2, 2013)

Long-Term Bar Chart Patterns with the Best Performance and the Lowest Risk of Failure

We have selected several patterns to highlight based on their combination of high gains and minimum failure rates. Other patterns can also be successful if monitored closely, but the "edge" appears to be in these patterns.

TABLE 8.1	Comparative 3-Month Results in Classic Bar Chart Patterns				
	Overall Performance	Failure to Reach 5%	Average Performance	Tendency to Retrace	Reaches Target Price
High and tight flag, break up	1 / 23	0%	69%	54%	90%
Head-and-shoulders top, complex, break down	3 / 21	4%	23%	67%	53%
Head-and-shoulders top, break down	1 / 21	4%	22%	50%	55%
Triangle, descending, break up	5 / 23	7%	47%	37%	84%
Diamond bottom, break down	1 / 21	10%	21%	71%	63%
Diamond top, break down	7 / 21	6%	21%	57%	76%
Rectangle bottom, break up	11 / 21	10%	46%	53%	85%

Source: Bulkowski (www.thepatternsite.com)

According to Bulkowski (2015), the best-performing patterns, considering gain and risk, are the high-and-tight upward breaking flag, the head-and-shoulders top, top islands breaking down, and upward breaking descending triangles. A summary of these patterns is shown in Table 8.1.

■ Conclusion

In summary, the profitable use of chart patterns is not easy. The potential problems with recognizing and acting upon chart patterns that we have discussed in this chapter highlight the need to know thoroughly what we are doing. There are many variables in price behavior—mostly human—and being human ourselves and subject to the same biases, we must be adaptable and recognize that chart patterns are flexible.

It is unlikely that researchers will ever be able to prove definitively that patterns exist because the mathematics are so complicated and because the marketplace is always changing. In addition, many different patterns have been recognized, and, right or wrong, they have been described in the literature with nothing more than anecdotal evidence as to their reliability. If you see a pattern described with no background statistical evidence as to its usefulness, it is best not to bother with it. Today, most writers describing patterns will give some realistic evidence. Although this evidence might be flawed, it at least shows that it has been the subject of some serious study and, thus, is not merely a superstition.

The most reasonable approach for any chart reader is to take the classic patterns described in this chapter and become experienced in their use. Although the performance of these patterns will differ with different securities and with different trends in the general market, the behaviors of these patterns have remained relatively consistent for more than 100 years. We have discussed general attributes of patterns that in several studies show promise, but the analyst must always adjust parameters to fit the peculiarities of the security being analyzed. Profitable chart pattern analysis is the result of determined study.

■ References

Bulkowski, Thomas N. *Encyclopedia of Chart Patterns*. 2nd ed. New York, NY: John Wiley & Sons, Inc., 2005.

Bulkowski, Thomas N. *Trading Classic Chart Patterns*. New York, NY: John Wiley & Sons, Inc., 2002.

Bulkowski, Thomas N. "Bulkowski's Free Pattern Research," http://www.thepatternsite.com, 2010.

Bulkowski, Thomas N. www.thepatternsite.com/bestpatterns.html, accessed 2015.

Burnham, Terry. *Mean Markets and Lizard Brains*. Hoboken, NJ: John Wiley & Sons, Inc., 2005.

Edwards, Robert, John Magee, and W.H.C. Bassetti. *Techincal Analysis of Stock Trends*. 9th ed. Boca Raton, FL: St. Lucie Press, 2007.

Hasanhodzic, Jasmina, Andrew W. Lo, and Emanuele Viola. "Is it Real, or Is it Randomized?" A Financial Turing Test." Unpublished manuscript, 2010 (available at http://web.mit.edu/alo/www/papers/arorassrn.pdf).

Johnson, Spencer. *Who Moved My Cheese?* New York, NY: Penguin Putnam, 1998.

Kahneman, D. and A. Tversky. "Prospect Theory: An Analysis of Decision Under Risk." *Econometrica* 47 (1979): 263–291.

Kahneman, D. "Variants of Uncertainty." In *Judgment Under Uncertainty: Heuristics and Biases* (512), D. Kahneman, P. Slovic, and A. Tversky, eds. Cambridge University Press, Cambridge, 1982.

Levy, Robert A. "Predictive Significance of Five Point Chart Patterns." *Journal of Business* 44, no. 3 (1971): 316–323.

Lo, Andrew W. and Craig MacKinlay. "Stock Market Prices Do Not Follow Random Walks: Evidence from a Simple Specification Test." *Review of Financial Studies* 1 (1988): 41–66.

Lo, Andrew W., Harry Mamaysky, and Jiang Wang. "Foundations of Technical Analysis: Computational Algorithms, Statistical Inference, and Empirical Implementation." *Journal of Finance* 55 (2000): 4.

Merrill, Arthur A. *Behavior of Prices on Wall Street*. Published privately by the author, 1997.

Merrill, Arthur A. *Filtered Waves*. Published privately by the author, 1997.

O'Neil, William J. *How to Make Money in Stocks*. 3rd ed. (2002). New York, NY: McGraw-Hill, 1988.

Schabacker, R. *Stock Market Theory and Practice*. New York, NY: BV.C. Forbes Publishing Company, 1930.

Schwager, Jack D. *Schwager on Futures: Technical Analysis*. New York, NY: John Wiley & Sons, Inc., 1996.

Schwager, Jack D. *Technical Analysis*. New York, NY: John Wiley & Sons, Inc., 1996.

Skinner, B.F. "Superstition in the Pigeon." *Journal of Experimental Psychology* 38 (1947): 168–172.

THEORY AND ANALYSIS

CHAPTER 9

Short-Term Patterns

From Charles D. Kirkpatrick II and Julie R. Dahlquist, *Technical Analysis: The Complete Resource for Financial Market Technicians*, 3rd Edition (Old Tappan, New Jersey: Pearson Education, Inc., 2016), Chapter 17.

Learning Objective Statements

■ Identify short-term patterns that can be used as a tool to identify reversals in longer-term trends
■ Recognize the types of gaps that occur on price charts
■ Explain the significance of various types of gaps
■ Compare and analyze wide-range days and narrow-range days to identify their implications for volatility
■ Describe and interpret the most common candlestick patterns

We now turn our attention to short-term patterns. In this chapter, our focus is on short-term patterns on bar charts and candlestick charts. These patterns concentrate on the configuration and characteristics of individual bars, such as the height of the bar and the position of opening and closing prices on the bar. Some patterns also compare one period's bar with the preceding bar. Despite what their title suggests, short-term patterns are not limited to a particular short-term period, like one day. In this instance, "short-term" means a small number of bars. For example, on a daily bar chart, short-term patterns may form from one or two days of trading data, but on an hourly bar chart, a two-bar short-term pattern would include two hours' worth of trading data.

Although the longer-term patterns we have considered can be useful by themselves, they occur less frequently than shorter-term patterns. On the other hand, the shorter-term patterns we consider in this chapter are not useful by themselves but are common. Why do short-term patterns occur more frequently than longer-term patterns? Think of a common bar chart; four pieces of data are represented on each bar: an open, close, high, and low. With only four pieces of information, the number of various combinations in which these variables can occur is small. Even though stretching out the pattern to several bars increases the number of possible combinations, the number is still relatively small, and these combinations occur frequently.

Unfortunately, frequent patterns often give false signals. Although most market turning points include one or more of the short-term patterns covered in this chapter, these same patterns also occur at places where a reversal fails to follow. As Schwager (1996) states when referring to the one-day reversal pattern, it "successfully call(s) 100 out of every ten highs" (p. 89). Like Schwager, many others have been skeptical about the validity of short-term patterns. Just how useful and effective are they? Although some empirical tests suggest that these short-term patterns are not effective, many of the tests have covered longer testing periods than would be seen in practice. In most successful tests, short-term pattern entry signals are closed either at the close of the same day, the opening of the next day, the first profitable opening (called the **bailout** by Larry Williams), or the first profitable closing, which usually is only a few days later, barring the position first being stopped out. The ability to test over these short periods requires high-frequency data on a tick-to-tick basis and is usually beyond the capability of the normal investor or academic.

Nevertheless, once fully understood, short-term patterns are useful not only for trading but also for entering and exiting longer-term positions at more favorable prices. Although the average investor would not usually have the time or computer equipment and data feed to watch for short-term patterns, the professional trader certainly has the ability to watch intraday price behavior and can improve job performance and profits by understanding the nature of short-term patterns.

The basis for short-term patterns is to anticipate a sudden move, similar to the breakout concept in larger patterns, to take advantage of a period when prices have reached an emotion extreme, or to enter into a trend at an advantageous price as on a pullback or throwback. The methods usually have what is called a **setup**. A setup occurs when certain known factors needed to establish the pattern have occurred, and the trader is waiting for the action signal to occur. In larger charts, we have seen this concept in patterns. When the pattern, such as a triangle, forms, the setup is the pattern formation. If this pattern formation does not abide by the rules of triangle formations during its creation, it is not a setup, and we ignore it. If it does form correctly, we wait for the breakout, which is the action signal. Traders use the short-term patterns in the same manner, but over shorter time horizons, and they use tighter stops and exit signals.

Because short-term patterns are relatively frequent and usually depend on the previous trend as well as other factors, the prior trend must be known before short-term patterns can be used. A top pattern in a downward trend is obviously meaningless, for instance, and, thus, all top patterns can be disregarded from consideration during a declining trend. This leaves only bottoming patterns to consider during a downward trend. Also, a short-term reversal pattern should only be considered necessary when prices are at some kind of support level, resistance level, or trend line. Whenever many bits of evidence occur at a particular price and time, it is called a **cluster** of evidence. Once a cluster of evidence begins to form, the analyst should begin looking for a short-term pattern. It then can be useful in signaling when and where to act as well as what the price risk might be.

Short-term patterns can also be used to determine when upward or downward momentum is slowing. Remember that instead of using a momentum signal for action, using short-term patterns can often signal more precisely when to act and what risk exists once momentum begins to slow.

Although short-term patterns are usually reversal patterns, they can be used as continuation patterns in corrections within a trend. For example, in a strong upward trend, when the price corrects or retraces in a normal manner and a cluster of evidence forms that indicates the earlier, longer trend may soon continue, a short-term bottom reversal or continuation pattern may signal when to act. Usually, however, short-term patterns are best when they occur right at a peak or trough. Minimum action should be taken, however, unless there is a cluster of evidence that a longer-term reversal is due or that a strong trend is due to continue. For example, in an uptrend, if a price is near previous resistance, under but close to an important moving average, and has reached a price target, a short-term reversal top pattern is likely valid and worth acting upon. If a short-term reversal pattern of any kind occurs without supporting evidence, it might or might not signal an actual price reversal; it might simply signal that a slight consolidation period is next.

Short-term patterns are also the first sign that a reversal is nearing. They act quickly, often occurring on the actual peak or trough day. As such, they lead most other patterns, which take time and further price action to develop. In a head-and-shoulders top pattern, for example, the analyst must wait for the actual breakout below the neckline before acting, but a short-term reversal pattern might have already indicated a potential reversal right at the top of the head.

In experimenting with short-term patterns, the technical analyst should consider several variables:

- The more complex the pattern, the less frequently it is going to occur. Some analysts have libraries of hundreds of patterns they have found useful in the past and through experimentation and use a computer-screening program that will pump out all the relevant patterns before each trading day. This gives them an edge but is impractical for most traders.

- The relationship between bars in a pattern need not be just a matter of the position of the high, low, open, and close to each other. The relation can be a proportional one rather than an exact one (Harris, 2000) where, for example, the close is in the lower 33% of the trading range, or the range that is three bars earlier is one-half the range of the last bar.

- The pattern may be split between two time periods, whereby one pattern appears at one time, and at some predetermined time later, another pattern must appear.

- The entry may be delayed by some predetermined time.

- The pattern may relate to another market entirely, whereby, for example, a pattern in the bond market may give a signal in the stock market or a currency.

These variables make the search for reliable patterns exceedingly complex and likely beyond necessity. The old principle of keeping things simple should be applied to any kind of pattern recognition search.

We divide the types of patterns into traditional bar chart patterns and candlestick patterns. Candlestick patterns portray the raw data of open, close, high, and low differently than a bar chart, but their patterns are similar to bar chart patterns. Part of the appeal of candlestick charts is not so much the patterns but the visual ease with which the analyst can "see" intraday pressures on price and the price trend. They also have peculiar but memorable names for specific patterns that make them engaging.

As in all patterns, experience will separate the winners from the losers. Anyone using such patterns should record in a notebook the successes and failures from interpreting short-term patterns. Reviewing this recording periodically will help the investor develop a better "feel" of his ability to act profitably and learn where mistakes more frequently occur. Every trading vehicle has its own "personality." Success is often a function of understanding the peculiarities of the trading vehicle most commonly traded.

■ Pattern Construction and Determination

The principal data used in short-term patterns—both traditional and candlestick, regardless of bar time—is open, close, high, and low. The opening price is traditionally considered the price established from any news, emotion, anticipation, or mechanical signals that have built up overnight. Most professional day traders, scalpers, and even swing traders prefer to avoid it. They wait for some action—a gap or opening range—to take place before judging the tone of the market.

Because the closing price is the final price of the day and the one at which most margin accounts are valued, it is like a summary of the bar's activity. If the close is up, the majority and most recent action was positive; if the close is down, the majority and most recent price action was to the downside. Professionals use it as a benchmark with which to compare the next day's price action. Most people reading the financial news remember and use it to value their accounts. The closing price becomes a benchmark for future action, both long and short term. Some traders consider it the most important price of the day, even though it is somewhat arbitrary.

The high is the upper extreme reached by buyers during the bar and is, thus, a measure of buying ability and enthusiasm. On the other hand, the low is the lower extreme reached by sellers during the bar and is, thus, a measure of selling ability and fear.

The configuration, length of the bar, position on the bar, preceding bar data, and price distance between each determine the pattern. As you might guess, there is a multitude of potential combinations, and all have been investigated for ways to profit. We present next just a few of the large array of short-term patterns that have shown promise in the past.

■ Traditional Short-Term Patterns

Let us look at some of the short-term patterns and their trading implications. These are patterns in use today that by themselves are warnings, at best, but not necessarily action patterns, that should be followed without a cluster of other evidence. You will notice that none of the patterns includes moving averages. Over short time periods, especially when the period is interrupted by inactivity, moving averages are not reliable. For example, when using five-minute data, the only moving average with any value would be short because the period from one day to the next is interrupted by a long period overnight when no trading activity occurs. In 24-hour markets, short-term moving averages have more value because the markets are open continuously.

Gaps

Gaps occur when either the low for the current bar is above the high for the previous bar or the high for the current bar is lower than the low of the previous bar. Figure 9.1 pictures a gap down. The "hole" or "void" created in the price history is a "price range at which no shares changed hands" (Edwards and Magee, 2007). A price gap might or might not have significance. We have seen them before in analyzing break-outs from classic patterns, trend lines, and support or resistance zones, and in those instances, the gaps were demonstrating the beginning of a new trend. However, gap types differ based on the context in which they occur. Some are meaningful, and others can be disregarded.

Gaps often do not occur in market averages that are not themselves traded. For example, the day following Saddam Hussein's capture on December 13, 2003, a majority of stocks opened strongly upward on gaps, while the Dow Jones Industrial Average showed an opening price roughly the same as that at the close of the previous day and then rose as the prices of the component stocks gradually opened. No gap existed in the DJIA because it is an average, not a security. On the other hand, the DJIA future showed a gap because it is a traded security.

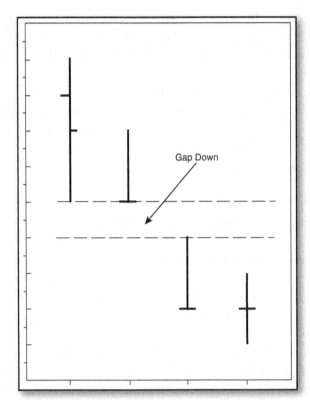

FIGURE 9.1　A gap down

Breakaway (or Breakout) Gaps　The most profitable gaps are those that occur at
the beginning of a trend, called **breakaway gaps**. We have seen these before when
prices suddenly break through a formation boundary and a major change in trend
direction begins. Breakaway gaps signal that a pattern is completed and a boundary
penetrated. The size of the gap—the space between the two extremes in which no
activity occurs—appears to be proportional to the strength of the subsequent price
move. Heavy volume usually accompanies upward gaps but not necessarily downward gaps. The best manner of trading breakaway gaps is to wait a short while for
the initial fading or profit-taking by the professionals to see if the gap is filled and, if
not, to enter in the direction of the gap with a stop at the point where the gap would
be filled. If the gap is filled immediately, a stop and reverse might be appropriate
because a sudden failure in a gap is often followed by a large move in the opposite
direction from the gap direction, similar to a Specialist's Breakout.

　　David Landry (2003) suggests a method of mechanizing the breakaway gap, known
as the "explosion gap pivot." A reversal point, often called a **pivot**, establishes not
only where prices have reversed direction but also where supply and resistance are
likely to occur in the future.[1] In Landry's method, a pivot low is the low of a bar that

---

[1] This reversal "pivot" should not be confused with the "pivot point" used in intraday trading for
anticipating potential support and resistance levels.

is surrounded on both sides by a bar with a higher low, as shown in Figure 9.2. This establishes a reversal point. Requirements that are more restrictive can be placed on the pivot point; for example, higher lows may be required for two or more bars on either side of the pivot point. For Landry's method, however, one on both sides is sufficient.

We know that a breakaway gap can be a false gap and that if it is "filled," the odds of it being false increase. Thus, we want a breakaway gap to establish a new high, for at least the past 20 days, and for the subsequent retracement not to fill the gap. If either of these requirements is not met, the gap is ignored. When the retracement does occur, eventually it will create a pivot low above the lower edge of the gap. Once this pivot low occurs, a buy entry stop is placed above the high of the next bar from the pivot low (the one that establishes the pivot), and a protective stop is placed just above the gap lower edge (or Landry suggests just below the pivot low). If the gap is then filled, the protective stop will exit the position. Occasionally, the pivot low will be penetrated again, but as long as the gap is not filled, the position should be kept. The reverse configuration is equally applicable to downward break-away gaps.

Opening Gap   When the opening price for the day is outside the range of the previous day, it is called an **opening gap**. After the opening, prices might continue in the direction of the gap, and the gap becomes a breakaway gap, or prices might retrace from the opening and fill the gap. Figure 9.3 shows an opening gap to the downside,

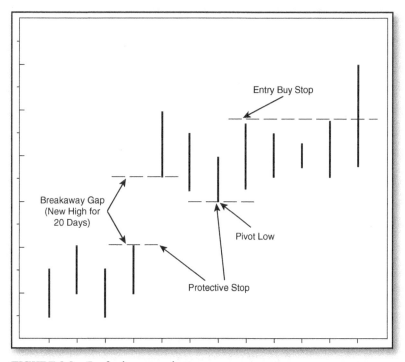

FIGURE 9.2   Explosion gap pivot

with prices retracing and filling the gap during the day. This type of pattern is sometimes useful in determining a short-term trend reversal. The history of opening gaps in index futures suggests that they should be "faded" (or sold into) on large upward openings because they most often "fill" (retrace through the price vacuum) during the day. In downward opening gaps, a fill is not as common (Kaufman, 1998). In individual stock issues and commodities, a fill is a sign of weakness and should not occur in a breakaway gap. If the gap is not filled, usually within the first half hour, the odds of the trend continuing in the direction of the gap increase.

One potential way to profit from an opening gap is to watch the first three five-minute bars (a three-bar range) and determine the high and low of this range. A breakout of that range in the direction of the gap often indicates that the trend will continue in the gap direction; a breakout that moves in the direction of filling the gap will often continue to fill the gap. A danger is that the first run from the gap can last longer than the three bars. The three-bar range must, therefore, be obvious, not a continued run in the gap direction. In addition, the breakout from the three-bar gap range in the direction of the gap may be false. A tight stop is necessary, or a wait for a pullback or throwback from the breakout, a narrow range bar break, or even a small cup and handle.

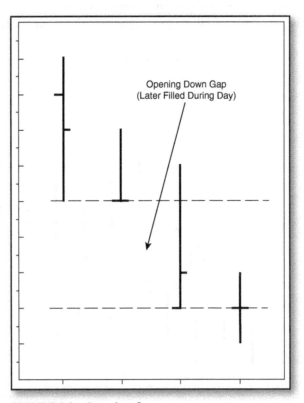

Opening Down Gap
(Later Filled During Day)

FIGURE 9.3 Opening down gap

If the price breaks the three-bar range in the other direction toward the fill, the previous day's close, the fill line, will likely be the target. A bounce between the fill line and the range breakout line suggests that the longer-term move will be in the direction of the fill, a reversal of the gap. On the other hand, if the prices after a range break in the direction of the fill turn and retest the outer extreme of the three-bar range, the odds increase that the longer-term move will be in the direction of the gap.

Runaway Gaps (or Measuring Gaps) Gaps that occur along a trend are called **runaway gaps**. They can appear in strong trends that have few minor corrections and just keep rising or declining without retracements or other interruptions. They are also called **measuring gaps** because, like pennants and flags, they often occur at about the middle of a price run, and, thus, the initial distance to them can be projected above them for a target price. An upward runaway gap occurs on average 43% of the distance from the trend beginning and the eventual peak, whereas a downward gap occurs on average 57% of the distance (Bulkowski, 2010).

Exhaustion Gaps Exhaustion gaps occur at the end of moves but are not recognized at the time because they have the same characteristics as runaway gaps. If a gap is later closed, it is likely an exhaustion gap. These gaps appear when a strong trend has reached a point at which greed or fear has reached its apex. Usually they represent latecomers to the trend who are anxious to jump on or jump off. They can occur on light volume but more often occur on heavy volume.

The sign that such gaps are not runaway gaps is an immediate fill within a few bars of the gap. Remember that a runaway gap often occurs midstream in a price run. Prices should not immediately reverse and fill a gap unless the end of the run is approaching. Exhaustion gaps occur at the end of a move and signal a potential trend reversal. Usually more evidence of an exhaustion gap is necessary before an action signal can be justified. Sometimes prices reverse immediately, and sometimes they enter a congestion area.

Other Minor Gaps Common gaps are those that occur frequently in illiquid trading vehicles, are small in relation to the price of the vehicle, or appear in short-term trading data. They are of no consequence. Pattern gaps occasionally appear within the formation of larger patterns, and generally they are filled. Their only significance is to suggest that a congestion area is forming. Ex-dividend gaps sometimes occur in stock prices when the dividend is paid and the stock price is adjusted the following day. These have no significance and must not be misinterpreted. Often gaps occur in 24-hour futures trading when one market closes and another opens, especially if one market is electronic and the other open outcry. These are called **suspension gaps** and are also meaningless unless they occur as one of the four principal gaps described previously.

Figure 9.4 contains daily bar charts for Apple Computer (AAPL) for September 2009 through May 2010. What actions might we have taken in this stock, given our knowledge of classic patterns and gaps? Each paragraph number that follows corresponds to a number on Figure 9.4.

1. First we see a small pennant formation with an upward breakout at $167.28. We buy the stock on the breakout. Because we don't have the past history, we can't at this point make a measured move projection of the eventual target, and we decide to just hold the stock with a protective stop below the pennant's lower bound at $164.11. Upward gap1 and gap2 appear next. We use them to place trailing stops as the price progresses upward. The pivot low after the gap1 is the first trailing stop at $169.70. We now have a locked-in profit even if the stop is triggered. Gap2 is a runaway gap. A runaway gap should not retrace back into the gap, or it is not a runaway. We, thus, raise the trailing stop to the upper edge of the gap at $177.88. Because this is a runaway gap, we can now project the target with the measured move method. We do this by measuring the price difference between the move beginning ($167.28) and the midpoint in the gap ($176.77). This $9.49 we add to the gap2 midpoint to arrive at an estimated objective of $176.77 + $9.49 = $186.26. This price is reached two days later, at which point we can sell or hang on with a close trailing stop so we don't lose the gain we have already achieved. If we sell at the target price, we will have profited by $18.97, about 11.3% in nine days.

2. The price then goes into a flag pattern, and when it breaks out at $187.30, we buy it again. This breakout is accompanied by gap3, which is later filled. We place the protective stop at the low price of the flag at $180.70.

3. Gap4 occurs and has the initial appearance of a breakout or runaway gap. In neither case should prices fill such a gap, so we move our stop to the upper limit of gap4 at $197.85.

4. Our trailing stop is triggered by an unexpected price decline that negates the earlier interpretation of gap4. We profit by $10.55.

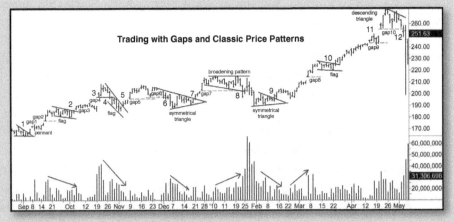

FIGURE 9.4   Case Study: Apple Computer

5. The price then forms a downward flag pattern, and volume confirms as it declines with price. The break upward from the flag triggers another buy at $190.73. This is followed by gap5, another likely runaway gap. The measured move projection from this gap is $200.73, which is reached on the day following gap5. We can sell at this level and reap another gain, this time of $10.00.

6. Had we not sold at the target price, we still would have placed a trailing stop at the upper level of gap5 at $196.26 and sold the stock on the retracement. We might also have sold the stock short on the trailing stop because the filling of what's thought to be a runaway gap is often an exhaustion gap and, therefore, a price trend reversal.

7. Whether we sold the stock short or not, the upward breakout from a symmetrical triangle would require another entry buy at $196.05. Following that triangle, breakout gap7 forms. This also has the appearance of a runaway gap (strong price move closing near high on increased volume), and we move a trailing stop from below the triangle to the upper edge of the gap at $203.35. We also calculate the measured move target of $209.68, which is reached two days later. If we sell at the target, we achieve on the trade a profit of $13.63.

8. If we don't sell at the target, we certainly are forced to sell when the price breaks below our trailing stop at the upper bound of gap7. This breakout is not only through the gap but also through the lower bound of a broadening pattern. Indeed, with this combination, we will short the stock at the breakout price of $203.35 and place a protective stop at the upper bound of the broadening pattern at $215.55. Following the breakout down, the price rallies in a pullback to the breakdown level but fails to penetrate back through it on the upside. However, it also fails to continue downward after the pullback and instead forms a symmetrical triangle. We place a buy stop each day along the upper bound of the triangle as our trailing stop.

9. We get stopped out with the trailing stop at $196.60, and we buy the stock on the basis of the triangle pattern confirmed with declining volume. We place a protective stop at the cradle of the triangle where the two bounds meet at $189.48 in case the breakout is false. Indeed, the price throws back shortly after the breakout but doesn't penetrate the cradle, and we remain long the stock. Gap8 comes after a healthy rise in the stock price. This also has the appearance of a runaway gap (high volume, large price move), and we move our trailing stop to the upper bound of the gap at $219.70. The measured move target from this runaway gap is $234.02. It is reached 18 days later.

10. We could sell at the target price, but before the target is reached, a flag pattern formed. We move our trailing stop up to the lower edge of the flag at $220.15 to protect our profit. A flag pattern is also a measured pattern that will give an additional price target. The calculation in this instance is to take the high point in the flag at $227.73 minus the starting price of the move ($196.60) for an estimated price distance of $31.13 that we add to the level at which the price breaks out of the flat ($224.64). But prices broke upward from the flag and, thus, projected $31.13 to a target of $255.77, our new target.

11. Our price target is reached 21 trading days after the upward breakout from the flag pattern on a large upward gap (gap10). There was a small gap9 preceding gap10 and a few others along the way. Each of these gaps failed to show the characteristics of a runaway gap and were, thus, ignored. But gap10, aside from reaching our objective, was substantial and also likely a runaway gap, just because of the size of the gap compared with others. If we don't sell at the target price, we at least move the trailing stop to the upper level of the gap at $255.73.

12. As it turns out, gap10 was an exhaustion gap—something that can only be recognized in retrospect. However, we were stopped out of our trade at the trailing stop and perhaps went short on the exhaustion gap breakdown because this type of breakdown often indicates a trend reversal. That the exhaustion gap occurred at the price target from the earlier flag formation confirmed the likelihood of a trend reversal. The sell stop produced a profit of $59.13, a 30% gain, in less than 3 months.

The preceding example shows what can be done with just technical analysis alone. We did not act on any news or outside market behavior. We simply watched the price very closely. Stops were an important part of our strategy. If we had not moved stops when we did, we would have suffered at the upward breakout from the symmetrical triangle and from the failure of gap10. Risk control is sometimes more important than entry technique. Technical analysis takes knowledge, patience, and close watching of price action, but profits can be made.

Spike (or Wide-Range or Large-Range Bar)

Spikes are similar to gaps except that the empty space associated with a gap is a solid line (in a bar chart). Should a breakaway gap occur intraday, for example, the daily bar would not show the discontinuity from the gap but instead would show a long bar. The importance of a spike, as in a gap, depends on the context surrounding it. A spike can occur on a breakout from a formation, midpoint in a strong, accelerating trend, and as the final reversal day at the end of a trend. In the earlier discussion of breakouts, we demonstrated the Specialist Breakout. This is often a spike because it usually occurs intraday. At the ends of trends when either gross enthusiasm or panic appears, the last few bars are often spikes. At the end of an accelerated trend, the last bar within the trend is often a spike called a **climax** (see Figure 9.5). Thus, spikes can represent the beginning or the end of a trend. On the other hand, some stocks and commodities, especially those awaiting a news announcement, will have wide-range bars that subside almost immediately within the next few days with little net change in trend direction. This behavior is generally associated with a stock or commodity that will not follow standard technical rules.

Dead Cat Bounce (DCB)

"Dead Cat Bounce" is a graceless term for a failed rally after a sharp decline. Although the term has been used for many years on Wall Street and in Chicago, it was probably first used in print either in a 1985 *Financial Times* article by reporter Chris Sherwell in a comment on the sharp decline in the Singapore stock market or by Raymond Devoe Jr., research analyst and professional cynic, who advocated using a bumper sticker "Beware the Dead Cat Bounce" in 1986.

The DCB is most profitable and more easily recognized after a large downward breakaway gap or downward breakaway spike. The sudden downward motion is

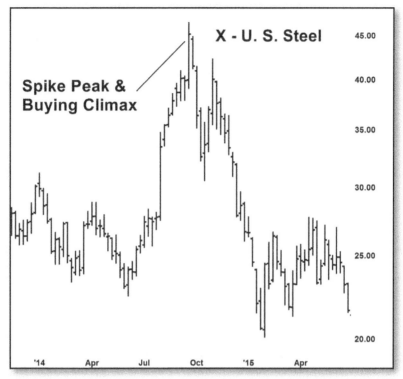

FIGURE 9.5 Spike peak and buying climax (X—U.S. Steel, weekly: November 8, 2013– June 26, 2015)

called an **event decline** because it usually occurs on an event such as a bad news announcement. It lasts just a few days (average of seven) and usually begins a longer-term downward price trend. The DCB's characteristics include a short rally of several days up to two weeks following the initial bottom from the sharp initial news event sell-off. Ideally, the rally should follow an event decline of more than 20%. Normally, the larger the first decline, the higher the bounce. A DCB is shown in Figure 9.6 of Hewlett Packard (HPQ). The "bounce" comes from bargain hunters and bottom-fishing traders who are second-guessing when the actual bottom will take place. It gathers momentum from short covering and momentum signals. The buyers are usually wrong. In more than 67% of DCBs (Bulkowski, 2010), the price continues to lower after the DCB and breaks the earlier news event low an average of 18%. The second decline in a DCB is characteristically less intense but equally deceiving. It also tends to be accompanied by much lower volume. Not all event declines include a DCB.

To trade the DCB, the event decline must first be recognized. This is usually easy because almost every day, somewhere, some bad news comes out about a company or commodity. Wait for the initial sell-off volume to decline and then look for a rally on lesser volume, sometimes back as far as the lower edge of the breakaway gap, and lasting only a few days. If the downward rush occurred as a spike rather than gap, look into the intraday trading to see where the news event gap occurred

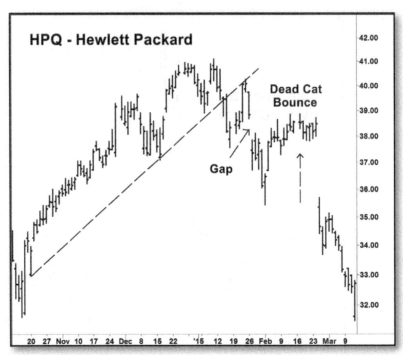

FIGURE 9.6 Dead Cat Bounce (HPQ—Hewlett Packard, daily: October 13, 2014– March 12, 2015)

use that gap just as if it had occurred between the daily bars. In the Hewlett Packard chart (refer to Figure 9.6), the rally filled the gap, just barely. The short-selling trading requirement then is for a topping of the bounce or a short-term top pattern, close protective stops above the entry, and a longer time horizon. For those wanting to purchase the stock, the odds are against profiting from a purchase for at least six months. Most bullish chart patterns fail during this period.

Island Reversal

An island reversal can occur at either a top or a bottom, and only after a relatively lengthy trend. It can happen in a congestion area, but only infrequently. It requires two gaps at roughly the same price: the first in the direction of the trend, an exhaustion gap, and the second in the reverse direction, a breakaway gap. The British Petroleum chart shown in Figure 9.6 shows an island reversal top within the context of a downward trend. The larger the gap, the more important is the formation. Between the gaps, low volatility trading can occur for a number of days or even weeks. Volume usually increases on the second gap from an island top but not necessarily from a bottom. The extreme price in the island must be either higher than previous highs at a top or lower than previous lows at a bottom. Pullbacks and throwbacks are frequent (65%–70%), and failures are low, around 13%–17%. This pattern is not common and has terrible performance results (Bulkowski, 2010).

One- and Two-Bar Reversal Patterns

The following one- and two-bar reversal patterns are common. Therefore, each of these patterns needs confirmation before use.

One-Bar Reversal (Also Reversal Bar, Climax, Top or Bottom Reversal Bar, Key Reversal Bar) When a trading bar high is greater than the previous bar high and the close is down from the previous bar close, it is called a **one-bar reversal**. It is sometimes preceded by a gap, at least an opening gap, and its bar length is not as extreme or intensive as in a spike. It is not a spike, because a spike is not necessarily a reversal, but a combination of spike and reversal can elevate its meaning. This pattern will occur in reverse at a bottom. It is common, but unfortunately, its top and bottom version will also occur within a trend, making it practically useless as a signal by itself. To be useful, but also cutting down on the number of profitable signals, it needs more stringent requirements. For example, rather than just closing down, the close may be required to exceed the previous bar low or even the low of the two previous bars. Kamich (2003) argues that a close is more reliable after a sustained advance than after a short rally. This may require that it be the highest high or lowest low over a specified period or that a series of higher highs or lower lows precede it. When combined with a cluster of other evidence, a close's significance improves. Whatever signal it gives is completely negated once prices exceed its reversal peak or trough.

Two-Bar Reversal (Also Pipe Formation) The two-bar reversal pattern, like the one-bar reversal, occurs at the end of a trend, upward or downward, but extends the reversal over two bars. Bulkowski calls it a **pipe formation**. A two-bar reversal formation is pictured in Figure 9.7. In the bottom pattern, the first bar usually closes in the lower half of the bar, and the second bar close ends near its high. Usually high volume is seen on both bars. In its extreme and more reliable version, it consists of two side-by-side spikes, but it can also be above-average length side-by-side bars of roughly equivalent length, peaking or bottoming at close to the same price, and occurring after a lengthy trend. Following and prior to the two-bar reversal, low bar prices should be in the vicinity of the top of the bars (in a bottom, the opposite for a top). It, thus, stands out quite easily in retrospect. It is preferable for the second bar to be slightly longer than the first bar, and volume is preferably higher on the left bar than on the right. Rarely this pattern acts as a consolidation area within a trend. Many pipes occur at the end of the retracement of a longer-term move. The directional clue is the direction of the breakout from it.

Failure rates are in the 5% range, which is low for a pattern (Bulkowski, 2010). Usually the failure occurs when the previous trend has been less than 5%. If the earlier trend is lengthy, the pattern rarely fails. Once the pattern has formed and prices have reversed direction, it is common for a test of the bars to occur soon thereafter. In most cases, the bars hold their extreme within a small percentage during the test, and this presents a good spot to place an initial protective stop. Both Kamich and

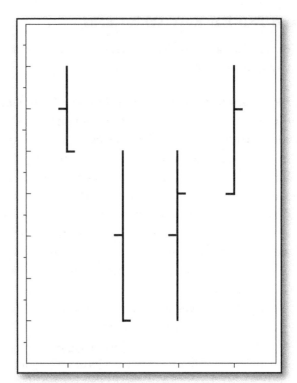

FIGURE 9.7 Two-bar reversal bottom (or pipe bottom)

Bulkowski maintain that the formation in weekly bars is more reliable than in daily bars. Bulkowski ranks it 2 out of 23 for performance in a bull market.

Horn Pattern Bulkowski describes the horn pattern as being almost identical in behavior to the pipe except a smaller bar separates the two lengthy bars. The two long bars become the "horns" of the formation (see Figure 9.8). As in the two-bar reversal, the formation is more reliable with weekly bars and otherwise has the same characteristics as the pipe. It is not as effective as the pipe at bottoms and tops, and its failure rate increases when the trend preceding the pattern is short.

Two-Bar Breakout The two-bar breakout is an extremely simple pattern. Indeed, it is so simple that it is hard to believe it will work, but the testing column in *Active Trader Magazine* (November 2003) tested it and found it to be successful for stocks and commodities (more so with commodities). The rules they used and that could easily be experimented with are for longs: the next day buy on a stop one tick above today's high if (1) today's low is less than yesterday's low, (2) today's high is less than yesterday's high, and (3) today's close is less than today's open. Exit on a stop at the then-current day's low. The sell side is just the opposite. Results should be tested against a better exit strategy, but as it is, the pattern produced reasonable profits in commodities and an extremely low drawdown. In stocks, the results were not as favorable but likely could be improved upon with money management and a better exit strategy.

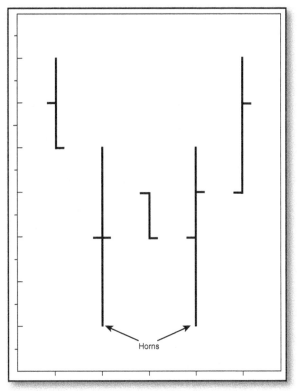

Horns

FIGURE 9.8 The horn pattern

Inside Bar An inside bar is a bar with a range that is smaller than and within the previous bar's range, as shown in Figure 9.9. It reflects a decline in momentum in a trend, a bar where a short-term congestion area is formed. As in most congestion areas, it reflects a pause, a period of direction-less equilibrium waiting for something to happen that will signal the next trend direction. During a larger congestion pattern, such as a triangle or rectangle, an inside bar has little meaning because it is just reflecting the lack of motion in the larger pattern. Some analysts plotting larger patterns delete inside bars, especially when determining pivots, because these bars fail to represent any important price action, similar to the way the point and figure chart eliminates dull periods. Within a trend, however, the inside bar provides some useful information and can generate profitable, short-term signals. As in the gap pattern, the context of the pattern's location is more important than the pattern configuration.

Toby Crabel (1989) found that without a cluster of other information, a number of inside bar combinations during the 1982–1986 period in the S&P futures achieved a better-than-average winning percentage. Crabel tested buying at the opening, if the opening price occurred above the earlier inside bar close, and selling at the opening, if it occurred below the earlier inside bar close (see Figure 9.10). This strategy produced a 68% winning percentage. This winning percentage could then be improved by adding even other requirements, mostly having to do with characteristics of the

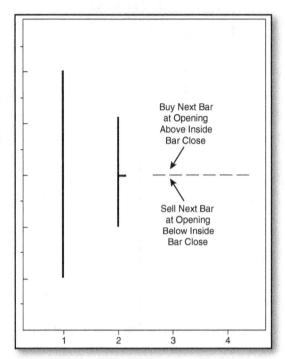

FIGURE 9.9 Inside bar

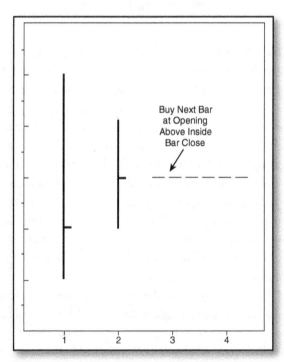

FIGURE 9.10 Inside bar with higher close

bars preceding the inside bar and with the preceding trend. One strategy, for example, is to buy if the inside bar close was higher than the previous day close and there is a higher open on the current bar. Likewise, you'd sell when the inside bar close was below the previous day close and the opening on the current bar is below the inside close. For this slightly more complex strategy, a 74% winning percentage occurred.

Crabel took his inside tests a little further, looking for a four-day pattern. If Day 2 had a higher low than Day 1, Day 3 was an inside day, and Day 4 opened lower than the midrange and close of the inside day, a sell signal was generated. This strategy is pictured in Figure 9.11. During Crabel's test period, this strategy had an 80% winning percentage. The opposite strategy would occur when Day 2 had a lower high than Day 1, Day 3 was an inside day, and Day 4 opened above the inside day close, triggering a buy signal. This strategy produced a 90% winning percentage. Although these strategies had extremely high winning percentages, they only occurred on average twice a year.

What Crabel was demonstrating, regardless of the percentages, was that the opening of a bar after an inside bar shows a strong bias toward the new price direction. Granted, his testing was done during a bull market in the late 1980s and is somewhat dated today, but nevertheless, the tests showed some correlation to the inside day breakouts and future performance. His exit criterion was to close the position on

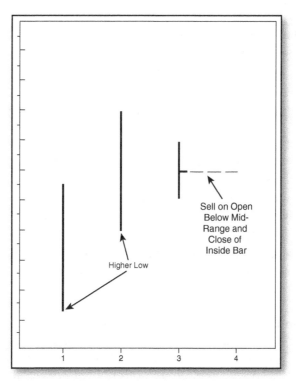

FIGURE 9.11 A four-bar sell pattern with an inside bar

the close of the day the trade was entered. This limits such trades to day traders. However, an inside bar can also occur on weekly bar charts and usually signifies a larger congestion area similar to a pennant or flag on a daily chart. In these cases, the inside week can be useful for longer-term trading.

Several other common patterns use the inside bar concept.

Hook Reversal Day   Hook is a common term for a quick loss when a profit was expected. It comes from the fishhook that the fish bites thinking that the bait is a free meal. As outlined by Kamich (2003) and Crabel (1989), a hook reversal occurs after a series of upward thrust bars, called **run bars** when they occur right after each other (Schwager, 1996). Then suddenly, a narrow-range bar occurs with specific characteristics. The narrow-range bar must open at above the previous high and close below the previous close. Kamich's variation is for an inside bar that opens at its high and closes at its low. This signals that the momentum built up during the run has reached a climax. A downward break would be an action signal.

Another hook formation occurs when traders are "hooked" into believing that the trend has reversed. This occurs when an open is above the previous high, but prices reverse direction and close down on the bar. This is the hook. It must have a narrower range than the previous bar, but it often fools traders into believing that a top has occurred. The action signal is when the price breaks back above the close of the first. It also works in reverse.

Naked Bar Upward Reversal   A variation of the hook, a naked bar is one that closes below a previous low (suggested by Joe Stowell and Larry Williams) and is a down bar (close less than open). It is the most bearish close possible. If an inside bar follows a naked bar with open greater than naked bar close, it is a sign that the downtrend is reversing. An upward break from the inside bar would suggest the bears are caught.

Hikkake   The hikkake is an inside bar signal that fails and becomes a signal itself (see Figure 9.12). As described by Daniel Chesler (2004), in Japanese, "hikkake" is a term meaning to trap, trick, or ensnare. It is a pattern that starts with an inside bar. When prices break one way or the other from an inside bar, the conventional belief is that they will continue in the same direction. The hikkake pattern occurs when the breakout fails to continue and prices in the following bars return to break in the opposite direction through the previous inside bar extreme. The reversal and opposite breakout must occur within three bars after the first breakout; the open and close of each bar seems to be unimportant.

Outside Bar   An outside bar occurs when the high is higher than the high of the previous bar and the low is lower than the low of the previous bar. It is a specific kind of wide-range bar that "covers" all the previous bar's price action. In other words, the outside bar is longer than the previous bar and contains the entire price range of the previous bar. Traditionally, an outside bar is thought of as a bar of increased volatility,

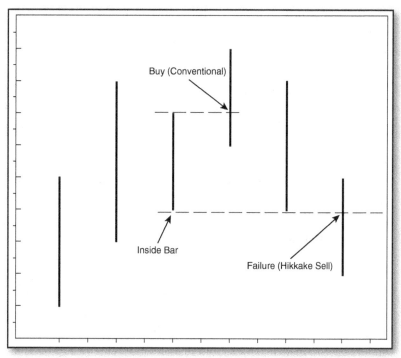

FIGURE 9.12 Hikkake buy failure

and, depending on the close, perhaps the beginning of a trend. Larry Williams (1988, 1995, 1999, 2000, and 2003) has done considerable study of outside bars, and the results are available in his various books.

When an outside bar closes near an extreme—that is, a high or low—and above or below the previous close and its current opening, it suggests further action in the direction of the close into the following bar. Bulkowski, using daily lows, observes that the close, if located within the upper or lower 25% of the range, tends to predict the future breakout upward about 66% of the time and downward 62% of the time. However, it often is a false signal. For example, one of the more reliable, although less frequently seen, setup patterns with an outside day is when the outside day closes at below the previous day's low and the next day opens lower than the outside day close. Buy the following day opening (Williams, 2000). Standard opinion would suggest that the series of lower closes was bearish, yet the setup is bullish.

Other Multiple-Bar Patterns

One- or two-day patterns are common, easily defined but not always reliable. Complex patterns are subject to interpretation by the analyst because their formation is not a perfect fit to the ideal. Between these pattern types are patterns with a few bars that have simple rules but require more price action than the short-term variety and are not as common as classic patterns.

Correction within a Trend Many studies have shown that acting in the direction of the trend is more advantageous after waiting for a correction to that trend. The reward of catching the trend at a cheaper price as well as having a closer stop level outweigh the potential opportunity loss of missing the trend.

There are at least two different types of trend correction patterns. One is to recognize a trend and act on a percentage pullback from that trend. *Active Trader Magazine* (March, 2003) tested on 18 stocks a long-only 6% pullback system. It demonstrated during the period 1992 through 2002, a generally rising period, that entering a buy at 6% below the previous bar close and exiting on the next open would produce an excellent equity curve when triggered. The gain over the period was the same as the buy-and-hold, but the market exposure was only 17% due to the limited number of trades and the quick exits.

Knockout Pattern The knockout (or KO) pattern is another trend correction method, used by David Landry (2003). (See Figure 9.13.) The first requirement for this pattern is that an extremely strong and persistent trend must be present. In an upward trend, Landry's criteria for a strong uptrend is that the stock must have risen at least ten points in the past 20 trading days and a trend line drawn through the prices touch almost all bars. Thus, if we think about a linear regression line, the bars should have a small deviation from that line, not wide swings back and forth. At some time, the stock will develop a throwback of two to five days in which two prior lows will be exceeded. Place a buy entry stop at the high of the bar with the second low. If

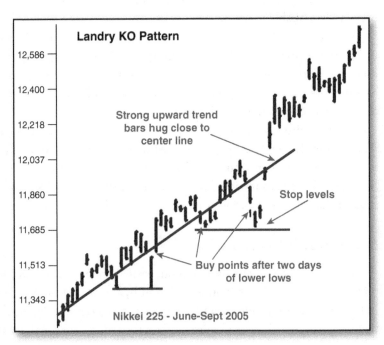

FIGURE 9.13 Landry KO pattern

the next bar is lower, move the buy stop to its high until the position is executed. Place a protective stop below the last low, or use any reasonable stop method. According to Landry, the reverse is equally as successful in a downtrend using the criteria in reverse. Figure 9.13 shows a steady downward trend in the Nikkei 225 with occasional two-day rallies that fulfill the requirements of the KO pattern.

Oops! Larry Williams (1979) uses the term **Oops!** to name an opening range pattern that profits from a sudden change in direction (see Figure 9.14). The setup for this pattern occurs when the opening price on today's bar is outside the previous day's range. Assume, for example, that a stock opens today at a price below yesterday's range. A buy stop is then placed just inside yesterday's range in case the market closes the gap, indicating a reversal. This pattern depends on other traders acting in the direction of an opening gap and being caught when prices reverse.

Larry Connors (1998) uses a 10% qualification variation of the Larry Williams Oops! pattern. The pattern is for the first day to have a close within 10% of the low. The second day must open on a downward gap. If these conditions are met, place a buy stop at the first day's low with a sell stop near the second day's opening. A sell pattern is just the reverse on a day when the close is within 10% of its high.

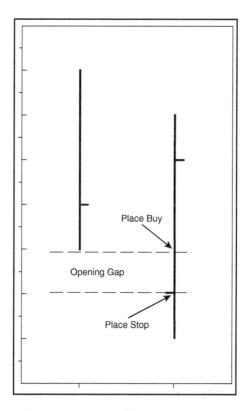

Place Buy

Opening Gap

Place Stop

FIGURE 9.14   Oops! buy pattern

Shark The shark pattern is a three-bar pattern. The most recent bar high must be lower than the previous high and the recent low above the previous low. In other words, the recent bar is an inside bar. The previous bar must also be an inside bar. The progression in bars, therefore, is one base bar and two successive inside bars, as shown in Figure 9.15. In effect, it is a small triangle or pennant. The name "shark" comes from the pattern's finlike shape.

In a *Stocks and Commodities* article, Walter Downs (1998) demonstrated that the short-term pattern called the **Shark-32** has implications for the longer-term as well as the immediate future. This study was an interesting approach to determining the success or failure of the pattern in that Downs questioned whether the symmetry of the pattern added to or detracted from its performance. Symmetry was measured by determining the amount by which the center of the final inside day range, called the **apex**, deviated from the center of the base day range. Although there can be many shark patterns, Downs limited his study to those patterns that fit a specified symmetry. The test was run on Harley Davidson stock from July 1986 to April 1998, a period of generally rising stock prices. The entry was to buy on the close of the first day after a day in which the close exceeded the widest point in the pattern—usually the base day. The exit was a trailing stop or a reversal on the opposite signal.

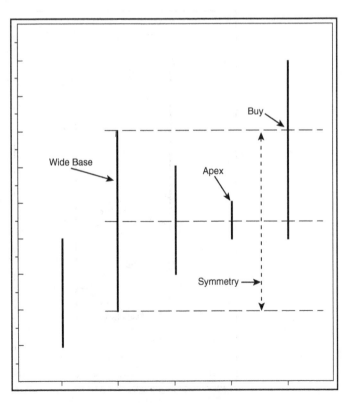

FIGURE 9.15 Shark pattern with break to the upside

The results of Downs' study were useful in that they suggested that the more symmetrical the shark formation, the more likely prices would continue in the same direction and improve performance at least out to 30 days thereafter. As the symmetry became tight, the results did not change, but the number of patterns that fit into the requirements declined. One example was that if the symmetrical variance of the apex midrange was within 12% either side of the center of the base day range, the trend continued in the same direction as the prepattern direction 91% of the time, strengthened in 36% of the instances, and increased in momentum 34% of the time within 30 days.

Volatility Patterns

Most short-term patterns rely on an expansion in volatility. The inside bar strategies, for example, are based on the notion that inside bars represent low volatility and that when prices break one way or another, volatility expands. To take this concept of volatility further, many patterns look directly at volatility itself—either historical volatility as defined in the option markets, changes in trading ranges, or indicators such as the ADX. An expansion in volatility is used as a signal for action in most patterns, but sometimes a contrary action is suggested when volatility becomes extreme. Following are examples of some of these patterns.

Wide-Range Bar A wide-range bar is a bar in which the range is "considerably" wider than the normal bar. The bars are relatively long compared with the previous bar. How large does the range have to be to be considered "wide," and how far back must the comparison be made? There are no definitive answers to these questions. In any case, a wide-range bar is usually a bar with increased volatility. Increased volatility can imply the beginning of a new trend as in a breakout bar, or if the trend has been in existence for a long time and is accelerating, the wide-range bar may act like an exhaustion gap and warn of the trend's end. As a sign of impending trend reversal, it is more often seen at panic lows, as the emotions of fear accelerate prices downward. Emotional spikes and two-bar reversals are often wide-range bars. Otherwise, it is usually found on a breakout from a pattern, small or large, or as the base for a pennant or flag, indicating that the trend reached a very short-term peak and is about to consolidate. On the other hand, not all wide-range bars are meaningful. Consideration of trend, areas of support and resistance, patterns, and the relative location of opens and closes are necessary before a judgment of the significance of the wide-range bar can be determined.

Larry Connors (1998) gives an example of a wide-range pattern. Connors first looks for a wide-range day in which a stock experiences a two-standard deviation decline. On the following day, if the opening is a downward gap, place a buy entry stop at the first day's close with a protection stop at the first day's low. If the buy is near the previous day's low, lower the stop to give some room for the pattern to develop. The reverse set of signals is valid on the sell side at a top. The exit is to sell on the close, or if the close on the action day is within 10% to 15% of the high, sell on the next day opening.

Narrow-Range Bar (NR)   Wide-range bars indicate high volatility; narrow-range bars indicate low volatility (see Figure 9.16). Determining narrow-range bars is useful because the low volatility will eventually switch to high volatility. As with the wide-range bar, the criteria for determining a narrow-range bar are not precise.

Toby Crabel designed one method of defining and using narrow-range days. In his method, he determines whether the current day has a narrower range than the previous day and, if so, over how many past days. For example, if the current day has a narrower range than the past three days, it is called an **NR4** day (to include the current day and the past three days); in other words, the current day represents the narrowest trading range of the four days. The common narrow days of this type are the NR4 and NR7 day. Their entry signal is a breakout from the most recent narrow-range day. Thus, if today is an NR7 day, we place a buy and sell entry stop on either side to be acted upon tomorrow or the next day.

Linda Bradford Raschke (www.lbrgroup.com) is one of the leading proponents of using narrow-range days to determine low-volatility setups. Raschke adds

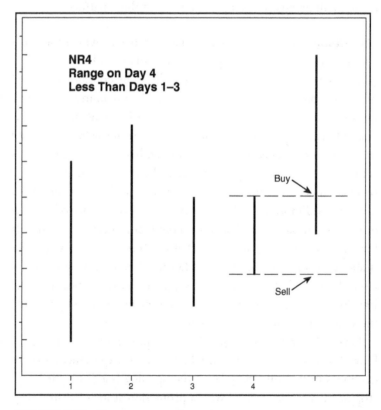

FIGURE 9.16   Narrow-range bar

another constraint to Crabel's method. She calculates the historic volatility of the vehicle over 6 days and over 100 days. If the 6-day historic volatility is 50% less than the 100-day, the conditions are right for either an NR4 day or inside day signal, provided today meets the criteria for each of these types of days. The buy and sell entry stops are placed at the high and low of the qualified NR4 or inside day. If the entry stop is executed, an additional exit stop is placed where the opposite entry stop currently exists. Exit the position at the close of the day if not already stopped out.

VIX Remember that the VIX is a reflection of anxiousness in the market. Traders and investors become anxious when the market declines and become complacent when the market advances. Thus, VIX becomes a sentiment indicator. Generally, when the market is bottoming, VIX is high because of the investor anxiousness. When the market is topping, VIX is generally low, indicating the complacency among investors.

Larry Connors (1998) introduced a number of short-term price patterns that were based on the behavior of the VIX. The principle behind these patterns was to watch for changes in VIX, as a measure of sentiment, at extremes, as for example, either after X number of days or combining with an oscillator formula to determine when VIX is overbought or oversold. A more general strategy for the VIX was to look at the deviation from a moving average (Connors, 2004). VIX has changed levels over the past decade, but a moving average dampens those changes. Connors used a 5% deviation from a 10-day simple moving average. If the VIX is below the SMA by 5% and the market is above its 200-day moving average, the odds favor a continuing upward trend but not necessarily a good time to buy except on throwbacks. When the ratio is above 5%, and even more so when it is above 10% of the SMA, the time is usually excellent to buy. Thus, the VIX in this instance gives general zones of when action in certain directions can be contemplated. The opposite relationship is valid when the market is below its 200-day moving average. Generally, bottoms are more reliably signaled by the VIX than tops.

Intraday Patterns

The opening range is the range of a daily bar that forms in the first few minutes or hour of the trading day (see Figure 9.17). It can be defined as either the high and low after a certain time, such as the high and low price that occur during the first 15 minutes of trading, or it can be a predetermined range about the opening price. A horizontal line is drawn at the opening range high and low on the intraday bar chart as a reference for the rest of the day. Other lines from the opening price, the close yesterday, the range yesterday, and so forth may also be drawn. These lines often become support or resistance levels during the day.

The opening range breakout (ORB) is a popular method of entering a position once a setup has been established from a previous short-term pattern. As reported in *Stocks & Commodities Magazine,* Toby Crabel experimented with NR days as setups

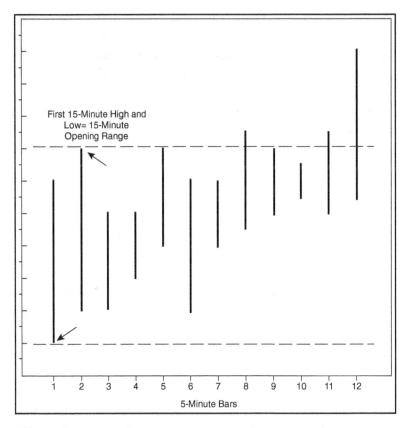

First 15-Minute High and
Low= 15-Minute
Opening Range

5-Minute Bars

FIGURE 9.17 Opening range

and used an ORB defined by a specified, predetermined amount above or below the opening range. He compared these results with using a wide-range day setup. He found, first, that the wide-range day setup over both four and seven days vastly underperformed the NR days over the same period, thus confirming that more profit can be obtained from an expansion in volatility than contraction. Second, he found that once the price had moved away from the open in one direction after an NR2, it normally did not return to the opening.

In a series of articles for *Stocks & Commodities Magazine*, Crabel describes methods of trading from an ORB in considerable detail. In the first article, he described how he calculates the specified amount, called the **stretch**, above and below the opening that establishes the ORB. Crabel uses the ten-day average of the past differences between the open for each day and its closest extreme to the open for that day. Analysts use a number of other methods for calculating stretch, including specifying a number of ticks or calculating a range based on the ATR over some past period.

Crabel found that the use of ORBs worked well with NR4, NR7, inside days, and hook days. He found that the earlier in the day the ORB was penetrated, the better the chance for success. Even without the previously mentioned setups, trading on the ORB within the first five to ten minutes would also work, but after that short interval, if the prices have not penetrated out of the range, all orders should be canceled because the day will likely revert to a listless trading day rather than a trending day.

By analyzing the action around opening range levels, a good trader can find ways to take advantage of the tendency for these levels to act as support and resistance. One method of accomplishing this is called the **ACD method**, developed by Mark Fisher (2002). This some-what complicated method uses the opening range determined over the initial minutes of trading, an additional filter that is added to the upper bound of the range, and another subtracted from the lower edge, as shown in Figure 9.18. Entry signals occur when the outer bounds are broken during the day, and exit signals occur when the range bounds are broken. Fisher's method is not quite this simple because he uses numerous other rules and confirmations. However, Fisher, who reportedly has a trading room of more than 75 day traders using this method to make their daily bread, has appeared to be very successful.

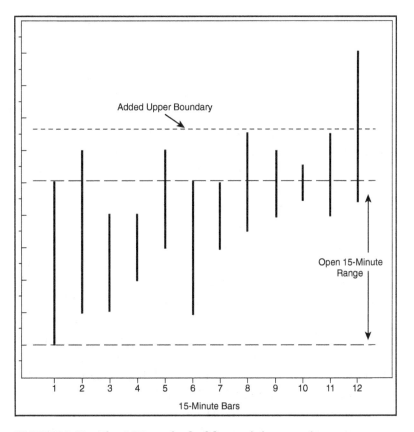

FIGURE 9.18 The ACD method of determining opening range

◼ Summary of Short-Term Patterns

Although there appears to be value in short-term patterns, they are not immediate sources of wealth without study, experience, and trial-and-error testing. We have only touched the edge of methods being used. Others include performance around national holidays, days of the week, time during the day, and even the new moon. There seems to be no limit. The point in this exercise, however, is to demonstrate the many ways that prices are analyzed over the short term. If interested, you can continue to experiment on your own.

◼ Candlestick Patterns

In "History and Construction of Charts," we learned how to construct a candlestick chart. As you will recall, the raw data used in the candlestick chart is the same as the raw data used in the bar chart: open, close, high, and low price per specific period.

The candlestick chart has become popular because it represents price action in a more striking way; furthermore, the patterns that result have interesting and novel names. One advantage of the candlestick chart is that it can still use the Western methods of analysis—patterns, trend lines, support, and resistance—yet it has a set of unique patterns of its own. These patterns are mostly short term of only one to five bars, and by themselves they have not tested well. Many patterns have their Western equivalents that we have seen before. They are generally reversal patterns and can reveal price reversals early in overbought or oversold conditions, at trend lines, or at support or resistance levels. However, they are tools, not a system. Their disadvantage is that one must wait for the close before a pattern can be recognized, and they are useless in markets that do not accurately report the opening prices. The best resource on candlesticks is *Japanese Candlestick Charting Techniques* by Steve Nison (2001), the person who introduced this ancient method to the West.

The principal analytical difference between candlestick patterns and Western bar patterns is the emphasis on the opening and close. Western traders have recognized the importance of the opening and close, but bar charts treat them without special weighting. In candlestick charts, the "real body" is the wider area between the open and close. The "shadow" is the vertical line from the real body up to the price high and down to the price low. A long shadow indicates the inability for prices to maintain their highs or lows and is, thus, a warning of trouble. The real body is a heavy color, such as black, when the close is lower than the open, and usually white when the close is higher than the open. A black body denotes, therefore, a "down" day, and a white body indicates an "up" day. (This definition is different than in the West, where a down day is a day in which the close is lower than the previous close.) A large body (in relative terms) indicates strength in the direction of the trend, and a small body indicates indecision and a potential reversal, especially after a meaningful prior trend.

Patterns are made by the relative position of the body and the shadow, the location of the candlestick in relation to its neighbors, and the confirmation the next day. Because candlestick patterns usually are defined as top or bottom patterns, the analyst must be sure that the preceding price action is in a trend, either up or down. A single pattern may or may not be meaningful depending on the direction of the previous trend. Similar to Western short-term patterns, a candlestick pattern cannot predict the extent of the subsequent move or the significance of the pattern—that is, whether it occurs at a major or minor reversal. Thus, the pattern should always be used with other evidence before action is taken. For example, candlestick patterns are often reversal patterns and thus identify support or resistance levels when they switch direction. At first, the analysis of these patterns seems to be filled with an endless set of rules and names, but as you become more familiar with the nomenclature, you will see that the basis of these patterns is not much different from the basis for Western short-term patterns.

There have been few tests on the effectiveness of candlestick patterns. This is odd because the patterns are easily computerized. As with tests of other short-term patterns, many of the existing studies are flawed in that the signal outcomes are often assumed to last longer than they should. Measuring the effectiveness of patterns over weeks or months is useless because these patterns are only useful in short-term situations. However, even over shorter periods, the patterns do not test well. Their profit factors are relatively low, and their drawdowns are high and in all cases greater than net profits. Some of the variables in each pattern can be tweaked to improve performance, but the basic patterns, by themselves, are not outstandingly profitable.

Two relatively recent studies with short-term results are by Caginalp and Laurent (1998) and by Schwager (1996). The Caginalp and Laurent tests included eight three-day patterns in S&P 500 stocks from 1992 to 1996. Their purpose was to demonstrate that the patterns had value above what could be expected from a random walk; however, drawdowns were not considered. Schwager tested six major patterns in ten commodities from 1990 to 1994 and included a momentum filter to account for trend, an important factor in candlestick pattern analysis. A criticism, however, is that Schwager estimated commissions and slippage to be $100 per trade, considerably higher than what can be achieved now. Both studies suffer from the type of exit method in that they depend on a holding period that is arbitrary and not based on the behavior of prices. The results could be considerably improved with testing of each pattern in combination with others and the use of protective stops. At least stops and other exit signals would reduce the extremely large drawdowns. In our presentation of the patterns covered by Schwager, we average the results from the ten commodities for each pattern and give the relative ranking rather than the raw percentages. This avoids, to some extent, the problem of commissions and slippage.

Following are some examples of the more common candlestick patterns.

One- and Two-Bar Candlestick Patterns

Candlestick patterns are short-term patterns. In fact, a number of candlestick patterns are formed by only one or two bars. Thus, on a candlestick chart of daily data, only one or two days' worth of data would be necessary to form the pattern.

Doji A doji pattern is formed when the open and close are identical, or nearly identical. This creates a candlestick with a real body that is simply a horizontal line, as shown in Figure 9.19. It suggests that the market is in equilibrium and affected by indecision. In some respects, it is like an inside bar in its meaning because in a trend, it shows a point at which the enthusiasm of the trend has stalled. It is, thus, often a warning of a reversal, but not necessarily a reversal pattern by itself. It can also occur about anywhere during a trend or within a trading range and is, thus, difficult to assess. As a result, its performance statistics were low (Schwager, 1996). It ranked at the bottom of our scale based on net profit, average trade, maximum drawdown, and percent winners.

Windows Windows are simply the gaps that we discussed earlier in this chapter. Nison believes they are the most reliable formations, and evidence from short-term bar patterns tends to confirm his opinion. Because the interpretation of candlestick windows is the same as for Western gaps, we will not spend time discussing them.

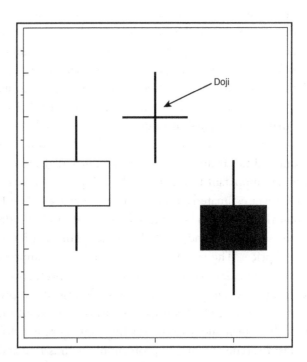

FIGURE 9.19 Doji candlestick

Harami A harami pattern is a two-day pattern consisting of a large body of either color followed by a small body of either color that is completely within the boundaries of the large body. The harami pattern is pictured in Figure 9.20. The second candlestick pictured in the harami pattern in Figure 9.20 is called a **spinning top**. This second candlestick can also be a doji (resulting in a harami cross pattern), a hammer, a hanging man, or a shooting star; the only requirement is that the second candlestick body is within the first candlestick body.

The harami pattern is similar to the inside bar pattern; however, with the harami, the range, or wick, of the second bar does not have to be within the range of the first bar. The real body of the second candle must be within the real body of the first candle. Thus, the open and close range, rather than the range, determines whether the harami criterion is met.

We know that the inside day demonstrates a contraction in volatility, and the same can be said for the harami pattern. We also know from studies of short-term bar patterns that low volatility turns into high volatility and often begins a new trend. Thus, a harami pattern can be a powerful way of signaling either the reversal of a trend or an increase in velocity of the current trend, depending on which direction prices break.

Hammer and Hanging Man Both the hammer and the hanging man are candlesticks in which the real body is located at the upper end of the trading range, as

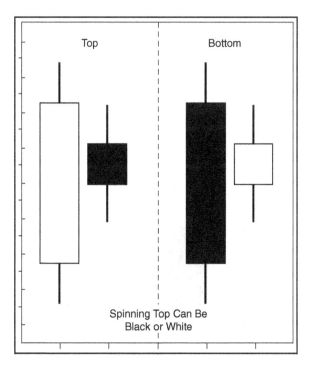

FIGURE 9.20 Harami candlestick pattern

pictured in Figure 9.21. For these formations, the lower wick is at least twice to three times as long as the body, and the upper wick is small or nonexistent. In other words, both the open and close occur within approximately the top one-third of the bar's trading range, and either the open or close is, or nearly is, the highest price of the bar. The color of the body is irrelevant.

If this formation occurs at a peak, it is called a **hanging man**. A variation is called the **kasakasa** or **paper umbrella** when the body is shorter than the shadow. When the same formation occurs at a trough, it is called a **hammer**. These formations ranked best in our scale and were close to a tie with morning and evening stars.

Shooting Star and Inverted Hammer   The shooting star and the inverted hammer can be thought of as an upside down hanging man or hammer. For these formations, the real body occurs in the lower end of the trading range. A shooting star occurs at peaks, and the inverted hammer occurs at bottoms. Both have long shadows above their bodies and short or nonexistent shadows below their bodies, as shown in Figure 9.22. Again, the color of the body is irrelevant. In our ranking of patterns, they fell into the middle, nowhere near the best-performing hammer and hanging man to which they are related.

THEORY AND ANALYSIS

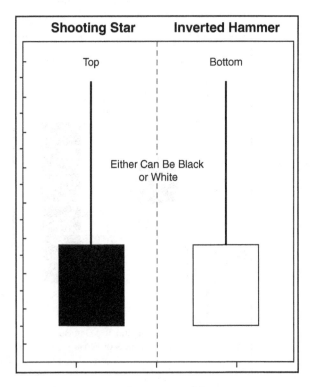

FIGURE 9.21   Hanging man and hammer

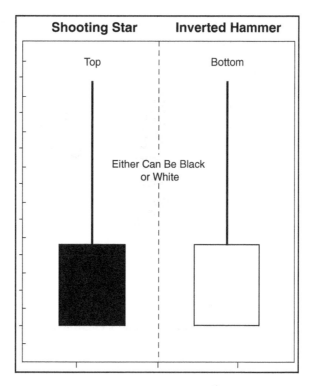

FIGURE 9.22 Shooting star and inverted hammer

Engulfing An engulfing pattern is a two-bar pattern in which the second body engulfs the first body (see Figure 9.23). This pattern is similar to an outside day reversal in bar patterns. Because this pattern is designed to recognize a trend reversal, there must be a clear trend preceding the engulfing pattern. In a market uptrend, a bearish engulfing pattern would indicate a market top. The bearish engulfing pattern consists of a small white-bodied candle followed by a black body that engulfs the white body. The bullish engulfing pattern would indicate that a downward trend is reversing. This bullish engulfing pattern consists of a candle with a small dark body on one bar followed by a candle with a larger white body that engulfs the dark body. For both the bearish and bullish engulfing pattern, the signal is much stronger when the first body is small and the second body is large. However, performance of engulfing patterns is near the bottom of the six pattern types tested by Schwager. They had the worst net profits and the largest maximum drawdowns.

Dark Cloud Cover and Piercing Line A dark cloud cover is a two-body pattern at a top. The first body is large and white, and the second body is large and dark. The second open should be above the upper shadow of the first bar, an opening gap upward, and the close well within the first bar's white body, preferably below the 50% level. The pattern resembles the Oops! pattern in bar charts. Performance

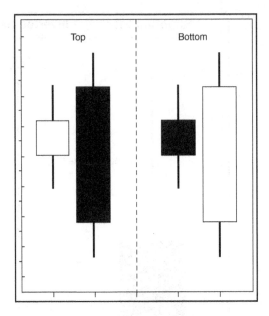

FIGURE 9.23   Candle engulfing pattern

of this pattern is supposedly enhanced by a deeper penetration of the white body. (A complete penetration would be an engulfing pattern.)

The opposite pattern, a piercing line pattern, would indicate market bottom. The piercing line follows the same rules as the dark cloud pattern, only in reverse. Both the dark cloud cover and piercing line formations are pictured in Figure 9.24. These patterns ranked in the lower half of the six types followed. They had the second to least drawdown, the lowest average profit per trade, and the lowest winning percentage.

Multiple-Bar Patterns

Multiple-bar candlestick patterns develop over a time period of more than two bars. A quick glance at names such as "three black crows," "three white soldiers," and "three outside up" reveals that many of the multiple-bar patterns are three-bar patterns.

Morning and Evening Star   The evening star is a three-bar candlestick pattern that occurs at market tops, and the morning star is a three-bar, market bottom pattern. In each of these patterns, the second bar, or middle candlestick, is known as a star. A star is a candlestick that has a small body that lies outside the range of the body before it. It implies an opening gap, as does a dark cloud and piercing line pattern, but it can later cover part of the previous bar's shadow. The important point is that its body does not overlap the previous bar's body at all. It is similar to a doji in that it represents a sudden halt in a trend and some indecision between buyers and sellers.

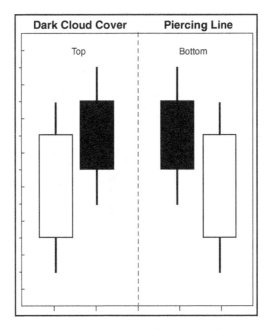

FIGURE 9.24 Dark cloud cover and piercing line

Indeed, a doji can be a star, called a **doji star**, if the doji body occurs outside the body of the previous bar's body.

The evening star pattern, pictured in Figure 9.25, starts with a long white body followed by a star of either color. If the third bar forms a large black body that closes well within the body of the first bar, the pattern is confirmed. Ideally, the third body should not touch the star's body, but this rarely occurs, and it is not a necessary condition for the pattern. The amount of penetration into the first white body is more important. The evening star is similar to the island reversal bar pattern without the necessary second gap.

The morning star, which occurs at a market bottom, is the opposite formation of the evening star. As shown in Figure 9.25, it begins with a black-bodied candlestick, followed by a star. The body of the star lies completely below the body of the previous candlestick. The pattern is then confirmed if, on the third bar, a white-bodied candlestick closes well within the range of the first candlestick.

The morning and evening stars were the second-best patterns in our ranking of Schwager's tests. They were first in net profits, had the least drawdowns, and were second in the percentage of winning trades. In the Caginalp and Laurent study, the morning and evening star pattern ranked third out of the four multibar types studied.

Three Black Crows and Three White Soldiers White soldiers are white bodies and black crows are black bodies. Three black crows is a pattern with three consecutive,

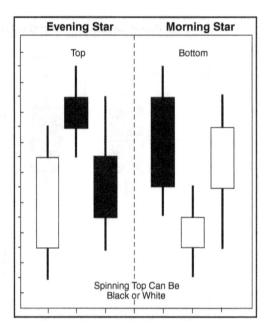

FIGURE 9.25 Evening star and morning star candlestick patterns

preferably long, black bodies, closing near their lows with openings within their previous day's body, and occurring after a meaningful upward trend. They are a top-reversal formation. As shown in Figure 9.26, three white soldiers is a bottom-reversing formation that requires the same parameters in the opposite direction.

Unfortunately, traders have difficulty profiting from these patterns because by the time they are recognized, a large portion of the new trend has already occurred. They are best played on a pullback or a throwback. Nison believes that the first or second bar in the pattern is the best location for entry on the retracement. That level is often accompanied by another pattern suggesting a short reversal in the direction of the trend signaled by the major pattern.

Three Inside Up and Three Inside Down   The three inside up pattern is a reversal pattern that occurs at the end of a declining trend. The first bar of this pattern has a large black body, and the second bar is a white spinning top (or doji) that forms a harami pattern. Then the third bar is a large, white candle that breaks and closes above the large black body of the first bar. Although the name may sound like it, the three inside up pattern does not imply that three inside bars in a row occur, as we saw with the NR3 pattern. Instead, the three inside up pattern is similar to an upward breakout from an inside bar in a bar pattern.

As shown in Figure 9.27, the three inside down pattern is the reverse of the three inside up pattern. The three inside down pattern consists of a large white bar

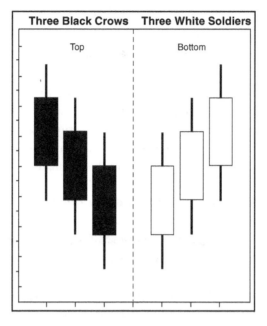

FIGURE 9.26 Three black crows and three white soldiers' candlestick patterns

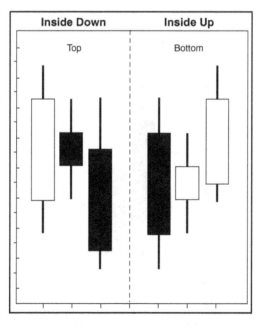

FIGURE 9.27 Inside down and inside up candlestick patterns

followed by a black spinning top and a downward break by a large black body. This pattern signals that an upward trend has ended. From the Caginalp and Laurent study, we ranked this pattern type the best. It had the highest percentage of winning trades of the four pattern types studied.

From our look at short-term bar patterns, we know that outside bars are less predictable and less profitable than inside bars because the volatility has already expanded and is open to contraction at any time soon thereafter. The results of the three outside bar pattern types show the same decreased performance and were ranked fourth in our interpretation of the Caginalp and Laurent study.

Three Outside Up and Three Outside Down   This pattern type starts with an engulfing pattern after a trend, just as the inside up and down started with a harami pattern. The three outside up version occurs at market bottoms. The first body is small, a spinning top, and the second body is large, engulfing the smaller previous body. The first is black and the second is white. A white body that closes above the second bar and reaches a new high above the previous two bars follows the engulfing pattern. This pattern is pictured in Figure 9.28.

Figure 9.28 also shows how the three outside down pattern is the same with opposite parameters. For the outside down pattern, the first bar is a small, white body, and the second bar is a black body that engulfs the first. The third bar is also a black body with prices moving lower than the second bar. Outside down bars occur at market tops.

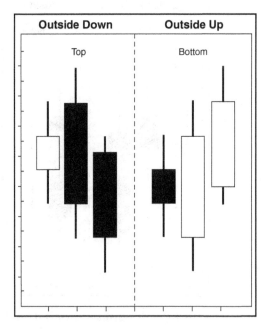

FIGURE 9.28   Outside down and outside up candlestick patterns

TABLE 9.1	Bulkowski Ranking of Candlestick Patterns—Ten Best (Some are not shown but may be accessed from www.thepatternsite.com.)	
Pattern	Reversal or Continuation	Percent Accurate
Three-line strike	Bullish reversal	84%
Three-line strike	Bearish reversal	65%
Three black crows	Bearish reversal	78%
Evening star	Bearish reversal	72%
Upside Tasuki gap	Bullish continuation	57%
Hammer, inverted	Bearish continuation	65%
Matching low	Bearish continuation	61%
Abandoned baby	Bullish reversal	70%
Two black gapping	Bearish continuation	68%
Breakaway	Bearish reversal	63%

Source: www.thepatternsite.com © 2008–2009 by Thomas N. Bulkowski

Candlestick Pattern Results

We have described several of the most popular candlestick patterns. Bulkowski maintains a Web site (www.thepatternsite.com) with an extensive list of candlestick patterns. Table 9.1 highlights Bulkowski's ranking of the ten best-performing candlestick patterns.

■ Conclusion

We have looked at a number of short-term patterns in this chapter on both bar charts and candlestick charts. To use these patterns successfully, a trader must be familiar with the underlying market trend. Remember that these short-term patterns are most often reversal patterns, giving the trader a hint that the underlying trend may be changing.

Short-term patterns forming as open, high, low, and close prices occur in particular combinations during a bar or over a few bars of trading. Particular short-term patterns occur frequently. Because of the frequency with which they occur, many times they are false patterns. Traders must be aware of this and not simply rely on a particular short-term pattern to make decisions. These short-term patterns can be useful indicators, but traders need to watch for a cluster of evidence instead of relying on a short-term pattern to make decisions.

Remember that the key to making money is riding a trend. Short-term patterns are a tool to help us determine when a new trend is beginning. These formations can also help us determine when a trend is ending. This allows us to participate in the trend as soon as possible and to exit the market as quickly as possible whenever the trend has ended. Using short-term patterns and protective stops can aid traders in maximizing their gains and minimizing their risk.

■ References

Bulkowski, Thomas N. "Bulkowski's Free Pattern Research, www.thepatternsite.com, 2008–2010.

Caginalp, Gunduz, and H. Laurent. "The Predictive Power of Price Patterns." *Applied Mathematical Finance* 5 (1998): 181–205.

Chesler, Daniel. "Trading Fallse Moves with the Hikkake Pattern." *Active Trader Magazine* 5, no. 4 (April 2004): 42–46.

Connors, Laurence A. *Connors on Advanced Trading Strategies*. Malibu, CA: M. Gordon Publishing Group, 1998.

Connors, Laurence A. "Larry Connors on How the Markets Really Work." Interview by Editor Jayanthi Gopalakrishnan. *Technical Analysis of Stocks & Commodities* 22, no. 12 (2004): 74–79.

Crabel, Toby. "Inside Day Patterns in the S&P." *Technical Analysis of Stocks & Commodities* 7, no. 11 (1989): 387–389.

Crabel, Toby. "Opening Range Breakout Parts 1–8." *Techincal Analysis of Stocks and Commodities* (1989–1990). The parts are in separate issues; 6, no. 9 (pp. 337–339); 6, no. 10 (366–368); 6, no. 12 (456–458); 7, no. 2 (47–49); 7, no. 4 (119–120); 7, no. 5 (161–163); 7, no. 6 (188–189); 7, no. 7 (208–210).

Downs, Walter T. "Combining Statistical and Pattern Analysis." *Technical Analysis of Stocks & Commodities* 16, no. 10 (1998): 447–456.

Edwards, Robert, John Magee, and W.H.C. Bassetti. *Techincal Analysis of Stock Trends*. 9th ed. Boca Raton, FL: St. Lucie Press, 2007.

Fischer, Mark B. *The Logical Trader*. New York, NY: John Wiley & Sons., Inc., 2002.

Harris, Michael. *Short-Term Trading with Price Patterns*. Greenville, NC: Traders Press, Inc., 2000.

Kamich, Bruce M. *How Technical Analysis Works*. New York, NY: New York Institute of Finance, 2003.

Kaufman, Perry J. *Trading Systems and Methods*. 3rd ed. New York, NY: John Wiley & Sons, Inc., 1998.

Landry, David. *Dave Landry's 10 Best Swing Trading Patterns and Strategies*. Los Angeles, CA: M. Gordon Publishing Group, 2003.

Landry, David. *David Landry on Swing Trading*. Los Angeles, CA: M. Gordon Publishign Group, 2003.

Nison, Steve. *Japanese Candlestick Charting Techniques*. New York, NY: New York Institute of Finance, 2001.

Schwager, Jack D. *Schwager on Futures: Technical Analysis*. New York, NY: John Wiley & Sons, Inc., 1996.

Schwager, Jack D. *Technical Analysis*. New York, NY: John Wiley & Sons, Inc., 1996.

Williams, Larry. *How I Made One Million Dollars Last Year Trading Commodities*. Brightwaters, NY: Windsor Books, 1979.

Williams, Larry. *The Definitive Guide to Futures Trading*. Brightwaters, NY: Windsor Books, 1988.

Williams, Larry. *Futures Millionaire*. Manual published by Karol Media, Wilkes-Barre, PA, 1995.

Williams, Larry. *Long-Term Secrets to Short-Term Trading*. New York, NY: John Wiley & Sons, Inc., 1999.

Williams, Larry. *Day Trade Futures Online*. New York, NY: John Wiley & Sons, Inc., 2000.

Williams, Larry. *The Right Stock at the Right Time*. New York, NY: John Wiley & Sons, Inc., 2003.

THEORY AND ANALYSIS

CHAPTER 10

Single Candle Lines

From Steve Nison, *The Candlestick Course* (Hoboken, New Jersey: John Wiley & Sons, 2003), Chapter 2.

Learning Objective Statements

- Interpret market psychology from candle shapes
- Identify and interpret spinning tops and high wave candles
- Identify and interpret the hammer and the hanging man
- Explain the importance of candle signals in the context of trends

SECTION ONE

Spinning Tops and High Wave Candles

In this very important chapter, we'll focus on single candle lines. (We refer to one candle as a candle line.) Section One focuses on spinning tops and high wave candles. Section Two reveals the potency of the doji. In Section Three, we'll explore bullish and bearish belt-hold lines.

Many candle signals consist of two and three candle patterns, but we can obtain volumes of valuable information from single candle lines. Don't let the simplicity of single candle lines fool you: They send compelling signals as to who is winning the battle between the bulls and bears.

In this section you will learn ...

- Interpreting market psychology, as indicated by small real bodies and long shadows
- Identifying and distinguishing between spinning tops and high wave candles
- How to use spinning tops and high wave candles in a box range
- How to identify the hammer and the hanging man
- The importance of candle signals in the context of trends

Key terms to watch for:

- Spinning tops
- High wave candles
- Hammer
- Hanging man
- Shooting star

■ Getting Started

Candle charts indicate early trend reversal, but they also have the advantage of displaying the force underpinning the move. Since nearly every candle line has a story to tell about the market's mood and manner, we'll start with how to use real bodies to gauge the force of the trend.

You may remember from a previous discussion that the Japanese call the candle's real body the essence of the price movement. Indeed, the length of the real bodies, in relation to their shadows, furnishes you with unique insights into the psychology of the stock market. Obviously, a tall white real body reflects a session when the bulls are dominant, whereas a black real body shows that the bears have greater control. However, when the real body shrinks (the real body can be black or white), it is a strong hint that the prior trend may be losing steam.

A *spinning top* (see Figure 10.1A) is the picturesque Japanese term for a candle with a small real body, either black or white. Spinning tops may have upper and lower shadows—or none at all. The important identifying trait of these candle lines is their diminutive real body. Later, you'll learn how spinning tops are components of candle formations such as morning and evening stars, harami, hammers, and shooting stars. In Section Two, we'll talk about a spinning top that has no real body, called a doji.

> **KEY POINT**
>
> For a small real body the color is not important. The diminutive size of the real body sends out the warning signal, not the color.

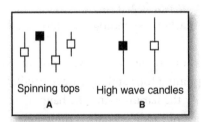

FIGURE 10.1 Spinning Tops and High Wave Candles

A small real body shows that the bulls and bears are battling it out in a tug-of-war, with neither the bulls or bears being able to take dominant control. Selling pressure (bears) pushes the real body down, but buying pressure (bulls) keep it from being a long black real body. In the other scenario for a spinning top, demand is stepping in but supply is counterattacking and, in doing so, keeps the market from forming a tall white candle.

Spinning tops have a sort of cousin named high wave candles. *High wave candles* also have diminutive real bodies, either white or black. To qualify as a high wave, however, these candle lines must not only have small real bodies but also long upper and lower shadows. The shadows of the high wave candles need not be the same size, but both the upper and lower shadows have to be unusually long.

If spinning tops translate into indecision on the part of the bulls and bears, high wave candles indicate downright confusion. As you can see by studying Figure 10.1B, the long upper shadows mean that some time after the session's open, buying pressure thrust the security's price to an extended high. During the same session, selling pressure drove the price to a protracted low. Yet, by the session's close, the price returned almost to the opening price. That's confusion!

Now, take spinning tops and high wave candles into the context of an uptrend or downtrend on a chart. In a solid uptrend, a market might rise, but the shape of the candle lines during the ascent is an important clue about the sustainability of the advance. Long white real bodies are like a green light showing that the prior rally is going strongly. However, if there are small real bodies (either black or white) during an ascent, caution is warranted from the long side. This is because the small real bodies imply that the bulls have less than full control—in spite of the advancing prices. Such spinning tops are a warning not to follow this market from the long side. Spinning tops become even more consequential in a market that is becoming overextended and perhaps nearing resistance: A trend shift or reversal may be in the offing.

KEY POINT

A high wave candle has the name because the Japanese compare the very extended upper and lower shadows to large ocean waves. Once again we get a sense of the pictorial representation the Japanese give to the names of the candle signals.

Conversely, if you see spinning tops moving sideways in a consolidation pattern or box range, they are not signaling a trend reversal or shift. The market is simply resting until it breaks up, or down, from that price zone. As such, spinning tops and high wave candles have no trading implications within a box range environment.

Three candle lines that contain spinning tops are the hammer, the hanging man, and the shooting star. These candle lines are shown in Figure 10.2. Let's first focus on the hammer and hanging man, since they have the same shape. We will then address the shooting star.

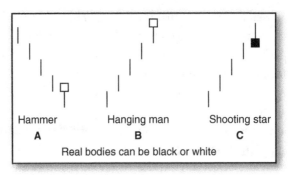

FIGURE 10.2 Hammer, Hanging Man, and
Shooting Star

The hammer and hanging man candle lines have small real bodies (either black or white), and these real bodies have to be at or near the highs of the session. Another criterion is that they need very long lower shadows (at least two to three times the height of the real body). Because of their identical shape, you identify them depending on where they appear in an uptrend or downtrend. As you can see in Figure 10.2A, a hammer will appear at or near the bottom of a decline, either brief or extended; thus the name *hammer*, which suggests that the market is hammering out a base. The hanging man (see Figure 10.2B) has the same shape as the hammer, except that it comes after an uptrend, preferably at a new high for the move. Because of the hanging man's bullish long lower shadow one must wait for a close under the hanging man's real body before becoming bearish.

> **KEY POINT**
> With the hanging man's bullish lower shadow, one might think that this line can only be bullish. Although the bullish shadow is a positive, the hanging man's small real body shows that there is some hesitation. And the long lower shadow, while it is a plus, shows that at some time during the session the market had sold off.

The *shooting star* is a top reversal line, just like the hanging man. A shooting star, however, displays a long upper shadow, and its small real body is at or near the lows of the session. We can see how the name describes the line, as it appears to be a shooting star, complete with long tail, soaring across the sky. The Japanese say that the shooting star shows "trouble overhead." Because of the shooting star's bearish long upper shadow, we don't need as much bearish confirmation with that line as we do with a hanging man.

As shown in Figure 10.2C, the shooting star is a bearish reversal signal, so it must appear during a rally. Shooting star real bodies can be either white or black.

A shooting star tells you that the market is rising in an uptrend and is perhaps becoming overbought. Finally, the bulls refuse to pay any more. The shooting star forms as the session opens near, or at, what will turn out to be the low. It rises, but the bulls cannot sustain the demand. Bears come in and drive the price back down. Remember, a long upper shadow on *any* candle means selling pressure.

The Japanese have an all-encompassing description for candle lines that form with long lower shadows and small real bodies near the top of their range: *umbrella lines*. In one Japanese book there was a line that looked like a hammer. The text related to this figure said, "Buy from below and sell from above." As with most candlestick wisdom in the original, this text required some mental gymnastics. I finally deduced that the author meant that we should feel bullish with a hammer shape line after a falling market ("buy from below") and bearish after a rising market ("sell from above"). Deciphering these secrets of the Orient presented a real challenge!

Source: "Analysis of Stock Price in Japan." Tokyo: Nippon Technical Analysts Association, 1986, pg. 82.

As you learn and review the different candle formations, you can see how each candle line tells a story. With small real bodies indicating indecision, long real bodies showing definite opinion, and buying and selling pressure being revealed by lower and upper shadows, it's no wonder your skill at reading candle charts will add to your success as a trader or investor.

In Section Two, we'll talk about a candle similar to a shooting star, called a gravestone doji. Its appearance in the context of an extended rally is more menacing than that of a shooting star. As a matter of fact, doji in general broadcast extremely important signals.

SECTION TWO

The Dangerous Doji

In this section we'll focus on the powerful single candle line known as the doji. The doji plays an important role in candle charting techniques. When it appears in the context of an uptrend, especially in a zone of prior resistance, it can signal a significant trend shift, or reversal. Naturally, candles subsequent to the doji's appearance confirm the potential turn.

In fact, the doji's ability to convey the market's message is echoed in a letter I received from a medical doctor. He wrote, "As a physician, I can most appreciate the simplicity and effectiveness of candlestick charting. Like a stethoscope, simplistic in design, but powerful in diagnosis, candlestick charting has shown me a form of technical analysis well suited to diagnosing the health of my stocks."

In this section you will learn . . .
- The definition of a doji
- How to identify different types of doji
- The importance of doji when they appear in uptrends and downtrends
- How to interpret a doji when it forms in a box range

- Doji
- Dragonfly doji
- Gravestone doji
- Northern doji
- Southern doji

■ Getting Started

The Japanese place great significance on the power of the doji. Especially in the context of a market experiencing a mature uptrend, this candle line, either alone or included in a two- or three-candle pattern, warns you that a trend shift may be in the offing.

The *doji* is a session in which the opening and closing prices are the same; therefore, it resembles a cross. Like the spinning top, the doji indicates a market in complete balance between supply and demand. Since a doji session represents a market at a juncture of indecision, it can often be an early warning that a preceding rally could be losing steam.

The ideal doji forms with the same opening and closing price, but this rule is flexible. When the opening and closing prices are only a few ticks from each other you can still consider the candle line as a doji.

Maybe you've heard the old saying, "The stock market hates uncertainty." The doji is synonymous with uncertainty. Consider the doji a warning that the framework built by the bulls may soon falter or crumble.

While doji are extremely valuable at calling market tops (especially after a long, white candle), they sometimes lose signal potential when defining market bottoms. The doji's possible negative influence at trend tops comes from its warning that the market is indecisive. As such, a close over the doji's high could be a signal that the bulls have regained a foothold.

Although a doji's appearance in a rally might signal an exhausted market, a doji's emergence in a downtrend may not portend a bottom. Other Western indicators, and certainly price environment, must confirm a market turning into a base. Why? Remember that a doji indicates indecision. Indecision and uncertainty in an oversold market may just be a resting place before another downturn resumes.

Depending on the placement of the open and close price on the session, some doji have nicknames. These doji are still reversal indicators, but they hint at more positive or negative outcomes. A few of these specially named doji are the dragonfly doji, the gravestone doji, the Northern doji, and the Southern doji. Figure 10.3 illustrates these special doji lines.

KEY POINT

The pronunciation of doji is *doh' gee*. The plural of doji is doji.

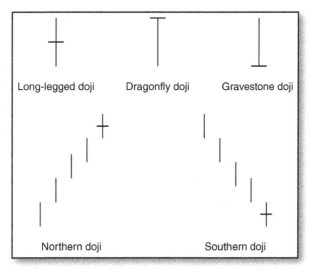

FIGURE 10.3 Doji

The *dragonfly doji* forms with the open and close near, or at, the high of the candle. This candle emits bullish implications. It's long lower shadow shows that the market fell sharply during the session, but buying pressure pushed the price back up to close at, or very near, the session's high. If you're thinking this doji resembles a hammer, but without the real body, you are correct.

Pay attention when you see the dragonfly doji emerging during declines that have become oversold. Normally doji in declines are not important, but the dragonfly doji is an exception.

The bearish counterpart to the dragonfly doji is the *gravestone doji*, also shown in Figure 10.3. The gravestone doji's open, low, and close all reside at the bottom of the candle. From the shape of this doji you can understand its name: It looks like a tombstone.

KEY POINT

The doji is more influential when it is a rare occurrence. If numerous doji have formed on a particular chart, do not view the development of a new doji as meaningful.

SIDE LIGHT

A Japanese proverb says, "Don't climb a tree to catch a fish." The gravestone doji has an ominous sound to its name and portends a potential uptrend reversal, but don't give it more import than it has. Even though its extended upper shadow and close at the low amplifies a trend change, candle signals don't forecast the scope of a possible decline. Remember, candle signals give you early reversal or change signals, but they don't predict future price targets. So, even if there are numerous gravestone doji, it doesn't perforce mean the market will fall that much steeper. It just means that the odds of a turn are greater than they would be with one gravestone doji.

The gravestone doji's strong point is in calling top reversals. Imagine an uptrend becoming overbought, rising on white real bodies. Perhaps a glance at the chart tells you that recent resistance at this same price level is also in place. Now, the gravestone doji appears. The market opens, rises to a much higher price (shown by the extended upper shadow), then falls to the low of the session to close. For the moment, at least, the bears have won control. If the next candle falls to the downside, the signal is complete.

Naturally, if the candle that forms after a gravestone doji rises above it and culminates in a long white real body, or other positive candle line, the potential trend reversal signal given by the gravestone doji is negated.

To differentiate between doji appearing in a rally and those materializing in a decline, I refer to the former as *Northern doji* and the latter as *Southern doji*. A doji with long upper and lower shadows is called a *long-legged doji*.

Like a pivotal word in a sentence, the doji gives optimum signals when taken in the context of a prior trend, when they confirm other technical indicators or patterns, and during consideration of follow-through action.

KEY POINT

When the market is rising and overbought, and then a doji appears after a tall, white candle, the Japanese say that the market is tired. What an appropriate way to view doji. A doji's emergence may not foretell an immediate price reversal. It may only suggest that the market is vulnerable and susceptible to change. A trader can use the highest high between the doji and the prior candle as resistance. If the market closes above that area, the Japanese say the bulls are refreshed.

In Section Three, we'll finish our discussion of single candle lines by exploring the messages displayed by bullish and bearish belt-holds and their long real bodies. We'll also talk about the psychology that underpins these candle lines "with an attitude."

SECTION THREE

Long Real Bodies, the Consummate Storytellers

In previous sections, we focused on single candle lines that incorporate small real bodies. These small real bodies project indecision on the part of market participants, especially when they form at support and resistance areas.

Now, we'll switch gears and talk about long real bodies. Candle lines with extended real bodies can also display strong signals, especially when they touch support and resistance zones. Toward the end of this section, we'll summarize market psychology as it pertains to single candle lines and their shadows, as well as their real bodies.

In this section you will learn . . .

- Market sentiment that underpins long white or black real bodies
- Bullish and bearish belt-holds, what they look like, and what they mean

- The importance of belt-hold lines when they develop at support and resistance areas
- How belt-hold lines add to your money management skills
- The significance of upper and lower shadows on all candle lines

Key terms to watch for:
- Bullish belt-hold
- Bearish belt-hold
- White opening shaven bottom
- Black opening shaven top
- Belt-hold candle line
- Blow-off

■ Getting Started

A candle chart displaying small real bodies at the culmination of an uptrend or down-trend—or even intermediate moves to the upside or downside—indicates that bulls and bears are fighting in a dead heat. The flip side of these small-bodied candle line reversals, which include spinning tops, high wave candles, and doji, are single candle lines incorporating long black or white real bodies. The Japanese refer to the candle line featuring this extended real body as a belt-hold.

As Figure 10.4 illustrates, the *bullish belt-hold* is a tall, white candle that opens on (or very near) the low of the session and closes at, or near, the high of the session. When it appears in a decline, it forecasts a potential rally. When it appears during an ascent, it keeps the bull trend intact.

> **SIDE LIGHT**
> The Japanese name for the belt-hold is derived from the sumo wrestling term, *yorikiri*. Yorikiri means "pushing your opponent out of the ring while holding onto his belt."

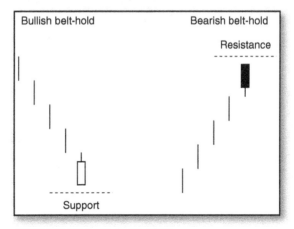

FIGURE 10.4   Belt-Hold Lines

As you can see in Figure 10.4, the bearish *belt-hold* is a long, black candle that opens at, or near, the high of the session, then tumbles lower as the session unfolds. If this candle line appears in the context of a mature uptrend, it may form a top reversal.

Generally speaking, the longer the height of the belt-hold candle line, the more important is the signal it gives. That makes sense, because an extended range culminating in a session's closing at the opposite end from the opening means that either the bulls or the bears dominate that session.

As you can see by the support and resistance lines in Figure 10.4, belt-hold lines that appear at prior support or resistance areas, thereby confirming the strength of those areas, are extremely valuable signals since they increase the chances of a reversal. Belt-hold lines also gain value as a reversal signal when they have not appeared regularly on the chart's recent time frame.

Like many candle trend reversal signals, bullish and bearish belt-holds can play an important role in sound money-management principles. Say you are long and your stock rises nicely in an uptrend. Soon, a doji or spinning top appears, then a bearish belt-hold forms. The doji was a warning to scale back on longs, but the bearish belt-hold completely confirms the reversal and could signal a time to consider closing your entire position and taking profits.

The reverse scenario occurs if you are holding a short position in the context of a downtrend. Perhaps the decline slows, and a bullish belt-hold forms at a prior support area. You may choose to cover part or all of your position, thus preserving your gains.

We've explored the size of real bodies thoroughly in previous pages. Still, the candle's upper and lower shadows—or lack of them—also tell a story. In the last section, we looked at the long lower shadows of hammers and the long upper shadows created by shooting stars. The long lower shadow of the hammer echoed the fact that at some time during the session the market had sold off sharply, but by session's end the market had regained all the lost ground and closed at or near the high of the session. In other words, the long lower shadow visually shows that the market had rejected lower price levels. A long upper shadow, such as that in a shooting star, illustrates a market that tests and then rejects higher prices.

Likewise, if there is a tall white candle that also has an extended upper shadow, that upper shadow offsets some of the bullish implications of the tall white candle. Conversely, the bearish implications of a long black candle are mitigated by a long lower shadow. Consequently, when analyzing candle lines, one should consider both the real bodies and shadows.

Conversely, imagine you see a market stabilizing at prior lows or a support zone, then stabilize. At that time, many of the shadows develop with definable long, lower bullish shadows—despite the size of the real body. That tells you that buyers are accumulating each time the price comes down to that support level. As a trader or investor, you might monitor that stock for a possible basing move and subsequent long entry, if and when it penetrates resistance on strong volume.

You've learned how powerful single candle lines can be. When they develop near support or resistance, they can become even more potent.

These patterns, constructed of two or more candle lines, give incredibly powerful signals that help foretell trend reversals. Like their single candle line colleagues, patterns come with highly descriptive names, including dark cloud cover, tweezers, and three white soldiers.

CHAPTER 11

Multi-Candle Patterns

From Steve Nison, *The Candlestick Course* (Hoboken, New Jersey: John Wiley & Sons, 2003), Chapter 3.

Learning Objective Statements

- Identify piercing and dark cloud cover
- Explain the importance of engulfing candles
- Recognize possible reversals through counterattack candles
- Identify candle confirmations of support and resistance

SECTION ONE

Close Cousins: Piercing, Dark Cloud Covers, Engulfing, and Counterattacks

Candle charts are most powerful when two or more candle lines combine in a candle pattern. Just as the Japanese endowed single candle lines with imaginative names, they also bestowed colorful descriptions on candle patterns. These descriptive monikers underscore the nature of the pattern's signals. For example, *dark cloud cover* is a bearish signal consisting of a two-candle pattern that indicates a top reversal. Of course, when dark clouds cover the sky, it is the warning before the storm.

In this unit, we'll discuss patterns that include two or three candle lines. We'll also discuss windows, which the Japanese call disjointed candles.

The section that follows explains dark cloud covers and engulfing, piercing, and counterattack patterns. Readily recognizable on charts, these candle patterns offer potent signals of possible trend changes and reversals. Use them in conjunction with Western indicators to find buy/sell setups and incorporate them into your money-management tactics.

In this section you will learn . . .

- An overview of multiple candle patterns
- How to recognize the bullish piercing pattern
- How to recognize the dark cloud cover pattern
- The importance of bullish and bearish engulfing patterns
- How bullish and bearish counterattack patterns can lead to quick trend changes

Key terms to watch for:

- Bullish piercing pattern
- Dark cloud cover
- Bullish engulfing pattern
- Bearish engulfing pattern
- Bullish counterattack pattern
- Bearish counterattack pattern

■ Getting Started

In earlier units, we learned about the power of single candle lines. Now we'll discuss why multiple candle patterns display even more intense signals.

Just as individual candle lines send important signals about the market's health, two- and three-candle patterns that emerge during uptrends and downtrends often presage a trend reversal, or change. Typically, a two-candle pattern begins with the topping or bottoming candle; the next candle confirms the reversal. A three-candle pattern may start with the formation of a candle in the context of a trend, followed by the topping or bottoming candle. The third candle's appearance verifies the reversal signal.

First, we'll discuss the two-candle pattern referred to as the *bullish piercing pattern* (Figure 11.1A), which appears in the context of a decline, or downtrend. Naturally, the more oversold the decline, the more significant the signal may be. The bullish piercing pattern consists of a black body forming in the downtrend; the next real

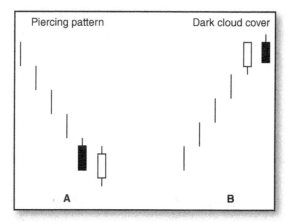

FIGURE 11.1 Piercing Pattern and Dark Cloud Cover

body culminates in a white real body that closes within the prior black body, preferably more than one-half of the black body's length. The white real body "pierces" the recent downtrend, with the bulls overwhelming the bears. Subsequent price action should confirm this pattern.

You might expect the counterpart to the bullish piercing pattern to be called a bearish piercing pattern. However, the opposite pattern is a powerful top reversal pattern known as *dark cloud cover*.

As illustrated in Figure 11.1B, a *dark cloud cover* forms a top reversal pattern. The first session should be a strong, white real body. The second session's price opens over the prior session's high (or above the prior session's close). By the end of the second session, it closes near the low of the session. The black candle should ideally close below the center of the prior white candle.

This foreboding pattern graphically indicates that the bears constrained the bulls. If the black real body does not close below the halfway point of the prior white candle, consider waiting for bearish confirmation on the following session. This could be a lower close on the next session.

SIDE LIGHT

If you're waiting for a good shorting setup, pay attention when a security in a steep uptrend that's overbought gets to a resistance area and forms dark cloud cover. When that scenario takes place, especially with high volume, you may wish to survey your other technical indicators to see if a shorting setup is at hand. Of course, a close over the highs of the dark cloud cover would be a reason to exit any shorts. Remember the concepts of stops!

Here's an example of how candle patterns add to your money-management skills by giving early warning of trend change. If you were holding a long position of a security in an uptrend and you saw the strong, white real body of the first candle soaring into the uptrend, you would surely remain bullish. On the next session, the security opens at a new high, confirming your bullishness. By the end of that session, however, the price has fallen well within the prior session's real body, indicating that the new price high failed to hold: Supply overcame demand. At this point, your bullishness may change to caution, and wisdom tells you to take profits. This is a prime example of how candle signals offer early reversal information and can aid you in locking in profits.

Next, we'll look at the two-candle pattern called the *bullish engulfing pattern*, illustrated in Figure 11.2. Like a piercing pattern, the bullish engulfing pattern typically appears at the culmination of a decline or a downtrend (see Figure 11.2A). The market falls, and a black candle forms. Next, a candle line develops with a real body that wraps around the prior session's black body. (The Japanese sometimes refer to this as a hugging line, for obvious reasons.) As the white real body opens under the prior black real body's close and closes above that session's open, it shows that buying pressure has overpowered selling pressure (i.e, the bulls have taken charge!) If the market is solid, the lows of the bullish engulfing pattern should be support. Thus, for those who are long based on this pattern, there should be a stop under the lows of this pattern.

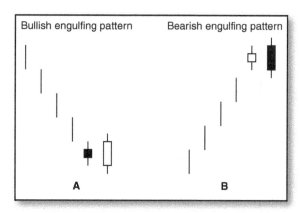

FIGURE 11.2 Engulfing Patterns

The flip side of a bullish engulfing pattern is the *bearish engulfing pattern,* which appears at the top of a market experiencing an uptrend. A white real body is engulfed by a black real body, suggesting a top reversal. As you can see in Figure 11.2B, the black real body gaps open above the prior white real body's close. Then the market falls to close below the prior session's open—a bearish signal. That movement indicates that supply has overpowered demand. Obviously, the bears have wrested control from the bulls. If the market is weak, the high of the bearish engulfing pattern should be a resistance area.

The next patterns we'll study are counterattack lines. Counterattack lines are formed when opposite-colored candles have the same close.

The *bullish counterattack line* occurs during a decline. As illustrated in Figure 11.3A, the initial candle in this pattern is usually a black candle. The next candle opens lower, which delights the bears. Suddenly, the bulls stage a counterattack by propelling prices to the prior candle's close. This causes the downtrend to stall.

The bullish counterattack pattern is similar to the bullish piercing pattern. The difference is that the bullish counterattack line does not move up into the prior candle's real body. Instead, it returns to the prior candle's close. The inability of the bullish counterattack formation to push into the former candle's real body tells you

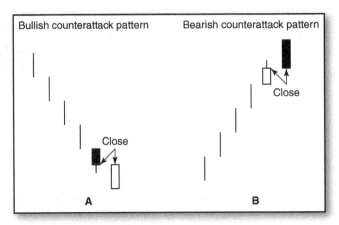

FIGURE 11.3 Counterattack Patterns

that it may not be quite as potent as the piercing pattern, nonetheless, the counterattack line should be respected. It shows a changing of the guard from bears to bulls, and that's always a significant event.

In a *bearish counterattack pattern* (see Figure 11.3B), the first white candle shows the bulls happily in control. The next candle gaps open higher, but the bears rush in to force the closing price down to the prior session's close. The surprised bulls have no doubt swallowed their recent optimism and now find themselves on shaky ground.

As you've probably surmised, the bearish counterattack pattern is similar to dark cloud cover, but again, the black counterattack candle does not penetrate the prior session's real body. Instead, it closes at the prior session's close. This suggests that dark cloud cover may display a slightly stronger signal, but again, whenever supply overwhelms demand, it significantly changes the market's texture.

Bearish counterattack lines send especially potent signals when the second session gaps open *much* higher than the previous session. This tells you that the market moved strongly in the direction of the prevailing trend, then made a sharp U-turn to close at the prior day's closing price. In other words, it shot up, only to end back down where it started.

You can imagine the same scenario, with directions reversed, for the bullish counterattack pattern.

Now you can see why the two-candle bullish and bearish engulfing pattern, bullish piercing pattern, dark cloud cover, and bullish and bearish counterattack patterns are such powerful indicators. Strong opinion drives the price in one direction, then suddenly that opinion reverts. Driven by a swift change in supply and demand, the price turns around and shoots in the opposite direction.

In the next section, we'll talk about additional two-candle patterns that presage trend change.

SECTION TWO

The Harami and Harami Cross, Morning and Evening Stars

In this section, we're going to discuss more candle patterns that are formed by a combination of single candle lines. First, we'll look at an interesting two-candle pattern called the harami, and a variation on that pattern known as a harami cross. Then we'll delve into a powerful three-candle pattern—the star pattern—renowned for calling bottom and top reversals. The star pattern incorporates spinning tops and doji. As you remember, we discussed the shooting star before. Now we'll explore morning stars, evening stars, and stars that include a doji, called morning doji stars and evening doji stars.

In this section you will learn . . .

- The importance of the harami and harami cross
- The differences between the harami and harami cross
- The power underpinning the harami cross
- How to differentiate between the harami and the engulfing pattern
- How the harami pattern compares to the Western inside day
- The criteria for morning and evening stars
- How morning and evening stars call bottom and top reversals
- How volume activity intensifies star signals

Key terms to watch for:

- Harami
- Harami cross
- Petrifying pattern
- Inside day
- Star
- Morning star
- Evening star

■ Getting Started

In previous sections, we talked about single candle lines called spinning tops. These small real lines are components in the reversal pattern referred to as the *harami*.

As shown in Figure 11.4, the first real body of this pattern is an unusually long black or white real body. The next candle consists of a small real body, which is completely within the prior real body.

The color of the real bodies in this pattern is unimportant: They can be opposite or the same.

SIDE LIGHT

The term *harami* is derived from a Japanese word that means pregnant. The first candle has a large body (the mother) with the small real body (the baby) inside it.

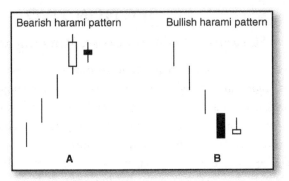

FIGURE 11.4 Harami

As you can see, like all candle patterns we've discussed so far, the harami is a reversal pattern. The Japanese say that when the harami pattern (Figure 11.4A) appears, a preceding rally or downtrend is losing its breath. The bearish harami tells us that despite the bullish white real body that moved the market higher, the tiny real body that follows indicates uncertainty and indecision. As you learned in previous sections, the limited price range of the small real body—especially when it follows a real body with a wide price range—shows that trend velocity has weakened.

On the other hand, when a bullish harami (Figure 11.4B) appears in a decline or downtrend, the selling pressure demonstrated by the first long, real body in the pattern is apparent. Then the second tiny real body forms. The bears suddenly lose momentum; they are unable to close the market at or below the prior candle's close. Uncertainty sets in, as the harami foretells a possible reversal and trend break. Do you understand how this pattern tells you an important story about market environment, with its accompanying change of sentiment? If the second real body is a doji instead of a spinning top, it is called a *harami cross* (Figure 11.5).

> **SIDE LIGHT**
>
> If both the first and second candles of a harami pattern are white, it is called a white-white harami. If the first is black and the second is white, it is called a black-white harami. I just call them both harami since the colors of the real bodies are not significant in this pattern.

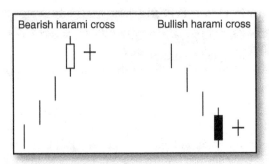

FIGURE 11.5 Harami Crosses

Next, we'll discuss an intriguing pattern known as the star. Indeed, this pattern is a star when it comes to calling top and bottom reversals!

A *star* is a small real body (think spinning top) that gaps away from the long real body preceding it in an uptrend or downtrend. The third candle in the formation also should gap away from the real body of the star, leaving the star's real body isolated at the top or bottom of an uptrend or downtrend. Ideally, the real bodies should not overlap, although the star's real body can intrude into the prior candle's shadow.

The star's real body represents a tug-of-war between the bulls and bears. It's a similar concept to that of the harami—a strong move in an uptrend or downtrend, directly followed by an indecisive time period. The star represents a stronger initial surge in the prevailing trend, however, before opposite forces arrive to quell it.

The star is the middle portion of two candle patterns called the morning star and evening star (Figure 11.6). The *morning star* is a bottom reversal pattern that derives its picturesque name from Mercury, the morning star that appears just before sunrise. Just as the morning star precedes daylight, the morning star candle pattern potentially presages higher prices.

Three candle lines form this pattern. First, in the context of a downtrend, a long, black candle develops, assuring the bears that they continue to be in command. Then a small real body or spinning top appears, gapping down at the open of its session and delighting the confident bears. The star (the middle portion of the morning star) completes its formation in a tight price range, without rising back to close into the prior black real body, although it may rise to an intraday high that infringes on the black candle's lower shadow. The final candle of the morning star pattern is

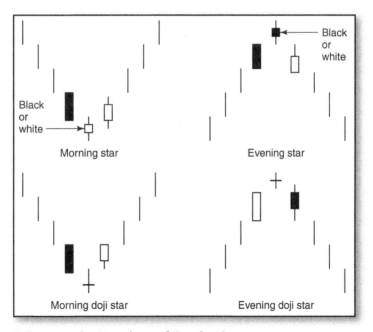

FIGURE 11.6 Morning and Evening Stars

a white real body that moves deeply into the first session's black candle. This panics the bears, as the white candle proves that the bulls have taken control and reversed the downtrend.

The morning star's bearish counterpart is the *evening star*. Three candle lines make up this top reversal signal. In the context of an uptrend, a long white candle appears, convincing the bulls that the rally will continue. Then the star appears in the form of a small real body that classically gaps up from the white candle's closing price. The star's real body (black or white) remains isolated as the next candle confirms the trend top by gapping away from the star and producing a long, black real body that pushes into the white candle's real body. The final candle seals the fate of the bulls as the bears grab control and push the market downward.

SIDE LIGHT

Certain volume signals infuse even more power into the star pattern. For example, imagine a setup in which light volume develops on the first candle line, followed by heavy volume on the third candle line. The light volume tells you that the force propelling the initial trend was weakening. The star materializes, showing uncertainty. Strong volume shooting into the third candle fuels the force that ignites the new trend.

If the middle portion of either the morning or evening star is a doji instead of a spinning top, the pattern is called a *morning doji star* or *evening doji star* (Figure 11.6).

The valuable harami, harami cross, and star patterns offer you more reversal patterns to place in your trader's toolbox. Your ability to recognize these patterns on charts of any time frame will add to your trend forecasting and money-management skills.

In the next two sections of this chapter, we'll discuss more candle patterns that signal top and bottom reversals. We'll also explore an entirely different concept, that of candles in continuation patterns.

SECTION THREE

Picturesque Storytellers: Tweezers, Crows, and Soldiers

In this section, we'll continue to explore interesting candle patterns that tell us more about the mood and manner of market environment. Although the recent price action of a chart is important, earlier price history can also contribute to our assessment of future price movement. The stories candle patterns tell us, present and past, all add to our ability to evaluate potential opportunities that will contribute to our success as traders and investors.

Now, on to the candle patterns known as tweezers, crows, and soldiers. The knowledge you've acquired in previous sections will make the following patterns easy to understand.

- The construction of the candle pattern the Japanese call tweezers
- How tweezers signal trend changes on long-term charts
- How tweezers incorporate other candle patterns
- The definition of *three black crows* and the signal they give
- The pattern known as three advancing soldiers and variations on the pattern
- Caveats pertaining to three advancing soldiers

Key terms to watch for:

- Tweezers
- Tweezers top
- Tweezers bottom
- Three black crows
- Three advancing soldiers

■ Getting Started

The candle pattern known as *tweezers* consists of two or more candle lines with matching highs or lows. The name is derived from the appearance of their formation. The *tweezers top* occurs in a rising market when two or more consecutive highs match each other, thus giving the image of the two prongs of a tweezers (Figure 11.7). (Since tweezers pinch, the connotation is that the trend is getting pinched.) A *tweezers bottom* takes place in a declining market, when two successive lows are equal.

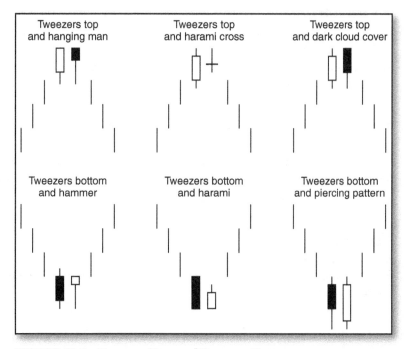

FIGURE 11.7 Tweezers Tops and Tweezers Bottoms

Ideally, the tweezers pattern should develop with the first session incorporating a long real body. In a declining market, this would probably be a long black candlestick; in a rising market, it would finalize as a long white candlestick.

The second session is interesting because it has many variations. It's best—but not absolutely necessary—when this session forms with a small real body. You are already familiar with the candle lines that may provide this component. For example, a tweezers top might finish with a hanging man, a shooting star, or a dark cloud cover pattern. A tweezers bottom could culminate with a hammer, harami cross, or piercing pattern.

With the first long real body and the second smaller real body integrating two consecutive highs, the tweezers top tells us that the bullish force of the long white candle began to dissipate with the small real body of the second candle line. Also, since the second candle cannot make a higher high than the first candle, the tweezers top adds to the outlook of a slakening of demand.

The tweezers bottom begins with a long black real body carrying the happy bears to victory. But the next candle, with the same lows and often completed with a small real body, switches victory to uncertainty. As buying bulls start nibbling, the bear's failure to press the second session to a lower low intensifies their angst. Naturally, the next candle will help confirm the potential reversal.

We assign little importance to two consecutive highs or lows shown on a daily or intraday chart unless other defining signals are present. In and of themselves, they are not noteworthy.

If you are a long-term trader or investor, you probably study weekly and monthly charts to obtain a longer perspective. So, as opposed to shorter time frames of intraday and daily charts, tweezers tops and bottoms that appear on weekly and monthly charts potentially indicate important reversal signals. For example, if a declining stock finished the current week by successfully holding last week's low, it could be the start of a base for a future rally. Conversely, if a 15-minute candle on an intraday chart successfully holds at the prior candle's low, it is not as significant.

The next candle pattern appears only at high price levels, or in the context of a mature uptrend. The Japanese gave it the quaint name, three black crows. Also called three winged crows, the *three black crows* pattern consists of three black candles that should close at or near their lows (Figure 11.8). The first candle appears near the top of an uptrend that's already starting to roll over, or move down. Each session's open should ideally take place within the previous session's real body.

The three black crows pattern sends useful signals for long-term traders and investors. By the time the pattern concludes with the completion of the third black

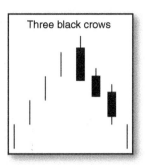

FIGURE 11.8 Three Black Crows

candle, it's already obvious that the market has fallen significantly from its recent high. Were you holding a prospective long-term position and a three black crows pattern appeared on a weekly chart, in conjunction with other indicators, it might warn you to take partial or all profits.

As we can see in Figure 11.9, *three white soldiers* appear as three long white candles exhibiting consecutively higher prices. This is a continuation pattern, and optimally, each candle should close at or near its high. The lines form an orderly, ongoing rise, with each candle opening within or close to the prior candle's real body. For this pattern, trend is not critical. The soldiers may begin an upward climb out of a downtrend reversal or may emerge during a rally. In these instances, the pattern suggests positive momentum ahead.

Pundits are fond of saying, "Trading is war." The patterns in this section— tweezers tops and bottoms, three black crows, and three white soldiers—provide you with extra ammunition to carry into battle. In the market combat zone, the more knowledge you have, the more likely you are to succeed. That's true now, more than ever, with volatility occurring as an everyday event.

KEY POINT

A caveat regarding the three white soldiers pattern: Although the candles display a healthy rise in the market, they do not necessarily give you a buy signal. When the candles move to an extended price range, be careful of entering long positions. Overbought markets usually consolidate or retrace after prolonged price rises. The proper long entry may appear after a pullback to price support.

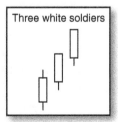

FIGURE 11.9 Three White Soldiers

In the next section, we will discuss the powerful candlestick continuation pattern known as windows. The window represents the Japanese version of the Western gap, and it provides us with a host of compelling signals.

SECTION FOUR

Disjointed Candles: Rising and Falling Windows

In previous sections, we've studied reversal patterns. These patterns have suggested we take action, whether to open a new position or apply money-management rules to close a position. Now we are going to explore a Japanese continuation pattern that implies the prior trend will continue. This pattern, called a window, is synonymous with the Western pattern known as a gap. We'll discuss the fundamental concepts of windows and how they apply in different patterns. We'll also talk about some general concepts as they apply to trends.

In this section you will learn . . .

- The definition of window
- How a rising window differs from a falling window
- How windows act as support and resistance areas
- Why closing prices are so important when closing windows
- Why size doesn't matter with windows
- Where key support areas are located in large windows
- Why it's important to trade with the trend

Key terms to watch for:

- Window
- Rising window
- Falling window
- Price vacuum

■ Getting Started

In technical analysis, we generally talk about two kinds of patterns: reversal patterns and continuation patterns. By now you are familiar with the action that takes place in a reversal pattern, meaning a change in direction. If you are a trader, you spend the majority of your time assessing charts and looking for potential trend reversals; that is where you typically enter and exit positions. Continuation patterns suggest that the trend before the pattern will continue, whether up or down.

A window is the same as a Western gap, but the Japanese have unique uses for windows (details follow in this section). A *window* means there is a price zone in which no trades take place, or a price vacuum. For example, stock XYZ has a high at $50. If the low of the next session is $52, there is a $2 *rising window*. If, however, stock XYZ has a low at $50, with the next session's high at $48, we would say it has gapped down $2 and therefore a $2 *falling window* exists.

A *rising window* is a bullish signal. The price vacuum between the prior candle's high and the current session's low means the bulls are in control and willing to pay up. A falling window is a bearish signal. The absence of price activity between the prior candle's low and the current session's high shows the bears are driving the market down, with no competition from the bulls.

The Japanese advise, "Go in the direction of the window." This makes sense, as windows are continuation signals. If the bulls are willing to skip several price levels and pay higher prices for a security, then they are indeed in control. Conversely, if prices are so weak that bears can force them to plunge below a certain range, then the selling pressure is not to be doubted.

SIDE LIGHT

For a quick demonstration of how gaps can be filled on an intraday basis, watch a stock that gaps up a point or more at the open. Since some market professionals make a living from *fading the gap*, or trading in the opposite direction from the gap move: If a stock gaps higher a substantial amount at the open, the pro will sell it short for a quick trade. If enough selling pressure occurs, the stock will drop enough to fill a portion, or all, of the price vacuum. (Please don't try this technique yourself, unless you are a very experienced trader. It involves extremely high risk.)

One of the most common misunderstandings about rising and falling windows is identifying the part of the candle session that constitutes a price limit. Some think that if real bodies do not touch, the space between is a window. This is incorrect. With rising and falling windows, there must be a space—whether narrow or wide—where candle highs and lows do not intersect. If shadows intersect, there is no window. There must be a *price vacuum,* or space between price levels, for a window to be valid.

One of the most useful signals offered to us by rising and falling windows is summed up by another Japanese saying: "Corrections stop at the window." That means windows often become support and resistance areas. You can see how this works in Figure 11.10, with windows acting as springboards of support and resistance.

When a rising window occurs, the *entire space* of that window is considered a support area. Therefore, if you have a long position that just developed a rising window, you can expect that window to act as support if the market pulls back. If the price retraces to the bottom of the window, but *does not close below it*, then support has not been broken. If, however, the market closes below the window's bottom, then support has been broken. Consequently, the most important area of a rising window is the bottom of that window.

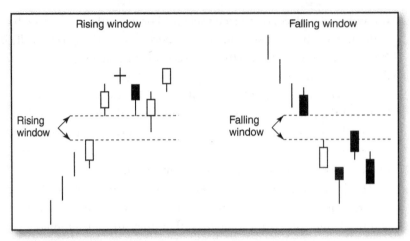

FIGURE 11.10 Rising and Falling Windows

The same is true for a falling window. When a falling window forms, the entire price vacuum establishes a resistance area. If you are considering a short sale, you can regard the window as price resistance when (if) the security rallies. If the price rallies to the top of the window, but *does not close above it*, that resistance stays intact. However, if the price rallies through the falling window and *closes* above it, the resistance area is broken; no short sale should be entered. Thus, the top of a falling window is its critical resistance area.

In "Forecasting and Trading Techniques," you will find many different examples of rising and falling windows to study. Just as a picture is worth a thousand words, these diagrams and real-world charts will help you understand more thoroughly how windows act as strong components of price patterns.

CHAPTER 12

Forecasting and Trading Techniques

From Steve Nison, *The Candlestick Course* (Hoboken, New Jersey: John Wiley & Sons, 2003), Chapter 4.

Learning Objective Statements

- Identify candle patterns that provide potential reversal signals
- Explain how to combine Western technical indicators with candles
- Explain techniques for using candles in multiple time frames
- Explain how to protect capital with candles

As the Japanese proverb states, "Make use of your opportunities." In this chapter I show some practical applications of how candle charts will let you take advantage of market opportunities. The examples in Section One of this chapter provide illustrations of the following real-world applications.

- Using candle charts to preserve capital
- How candle charts give early reversal signals
- How candle charts can confirm support or resistance areas
- Using a confluence of candle signals to confirm support or resistance
- The ease of combining Western technical tools with candle charts
- Obtaining a price target
- Harnessing the insights of the candles to enter and exit a trade
- Using intraday trading signals
- The technique of using a longer time frame chart to get support or resistance and a short time frame to issue the buy or sell signal

Keep in mind that the techniques shown in the rest of this chapter can be applied to any market you are trading—futures, equities, fixed-income—and any time frame—from a 1-minute to a monthly chart. In addition, option traders can also use candle signals as a timing mechanism. The exception to this universality of use for candles is that the market has to have an open, high, low, and close. Tick charts and daily mutual funds, for example, can't have candle charts, since both only have closes.

SECTION ONE

Candle Chart Applications

Properly used, candle charts not only help improve profits, but they also assist in preserving capital. They do so by helping you avoid a potential losing trade or exiting a profitable trade early. Figure 12.1 shows an example of the latter. The dashed lines in Figure 12.1 show a resistance area near 135. A tall white candle pierces this resistance in early March. For those who were already long this index, this was a green light to remain long. But observe what unfolded the next session—the doji. This doji line hinted that the bulls had lost full control of the market (however, it does not mean that the bears have taken control). With this doji, one should consider taking profits, moving up protective sell stops, or selling calls. This is a classic example of the power of candle charting techniques: Within one session we were able to glean the visual clue via the doji that while the market was maintaining its highs, the doji shouted that the bulls were not in complete control. So while the market looked healthy from the outside, the internals (as shown by the doji) were relaying the message that the market was not

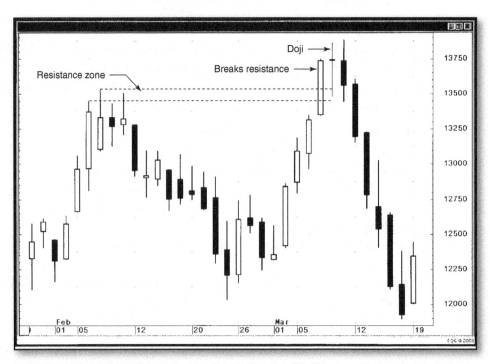

FIGURE 12.1 Oil Service Index: Daily (Using Candle Charts to Preserve Capital)
© CQG Inc. used by permission.

FIGURE 12.2 Semiconductor Index: Daily (Using Candle Charts to Confirm Resistance)

© Aspen Graphics. Used by permission.

as healthy as it seemed. This market was, as the Japanese proverb states, "Like a leaking boat brightly painted."

A key concept is that the more technical signals that emerge at the same support or resistance level, the higher the likelihood of a reversal. This convergence concept can be applied with candles and Western techniques. That is, if a candle signal confirms a Western technical signal, as the Japanese proverb says, like the right hand helping the left. The charts in Figures 12.2 and 12.3 are examples of the ease and power with which one can merge candle and Western charting techniques. Figure 12.2 shows how candles can confirm support and how we can use Western technical tools to get a price target. Figure 12.3 displays how a candle signal helped confirm a base.

Figure 12.2 shows how a gravestone doji helped reinforce a resistance zone near 420. Another technical signal at or near the same price area of the gravestone doji amplifies the candle signal's significance. A limitation of candle charts is that they normally don't provide price targets. This is why classic Western techniques, such as looking at support or resistance lines or pivot highs or lows, is so important, since you use these levels as targets. With this in mind, let's turn our attention to the same chart. Observe how this market was in a box range of about 420 to 370. Once the gravestone doji confirmed the top end of the box range at 420, a trader could consider selling short with that signal (with a stop over the top end of the box range) with a target to the bottom end of the box range near 370. This objective was quickly met.

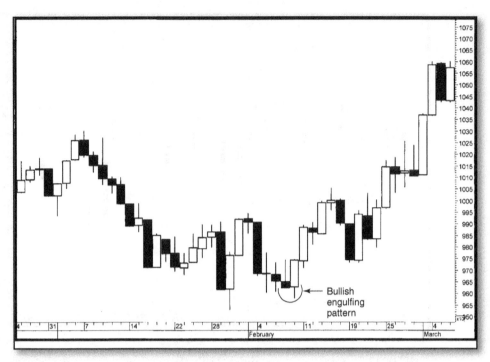

FIGURE 12.3   Dow Jones Industrials: Daily (Using Candle Charts to Confirm Support)
© Charts powered by MetaStock. Used by permission.

In Figure 12.3 a bullish engulfing pattern that took on extra importance as a turning signal is highlighted for two reasons. The first was that the lows of that bullish engulfing pattern confirmed a potential support level set by the lows made in late January. The second consideration is that, although a classic bullish engulfing pattern has a white candle wrapping around a prior black candle, this bullish engulfing pattern had a white candle that engulfed the three prior small real bodies (one of which was a doji). Though this aspect doesn't forecast that the market will move much higher than it would with a regular bullish engulfing pattern (remember, candles don't give targets), it does greatly improve the chances of a turn and thus makes a buy more attractive.

In Figures 12.2 and 12.3 I touched upon combining candle charting tools with Western technical analysis (please note that this book only touched the tip of the iceberg with this concept. Please see conclusion for more source material on ways to combine moving averages, volume, Bollinger bands, etc with candle charts).

Candle signals converge, just as Western technical indicators do. This means that if you see more than one candlestick signal confirming support or resistance set by another candle pattern, such as a hammer confirming a support area set by a bullish engulfing pattern, the likelihood of a turn increases. Figure 12.4 illustrates what I call a confluence of candles. This chart also shows that candle charting techniques are easily applicable to intraday charts.

FIGURE 12.4 American Express: 60 minute (Confluence of Candles)
© Aspen Graphics. Used by permission.

Figure 12.4 shows a bearish falling window, or resistance zone, from $39.80 to $40.20. Thus, one could consider selling on a move up to that window. The stock got to that level at candle line A. But although the stock was at resistance, would one sell short with a tall white candle? I wouldn't recommend that, even if the market is at a resistance level! Notice what unfolded after candle line A: As shown at area B, the market formed a series of small real bodies (aka spinning tops). These small real bodies tell us that the bulls were tired, confirming the market's hesitation at the resistance zone set by the falling window. This could be a good time to sell short. Of course, if the market closed over the top of the falling window (i.e., $40.20), one should reconsider being short. As such we had one candle signal (the falling window) set the resistance area and another candle signal (the small real bodies) reinforcing that supply was stepping in at the window's resistance.

Because candle charts often send out reversal signals much sooner than bar charts, candles will shine at helping you improve market timing. Indeed, some of our advisory clients use fundamentals to decide which markets to buy or sell and then use the candles for timing these buy or sell times. Figure 12.5 illustrates how a trader might use the candles to enter or exit trades.

A hammer forms on May 7 (the upper shadow was small enough to make this a hammer). This, in combination with the series of bullish shadows shown at A and B, was a strong indication that the market was trying to build a foundation for a rally. One could buy on that hammer with a stop under the low of the hammer. In the next

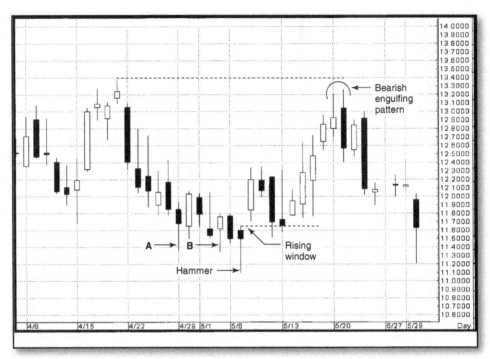

FIGURE 12.5 Converse Technology: Daily (Using Candle Signals to Enter or Exit Trades)

© Aspen Graphics. Used by permission.

session the market formed a rising window, which was another positive signal. A few days after this rising window the stock descended, but the bottom of the rising window maintained itself as support based on the close (remember that it takes a *close* under the bottom of a rising window for the window's support to be broken). Since this support held, we would stay long. In the week of May 13, the market moved north. The emergence of a bearish engulfing pattern near $13.30 at a resistance level defined by the highs of April 19 (shown by the dashed line) was a strong indication to take profits from the longs purchased on the hammer session.

In Figures 12.6A and 12.6B I show just one of the many ways a trader can harness the power of intraday candle charts to get a leg up on the competition.

In Figure 12.6A we see a solid band of support near $43.25 underpinned by the dual bullish engulfing patterns on the week of June 3. The lows set by these two bullish engulfing patterns was successfully defended on June 14. The rally that began on June 14 stalled with a shooting star near $47. As the price dip from this shooting star approached the aforementioned support area toward $43.25 on June 26, you might consider buying on the session. To help improve our timing we can turn to an intraday chart to see if there are any buy signals as the stock approached $43.25 intraday. We now turn to the 5-minute chart of this stock at Figure 12.6B.

On this June 26 5-minute chart, the horizontal line shows the support area obtained from the daily chart (Figure 12.6A) near $43.25. This level was confirmed

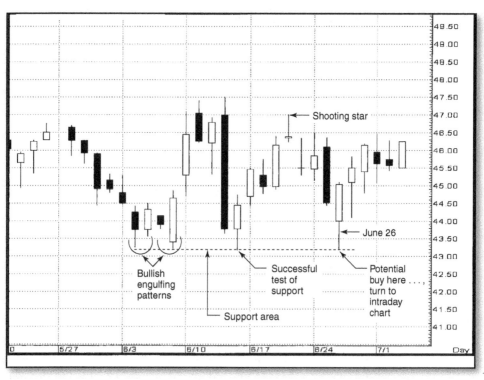

FIGURE 12.6A H and R Block: Daily (Using Intraday Candle Signals)

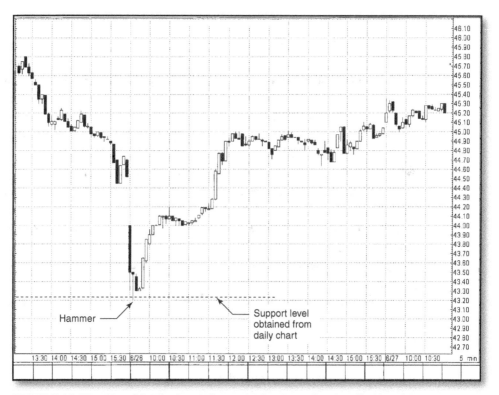

FIGURE 12.6B H and R Block: 5 Minute (Using Intraday Candle Signals)

by a hammer. Therefore we can buy on that hammer based on this 5-minute chart because it confirmed a support level derived from the longer-term daily chart. These two figures illustrate the concept of using a longer time frame (daily) to obtain support or resistance and then a shorter time frame's candle signal (a 5-minute chart) to place the trade. This concept can be expanded to any two time frames. Thus, for example, you could use a weekly chart to get a support level and see if there are any bullish candle signals on a daily chart as the stock gets to this support.

SECTION TWO
Trading Guidelines

In Section One of this chapter I gave some real-world examples so you could get a feel for how to apply the tools and techniques of using candlestick charts. Now we take the next step by listing the pivotal trading concepts.

A note of caution: Market conditions affect some of the precepts listed below. According to one of the guidelines below, northern doji are normally more significant than southern doji. While this is generally true, if there's a southern doji confirming a major support area, you can be assured that I would pay close attention to that southern doji. This brings to the fore the importance of looking at all candle signals and trading guidelines in the context of the market environment.

■ The Guidelines

- As the real body gets smaller, it implies that the prior trend is losing steam.
- The larger the real body, the greater the force underpinning the move.
- The more technical signals, whether Eastern (candles) or Western, that confirm the same support or resistance level, the greater the chance for a bounce from support or decline from resistance.
- Northern doji are normally more significant than southern doji.
- A series of long upper shadows as the market is ascending implies that the bulls do not have full control.
- A series of long lower shadows as the market is falling hints that the bears do not have full control.
- The rising and falling windows are, respectively, bullish and bearish continuation indicators.
- Doji in the middle of a box range are not a trading signal, since there is no trend to reverse.
- Candle charts are best used as a tool, not a system.
- Resistance or support is not considered broken unless by a close.
- If you see a reversal signal, consider initiating a new position only if that signal is in the direction of the major trend.

- Never place a trade with a candle signal until you have considered the risk/reward of the potential trade.
- Candle signals can denote areas of support and resistance.
- Candle indicators do not offer price targets.
- You should wait for the session's close to confirm a candle signal.
- A hanging man needs bearish confirmation by a close under the hanging man's real body.
- When analyzing a single candle line, one should consider both the real body and the shadows.
- Remember the importance of stops.
- The entire space of the rising window is a support area, with the most important area the bottom of the rising window.
- The entire area of the falling window is a resistance zone, with its most important area the top of the falling window.

RISK MANAGEMENT

This short section revisits the basic understanding of option pricing, implied volatility, and calculation of the VIX index. These chapters include the same content found in the CMT Level I text. They are included in CMT Level II for two reasons: first, for the convenience of study within a single book; second, so that candidates can reconsider this information in a new light. Astute analysts and traders can use option prices and implied volatility calculations to signal when the anticipated volatility in price movement implies an elevated threat to an existing trend.

■ What Candidates Need to Know

For CMT Level II, candidates will be expected to not only understand what implied volatility is and how to calculate it, but also how to apply it as part of a forecast. Candidates should know how to calculate implied volatility over a 30-day time frame and recognize the procedure for calculating any other time frame as well.

CHAPTER 13

Option Pricing Basics

From Edwin J. Elton, Martin J. Gruber, Stephen J. Brown, and William N. Goetzmann, *Modern Portfolio Theory and Investment Analysis*, 9th Edition (Hoboken, New Jersey: John Wiley & Sons, 2014), Chapter 23, Option Pricing Theory.

Learning Objective Statements

- Recognize the basic characteristics of call and put options
- Differentiate between call options and put options

The markets for options are among the fastest-growing markets for financial assets in the United States. While option trading is not new, it experienced a gigantic growth with the creation of the Chicago Board Options Exchange in 1973. The listing of options meant more orderly and thicker markets for these securities.

The growth in option trading has been accompanied by a tremendous interest among academics and practitioners in the valuing of option contracts. In this chapter we discuss alternative types of options, examine the effect of certain characteristics on the value of options, and present explicit models for valuing options.

■ Types of Options

An option is a contract entitling the holder to buy or sell a designated security at or within a certain period of time at a particular price. There are a large number of types of option contracts, but they all have one element in common: the value of an option is directly dependent on the value of some underlying security. Options represent a claim against the underlying security and thus are often called contingent claim contracts. The two least complex options are called puts and calls. These are the most widely traded options. In addition, most other options either can be valued as combinations of puts and calls or can be valued by the methodology developed to value puts and calls. Consequently, we begin this section with a discussion of puts and calls, and then we discuss other types of options and combinations of basic options.

Calls

The most common type of option is a call. A call gives the owner the right to buy a fixed number of shares of a stock at a fixed price, either before or at some fixed date. It is common to refer to calls that can be exercised at only a particular point in time as European calls and calls that can be exercised at any time up to, and including, the expiration date as American calls. Take, for example, a November 20 American call on Mobil at $70. This call gives the owner the right to buy a certain number of shares of Mobil at $70 a share anytime on or before November 20. Calls are normally traded in units of 100 shares. Thus one call would be a right to buy 100 shares of Mobil. Each characteristic of the call has a name. For example, the $70 price is called the exercise price. The final date at which the call can be exercised is the expiration date.[1]

One of the distinguishing characteristics of a call is that if it is exercised, the exchange of stocks is between two investors. One investor issues the call (termed the *call writer*) and the other investor purchases the call. The call is a side bet between two investors on the future course of the security. Figure 13.1*a* shows the profit per share of stock for the holder of a call at the expiration date. The figure represents the pattern for a call originally purchased for $5 with an exercise price of $50. For a stock price below $50, it would not pay to exercise the call because shares could be purchased in the open market for less than the exercise price. For share prices above $50, it would pay to exercise the call and gain by the difference between the share price and exercise price. For example, if the share price is $54, then the holder of a call benefits from the ability to purchase the stock at $50 rather than $54. For share prices up to $55, the owner of the call loses money since the payoff from the stock purchase is less than the cost of the call. For a stock price above $55, there is a profit.

The position of the call writer is depicted in Figure 13.1*b*. The pattern of the profit is exactly opposite that of the call purchaser. For a stock price below $50, the call writer makes a profit equal to the $5 per share received from the issuance of the call; from $50 to $55, part of the $5 is lost by having to furnish the stock at a price below the market price; above $55, the call writer loses more than was received by selling the call.

Up to now, we have referred to shares being traded between individuals as a result of exercise at the expiration of a call. We could have also discussed the exercise of a call before the expiration date. However, we have not done this so far because calls (even those that have an exercise price below the price of the stock) are rarely

---

[1] In the example, we use an arbitrary date for expiration. For options not listed on the exchanges, any date is possible. However, options trading on the Chicago Board Options Exchange have standardized expiration dates. Any single security will normally have options outstanding with three different expiration dates. These dates are three months apart (e.g., April, July, and October). These options expire at 10:59 A.M. Central Time on the Saturday after the third Friday of the month.

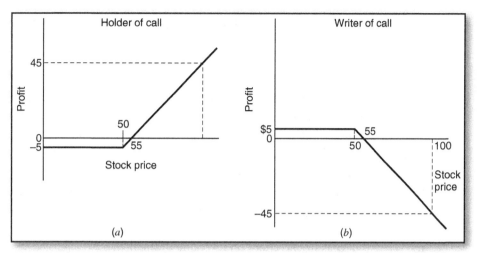

FIGURE 13.1 Profit from call.

exercised before the expiration date. For example, assume the share price is $60 and the exercise price is $50. Clearly, a profit can be made by exercising the option. There is a third alternative. Instead of exercising the option, sell it.

The sale may be to someone who does not currently maintain a position in the option or it may be to an investor who wrote an option and also wishes to liquidate his position.[2] The listing of options on exchanges facilitates these sales. With options listed on the exchange, the mechanics of the purchase or writing of an option becomes identical to the mechanics of the purchase or sale of a stock, except for differences in margin requirements.

There are actions that a firm might take that will affect the value of its shares. For example, a two-for-one stock split would be expected to cut the price of a share in half. Stock dividends and cash dividends are two other examples. The value of an option is affected by these actions of the firm. Clearly, if there were no adjustment in the exercise price when a stock splits, the value of an option would be substantially reduced. Most options are protected against stock dividends and stock splits by automatic adjustments in the exercise price and the number of shares that can be purchased with one option. Cash dividends are not as frequently protected against. For example, there are no adjustments for cash dividends for options traded on the exchanges. The price of a stock on average decreases by slightly less than the amount of the dividend when a stock goes ex-dividend. Thus, all other things being equal, the price of an option should be lower on a stock that will go ex-dividend before the expiration date.

---

[2] When an individual sells an option, the person purchasing it need not be the original writer. Rather, the individual purchasing the option is whoever happens to wish to buy the option on the day of sale. This is identical to what happens with any other security. When you buy a share of stock and subsequently sell it, the individual from whom you buy or to whom you sell is unknown and normally different.

The next most common type of option is a put, which we will discuss in the next section.

Puts

A put is an option to sell stock at a given price on or before a particular expiration date. Consider, for example, a $50 General Electric put of December 18. The person who owned such a put would have the right to sell the General Electric stock to the person who issued the put at $50 a share on or before December 18. Puts, like calls, are traded in units of 100 shares. Thus one put involves the right to sell 100 shares. If the exercise can take place only at the expiration date, it is called a European put. If the exercise can take place at any time on or before the expiration date, it is called an American put. A put, like a call, involves a transaction between two investors. Thus the writing of puts has no effect on the value of the firm.

Figure 13.2 shows the profit at the expiration date for a put with an exercise price of $50 that originally cost $5. Figure 13.2*a* shows the profit to the owner of the put. Figure 13.2*b* shows the profit to the writer of a put. Consider Figure 13.2*a*. For prices above $50, the owner of the put would prefer to sell shares in the regular market rather than to the writer of the put, because the price received is greater. Thus, for prices above $50, the exercise value is zero. For prices above $45 but below $50, the owner of the put would prefer to exercise her option instead of selling her stock on the open market. However, the owner of the put loses money, because she paid more for the put than she gains from the sale at a higher price. Below $45, the owner of the put makes money, because the amount she gains from the sale at a more attractive price more than compensates for the cost of the put. The payoff pattern for the writer of the put is the exact opposite of the payoff pattern for the owner. For prices above $45, he makes money, and for prices below $45, he loses.

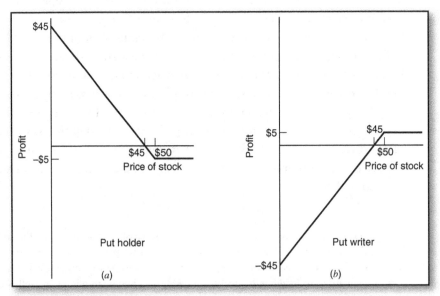

FIGURE 13.2 Profit from put.

Puts, like calls, are rarely exercised before expiration. Assume the share price in our example declined to $40. At $40, it clearly pays to exercise rather than to let the option expire. Instead of exercising the option, the owner could sell the right. Although an American put is more likely to be exercised before expiration than an American call, we will show that it generally pays to sell rather than exercise a put, for the sale price will almost always be higher than the exercise value. The exception can occur when the put is deep in the money.

Warrants

A warrant is almost identical to a call. Like a call, it involves the right to purchase stock at an exercise price at or before an expiration date. A warrant differs from a call in one way: a warrant is issued by the corporation rather than another investor. This seemingly small difference is very important. There are two instances when this difference has an effect on the value of the firm that issues the warrant. First, when the warrants are issued, the company receives the money for the warrant. Second, when the warrants are exercised, the following occurs:

1. The company receives the exercise price.
2. The number of shares of the firm that are outstanding goes up by the number of shares that are exercised.
3. The number of warrants still outstanding goes down.

Calls and puts are side bets by market investors, and the corporation has no direct interest in transactions involving these options, either when they are created or when they are exercised. Warrants, on the other hand, are used by the corporation to raise capital. The corporation and its shareholders have a definite interest in their issuance and exercise, because these transactions affect both the amount of cash the firm has raised and the ownership interest of its shareholders. Because the issuance and exercise of warrants affect the value of the security on which the warrant represents a contingent claim, the valuation of warrants becomes a more complex problem than the valuation of calls.

Combinations

Part of the fun of reading the options literature is the colorful terminology. One of the areas where it is especially colorful is the naming of combinations of options. An infinite number of combinations of puts and calls can be considered. A combination of a put and call with the same exercise price and expiration date is called a *straddle*. A similar combination of two puts and a call is a *strip*. If the combination is two calls and a put, it is called a *strap*. The payoff pattern at expiration is easy to determine using the techniques discussed earlier. Similarly, the valuation can be accomplished using the techniques discussed later in this chapter.

Consider a straddle. Figure 13.3*a* shows the profit at expiration from the point of view of the purchaser of the option. Figure 13.3*b* is the profit from the point of view of the writer. As we can see from examining these diagrams, a straddle should be purchased

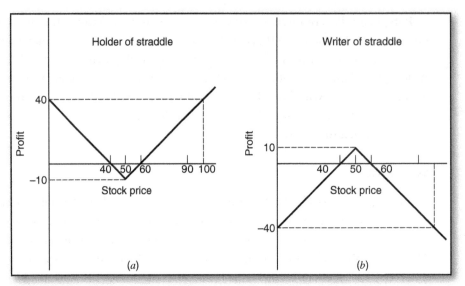

FIGURE 13.3   Profit from straddle.

by someone who believes the price of the shares will move substantially either up or down, without being sure of the direction, and who also believes that other investors have underestimated the magnitude of future price changes. For example, a straddle could be purchased by someone who knew that major information was about to be announced that would seriously affect the company's fortune, was unsure whether the information would be good news or bad news, and believed that other investors were unaware of the existence of this information. In contrast, the writer of a straddle is an investor who believes that the share price will trade at close to the exercise price, while others believe differently.

One of the interesting ways to trade options is in combination with the stock on which they represent a claim. The investor who combines stocks with contingent claims on the stocks has two assets with very strong correlations. Consider the writer of a call who also owns the shares.[3] Figure 13.4 shows the payoff pattern at expiration. The exercise price is assumed to be $50, the cost of the stock to the holder is also assumed to be $50, and the call is assumed to cost $5. Three separate lines are shown: one for the stock, one for the call, and one for the combination. As Figure 13.4 shows, an investor who writes a call and owns the stock rather than simply owning the stock increases the return at low stock prices at the expense of returns at the higher share prices.

As a final example, consider the ownership of a put plus the ownership of stock. Once again, assume an exercise price of $50, a stock cost of $50, and a put cost of $5. Figure 13.5 shows the payoff pattern. This combination reduces the return at higher stock prices in exchange for guaranteeing that if the stock declines in price, the portfolio will not decline below a lower limit.

Another type of combination is an option that can be purchased only in combination with another security. A convertible bond is an example of this combination. A

---

[3] The writing of a call while owning the stock is called *writing a covered call*.

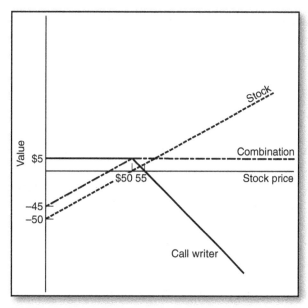

FIGURE 13.4 The value of a combination of common stock and a call.

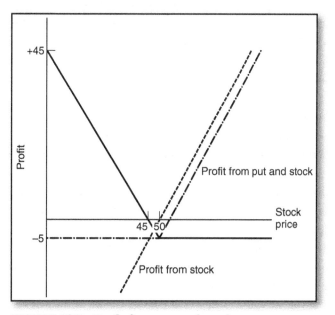

FIGURE 13.5 Profit from put and stock.

convertible bond has the same characteristics as a normal bond and in addition can be converted into the shares of a company. Thus the convertible bond can be considered a bond plus a call. However, the call has a special feature. Conversion of the bond into shares of stock involves giving up the bond, plus sometimes cash for the stock. Because the value of the bond changes over time, the exercise price changes over time.

We have discussed a number of combinations of options and options plus security positions in this section. Many others are possible. We leave it to our readers to determine the payoff patterns for those they find interesting.

■ Some Basic Characteristics of Option Values[4]

We can infer the manner in which certain characteristics of options should affect their value in a rational market. Not only are these relationships interesting in themselves, but they will also prove useful as a check on valuation models. Any valuation model should be consistent with these basic relationships. It is interesting to note that some of the earlier option valuation models that were later proved incorrect were not consistent with these basic relationships.

Relative Prices of Calls with Alternative Characteristics

Recall that the European call gives the holder the right to purchase stock at the exercise price on a particular date (the expiration date). The American call differs from the European call in that it can be exercised at any time up to the expiration date. Because the American call is a European call with the added opportunity to exercise before the expiration date, it cannot be worth less than the European call. Thus the first relationship established is that a European call with the same expiration date and exercise price as an American call cannot sell for more than the American call.

Consider two American calls with the same exercise price and assume both calls are on the same stock. The one with the longer life offers the investor all the exercise opportunities of the one with the shorter life, plus some additional opportunities. Hence it cannot be worth less. It might bother the reader that we do not simply say that the longer-lived call is more valuable. In general, this is true, but in some extreme cases (e.g., when both calls are worthless), this is not true. Hence the more cautious statement.

The next relationship concerns the exercise price. Consider two calls with the same expiration date written on the same stock. The one with the higher exercise price cannot be more valuable than the one with the lower exercise price. This is obvious, because the holder of the latter can be in the same position as the holder of the former, upon exercise, except that she will have cash left over.

While these relationships seem quite simple, as discussed earlier, not all valuation models that have been developed were consistent with these principles; hence they are worth keeping in mind.

---

[4]The results in this section were developed by Merton (1973).

Minimum Value of a European Call

In this section we will show that the value of a European call on a non-dividend-paying stock is at least the greater of zero and the difference between the stock price and the present value of the exercise price. To see this, consider two different portfolios. Portfolio A involves the purchase of a call and a bond that matures at the expiration date of the call and which at that date will have a value equal to the exercise price. If R is the interest rate between the time the call is valued and the expiration date, and if E is the exercise price, then bonds in the amount of $E/(1+R)$ should be purchased. An alternative to portfolio A is the purchase of stock directly. Call this portfolio B. The key characteristics to these investments are shown in Table 13.1. S_1 is the stock price at expiration, S_0 is the current stock price, E is the exercise price, and C is the current price of the call. The payoffs at the expiration date are shown in the last two columns of the table.

If $S_1 > E$, then the payoffs from both portfolios are the same. However, if $S_1 \leq E$, the payoff from portfolio A is larger. Thus portfolio A is at least as desirable as portfolio B, and if $S_1 \leq E$ at expiration is possible, A is more desirable. Given that portfolio A is at least as desirable as B, it cannot cost less than B; otherwise no one would purchase the stock (portfolio B). Therefore

$$C + \frac{E}{1+R} \geq S_0$$

or

$$C \geq S_0 - \frac{E}{1+R}$$

The European call cannot sell for less than the stock price less the present value of the exercise price. Because the call cannot sell for a price below zero, we have completed the proof.

TABLE 13.1 **Payoffs from Alternative Holdings**

Action	Investment	Value at Expiration Date	
		If $S_1 > E$	If $S_1 \leq E$
Portfolio A			
Buy call	$-C$	$S_1 - E$	0
Buy bonds	$\dfrac{-E}{1+R}$	E	
Total	$-C - \dfrac{E}{1+R}$	S_1	E
Portfolio B			
Buy stock	$-S_0$	S_1	S_1

Early Exercise of an American Call

Probably the most surprising conclusion of modern option pricing theory is that it never pays to exercise an American call before the expiration date on a stock that does not pay dividends or whose exercise price is adjusted for dividend payments. Later we will present a simple proof. But before we do, it is worthwhile to discuss why this holds. The reason is simple but subtle. The American call is worth more alive than dead. It is worth more keeping the American call alive by not exercising it than killing it through exercise. Thus an investor no longer wishing to hold the call is better off selling it than exercising it. Consider an example. Assume a stock is selling for $60 and an investor holds an American call with an exercise price of $50. Furthermore, assume this investor believes that the stock price will decline between now and the expiration date. Clearly the investor would prefer to exercise the call now rather than hold it and exercise it at a later date. There is another option: sell the call to another investor.

If the call has a market price higher than the $10 the investor makes on exercise ($60 stock price − $50 exercise price), selling the call is preferable. Why should the price of the call be more than $10? The American call has two sources of value: the value of an immediate call ($10) plus the value of the chance to call from now to the expiration date. As long as this latter opportunity has value, the American call should sell for more than $10. You might well ask why someone would wish to buy the call when the investor believes the stock price will decline. The answer is that this cannot be the general market belief or the stock price would have already declined. In other words, the aggregate market belief must be that the correct price is $60 and that at $60 the total return from the stock is competitive with securities of similar risk. Thus the market must believe the return on the stock will be positive.

Now for the proof. Earlier, we argued that an American call cannot be worth less than a European call. We also showed that the European call was worth more than the maximum of zero and the difference between the stock price and the present value of the exercise price $[S_0 - E/(1 + R)]$. Thus the value of the American call must be greater than the maximum of zero and $S_0 - E/(1 + R)$. However, if the call is exercised, its value is $S_0 - E$. Because $S_0 - E/(1 + R) > S_0 - E$, the call sells for more than its value if exercised.

The foregoing discussion assumed that the stock did not pay a dividend before the expiration date or that the call was protected against dividends by having the exercise price adjusted by the amount of the dividend. If the stock is dividend paying or the call is not protected, early exercise is possible. Consider the example discussed earlier with a $60 stock price and a $50 exercise price. If the stock was about to pay a large dividend, then investors could rationally believe that the share price should be lower than $60 between the ex-dividend date and the expiration date and thus that the current difference is the best that can be obtained.[5]

---

[5] Stock prices are expected to drop by slightly less than the amount of the dividend when a stock goes ex-dividend.

Put Call Parity

A put and the underlying stock can be combined in such a way that the combination has the same payoff pattern as a call. Similarly, a call and the underlying equity can be combined so that they have the same payoff pattern as a put. This allows the put or call to be priced in terms of the other security.

This relationship is easiest to derive for European options. Furthermore, it is convenient to assume that the common equity will not pay a dividend in the period before the option expires. Define

S_0 as the current stock price
S_1 as the stock price at the expiration date
E as the exercise price
C as the call price
P as the put price
R_B as the borrowing rate
R_L as the lending rate

Now consider a combination of a share of stock, a put, and taking a loan for an amount $E/(1+R_B)$. If $E/(1+R_B)$ is borrowed and if the interest rate between the purchase of the combination and the expiration date is R_B, then $[E/(1+R_B)](1+R_B) = E$ will have to be paid back. Thus, if $E/(1+R_B)$ is borrowed, an amount equal to the exercise price will have to be paid back at the expiration date. The payoff of this combination at the expiration date is shown in Table 13.2. The payoff pattern is, of course, exactly the same pattern as for a call.

The investor has two possible investments: the call or the portfolio being discussed. Each investment has the same value at the expiration date. If they sell at different prices currently, then the investor can purchase the least expensive investment and issue the more expensive investment. Because they have the same payoff pattern at the expiration date, the investor can use the proceeds of the one investment to meet the obligations of the other. If they have different costs, a guaranteed profit can be made. Assuming the portfolio is less expensive than the call, then the investor would write the call and purchase the portfolio. If the call is more expensive than the portfolio, this combination then yields a guaranteed profit. The guaranteed profit is immediate and

TABLE 13.2 Payoffs of Portfolios Involving Puts

	Value at Expiration Date	
Security	If $S_1 > E$	If $S_1 \leq E$
Portfolio A		
Buy stock	S_1	S_1
Buy put	0	$E - S_1$
Borrow	$-E$	$-E$
Total	$S_1 - E$	0
Purchase of call		
Buy call	$S_1 - E$	0

has zero risk. Such a possibility cannot last long in any efficiently functioning market. Thus the call cannot be more expensive than the portfolio, and writing the call plus purchasing the portfolio cannot be profitable. Writing a call involves a cash inflow of C and purchasing portfolio A involves flows of $-S_0 - P + E/(1 + R_B)$. This implies

$$C - S_0 - P + \frac{E}{1+R_B} \leq 0$$

or

$$S_0 + P - \frac{E}{1+R_B} \geq C$$

Consider what happens if the call is less expensive than the portfolio. In this case, the investor would wish to issue the portfolio and buy the call. The flows would be $-C$ for the call and $S_0 + P - E/(1 + R_L)$ for portfolio A.

These flows closely resemble those discussed earlier, but R_L has replaced R_B. Because we assume the investor is short selling the portfolio rather than purchasing it, the investor is lending rather than borrowing, and R_L is assumed to be the lending rate.

If the call is less expensive than the portfolio, then this combination yields a guaranteed profit. A guaranteed profit with no risk can't last long in the market, so buying the call and issuing the portfolio cannot be a profitable combination. This implies that

$$S_0 + P - \frac{E}{1+R_L} - C \leq 0$$

or

$$C \geq S_0 + P - E/(1+R_L)$$

Putting the equations together yields

$$S_0 + P - \frac{E}{1+R_B} \geq C \geq S_0 + P - \frac{E}{1+R_L}$$

If $R_L = R_B$, the preceding inequalities become equalities, and we have the put call parity relationship.

Some comment on the two different arbitrage combinations is in order. The first combination was appropriate if the call was more expensive than the portfolio. This strategy involved buying stock and a put, borrowing, and writing a call. All of these are feasible, and the combination is a full description of the necessary actions.[6] The other combination was appropriate when the call was less expensive than the

------

[6] The only margin required is the margin on the call. The ownership of the stock is sufficient to meet this requirement.

portfolio. This involved selling the stock short, writing a put, lending, and buying a call. The analysis assumed that the proceeds of the short sale were immediately available. This is unrealistic in general, as discussed earlier. However, it would represent a realistic situation for an investor who currently owned the shares and who engages in a transaction identical to a short sale by selling his existing shares. Because there are likely to be many of these investors, the put call parity theorem should hold reasonably well.

The previous analysis examined the payoff pattern at the expiration date of the option. This is, of course, the only relevant date to examine for European options. With American options, other dates are potentially relevant. One of the components of the portfolio is a put. It can be shown that it may pay to exercise a put before expiration, and the value of the American put may be higher than shown in the prior tables.[7] The issuance of an American put involves the risk of premature exercise, and the arbitrage discussed earlier need no longer hold. Another problem with applying the prior analysis is the possibility of the payment of dividends. The payment of dividends would, of course, affect the payoffs depicted earlier. If the dividends are already announced, then the stock price can be adjusted by reducing it by the present value of the dividends. With this adjustment, dividends do not affect the prior analysis, except insofar as they affect the probability of exercising a put. If dividends are not announced, then adjusting by the expected dividends is reasonably satisfactory. All these issues mean that the put call parity relationship may not hold perfectly for American options. Nevertheless, it should be a close approximation to market relationships. This is exactly what the empirical results (see Klemkosky and Resnick, 1979; Gould and Galai, 1974) have shown.[8]

■ Bibliography

Arditti, Fred D., and Kose, John. "Spanning the State Space with Options," *Journal of Financial and Quantitative Analysis*, XV, No. 1 (March 1980), pp. 1–10.

Ball, Clifford A., and Torous, Walter N. "Bond Price Dynamics and Options," *Journal of Financial and Quantitative Analysis*, XVIII, No. 4 (Dec. 1983), pp. 517–532.

———. "Futures Options and the Volatility of Futures Prices," *Journal of Finance*, 41, No. 4 (Sept. 1986), pp. 857–870.

Barone-Adesi, Giovanni, and Whaley, Robert E. "Efficient Analytic Approximation of American Option Values," *Journal of Finance*, 42, No. 2 (June 1987), pp. 301–320.

Bhattacharya, Mihir. "Empirical Properties of the Black–Scholes Formula under Ideal Conditions," *Journal of Financial and Quantitative Analysis*, XV, No. 5 (Dec. 1980), pp. 1081–1106.

---

[7] See Merton (1973).

[8] The arbitrage involving the short sale of stock is sometimes profitable empirically. This part of the put-call relationship has less empirical support.

Black, Fischer, and Scholes, Myron. "The Pricing of Options and Corporate Liabilities," *Journal of Political Economy*, 81, No. 3 (May/June 1973), pp. 637–654.

Blomeyer, Edward C., and Johnson, Herb. "An Empirical Examination of the Pricing of American Put Options," *Journal of Financial and Quantitative Analysis*, 23, No. 1 (March 1988), pp. 13–22.

Bookstaber, Richard, and Clarke, Roger. "Problems in Evaluating the Performance of Portfolios with Options," *Financial Analyst Journal*, 41, No. 1 (Jan./Feb. 1985), pp. 48–62.

Bracken, Jerome. "Models for Call Option Decisions," *Financial Analysts Journal*, 24, No. 5 (Sept.–Oct. 1968), pp. 149–151.

CHAPTER 14

Understanding Implied Volatility

From Russell Rhoads, *Trading VIX Derivatives: Trading and Hedging Strategies Using VIX Futures, Options, and Exchange Traded Notes* (Hoboken, New Jersey: John Wiley & Sons, 2007), Chapter 1.

Learning Objective Statements

- Identify effective measures of volatility risk
- Identify volatility risk from given charts and data
- Compare volatility behavior with corresponding price behavior

In this chapter, we will discuss the ins and outs of a popular market indicator, or index, that is based on implied volatility. The indicator is the CBOE Volatility Index®, widely known by its ticker symbol, VIX. It should come as no surprise that a solid understanding of the index must begin with a solid understanding of what implied volatility is and how it works.

Implied volatility is ultimately determined by the price of option contracts. Since option prices are the result of market forces, or increased levels of buying or selling, implied volatility is determined by the market. An index based on implied volatility of option prices is displaying the market's estimation of volatility of the underlying security in the future.

■ Historical Versus Forward-Looking Volatility

There are two main types of volatility discussed relative to securities prices. The first is historical volatility, which may be calculated using recent trading activity for a stock or other security. The historical volatility of a stock is factual and known. Also, the historical volatility does not give any indication about the future movement of a stock. The forwardlooking volatility is what is referred to as the implied volatility. This type of volatility results from the market price of options that trade on a stock.

The implied volatility component of option prices is the factor that can give all option traders, novice to expert, the most difficulty. This occurs because the implied volatility of an option may change while all other pricing factors impacting the price of an option remain unchanged. This change may occur as the order flow for options is biased more to buying or selling. A result of increased buying of options by market participants is higher implied volatility. Conversely, when there is net selling of options, the implied volatility indicated by option prices moves lower.

Basically, the nature of order flow dictates the direction of implied volatility. Again, more option buying increases the option price and the result is higher implied volatility. Going back to Economics 101, implied volatility reacts to the supply and demand of the marketplace. Buying pushes it higher, and selling pushes it lower.

The implied volatility of an option is also considered an indication of the risk associated with the underlying security. The risk may be thought of as how much movement may be expected from the underlying stock over the life of an option. This is not the potential direction of the stock price move, just the magnitude of the move. Generally, when thinking of risk, traders think of a stock losing value or the price moving lower. Using implied volatility as a risk measure results in an estimation of a price move in either direction. When the market anticipates that a stock may soon move dramatically, the price of option contracts, both puts and calls, will move higher.

A common example of a known event in the future that may dramatically influence the price of a stock is a company's quarterly earnings report. Four times a year a company will release information to the investing public in the form of its recent earnings results. This earnings release may also include statements regarding business prospects for the company. This information may have a dramatic impact on the share price. As this price move will also impact option prices, the option contracts usually react in advance. Due to the anticipation that will work into option prices, they are generally more expensive as traders and investors buy options before seeing the report.

This increased buying of options results in higher option prices. There are two ways to think about this: the higher price of the option contracts results in higher implied volatility, or because of higher implied volatility option prices are higher. After the earnings report, there is less risk of a big move in the underlying stock and the options become less expensive. This drop in price is due to lower implied volatility levels; implied volatility is now lower due to lower option prices.

A good non-option-oriented example of how implied volatility works may be summed up through this illustration. If you live in Florida, you are familiar with hurricane season.

The path of hurricanes can be unpredictable, and at times homeowners have little time to prepare for a storm. Using homeowners insurance as a substitute for an option contract, consider the following situation.

You wake to find out that an evacuation is planned due to a potential hurricane. Before leaving the area, you check whether your homeowners insurance is current. You find you have allowed your coverage to lapse, and so you run down to your agent's office. As he boards up windows and prepares to evacuate inland, he informs you that you may renew, but the cost is going to be $50,000 instead of the $2,000 annual rate you have paid for years. After hearing your objections, he is steadfast. The higher price, he explains, is due to the higher risk associated with the coming storm.

You decide that $50,000 is too much to pay, and you return home to ride out the storm. Fortunately, the storm takes a left turn and misses your neighborhood altogether. Realizing that you have experienced a near miss, you run down to your agent's office with a $50,000 check in hand. Being an honest guy, he tells you the rate is back down to $2,000. Why is this?

The imminent risk level for replacing your home has decreased as there is no known threat bearing down on your property. As the immediate risk of loss or damage has decreased tremendously, so has the cost of protection against loss. When applying this to the option market, risk is actually risk of movement of the underlying security, either higher or lower. This risk is the magnitude of expected movement of the underlying security over the life of an option.

When market participants are expecting a big price move to the upside in the underlying security, there will be net buying of call options in anticipation of this move. As this buying occurs, the price of the call options will increase. This price rise in the options is associated with an increase risk of a large price move, and this increase in risk translates to higher implied volatility.

Also, if there is an expectation of a lower price move, the marketplace may see an increase in put buying. With higher demand for put contracts, the price of puts may increase resulting in higher implied volatility for those options. Finally, if put prices increase, the result is corresponding call prices rising due to a concept known as put-call parity, which will be discussed in the next section.

■ Put-Call Parity

Put and call prices are linked to each other through the price of the underlying stock through put-call parity. This link exists because combining a stock and put position can result in the same payoff as a position in a call option with the same strike price as the put. If this relationship gets out of line or not in parity, an arbitrage opportunity exits. When one of these opportunities arises, there are trading firms that will quickly buy and sell the securities to attempt to take advantage of this mispricing. This market activity will push the put and call prices back in line with each other.

TABLE 14.1	Put, Call, and Stock Pricing to Illustrate Put-Call Parity
Stock/Option	**Price**
XYZ Stock	$50.00
XYZ 50 Call	$1.00
XYZ 50 Put	$2.00

Put and call prices should remain within a certain price range of each other or arbitragers will enter the market, which results in the prices coming back into parity. Parity between the two also results in a similar implied volatility output resulting from using these prices in a model to determine the implied volatility of the market.

Stated differently, increased demand for a call option will raise the price of that call. As the price of the call moves higher, the corresponding put price should also rise, or the result will be an arbitrage trade that will push the options into line. As the pricing of the option contracts are tied to each other, they will share similar implied volatility levels also.

For a quick and very simple example of how put-call parity works, consider the options and stock in Table 14.1.

Using the XYZ 50 Put combined with XYZ stock, a payout that replicates being long the XYZ 50 Call may be created. The combination of owning stock and owning a put has the same payout structure as a long call option position. With the XYZ 50 Call trading at 1.00 and the XYZ 50 Put priced at 2.00, there may be a mispricing scenario. Table 14.2 compares a long XYZ 50 Call trade with a combined position of long XYZ stock and long a XYZ 50 Put.

The final two columns compare a payout of owning XYZ stock from 50.00 and buying the XYZ 50 Put at 2.00 versus buying an XYZ 50 Call for 1.00. Note that at any price at expiration, the long call position is worth 1.00 more than the combined stock and put position. With this pricing difference, there is the ability to take a short position in the strategy that will be worth less and buy the strategy that will be worth more at expiration. The payout diagram in Figure 14.1 shows how the two positions compare at a variety of prices at expiration.

The lines are parallel throughout this diagram. The higher line represents the profit or loss based on buying the 50 call. The lower line represents the payout for the spread combining a long stock position and a long 50 put position. At any price at

TABLE 14.2	Payout Comparison for Long Call and Long Stock + Long Put Trade			
XYZ at Expiration	**Long XYZ Stock**	**Long XYZ 50 Put**	**Long Stock + Long Put**	**Long XYZ 50 Call**
45.00	−5.00	3.00	−2.00	−1.00
50.00	0.00	−2.00	−2.00	−1.00
55.00	5.00	−2.00	3.00	4.00

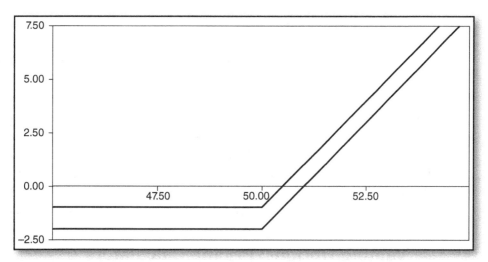

FIGURE 14.1 Payout Diagram Comparison.

expiration, the combined position has less value than the long 50 call. Knowing this outcome, it is possible to benefit from the 1.00 spread, which will exist at any price at expiration for two positions that are basically the same.

Due to put-call parity and the mispricing between the 50 Call and 50 Put, the call may be purchased combined with a short position in the stock and put option. A quick transaction using the prices in the example would result in a profit of 1.00 upon options expiration. This 1.00 profit would be realized regardless of the price of the stock at expiration. Firms would attempt to take advantage of this opportunity through buying the cheaper call option and selling the comparable more expensive put option. The market activity of these participants is what keeps put and call option prices in line with each other and the implied volatility of both put and call contracts at the same level.

■ Estimating Price Movement

What the implied volatility of an option projects onto the underlying security is the expected range of price movement over a certain period of time. This estimation of price movement is based on statistics and the bell curve. The implied volatility of an option is the projection of an annualized one standard deviation move in the underlying stock over the life of the option. According to statistics and using implied volatility as a guide, the price of a stock should land between up and down one standard deviation at option expiration. The closing price should land in this range 68.2 percent of the time.

This 68.2 percent comes from statistics and what is referred to as a normal distribution. Statistics like this reveal that 68.2 percent of the time a stock should be between up one standard deviation and down one standard deviation a year from today. A formula may also be used to take this annualized number and narrow down the projection to a single day. The normal distribution also indicates that there is a 95.4 percent expectation of the stock landing between up two standard deviations and down two standard deviations. Finally, at three standard deviations, the probability reaches 99.7 percent.

With a stock trading at $50 and the underlying option prices indicating 20 percent implied volatility, the result is a one standard deviation price move equal to $10 (20 percent of $50). In other words, the stock is expected to close between $40 (down $10) and $60 (up $10) with 68.2 percent certainty a year from today. A two standard deviation price move would be equal to $20. This is calculated by simply multiplying 2 times a single standard deviation. Using two standard deviations, it can be projected out that the stock should land between $30 and up $70, with a confidence of 95.4 percent. At three standard deviations, there is a 99.7 percent chance of the stock closing between $20 and $80 a year from the date of the calculation.

■ Valuing Options: Pricing Calculators and Other Tools

An option pricing calculator is a tool that allows a user the ability to input the pricing variables that determine the value of an option with the result being a theoretical option price. Ultimately the market determines the price of an option through buying and selling forces. However when analyzing and investigating option trades, using an option pricing calculator with certain assumptions gives an idea where an option may be trading in the future. Also, using an option pricing calculator is an excellent way to become familiar with the price action of option contracts. The CBOE has a free option calculator available on its website at www.cboe.com/tradtool; it is a valuable tool for option pricing.

The value of an option contract is derived from a variety of inputs. Inputs into an option pricing model include the price of the underlying security, the strike price of the option, the type of option, dividends, interest rates, and time to option expiration. The final input into an option pricing model is the implied volatility of the option. These inputs may be used in a model to determine the value of an option.

Table 14.3 demonstrates how an option pricing model is used to determine the value of an option. The inputs are at the top of the table, with the value of the option showing up as the only output. Option pricing models calculate a variety of pieces of useful information, such as the impact of changes in pricing factors. These outputs are known as the option Greeks. However, to keep focus on the topic at hand, implied volatility, only the necessary outputs are going to be demonstrated in this example of an option calculator.

The option price in the model is determined from a stock trading at 44.75 with implied volatility of 30 percent and a risk-free interest rate of 1.00 percent. The result is a call option value with a strike price of 45 and 30 days to expiration would be valued at 1.45 based on the inputs used in this model. Keep in mind that this is a pricing model, not the actual market trading price of the option. Again, the inputs in the model are assumptions, not just the market price. Just because using these inputs results in a value of 1.45 for this 45 Call does not mean it can be traded at this level.

TABLE 14.3 Option Pricing Calculator–Option Value Output

Factor	Input
Call/Put	Call
Underlying Price	44.75
Strike Price	45.00
Implied Volatility	30%
Days to Expiration	30
Interest Rate	1.00%
Dividends	0.00%
Output	**Result**
Option Value	1.45

In fact, the market price of this option will vary if the market consensus differs from the inputs used in this model.

The real value of an option at any given time is actually determined by the price that it may be bought or sold in the market. In the case of this 45 Call, even though the inputs into the model result in a 1.45 value, when checking market quotes for this option we find that the current trading price is 1.70. The reason for the difference between our model's value and the market price is the result of different implied volatility levels being used. The previous model, in Table 14.3, takes inputs and the result in a difference in option values based on the inputs.

The pricing factors in an option pricing model are for the most part set in stone. The exception of this is the implied volatility input. For the model, the assumption of 30 percent implied volatility was used. However, the market is pricing in a higher implied volatility level. This is determined before any numbers or formulas have been run just by comparing the option market price and the option value assumption that resulted from the model. The market price of the option is higher than the pricing model output. Seeing this, it is pretty certain that the implied volatility based on market prices is higher than what was entered into the model. There is a direct correlation between high and low relative option prices and higher or lower implied volatility.

Table 14.4 is an option pricing model that uses the market price as an input with the sole output being implied volatility. This implied volatility level is being indicated by the 1.70 market price of the 45 Call. The higher option price here is a higher implied volatility than what was used in the first pricing model. As the option price in this model is higher than the option value that resulted from a 30 percent implied volatility, the expectation would be a higher implied volatility result. Using 1.70 as the price of the option actually results in the implied volatility that is being projected by this option price to be 35 percent. Professional traders generally start with the market price of an option to calculate implied volatility as that is where the implied volatility of an option is ultimately determined.

Another method of demonstrating the impact of different implied volatility levels on option prices appears in Table 14.5. Instead of a comparison of what the model

TABLE 14.4	Option Pricing Calculator—Implied Volatility Output
Factor	**Input**
Call/Put	Call
Underlying Price	44.75
Strike Price	45.00
Option Price	1.70
Days to Expiration	30
Interest Rate	1.00%
Dividends	0.00%
Output	**Result**
Implied Volatility	35%

TABLE 14.5	Impact of a 5 Percent Increase in Implied Volatility	
Implied Volatility	30%	35%
Option Price	1.45	1.70

output was versus the option price based on model outputs, consider the previous option prices in a different way. Consider the two option prices and implied volatility differences as changes based on an increase in demand for the option. Both prices represent the market and the option price increases from 1.45 to 1.70. This option price rise occurs due to an increase in buying of the call option while all other factors that influence the option price stay the same.

Since the price of the option contract has increased, the resulting implied volatility output from an option model has also increased. Higher option prices, whether put or call prices, will result in a higher implied volatility output with no changes in any of the other option pricing factors.

To recap, there is a direct link between the demand for option contracts and their prices in the marketplace. This is regardless of changes occurring in the underlying stock price. With demand in the form of buying pressure pushing option prices higher or an increase in selling occurring due to market participants pushing option prices lower, the implied volatility of an option is dictated by market forces.

■ Fluctuations Based on Supply and Demand

As mentioned in the first section of this chapter, implied volatility does fluctuate based on supply and demand for options. This leads to the question, "What exactly causes the supply and demand for options to fluctuate?" The short answer is the near-term expected price changes that may occur in the underlying stock. These moves are usually the result of information that has influenced the fundamental outlook for a stock. The best example of this type of information would be a company's quarterly earnings reports.

Every publicly traded company in the United States reports its earnings results four times a year. The date and timing (generally before the market open or after the market close) are usually known well in advance of the actual announcement. Along with the earnings results, other information is disseminated, such as the company's revenues and the source of those revenues. Many companies offer a possible outlook regarding the prospects for their business conditions, and most will hold a public conference call to answer professional investors' questions. These events often have a dramatic impact, either positive or negative, on the price of a stock.

Again, the date that these results are announced is public knowledge and often widely anticipated by analysts and traders. As the date draws near, there is usually trading in the stock and stock options that is based on the anticipated stock price reaction to the earnings announcement. The result is usually net buying of options as there is speculation regarding the potential move of the underlying stock. The net option buying results in higher option prices and an increase in the implied volatility projected by the options that trade on this stock. Usually this increase impacts only the options with the closest expiration and strike prices that are close to where the stock is trading. An excellent example of this can be seen in the option prices and resulting implied volatility levels for Amazon stock shown in Table 14.6.

These are market prices from just before the close of trading on July 22, 2010. Amazon's earnings were reported after the market close on the 22nd with weekly options that expire on the 23rd having only one trading day until expiration after the news was released. The difference in implied volatility between the options that have one trading day left and those that have just under a month left is pretty significant.

This difference stems from the options that market participants would use as a short-term trading vehicle related to Amazon's earnings announcement. This would be the same for hedgers and speculators alike. Both would focus on the strike prices that are closest to the trading price of the stock as well as the options with the least amount of time to expiration.

TABLE 14.6	Amazon Option Implied Volatility and Option Prices Minutes Prior to an Earnings Announcement			
	AMZN @ 120.07			
Call Strike	July 23 Call	July 23 Call IV	Aug 21 Call	Aug 21 Call IV
115	7.00	163%	9.25	48%
120	3.92	156%	6.25	45%
125	1.82	148%	4.05	45%
Put Strike	July 23 Put	July 23 Put IV	Aug 21 Put	Aug 21 Put IV
115	1.92	159%	4.05	48%
120	3.82	155%	6.20	47%
125	6.75	148%	8.90	45%

Option contracts that have the closest expiration to a known event that occurs after the event are the contracts that will have the most price reaction before and after the event occurs. With Amazon reporting earnings the evening of July 22 and an option series expiring on July 23, the July 23 options are the contracts that will see the most price action based on the stock price reaction to the earnings release.

The stock price is very close to the 120 strike price when the option first listed and just before the earnings announcement. Using the 120 strike options, implied volatility for both the put and call options that expire the following day is around 155 percent. This indicates that on an annualized basis the option market is pricing in a 155 percent price move over a single day. This is much more dramatic sounding that it is in reality. Annualized implied volatility of 155 percent for an option with a single trading day left translates to a one-day move of around 9.76 percent. The math behind this is (see the following feature on calculating single day implied volatility):

$$9.76\% = 155\%/15.87$$

This single-day implied volatility can be interpreted as being a single standard deviation range of expected price movement of the stock on that day.

CALCULATING SINGLE-DAY IMPLIED VOLATILITY

Assuming there are 252 trading days in a year, the denominator of this formula turns out to be the square root of the number of trading days for the year.

1 Day Movement = Implied Volatility/Square Root of 252

Amazon did report its earnings, and the initial price reaction was pretty close to what the option market was pricing in. The NASDAQ opening price the day after the company reported earnings was down 11.76 percent from the previous day's close. The market was forecasting a 9.76 percent move based on option pricing.

As a refresher from college statistics: One standard deviation in statistics indicates there is a 68.2 percent chance that an outcome is going to land between up and down one standard deviation. So this single-day implied volatility indicates the market is expecting Amazon's stock to trade within up or down 9.76 percent with a 68.2 percent level of confidence in the next day.

Table 14.7 shows the increase in the implied volatility of the 120 Call projected by Amazon option prices as the earnings announcement approaches. Implied volatility for other options rises in the same way, since 120 is the closest strike to the stock price when the option started trading and just before earnings were announced. Also, the options contract is a weekly expiration option that begins trading on a Thursday morning and expires on the following week's Friday close. This particular option started trading on July 15 with the last trading day being July 23 or is what is called a weekly option that has only eight trading days from listing to expiration.

TABLE 14.7	Implied Volatility Changes Approaching Amazon Earnings		
Date	AMZN	120 Call	120 Call IV
July 15	120.13	4.80	71%
July 15	122.06	5.92	78%
July 16	118.49	4.00	84%
July 19	119.94	4.33	87%
July 20	120.10	3.95	90%
July 21	117.43	2.73	111%
July 22	120.07	3.92	155%

The first row is the opening price for the weekly option and underlying price for the option. When the option first traded it had an implied volatility level of 71 percent. This compares to non-earnings-period implied volatility levels, which are usually in the mid 30 percent range for Amazon options.

Over the next few days, the earnings announcement draws closer and the stock stays in a fairly tight range. The implied volatility of the option contracts continues to rise as time passes. By the time the announcement is imminent, the implied volatility of the 120 Call has more than doubled.

This illustration of how implied volatility climbs in front of a potentially market-moving event is a bit magnified by the options only having one day of time value remaining before the announcement. However, it is a good illustration of how option prices, through the implied volatility component, discount a potential market-moving event when the timing of this event is a known entity.

■ The Impact on Option Prices

Implied volatility is commonly considered an indication as to whether an option is cheap or expensive. This determination may be made through examining past implied volatility levels for the options of a particular stock or index and comparing present values.

Demand for options pushes up the price of an option contract and results in higher implied volatility. However, other factors such as the underlying price, time to expiration, and interest-rate levels also determine the price of an option. These other factors are not impacted through the buying and selling pressure on option contracts. Only implied volatility will fluctuate based on market buying and selling pressure.

The goal of any directional trading strategy should be to buy low and sell high. If themarket considers any trading vehicle inexpensive, there will be participants that take advantage of this through purchasing the instrument. On the other hand, if something appears expensive it may be sold. Implied volatility is a measure that option traders use to define whether options are overvalued or undervalued.

TABLE 14.8	Implied Volatility Levels and Option Prices	
Stock Price	25 Call	Implied Volatility
24.00	0.80	20%
24.00	1.05	25%
24.00	1.30	30%

As a simple example, take the option prices and implied volatility levels in Table 14.8. The data in this table represent a stock trading at 24.00 per share, and the value of a 25 Call with 90 days until expiration. The different option prices are based on various implied volatility levels. Note that as the option price increases so does the implied volatility of the 25 Call.

If options for the underlying stock usually trade with an implied volatility of 25 percent, then when the option could be purchased for 0.80 it may be considered undervalued or inexpensive. At 0.80 the option had an implied volatility level of 20 percent. When implied volatility rose to 30 percent and the option was trading for 1.30, the option may be considered expensive. At 1.05 with an implied volatility of 25 percent, the historical norm, the 25 Call may be considered fairly valued.

Of course, using implied volatility as a measure of how expensive or cheap an option is must be done in the context of some external factors. Remember, if the company is preparing to announce quarterly earnings, the implied volatility would be expected to be high relative to other periods of time. In that case, a comparison to implied volatility behavior around previous earnings announcements would be a more accurate analysis of whether the options appear cheap or expensive.

■ Implied Volatility and the VIX

The VIX will be further defined, but the concepts in this chapter should be tied to the VIX before moving forward. The VIX is a measure of the implied volatility being projected through the prices of S&P 500 index options. The VIX can be used to indicate what type of market movement option prices are projecting on the S&P 500 over the next 30 days or even a shorter time. Since the VIX is measuring implied volatility of S&P 500 index options and since implied volatility is a measure of risk projected by option pricing, the VIX is considered a gauge of fear in the overall market.

The remainder of this book explores the VIX index which is based on the concept of implied volatility. With a solid understanding of implied volatility, exploration of the VIX index, methods of using the VIX for market analysis, and ways to directly trade volatility should be easier to comprehend.

CHAPTER 15

About the VIX Index

From Russell Rhoads, *Trading VIX Derivatives: Trading and Hedging Strategies Using VIX Futures, Options, and Exchange Traded Notes* (Hoboken, New Jersey: John Wiley & Sons, 2007), Chapter 2.

Learning Objective Statements

- Calculate expected 30-day movement of an index or a stock
- Explain the relationship between the VIX and market movement
- Interpret volatility signals as part of a market forecast

Officially known as the CBOE Volatility Index, the VIX is considered by many to be a gauge of fear and greed in the stock market. A more accurate description of what the VIX measures is the implied volatility that is being priced into S&P 500 index options. Through the use of a wide variety of option prices, the index offers an indication of 30-day implied volatility as priced by the S&P 500 index option market.

Before diving further into the calculation that results in the VIX, this chapter will cover the history of exactly how this index was developed followed by an overview of how the VIX is determined. Then for interested parties there is a more in-depth discussion of how the VIX is calculated. The VIX index has historically had an inverse relationship to performance of the S&P 500, and this often results in questions from traders who are new to the VIX. This relationship will be discussed in the context of put-call parity.

Finally, there are a handful of VIX-related indexes based on other equity-market indexes. The S&P 100–related VIX is still calculated using the old method to maintain some continuity for historical comparisons. Finally, there are also VIX indexes calculated on options based on the NASDAQ 100, Russell 2000, and Dow Jones Industrial Average, which are discussed toward the end of the chapter.

■ History of the VIX

The concept behind the VIX index was developed by Dr. Robert Whaley of Vanderbilt University in 1993. His paper "Derivatives on Market Volatility: Hedging Tools Long Overdue," which appeared in the *Journal of Derivatives*, laid the groundwork for the index. The original VIX was based on pricing of S&P 100 (OEX) options and used only eight option contracts to determine a volatility measure.

At the time, OEX options were the most heavily traded index option series that reflected performance of the stock market in the United States. This volatility index was based on a limited number of options and was slightly disconnected from the overall stock market due to the narrower focus of the S&P 100 versus the S&P 500.

In 2003 there was a new methodology for calculation of the VIX index that was developed through work done by the CBOE and Goldman Sachs. Although the calculation was altered, the most important aspect to this change for individuals is that the underlying options changed from the OEX to options trading on the S&P 500. Another significant change was an increase in the number of options that were used in the index calculation. Through a wider number of option contract prices feeding the formula to calculate the VIX, a true 30-day implied volatility level that is being projected on the S&P 500 by the options market is realized.

The S&P 500 index is considered by professional investors to be the benchmark for the performance of the stock market in the United States. The members of the index are 500 of the largest domestic companies in the United States that meet criteria based on market capitalization, public float, financial viability, liquidity, type of company, and industry sector. Companies are usually dropped from the index when they have violated membership criteria or have ceased to operate due to a merger or acquisition.

The industry representation of the S&P 500 index appears in Table 15.1. With a broad distribution of companies in the index, there is no industry that dominates the index's performance. This diversification across industries is a major reason the S&P 500 is considered a performance benchmark by most professional investors.

TABLE 15.1 **S&P 500 Industry Weightings**

Industry	Weighting
Consumer discretionary	9.10%
Consumer staples	11.70%
Energy	11.40%
Financials	15.40%
Health care	13.40%
Industrials	10.00%
Information technology	18.50%
Materials	3.40%
Telecom services	3.30%
Utilities	3.80%

■ Calculating the VIX

After the VIX index was introduced, the CBOE moved forward with the first exchange listed volatility derivative instruments. Through the CBOE Futures Exchange (CFE®), the CBOE introduced futures contracts based on the VIX. Other instruments have followed, and more are in development.

There are two ways to explain how the VIX is determined. First, it can be explained using simple nonmathematical terms. Then, for those interested in an in-depth discussion of the formula and calculation, a more detailed overview will follow. Having a basic understanding of how the VIX is determined is more than enough to move forward with trading. However, for those with more interest in the VIX calculation, the more comprehensive description is included.

The Nonmathematical Approach

The VIX is an indicator of 30-day implied volatility determined through the use of S&P 500 index option prices. The option price used in the formula is actually the midpoint of the bid-ask spread of relevant at and out of the money actively traded S&P 500 index options. Using the midpoint of the spread is a more accurate price description than the last price for an option contract. Also, the contracts used are the S&P 500 index options that trade to the next two standard expirations with at least eight days to expiration. When a series reaches this eight-day point, it is not used anymore in the calculation and the options that expire farther in the future then start to contribute to the VIX calculation.

All of these S&P 500 options are then used to create a synthetic at the money option that expires exactly 30 days from the very moment of the calculation. This time variable to the formula is constantly being updated to weight the balance of the two expiration series in the formula. Using a wide number of actively quoted S&P 500 index options, a synthetic 30-day option is created and the VIX is the implied volatility of that option. This results in implied volatility of the synthetic option contract, which is then reported as the VIX.

The Formula and Calculations

It is possible to trade the VIX with a cursory understanding of how the index is determined. Those who are satisfied with their understanding of the VIX and what it represents may skip ahead. However, readers who are more interested in how the VIX is calculated should be interested in the remainder of this section.

The input for calculating the VIX index comes from all actively quoted S&P 500 index options for the next two standard option expirations that have at least eight days remaining until expiration. Eliminating the nearer term expiration options that have only a week to expiration takes out some of the end-of-contract volatility that can occur in the market.

The option contracts from these two expiration series are the at and out of the money put and call options. The series of options used extends out of the money until there are two consecutive option strikes that have no bid-ask market posted. Again, the midpoint of the bid-ask spread for the options is used in the calculation.

The time to expiration part of the calculation is very specific, down to the second. This is constantly being updated to change the weighting between the two series of options feeding into the calculation. Although S&P 500 index options cease trading on a Thursday for Friday morning settlement, the time to expiration is based on the market opening time, 8:30 A.M. central time, on the Friday of expiration.

There is also a forward price for the S&P 500 that is calculated using the closest at the money options in conjunction with put-call parity. This S&P 500 forward price is the underlying security price and strike price used to price the synthetic option used in the calculation. The implied volatility of that option is what is quoted at the VIX. that option is what is quoted at the VIX.

Finally if there is interest in using Microsoft Excel© to replicate calculating the VIX, a paper produced by Tom Arnold and John H. Earl Jr. of the University of Richmond is useful. In a very short study, 10 pages, they lay out the groundwork for using Excel to replicate the calculation of the VIX (to read the full paper, go to http://papers.ssrn.com/sol3/papers. cfm?abstract id=1103971). Also, once the template has been set up, changing the time frame and underlying instrument is simple. Using the template, the VIX methodology may be applied to a variety of instruments or time frames with little effort.

THEORY AND ANALYSIS

■ The VIX and Put-Call Parity

Many traders and investors often ask why there appears to be an inverse relationship between the direction of stock prices and the VIX. The relationship may be broken down to the nature of purchasing options. When the market is under pressure, there is a net buying of put options, which will result in higher implied volatility. This rapid increase in demand for put options pushes the implied volatility for both put and call contracts higher; the reason behind this is called put-call parity.

Put-call parity states that the prices of put and call options that have the same strike price and expiration are related. This relationship exists due to the ability to create synthetic positions in one option through combining the other option with the underlying stock. With this possibility, if the price of one option differs enough from the price of the other, an arbitrage opportunity may present itself.

For instance, in a zero-interest-rate environment, a put and call price should have the same value if the stock is trading at the strike price. As the options are related in price, the implied volatility of these options is also related. This is unrealistic, but it is a good method of demonstrating putcall parity. The prices in Table 15.2 may be used to demonstrate what can happen when put-call parity breaks down.

It is possible to replicate the payout of a long call through combining a put option and a stock position. Stated another way, a long stock position along with owning a put will result in the same payout structure as being long a call option. So, if the same payout may be created in two methods, the pricing of these two

TABLE 15.2	Prices to Demonstrate Put-Call Parity
Security	Price
XYZ Stock	45.00
XYZ 45 Call	2.50
XYZ 45 Put	2.00

should be equivalent. If they are not equal, the lower priced one may be bought while the higher priced one is simultaneously sold. This is known as an arbitrage trade, in which an instant profit may be realized through a pricing difference in two equivalent securities.

If the XYZ 45 Put is purchased and shares of XYZ stock are also bought, the resulting position at expiration will be the same as owning the XYZ 45 Call. Above 45.00, the call option would result in a long position in XYZ; below 45.00, the call would not be exercised and there would be no position in XYZ. With a long 45 put position combined with a long position in the stock, if the stock is below 45.00 at expiration the put option will be exercised and the stock sold. The result would be no position in XYZ. Above 45.00, the stock would still be owned, as the XYZ 45 Put would not be exercised. Regardless of the stock price at expiration, the resulting position in XYZ will be the same. Due to the different prices between the 45 Call and 45 Put, there is a difference in profit or loss of the position at expiration. Table 15.3 demonstrates this at a variety of price points at expiration.

The column Long Stock + Long Put represents the position payout at expiration of the combined long stock–long put position. Note at all price levels the combined long stock and long put position is worth 0.50 more than the long call position. If at all price levels at expiration the long call position will be worth less than stock plus put position, then an arbitrage opportunity exists.

The arbitrage trade would be to purchase the stock and put option while taking a short position in the call option. At any price level for XYZ at expiration, this trade would result in a profit of 0.50. Table 15.4 displays the outcome through buying XYZ at 45.00 and purchasing the XYZ 45 Put for 2.00 along with selling the XYZ 45 Call at 2.50.

Admittedly this is an overly simplistic example, but the hope here is to get across the idea of put-call parity and what happens when put and call prices get out of line relative to each other. Execution of this combined position with the result of a

TABLE 15.3	Long XYZ 45 Call versus Long XYZ 45 Put + Long XYZ at Expiration			
XYZ	Long XYZ Stock	Long XYZ 45 Put	Long Stock + Long Put	Long XYZ 45 Call
35	−10.00	8.00	−2.00	−2.50
40	−5.00	3.00	−2.00	−2.50
45	0.00	−2.00	−2.00	−2.50
50	5.00	−2.00	3.00	2.50
55	10.00	−2.00	8.00	7.50

XYZ	Long XYZ Stock	Long XYZ 45 Put	Short XYZ 45 Call	Combined Profit/Loss
35	−10.00	8.00	2.50	0.50
40	−5.00	3.00	2.50	0.50
45	0.00	−2.00	2.50	0.50
50	5.00	−2.00	−2.50	0.50
55	10.00	−2.00	−7.50	0.50

TABLE 15.4 Long XYZ Stock + versus Long XYZ 45 Put + Short XYZ 45 Call at Expiration

riskless profit would involve transaction costs and a cost of capital. For individuals this might be prohibitive, but for professional trading firms this is an opportunity. When option prices get out of line to a point where a professional firm may take advantage through placing orders to buy and sell the instrument that are mispriced, then orders to take advantage of this mispricing will be executed. These trades will quickly push markets back into line and eliminate the arbitrage profit.

Figure 15.1 is a payoff diagram that compares the payout of the long call and combined long put–long stock position. The higher line represents the combined long put–long stock position. The lower line shows the profit or loss for the long call position. Note the lines are parallel—the only difference is the profit or loss. This difference shows an arbitrage profit that may be realized by shorting the long call and buying the other two instruments, then holding the positions to expiration.

The put-call parity formula has many components and is beyond the scope of this book. However, the formulas in Table 15.5 illustrate on a position basis what the equivalent single-position result is from different combinations of a put, call, or stock.

A comparable payout of any single long or short position with a put, call, or stock may be created using a combination of the other two securities. Although it may seem like this does not relate to the VIX, there is a point to this exercise.

THEORY AND ANALYSIS

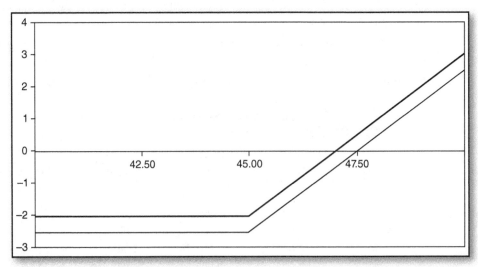

FIGURE 15.1 Payoff Comparison.

TABLE 15.5	Variety of Positions Created through Put-Call Parity
Position	Combination
Long call	Long stock + long put
Short call	Short stock + short put
Long put	Short stock + long call
Short put	Long stock + short call
Long stock	Long call + short put
Short stock	Short call + long put

The relationship between put and call prices that results in put-call parity does have an impact on the VIX index. The level of the VIX is based on the implied volatility of a variety of both put and call options. The indicated implied volatility of option contracts rises and falls based on market forces. The specific market force that impacts implied volatility is the net buying or selling of options. This increase in demand is not necessarily purchase of either all call or all put options buy just net buying of option contracts. Since strong demand for call options will result in higher put prices and demand for puts will result in higher call prices, higher demand for either type of contract results in higher implied volatility for both put and call contracts.

The VIX has historically had an inverse relationship with the S&P 500 index. The reason behind this inverse relationship relates to the type of option activity that occurs during bullish markets versus bearish markets. When markets rally, there is rarely a rush by investors to purchase call options. Therefore when the market is rising, there is rarely dramatically higher option purchasing versus options selling.

When the S&P 500 comes under pressure, especially in very turbulent times, there is often a panic-like demand for put options. This demand for protection results in increased purchasing of put options. The result is a fast move higher in implied volatility for both S&P 500 put and call options. This higher demand then results in an increase in implied volatility and finally a move higher in the VIX index.

In summary, the VIX moves higher when there is more demand for S&P 500 options, this demand tends to increase when there is nervousness about the overall market. This concern about the market will result in increased demand for put options. Put-call parity is the reason the implied volatility of both types of options moves together. The result of this increased demand for puts is higher implied volatility indicated by the pricing of S&P 500 options and a move higher in the VIX.

■ The VIX and Market Movement

Again, the VIX is a measure of 30-day implied volatility as indicated by the pricing of S&P 500 index options. The VIX is expressed as an annualized volatility measure, but it may actually be used to determined shorter-term market-price movements. Recall the example with Amazon reporting earnings. The implied volatility of the at the money options that only had a day left to expiration could be used to determine the magnitude of movement expected from Amazon stock the day following the company's earnings release. The implied volatility of those options was expressed as an annualized number.

The VIX is the 30-day implied volatility of the S&P 500, but it is also expressed as an annual figure. When the VIX is quoted at 20, this can be interpreted as SPX options pricing in an annualized move, up or down, of 20 percent in the S&P 500 index over the next 30 days. Using the VIX index, the anticipated movement of the underlying market may also be interpreted. The formula for determining the expected magnitude of market movements based on the VIX index is shown in the section following.

CALCULATING EXPECTED 30-DAY MARKET MOVEMENT

The formula for determining expected 30-day market movement is simple:

30-Day Movement = VIX/Square Root of 12

Determining the anticipated 30-day movement of the stock market as defined by the VIX involves dividing the VIX by the square root of 12. The implied volatility for a stock is used to interpret the expected one-day move for the stock. The square root of 12 is a convenient number as 30 days is the average month and there are 12 months in the year. In a similar manner to breaking down what implied volatility was indicating about movement in Amazon stock, the VIX may be used to determine the anticipated 30-day move for the S&P 500.

If the VIX is quoted at 20, the result would be the market expecting movement of about 5.77 percent over the next 30 days. Following the formula for determining 30-day market movement, the math would be:

$$5.77\% = 20/3.46$$

At times the VIX has reached some extreme points with the index actually reaching over 100 intraday. Table 15.6 shows what different VIX levels indicate about anticipated stock market movement.

The VIX may also be used as an indication of what magnitude of daily price movement is being expected for the S&P 500. The VIX can be taken down to a single-day estimate of market movement.

In the VIX trading arena, the option and futures traders take the level for the VIX and divide it by 16 to get a rough estimate of what sort of daily move is expected in the stock market based on the level of the VIX. The denominator of the formula is the square root of 252 or about 15.87. The traders round this up to 16 to get their denominator. So the VIX at 16 would indicate S&P 500 index options are anticipating daily pricemovement of 1 percent (16/16). A VIX of 32 would be interpreted as the S&P 500 option market anticipating a daily price move of 2 percent (32/16).

The math behind this method is not exact, but this is a pretty good rule of thumb. In 2008 when the VIX was trading in the mid-60s, this may be taken as the option market expecting a daily price move of 4 percent. Using a more common stock market index, this translates to the Dow Jones Industrial Average (DJIA) at 10,000 points being expected to

THEORY AND ANALYSIS

TABLE 15.6	VIX and Expected 30-Day Movement of the S&P 500	
VIX	**Expected 30-Day Move**
3.46	1%
6.92	2%
10.40	3%
13.85	4%
17.32	5%
20.78	6%
24.25	7%
27.71	8%
31.18	9%
34.64	10%

trade in a 400-point range on a daily basis. Four-hundred-point days in the DJIA usually result in the stock market getting more than just professional investor's attention during the day. Those sort of moves generally grab headlines.

■ Equity Market Volatility Indexes

In addition to an index based on S&P 500 volatility, the CBOE has developed a handful of other volatility measures based on other common stock market indexes. Table 15.7 is a list of indexes based on index volatility that the CBOE has developed. There are also some quotes and strategybased and alternative-asset-based volatility indexes the CBOE has developed.

CBOE DJIA Volatility Index

The CBOE DJIA Volatility Index is calculated in a similar fashion as the VIX. Quotes for this index are disseminated using the symbol VXD. The index was created in 2005, and the index was introduced on March 18 of that year. The index indicates the market's expectation of 30-day implied volatility based on index option prices on the Dow Jones Industrial Average (DJX).

TABLE 15.7	CBOE Equity Market Volatility Indexes		
Index	**Ticker**	**Underlying**	**Website**
CBOE Volatility Index	VIX	SPX	www.cboe.com/vix
CBOE DJIA Volatility Index	VXD	DJX	www.cboe.com/vxd
CBOE NADSAQ-100 Volatility Index	VXN	NDX	www.cboe.com/vxn
CBOE Russell 2000 Volatility Index	RVX	RUT	www.cboe.com/rvx
CBOE S&P 100 Volatility Index	VXO	OEX	www.cboe.com/vxo
Amex QQQ Volatility Index	QQV	QQQ	www.nyse.com

Sources: www.cboe.com and www.nyse.com.

The DJX is one of the oldest stock indexes and is one of the most commonly quoted indicators of the overall stock market. Charles Dow, the publisher of the *Wall Street Journal*, created the index in order to bring more attention to his newspaper. The DJIA was first quoted on May 26, 1896. On days the stock market is open, at some point on the national news how the DJX did on the day will be mentioned. Some other common names for the DJX are the DJIA, Dow Jones, or just the Dow. For a person who pays little attention to the stock market or even for most investors, the Dow Jones Industrial Average is what they think of when they think of the stock market.

The DJX is composed of 30 stocks that represent a wide variety of industries and some of the largest companies in the United States. The stocks appear in Table 15.8. The small

TABLE 15.8 **Members of the Dow Jones Industrial Average**	
Company	**Symbol**
Alcoa Inc.	AA
American Express Company	AXP
AT&T Corp.	T
Bank of America Corp.	BAC
Boeing Co.	BA
Caterpillar Inc.	CAT
Chevron Corp.	CVX
Cisco Systems	CSCO
Coca-Cola Co.	KO
E.I. Du Pont de Nemours	DD
Exxon Mobil Corp.	XOM
General Electric Company	GE
Hewlett-Packard Co.	HPQ
Home Depot Inc	HD
Intel Corp.	INTC
International Business Machines Corp.	IBM
Johnson & Johnson	JNJ
J. P. Morgan Chase Company	JPM
Kraft Foods Inc.	KFT
McDonald's Corp.	MCD
Merck & Co. Inc.	MRK
Microsoft Corp.	MSFT
Minnesota Mining & Mfg. Co.	MMM
Pfizer Inc.	PFE
Procter & Gamble Co.	PG
The Travelers Companies	TRV
United Technologies Corp.	UTX
Verizon Communications Inc.	VZ
Wal-Mart Stores Inc.	WMT
Walt Disney Co.	DIS

TABLE 15.9	Dow Jones Industrial Average Industry Weightings	
Sector	**Weighting**
Basic materials	3.75%
Consumer goods	10.52%
Consumer services	13.24%
Financials	10.80%
Health care	7.78%
Industrials	22.46%
Oil and gas	9.83%
Technology	17.64%
Telecommunications	3.98%

concentration of companies does take something away from the index being representative of the overall economy, but it continues to be the most commonly quoted index.

Note that although the index is referred to as an industrial index, a variety of industries are represented by the DJX. For example, Wal-Mart and Home Depot are major retailers, Pfizer is a pharmaceutical company, and The Travelers Companies specializes in financial services. The industry weightings for the DJX appear in Table 15.9.

The highest weighting of stocks in the DJX is represented by industrial companies, but only about a quarter of the performance of the index will be attributed to this market sector. A variety of other industries contribute to the DJX, which does result in an index that is representative of the overall economy in the United States. For instance, when consumer goods and services are combined, this area of the market represents about another quarter of the index's performance.

Finally, the CFE does not currently trade futures based on the VXD. However, from April 2005 to the middle of 2009 futures contracts based on this index did trade at the exchange.

CBOE NASDAQ-100 Volatility Index

Using quotes for options that trade on the NASDAQ-100 Index (NDX), the CBOE NASDAQ-100 Volatility Index is an indication of implied volatility on the NASDAQ-100 index. Trading with the symbol VXN, the index displays 30-day implied volatility for the NDX.

The NASDAQ-100 is an index composed of the 100 largest companies not involved in the financial sector that trade on the NASDAQ. The NASDAQ marketplace opened in 1971 as an alternative exchange to the traditional floor-based exchanges like the New York Stock Exchange. In 1985 the NASDAQ developed two market indexes to promote their exchange, one of which is the NASDAQ-100.

Table 15.10 shows the industry sector weightings that comprise the NDX. What is unique regarding this market index is the lack of financial and health care stocks in the index. The result is a focus on other industries with a very large weighting in the technology sector. In fact, the index is dominated by technology- and communications-oriented stocks, which when combined make up almost 75 percent of the index.

TABLE 15.10	NASDAQ-100 Sector Weightings
Sector	Weighting
Basic materials	0.40%
Consumer cyclical	8.40%
Communications	24.40%
Consumer noncyclical	16.80%
Energy	0.50%
Industrial	3.10%
Technology	46.40%

Also, the SPX has approximately a 20 percent weighting in the financial sector, which results in the NDX and SPX having disparate performance at times.

Futures were also traded on the VXN from 2007 to 2009. As this index may experience higher volatility than some other market indexes, the demand for a return of these contracts may result in them being relisted at some point.

CBOE Russell 2000 Volatility Index

The Russell 2000 Index is composed of the 2,000 smallest companies that are in the Russell 3000 Index. Although representing two-thirds of the companies in the Russell 3000, which is composed of 3,000 of the largest publicly traded companies in the United States, the Russell 2000 only represents about 8 percent of the market capitalization of the Russell 3000. The Russell 2000 index is composed of small-cap companies, which mostly focus on domestic markets. This index has a great niche as a representation of domestic economic trends in the United States.

Russell Investments also calculates the Russell 1000 index, which consists of the 1,000 largest companies in the Russell 3000. The top third of those companies represents 92 percent of the market capitalization of the Russell 3000.

The ticker symbol RUT represents option trading on the index and, like the previous volatility related indexes, the Russell 2000 Volatility Index (RVX) attempts to show what the market is pricing in 30-day implied volatility for the index. At times the Russell 1000, Russell 2000, and Russell 3000 names are not entirely accurate. When, due to an acquisition, merger, or dissolution, a company ceases to exist as it had in the past, it may be replaced by a new company in a market index. These Russell indexes are actually reconfigured once a year at the end of June, with the number of stocks in each index taken back to the proper number.

Also, there is a minimum capitalization level for a company to be a member of the Russell 1000. When the indexes are rebalanced, the number of stocks in the Russell 1000 and Russell 2000 is very close to their respective numbers, but it may not be equal to the expected number of stocks in each index. For instance, after the 2010 rebalance the Russell 1000 consisted of 988 stocks and the Russell 2000 consisted of 2,012 stocks. The total of the two indexes results in all the stocks that make up the

Russell 3000. The Russell 3000 makes up 99 percent of the market capitalization of the U.S. stock market.

Between the index restructuring dates, companies that cease to exist will be deleted from the indexes, but no replacement will necessarily be put in their place. However, company spinoffs and initial public offerings may be added between the June reconstruction dates. Those stocks are added on a quarterly basis.

RVX futures traded at the CBOE from 2007 through early 2010.

CBOE S&P 100 Volatility Index

When the VIX was originally quoted by the CBOE, the calculation was based on the implied volatility of the S&P 100 Index (OEX), not the S&P 500. When the calculation was altered in 2003, it was done so with part of the revision resulting in a focus on the S&P 500 as opposed to the S&P 100 index.

The CBOE S&P 100 Volatility Index (VXO) is actually the original VIX index, which was created in 1993. It continues to be calculated using the original methodology based on OEX options. Introduced in 1983 by the CBOE, OEX was the first equity index option product. Originally the index name was the CBOE 100 Index. Loosely translated, OEX could mean Option Exchange 100. The OEX and options listed on the index were so innovative that entire books were written on trading OEX options.

The OEX represents 100 of the largest companies in the United States. This results in the combined components of the OEX being close to 45 percent of the total market capitalization of publicly traded stocks in the United States. Also, almost 60 percent of the S&P 500 market capitalization is represented by the 100 stocks in the OEX.

Even with just 100 names, the OEX is a diversified index with all industry sectors being covered. Table 15.11 is a summary of the industry weightings of the OEX. Note the industry weightings of the OEX are as diversified as the S&P 500 even though there are fewer stocks in the index.

TABLE 15.11	S&P 100 Index Industry Weightings
Industry	**Weighting**
Consumer discretionary	6.25%
Consumer staples	15.32%
Energy	15.86%
Financials	11.06%
Health Care	15.40%
Industrials	10.59%
Information technology	17.35%
Materials	1.03%
Telecom services	5.30%
Utilities	1.86%

■ Amex QQQ Volatility Index

The Amex QQQ Volatility index is another measure of implied volatility of the Nadsaq market. The method behind this index is similar to the original volatility index calculation used for the VXO. The index indicates the forward-looking volatility for the QQQ based on option prices. To get a true option contract value, the midpoint of the bid-ask spread is used as the option price input for the calculation.

The CBOE and CFE currently trade options and futures only on the VIX index. However, these alternate VIX indexes may be used to gain insight into market activity. The VIX and other index-related volatility indexes are excellent representations of what sort of near-term volatility is expected from the overall stock market according to the implied volatility of index options. Each of the indexes that have VIX representation have slightly different components and may indicate that there is higher expected volatility in one sector as opposed to others.

TECHNICAL INVESTMENT STRATEGIES

Candidates for the CMT certification need to understand how to use technical analysis not only to interpret a single chart of a single security or asset, but also to recognize how technical measures can help identify valuable investment strategies and methods for selecting individual securities into a portfolio. This includes an understanding of intermarket analysis, cycle studies, business cycles, and an understanding of sector rotation.

Additionally, this section includes sample models for selecting stocks and bonds. These models are not meant to be considered singular standards to the exclusion of all others, but rather to be considered examples of what valid models might look like. Candidates should learn from these models what components might be valuable in constructing their own models for selecting assets and securities.

■ What Candidates Need to Know

Candidates should recognize how to properly interpret signals from disparate markets in a strategic way. They should be able to apply technical analysis tools to generate a selection process or a model for selecting the proper assets to add to a portfolio.

CHAPTER 16

Selection of Markets and Issues: Trading and Investing

From Charles D. Kirkpatrick II and Julie R. Dahlquist, *Technical Analysis: The Complete Resource for Financial Market Technicians*, 3rd Edition (Old Tappan, New Jersey: Pearson Education, Inc., 2016), Chapter 21.

Learning Objective Statements

- Explain the major factors to consider when choosing a security to invest in or trade
- Describe the relationship between markets for hard assets and soft assets
- Explain the basic concepts of intermarket analysis
- Analyze various securities and investment vehicles using relative strength
- Identify the relative strength of an individual stock compared to a benchmark

We have now reached the stage in technical analysis where we become more practical. After learning how to analyze the long-term stock market and how to use various technical tools to determine the best entry and exit points in individual issues, we now focus on exactly what issues to consider for trading or investment goals. Those interested in using technical methods in markets must determine whether they have the time, inclination, and facilities to trade issues or whether they want to consume less time and utilize technical methods for investing over longer periods.

■ Which Issues Should I Select?

Investment requires a certain aspect of the investor's time and energy, not to mention knowledge and psychological makeup, to profit. Investing, including trading, breaks down into four general categories: 1) buy-and-hold, 2) position trading, 3) swing trading, and 4) day trading. The amount of time and skill necessary increases as you go down the scale from buy-and-hold to day trading. Buy-and-hold, basically a fundamental exercise in company and economy analysis, can be done once a year if necessary but more likely once a month, and drawdowns are of little concern because if the portfolio is properly diversified, whatever price declines that occur will likely be reversed over time. Position trading takes more fundamental and technical research because the positions will turn over more frequently and usually an exit strategy is necessary, forcing the investor to watch positions more closely, say once per month or every few weeks. Weekly charts are the most productive technical charts because the position investor or trader is not interested in the daily price oscillations. Swing traders hold a position between one day and several months but mostly for only a few days or weeks. This method requires daily charts and daily inspection for patterns and leadership. Finally, day trading is completely technical and based on technical criteria such as price, volatility, tendency to trend, liquidity, volume, and a myriad of other technical evidence. Before you select issues, you must decide what kind of investor/traders you want to become. Other considerations are discussed next.

Trading (Swing and Day)

Day trading requires a complete commitment to the markets. It requires time every day and night, whereas swing trading requires a daily commitment that can still allow time for a job. Day trading requires constant attention, excellent execution abilities, and high-speed price reporting. It is not for everyone, and it is not advisable for people who have other jobs and limited time to commit. Day trading can be accomplished through mechanical systems that are developed for that purpose, but even then, a heavy time commitment is necessary to perform the executions, to monitor the system, and perhaps to develop new systems.

The wise swing and day traders will select more than one issue to trade. In the stock market and the futures market, diversification is a necessity for many reasons. First, when a single issue becomes dormant in a small trading range and is difficult to trade, other issues with which the trader is already familiar can take its place. Second, following more than one issue increases the odds that a profitable trend will not be missed. Third, diversification, especially in issues that are not correlated, reduces risk. Thus, when screening markets with the criteria discussed next, anywhere from three to ten issues should be selected, watched, and traded. Trading only one issue, and using more than the suggested initial capital in that one issue, substantially increases risk of failure.

Some traders, rather than concentrating on just a few issues, would prefer to screen through the entire marketplace for issues showing signs of an impending trend change. They program their computers to search for new highs and lows, gaps, one- and two-day reversal patterns, range and volatility changes, volume changes, moving average crossovers, and any number of other short-term indicators of possible trend change in individual stocks and contracts. From this information, they glean issues to trade over short periods and then go on to the next selected issues.

Choosing Between Futures Markets and Stock Markets

A swing or day trader must also make a choice about whether to trade in the stock market or the futures market or both. This choice is a personal one. The trader must consider a number of factors when making this decision. These factors include costs, personal risk preferences, preferred time horizon for trading, familiarity with each market, access to the proper equipment, and execution capability. Let us look at these factors in a little more detail.

Costs Trading is a grueling, time-consuming process. It is not as glamorous as some recent movies make it out to be. Aside from the emotional strain of having to make instant decisions and instant executions, trading has numerous hidden costs that add up because of the many transactions necessary to profit. These transaction costs go beyond the commissions paid to the executing broker. The first cost is the initial setup of equipment. To trade, you must have not only a high-speed computer, excellent data feeds, and reliable, quick execution capability, but also a backup. You cannot afford to have your system go down during a short-term, especially intraday, trade. Other costs are commissions, slippage, missing the intended price during a fast market, limit days, and unexpected events, seemingly always occurring at a critical juncture. (The dog pulls the wires out of the computer, the cat walks across the keyboard and executes several orders, and so on.)

Risk Each trader must determine her own level of risk tolerance. Futures are considerably more risky than stocks because they are usually traded with high leverage. Leverage is the amount of capital that can be borrowed to initiate and carry a position. Because futures can be entered into with a relatively small amount of personal capital, a trade can lose all its capital with a small adverse move. With futures, the danger always exists that an adverse move will eliminate the trader's protective margin, requiring the trader to come up with more funds or be "stopped out."

Stocks can also be leveraged, but usually not to the degree that futures can, and are, thus, not as risky to capital. This is not to say, however, that a stock trader cannot go broke as quickly as a futures trader can. Capital risk depends on many other factors than just leverage.

Suitability Your experience in the markets determines the issues with which you are most comfortable. For beginners in technical trading, the slowest and least risky markets are the best. Once your trading experience provides enough confidence, you can enter other faster and more risky issues. Suitability also encompasses time available, how much should be invested in fancy quote and execution equipment, and so on. It is based on personal choice and preference.

Time Horizon Day trading has many methods: scalping; using patterns, trend lines, or support and resistance; and analyzing short-term patterns.

Scalping involves taking small profits between the bid and ask prices of a stock. It requires close attention, excellent execution, fast-feed charting equipment, and communications, in addition to considerable experience. The competition is fierce between the scalper and the market makers, specialists, desk traders, and those others closely connected with the issues being traded. This type of trading is not for amateurs.

Regular day trading is trading an issue and closing all positions by the end of the day. It has an advantage in that there is no overnight risk because no position is held overnight. A variation of day trading is called **screen trading**. Screen trading uses technical analysis intraday shown on a computer screen to give signals. The bar lengths are determined by the trader's ability to react quickly and accurately. Most commercial intraday technical analysis software divides trading into anywhere from single tick-by-tick, to 5-, 10-, 15-, and 60-minute bar lengths. From this data and software, almost any indicator or pattern can be programmed and used to identify opportunities. Again, however, it requires the time to watch positions all day and the equipment necessary to execute and watch entries and exits. Nevertheless, day trading has become popular. The new automated electronic exchanges where trades are executed immediately against the trading book have revolutionized day trading and made markets more accessible to nonprofessionals. The advent of the e-mini S&P 500 futures at the Chicago Mercantile Exchange is an excellent example of a futures contract that is executed almost instantly and has a margin requirement considerably less than its earlier, larger version.

Swing trading is more easily accomplished by amateurs. It is the holding of positions over several days or weeks, attempting to catch the small trends accompanying or counter to a longer trend. The swing trader can determine entry and exit prices during nontrading hours and can judiciously place orders for the next trading day to enter or exit positions. Many swing traders watch the market throughout the day, but it is often not necessary.

Of course, professional traders are active in all the preceding trading methods because they are intimately in tune with the markets.

Volatility As we saw in some of the short-term trading patterns, low volatility is a difficult world in which to make profits. The breakout from low volatility to high volatility is where most of the profit is derived. Therefore, futures or stocks with low volatility are generally not good choices for trading. The transaction costs of exit and entry, the possible mistakes in execution, and other costs demand that the issue traded has enough price change to make a profit despite these problems.

Liquidity Volatility, however, must be accompanied by liquidity. Price changes may be large (high volatility), but if no size is available for trading, this volatility is of no use to the trader. Liquidity is the ability to transact a meaningful number of shares or contracts easily and without bringing about a large price change. The difference between the quote price and the execution price is called **slippage**. Larger slippage is generally found in thinly traded stocks but may also occur with volatile, heavy volume stocks if the volume only occurs sporadically within the trading horizon or is the product of high-speed trading systems buying and selling the spread for large investment firms. For stocks, volatility can be measured using the ATR14. A more complicated formula is necessary for futures because of the different dollar value of point moves and the different margin requirements for each market contract.

Volatility usually is related to the consistent size of the bid and ask and the spread between bid and ask. A narrow spread does not guarantee liquidity because the bid and ask may be small. For easy entry and exit, high liquidity is a requirement. Trading is difficult enough without having to worry about whether an order will be executed close to the desired price. Each month, a section of *Technical Analysis of Stocks & Commodities* called "Futures Liquidity" shows a list of the most popular futures markets with their respective relative liquidity. These figures are based on the number of contract expirations that are traded, the total open interest, and the volume. The list also displays the margin and effective margin for each contract series.

Volume Issues with constant heavy volume are usually issues that have liquidity, but they might not have sufficient volatility to profit. Volume is, therefore, a requirement for a trading issue, but it is not the final determinant. Liquidity and volatility are also required.

■ Which Issues Should I Select for Investing?

When investing, the universe of potential investments is enormous. This means that some method must be used to cull out the investments, determining those most likely to outperform the markets. Usually, the investor only goes long investments or in cash, rarely short, although in the commodities markets, long one currency, for example, may be equivalent to being short the other. Let us look at some of the items you need to consider when choosing investment securities.

In the futures markets, selection is usually based on a ratio analysis of each future versus a basket of futures or against another investment vehicle. In the stock market, selection uses two different methods. The first method is the top-down method whereby the prospects for the market and sectors are first determined, the prospects for groups (such as industry groups or countries) are determined, and finally—after the decision is made that a particular market is favorable and certain groups are favorable for investment—specific stocks are selected from within the groups. This method is more common in fundamental analysis and in professional management of buy-and-hold portfolios where there may be little choice as to whether to be in the stock market or not. It is often called **asset allocation**, and the method we will look at is the observation of intermarket relationships.

The second method is the bottom-up method, whereby stocks are selected, usually based on their price behavior, but also on their earnings, cash flow, and general business prospects. This method is more technically oriented because it uses relative price strength as one of its primary selection criteria. By selecting stocks first, regardless of their group affiliations, the investor can assess what groups are performing well and whether the entire market is favorable or not. If few stocks come through the screens for performance, it is clear that the market is in difficulty, for example, and if many stocks meet the investment criteria, the market is favorable.

■ Top-Down Analysis

Top-down analysis begins with a study of the major markets such as interest rates, currencies, commodities, and stock market to determine which market has the highest possibility of profit in the future. Once a market has been selected, the next level of decision making is the groupings of issues in that market and, finally, the individual issues within those groupings. In the currency markets, the breakdown for U.S. investors is basically whether to invest in the dollar or in a foreign currency. If it is to be a foreign currency, the selection is large and can be broken into further groups—for example, the resource-producing countries and the emerging countries. If the bond market is chosen, the groupings can be on length to maturity, country and currency, and level of default risk. In the stock market, of course, industry groups are the standard sectors, but others are used such as capitalization, foreign origin, investment style, and interest-rate related. First, though, the investor must decide the long-term, secular trend in the various markets. As in trading, the trend is the most important aspect of any price change and the major determinant of whether the investor will profit from investing. Bucking the trend in investing is just as dangerous as it is in trading.

The technical method used to determine markets' relative attractiveness is called **ratio analysis**. It compares different markets with each other to see which is performing most favorably. After a market has been selected that fits the investor's objectives, further comparisons are made with components of that market, such as by industry group, capitalization, or quality.

Secular Emphasis

John Murphy, in his book *Intermarket Technical Analysis* (1991), discussed the concept of alternating emphasis in the markets on hard assets and soft assets over long secular periods. **Secular** is a term used for any period longer than the business cycle. **Hard assets** are solid commodities such as gold and silver; these assets traditionally are considered an inflation hedge. **Soft assets** are financial assets, called **paper assets**, which primarily include stocks and bonds.

The reason for the inverse relationship between the value of hard assets and of soft assets is that a close correlation exists between material prices and interest rates. Inflation, or higher material prices, is generally associated with higher interest rates. When inflation becomes a threat, paper assets, which decrease in value as interest rates rise, are undesirable as investments. Likewise, when hard asset prices decline, interest rates usually decline, and soft assets increase in value. The theory that one or the other of these kinds of assets becomes popular for substantial periods is not a new one.

As the theory states, when hard assets rise in value, soft assets decline. However, between 1998 and 2012, this relationship has not always held. Gold is traditionally the measure of hard asset prices because of its universal appeal as an inflation hedge, and the stock market is a soft asset. Figure 16.1 shows the history of gold prices and the Dow Jones Industrial Average since 2000. Except during the major decline in stock prices from 2000 through 2009 and a few other "bumps," these two markets uncharacteristically headed in the same directions. Indeed, over this period, gold outperformed the stock market. This action dispels the theory that they will travel in opposite directions.

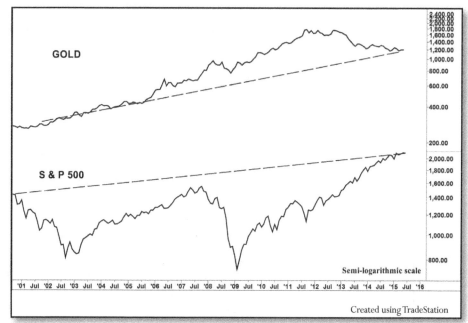

FIGURE 16.1 Gold price and the Dow Jones Industrial Average (May 2000–May 2015)

Looking at a ratio chart of gold to the stock market, we see that clear trends develop in the relationship between these two types of assets. Figure 16.2 shows a graph of the ratio of gold to the stock market. A decline in the gold/stock market ratio indicates that gold is underperforming the stock market and, in relationship to the stock market, is not a wise investment.

In this case, the broad signal as to when to switch from one asset class to another is given when the ratio crosses its 24-month SMA. This is a crude method of signaling and requires considerable refinement but here is used for illustrative purposes. In Figure 16.2, the last signal to switch from hard assets to soft assets occurred around May 2012 when gold was trading at 1,300/oz. and the S&P 500 was around 1,585. Until then, gold had been outperforming stocks.

Although these signals are not precise by any means, they do indicate over long periods in what asset type the investor should be invested. Once a definite trend toward one or the other asset type is clear, it usually remains in place for many years.

Even though we have used gold as an example of a hard asset thus far, gold is not necessarily the best hard asset. Others exist, such as silver, oil, copper, and aluminum. These are called **industrial raw materials** or **industrial metals** and are normally associated with the business cycle. An increase in industrial metals prices generally indicates business expansion. Along with gold, these industrial prices have a long-term component that coincides with the gold price and gives more options for investment during a period of hard assets.

Figure 16.3 shows the relationship between industrial metals prices and the stock market since 2005. We used old-fashioned trend lines for signals, and the last one in March 2012 coincided almost exactly at the sell signal for gold.

FIGURE 16.2 Ratio line of gold to the S&P 500 (May 2000–May 2015)

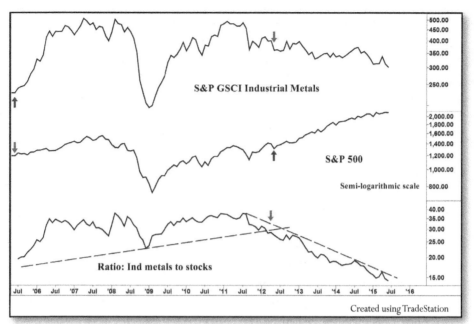

FIGURE 16.3   Ratio of industrial raw material prices to the DJIA versus the DJIA

What does this mean for investment selection? Being in the time period following the 2012 signal for the switch to soft assets suggests that analysis should be concentrated on those investments concerned with the stock market or bond market.

Cyclical Emphasis

Within the longer secular economic trend are a number of business cycles. These business cycles are of varying length but usually average around four to five years. These business cycles are the normal horizon for most economists, business managers, and investors. It is well recognized that leadership in the trading markets often switches within the business cycle. There appears to be a standard pattern that is worth watching. Murphy maintains that although the markets may appear independent, they are interrelated and follow certain patterns. For that reason, he suggests that investors should be aware of all these markets and their interactions. The activity in all of these markets might offer suggestions about investment prospects.

Martin Pring (2002) classifies investment markets into three categories: commodities, bonds, and stocks. Murphy adds currencies and, to some extent, foreign stock markets, to this list. The business cycle affects each of these markets but in different ways. Let us look at the normal sequence of leadership among these investments and see how to recognize when a change in leadership has occurred. We will look in sequence at the dollar exchange rate to gold, using gold as a proxy for inflation and commodity prices, gold futures contract to the long-term bond (U.S. Treasury 30-year futures contract), a proxy for interest rates, the long-term bond to the stock market (Standard & Poor's 500), and, finally, the stock market back to the dollar exchange rate (U.S. Dollar Index—DXY).

U.S. Dollar and Gold Murphy maintains that currency rates influence industrial prices but sometimes with a considerable lead. The dollar is important in that it is the pricing currency for many of the world's raw materials such as oil, gold, and other precious metals. When the dollar declines, it makes these commodities cheap in foreign currencies but expensive in dollar terms. Thus, there is a leading inverse relationship between the U.S. dollar and raw materials prices in the United States. In Figure 16.4, we use gold as a proxy for industrial prices because gold has a well-defined price, whereas most indexes of material prices have different weightings for their components and are, thus, biased toward the interest of the respective index compilers. Figure 16.4 shows the ratio of the dollar to gold and gold itself. When the ratio is rising, or the dollar is stronger than gold, gold tends to decline, and vice versa.

We use the trend line as the means of generating a crossover signal. In Figure 16.4, the most recent ratio line crossed upward through a trend line in December 2011, suggesting a rise in the dollar versus gold. At that time, the dollar was in a long downward trend, blocking any purchase until it turned up in August 2014 when it broke upward through its own downward trend. This raises an important point about investing on ratios. Because a ratio can be tilted one way or the other even when both components are declining, the investor must never enter the favored market until it also is advancing on an absolute basis. In the current instance, although the dollar

THEORY AND ANALYSIS

FIGURE 16.4 Ratio of U.S. dollars to gold (monthly, 1996–2015)

was favorably compared to gold, it should not have been bought until August 2014 when it finally turned up. Had it not turned up and then underperformed gold later, the investor would have saved his portfolio from loss in each asset class by not acting based solely on the ratio crossover.

Gold and Bonds (Long-Term Interest Rates)   The next sequence is typically for industrial prices to lead long-term U.S. interest rates. This was not the case in the period between 2005 and 2012 when both asset classes rose, gold outperforming bonds. Thus, the assumed relationship did not occur, raising questions about future assumed relationships. It doesn't help portfolio performance by arguing that the FED kept interest rates low and thus upset the normal relationship. Excuses don't save money, but research, flexibility, and skepticism do.

By taking a ratio of the gold price to the U.S. Treasury bond futures, we see that at certain times, a signal is given by the ratio as to when to enter or exit the long-term bond market. The ratio is shown in Figure 16.5. The most recent signal of trend change is occurring at the time of this writing, June 2015, and like many signals, it is not yet clear. The reason is that the upward crossover in the ratio is not confirmed yet by an upward crossover in the favored gold price. On the other hand, the bond

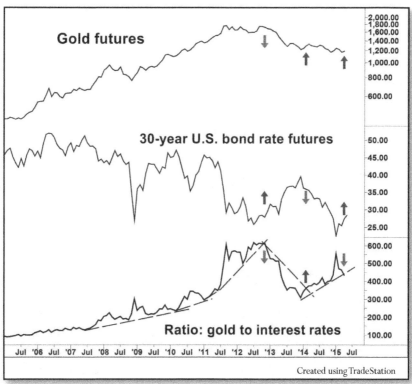

FIGURE 16.5   Gold to bonds (U.S. ten-year note) versus bonds, monthly

market is edging slightly below its upward trend line and is in a position to be sold. The bottom line is that the gold futures need to progress higher to confirm their relative strength, but bond futures can likely be sold right now.

Bond Market and Stock Market Ideally, in the normal business cycle sequence, the next switch in markets is from the bond market to the stock market. Murphy argues that this is because for the first time since the 1930s, actual deflation has become a threat and has upset the previous balance between interest rates and the stock market. Nevertheless, a plot of the ratio of bonds to stocks, as shown in Figure 16.6, shows definite times when one or the other has the advantage.

The ratio in Figure 16.6 shows wide swings in the relationship between stocks and bonds. From after the 2003 stock market bust, stocks outperformed bonds handily. However, in November 2007, almost at the peak of the stock market, the ratio turned up, suggesting that stocks be sold in favor of bonds. And again, at the bottom of the market crash, the ratio swung the other way and suggested a return to the stock market again. This suggests that the bond to stock ratio has an excellent history of timing the stock market.

FIGURE 16.6 Ratio of bonds (U.S. Treasury 10-year note) to the DJIA versus the DJIA

U. S. Dollar and the Stock Market   The final analysis is to return to the beginning and see how the dollar and the stock market have interacted. The dollar usually leads the industrial raw material market, which in turn generally leads the bond market, which in turn leads the stock market. By connecting the loop, nothing is accomplished because there seems to be only a slight relationship between the stock market and the dollar. This may have changed also, because Figure 16.7 shows the dollar now has an excellent timing relationship with the stock market. The dollar to stocks ratio gave a buy signal for the dollar and a sell signal for the stock market in December 2007, right at the peak in the stock market. Roughly a year later in March 2009, the reverse occurred when the ratio suggested a switch from the dollar back into stocks, right at the stock market bottom.

A little disconcerting right now is that the signal occurred again to buy the dollar and sell the stock market in September 2014. As of this writing, the stock market has not confirmed the signal by breaking its trend, but the dollar is completing a strong rally.

Implications of Intermarket Analysis   From the previous analysis, it appears that around 2001, the investor should have been looking at the raw materials markets and the stock market. Because both markets appeared favorable, the raw material market stocks would likely have been the best investments. The signals given by the various ratios are usually long-term signals, in the sense that they are operating within the business cycle. They are neither trading signals nor mechanical signals. Their purpose

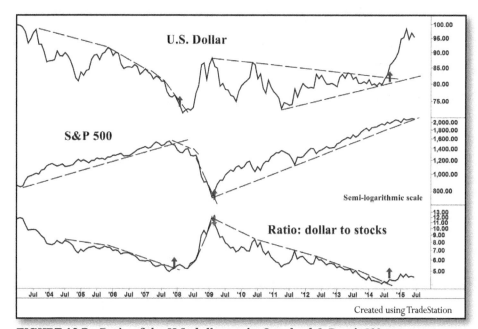

FIGURE 16.7   Ratio of the U.S. dollar to the Standard & Poor's 500

is to inform the investor in which markets to invest solely from the way the marketplaces are behaving. When certain sectors become strong, they tend to remain strong, just as when a trend begins, it tends to remain. Eventually these ratios will suggest changes in the investment mix, but only rarely do they err, and often that miscalculation comes from the investor impatience and greed, treating the signals as mechanical rather than waiting to be sure they are real.

Create an Array   One method of consolidating all the relationships mentioned earlier and lessening the difficulty in keeping straight the current situation with these asset classes is to periodically draw an array that includes the classes and gives a hint as to where investment assets should most likely be placed. In Table 16.1 is an array of the current readings of the preceding charts and their summary.

The array in Table 16.1 suggests that investments should be half invested in dollar assets and none in the bond market, leaving a split between gold and the stock market, with more emphasis on the stock market. Investments in dollars suggests selling foreign currencies and buying dollar-producing entities such as companies that produce overseas and sell exclusively to Americans. The point in this exercise of determining what asset classes have the most promise during the business cycle is to provide a framework for determining with some degree of certainty just where investment funds should go. Once the overall plan is established, the nitty-gritty of deciding of sectors, groups, and so on becomes a study of specific areas for direct investment. At that point, the analyst can use his technical skills to sort out the issues worth playing.

Finally, this analysis is not intended to forecast the economy. It is useful primarily in determining where the best market for investment might be at any time. Because most indicators lead the economy, forecasting the economy is unfruitful. From this information, certain aspects of the economy are obvious, but investment is best left to the analysis of price than to the analysis of the lagging economy.

TABLE 16.1   **Combinations of Relative Asset Class Strength**

Sell/Buy	Dollar	Gold	Stocks	Bonds
Dollar		No	No	No
Gold	Yes		Yes	No
Stocks	Yes	No		No
Bonds	Yes	Yes	Yes	
Total	3	1	2	0

BOX 16.1   LAW OF PERCENTAGES

A relative loss of 20% can be made back with a relative gain of 20%, but an absolute 20% loss requires a 25% gain to break even. This is called the **law of percentages**. In investing, it suggests that all absolute losses must be kept to a minimum. As the old adage goes,

"You can't spend a relative return." For example, if you have $100 in capital and sustain a 20% loss, you are left with $80. You must earn a 25% return on the $80 to return to the break-even level of $100. For any particular loss amount, the percentage amount that must be gained to break even is calculated using the formula %gain necessary = %loss ÷ (1 − %loss). As an extreme example, a 50% loss requires a 100% gain to break even. Considering the difficulty of investing for a 100% gain, the investor is better off cutting losses before reaching such an extreme that is unlikely to be recouped.

Stock Market Industry Sectors

Should the stock market become a potential favorite from the business cycle analysis above, the next step is to either go downstream to industries or groups and then to specific issues or just start at the bottom with stocks and let their strength tell the investor where the opportunities lie. On the former method, some analysts have proposed theories of industry group and sector rotation during the stock market cycle. These rule definitions, however, are too strict, and often the markets do not accommodate them. For example, some models suggest that utilities, generally considered interest-related stocks, should be bought at certain stages of the market cycle when interest rates are expected to decline. However, as we have seen previously, when an inflationary environment exists, anything to do with interest rates will generally underperform. In other words, any system of following specific models of business cycles is not flexible enough to account for changes in the major market segments.

For some individuals, like stock mutual fund managers, investment in the stock market is a requirement. In these instances, the best manner of screening out the most likely sectors to outperform is the use of ratio analysis between the sector performance and the stock market as a whole. For example, Figure 16.8 shows a three-point reversal, point and figure plot of the Dow Jones Utilities Sector to the Dow Jones Industrials. Figure 16.9 shows a three-point reversal, point and figure plot of the Dow Jones Energy Sector to the Dow Jones Industrials.

Plotting the relative strength ratio of an industry and often a stock to some underlying average, we often see an irregular line that is difficult to interpret. By plotting these ratios on a point and figure chart, the minor, less significant oscillations are eliminated, and the overall relationship of the two indices becomes more obvious. In Figure 16.8, for example, it is clear that underperformance of utility stocks began in 2009. These charts are much more informative than a line chart. Remember, however, when deciding whether to act on any of the ratio analyses, the absolute price action of the stock in the numerator always must be analyzed as well. When both charts demonstrate a trend, one can act with more confidence.

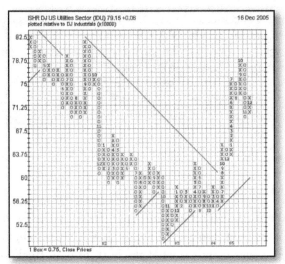

FIGURE 16.8   Three-point reversal, point and figure chart of the ISHR U.S. Dow Jones Utility Sector Index (IDU) to the Dow Jones Industrial Average

Source: Investors Intelligence

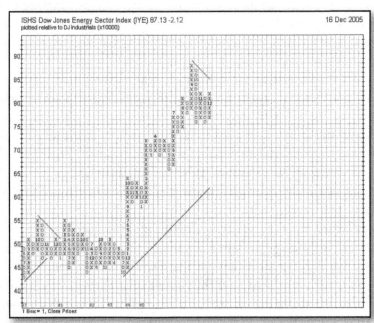

FIGURE 16.9   Three-point reversal, point and figure chart of the ISHS Dow Jones Energy Sector Index (IYE) to the Dow Jones Industrial Average

Source: Investors Intelligence

Bottom Up—Specific Stock Selection and Relative Strength

At present, almost 8,000 stocks trade in the active stock markets in the United States. This number is too large for an analyst to screen at frequent intervals. Some technical analysts briefly inspect the chart of every stock in their universe, using a bar, candlestick, or point and figure chart. This is a laborious process that's far from objective. Others screen through relative strength ratio charts. The least time-consuming and most objective method is to screen all stocks on a periodic basis for relative price strength using one of the methods described next. Relative strength provides evidence that a particular stock is outperforming the market and is likely in a strong, upward trend. These methods have also been used successfully in mutual funds, ETFs, industry group selection, commodities, and foreign securities.

Relative Strength

Most technical screening methods use a concept called **relative strength** to judge which securities have the most promise. Relative strength is a reliable concept that has been demonstrated academically and practically to have value. Indeed, because the method is so successful, it is the primary argument against the Random Walk and Efficient Markets Hypotheses. The presumption behind the concept of relative strength is that strength will continue, similar to the way trends will continue, and that by recognizing the strongest trends, an edge can be obtained by investing in them until their strength abates. If the strongest stocks remain strong, the market cannot be random or efficient.

The most common means of establishing relative strength is called the **ratio method.** It is merely the ratio between two investments, sectors, industry groups, averages, commodities, and so on to see which is outperforming the other. Usually a line chart is drawn that shows the item of interest, say a steel stock, and a ratio of the item to an average, say a steel industry average. If the line of the ratio is rising, it is simply showing that the particular stock is stronger than its industry average. Interpretations of behavior are similar to those used in price and other oscillators. Divergence analysis, trend lines, and even patterns appear in the ratio lines. The item can also be plotted in a point and figure chart along with a point and figure chart of the ratio similar to what is shown in the sector charts shown in Figures 16.8 and 16.9.

Academic Studies of Relative Strength

In 1967, Robert Levy, PhD, published a paper in the *Journal of Finance* in which he argued that relative price strength tended to remain for a long-enough period that it could be profitable and that the concept of random walk was, therefore, dead.

His paper received considerable opposition at that time when the Efficient Markets Hypothesis (EMH) and the Random Walk Hypothesis (RWH) were relatively new and highly favored among academics.

Not until 1993 was another major paper published on the subject of relative price strength, or **momentum** as it is commonly called. This paper, "Returns to Buying Winners and Selling Losers: Implications for Stock Market Efficiency," was also published in the *Journal of Finance*. The authors, Professors Narishimhan Jegadeesh and Sheridan Titman, demonstrated how stocks with high returns over a 3- to 12-month period earned excess profits of about 1% per month for the following year. However, they also found that these stocks on average had losses 13–60 months later, thus proposing the theory that relative price strength was not permanent but more likely a temporary phenomenon. They clearly stated that the t-test statistical evidence forced them "to conclude that the hypothesis of market efficiency can be rejected at even the most conservative levels of significance."

In a study of 150 momentum (relative strength) and contrarian strategies, Conrad and Kaul (1998) also found that the optimum profit occurred during the 3- to 12-month horizon. In addition, they found that a contrarian strategy (buying the lows) only had statistically significant profits during the period 1926–1947.

Of course, other academics immediately criticized the study for any number of possible reasons, but by the time of Conrad and Kaul's paper, other doubts about market efficiency had also been demonstrated, and the evidence was not rejected immediately as it had been with Levy in the 1960s. Since then, the basis of their paper has been proven correct not only in foreign countries but also in the period following the original paper in the United States, as reported in a subsequent paper by Jegadeesh and Titman in 2001 in the *Journal of Finance*.

In 1998, Professor K. G. Rouwenhorst showed that momentum was successful in 12 European stock markets, and in 1999, he demonstrated that momentum was most strong in emerging markets. Other studies confirm the existence of profitability from relative strength in China, Germany, eight different Asian markets (without Japan), and Switzerland. Even Professor Eugene Fama, one of the originators of the EMH, found that momentum was the only anomaly to survive a multitude of tests (Fama and French, 1996). Academia has, thus, concluded that the theory of relative price strength shows success not only in producing profits but also in debunking part of the EMH.

Various reasons have been proposed for the existence of relative strength, none of which has been proven. The most logical has to do with behavioral tendencies of investors and the flow of information. An excellent discussion of the behavioral model describing investor underreaction and overreaction is Barberis, Shleifer, and Vishny (1997). However, we are not concerned with why relative strength is valid. Our only concern is that over a period of three to six months, using relative strength is a viable strategy and is, thus, a reliable means of selecting stocks.

Measuring Relative Strength

Given the importance of relative strength, the technical analyst needs a method for measuring it. A number of methods of measuring relative strength exist, the most popular being the percentage change, the alpha, the trend slope, and the Levy methods.

Percentage Change Method In their study, Jegadeesh and Titman used a six-month price change as their basic lookback calculation. **Lookback** is the period over which relative price strength is calculated. The stocks then were sorted based on these rates of change. They found that the higher decile stocks continued to be strong for the next three to ten months. Their sample included both large capitalized and thinly capitalized and both high-priced and low-priced stocks. All performed similarly both in the original experiment and in the subsequent out-of-sample tests.

Alpha Method A number of different methods of calculating relative strength have been developed. One is the alpha method. In the beta theory of Modern Portfolio Theory (MPT), stock prices are compared with an average, usually the S&P 500, weekly, over a year (and sometimes with different time intervals and period). The weekly percentage change in the stock price is plotted versus the weekly percentage change in S&P 500, and a linear regression line is drawn through these plots on a best-fit basis. The line so defined is expressed using the slope of the line, called the **beta**, and the intercept with the vertical axis, called the **alpha**. Thus, each stock over a specified period has an alpha and a beta. Traditionally, beta has been used as a measure of volatility relative to the S&P 500 and considered a definition of market risk. Stocks that have a steep slope in their regression line and have a high beta demonstrate a proclivity to have higher gains than the S&P 500 when the market is higher but, also, larger losses than the S&P 500 when the market is lower. The alpha describes the value when the regression line crosses the 0% change in the S&P and is, thus, a measure of the trend relative to the S&P 500. MPT suggested that high beta stocks would be more profitable but would also be more risky. What they missed is that high beta stocks could also have negative alphas, suggesting that,

---

BOX 16.2   CALCULATION OF ALPHA FOR AAPL

The graph in Figure 16.10 shows the scatter plot of weekly changes in AAPL (Apple Computer stock) and the S&P 500 index. The linear regression line through the scatter plot can be defined by its beta (1.60) and its alpha (1.55). Beta represents how volatile AAPL is relative to the S&P. AAPL's beta of 1.6 implies that AAPL stock will, on average, move 60% more than the S&P 500 on a weekly basis. The alpha of 1.55 indicates that AAPL has been outperforming the S&P by 1.55% on average over the 52 weeks in the plot. It thus has a positive alpha and is a strong stock. Comparing AAPL's alpha to that of other stocks is a way to determine the strongest and best candidates for investment.

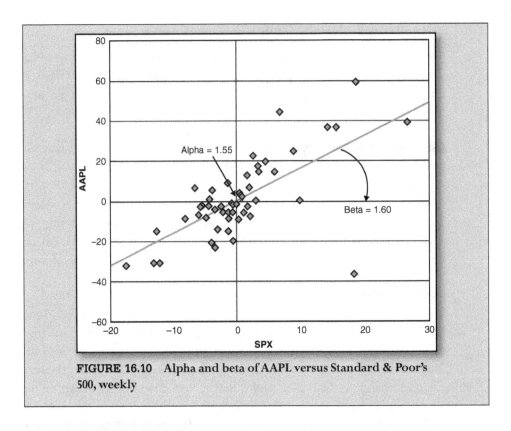

FIGURE 16.10 Alpha and beta of AAPL versus Standard & Poor's 500, weekly

although more volatile, their trends relative to the S&P could be downward. In MPT, the alpha must always either approach or be close to zero because, in theory, no systemic gain can come from the market (the S&P 500) itself. In other words, a stock's price motion is determined by beta, not alpha. Alpha is not considered of any importance. However, in actual markets, alpha does not remain at the zero level and has, thus, become a measure of how much better or worse the stock is performing relative to the S&P. When alpha is compared among stocks, it provides a relative strength measure, and stock lists can be ranked by alpha to show which issues are the strongest. Alpha will change more frequently and more widely than beta, but beta is somewhat irrelevant to the relative price strength and has been largely discarded, even as a measure of volatility.

Trend Slope Method Rather than go through the more complicated calculation of alpha and beta, another method of screening for relative price strength is to calculate the slope of the price curve in percentage terms over a specified period through a linear regression formula for each stock. The stocks can then be ranked by the slopes of their price curves. This method is similar to the alpha method and to the Jegadeesh and Titman method. It is easier to calculate than the alpha method and does not suffer from the drop-off effect of a rate-of-change calculation beginning at an arbitrary price.

Levy Method Robert Levy introduced a method of calculating relative strength in his 1965 paper. Levy first calculated the ratio of the stock's current price to its 131 trading-day moving average. He then ranked this ratio against the same ratio for all other stocks.

Levy found, as did Jegadeesh and Titman later, that the screen for relative strength should be calculated on performance of the stock over a six-month lookback period. Anything shorter tended to give multiple whipsaws in postcalculation performance, and anything longer tended to be too close to when the performance began to regress back to its mean. Levy also found that when the overall stock market headed downward into a lengthy bear market, relative strength continued to be reliable but gradually lost its ability to pick winning stocks, and when the final decline, the washout, occurred, those stocks having been relatively the strongest usually declined the most. In his estimation, relative strength was, thus, a bull market selection process and should not be used when the stock market declines.

One of the authors has tested the method live over 17 years (Kirkpatrick, 2001) using 26 weeks as the lookback period. He found it still provides a consistent list of winning stocks. Twenty-six weeks is close enough to Levy's original 131 days and can be substituted in the ratio to make the calculation easier.

■ Examples of How Selected Professionals Screen for Favorable Stocks

Different analysts develop different methods for screening for favorable stocks. Let's look at ways a few selected professionals go about this task.

William O'Neil CANSLIM Method

CANSLIM is an acronym for a method of picking stocks to buy, devised by William O'Neil (2002), publisher of *Investor's Business Daily*. The data and ratings for each stock are included in a subscription to that newspaper. The breakdown of CANSLIM is as follows:

C—Current quarterly earnings per share versus a year earlier
A—Annual earnings increases
N—New products, management, and stock price highs
S—Supply and demand of stock
L—Leader or laggard I—Institutional sponsorship
M—Market direction

We, as technical analysts, are only concerned with L and M. The other selection criteria are useful but not in the domain of this book. To determine L, leader or laggard, O'Neil calculates the 12-month percentage price change of every stock, weighted more heavily over the most recent 3 months, and ranks each stock in percentiles from 99 to 0, with 99 being the strongest. He has not divulged the exact formula, but as we know from academic studies and others, the exact calculation is less important than the lookback time over which price change is measured. This method is on the long side at 12 months, about the time when a strong stock begins to revert to its moving average. The weighting over the past 3 months reduces the overall time for comparison and, therefore, improves the prospects of price strength continuing. O'Neil found that the average relative strength percentile, by his calculation, was 87 before large upward moves.

For M, market direction, O'Neil refuses to listen to newsletters and "gurus" and refuses to use economic data because it lags behind the market. He has a number of specific indicators and patterns he watches for signs that a market is bottoming. He believes that the buy-and-hold method is faulty because the widely held belief that all stocks will recover after a bear market is a myth.

James P. O'Shaughnessy Method

Not surprisingly, James O'Shaughnessy, the president of O'Shaughnessy Capital Management in Greenwich, Connecticut, found in studying 43 years of fundamental and price data that most investment strategies are mediocre at best and that traditional investment management does not work. He studied market capitalization, price-to-earnings ratios, price-to-book ratios, price-to-cash flow ratios, price-to-sales ratios, dividend yields, earnings changes, profit margins, and return on equity. He found that relative price strength, out of all the possible variables, fundamental and technical, was the only "growth variable that consistently beats the market" (1997).

O'Shaughnessy's calculation of relative strength is similar to O'Neil's in that it takes a ratio of the year-end price to the price one year prior. It is, thus, a 12-month relative price strength measure, a slightly longer-term calculation considering the history of relatively strong stocks remaining strong. O'Shaughnessy developed from his testing of data from December 31, 1954, through December 31, 1995, a multifactor investment strategy model called the Cornerstone Growth Strategy. It includes a primary screen for stocks with a price-to-sales ratio below 1.5, earnings greater than the previous year, and of those selected so far, the top 50 stocks in relative price strength.

Charles D. Kirkpatrick Method

Charles Kirkpatrick (2001), coauthor of this book, has long had a model similar to that of O'Shaughnessy. The principal differences are twofold. First, in working with Robert Levy in the late 1960s, he discovered the importance of relating all ratios to each other. Thus, in using the stock price, he calculates the ratio of the closing price to the stock's moving average and then ranks all stocks by their ratio. Second, Kirkpatrick uses the Levy calculation of relative price strength over six months in line with Levy's original work and that of later studies showing the importance of that period for postcalculation continuation of price strength (see Figure 16.11).

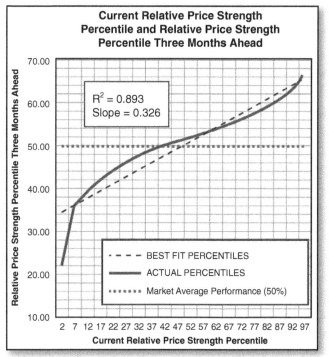

FIGURE 16.11 Relative three-month performance of stocks selected by relative price strength using the Kirkpatrick (2008) method

Source: Kirkpatrick (2008)

Figure 16.11 is a chart of the relationship between the current relative price strength percentile (independent variable) and relative price strength percentile three months later (dependent variable). The relationship is strong. The dark, straight line (actual data) fits closely to the dark, dashed line (expected data) and has a relatively steep slope of 0.326. This suggests that for every increased point in relative price strength percentile, the results increased by close to a third of a point. Its R^2 is high at 0.893, suggesting that the relationship is relatively close to perfect, which would be 1.000. It is positive, which suggests the higher the current relative price strength percentile, the higher will be the relative price strength percentile three months later. The best three-month performance comes from the highest level of current relative price strength percentile.

Value Line Method

The Value Line Ranking System (www.valueline.com) has an extraordinary history of outperforming the stock market. Value Line claims that its Timeliness Ranking system has outperformed the Standard & Poor's 500 by 16 to 1 since 1965. Although the company will not divulge its method of calculation, it does admit that a significant portion of it includes a calculation of relative price strength. Other factors include earnings trends, recent earnings, and earnings surprises. Value Line charges a fee for its stock services.

Richard D. Wyckoff Method

A method of profiting from the stock market using technical analysis and relative price strength that has stood the test of more than 80 years is the method that has been taught by Richard DeMille Wyckoff since 1931.

Richard Wyckoff, now considered a legend and one of the most important proponents of technical analysis, began his long career in Wall Street as a runner in 1888 when he was only 15 years old. He organized his own brokerage firm by the time he was 25. From his brokerage firm, he published a daily newsletter that evolved into a magazine called the *Magazine of Wall Street*. Motivated by seeing "appalling losses in securities suffered annually by millions of people who do not realize what they are risking and have an amazingly small knowledge of the market" (Hutson, 1986), in 1910, under the pen name "Rollo Tape," Wyckoff described many important aspects of the stock market in a book titled *Studies in Tape Reading*. His observations then are still valid today. Before retiring for health reasons in 1928, his subscriber list exceeded 200,000 names, and later, when he returned to Wall Street in the early 1930s, he wrote many books on the subject of profiting from the stock market and developed a correspondence course.

Wyckoff believed most strongly that stock prices were determined solely by "supply and demand." He had little use for "tips, rumors, news items, earnings analyses, financial reports, dividend rates, and the myriad of other sources of information" or the "half-baked trading theories expounded in boardrooms and popular books on the stock market" (Wyckoff in Hutson, 1986). He was a true technical analyst, and a successful one. He believed that the markets were influenced mostly by wealthy individuals and informed insiders. Substituting "institutions" today for these players, we find that the situation has not changed. By understanding what these capital pools were doing in the markets, one could profit by following them. Their capital moved the markets, right or wrong, and the small investor could take advantage of this movement by understanding how to gauge it.

Wyckoff's tools were many of the methods described in this book. He used bar charts (called **vertical charts**) and point and figure charts (called **figure charts**). He measured relative strength for both long and short positions, used volume as a means of testing the best time to consider acting, required stop orders be entered with any action order, used trend lines to determine direction, used composite indexes, used group indexes, and believed that timing of entry and exit was the most important variable in success. Support and resistance, reversal points (called **danger points**), and horizontal counts from figure charts were important to his method. In short, he used about everything you have learned so far. He believed that attempting to fit the market into a formula or specific pattern was futile because no two markets are the same. The market, he believed, traveled in waves—small ones evolving into larger ones in either direction. He believed that these waves could be detected and even anticipated, but they followed no certain, mathematical path. Consequently, although his method had some organization, it required judgment and experience.

Wyckoff's progression of selecting stocks was as follows:

1. To determine the direction of the entire market, Wyckoff devised an index called the **Wyckoff Wave** that was a composite of the most widely held and active stocks. This was his proxy for the market. Preferably, the stocks in the index were the ones that the investor or trader was interested in trading. His concept of trend was to watch trend lines drawn on the Wave chart and on charts of the composite market.

2. To select the stocks in harmony with the market, Wyckoff selected stocks that were strong in upward trends and weak in downward trends. He believed it was futile to act against the trend. His calculation of relative price strength used the percentage changes from wave highs to lows and lows to highs of each stock versus those of the Wyckoff Waves. Those stocks that consistently outperformed in each wave in the direction of the longer wave trend were the ones to analyze further.

3. To determine the potential of those selected so far, Wyckoff used the point and figure horizontal count. At the same time, a stop level was established, and for the stock to be considered further, a three-to-one ratio of potential gain to potential stop loss was necessary.

4. To determine if the stock is ready to move, shorter-term considerations were needed to analyze the nature of its price action. To do this, Wyckoff relied on volume, range, and to some extent, short-term momentum. This portion of his method relied heavily on experience and judgment.

5. To time the entry, Wyckoff based his decision on the turning in the overall market. His basis for this principle was that most stocks move with the market direction, and timing with the market change reduces the risk of error.

■ Conclusion

Trading is often focused on few issues because each must be watched closely and intently. Selecting the issues most suitable for a trader depends on many factors having to do with the trader's time horizon, liquidity, volatility, preferred market, technical methods, operating costs, and risk tolerance. Those traders who look for special opportunities in the market rather than concentrate on a small number of issues are often swing traders who hold their positions for a few days or weeks. They use screens based principally on technical action such as patterns, gaps, breakouts from prior highs and lows, and changes in volume or volatility to select issues. Their equipment is able to scan through large numbers of issues looking for such indications of trend change. As might be expected, these methods are not often used by amateurs because they must be followed each day all day, although swing trading setups can often be recognized at night and orders placed for the next day while the trader is otherwise occupied.

In investment selection, as in fundamental screening for issues in which to invest, technical screening can begin with the overall picture—the top-down approach—or it can begin right with the individual issues in the markets that the investor is most interested in—the bottom-up approach. Of course, rather than analyze economics and company financial data, the technical analyst regards the price action of the areas of interest. In the top-down approach, the analyst begins with the long, secular period of economic activity and studies the relative action of the four basic investment segments—currencies, materials prices, interest rates, and stock markets. From the results of that analysis, the analyst can then further analyze the sectors of those markets showing the most promise. At all times, focus is placed on the best-acting areas for investment because they have consistently been shown to continue with such strength, similar to the behavior of trends on an absolute basis. The bottom-up approach is most often accomplished specifically for the stock markets because they have so many different issues from which to choose. This analysis is likewise centered around what is called relative strength to determine the best acting issues over a specified past lookback period, usually around six months, with anticipation that those selected issues will continue to outperform over the following year. Relative strength has been widely tested both in academia and in practice and has shown consistent reliability.

■ References

Barberis, Nicholas, A. Shleifer and Robert W. Vishny. "A Model of Investor Sentiment." Working paper no. 5926, National Bureau of Economic Research, Cambridge, MA, 1997.

Conrad, Jennifer and Guatam Kaul. "The Anatomy of Trading Strategies." *The Review of Financial Studies* 11, no. 3 (1998): 489–519.

Fama, E.F. and K.R. French. "'Multifactor Explanations of Asset Pricing Anomalies." *Journal of Finance* 51 (1996): 55–84.

Hutson, Jack K. *Charting the Stock Market: The Wyckoff Method.* Seattle, WA: Technical Analysis, Inc., 1986.

Jegadeesh, Narisimhan and Sheridan Titman. "Returns to Buying Winners and Selling Losers: Implications for Stock Market Efficiency." *Journal of Finance* 48 (1993): 65–91.

Jegadeesh, Narisimhan and Sheridan Titman. "Profitability of Momentum Strategies: An Evaluation of Alternative Explanations." *Journal of Finance* 56 (2001): 699–720.

Kirkpatrick, Charles D. "Stock Selection: A Test of Relative Stock Values Reported over 17 1/2 Years." *Journal of Technical Analysis* (formerly *The Market Technicians Association Journal*) 57 (2001): 30–34.

Kirkpatrick, Charles D. *Beat the Market: Invest by Knowing What Stock to Buy and What Stocks to Sell.* Short Hiills, NJ: FT Press, 2008.

Levy, Robert. "Relative Strength as a Criterion for Investment Selection." *Journal of Finance* 22, no. 4 (1967b): 595–610.

Levy, Robert. *The Relative Strength Concept of Common Stock Price Forecasting.* Larchmont, NY: Investors Intelligence, 1968.

Murphy, John J. *Intermarket Technical Analysis: Trading Strategies for the Global Stock, Bond, Commodity and Currency Markets.* New York, NY: John Wiley & Sons, Inc., 1991.

O'Neil, William J. *How to Make Money in Stocks.* 3rd ed. (2002). New York, NY: McGraw-Hill, 1988.

O'Shaughnessy, James P. *What Works on Wall Street.* New York, NY: McGraw-Hill, 1997.

Pring, Martin J. *Technical Analysis Explained.* 4th ed. New York, NY: McGraw-Hill, 2002.

CHAPTER 17

Intermarket Analysis

From Markos Katsanos, *Intermarket Trading Strategies* (Hoboken, New Jersey: John Wiley & Sons, 2008), Chapter 3.

It's not that I am so smart; it's just that I stay with the problems longer.

—Albert Einstein

Learning Objective Statement

■ Recognize confirmation signals inferred from intermarket analysis

The basic premise of intermarket analysis is that there is both a cause and effect to the movement of money from one area to another. Consider, for example, the price of gold and the dollar. Because gold is denominated in US dollars, any significant fluctuation of the dollar will have an impact on the price of gold, which in turn will affect the price of gold mining stocks.

The strength and direction of the relationship between two markets is measured by the correlation coefficient which reflects the simultaneous change in value of a pair of numeric series over time.

Highly positively correlated markets can be expected to move in similar ways and highly negatively correlated markets are likely to move in opposite directions. Knowing which markets are positively or negatively correlated with a given market is very important for gaining an understanding of the future directional movement of the market you propose to trade.

Advancements in telecommunications have contributed to the integration of international markets. Sophisticated traders are starting to incorporate intermarket analysis in their trading decisions through a variety of means ranging from simple chart analysis to correlation analysis. Yet the intermarket relationships hidden in this data are often quite complex and not readily apparent, while the scope of analysis is virtually unlimited.

But what is intermarket analysis?

The financial markets comprise more than 500,000 securities, derivatives, currencies, bonds, and other financial instruments – the size of a small city. All interact with each other to some extent and a seemingly unimportant event can cause a chain of reactions causing a landslide of large-scale changes to the financial markets.

Consider the following example: Let's suppose that the Bank of Japan dcides to buy dollars in order to push the yen down. As a result Japanese stock prices will go up as a weak yen will help boost profits for exporters. A sharp rise of the Nikkei will in turn have a positive effect on all other Asian markets. The next morning European markets, in view of higher Asian markets and in the absence of other overnight news, will open higher. This will in turn drive US index futures higher and boost US markets at open. In addition lower yen prices will encourage the "yen carry trade", i.e. borrowing yen at lower or near zero interest rates and buying higher yielding assets such as US bonds or even emerging market equities, which in turn will push bonds and equities higher. On the other hand, a scenario for disaster will develop if the opposite happens and the yen rises sharply against the dollar. This will cause a sharp unwinding of the "yen carry trade", triggering an avalanche of sharp declines in all financial markets.

But what might cause the yen to rise? The following is a possible scenario: As we head into the economic slowdown, the carry trade money that has flowed into risky cyclical assets is likely to fall in value. As a result, speculators in these assets will cut their losses, bail out and repay their yen debts. This is a scenario for disaster because when the yen rebounds against the dollar, it often snaps back very fast and carry trades can go from profit to loss with almost no warning.

A popular chaos theory axiom (known as the "butterfly effect" because of the title of a paper given by the mathematician Edward Lorenz in 1972 to the American Association for the Advancement of Science in Washington, D.C. entitled "Predictability: Does the Flap of a Butterfly's Wings in Brazil Set Off a Tornado in Texas?") stipulates that a small change in the initial condition of the system (the flapping of the wing) causes a chain of events leading to large-scale phenomena. Had the butterfly not flapped its wings, the trajectory of the system might have been vastly different.

A financial series would appear to be chaotic in nature, but its statistics are not because, as well as being orderly in the sense of being deterministic, chaotic systems usually have well defined statistics.

The rapid progress of global communications has contributed to the integration of all international financial markets as the world has gotten smaller due to the ability to communicate almost instantaneously. Relationships that were dismissed as irrelevant in the past cannot be ignored any more as the globalization of the markets contributes to a convergence of formerly unrelated markets.

Take a look at the comparison chart in Figure 17.1. The S&P 500 is depicted with a bold thick line. The second one however is not even a stock index. It is the Japanese yen exchange rate (USD/JPY).

The next composite chart in Figure 17.2 is of three stock indices. The first two (depicted with a bar chart and thick line) are of the S&P 500 and the Nasdaq Composite respectively. The third chart (thin line) is the Athens General Index which, surprisingly, correlates better with the S&P 500 than its compatriot, the Nasdaq Composite.

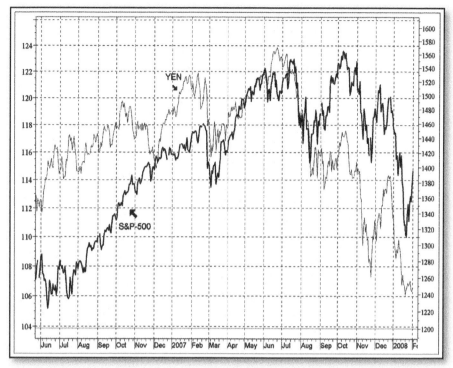

FIGURE 17.1 Comparison Chart of the S&P 500 (in Bold with the Scale on the Right Y-axis) and the Yen (USD/JPY) (with the Scale on the Left Axis) from June 2006 to January 2008.

FIGURE 17.2 Weekly Comparison Chart of the S&P 500 (Thick Line with the Scale on the Right Y-axis), the Nasdaq (in Bold with the Scale on the Left Axis) and the Greek Athens General Index (ATG) from 1999 to 2008.

The above examples are included to illustrate that the integration of global markets can extend beyond the obvious relations.

I often hear CNBC guests suggesting investing in international markets as a means of diversifying one's portfolio away from the US equity markets. Although some emerging markets may have relatively medium to low correlation with US markets, one important question to ask is whether diversification works when it is needed most. Evidence from stock market history suggests that periods of negative shocks and poor market performance were associated with high, rather than low, correlations. The events of 21 January 2008 are still fresh in my mind, when a 2.9% correction in the S&P 500 was followed the next day by a devastating 7.2% drop in the German DAX, wiping out nine months of profits in a day. Emerging markets sunk even more with the Jakarta Composite falling more than 12% in two days while Brazil's Bovespa lost more than 8.5%. Indeed, investors who have apparently relied upon diversification in the past to protect them against corrections of the market have been frequently disappointed.

The only effective method of diversifying one's portfolio is by including asset classes with low or negative correlation to stocks such as cash, foreign exchange or commodities. Whatever the relationship is – leading, lagging, or divergent responses to economic conditions – a strong negative correlation coefficient between two markets is a suggestion that these markets will move against each other sometime in the future. And, of course, the higher the absolute value of the coefficient of correlation, the higher the diversity of their performances.

Although intermarket analysis has been classified as a branch of technical analysis, it has not been embraced fully by analysts. The majority of traders continue to focus on only one market at a time and they tend to miss the forest for the trees. No market exists in a vacuum, and traders who focus on the bigger picture portrayed through all international markets tend to be the ones that deliver better performance.

Traditional technical analysis indicators such as moving averages are lagging indicators calculated from past data and are limited in assessing the current trend. Regardless of the hours spent in back-testing, there is a limit beyond which a system based on a lagging indicator can be improved further. Thus the addition of leading indicators that anticipate reversals in trend direction is essential and beneficial to the system's performance. These can only be created by taking into consideration directional movements of correlated markets.

The use of intermarket correlation analysis can help you improve on your trading system by avoiding trades against the prevailing direction of correlated markets, but can also be used on its own to develop a complete system based on divergences between two or more highly correlated markets. Knowing the correlation of the market you propose to trade with other markets is very important for predicting its future direction. In addition, short-term traders can take advantage of the time difference between world markets and anticipate the next day's movement. Asian markets are the first to start trading, followed by the European markets. For a US trader the insight gained from all preceding markets is a valuable tool in predicting at least the opening in his local market.

I have found that the most accurate economist is the market itself. It is far easier to forecast economic activity from the behavior of markets themselves than it is to forecast the capital markets from lagging economic statistics such as the unemployment index. The market is a discounting mechanism. It interprets the impact of economic news some time in the future. Of course, this is only a guess and guesses are not always right. But the truth is that the market is a much better guesser than any of us are, as it represents the average opinion of all the economists in the world.

There appears to be no end to the conclusions that can be drawn if a little understanding, imagination, and pure common sense are applied. Major changes in commodity prices affect the bond markets of different countries in different ways, depending upon their economic structure.

What sectors are affected first? Which asset class will provide the best potential profits? If opportunities dry up in one sector, where is the money heading to take advantage of the next cycle? This is what intermarket analysis can tell you if you learn what to look for, which makes it a grand endeavor and a continuing challenge but always worth the effort.

Intermarket analysis can also be useful in estimating the duration and state of the business cycle by watching the historic relationship between bonds, stocks and commodities as economic slowing favors bonds over stocks and commodities.

Near the end of an economic expansion bonds usually turn down before stocks and commodities and the reverse is true during an economic expansion. Bonds are usually the first to peak and the first to bottom and can therefore provide ample warning of the start or the end of a recession. Bonds have an impressive record as a leading indicator for the stock market, although this information cannot be used in constructing a trading system as the lead times can be quite long, ranging from one to two years.

You can see in Figure 17.3 that bonds peaked in October 1998, 18 months before stocks peaked in March 2000 and 29 months before the official start of the recession in March 2001. The Commodity Research Bureau (CRB) index was the last to peak, making a complex triple top formation with the last peak coinciding with the start of the recession.

Bonds were also the first to bottom in anticipation of the recovery, followed by commodities and then stocks. From the beginning of 2003 until the middle of 2005 all three were rising together. Commodities are usually the last to bottom during a recovery but this was not the case here as they were boosted by the weakness in the dollar. The dollar made a final peak in January 2002 and reversed direction, dropping like a rock against the euro and other major currencies. This triggered a secular bull market in gold which spread to the rest of the commodities and has continued until the end of June 2008, almost nine months after stocks peaked in September 2007.

More information on the business cycle, including sector rotation during economic cycles, can be found in John Murphy's excellent book *Intermarket Analysis: Profiting from Global Market Relationships*.

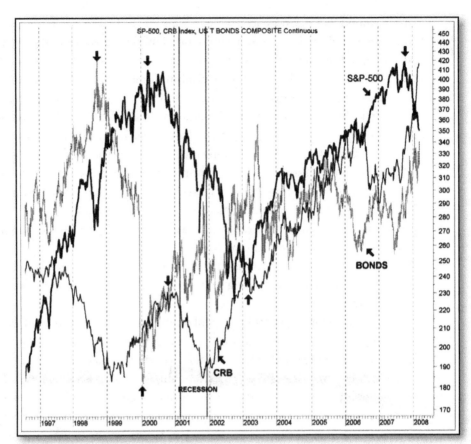

FIGURE 17.3 Weekly Composite Chart of the S&P 500 (Thick Line), the CRB Index (Thin Line with the Scale on the Right Y-axis) and US Treasury Bonds (Grey Bar Chart) from 1997 to 2008. Down arrows indicate major tops in stocks and bonds and up arrows bottoms.

■ 17.1 Determining Intermarket Relations

The simplest and easiest method of intermarket analysis is a visual inspection of a comparison chart of one security superimposed on the chart of another. A custom indicator can also be calculated from the ratio of prices, to help assess their past relation and anticipate future direction. Both of the above methods, however, are limited to two markets and the use of the correlation coefficient is essential for an analysis of multiple markets. For predictive purposes, we wish to detect correlations that are significantly different from zero. Such relationships can then be used to predict the future course of events in trading systems or forecasting models.

In addition, linear regression can be used to predict the future price trend of a market based on its correlation with multiple related markets.

When assessing intermarket relations you should always keep in mind that these are neither fixed nor static in time. Instead they fluctuate continuously in strength and time. It is usually very difficult to determine which market is leading or lagging. A lead can shift over time and become a lag, with the markets switching positions as follower and leader. In addition, a weak positive correlation can sometimes become negative and vice versa. For this reason it is always prudent to look at the prevailing rate of change of the correlation between two related markets before reaching any important conclusions or trading decisions.

The variability of the correlation over time is more evident in Figure 17.4, where yearly correlations between the S&P 500 and four major international indices are plotted against time from 1992 up to the end of 2007. You can see that correlations before 1996 were inconsistent and unpredictable but started to converge during the last ten year period. The most incongruous relationship is that between the S&P 500 and Japan's Nikkei (in white) as it fluctuated from negative to positive values over time.

The recent integration of global markets has also been accelerated by a flurry of mergers, acquisitions and alliances between international exchanges, the most important being the merger between the New York Stock Exchange and Euronext, Europe's leading cross-border exchange, which includes French, Belgian, Dutch and Portuguese national markets. A few months later the Nasdaq, after a failed bid for the London Stock Exchange, announced a takeover of the OMX, which owns and operates stock exchanges in Stockholm, Helsinki, Copenhagen, Reykjavik (Iceland) and the Baltic states.

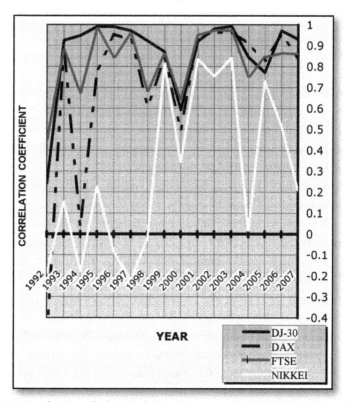

FIGURE 17.4 **Yearly Correlation Variation Between the S&P 500 and Leading International Indices from 1992–2007.** The correlation with the DJ-30 is depicted by a black line, with Germany's DAX by a dashed line, with the FTSE by a grey line, and with the Nikkei by a white line. Notice the correlation volatility, especially before 1996. The Nikkei had the weakest and most volatile correlation with the S&P 500.

■ 17.2 Using Intermarket Correlations for Portfolio Diversification

The benefits of diversification are well known: most investment managers diversify by including international equities, bonds and cash in their US stock portfolio. Less common, however, is the diversification into other asset classes such as commodities or foreign currencies (forex).

There is a widely held belief that, because commodities and currencies are traded on very thin margins, they are just too risky and can lead to financial ruin. Visions of wheat being delivered to the trader's front yard, margin calls or stories of consecutive "limit down days" add fuel to the fire. Claims that "over 90% of all futures traders lose money over time" do not help either.

Because of their low correlation to equities, most commodities are attractive diversification candidates as they can lead to a large increase in returnwhile simultaneously reducing risk. Furthermore, futures diversification is particularly effective in declining stock markets, just where it is needed most.During periods of very lowor negative stock returns, commodities (except industrial metal futures) dominate the portfolio return, acting as a hedge, or buffer, in fallingmarkets. The benefit of including foreign stocks is not so clear as the world has gotten smaller due to the ability to communicate almost instantaneously.

Unfortunately, the approach of most novice investors or even fund managers is to have no risk management at all and it becomes obvious too late that this is an extremely dangerous omission. A fund or portfolio manager should not be evaluated only by the return he has achieved. Another important criterion of his performance is the portfolio risk exposure over time. A good benchmark of that risk is the standard deviation of returns. This is a measure of how far apart the monthly or yearly returns are scattered around the average.

Correlation is a relatively simple concept but absolutely mandatory in the use of investments. It basically refers to whether or not different investments or asset classes will move at the same time for the same reason and in the same direction. To be effective, diversification must involve asset classes that are not correlated (that is, they do not move in the same direction at the same time). High positive correlation reduces the benefits of diversification. On the other hand, selecting uncorrelated or negatively correlated asset classes not only reduces the downside volatility in the performance curve of the portfolio to a minimum but can also increase overall profitability as well. An example will help illustrate the basics of diversification.

Suppose you are considering diversifying your stock portfolio by adding an uncorrelated commodity future from the energy complex. If you invest your entire equity in either stocks or crude oil futures, and returns vary in the future as they have in the past, your equity line (in points) will be similar to the charts in the bottom window of Figure 17.5. If, however, you invest 70% of your initial capital in stocks and 30% in crude oil futures, your equity line will be similar to the top chart in Figure 17.5. You can clearly see that the portfolio's returns are not nearly as volatile as are those of the individual investments.

FIGURE 17.5 Monthly Comparison Chart of the S&P 500 (Bar Chart with the Scale on the Right Y-axis) and Light Sweet Crude Oil Futures Continuous Contract (NYMEX:CL) (Line Chart Below) from January of 1994 to January of 2008. The equity line of a composite portfolio consisting of 70% equities (represented by the S&P 500) and 30% oil futures is plotted in the top window. The composite portfolio produced better returns with less volatility.

The reason for the reduction in volatility is that stocks did not move in the same direction at the same time with crude oil futures. Thus, a crucial factor for constructing portfolios is the degree of correlation between investment returns. Diversification provides substantial risk reduction if the components of a portfolio are uncorrelated.

In fact, it is possible to reduce the overall risk of the portfolio to almost zero if enough investment opportunities having non-correlated returns are combined together!

Maximum return, however, is also proportional to risk. Low risk investments produce low returns and speculative or riskier investments can produce higher returns. Thus reducing risk can also reduce return. Like everything else in life, the best solution is a compromise between risk and return.

The problem is therefore reduced to finding an efficient portfolio that will maximize expected return according to one's individual risk preferences. The following example will help illustrate the basics of selecting an appropriate portfolio of securities or asset classes.

Let's suppose that we want to invest in international equities but also diversify into futures and forex. For simplicity's sake I include only one sample from each asset class, for example crude oil futures to represent commodities, gold to represent precious metals and the British pound to represent foreign exchange. International

TABLE 17.1	All Stock Index Returns Include Dividends. Also foreign index returns were converted to US dollars. The bond returns were obtained from the Lehman Brothers website (http://www.lehman.com/fi/indices/) and concerned aggregate returns of the US Bond Index. British pound (GBP/USD) returns include price appreciation versus the USD and also interest income. Oil returns were obtained from the historical continuous light sweet crude oil contract (NYMEX:CL).

Annual Returns

Year	S&P 500	FTSE	Hang Seng	Bonds	GBP	Gold	Crude Oil	Cash
1997	33.36	23.98	−17.3	9.65	2.31	−21.8	−31.9	5.25
1998	28.58	17.02	−2.15	8.69	6.47	−0.26	−31.7	5.06
1999	21.04	17.22	71.51	−0.82	2.37	0.00	112.4	4.74
2000	−9.10	−15.6	−8.96	11.63	−1.85	−5.55	4.69	5.95
2001	−11.9	−17.6	−22.0	8.44	1.39	2.48	−26.0	4.09
2002	−22.1	−8.79	−15.1	10.26	13.56	24.80	57.3	1.70
2003	28.68	27.60	38.55	4.10	14.35	19.09	4.23	1.07
2004	10.88	18.43	16.30	4.34	12.25	5.58	33.61	1.24
2005	4.91	9.70	7.82	2.43	−5.78	18.00	40.48	3.00
2006	15.79	27.77	37.35	4.33	18.85	23.17	0.02	4.76
Mean	10.02	9.97	10.61	6.31	6.39	6.55	16.31	3.69
St Dev	19.14	17.53	30.35	4.00	8.02	14.73	45.67	1.80

equities are represented by the S&P 500 (or a stock selection tracking the S&P), one European (the FTSE 100) and one Asian (the Hang Seng) index. In Table 17.1, I have prepared the average yearly percentage returns and standard deviation of returns. I have also calculated, at the bottom of the table, the total average 10-year return and the standard deviation of returns using Excel's STDEV function.

The correlation coefficients between the selected asset classes or indices are listed in Table 17.2. These coefficients are based on monthly percentage yields and are calculated, as part of this study, over the same 10-year period. As discussed later, the correlation coefficients play a role in selecting the asset class allocation.

TABLE 17.2	Pearson's Correlation of Monthly Percentage Yields for the 10-year Period from 1997 to 2006

Correlation of Monthly Returns

	S&P 500	FTSE	Hang Seng	Bonds	GBP	Gold	Crude Oil
S&P 500	1	0.81	0.57	−0.06	−0.09	−0.04	−0.03
FTSE	0.81	1	0.57	−0.02	−0.30	−0.06	0.03
Hang Seng	0.57	0.57	1	0.05	0.00	0.11	0.18
Bonds	−0.06	−0.02	0.05	1	0.10	0.08	0.11
GBP	−0.09	−0.30	0.00	0.10	1	0.36	0.00
Gold	−0.04	−0.06	0.11	0.08	0.36	1	0.18
Oil	−0.03	0.03	0.18	0.11	0.00	0.18	1

You can see from Table 17.2 that the S&P 500 is correlated only with international indices. Among the other asset classes, the British pound is weakly correlated with gold ($r = 0.36$) and negatively correlated with the FTSE ($r = -0.30$) so it might be beneficial to include the pound together with the FTSE but not with gold. Gold is also very weakly correlated with crude oil ($r = 0.18$). As you will see later, however, in the case of low correlations the volatility and not the correlation coefficient is the dominant factor to consider in reducing portfolio risk. Bonds had very low correlation with the British pound ($r = 0.10$) and crude oil ($r = 0.11$) but were not particularly correlated with the others.

A comparison of the returns, standard deviation and risk adjusted return of the four hypothetical passive portfolios shows the real effect of diversification (Table 17.3). The first portfolio (in the third column of Table 17.3) contained a typical allocation of asset classes found in an average US fund, i.e. 70% equities, 20% bonds and 10% money market. By including uncorrelated assets such as bonds and cash (with zero correlation with the S&P), a risk reduction of 31% was achieved with only 1.4% reduction in returns. A further 5% risk reduction was accomplished by including international equities (10% British and 10% Hong Kong equities). The main reason for including international equities was to improve on US equity returns, but this was not the case in the hypothetical portfolio as the Hang Seng underperformed the S&P 500 during the 1997–1998 Asian financial crisis. Commodities, however, were the real star of the show as they played an important role in significantly reducing risk and, at the same time, increasing return.

TABLE 17.3 Risk Reduction Associated with Asset Allocation and Correlations. The standard deviation of each portfolio was calculated in a separate spreadsheet by adding the annual returns of each asset class according to their percentage weights in the portfolio and then calculating the standard deviation of the annual returns for the entire 10-year period of the study.

Portfolio Allocation	US Stocks Only	Stocks & Bonds	International Stocks & Bonds	Stocks, Bonds & Futures	Minimum Risk	Maximum Return
S&P 500	100%	70%	50%	40%	10%	60%
Cash		10%	10%			
FTSE			10%			
Hang Seng			10%			10%
Bonds		20%	20%	40%		
GBP					55%	
Gold				10%		
CRB						
Oil				10%	15%	30%
Average % Return	10.0	8.64	8.69	8.81	8.92	11.96
Standard deviation	19.1	13.1	12.5	6.86	6.38	18.70
Risk adj. return	0.52	0.66	0.70	1.28	1.40	0.64

This is evident from the standard deviation of returns of the third hypothetical portfolio. A huge 64% reduction in risk was achieved by including gold (10%) and crude oil futures (10%), even though the standard deviation (and risk) of investing in crude oil alone was more than double that of the S&P.

The fourth portfolio was obtained by finding the best allocation (highest return) with the minimum risk. This produced a portfolio consisting of 30% US equities, 55% bonds and 15% oil futures. The relatively high percentage allocation of bonds was to be expected as their standard deviation was the lowest of the group. The presence of the highly volatile oil futures in the minimum risk portfolio, however, was certainly a surprise.

This portfolio reduced risk by an astonishing 64%, sacrificing only 1.2 percentage points in return compared to the equities only portfolio. The relatively low performance of this portfolio was no surprise as the standard deviation is proportional to returns: the smaller the standard deviation, the smaller the risk and, of course, the smaller the potential magnitude of the return. There is therefore a limit beyond which the expected return cannot be increased without increasing risk.

Finally I used Excel's Solver to maximize return without increasing the risk more than the first (equities) portfolio. This portfolio (last column in Table 17.3) included 60% US stocks, 10% international equities and 30% crude oil futures. It outperformed the S&P 500 by almost 2 percentage points with slightly less risk. Typically, futures can be added up to a maximum 30% allocation while maintaining a risk advantage over a portfolio without futures.

In maximizing the return I had to constrain the risk to lower than the first portfolio, otherwise the solver produced a portfolio consisting of 100% oil futures which is unacceptable. Similarly in minimizing risk (fourth portfolio) I had to specify a minimum return otherwise the solution also produced an unacceptable portfolio consistingmostly of cash and bonds. I also had to constrain the allocation percentages to positive values otherwise the solution occasionally included negative allocations indicating selling the asset short rather than buying.

Of course future performance rarely measures up fully to past results. While historical relations between asset classes may provide a reasonable guide, rates of return are often less predictable. In addition, as you can see from Figure 17.4, correlations can also change over time.

One solution is to rebalance the portfolio on a set time period to take into account the most recent correlations in order to maintain the desired level of risk exposure. This method of asset allocation, is not the only one, however.

A different, dynamic rather than static, approach would involve changing asset weights depending on market conditions. This can be accomplished by reducing the allotment of equities in favor of cash, precious metals or foreign exchange in a down market.

CHAPTER 18

Cycle Analysis

From Perry J. Kaufman, *Trading Systems and Methods,* + *Website,* 5th Edition (Hoboken, New Jersey: John Wiley & Sons, 2013), Chapter 11.

Learning Objective Statements

- Identify potential trading opportunity and risk based on seasonal cycle information
- Define methods for applying cycle studies
- Explain how to identify a cycle by removing the trend from a price series
- Identify entry and exit signals given by the standard forms of the following technical studies: Hilbert Transform, Fisher Transform, Cycle Channel Index, Short Cycle Indicator

The cycle is another basic element of price movement, along with the trend and seasonality, but as a mathematical problem it can be more difficult to evaluate and is often avoided. But there are many different types of cycles, from agricultural to presidential election, and many of them are simple to evaluate and can improve trading.

Cycles come in many forms—seasonality, production startup and shutdown, inventory or stocks, behavioral, and even astronomical. Seasonality is a special case of a calendar or annual cycle. Some of the cycles are clearly *periodic,* having regular intervals between peaks and valleys; others are more uniform in their *amplitude* or height but irregular in period. The most definitive and regular cycle remains the seasonal, which is determined by periodic physical phenomena, the changing of the year.

This chapter will discuss the major commodity and financial cycles that most likely result from business decisions, government programs, and long-term market characteristics and phenomena. Short-term cycles are usually attributed to behavior.

There are a few important ways to find the cycle, the most common being *trigonometric curve fitting* and *Fourier (spectral) analysis.* Both will require a computer and will be explained in the following sections. John Ehlers introduced *Maximum Entropy Spectral Analysis* (MESA), which finds price cycles based on small amounts of data, at the same time avoiding some of the problems inherent in other methods. Examples of solutions will be included in the explanation of the methods and applications that follows.

■ Cycle Basics

The cycle, along with the trend and seasonality, comprise the three orderly components of price movement. The fourth is noise, which includes everything not accounted for in the first three. To find any one component, we must remove the others. We found that we can eliminate the trend by taking the first differences of the data; that is, subtracting the previous value from the current value. Alternatively, statistical software will subtract this month's average price from that of 12 months ago, or today's daily price from that of 252 days ago in order to detrend the data. By finding the first differences and then subtracting the 1-year average, or by removing the 1-year differences, we are left with the cycle and the unaccountable price movement, which we call *noise*.

Even when the seasonal pattern is eliminated, most cycles are still based on the periodic effects in our Universe. After the 1-year orbit of our planet around the Sun, there is the 28-day lunar cycle; converted to business days, this gives the very familiar 20-day reference that remains overwhelmingly popular among all analysts (also corresponding to four weeks). The possibility cannot be eliminated that planetary motion may account for, besides seasonality, the effects of mass behavior, which can produce a consistent cycle that repeats with a fixed period.

Cycles can be complex and difficult to see because there is often a combination of larger and smaller patterns, and cycles within cycles, all acting at the same time. Nevertheless, they exist, and they are real. The cycles that appear to be most important are either long-term or the sum of a number of subcycles that come together at peaks or valleys. This gives us a way to identify one point on a cycle; we must remember that, when the individual components are found, there may be a number of smaller patterns that cause this effect. Thinking about it as *harmonics*, just as in music, means that a smaller cycle is a fraction of the larger cycle, for example, its cycle length is ½, ⅓, ¼, . . . of the larger. When two cycles are *synchronized*, their peaks or valleys occur at the same time. Any price series can be decomposed into individual cycles, and represented as the sum of multiple cycles.

Observing the Cycle

Before selecting a market for cycle analysis, it is necessary to observe that a dominant cycle exists; it is also useful to know why it exists in order to avoid uncovering spurious patterns. This is most easily done for markets in which you can clearly identify the fundamental or industrial reasons for cycles. The basis for a cycle could be a pattern of holding inventory, the fixed time needed for breeding and feeding of livestock, seasonality, the time necessary for closing a mining operation then starting it up again, expansion or contraction of business based on disposable income, the effects of government interest rate policy, or other economic factors.

The Cattle Cycle   Using cattle as an example, Figure 18.1a shows a clear 9- to 11-month cycle in futures prices[1] over a 6-year period from 1980 through 1985. The peaks and valleys vary by up to one month, making the pattern reliable for use as part of a long-term trading strategy. Although feedlots in the Southwest have made the supply of cattle more evenly distributed throughout the year, there are still a large number of ranchers in the North who send their cattle to market in the early fall to avoid the difficulties of feeding during a harsh winter. This causes generally lower prices in the Fall and higher prices in the mid-Winter when supplies are low.

A similar pattern can be seen more recently in Figure 18.1b. During the past six years the peaks of the cycle are consistently 12 months apart, although the valleys are not as consistent, most often coming within a few months after the peaks. The overall picture shows that cattle prices continue to have a clear cycle, driven by the fundamentals of production.

The Swiss Franc Cycle   The Swiss franc cycle (denominated as Swiss francs/ U.S. dollars on Chicago's International Monetary Market) shown in Figure 18.2a is quite different.[2] There are two likely cycles: the primary one (shown using letters at the peaks and valleys) and a subcycle (marked with numbers). The subcycle ranges from 24 to 35 weeks with a 40% variance compared to 20% for cattle. Most important, the cycle in the Swiss franc cannot be attributed to any specific fundamental cause. There is certainly a long-term cycle based on the strength and weakness of the U.S. economy with respect to the Swiss economy, or the relative attractiveness of U.S. interest rates. There is also the general ebb and flow of the U.S. trade balance and, of course, investor behavior. Unlike cattle, these patterns do not need to be rigid.

Looking at Swiss franc prices from 1997 through 2002 there are obvious peaks and valleys that continue a cyclic pattern (see Figure 18.2b). Although they are crisp in appearance, the cycle now has an average period of about 38 weeks with a range from 30 to 52 weeks. The new cycle falls about midway between the periods of the previous primary and subcycles. Although the cycles seem clear, the change in period and the variance between cycle tops will make a systematic strategy difficult.

Basic Cycle Identification

A simple way to begin the search for major cycles is to look at a long-term chart, displayed as weekly rather than daily prices. The dominant half-cycle can be found

[1] Jacob Bernstein, "Cycle and Seasonal Price Tendencies in Meat and Livestock Markets," in Todd Lofton, ed., *Trading Tactics* (Chicago: Chicago Mercantile Exchange, 1986).

[2] Jacob Bernstein, *The Handbook of Commodity Cycles* (New York: John Wiley & Sons, 1982).

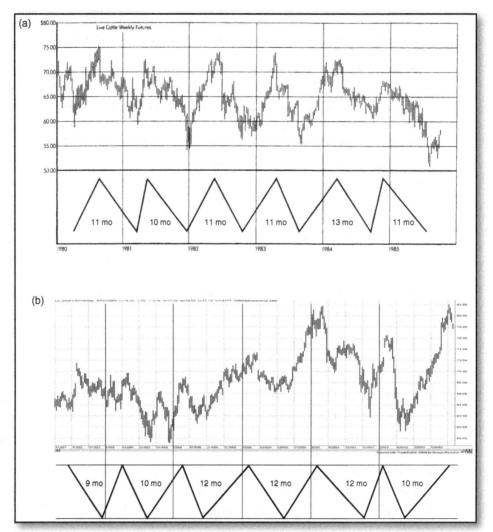

FIGURE 18.1 (a) 9- to 11-Month Cycle in Live Cattle, 1980–1985 Futures Prices.
(b) The Cattle Cycle, 1997–2002.

by locating the obvious price peaks and valleys, then averaging the distance between them. A convenient tool for estimating the cycle length is the Ehrlich Cycle Finder.[3] Developed in 1978, it is an expanding device with evenly spaced points, allowing you to align the peaks and valleys and to observe the consistency in the cycle. For finding a single pattern, it is just as good as some of the mathematical methods that follow. It is best to have at least eight cycle repetitions before concluding that you have a valid cycle.

Cycles can be obscured by other price patterns or market noise. Strong trends, such as the ones in Swiss francs (Figure 18.2a) or the seasonal movement of crops, may overwhelm a less pronounced cycle. Classic cycle identification requires that

---

[3] More information and a cycle-finding tool can be found on www.stanehrlich.com.

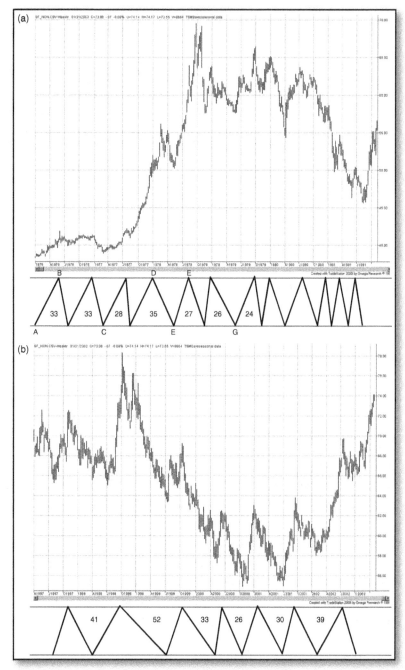

FIGURE 18.2 (a) Cycle in Swiss franc futures, 1975–1979. The lettered peaks and valleys show the choice for a primary cycle; the numbered peaks and valleys show a likely subcycle. (b) Cycle in Swiss franc futures, 1997–2002.

these noncycle factors first be removed by detrending and then by deseasonalizing. The resulting data will then be analyzed and the trend and seasonal factors added back once the cycle has been found. To find a subcycle, the primary cycle should be removed and a second cycle analysis performed on the data. This can be a tedious

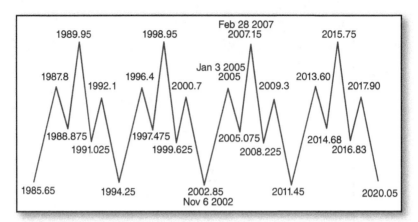

FIGURE 18.3 The 8.6-Year Business Cycle.

Source: The Princeton Economic Institute, available on www.financialsense.com.

process. In order to bypass these steps, the methods that follow (trigonometric regression and spectral analysis) can locate the dominant cycle and subcycles at one time using an integrated process.

The Business Cycle

The global business cycle, as distinguished from industry cycles, is the result of macroeconomic events, such as recessions, inflation, and government economic policy. Figure 18.3, a product of the Princeton Economic Institute, shows that this cycle is about 8.6 years, or about 4 years from top to bottom in each cycle. Although this chart dates from 1997, it seems remarkably accurate in capturing the tech bubble that ended in 2000, the downturn that followed, ending in 2003, the rally preceding the 2008 subprime crisis, and the extreme fall of the market and the economy afterward. It shows the bottom of this cycle in 2011, which we all hope is true.

The Kondratieff Wave

Much of the popularity of cycles is due to the publicity of Nicolai Kondratieff's 54-year cycle, known as the *K-wave*, or more recently, the *long wave*. During its documented span from about 1780 to the present, it appears to be very regular, moving from highs to lows and back again. In Figure 18.4 the Kondratieff wave is shown with major events (particularly wars) that have contributed to its pattern.[4] With only three full cycles completed, it is difficult to tell if the overall trend is moving upwards, or whether the entire pattern is just a coincidence.

The forecast of the *K-wave*, shown in Figure 18.4, corresponds to a sharp decline in wholesale prices due at about the year 1990, the millennium's equivalent to the depression of the 1930s. In fact, the 1990s posted remarkable gains in the stock market, peaking at the beginning of 2000. According to the chart pattern, this peak should be followed by 10 to 20 years of downturn in the economy, in which case we

---

[4] Jeff Walker, "What K-Wave?" *Technical Analysis of Stocks & Commodities* (July 1990).

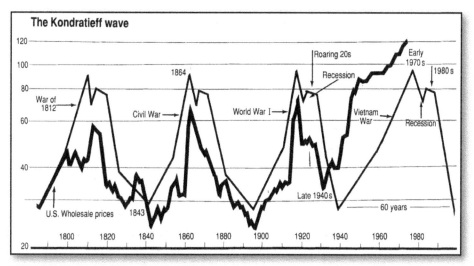

FIGURE 18.4   The Kondradieff Wave.

Source: Walker, Jeff, "What K-Wave?" *Technical Analysis of Stocks & Commodities* (July 1990).

are in the middle, having experienced a major correction in 2008. It should be noted that the peaks of the four waves are of different duration, 1870 being the shortest and the recent one in 2000 the longest.

Although we all accept the existence of an economic cycle, pinpointing the peaks and valleys is impractical. Even if the 54-year period varied only by 10%, we could be entering an investment position 5 years too soon or too late. Determining long-term cycles for any market has the same problem—the actual price pattern will never correspond exactly to the predicted peaks and valleys that most often come at regular intervals. Fortunately, there are other choices. Shorter-term cycles do not need to have the same constant period, and the way in which cycles interact with other strategy components will make them more flexible. However, some investors will want to keep this big picture concept, both the business cycle and the Kondratieff wave, as a general guide to investment timing.

Presidential Election Cycle

Of all the events that move the market, the presidential elections have been the most consistent. The patterns stem from the motivation of the incumbent party to provide good economic news to the voters prior to the election year, and as far into the election year as possible. Stock market action during the election year is always more erratic, as parties battle over the value of each other's actions.

Typically, the year preceding the election (year 3 in the president's term) posts the strongest gains for the market, followed by a reasonably strong election year. (See Table 18.1.) Some analysts have been more specific by starting on October 1 of the previous year. The two years after the election show returns below average as the reality of politics reasserts itself and the new administration tries to implement campaign promises that turn out to be unpopular. More recently, it is only in the first

TABLE 18.1	The Presidential Election Cycle, 1912–1992, Based on the Percentage Returns of the Dow Jones Industrial Averages	
Pre-election year	(Yr 3 in Prez term)	11.0%
Election year		7.0
Post-election year		4.7
Mid-term year		2.3
Average year		6.3%

Source: Adam White.

year that the president can push for serious reform. Beginning in the second year, the mid-term elections of members of Congress become more important.

There is the additional possibility that there is an eight-year cycle that should be watched;[5] however, the eight-year period should be most informative if it represented only those years in which the same president was in office. Actions by a president who cannot be reelected are likely to be different from one who seeks another term; therefore, we should expect a different pattern. This can be made more intricate by studying the patterns preceding and following a change of party, all of which have a fundamental basis in the behavior of the political parties and the voters.

More sophisticated computer software, such as that provided by Logical Information Machines,[6] a Chicago firm, can produce a very interesting, closer view of how voters respond to election politics. Table 18.2 breaks the election year into seven periods between the key events for those years in which the stock market began the election year within 8% of its 2-year high price (*days* refer to business days):

1. The returns of the year preceding the election year.
2. The first 10 days of the new year, typically a strong period (days 0–10).
3. Through the State of the Union address and the primaries (days 10–83).
4. Waiting for the conventions (days 83–161).
5. Preelection blahs: the actual campaign (days 161–195).
6. The election to year-end reaction (days 195–253).
7. Combined periods (2) + (4) + (6).

Combining the three periods (2), (4), and (6), which have strong upward biases, gives consistently positive results. Even if the newly elected party fails to deliver on its campaign promises, traders could have already converted those marketing gimmicks into stock market profits.

---

[5] Articles by Adam White, "The Eight-Year Presidential Election Pattern," *Technical Analysis of Stocks & Commodities* (November 1994); Arthur Merrill, "The Presidential Election Cycle," *Technical Analysis of Stocks & Commodities* (March 1992); and Michael J. Carr, "Get out the Vote and into Stocks," *Futures* (February 1996), all show very similar results for the four-year election pattern.

[6] See www.lim.com.

TABLE 18.2 Election Year Analysis for Years in Which the Stock Market Began the Year within 8% of the Previous 2-Year Highs

Year	1. Previous Year	2. First 2 weeks (1–10)	3. Primaries (10–83)	4. Pre-convention (83–161)	5. Pre-election (161–195)	6. Election to year-end (195–253)	7. (2) + (4) + (6)
1936	41.82	2.76	4.64	11.91	−0.62	5.85	20.52
1944	19.45	1.63	−0.84	9.27	−0.86	3.14	14.04
1952	16.15	1.60	−2.82	8.02	−2.49	5.47	15.10
1956	27.25	−1.78	5.42	3.16	−6.65	2.38	3.76
1960	8.48	−2.49	−5.75	2.94	−7.13	8.49	8.95
1964	18.89	1.79	4.44	3.03	2.52	0.06	4.88
1968	20.03	0.26	−0.10	1.44	4.39	4.25	5.95
1972	10.82	1.41	3.39	5.30	−1.78	4.88	11.59
1980	12.31	2.26	−5.42	18.57	−0.20	7.66	28.49
1984	17.53	1.27	−5.01	4.27	0.41	0.63	6.17
1992	26.30	0.80	−2.72	2.14	−0.23	5.87	8.82
Average	19.91	0.86	−0.44	6.37	−1.15	4.43	11.66

Source: Michael Carr, Logical Information Machines.

Presidential Cycle from 1983 to 2010   In our rapidly changing world, it is always interesting to see if the market reality continues to support expectations. In fact, using the S&P futures and calculating the year-end returns, the results (in Table 18.3) confirm our new expectations of the presidential cycle. There are moderately good returns in the preelection year, but excellent returns in the year of the election as all candidates and parties promise whatever is necessary to get elected.

Reality follows in the first year of office, when the president attempts to fulfill campaign promises but also takes this one opportunity for economic reforms that are likely to be unpopular, such as budget reductions and tax increases. A better year follows ahead of the mid-term elections, which have become a more important political event than in the past.[7]

TABLE 18.3   Updated Presidential Election Cycle Based on S&P Futures

Cycle	S&P Total Returns
Preelection	16.4
Election	69.5
1st year	(30.0)
2nd year	48.3

[7] Gerald Appel states, "There is a clear election-year cycle, where the election year is +10%, year after +4.5%, 2 years before next −1.25%, and the year before +20%." *Technical Analysis: Power Tool for Active Traders* (Upper Saddle River, NJ: FT Prentice Hall, 2005), 94.

■ Uncovering the Cycle

Before resorting to the highly mathematical methods for finding cycles, there are some simple approaches that may serve many traders. For example, if you believe that the dominant cycle has a 20-day period, then you simply create a new price series by subtracting the current data from a 20-day moving average. This removes the trend that may obscure the cycle. This is the same method used for removing seasonality, which subtracted the values of a one-year trend from the corresponding prices. Alternatively, you can take the 20-day differences $(pt - pt_{-20})$, which effectively removes the 20-day trend.

Most oscillators, such as a stochastic or RSI, can also serve to identify a price cycle; however, if you want to see the peaks and valleys of a 20-day cycle, you will need to use a calculation period for the oscillators that is no more than 10 days.

Removing the Trend

The cycle can become more obvious by removing the price trend. While we traditionally only use one trendline to do this, the use of two trendlines seems to work very well in most cases.[8] First smooth the data using two exponential moving averages, where the longer average is half the period of the dominant cycle (using your best guess), and the shorter one is half the period of the longer one. Then create an MACD indicator by subtracting the value of one exponential trend from the other; the resulting *synthetic* series reduces the lag inherent in most methods while removing the trend.

Using Triangular Weighting One method for enhancing the cycle is the use of *triangular weighting* instead of exponential smoothing. The weighting is *triangular* because it creates a set of weighting factors that are smallest at the ends and largest in the middle, and typically symmetric. You must first decide the calculation period and the weighting factor for the center price. For practical purposes, it is only necessary to give the center price the weight of 2.0. Because there needs to be a center price, the triangular weighting method will eliminate the oldest price if the calculation period is an even number.

The weighting factors begin with the value $2.0/(P/2)$, and increase by the same value. If the calculation period $P = 10$, the weighting begins at $t - P + 2$, or $t - 8$, eliminating the oldest value in order to have an odd number of prices. The weighting factors, w_i, are then 0.4, 0.8, 1.2, 1.6, 2.0, 1.6, 1.2, 0.8, and 0.4. The triangular average is

$$TMA_t = (w_1 \times P_{t-P+2} + w_2 \times P_{t-P+3} + \cdots + w_{P-1} \times P_t) / P$$

Enhancing the cycle requires that you calculate two triangular averages, one of which is half the period of the other, then take the difference of the two. The smooth curve of the *triangular MACD* in Figure 18.5 shows the enhanced cyclic pattern of IBM (shown for one year) based on 63 days (about the number of days in a calendar quarter) under the assumption that cycles are likely to be related to periodic

---

[8] In his article "Finding Cycles in Time Series Data," *Technical Analysis of Stocks & Commodities* (August 1990), A. Bruce Johnson credits John Ehlers for his work in the use of two exponential trends. See John Ehlers, "Moving Averages, Part 1" and "Moving Averages, Part 2," *Technical Analysis of Stocks & Commodities* (1988).

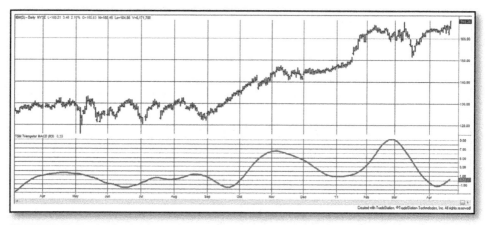

FIGURE 18.5   A 20-10 Triangular MACD Applied to IBM.

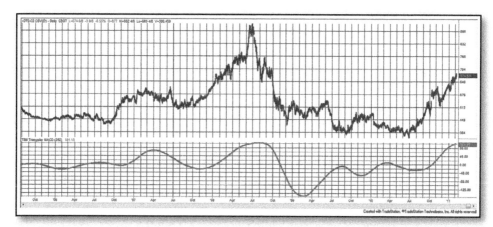

FIGURE 18.6   A 252-126 Triangular MACD Applied to Back-Adjusted Corn Futures.

earnings releases. Figure 18.6 uses a full year, 252 days, as the primary cycle, with back-adjusted corn prices covering more than five years.

While this method creates a smooth representation of cyclic movement, it has the characteristics of a momentum indicator because the peaks and valleys are not quite evenly spaced and the amplitude of the cycles varies considerably. However, the smoothness of the indicator allows you to anticipate the major changes in the direction of prices. A program, *TSM Triangular MACD*, is available on the Companion Website.

Terminology

Before getting technical about the measurement and calculation of cycles, there are a few terms that describe most of the concepts discussed throughout this chapter. Note that the use of *wave* and *cycle* are interchangable.

Cycle or wave. A recurring process that returns to its original state.
Amplitude (a). The height of the wave from its horizontal midpoint (the x-axis).
Period (T). The number of time units necessary to complete one wavelength (cycle).

Frequency (ω). The number of wavelengths that repeat every 360°, calculated as $\omega = 1/T$.

Phase. A measurement of the starting point or offset of the cycle relative to a benchmark wave.

Phase angle. Locates the position within the cycle measured as the minute hand of a clock moving clockwise, where 0° is three o'clock.

Left and right translation. The tendency for a cycle peak to fall to the left or right of the center of the cycle.

Finding the Cycle Using the Hilbert Transform

Ehlers is able to recognize the cyclic component of price movement using very little data as contrasted with the traditional regression methods. In one technique, using the *Hilbert Transform,*[9] only a small part of one cycle is needed to form a picture of the entire process, as little as 4 bars. This allows the cycle to be shown as an indicator with only a modest amount of lag.

The Hilbert Transform is based on the separation of the cycle phase, represented by a *phasor,* into two components, the *Quadrature* and *InPhase,* shown in Figure 18.7. The left circle with a single arrow points to the current position of the cycle based on the phasor being straight up (270°) at the cycle peaks and straight down (90°) at the cycle valleys. The cycle begins when the phasor is pointing to the right (0°). The right circle separates the phasor into its horizontal and vertical components, InPhase and Quadrature, respectively. The *phase angle,* shown as θ (theta), is the arctangent of the ratio of the Quadrature and InPhase components. Ehlers reduces the equations for the Hilbert Transform to:

Quadrature
$$Q = 0.0962 \times price_t + 0.5769 \times price_{t-2} - 0.5769 \times price_{t-4} - 0.0962 \times price_{t-6}$$
InPhase
$$I = price_{t-3}$$

These equations make it possible to write simple program indicators (*TSM Hilbert Transformation* and *TSM Hilbert Transformation V2,* available on the Companion Website) to plot the results of the Hilbert Transform for any data series. Although there are

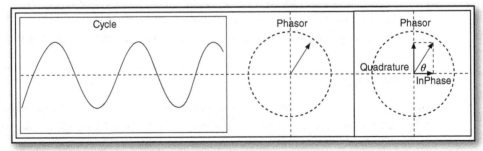

FIGURE 18.7   A Cycle with the Phasor and Phase Angle.
Source: Adapted from John F. Ehlers, *Rocket Science for Traders* (New York: John Wiley & Sons, 2001).

---

[9] John F. Ehlers, *Rocket Science for Traders* (New York: John Wiley & Sons, 2001), Chapter 6.

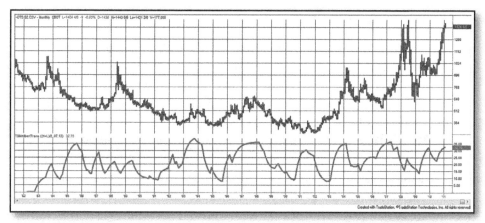

FIGURE 18.8 Back-Adjusted Soybean Futures from 1982 with the Hilbert Transform in the Lower Panel.

some penalties for truncating the Hilbert Transform, which is an infinite series, those penalties should not affect the use of this method for trading.

Applying the Hilbert Transform to soybean monthly prices gives the results shown in Figure 18.8. The continuous, back-adjusted series is shown at the top of the chart. Continuous data is preferable in this case to avoid any odd jumps in prices when one contract is rolled to another at expiration.

The bottom panel in Figure 18.8 is the result of first detrending the monthly data (part of the calculation process), then applying the Hilbert Transform with *alpha* = 0.07. The Hilbert Transform creates sharp peaks and valleys at the points where the cycle is expected to be at maximum and minimum value. There is usually one peak and one valley each year, and the minimum level often coincides with late summer or early fall, when the harvest yield is known and there is usually a surplus (or anticipated surplus) of soybeans. Sharp peaks are particularly good for mean reversion trading compared to indicators that reach maximum or minimum values and stay there while prices continue in the same direction. However, as we saw when comparing the results of cash and back-adjusted futures, these extremes will vary due to forward discounting of prices. Peaks tend to be earlier in the year using futures data; nevertheless, futures data are the only practical means of trading. In addition, geopolitical events have been much more influential in the past 10 years, and these are more likely to affect the high prices than the lows. The same method can be applied to weekly data. If the obvious major cycle is yearly, then a 52-period average can be used to detrend the data.

The Hilbert Transform indicator does a very good job of locating relative peaks and the highest and lowest values of the indicator could be used for sell and buy signals. However, the chart of the indicator does show characteristics similar to momentum indicators; that is, larger peaks in the indicator follow periods of low volatility in prices because the subsequent peaks will be seen as *relative highs*. While the peak to valley might be an ideal trade, the net returns will vary due to individual market volatility.

The Fisher Transform

It is well known that prices are not normally distributed; that is, the distribution of price changes, or price minus a trendline (detrended prices), does not appear to be a bell-shaped, symmetric curve. We have already discussed some of the idiosyncrasies of price movement, including the fat tail of trend-following performance, or the increase in volatility with price. The distribution of prices is called a *probability density function* (PDF), and the normal, bell-shaped curve is a *Gaussian PDF*.

The way in which prices move between two bands is very similar to the probability density function of a sine wave,[10] which spends more time in the vicinity of the peaks and valleys (where it changes direction) than in the middle (where it moves the fastest). Figure 18.9a shows two cycles of a sine wave with the PDF to the right (Figure 18.9b). Although the PDF is normally shown with the phasor angle along the bottom, as in (Figure 18.9c), this chart is drawn to represent a typical frequency distribution. The peaks of the sine wave occur when the phasor angle is 270° and the lowest points when the angle is 90°. The frequency of the peaks (the top of the chart) and valleys (the bottom of the chart) are much greater than the frequency of the other angles, especially 0° and 180°.

The same PDF can be seen in price movement if we form a channel around the prices and measure the relative position of prices within that channel. The channel high

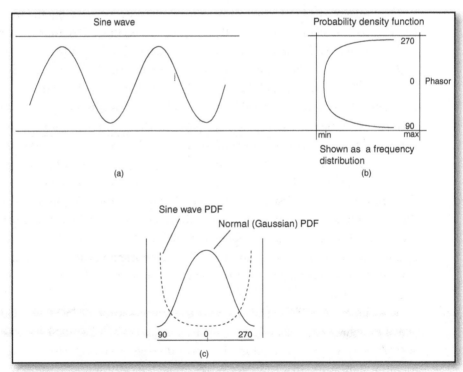

FIGURE 18.9 Probability Density Function (PDF) of a Sine Wave.

[10] This section is adapted from John Ehlers, *Cybernetic Analysis for Stocks & Commodities* (Hoboken, NJ: John Wiley & Sons, 2004), Chapter 1.

(*MaxH*) is simply the maximum price during period *p*, and the channel low (*MinL*) is the minimum price during the same period *p*. The value used in the distribution is calculated

$$X_t = 0.5 \times 2 \times ((P_t - MinL)/(MaxH - MinL) - 0.5) + 0.5 \times x_{t-1}$$

The Fisher Transform takes this distribution and changes it to one that is approximately Gaussian with the following formula:

$$y = 0.5 \times \ln\left(\frac{1+x}{1-x}\right)$$

where x = the input
        y = the output
        $\ln$ = the natural log

The result of applying the Fischer Transform to AMR monthly data can be seen in the second panel of Figure 18.10. For comparison, the Hilbert Transformation is in the third panel. In this case, the period for the calculation of the bands was 12 months, in order to allow a better comparison with other methods. An alternate choice would be 3 months to correspond to calendar quarters and earnings reports. Values for the Fisher Transform range from +1.0 to −1.0. The peaks of the Fisher Transformation are remarkably in line with the price peaks, and show very little lag compared to the Hilbert Transformation, although they occasionally peak out early and hold that level until prices reverse. The bottoms are also good, although there is an occasional lag. The Fisher Transform produces clearer, sharper turning points than a typical momentum-class indicator. A *trigger* is also included that corresponds to the MACD *signal line*. A sell signal occurs when the Fisher Transform value crosses the trigger moving lower. Experience shows that the best signals are those occurring just after an extreme high or low value and not after a turning point where the value is near zero, similar to MACD rules. Programs for creating the Hilbert, Fisher, and Inverse Fisher transforms are *TSM Hilbert Transform, TSM Fisher Transform,* and *TSM Fisher Inverse*, which can be found on the Companion Website.

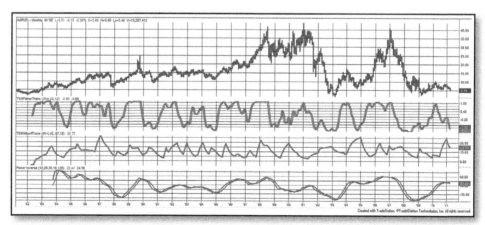

FIGURE 18.10   **Monthly AMR (Top) Prices from 1982 with the Fisher Transform (2nd Panel), Hilbert Transform (3rd Panel), and Inverse Fisher Transform (Lower Panel).**

Inverse Fisher Transform   One more variation produces a very credible momentum indicator, the _Inverse Fisher Transform_.[11] While the Fisher Transform uses the price to solve for the distribution, the Inverse Fisher Transform does the opposite,

$$x = \frac{e^{2y} - 1}{e^{2y} + 1}$$

However, implementation of this is wrapped around the RSI indicator as follows (shown in TradeStation code):

```
series = close - close[mom];
x1 = 0.1*(RSI(series,RSIper) - 50);
x2 = WAVERAGE(x1,waper);
invfisher = 100*(EXPVALUE(2*x2) - 1.0)/(EXPVALUE(2*x2) + 1);
```

using the input values, _mom_ = 10, _RSIper_ = 20, and _waper_ = 30. Note that _RSI_ and _WAVERAGE_ are the functions for the RSI and the linearly weighted average.

This process gives a bipolar distribution, where results are most likely to cluster near the extremes, +1 and −1. Based on monthly data of AMR, the results of the Inverse Fisher Transform are shown in the bottom panel of Figure 18.10.

■ Cycle Channel Index

A trend-following system that operates in a market with a well-defined cyclic pattern should have specific qualities that do not exist in a basic smoothing model. In order to confirm the cyclic turning points, which do not often occur precisely where they are expected, a simple moving average should be used, rather than an exponentially smoothed one. Exponential smoothing always includes some residual effect of older data, while the moving average uses a fixed period that accommodates the characteristics of a cycle. The cyclic turning point will use part of the data that represents about ¼ of the period, combined with a measure of the relative noise in the series which may obscure the turn.

These features have been combined by Lambert[12] into a _Commodity Cycle Index_ (CCI), which is calculated as:

$$CCI_t = \frac{x_t - \overline{x}_t}{0.015 \times MD_t}$$

where $x_t = (H_t + L_t + C_t)/3$ is the average of the daily high, low, and close

$$\overline{x}_t = \sum_{i=1-N+1}^{t} x_i, \text{ the moving average over the past } N \text{ days}$$

---

[11] See www.mesasoftware.com/papers/ and follow the link.
[12] Donald R. Lambert, "Cycle Channel Index," _Commodities_ (1980), reprinted in _Technical Analysis of Stocks & Commodities_.

$$MD_t = \sum_{i=1-N+1}^{t} |x_i - \bar{x}|, \text{ the mean deviation over the past } N \text{ days}$$

N = the number of days selected (less than ¼ cycle)

Because all terms are divided by N, that value has been omitted in the final formula. In the CCI calculations, the use of $0.015 \times MD$ as a divisor scales the result so that 70% to 80% of the values fall within a +100 to −100 channel. The rules for using the CCI state that a value greater than +100 indicates a cyclic turn upward; a value lower than −100 defines a turn downward. Improvements in timing rest in the selection of N as short as possible but with a mean-deviation calculation that is a consistent representation of the noise. The CCI concept of identifying cyclic turns is good because it accounts for the substantial latitude in the variance of peaks and valleys, even with regular cycles.

■ Short Cycle Indicator

In an excellent article,[13] Francisco Lorca-Susino presents the *Short Cycle Indicator*. This method is expected to correct some of the difficulty in financial time series, which are said to have a *long memory*, obscuring some of the patterns. It is applied to intraday bars and is best interpreted over multiple time frames.

The formula is based on the squared difference of two exponential moving averages, and the relationship of those trendlines with the highest low and lowest high of the slower period, a form of stochastic indicator. The term $(XF - XS)/XF$ addresses the convergence of the two trends. The combination of squaring and the stochastic is intended to smooth while still retaining the most important aspects of sensitivity.

$Slow = 20$

$Fast = 8$

XF = fast exponential smoothing (*Fast*)

XS = slow exponential smoothing (*Slow*)

LH = Lowest (*High, Slow*)

HL = Highest (*Low, Slow*)

$SF_1 = 1,000,000$

[13] Francisco J. Lorca [Susino], "Exploiting Stock Market Cycles," *Futures* (April 2009). The author appreciates the help of Mr. Lorca-Susino in this section. He can be reached at franlorcasusino@gmail.com.

$$SF_2 = 100$$

$$SF_3 = 1000$$

$$Lorca1 = \left(\frac{\left(XS - LH \right)^2 + \left(XS - HL \right)^2}{XS} \right) \times \frac{XF - XS}{XF} \times SF_1$$

$$Lorca2 = \frac{\left(XS - LH \right)^2 + \left(XS - HL \right)^2}{XS} \times SF_2 \times \frac{\dfrac{XF - XS}{XF} \times SF_3}{c^2} \times SF_1$$

As seen in Figure 18.11, the indicator tends to stay above or below the trigger line but reacts to changing volatility, recognized as divergence of the trendlines and the price extremes. These usually occur before prices change direction. It is interesting to note the multiple divergence signals that occur as prices rally on the first part of the chart, and that the indicator posts its lows in advance of the lows on April 5.

To generate a *sell* signal, Lorca looks for volatility to expand in a particular pattern. One of the three conditions must be satisfied:

1. $Lorca1_t > 0$ and $Lorca1_t < Lorca1_{t-12}$ and $Lorca1_t < Lorca1_{t-14}$ and $Lorca1_t < Lorca1_{t-16}$ and $H_t - L_t > H_{t-1} - L_{t-1}$ and $H_t = \text{Highest}(H, 12)$
2. $Lorca1_t > 0$ and $H_t = \text{Highest}(H, 16)$ and $Lorca1_t = \text{Lowest}(Lorca1, 32)_{t-1}$
3. $Lorca1_t > 0$ and $H_t = \text{Highest}(H, 16)$ and $Lorca1_{t-2} = \text{Lowest}(Lorca1, 32)_{t-1}$

In case 1, the indicator is rising but it is lower than the interval from 12 to 14 bars ago. In addition, the trading range of the current bar must be greater than the range of the previous bar and confirmed by a new 12-bar high, both measures of expanding volatility.

Cases 2 and 3 are simpler, requiring that the indicator is rising and that this is a 16-bar high. Then a *sell* signal occurs if either the current indicator value is the lowest of the past 32 bars or the indicator 2 bars ago is the lowest of the past 32 bars.

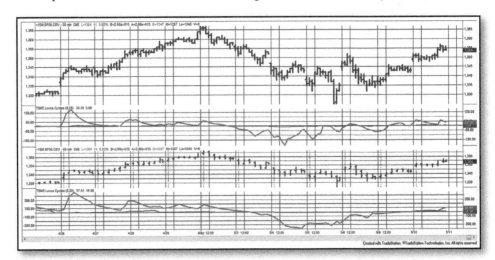

FIGURE 18.11 The Short Cycle Indicator Applied to the emini S&P 30- and 60-Minute Bars, May 2011.

■ Phasing

One of the most interesting applications of the cyclic element of a time series is presented by J. M. Hurst in *The Profit Magic of Stock Transaction Timing*.[14] He uses *phasing*, the synchronization of a moving average, to represent cycles. This section highlights some of the concepts and presents a simplified example of the method. It is already known that to isolate the cycle from the other elements, the trending and seasonal factors should be subtracted, reducing the resulting series to its cyclic and remaining noise parts. In many cases, the seasonal and cyclic components are similar but the trend is unique. Hurst treats the cyclic component as the dominant component of price movement and uses a moving average to identify the combined trend-cycle.

The system can be visualized as measuring the oscillation about a straight-line approximation of the trend (a best-fit centered line), anticipating equal moves above and below. Prices have many long- and short-term trends, depending on the interval of analysis. Because this technique was originally applied to stocks, most of the examples used by Hurst are long-term trends expressed in weeks. For futures the same technique could be used with continuous back-adjusted data.

As a simple example of the concept, choose a moving average of medium length for the trending component. The *full-span* moving average period may be selected by averaging the distance between the tops on a price chart (a rough measure of the cycle). The *half-span* moving average is then equal to half the days used in the full-span average.

The problem with using moving averages is that they always lag. A 40-day moving average is considered to be 20 days behind the price movement. The current average is normally plotted under the most recent price, although it actually represents the average of the calculation period and could be lagged by one-half the period. Hurst's method applies a process called *phasing*, which aligns the tops and bottoms of the moving average with the corresponding tops and bottoms of the price movement. To phase the full- and half-span moving averages, lag each plot by half the days in the average; this causes the curve to overlay the prices (Figure 18.12). Then project the phased full- and half-span moving averages until they cross. A line or curve connecting two or more of the most recent intersections will be the major trendline. The more points used, the more complicated the regression formula for calculating the trend. Once the trendline is calculated, it is projected as the center of the next price cycle.

With the trend identified and projected, the next step is to reflect the cycle about the trend. When the phased half-span average turns down at point *A* (Figure 18.13), measure the greatest distance *D* of the actual prices above the projected trendline. The system then anticipates that prices will cross the trendline at point *X* and decline an equal distance *D* below the projected centered trendline. Once the projected

---

[14] J. M. Hurst, *The Profit Magic of Stock Transaction Timing* (Upper Saddle River, NJ: Prentice Hall, 1970), reprinted in trade paper by Traders Press, 2000.

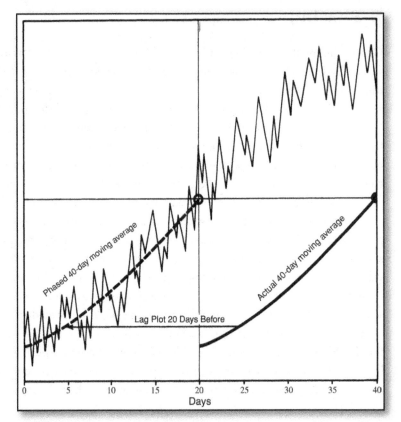

FIGURE 18.12 Hurst's Phasing.

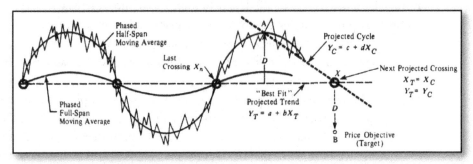

FIGURE 18.13 Finding the Target Price.

crossing becomes an actual crossing, the distance D can be measured and the exact price objective specified. The rules for using this technique are:

1. Calculate the full-span moving average for the selected calculation period; lag the plot by half the days. If the full-span moving average uses F days, the value of the average is calculated at $t - F/2$, where t is the current day. Call this phased point PH_t.

2. The half-span moving average is calculated for H days and plotted at $t - H/2 + PH_t$.

3. Record the points where the two phased averages PH_i and PF_i cross and call these points X_n, X_{n-1}, ...

4. Find the trend by performing a linear regression on the crossing points X_n, X_{n-1}, ... For the straight line, $Y_T = a + bX_T$.

5. Record the highest (or lowest) values of the price since the last crossing, X_n.
6. Calculate the projection of the half-span by creating a straight line from the highest (or lowest) half-span value since the last crossing A to the last calculated half-span value. This equation will be $Y_c = c + dX_c$.
7. Find the point at which the projected trendline crosses the projected cyclic line by setting the equations equal to one another and solving for X and Y. At the point of crossing $(X_T, Y_T) = (X_c, Y_c)$, giving two equations in two unknowns, which is easily solvable (X is time in days; Y is price).
8. If the half-span is moving down, the maximum price reached since the last crossing is subtracted from the Y coordinate of the projected crossing to get D. This distance D is subtracted again from the Y coordinate to determine the price objective, equidistant below the best-fit line. If the half-span is moving up, the price objective uses the minimum price and reflects the distance above the projected crossing. It should be noted that this calculation of distance is simplified because the trend is established by a straight line; for nonlinear fits, the measurement of D will be more complicated.
9. Recalculate the moving averages (Step 1), the half-span projection (Step 6), the projected crossing (Step 7), and price objective (Step 8) each day until the actual crossing occurs. At that time D is fixed.
10. Follow the trading rules:
    a. *Enter a new long position* when the half-span moving average turns up; cover any existing short positions regardless of the price objective.
    b. *Enter a new short position* when the half-span moving average turns down; close out any long positions.
    c. *Close out both long and short positions* if the price objective is reached. An error factor of 10% of the height of the full cycle (lowest to highest point) should be allowed. Therefore, the price objective should be closer by 10%.

Hurst's approach is a good example of a complex problem solved using elementary mathematics. There are many techniques for determining trends and a number of seasonally oriented systems, but a cyclic approach is rare. Hurst's explanation is more complete and the interpretation presented in this section should be considered only as a reasonable approximation.

CHAPTER 19

Relative Strength Strategies for Investing

From Mebane T. Faber, Portfolio Manager,
Cambria Investment Management, Inc.
(White Paper), April 2010.

Learning Objective Statement

- Describe two solutions to the drawbacks inherent in relative strength systems

■ Abstract

The purpose of this paper is to present simple quantitative methods that improve risk-adjusted returns for investing in US equity sector and global asset class portfolios. A relative strength model is tested on the French-Fama US equity sector data back to the 1920s that results in increased absolute returns with equity-like risk. The relative strength portfolios outperform the buy and hold benchmark in approximately 70% of all years and returns are persistent across time. The addition of a trendfollowing parameter to dynamically hedge the portfolio decreases both volatility and drawdown. The relative strength model is then tested across a portfolio of global asset classes with supporting results.

■ Momentum

Momentum based strategies, in which we group both trendfollowing and relative strength techniques, have been applied as investment strategies for over a century. Momentum has been one of the most widely discussed and researched investment strategies (some academics would prefer the term "anomaly").

This paper is not an attempt to summarize the momentum literature. There are numerous sources that have done a fine job on that front already including:

On the Nature and Origins of Trendfollowing—Stig Ostgaard
The Case for Momentum Investing—AQR Website
Bringing Real World Testing to Relative Strength—John Lewis
Global Investment Returns Yearbook—Dimson, Marsh, Staunton
Appendix in *Smarter Investing in Any Economy*—Michael Carr
Trendfollowing—Michael Covel
The Capitalism Distribution—BlackStar Funds
Annotated Bibliography of Selected Momentum Research Papers—AQR Website

Nor is this paper an attempt to publish an original and unique method for momentum investing. Similar systems and techniques to those that follow in this paper have been utilized for decades. Rather, our intent is to describe some simple methods that an everyday investor can use to implement momentum models in trading. The focus is on the practitioner with real world applicability.

■ Data

This research report utilizes the French-Fama CRSP Data Library since it has the longest history and is widely relied upon and accepted in the research community. Specifically, we are using the 10 Industry Portfolios with monthly returns from July 1926 through December 2009, encompassing over eight decades of US equity sector returns. Our study begins in 1928 since a year is needed for a ranking period. We utilize the value weighted groupings rather than the less realistic equal weighted portfolios, and the sectors are described below:

Consumer Non-Durables—Food, Tobacco, Textiles, Apparel, Leather, Toys
Consumer Durables—Cars, TV's, Furniture, Household Appliances
Manufacturing—Machinery, Trucks, Planes, Chemicals, Office Furniture, Paper, Commercial Printing
Energy—Oil, Gas, and Coal Extraction and Products
Technology—Computers, Software, and Electronic Equipment
Telecommunications—Telephone and Television Transmission
Shops—Wholesale, Retail, and Some Services (Laundries, Repair Shops)
Health—Healthcare, Medical Equipment, and Drugs
Utilities Other—Mines, Construction, Transportation, Hotels, Business Services, Entertainment, Finance

Data for the global asset classes are obtained from Global Financial Data and described in the Appendix.

■ Sector Returns

In the United States the 20th century experienced strong returns for an equity investor.

BUY AND HOLD	Non-Durab	Durab	Manuf	Energy	Tech
CAGR	10.35%	9.04%	9.74%	11.30%	9.71%
STDEV	16.38%	27.06%	22.25%	20.95%	25.94%
SHARPE (3.81%)	0.40	0.19	0.27	0.36	0.23
MAXDD	(65.88%)	(90.07%)	(88.66%)	(75.66%)	(91.06%)
BUY AND HOLD	Telecom	Shops	Health	Utilities	Other
CAGR	8.66%	9.66%	11.03%	8.58%	8.20%
STDEV	16.22%	20.46%	20.11%	19.79%	22.88%
SHARPE (3.81%)	0.30	0.29	0.36	0.24	0.19
MAXDD	(71.89%)	(84.14%)	(74.94%)	(85.90%)	(90.28%)

FIGURE 19.1   US Equity Sector Total Returns, 1928–2009

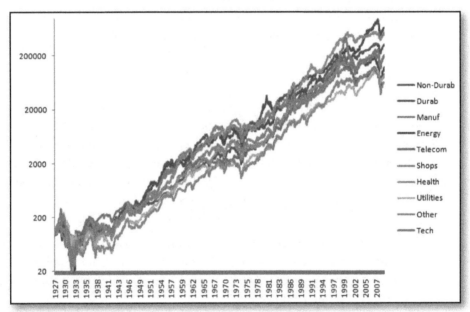

FIGURE 19.2   US Equity Sector Total Returns, 1928–2009

For comparison we have included a portfolio that is equal weighted among the ten sectors, rebalanced monthly, as well as the S&P 500.

BUY AND HOLD	S&P500	Equal Weight
CAGR	9.39%	10.28%
STDEV	19.39%	18.38%
SHARPE (3.81%)	0.29	0.35
MAXDD	(83.66%)	(81.67%)

FIGURE 19.3   US Equity Total Returns, 1928–2009

Investors received strong returns for equities, but they were not without risk. Volatility and massive drawdowns were commonplace. Below we will examine a method for momentum investing, specifically relative strength. Below are the buy and sell rules for the system.

Ranking

Each month the ten sectors are ranked on trailing total return including dividends. We use varying periods of measurement ranging from one to twelve months, as well as a combination of multiple months.

For example: If we are examining relative strength at the one month interval on December 31 2009, we would simply sort the ten sectors by their prior month (December 2009) total returns including dividends. For the three month period, we would sort the ten sectors by their three month (October 2009-December 2009) total returns including dividends.

Buy Rule

The system invests in the top X sectors. For Top 1, the system is 100% invested in the top ranked sector. For Top 2, the system is 50% invested in each of the top two sectors. For Top 3, the system is 33% invested in each of the top three sectors.

Sell Rule

Since the system is a simple ranking, the top X sectors are held and if a sector falls out of the top X sectors it is sold at the monthly rebalance and replaced with the sector in the top X.

1. All entry and exit prices are on the day of the signal at the close. The model is only updated once a month on the last day of the month. Price fluctuations during the rest of the month are ignored.
2. All data series are total return series including dividends, updated monthly.
3. Taxes, commissions, and slippage are excluded (see the Real World Implementation section later in the paper).

Below are summaries of the various ranking periods and returns for the portfolios. The 1, 3, 6, 9, and 12 month combination simply takes an average of the five rolling returns for each sector every month to sort the 10 sectors.

	Top1	Top2	Top3	Top4	Top5	Top6	Top7	Top8	Top9	EQ-Weight
CAGR	12.63%	13.74%	14.43%	13.88%	12.91%	12.47%	12.01%	11.85%	11.22%	10.28%
STDEV	23.00%	20.46%	19.79%	19.17%	18.81%	18.80%	18.62%	18.51%	18.43%	18.38%
SHARPE (3.81%)	0.38	0.49	0.54	0.53	0.48	0.46	0.44	0.43	0.40	0.35
MAXDD	(81.69%)	(74.21%)	(74.65%)	(76.36%)	(76.53%)	(78.31%)	(78.66%)	(79.49%)	(80.62%)	(81.67%)

FIGURE 19.4   1 Month Relative Strength Portfolios, 1928–2009

	Top1	Top2	Top3	Top4	Top5	Top6	Top7	Top8	Top9	EQ-Weight
CAGR	13.32%	13.83%	13.44%	13.08%	12.43%	11.79%	11.40%	10.84%	10.62%	10.28%
STDEV	20.79%	19.52%	18.55%	18.40%	18.29%	18.07%	18.14%	18.15%	18.38%	18.38%
SHARPE (3.81%)	0.46	0.51	0.52	0.50	0.47	0.44	0.42	0.39	0.37	0.35
MAXDD	(64.50%)	(70.20%)	(73.92%)	(75.80%)	(77.52%)	(79.23%)	(78.92%)	(80.29%)	(80.57%)	(81.67%)

FIGURE 19.5   3 Month Relative Strength Portfolios, 1928–2009

	Top1	Top2	Top3	Top4	Top5	Top6	Top7	Top8	Top9	EQ-Weight
CAGR	12.86%	14.10%	13.18%	12.60%	12.51%	11.72%	11.62%	11.01%	10.71%	10.28%
STDEV	21.60%	19.20%	18.29%	18.02%	17.87%	17.77%	17.87%	18.01%	18.24%	18.38%
SHARPE (3.81%)	0.42	0.54	0.51	0.49	0.49	0.45	0.44	0.40	0.38	0.35
MAXDD	(90.53%)	(84.30%)	(80.97%)	(76.81%)	(76.19%)	(77.68%)	(77.87%)	(78.86%)	(80.41%)	(81.67%)

FIGURE 19.6   6 Month Relative Strength Portfolios, 1928–2009

	Top1	Top2	Top3	Top4	Top5	Top6	Top7	Top8	Top9	EQ-Weight
CAGR	14.80%	14.17%	12.60%	12.28%	12.07%	11.80%	11.48%	11.13%	10.74%	10.28%
STDEV	22.21%	19.70%	19.00%	18.59%	18.36%	18.29%	18.06%	18.14%	18.22%	18.38%
SHARPE (3.81%)	0.50	0.53	0.46	0.46	0.45	0.44	0.42	0.40	0.38	0.35
MAXDD	(83.52%)	(75.94%)	(72.53%)	(75.26%)	(76.35%)	(76.86%)	(77.56%)	(79.10%)	(81.35%)	(81.67%)

FIGURE 19.7   9 Month Relative Strength Portfolios, 1928–2009

THEORY AND ANALYSIS

	Top1	Top2	Top3	Top4	Top5	Top6	Top7	Top8	Top9	EQ-Weight
CAGR	16.05%	14.75%	13.94%	13.41%	12.96%	12.50%	11.67%	11.48%	10.82%	10.28%
STDEV	21.79%	19.57%	18.38%	18.18%	17.92%	17.87%	17.94%	18.16%	18.23%	18.38%
SHARPE (3.81%)	0.56	0.56	0.55	0.53	0.51	0.49	0.44	0.42	0.39	0.35
MAXDD	(76.91%)	(76.27%)	(71.29%)	(74.01%)	(74.18%)	(74.23%)	(77.70%)	(79.72%)	(81.07%)	(81.67%)

FIGURE 19.8   12 Month Relative Strength Portfolios, 1928–2009

	Top1	Top2	Top3	Top4	Top5	Top6	Top7	Top8	Top9	EQ-Weight
CAGR	16.13%	14.87%	13.75%	13.08%	12.68%	12.47%	12.19%	11.47%	10.78%	10.28%
STDEV	21.74%	19.16%	18.45%	18.17%	18.14%	18.22%	18.30%	18.18%	18.31%	18.38%
SHARPE (3.81%)	0.57	0.58	0.54	0.51	0.49	0.48	0.46	0.42	0.38	0.35
MAXDD	(77.21%)	(77.96%)	(72.65%)	(73.26%)	(75.63%)	(75.82%)	(76.78%)	(79.54%)	(81.07%)	(81.67%)
BEST YEAR	95.33%	105.28%	89.18%	65.50%	60.65%	62.53%	65.98%	55.96%	57.89%	53.38%
WORST YEAR	(31.64%)	(31.30%)	(31.73%)	(30.70%)	(30.47%)	(30.14%)	(32.83%)	(35.01%)	(36.70%)	(38.21%)
% YEARS OUT	73.17%	70.73%	67.07%	71.95%	75.61%	73.17%	76.83%	74.39%	67.07%	-
Turnover	378%	331%	281%	235%	190%	197%	150%	119%	86%	0%

FIGURE 19.9   Combination 1, 3, 6, 9, and 12 Month Relative Strength Portfolios, 1928–2009

From the above tables it is apparent that the relative strength method works on all of the measurement periods from one month to twelve months, as well as a combination of the 1, 3, 6, 9, and 12 month time periods. More interesting is that the system outperforms buy and hold in roughly 70% of all years. Below is an equity curve for the combination measurement system. A rough estimate of 300-600 basis points of outperformance per year is reasonable.

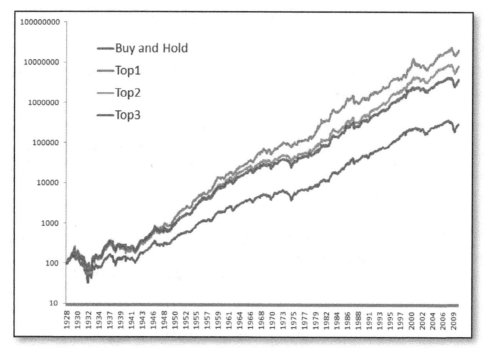

FIGURE 19.10   Relative Strength Portfolios, 1928–2009

Figure 19.11 shows the outperformance by decade for the relative strength strategy on a yearly compounded basis. For example, the Top 1 beat the buy and hold portfolio by 2.68% a year in the 1930s.

	Top 1	Top 2	Top 3
1930s	2.68%	2.61%	4.12%
1940s	5.61%	3.21%	2.00%
1950s	11.29%	9.77%	7.06%
1960s	8.11%	5.68%	4.19%
1970s	5.16%	2.29%	1.94%
1980s	2.27%	0.82%	1.14%
1990s	6.50%	6.65%	3.74%
2000s	3.85%	4.86%	1.76%
Average	5.68%	4.48%	3.24%

FIGURE 19.11   Relative Strength
Portfolios, CAGR Outperformance by
Decade 1928–2009

■ Solutions to the Drawbacks of Relative Strength Systems

The biggest drawback of a relative strength system is that the portfolio is long-only and fully invested, thus leaving the portfolio exposed to the risks of that particular asset beta. In this case the investor is exposed primarily to US stock risk. This detail can be seen in the volatility and drawdowns of all of the portfolios. There are two possible solutions to control for the losses and drawdowns while using a relative strength rotation system: (1) hedging and (2) adding non-correlated asset classes.

Solution 1: Hedging (either moving to cash or hedging with shorts). Hedging can be done on a sector basis or on a portfolio wide asset class basis. An investor could utilize a static hedge that always hedges a percentage of the portfolio, or possibly the entire portfolio (market neutral). This hedging technique has the drawback of hedging the portfolio when the market is appreciating, but also protects against all declines and shocks. An investor could also use options to gain short exposure (essentially acting as insurance), with a cost to the portfolio.

Another hedging option is a dynamic hedging technique that attempts to hedge when conditions are more favorable to market declines. Consistent with research we published in "A Quantitative Approach to Tactical Asset Allocation," using a long term moving average to hedge a portfolio results in a reduction in volatility and drawdown versus buy and hold. This approach can be seen in this research piece we published on trading Fidelity Sector Funds, "Combining Rotation and Timing Systems." Below we examine the combination of the 1, 3, 6, 9, and 12 month sector rotation portfolios when they are dynamically hedged. The portfolios move entirely to 100% cash (T-Bills) when the S&P 500 is below its 10 month Simple Moving Average (SMA). (Note: This system could also be run individually on the sectors with similar results.)

	Top1	Top2	Top3	Top4	Top5	Top6	Top7	Top8	Top9	EQ-Weight
CAGR	14.67%	14.42%	13.28%	12.53%	12.38%	11.94%	11.61%	11.10%	10.75%	10.40%
STDEV	17.94%	15.32%	14.26%	15.21%	13.48%	13.02%	12.77%	12.51%	12.32%	12.14%
SHARPE (3.81%)	0.61	0.69	0.66	0.57	0.64	0.63	0.61	0.58	0.56	0.54
MAXDD	(54.69%)	(51.36%)	(49.42%)	(54.65%)	(48.55%)	(45.74%)	(43.69%)	(43.29%)	(42.20%)	(42.27%)

FIGURE 19.12 Dynamically Hedged Combination 1, 3, 6, 9, and 12 Month Relative Strength Portfolios, 1928–2009

By adding the dynamic hedge, most portfolios preserve their returns (although the Top 1 takes a 150 basis point hit), but have the added benefit of reduced volatility and drawdowns. While an approximate 40–50% drawdown is still large, it is more tolerable than a 70–80% drawdown.

Solution 2: Addition of non-correlated asset classes. The second possible solution to the drawback of single asset class exposure inherent in the US sector rotation strategy is to add non-correlated global asset classes to the portfolio. Just as we have demonstrated above that a momentum strategy works in US equity sectors, so too does momentum work across global asset classes. We detailed this method in our book *The Ivy Portfolio* with a global rotation system that adds foreign stocks, bonds, REITs, and commodities to the portfolio. Other asset classes and spreads could be included to further diversify the portfolio, but examining this simple five asset class portfolio is instructive.

Below are the returns of the five asset classes we examine in this paper since 1973. The buy and hold benchmark is an equal-weighted portfolio of the five asset classes, rebalanced monthly.

	BUY & HOLD	S&P 500	EAFE	10 YR	GSCI	NAREIT
CAGR	10.01%	9.69%	9.62%	8.16%	8.82%	9.02%
STDEV	10.15%	15.75%	17.45%	9.07%	20.57%	18.23%
SHARPE (5.9%)	0.41	0.24	0.21	0.25	0.14	0.17
MAXDD	(46.02%)	(50.77%)	(56.40%)	(18.79%)	(67.64%)	(67.88%)

FIGURE 19.13 Global Asset Class Total Returns, 1973–2009

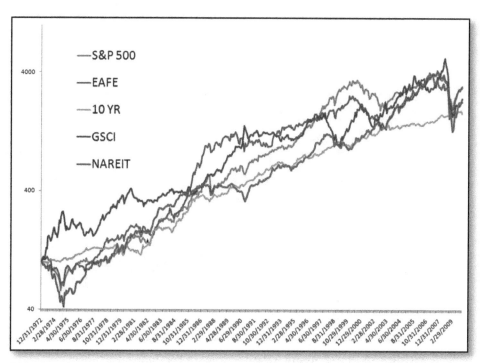

FIGURE 19.14 Global Asset Class Total Returns, 1973–2009

Below are summaries of the various ranking periods and returns for the portfolios.

	Top 1	Top 2	Top 3	Top 4	BUY & HOLD
CAGR	17.01%	14.79%	12.74%	10.93%	10.02%
STDEV	17.19%	12.26%	10.92%	10.60%	10.15%
SHARPE (5.9%)	0.65	0.72	0.63	0.47	0.41
MAXDD	(22.41%)	(29.39%)	(33.15%)	(44.04%)	(46.02%)

FIGURE 19.15　1 Month Relative Strength Portfolios, 1973–2009

	Top 1	Top 2	Top 3	Top 4	BUY & HOLD
CAGR	14.27%	13.23%	13.01%	10.72%	10.02%
STDEV	18.97%	12.75%	10.75%	10.40%	10.16%
SHARPE (5.9%)	0.44	0.58	0.66	0.46	0.41
MAXDD	(43.02%)	(31.46%)	(38.67%)	(41.85%)	(46.02%)

FIGURE 19.16　3 Month Relative Strength Portfolios, 1973–2009

	Top 1	Top 2	Top 3	Top 4	BUY & HOLD
CAGR	13.55%	16.13%	12.92%	10.87%	10.02%
STDEV	19.08%	12.29%	10.91%	10.28%	10.16%
SHARPE (5.9%)	0.40	0.83	0.64	0.48	0.41
MAXDD	(50.19%)	(34.22%)	(40.22%)	(43.63%)	(46.02%)

FIGURE 19.17　6 Month Relative Strength Portfolios, 1973–2009

	Top 1	Top 2	Top 3	Top 4	BUY & HOLD
CAGR	15.31%	15.00%	14.31%	11.20%	10.02%
STDEV	18.73%	12.77%	10.93%	10.57%	10.16%
SHARPE (5.9%)	0.50	0.71	0.77	0.50	0.41
MAXDD	(38.91%)	(35.14%)	(39.84%)	(43.34%)	(46.02%)

FIGURE 19.18　9 Month Relative Strength Portfolios, 1973–2009

	Top 1	Top 2	Top 3	Top 4	BUY & HOLD
CAGR	15.41%	14.83%	13.32%	11.48%	10.02%
STDEV	18.89%	12.64%	11.05%	10.70%	10.15%
SHARPE (5.9%)	0.50	0.71	0.67	0.52	0.41
MAXDD	(48.74%)	(39.65%)	(43.56%)	(46.82%)	(46.02%)

FIGURE 19.19　12 Month Relative Strength Portfolios, 1973–2009

	Top 1	Top 2	Top 3	Top4	BUY & HOLD
CAGR	16.30%	16.47%	14.49%	11.06%	10.02%
STDEV	18.58%	12.62%	11.00%	10.47%	10.15%
SHARPE (5.9%)	0.56	0.84	0.78	0.49	0.41
MAXDD	(30.87%)	(33.38%)	(39.84%)	(47.20%)	(46.02%)
BEST YEAR	74.96%	37.89%	36.08%	32.46%	26.58%
WORST YEAR	(15.18%)	(8.63%)	(22.26%)	(31.07%)	(30.09%)
% YEARS OUT	70.27%	70.27%	78.38%	59.46%	-

FIGURE 19.20 Combination 1, 3, 6, 9, and 12 Month Relative Strength Portfolios, 1973–2009

From the above tables it is apparent that the relative strength method works on all of the measurement periods from one month to twelve months, as well as a combination of time periods. More interesting is that the system outperforms buy and hold in roughly 70% of all years. A rough estimate of 300-600 basis points of outperformance per year is reasonable. Below is an equity curve:

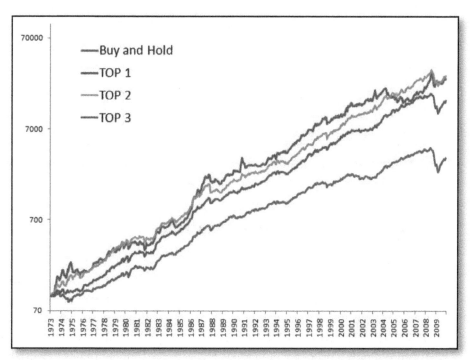

FIGURE 19.21 Combination 1, 3, 6, 9, and 12 Month Relative Strength Portfolios, 1973–2009

Figure 19.22 shows the outperformance by decade for the relative strength strategy on a yearly compounded basis. For example, the Top 1 beat the buy and hold portfolio by 6% a year in the 1990s.

	TOP 1	TOP 2	TOP 3
1970s	11.98%	12.94%	5.94%
1980s	4.70%	1.46%	3.04%
1990s	5.75%	4.96%	5.00%
2000s	4.46%	8.28%	4.29%
Average	6.72%	6.91%	4.57%

FIGURE 19.22 Combination 1, 3, 6, 9, and 12 Month Relative Strength Portfolios, CAGR Outperformance by Decade 1973–2009

What about combination both solutions? Below we report the results of rotation among global asset classes but only investing in the asset class if it is trading above its 10 month SMA (otherwise that portion is invested in T- Bills).

The results are slightly improved Sharpe Ratios and similar absolute returns, but with marked reductions in drawdown. The effect is most seen in the portfolios that utilized more asset classes.

	Top 1	Top 2	Top 3	Top4	BUY & HOLD
CAGR	15.97%	16.50%	15.00%	12.94%	10.02%
STDEV	18.40%	11.94%	9.60%	8.14%	10.15%
SHARPE (5.9%)	0.55	0.89	0.95	0.86	0.41
MAXDD	(31.17%)	(21.67%)	(12.95%)	(12.46%)	(46.02%)
BEST YEAR	74.96%	38.04%	36.08%	32.46%	26.58%
WORST YEAR	(15.18%)	(1.21%)	(3.49%)	(1.10%)	(30.09%)
% YEARS OUT	72.97%	72.97%	78.38%	64.86%	-

FIGURE 19.23 Combination 1, 3, 6, 9, and 12 Month Relative Strength Portfolios, 1973–2009

■ Real World Implementation

While this paper is meant to be an instructive base case scenario, care must be observed when translating theory into real world trading. While most industries over the period examined were represented by a robust amount of underlying companies, a few (Telecom and Health specifically) had less than twenty companies until the 1950s. The persistence of the momentum strategy by decade goes to show that this was not simply a property of markets 80 years ago, but continues to work today.

Obviously US sector funds did not exist in the 1920s. Attempting to transact in shares of the underlying companies would have been far too expensive to actively manage the portfolio in the early part of the 20th Century as turnover of 100% to 400% is very high for transactions in exchange traded securities. However, even assuming a round trip cost of 1% to the portfolio would still allow for excess momentum profits to the portfolios.

The practitioner today can choose from thousands of mutual funds, ETFs, and closed-end funds. Many of these funds can be traded for $8 a trade or less, and many mutual funds and ETFs are now commission free at some online brokers. Mutual funds also avoid any bid ask spread and market impact costs, but also typically have higher management fees than ETFs and can be subject to redemption fees if held for short periods of time (many Fidelity funds require a holding period of 30 days). Some ETFs can be painfully illiquid so care must be taken when selecting funds.

To reduce trading frequency and possible transaction costs an investor could implement a sell filter. Assuming a universe of ten funds, the investor could buy the top three funds and sell them when the funds drop out of the top five funds. This approach would lower the turnover to sub-100% levels.

As with any strategy, taxes are a very real consideration and the strategy should be traded in a tax deferred account. It is difficult to estimate the impact an investor would experience due to varying tax rates by income bracket and over time, but an increase from 5–20% turnover to 70–100% turnover could result in an increase in taxes of 50-150 bps.

■ Conclusion

The purpose of this paper was to demonstrate a simple-to-follow method for utilizing relative strength in investing in US equities and global asset classes. The results showed robust performance across measurement periods as well as over the past eight decades. While absolute returns were improved, volatility and drawdown remained high. Various methods were examined that could be used as solutions to a long only rotation system including hedging and adding non-correlated asset classes.

■ Appendix A—Data Sources

From the French-Fama website:

Detail for 10 Industry Portfolios

Daily Returns:	July 1, 1963–December 31, 2009
Monthly Returns:	July 1926–December 2009
Annual Returns:	1927–2009
Portfolios:	*Download industry definitions*

We assign each NYSE, AMEX, and NASDAQ stock to an industry portfolio at the end of June of year t based on its four-digit SIC code at that time. (We use Compustat SIC codes for the fiscal year ending in calendar year t–1. Whenever Compustat SIC codes are not available, we use CRSP SIC codes for June of year t.) We then compute returns from July of t to June of t+1.

Fama and French update the research data at least once a year, but we may update them at other times. Unlike the benchmark portfolios, (1) we reform almost all these portfolios annually (UMD is formed monthly), (2) we do not include a hold range, and (3) we ignore transaction costs. In addition, we reconstruct the full history of returns each time we update the portfolios. (Historical returns can change, for example, if CRSP revises its database.) Although the portfolios include all NYSE, AMEX, and NASDAQ firms with the necessary data, the breakpoints use only NYSE firms.

S&P 500 Index—A capitalization-weighted index of 500 stocks that is designed to mirror the performance of the United States economy. Total return series is provided by Global Financial Data and results pre-1971 are constructed by GFD. Data from 1900-1971 uses the S&P Composite Price Index and dividend yields supplied by the Cowles Commission and from S&P itself.

MSCI EAFE Index (Europe, Australasia, Far East)—A free float-adjusted market capitalization index that is designed to measure the equity market performance of developed markets, excluding the US and Canada. As of June 2007 the MSCI EAFE Index consisted of the following 21 developed market country indices: Australia, Austria, Belgium, Denmark, Finland, France, Germany, Greece, Hong Kong, Ireland, Italy, Japan, the Netherlands, New Zealand, Norway, Portugal, Singapore, Spain, Sweden, Switzerland, and the United Kingdom. Total return series is provided by Morgan Stanley.

U.S. Government 10-Year Bonds—Total return series is provided by Global Financial Data.

Goldman Sachs Commodity Index (GSCI)—Represents a diversified basket of commodity futures that is unlevered and long only. Total return series is provided by Goldman Sachs.

National Association of Real Estate Investment Trusts (NAREIT)—An index that reflects the performance of publicly traded REITs. Total return series is provided by the NAREIT.

CHAPTER 20

A Stock Market Model

From Ned Davis, *Being Right or Making Money,*
3rd Edition (Hoboken, New Jersey: John Wiley &
Sons, 2014), Chapter 3.
Loren Flath

Learning Objective Statements

- Generalize the model in this chapter to show how it could be adapted to work with anyone's own trading or investing system
- Identify the five points any environmental model should take into account
- Give an example of an indicator or study that could reasonably be substituted for one item in each of the three components covered in the Fab Five model

■ A Stock Market Model

I can almost hear Ned telling his partner, Eddie Mendel, at the dawn of Ned Davis Research back in 1979, that he would need only one programmer for one year. For over a decade, Ned had been charting his favorite indicators by hand, and the work was becoming overwhelming. There were many more indicators to chart and not enough time in the day to do so. And as Ned has pointed out, he not only needed better charting, but more importantly, he needed to replace subjective trading decisions with a more objective approach. So he hired a programmer and challenged him to create software that could not only draw effective charts, but could also analyze markets in a rather unusual way. Together they developed the concept of *timing models,* and these models formed the basis of NDR's core positions in a variety of markets and economies. It turns out, however, that predicting that he'd need just one programmer for one year was Ned's worst call. Today we have an IT staff of nearly 30!

   As Ned has pointed out many times, the bane of the investor is the Big Mistake. On the following pages I detail the makeup of one of our major models, the Fab Five. The goal of any NDR model is to keep us open-minded and disciplined, and to let our profits run while avoiding big mistakes. We realize models can be quite fickle, no matter what their ingredients are or how they are built. This model is no exception (there are no exceptions!). The game is to recognize potential capriciousness and pay attention to the effectiveness of each individual component and to the overall mix of indicators. One must always be vigilant when depending on models.

The Fab Five is an environmental model that uses what we call modes. Its job is to assemble the major internal and external factors that affect markets and combine them to produce a single objective verdict: bearish, neutral, or bullish. Offering only three possibilities might seem a bit too simplistic, like asking someone to rate a product on a scale of 1 to 3, instead of 1 to 10. But the goal is to keep things simple, and as you will see later, each mode can be open to subtle interpretation. To quote Ned, "The evidence is rarely black or white—rather, shades of gray."

Just what is an environmental model? In essence, it's one that can keep risk at arm's length without sacrificing too much on the long side. Such models effectively gauge how good conditions are for investing: do we have calm waters or are we about to enter the lower 40 latitudes? An environmental model takes into account what the Federal Reserve is doing, what the so-called smart money is doing, how speculators are feeling, what interest rates and inflation are doing, and, above all else, what the primary trend is. Using a weight-of-the-evidence approach gives us an educated feel for the risks in the market. The environmental model's job is not necessarily to give concrete buy and sell signals. Its job is to measure the level of risk in the market.

Before we examine the Fab Five in detail, let's briefly discuss some of the indicators we use to build models.

We look at two types of indicators: internal and external.

Internal indicators relate to the price action of a market or index and include the usual list of suspects, along with a multitude of variations: moving averages, momentum, advances and declines, and volume trends. All of these can be found in the bottomless bag of tools used by the creative technical analyst. I've seen enough momentum tricks alone to last a career. Ditto for moving averages. There seems to be no end of possibilities when it comes to manipulating an index or its components in order to come up with a so-called objective opinion on a market's direction.

We break down internal indicators into two distinct types: trend following and trend sensitive.

Trend-following indicators keep us in harmony with the market's primary trend, and with enough weight in a model they act as our stop-loss when needed. Used well, they can help investors let profits run and cut losses short. These indicators include moving-average crosses and slopes and some measures of momentum, used either alone or aggregated. Trend-following indicators are rarely neutral and can generate great returns, but sometimes give notoriously false signals. By their very nature they are late. Consequently, they require patience.

Trend-sensitive indicators, also known as overbought-oversold indicators, include mean reversion, momentum variations, and deviation from the trend. These indicators have a tendency for picking tops and bottoms and can influence models when price trends reach extremes. They are very accurate but not adept at generating significant gains. Since they spend a good part of the time in the neutral zone they tend to work well in multi-indicator models asserting themselves only at potential extremes.

Rounding out internal indicators is market breadth, an extremely useful tool in determining the technical environment. At NDR we gauge this by watching A/D data (advances, declines, unchanged), new highs and lows, the percent of stocks in a universe meeting a specified criteria (e.g., above or below a moving average), volume data (advancing and declining volume), and combinations of A/D and volume. Over the years we've developed our own stock database. We use only common shares for our calculations in order to get a pure view of the stock market that's unsullied by closed-end funds, preferred stocks, structured products, and so on. One day recently, 3,164 securities were being actively traded on the New York Stock Exchange but only 1,965 of them were common stocks. In fact, nearly 40 percent of the actively traded securities listed on the Big Board aren't common stocks.

External indicators include anything outside of price action: the monetary environment, crowd psychology, valuation, and economic conditions. At NDR we tend to lump valuation and crowd psychology in the sentiment category. We also tend to include economic indicators that can influence markets (e.g., inflation) in the monetary category and sometimes, to a lesser extent, the sentiment category. So basically we're looking at two sets of external indicators: monetary and sentiment. To analyze them, we can use the identical arsenal of measures we use for internal indicators, including moving averages, momentums, and deviations from trend.

My introduction to model building started in 1984, when Ned taught me the basics of creating what he called timing models. I was introduced to his major models with names like Big Mo, Little Mo, Lexi, Bondito, and Bondo Grande. There was also the Economic-Timing Model and the Inflation-Timing Model. He had models on 600 stocks, on gold, all the major currencies, crude, you name it. I was dizzy looking at all these models, and yet his approach to constructing them was amazingly simple: find some indicators that work, give them all equal weight by assigning +1, 0, or −1 to each, and add them up. I had cut my teeth on much more complicated systems. This was a whole new ball game. I came to believe that Ned had invented a simplified version of multiple linear regression, which makes predictions based on the relationships between dependent and independent variables. And the beauty was not only in the methodology but in the results. Here, I thought, was the ultimate KISS—keep it simple, stupid—system. But as it turns out, although the concept is quite uncomplicated the process can be complex and time-consuming. The devil is in the details. Done poorly, it's garbage in, garbage out.

I quickly learned the ropes and spent some serious time tweaking software and acquiring faster and faster computers (the difference in computing power between the machines back then and those available now is roughly a factor of 3,500—and today's computers are a whole lot cheaper!). My objective was to keep several computers busy crunching models 24/7, in the hope of building more and better models while expanding our universe of trading vehicles. All of this was fine, but no matter how much output the computers generated, the process still required a researcher to hand pick the indicators and the final model. Obviously this was a limiting factor. By the late 1980s I had written software to do the actual picking, which paved the way for a soup-to-nuts system for cranking out models. I was quite proud of myself and began building individual equity models.

However, a number of these models didn't hold up very well; some incurred pretty big losses. To remedy the problems I tweaked the programs. For example, we limited the amount of relative-strength indicators because even as a stock's price is falling, an RS (relative strength) line can rise. Another problem was insufficient diversity in the mix of indicators, which led to an overweighted indicator theme going bad and taking the model with it. In addition, too many models were accurate but lost money. And then there was the occasional so-called creative researcher who thought that making calls by pairing, say, IBM stock with COMEX (Commodity Exchange) gold was a cool idea (the old throw-it-at-the-wall-and-see-what-sticks approach).

Finally, I realized that to build a truly diverse, objective model requires finesse, diligence, a bit of artistic panache, and a strong knowledge of macroeconomic relationships, ranging from company fundamentals to macroeconomic fundamentals to Fed watching. Ironically, computing power takes a back seat in building good models.

■ Overview of the Fab Five

To create the Fab Five, we combined individual models covering our favorite areas of the market. The name comes from the famous basketball team that my alma mater, the University of Michigan, had in the early 1990s. (Ned is a huge basketball fan; we joke that if he fell and cracked open his head little basketballs would bounce out.) However, the model has only four components—sentiment, monetary readings, Combo, and the tape—but the tape is given double weight. I'll start with it because it accounts for two-fifths of the Fab Five.

Figure 20.1 shows the past 10 years of the Fab Five model. In the following pages, each component of the model is presented in the same fashion. The mode boxes at the bottom summarize the results for the full date range as well as for the past 10 years. The top clip has an additional series on it that represents an equity line based on going long the S&P 500 when the model is above the upper bracket, going into T-bills when the model is between the brackets, and shorting the S&P 500 when the model is below the lower bracket. This equity line is only for perspective; it's there to give a close-up view of how the model has behaved in the past. The stats tell a story, but not the whole story.

■ Tape Component

There are seven individual indicators in the tape component. As with all the other Fab Five components, and in keeping with our KISS philosophy, these indicators are each assigned −1, 0, or +1, and the result is produced through simple addition.

The first indicator in the tape component is shown in Figure 20.2. This simple, trend-following indicator is what technical analysts call a golden cross (a point at which a short-term moving average breaks above a long-term average, signaling a bull market to come). It is positive when the 50-day moving average of the S&P 500 is above its 200-day average and negative otherwise.

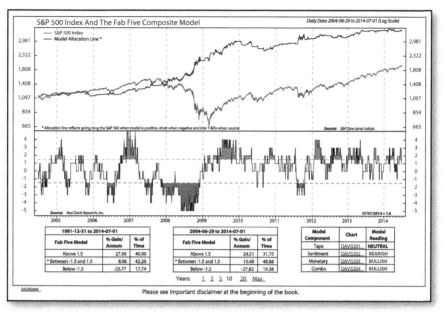

FIGURE 20.1 *Top*, S&P 500 Index and Model Allocation Line; *Bottom*, Fab Five Composite Model.

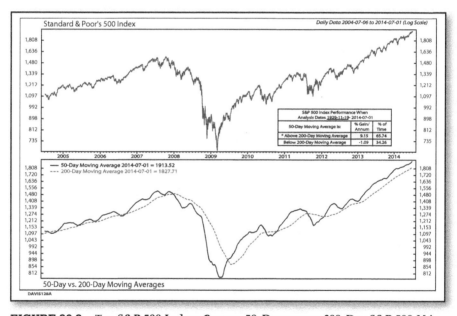

FIGURE 20.2 *Top*, S&P 500 Index; *Bottom*, 50-Day versus 200-Day S&P 500 MA.

The box on the top part of the chart summarizes the indicator's performance since 1929. At Ned Davis Research the box is called a mode bat. Ned invented this in the late 1980s, and it shows what the returns have been when buying during the bullish mode (when the 50 is above the 200) or the bearish mode (when the 50 is below the 200). It tells us that the 50-day has been above the 200-day nearly two-thirds of the time and that during those times the S&P 500 on a price-only basis has returned 9.1 percent per annum. When the 50-day has been below the 200-day the market has retreated at a

1.1 percent annual rate. Not shown in the mode bat are two other interesting statistics: a buy-and-hold approach would have generated a 5.5 percent yearly return, and reinvesting dividends while in the bullish mode would have produced a 13 percent return. Obviously an indicator like this is long-term: designed to catch the major moves.

The indicator in the chart in Figure 20.3 is a typical trend-sensitive indicator and is called a stochastic, which measures variation in momentum. The idea is to look back a set number of market days, pick the low and the high in that period, and calculate where the market's current value is relative to that range. The result is a percent; 100 percent is a new high, while 0 percent is a new low. The ambivalence of this indicator is reflected in whether you want to catch a thrust early and go long (called a bracket) or wait until the thrust is over and go short when it starts to fall (called a reverse bracket). It can be used either way, depending on the number of market days being looked at, whether a moving average is applied, and how wide the brackets are.

This chart's signals are summarized in what's known as a batting average, or bat. NDR, since its inception in 1980, has been using bats to evaluate indicators. The factors used include how accurate the long signals have been and what the overall annualized return has been. To illustrate a practical use of this indicator, Figure 20.3 assumes that on sell signals for stocks an investor will buy T-bills rather than short the market.

This 85-day stochastic is derived from NDR's All-Cap Equal-Weighted Index, based on our full Broad Market Equity Series universe. It is equally weighted and rebalanced quarterly. The result is smoothed with a five-day moving average and has brackets at 11 and 65. As the chart points out, a buy signal is generated when the smoothed result dips below then rises above 11, while a switch to T-bills is signaled when the indicator crosses above and then below 65. At NDR we call this method of signal generation a reverse bracket.

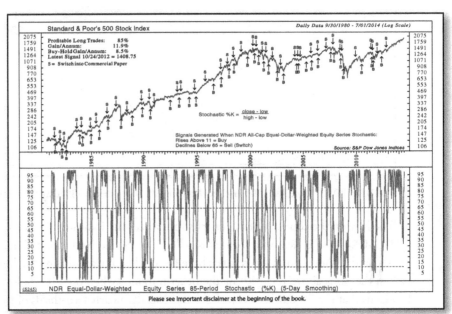

FIGURE 20.3 *Top*, S&P 500 Index with Stochastic Indicators; *Bottom*, 85-Period Stochastic NDR Equal-Dollar-Weighted Equity Series (Five-Day Smoothing).

To generate a signal, the indicator either has to cross above the upper bracket and then cross below the upper bracket (sell) or cross below the lower bracket and then cross above the lower bracket (buy).

The indicator also can go neutral: if a signal is given across the upper bracket, that signal stands until either the indicator drops below the bottom bracket and then crosses back above the bottom bracket, or the indicator crosses back above the upper bracket before crossing the lower bracket. If the latter happens, the indicator becomes neutral. I call that an *oops* signal. The bottom bracket is treated the same way.

As it turns out, the reverse bracket indicator has been negative only 19 percent of the time (it throws out a lot of oops signals), neutral 25 percent of the time (mostly from the sell side), and positive 56 percent of the time. As of this writing, the indicator is neutral and therefore has no influence on the tape component.

Moving away from direct price action, we turn to one of our favorite broad-market tool sets: breadth. This indicator is one of Ned's favorites. It's based on another fairly simple yet effective concept: evaluating the impact of volume supply and volume demand.

If a stock advances on the day, we consider all of the volume traded on that day to be advancing volume—this is the demand side. If a stock falls on the day, the volume is tallied on the declining, or supply side. If a stock's price stays steady, all of its trading volume is considered unchanged and is discarded in our calculations. (The percentage of unchanged stocks on a typical day has fluctuated around 1.5 percent since decimalization in 2001. Prior to 1997, when stocks traded in eighths, nearly one in five stocks were unchanged on the day!)

To stabilize the volatility and gain a useful perspective, we typically sum both supply and demand over a substantial period ranging from days to months. The percent of summed supply volume plus the percent of summed demand volume always adds to 100. They meet in the middle at 50 percent. The universe we are using for these calculations is the NDR Broad Market Equity Series All-Cap Index. This index represents 99 percent of the market value of the common shares trading on the big three exchanges. Its history goes back to September 1980.

The mode box in Figure 20.4 shows that when demand has been above supply, as it has been 79.0 percent of the time, the S&P 500 has advanced at 11.8 percent a year. But when supply is above demand, the market retreats 1.2 percent per annum. This indicator's contribution to the Fab Five tape component is +1 when demand is above supply and −1 otherwise.

There are many ways to look for excitement in the stock market: exuberance, whether rational or irrational, can be measurable. A couple of our favorite indicators look at the relationship between advancing and declining volume, or advances versus declines. Figure 20.5 evaluates the ratio of advances to declines. The ratio is actually a 10-day sum of NDR Multi-Cap advancing issues divided by a 10-day sum of declining issues. The NDR Multi-Cap universe covers the top 97 percent of tradable market cap and includes the NDR Large Cap plus the NDR Mid-Cap plus some of the NDR Small Cap (enough to get the market cap to 97 percent).

When the advance/decline ratio exceeds 1.9, we call that a *breadth thrust*. The table in Figure 20.5 shows the history of this indicator back to 1947. Now I know

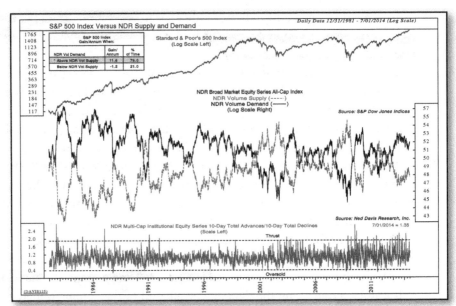

FIGURE 20.4 **S&P 500 Index versus NDR Supply and Demand.**

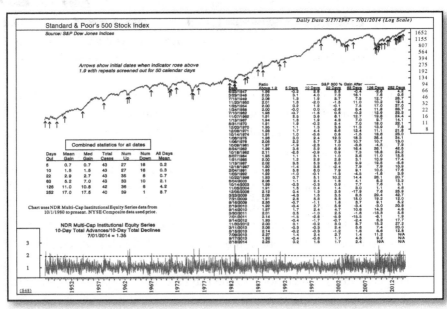

FIGURE 20.5 **S&P 500 Index with Advance/Decline Breadth Thrust.**

what you're thinking: Hold on—if the Multi-Cap started in 1980, just exactly
how did you do this? Especially given that lecture about following only common stocks on the NYSE? Well, we consider ourselves market historians, and
we love historical data—as much as we can get. So yes, we borrowed the NYSE
advance/decline data going back to 1947 to help illustrate the point that breadth
thrusts can be quite significant. It also turns out that, according to our database, stocks other than common stocks made up only 20 percent of listed NYSE
issues in 1980.

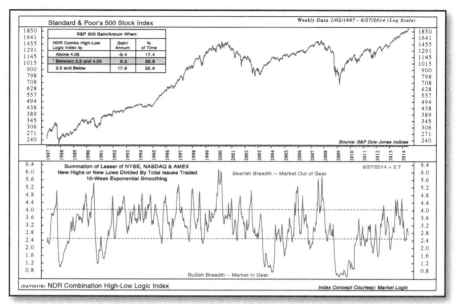

FIGURE 20.6 *Top*, S&P 500 Index; *Bottom*, NDR Combination High-Low Logic Index.

Now how exactly do we get these thrusts to work for us? Typically, we try to determine how long initial momentum is likely to last based on history and then refine our prediction from there. In the case of the indicator shown in Figure 20.5, 80 market days seemed to work well. But what if a signal is repeated in that period? One could approach it in at least two ways: either by simply resetting the count every time a new signal occurs in the 80-day window or by ignoring that signal. After some quick testing we decided on the latter.

The contribution of this indicator to the Fab Five tape component is either +1 or 0. It can never go negative.

If there ever was a cool breadth gauge, the *high-low logic indicator*—developed by Norman Fosback and shown in Figure 20.6—is it. It's basically a measure of how in gear, or bullish, the market is. I'll admit I was quite baffled by this at first. How could a single indicator with opposite messages give the same signal, regardless of the message?

Well, the market is considered in gear when new 52-week highs overwhelm new 52-week lows; it is also in gear when new 52-week lows overwhelm new 52-week highs. The rest of the time, this indicator is either neutral or out-of-gear (bearish).

The high-low logic is calculated by taking the ratio of either new 52-week highs or new 52-week lows, whichever is less, to the total number of issues and then smoothing this ratio with a 10-week exponential moving average.

Fosback's original work used NYSE data back to 1941. Here we use the NYSE in combination with the NASDAQ and the AMEX for a broader look. This also helps us get past our issue with the NYSE listings by adding in higher concentrations of common stocks.

Here's Ned's view of the concept:

> Since market tops are typically slow to form, the increased risk of a peak
> is evident when the quality market averages are reaching higher levels

without confirmation from increasing numbers of 52-week new highs. Whereas a churning, out-of-gear market is most effective as an indicator of tops after rallies, upside confirmation indicates that the market is in gear and that the current uptrend is healthy. Since market bottoms are usually formed relatively quickly, it is also bullish when the market is in gear at selling extremes characterized by new lows on the vast majority of stocks, a sign that a selling climax has left the market oversold.

When many stocks are making new highs at the same time that many are making new lows, the index reading is high, indicating a divergent market. When very few stocks are diverging from the prevailing trend, the index reading is low, a reflection of confirmation.

In other words, high index readings reflect widespread divergence, which is bearish, whereas low index readings point to one of two bullish conditions: a selling panic with almost no new highs, the sign of an extremely oversold market; or a selling vacuum with almost no new lows, the sign of a market with strong upside momentum. The indicator is able to identify new bull markets with buy signals, while remaining on sell signals during bear market rallies or the blow-off moves that tend to occur near the end of bull markets.

Another of our favorite breadth indicators is the diffusion index. It's more or less a consensus of certain measures for a host of similar vehicles; in this case, world stock markets relative to their 50-day moving averages. Why 50 and not 83 or 27? We like to keep things simple, and virtually everyone is familiar with the 50-day moving average.

Figure 20.7 shows the relationship between global equity markets and the U.S. market. If 71 percent or more of global markets are above their 50-day moving averages,

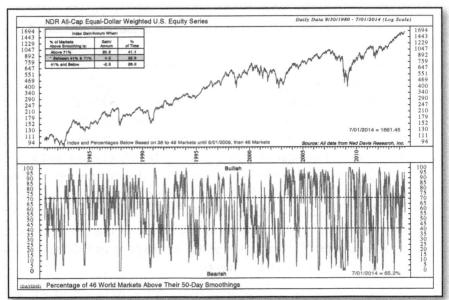

FIGURE 20.7 *Top*, NDR All-Cap Equal-Dollar Weighted U.S. Equity Series; *Bottom*, Percentage of 46 World Markets above Their 50-Day Smoothings.

the U.S. market, as represented by the NDR All-Cap Index, appreciates at 20.2 percent per annum. Since 1980, this has occurred 41.1 percent of the time. Conversely, when the percent of markets drops below 41 percent, the NDR All-Cap retreats at 2.3 percent per annum. The contribution to the Fab Five tape component is −1, 0, or +1.

The 46 world markets are MSCI (Morgan Stanley Capital International) All Country World Index members—23 developed economies and 23 emerging ones.

A long-standing tenet of NDR is to *go with Mo.* If the market's momentum is up, we're in; if it's down, we're out. We use this model as a gauge of technical health. Big Mo is a diffusion index that represents the percentage of bullish individual trend and momentum indicators taken from 96 of our own BMES subindustry indices. The trend indicators are based on the direction of a subindustry's moving average, while the momentum indicators are based on the rate of change of the subindustry's price index. The ratio of momentum to trend indicators is around two to one.

In the past we have had several versions of Big Mo. The first one I remember, from 1982, used industry groups that were defined by S&P. (We also had a daily version called Little Mo, built with individual stocks.) After developing our own geometric industry groups in the late 1980s, we rebuilt Big Mo. By the mid-1990s, having added to our stock database, developed our industry work even further, and added new analytical techniques, we took another shot at it. The current version was created in January 2013. As fate would have it, we were forced into a rebuild due to a data vendor technicality; we liked the old model but had no choice but to rebuild.

The indicator shown in Figure 20.8 introduces a modification of our standard mode bat: the directional mode bat. The two mode boxes in the upper left show results based on whether Big Mo is higher or lower than it was six weeks earlier. In the bottom section, the brackets are fixed at 56 and 79, and the results are quite different depending on Big Mo's direction. Whether the model is improving (rising) or

A STOCK MARKET MODEL

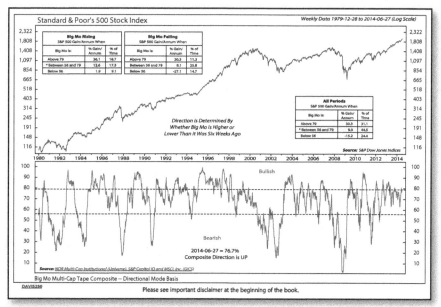

FIGURE 20.8 *Top*, S&P 500 Index; *Bottom*, **Big Mo Multi-Cap Tape Composite (Directional Mode Basis).**

weakening (falling) can give valuable information in addition to the model's current level: when Big Mo Tape has been high and rising, the returns have tended to be best, while a low and falling model reading has been associated with the weakest returns.

The weight of this indicator in the tape component of the Fab Five is tricky but sensible. When Big Mo is rising and above 56 we assign a +1; when it's rising and below 56, it gets a 0; falling and above 79 is another +1; falling and between the brackets is a 0, while falling and below 56 gets the only −1 reading. If Big Mo is unchanged on a six-week basis the reading from the prior week is used.

■ The Final Tape Component

Now that we have all of our indicators, it's a simple matter to add them up to produce a result (see Figure 20.9).

Since there are seven components to the model, the range should be −7 to +7. But remember, the thrust indicator can't go negative, so the overall sum ranges from −6 to +7. The brackets for the model are set at −1.5 and 25.5 (bottom chart section). As with all of the components of the Fab Five, this model is designed to work in four separate time frames. Its contribution to the overall Fab Five is −2, 0, or +2 (remember, it gets double weight).

■ The Sentiment Component

During my initial interview with Ned back in 1984 I was a bit nervous, to say the least. I really had no idea what Ned Davis Research was, and I had never heard of Ned Davis himself. Being new to Florida, I had been scanning the want ads when I came upon a two-line blurb for a statistical researcher. When I phoned the employment agency

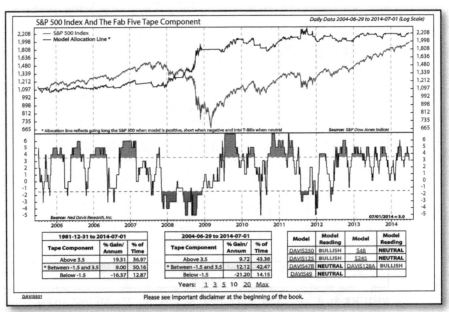

FIGURE 20.9 *Top*, S&P 500 Index; *Bottom*, Fab Five Tape Component.

that had placed the ad, the woman there told me that the client was looking for some-one with an MBA who could program in Basic, a once-popular computer language. After I told her I had an MS, had recently worked for a research organization, and could program in Basic, she set up an interview. No information about the company was forthcoming; I went in blind. The address was a house in a semiresidential area. I thought I had the wrong place until I saw a small weather-beaten sign out front that simply said, Ned Davis Research, Investments. I noticed a gleaming maroon Jaguar out back under a carport. My initial interview was in a converted bedroom. When I met Ned, he was wearing shorts, a T-shirt, and boat shoes. I felt a little out of place in my spanking new suit. As I sat there, Ned asked me if I knew the difference between a stock and a bond. My life flashed before my eyes. I had never read a newspaper's busi-ness section in my life. I had studied biology, chemistry, and statistics, and generally viewed business majors the way I viewed psychology majors—students from another planet. When I answered with a no, I thought it was curtains for my chances of getting the job, but as it turned out Ned viewed my ignorance as a plus, because it meant I had no preconceived notions about stocks or bonds. I was a bias-free blank slate.

After several months of working for Ned, I began to perceive the relationship be-tween investor psychology and markets. I realized I had gone from analyzing seasonal zooplankton populations to analyzing what basically amounted to fear and greed.

It's hard to find an investor or a trader, or anyone for that matter, who doesn't have an opinion on the direction of the stock market. From blogs to books to PhD dissertations to (above all else) the media, we find no end to sentiment-indicator pay dirt. The terms *irrational exuberance* and *the madness of crowds* reflect the fact that we humans have a flair for exposing our hand. And what better place to show what we're made of than in the stock market?

Fortunately, analysts and market historians have access to a smorgasbord of senti-ment indicators. These include polls of investors, newsletter writers, professionals, nonprofessionals, and so on; people who put their money where their mouths are. In addition, there are other ways of determining sentiment. For example, a high price/ earnings or price/dividend ratio reflects optimistic investors, while a low P/E or price/dividend ratio shows fearful investors. We can also say the same thing about market momentum in the context of optimism or pessimism. The whole idea is to look for extremes in these indicators. When investors are at their maximum bullish level (when virtually everyone is invested) that indicates a market top. When the vast majority of investors are bearish or have sold whatever they can sell, we generally find market bottoms. The trick, of course, is to detect these extremes.

The sentiment component of the Fab Five uses some of these concepts in its seven indicators. Each indicator delivers +1, 0, or −1 to the overall component, with one exception: our Daily Sentiment Composite (shown later in Figure 20.16), which gets double weight.

I wouldn't go so far as to call its name an oxymoron, but Investors Intelligence has been producing the Advisors' Sentiment Report for over 40 years. This survey is one of our favorites. The firm tracks more than 100 independent market newsletters, classifying each as bullish, bearish, or on the fence. In Figure 20.10, we're interested

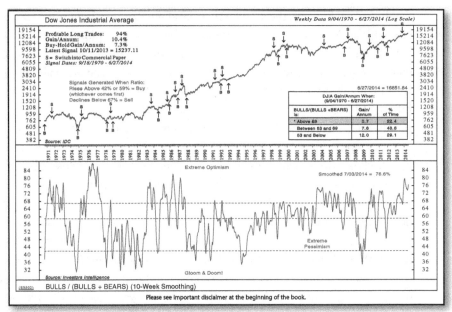

FIGURE 20.10   *Top,* DJIA with Buy/Sell Signals; *Bottom,* Bulls/(Bulls + Bears) with 10-Week Smoothing.

in bullish advisors as a percentage of those with an opinion (bullish + bearish). This presents a longer-term picture of how advisors are feeling, given that it's weekly and the ratio is smoothed over 10 weeks. The presence of too many bulls indicates a market top, while too few bulls points to a market bottom. Again, the trick is discovering how many are too many or too few.

There are three brackets and two analyses on the chart, adding a bit of complexity to this fairly straightforward concept. Let's deal with the signals first. In the bottom section of the chart, excessive optimism is evident when the indicator moves above the upper bracket. Using our reverse-bracket trick, the sell signal comes on the reversal as the indicator drops back below the upper bracket. This provides confirming evidence that a bullish extreme has been reached.

There are two ways to get buy signals, and both use reverse brackets. The most obvious comes when the indicator drops below the very bottom bracket and then reverses back above it. This confirms the bearish extreme. The second way to obtain a buy signal is for the indicator to drop below the middle bracket and reverse back above that bracket (without going below the bottom bracket) while on a sell. Obviously, there is quite a difference in bearish extremes between the middle and bottom brackets, but this only works directly after a period of extreme bullishness.

The second analysis is the mode bat on the bottom right of the top clip. This mode bat shows a straightforward perspective using brackets at 53 and 69. This indicates that the market does well when the reading is below 53 and not so well when it's above 69. It also hints that the indicator is neutral nearly half of the time.

This indicator's contribution to the Fab Five sentiment component is essentially the signals just described but with neutrals thrown in. Having a sentiment indicator that's always on can be a problem, so we employ the reverse-bracket oops trick I

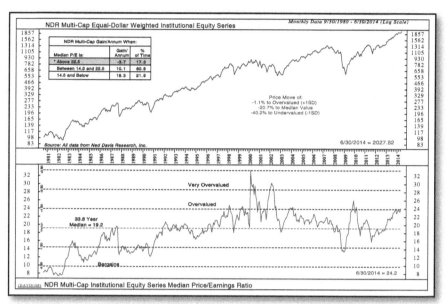

FIGURE 20.11 *Top,* NDR Multi-Cap Equal-Dollar Weighted Institutional Equity Series; *Bottom,* NDR Multi-Cap Institutional Equity Series Median P/E Ratio.

mentioned earlier. Doing this has the indicator in a neutral mode roughly 28 percent of the time, keeping it agnostic during repeat extremes.

The P/E ratio indicator shown in the bottom clip of Figure 20.11 is equally comfortable in the valuation or sentiment camp. Even if you know absolutely nothing else about stocks, no one will realize it if you can work P/E into a conversation. The ratio is calculated by dividing the stock price by the latest earnings per share. The P/E shown here is based on the median earnings yield of the stocks in the NDR Multi-Cap Equity Series. (In our calculations, we invert the median yield.) We use the median earnings yield because it's less likely to be influenced by questionable earnings reports.

When Ned explained the concept of P/E to me for the first time, he basically said that it's what investors are willing to pay for one dollar of a company's earnings; in other words, a P/E of 20 indicates that investors are willing to pay 20 times earnings. This chart shows us that over the long term, investors have been willing to pay $19.20 for one dollar in NDR Multi-Cap profits. When the P/E ratio goes beyond a factor of 24 or one standard deviation, we're getting into optimism and as it breaches the next bracket up, we're looking at pure euphoria.

The mode bat reveals our actionable levels. The indicator shows excessive optimism or overvaluation at a P/E of 22.5. In that zone, the NDR Multi-Cap Index has fallen at a rate of 14.7 percent per annum. Dropping below 14.5 takes the indicator into too much pessimism or undervaluation. At that position, the Multi-Cap has appreciated at 18.3 percent a year.

This indicator's contribution to the Fab Five sentiment component is +1 below 14.5, 0 from 14.5 to 22.5, and −1 above 22.5. This is one of the few Fab Five indicators that is calculated monthly.

In Figure 20.12 we have a sentiment indicator that could also fit into the valuation category or even the monetary category. This one is a relative measure of earnings to

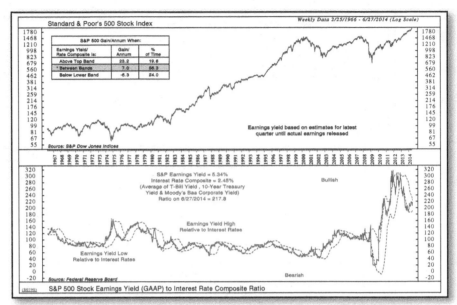

FIGURE 20.12 *Top*, S&P 500 Index; *Bottom*, S&P 500 Stock Earnings Yield (GAAP) Compared to Interest Rate Composite Ratio.

interest rates. While it's true that absolute valuation indicators can be at odds with relative valuation indicators, both can be extremely useful. In this case, very low interest rates can cause this particular indicator to be more bullish than the absolute P/E in Figure 20.11.

The interest-rate component is a composite calculated as the average yield of 91-day T-bills, 10-year Treasury notes, and Moody's Baa corporates. This gives us a more general view of the interest-rate situation.

To find extremes, we use a 60-week moving standard deviation, with plus or minus 1.3 standard deviations as the brackets. We examine earnings in two ways—relative to interest rates, and relative to time.

The contribution to the Fab Five sentiment component is −1 below the bottom bracket, 0 in between the brackets, and +1 above the upper bracket.

We first started using "moving standard-deviation brackets" in the late 1980s. This developed along with our use of reverse brackets, and indeed, they go well together (although this particular indicator uses regular brackets). An indicator that should be confined to some range but occasionally gets excited is difficult to pin down with absolute brackets. I have seen indicators that spent years in a well-defined range suddenly get trend-happy and then spend years above or below the magic range. Basically, the brackets adjust automatically to changing conditions, creating a new normal as indicators move strongly up or down. This also helps to correct for volatility. To illustrate this point, Figure 20.13 shows the Big Block Index, whose very nature has shifted dramatically over time due to changes in the size of the blocks, the move to decimals, and other factors. So moving standard-deviation brackets have kept this indicator relevant.

In Figure 20.14 we have an indicator whose basic components are more associated with breadth than sentiment. The TRIN (also known as MKDS or the Trading Index)

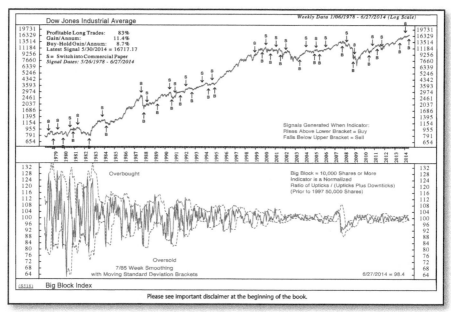

FIGURE 20.13 *Top*, DJIA with Buy/Sell Signals; *Bottom*, Big Block Index.

compares upside volume to downside volume and shows whether trading is concentrated in advancing or declining issues (i.e., it indicates whether the path of least resistance is upward or downward). It is calculated by dividing the ratio of advancing issues to declining issues by the ratio of advancing volume to declining volume.

TRIN's normal 10-day moving average is calculated by adding up individual daily readings and dividing the result by 10. In contrast, the Open 10 Trading Index uses the 10-day totals of each TRIN component (up stocks, down stocks, up volume, and down volume) rather than using individual daily computations. Once these component

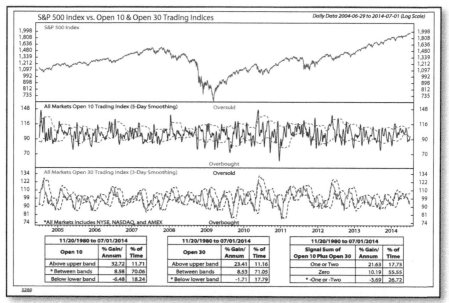

FIGURE 20.14 S&P 500 Index versus Open 10 and Open 30 Trading Indices.

totals are determined for 10 days, they are inserted in the usual TRIN formula: (up stocks/down stocks)/(up volume/down volume). The Open 30 TRIN is derived in the same fashion, but with 30-day totals.

High levels in the Open 10 and Open 30 Trading Indices indicate an oversold market and a cash build-up by the big money. They occur just prior to significant market upswings. The mode boxes show that the market tends to post much better gains when the Open TRINs are high (above the upper dashed lines) and poor results when the Open TRINs are low (below the lower dashed lines). If an investor followed just one of these indicators, he'd be in the market 30 percent of the time. But combining the two would increase that to about 45 percent.

Contribution to the sentiment component is −1 when both TRINs are negative or one is negative and the other is neutral, 0 when they sum to 0, and +1 when both are positive or one is positive while the other is neutral.

Back in the 1980s, Ned conducted weekly research meetings. He was a huge Value Line fan; he loved that firm's approach to research and loved its indicators. One day he told us a story about Arnold Bernhard, the founder of Value Line, who had built a hugely successful investment research firm that ultimately stood on its own two feet, independent of him. When Arnold Bernhard died in 1987 his death was widely reported but had no effect on the company; it was business as usual, and Value Line is still very strong and well-respected. Ned's point was that he hoped Ned Davis Research, the firm he founded, would someday have the same foundation. (Granted, Arnold Bernhard's firm was called Value Line and not Arnold Bernhard Research, but. . . .)

The indicator shown in the bottom clip of Figure 20.15 is one of Value Line's key fundamental indicators and is based on its analysts' three- to five-year P/E projections for the stocks in their universe. The estimate of the median price appreciation

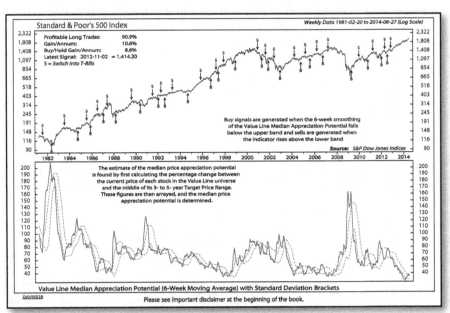

FIGURE 20.15 *Top*, S&P 500 Index with Buy/Sell Indicators; *Bottom*, Value Line Median Appreciation Potential (VLMAP) with SD Brackets (Six-Week Moving Average).

potential is found by multiplying each stock's current earnings by its future P/E projection as determined by Value Line analysts. Each stock gets a value and the median of these values is the VLMAP. As Value Line points out, though, the VLMAP tends to be a bit high (earnings estimates tend to be a little optimistic, to say the least).

We have applied the NDR moving standard-deviation reverse bracket solution to this indicator. The standard deviation is nine months and the brackets are asymmetric at −1.0 and +0.6. Although it can't be seen on the chart, we allow the signal to go neutral in typical oops fashion. The contribution to the Fab Five sentiment component is +1 when the six-week smoothing of the VLMAP drops below the upper bracket and −1 when it moves from below to above the lower bracket. That sell signal at the end of 2012 looked bad, but in Fab Five reality, it was negative for only seven weeks before it hit oops, or neutral, mode.

Although the Daily Trading Sentiment Composite shown in Figure 20.16 is just an indicator to the Fab Five, in reality this is a model composed of 27 individual indicators from six areas:

1. Advisory Service Sentiment (44.4 percent) is based on results from various polls, including those from the National Association of Active Investment Managers, Investors Intelligence, the American Association of Individual Investors, Mark Hulbert, and others.
2. Asset flows (13.3 percent) looks at the commitment of traders reports and mutual-fund flows.
3. Overbought/oversold (13.3 percent) includes various volume-related indicators as well as A/D indicators.
4. Valuation/sentiment (8.9 percent) looks at earnings relative to interest rates.
5. Volatility (8.9 percent) is based on the VIX (the Chicago Board Options Exchange's volatility index, which analysts use to help gauge how worried or

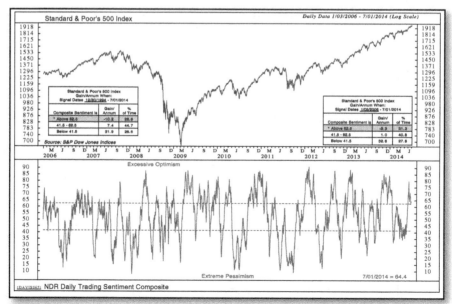

FIGURE 20.16 *Top*, S&P 500 Index; *Bottom*, NDR Daily Sentiment Composite.

479

A STOCK MARKET MODEL

confident investors are) and SKEW (an index that essentially tries to show the probability of an extreme market event, such as a crash).

6. Put/call options ratios (11.1 percent) include various ISE (International Securities Exchange) and CBOE ratios.

Each of the 27 indicators uses moving standard deviation brackets (not reverse brackets). During testing, each indicator had to work in all four predetermined time frames before being selected for inclusion. For an indicator to make the final model there had to be plenty of good results to pick from. This is true for any indicator in any Ned Davis Research model—if you have a feeling that an indicator has a strong relationship to the market and you're using the appropriate techniques, then you should get piles of output that reflect your perception of the indicator. If an analysis turns up only a small percentage of decent results then either (1) the indicator isn't any good, or (2) the analytical technique needs refinement. If there are only a handful of acceptable results after exhausting all possibilities for analysis, chalk those results up to luck, toss the indicator, and move on. In the case of the Daily Trading Sentiment Composite, virtually all of the indicators had plenty of acceptable results.

The composite itself is basically an inverted diffusion index: inverted so that high numbers are excessively optimistic and therefore bearish, and low numbers are pessimistic and therefore bullish.

The three charts that follow illustrate several components. The first is the Hulbert Newsletter Stock Sentiment Index (Figure 20.17). Mark Hulbert measures average equity exposure among a subset of advisors who focus on timing the overall stock market's short-term gyrations. This is a typical Daily Trading Sentiment Composite indicator, showing the moving standard deviation brackets in the middle clip with the bottom clip reflecting the same thing but in a form called a z-score. Doing this allows us to compare one z-score with another without the fog of periods and brackets. When most of the advisors move to the bullish side that's negative for the market, and vice versa.

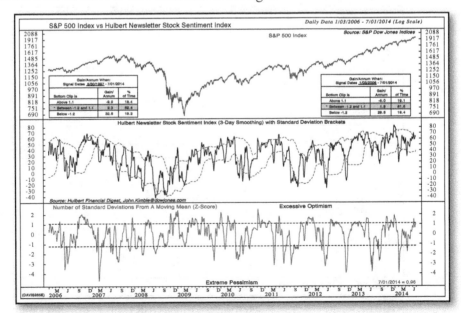

FIGURE 20.17 S&P 500 Index versus the Hulbert Newsletter Stock Sentiment Index.

The classic overbought-oversold indicator shown in Figure 20.18 is based on extreme volume movements. We have taken the NDR Multi-Cap universe and presented advancing volume as a percentage of advancing and declining volume combined. When advancing volume reaches an extreme by violating the upper bracket of the standard-deviation window it's typically negative for the market. This is another one of Ned's favorite get-ready-to indicators.

Volatility is sentiment in motion; Figure 20.19 shows the VIX to be bearish during low volatility periods and bullish during high volatility periods. The reversals are when most of the gains are made.

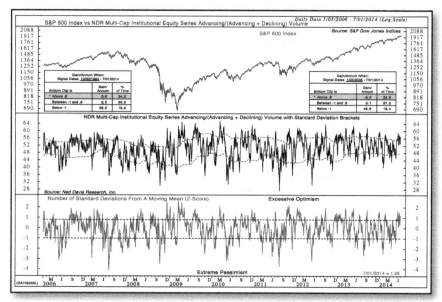

FIGURE 20.18 S&P 500 Index versus Multi-Cap Institutional Equity Series Advancing/(Advancing + Declining) Volume.

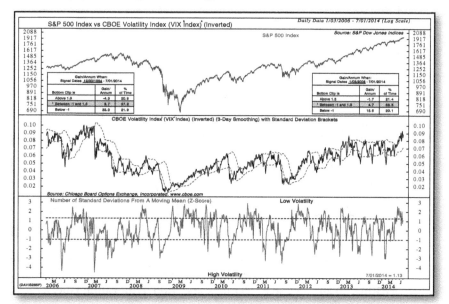

FIGURE 20.19 S&P 500 Index versus CBOE VIX (Inverted).

The contribution to the Fab Five sentiment component is +2 when the daily sentiment composite is below the lower bracket, 0 in between the brackets, and −2 when above the upper bracket.

Sentiment Summary

The final sentiment component, shown in Figure 20.20, is a sum of the indicators discussed (plus one more P/E indicator) for a range of -8 to +8 (remember, the daily sentiment composite has double weight). The brackets are set at −1.5 and 1.5.

The Monetary Component

Our third major piece is the Fab Five monetary component. The adage "money moves markets" is probably as old as the markets themselves; without demand in some form of purchasing power, there would be no markets. The availability of money equates to liquidity, and measures of liquidity help us get a handle on risk. Of course, the source and quality of money also matter, and our view of the monetary situation comes from two major sources: (1) the price of money, meaning interest rates; and (2) the supply of money.

Rates of change in interest rates—regardless of what maturities we're looking at or whether we're examining government or corporate securities—yield consistently good results against the stock market. My first real look at this was in 1987, when Ned came up with the idea of bulls/(bulls + bears) in the context of the monetary environment. He thought that when a bull market was under way it would take a much higher percentage of bulls to send a bearish signal than it would in a bear market. He

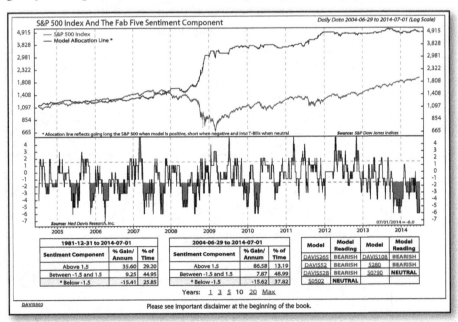

FIGURE 20.20 *Top,* S&P 500 Index and Model Allocation Line; *Bottom,* Fab Five Sentiment Component.

hypothesized the same should be true for buying the market under favorable conditions: the percentage of bulls shouldn't have to drop as far as it would have to under bear market conditions. To test this, we used a 26-week rate of change in intermediate government bond prices as a proxy for bull and bear markets. Bond momentum above a certain level would indicate a bull market, while momentum below a lower level would indicate a bear market. I can remember Ned standing behind me, tossing out ideas while I sat at my desk doing my best to program them into a computer. Sure enough, the concept worked, and thus Ned's dynamic brackets were hatched. This led to our embracing moving standard deviation brackets the following year.

The indicator shown in Figure 20.21 presents Moody's corporate Baa yields as a 26-week percent change. It's just that simple: when interest rates are heating up, it's bad for stocks. When interest rates are coming down, it's good for stocks. The brackets are set for the NDR Multi-Cap Geometric Total Return Index, but they work just as well for the S&P 500. The contribution to the monetary component is +1 below −3 percent, 0 between −3 and 6 percent, and −1 above 6 percent.

Figure 20.22, which shows the annual rate of growth of industrial production and the commodity price component of the producer price index (PPI) subtracted from the 12-month change of the M2 money supply, illustrates the relationship between monetary and economic environments, with industrial production and PPI commodities representing the economy and what is produced with available money.

Liquidity is represented by the current-dollar M2 money supply, a measure of the money available for spending. When M2's rate of growth exceeds that of industrial production and PPI commodities, there is excess liquidity in the system, some of

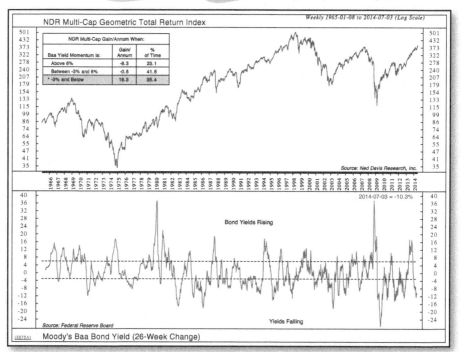

FIGURE 20.21 *Top*, NDR Multi-Cap Geometric Total Return Index; *Bottom*, Moody's Baa Bond Yield (26-Week Change).

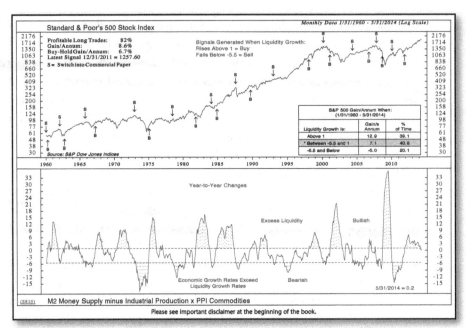

FIGURE 20.22 *Top,* **S&P 500 Index with Liquidity Signals;** *Bottom,* **M2 Money Supply—(Industrial Production × PPI Commodities).**

which flows into stocks. The periods of excess liquidity shown on this chart correspond well with stock-market uptrends.

When economic growth far exceeds the growth rate of liquidity, a rapidly expanding economy is siphoning liquidity away from financial assets and placing downward pressure on the stock market. Nearly all past bear markets have occurred when economic growth outstripped liquidity growth.

The mode box in the top clip of Figure 20.22 shows us that bullish conditions are best indicated when this indicator rises above the top bracket, while bearish conditions occur when the indicator falls below the lower bracket. The contribution to the Fab Five monetary component is –1 below the lower bracket, 0 between the two brackets, and +1 above the upper bracket.

Figure 20.23 uses a variation on a deviation-from-trend calculation to create an interest-rate indicator for the stock market using the benchmark 10-year Treasury note's yield. Instead of being represented by a longer term moving average, the trend is defined by a 70-week moving simple linear regression of the yield against time. The regression line represents the interest rate trend and the difference between the prediction and the actual result represents the deviation (see bottom clip).

To determine whether a given differential should be considered high or low, we plot moving standard deviation brackets around a three-year (156-week) moving average of the differential (+/– 0.4 standard deviation above and below). By doing this, roughly a third of the time historically is spent above the upper bracket (indicating rising interest rates), a third of the time is spent below the lower bracket (falling interest rates), and a third of the time is spent between the brackets (neutral rates). The three-year time frame gives us a longer term perspective in the level and volatility of the

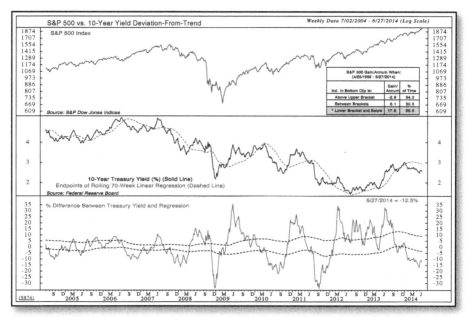

FIGURE 20.23 S&P 500 Index versus 10-Year Yield Deviation-from-Trend.

indicator. The mode box in the top clip summarizes the results from 1969–2014. It shows that the S&P 500 has had subpar returns, on average, when the differential has been above the upper bracket, while it has posted strong annualized gains when the differential has been below the lower bracket. Neutral readings have been associated with average returns. Only the latest 10 years of data are plotted for better visibility.

The concept behind the chart is that the rolling regression trend line could reflect a simplistic estimate of where investors might think interest rates should be, and incorporates their tendency to extrapolate an uptrend or downtrend in rates into the future, which a simple moving average doesn't do. This indicator thus gives a different perspective on where current bond yields are relative to their recent trend. This is a useful timing indicator for the stock market.

The contribution to the Fab Five monetary component is –1 above the upper bracket, 0 in between the brackets, and +1 below the lower bracket.

Early in my tenure at NDR, Ned mentioned the classic definition of inflation: too much money chasing too few goods. With the possible exception of interest rates, inflation is his favorite macro indicator; its effect on stocks has been featured in his *Hotline* many times. In the indicator shown in Figure 20.24 we use the rate of change of the Reuters Continuous Commodity Index (CCI) as a proxy for inflation. Since this is a weekly chart, updates are more timely than official consumer price data, so in a sense this gives us an early heads-up on inflation trends.

Rising commodity prices indicate inflationary pressures. When the year-to-year change in the three-week moving average of the Reuters CCI is above 8.2 percent, it has a negative effect on the stock market. When the year-to-year change drops by 4 percent or more, the market surges ahead.

The contribution to our Fab Five monetary component is +1 below 96, 0 between 96 and 108.2, and –1 above 108.2.

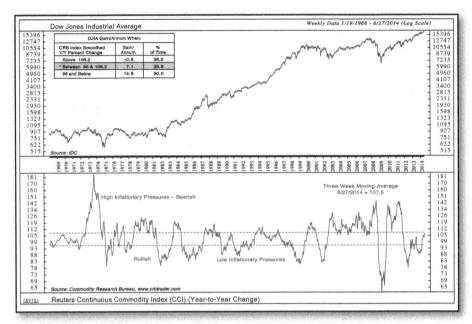

FIGURE 20.24 *Top*, DJIA; *Bottom*, Reuters CCI (Year-to-Year Change).

In Figure 20.25 we have the AMEX Securities Broker/Dealer Index, which tracks interest rate–sensitive financial stocks. The operative phrase is "interest rate–sensitive." These stocks do well when interest rates are falling and poorly when they're rising. They also tend to lead markets. If there are systemic risks, Financials generally will ferret them out. This is why Financials nearly always turn down on a relative basis before the overall stock market goes into a bear market. By smoothing the index over 10 days and employing moving standard deviation brackets, we can get a preview of

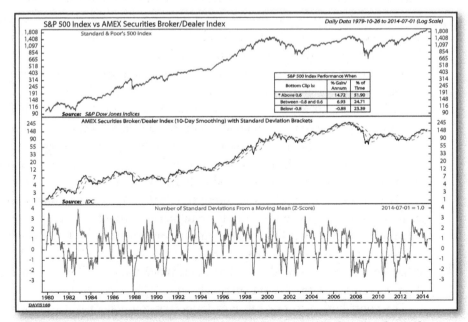

FIGURE 20.25 S&P 500 Index versus AMEX Securities Broker/Dealer Index.

where the market thinks interest-rate risk is headed. The standard deviation is done over 200 days, and brackets are just under plus or minus one standard deviation.

During and just after the Great Recession, we were looking for new monetary indicators that had weathered the storm. Ned thought this might work, and indeed it did and continues to do so.

The contribution to the monetary component is +1 when the smoothed price is above the upper standard deviation, 0 between the upper and lower deviations, and −1 when below the lower deviation.

As we know, liquidity or lack of liquidity helps to move markets. One way to tell whether the Fed's monetary policy is easy or tight is to follow the trend of free reserves (called *net borrowed reserves* when negative).

Most banks must keep a certain percentage of their deposits with the Federal Reserve. Since the banks can use excess reserves (total reserves less required reserves) to make investments, a free reserve position (excess reserves less borrowed reserves) usually indicates easy money. On the other hand, when money is tight banks often must borrow to meet the Fed's reserve requirements.

For the indicator shown in Figure 20.26, we take Federal Reserve Board data and normalize it by calculating the spread between the three-week moving average and the 52-week moving average. This shows us any deviations from the longer term trend. When the three-week rises faster than the 52-week, the chart indicates that Fed ease is accelerating. When the opposite occurs, this suggests that the Fed is becoming increasingly restrictive.

While the trend of free reserves is important, so is the level. As a rule, the market is in good shape when the normalized level of free reserves exceeds $200 million

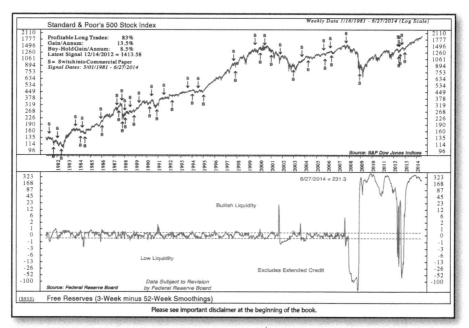

FIGURE 20.26 *Top,* S&P 500 Index with Buy/Sell Signals; *Bottom,* Free Reserves (3-Week minus 52-Week Smoothings).

($0.2 billion on the chart). When the normalized level of free reserves drops below −$180 million (−$0.18 billion on the chart), it indicates that the market is in trouble. As occurred in 1984, however, extremely low liquidity levels suggest that Fed easing is likely, a positive for stocks.

The Federal Reserve Board's actions can be inferred from the trend and level of free reserves. When free reserves are negative and falling, the Fed is putting the brakes on monetary policy. When they are positive and rising, the central bank is stepping on the accelerator.

The break we see in 2009 reflects the massive liquidity programs designed to ease strains in the banking system during the financial crisis and changes in reserve requirements. It also suggests that the Fed's policy of paying 0.25 percent interest on reserves had a longer term effect on this indicator. There is an obvious new normal here that begs the question: Is it time to reanalyze this indicator using our moving standard deviation tool? At some point, we will revisit this indicator.

The contribution to the Fab Five monetary component is +1 above the upper bracket, 0 between the two brackets, and −1 below the bottom bracket.

Figure 20.27 shows that growth in M1 can be so good, it's bad. But it also can be so bad, it's good. This is a reflection of the Fed's influence on the monetary base. Theoretically, an increasing monetary base and money supply should help depress the cost of money—interest rates. When the growth rate reaches an extreme, however, a change in Fed policy is likely. Extremely high money supply growth rates tend to be bearish for stocks, since they indicate that the Fed may tighten its monetary policy (due to inflationary pressures) and send interest rates upward. Conversely, extremely low money supply growth rates are actually bullish for stocks, since they indicate that the Fed may ease its monetary policy and allow interest rates to fall.

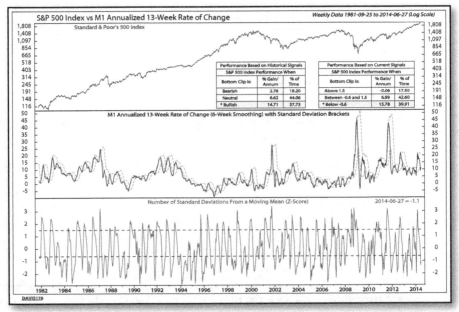

FIGURE 20.27 S&P 500 Index versus M1 Annualized 13-Week Rate of Change.

Extremes are determined by moving standard deviation brackets with the monetary component getting +1 below the bottom bracket, 0 in between the brackets, and −1 above the upper bracket.

■ Monetary Component Summary

The final monetary component in Figure 20.28 is a sum of the indicators discussed in the preceding section (plus an additional interest rate indicator, not discussed) for a range of −8 to +8. The brackets are set at −1.5 and 2.5. Because the brackets are asymmetric, it's easier to get a sell than it is to get a buy. As with all of our other Fab Five components, this model was constructed to work in all four of our preset time frames.

■ Fab Five Combo Component

We now come to the Fab Five's final component. We call it Combo because it's composed of six stock-market models, each with a different mix of indicators. The six range from the very simple to the very complex, but they each have the same weight. In choosing them, we simply grabbed models that Ned is comfortable with and watches every day (he watches a lot each day, and I still don't know how he does it). We've found that it helps to have a variety of models, each with its own indicator mix. Aggregating these models produces a consensus to help clarify risk and reward. Adding to our comfort level is that some of our best researchers have worked on these models over the years. And we've had some very smart, very creative analysts at what we sometimes call NDR University.

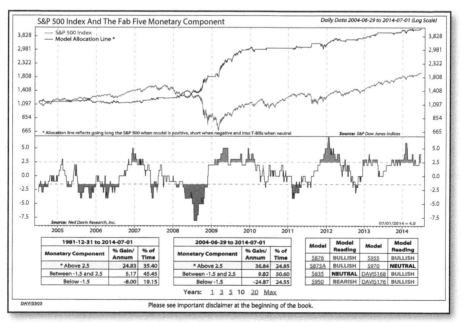

FIGURE 20.28 *Top,* **S&P 500 Index and Model Allocation Line;** *Bottom,* **Fab Five Monetary Component.**

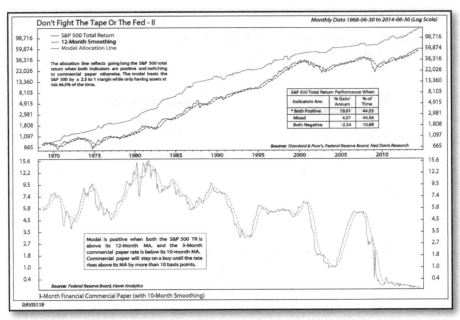

FIGURE 20.29 *Top,* S&P 500 Total Return with Model Allocation Line; *Bottom,*
Three-Month Financial Commercial Paper (with 10-Month Smoothing).

The model shown in Figure 20.29 is far and away the simplest; we call it Don't
Fight the Tape or the Fed II, which says it all. It has only a tape indicator and a monetary indicator. Adding to its simplicity is that it's monthly (and thus a longer term
indicator). The tape indicator is a 12-month moving average cross of the S&P 500
Total Return Index. It's positive when the total return is above the moving average,
and negative when it's below. The second indicator is also a moving-average cross.
It's positive when the 90-day commercial paper rate drops below its 10-month moving average, and negative when the yield moves above its average by 10 basis points
(each equal to 1/100th of a percentage point). When both indicators are positive (as
they are 44 percent of the time), the market cranks at a nearly 19 percent rate. When
they're both negative, it's best to be out of the market. The allocation line in the top
clip is a good reflection of what has happened going long the S&P 500 Total Return
when both indicators are positive, and holding 90-day commercial paper otherwise.

The contribution to the Fab Five Combo component is −1 when both are negative, 0 when mixed, and +1 when both indicators are positive.

Figure 20.30 is a mix of trend-sensitive, monetary, and sentiment indicators
(sound familiar?). Half of the model is trend-sensitive (based on breadth, to be specific) and half is external. This model was highlighted in Tim Hayes' 2000 book *The
Research Driven Investor*. Back then it was called the Nine-Indicator Model, and the
only change to it has been the dropping of the NYSE Member Short Ratio. This is a
case of a decent indicator no longer being published. There have been many over the
years. Here's a quick list of the eight:

1. NYSE weekly new lows is a simple indicator based on new 52-week lows as a percentage of total issues. Very low values are positive, while high values are negative.

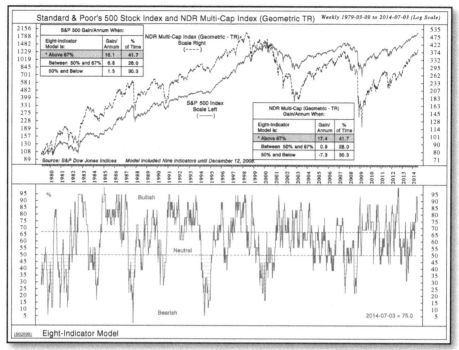

FIGURE 20.30 *Top,* **S&P 500 Index and NDR Multi-Cap Index (Geometric TR);** *Bottom,* **Eight-Indicator Model.**

2. Net new highs is basically NYSE weekly new highs minus new lows, as a percentage of total NYSE issues. High values are positive, while low values are negative.

3. S&P 500 reversals is a simple slope of the S&P 500. When the S&P 500 falls from a high by a certain percentage, this indicator goes negative. When it rises from a low by a certain percentage, it goes positive.

4. All Markets Open 40 Trading Index is an indicator that combines breadth data from all three U.S. markets (AMEX, NASDAQ, and NYSE) and calculates TRIN on a 40-day basis. This TRIN is then treated with a 6-month moving standard deviation with brackets. It's very similar to the TRIN indicator in the Fab Five sentiment component (which combines a 10 and a 30).

5. Bond yield/earnings yield change is a relative valuation indicator that compares bond yields to earnings yields. When the 6-month change in this ratio is high, the indicator is negative, while low is positive.

6. Composite bond yield reversals is another slope indicator; in this case the slope is applied to the long-term Treasury bond yield. A drop in the yield by a certain percentage is positive, while a rise is negative.

7. Prime rate reversals is another great Don't Fight the Fed indicator. When the prime rate falls by a certain percentage it's time to buy; when it rises by another percentage it's time to sell.

8. CCI momentum was discussed in the Fab Five monetary component.

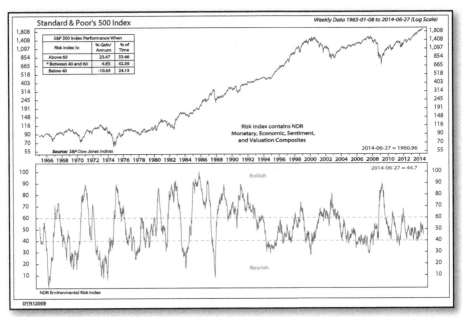

FIGURE 20.31 *Top*, S&P 500 Index; *Bottom*, Environmental Risk Index.

The contribution to the Fab Five Combo component is −1 below 50 percent, 0 between 50 percent and 67 percent, and +1 above 67 percent.

The Environmental Risk Index shown in Figure 20.31 is a composite of four external components, including monetary, economic, sentiment, and valuation. There are 71 total indicators in the model. It's another Ned Davis Research original and is designed to reflect the investing environment, but is not meant as a trading model. The seeds of the model go back to the 1980s, and although it has been reworked over the years it has remained essentially unchanged since 1995. However, we have had some attrition in the indicator mix: we lost a *BusinessWeek* index in 2009 and our big favorite, the Zweig sentiment indicator, in 2004.

The contribution to the Fab Five Combo component is −1 below 40 percent, 0 between 40 and 60 percent, and +1 above 60 percent.

The model shown in Figure 20.32 was built to call the MSCI Europe ex UK Index (which captures 14 developed markets in Europe excluding the United Kingdom), and it turns out, does a decent job calling the S&P 500 as well. It combines eight trend-sensitive indicators, and it's presented as a diffusion index. This adds a bit more diversity to the Combo component and cements the fact that big moves in stocks tend to be global, and that U.S. corporations have become more tied to world markets.

The contribution to the Fab Five Combo component is −1 below 40 percent, 0 between 40 percent and 75 percent, and +1 above 75 percent.

I discussed Big Mo Tape in the Fab Five tape section; now it's time to discuss this model's other half shown in Figure 20.33. As with a number of our external composites, this contains a thematic mix of indicators: economic, interest rates, sentiment, and valuation. The overlap with other external composites is pretty small. Three of these indicators are used elsewhere in the Fab Five, but that shouldn't pose

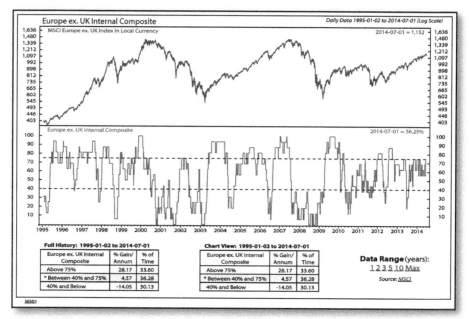

FIGURE 20.32 *Top*, MSCI Europe ex UK Index in Local Currency; *Bottom*, Europe ex U.K. Internal Composite.

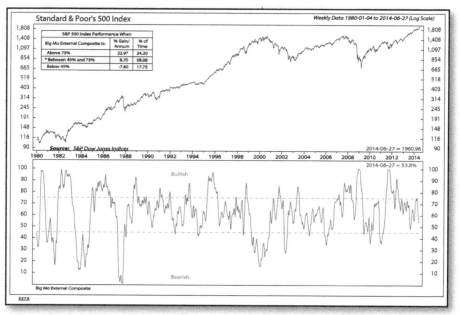

FIGURE 20.33 *Top*, S&P 500 Index; *Bottom*, Big Mo External Composite.

a problem since they make up just 15 percent of this model. There are five indicators in each theme (for a total of 20 indicators), and they are added up to create the Big Mo External Diffusion Index. As with all of our models, each indicator is monitored periodically, and we replace any that are misbehaving.

The contribution to the Fab Five Combo component is −1 below 45 percent, 0 between 45 and 75 percent, and +1 above 75 percent.

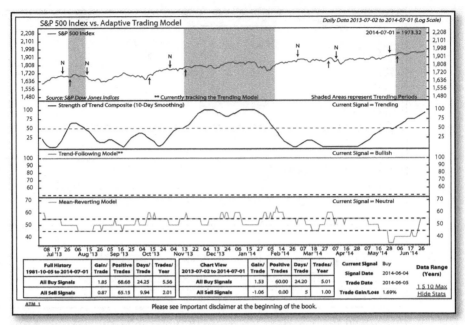

FIGURE 20.34 S&P 500 Index versus the Adaptive Trading Model.

We now come to the last piece of the puzzle—the Adaptive Trading Model in Figure 20.34. It consists of three components. Component number one is designed to distinguish between a trending market and a mean-reverting market (that's the adaptive part). In a trending market, component number two, the ATM Trend Model, takes over. And in a mean-reverting market, component number three, the Mean-Reverting Model, takes the helm.

While this all sounds complicated, it's really quite straightforward. The ATM Trend Model has only four fairly uncomplicated indicators, while the Mean-Reverting Model has five. The model controlling the switch has four. Still, this model has the same weight as the other six in the Fab Five Combo component and the contribution can be −1, 0, and +1. The Trend Model is never neutral, but the Mean-Reverting Model can be.

■ Combo Model Summary

Since there are six total indicators, the range of the model shown in Figure 20.35 is −6 to +6. The brackets are set at −1.5 and 2.5, and to be consistent with the other major Fab Five components, the model is designed to work in four preset date ranges.

■ Summing Up the Fab Five

Now that we've seen the components of the Fab Five, it's (finally!) time to add them together. Each component model is reduced to +1, 0, or −1 (with the exception of the tape component, which gets +2, 0, or −2), and the result is a simple sum. This

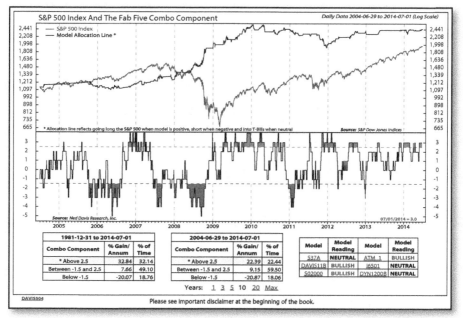

FIGURE 20.35 *Top,* S&P 500 Index and Model Allocation Line; *Bottom,* Fab Five Combo Component.

leaves the overall model's range at −5 to +5, with the brackets set at −1.5 and 1.5 (see Figure 20.1).

■ How We Use the Fab Five

I opened this chapter explaining that the Fab Five is an environmental model that provides a unified view and ties together sometimes opposing investment themes. If the model is outright bullish then our outlook will be on the bullish side. If it's merely flirting with the upper bracket we might temper our bullishness. We might make a distinction between high neutral and low neutral, depending on whether the model is moving up or down. For example, if it shifts from bearish to neutral, we might consider that hopeful. But going from bullish to neutral could make us cautious. We would never deviate too far from the Fab Five's basic verdict. If it's bullish we won't be bearish: we might be mildly bullish, but never bearish. Even though this model isn't designed for trading, traders can still use it to make decisions about whether they should have a bullish or bearish bias. If the short side is your thing then you should be a little more careful if the Fab Five is in bullish mode, and vice versa. At any rate, we still look to other inputs when evaluating our market position, but always in the context of the Fab Five.

CHAPTER 21

A Simple Model for Bonds

From Ned Davis, *Being Right or Making Money,*
3rd Edition (Hoboken, New Jersey: John Wiley &
Sons, 2014), Chapter 4.

Loren Flath

Learning Objective Statements

- Identify the five indicators used in the modified form of the Zweig Bond Model
- Explain one reason why this model might work well with mutual funds

About 10 years ago Ned got wind of a TradeStation seminar at the Venetian Hotel in Las Vegas. He is always looking for new ideas on markets and trading, and he thought I might learn something about new software or new analytical techniques. It was a three-day ordeal, with workshops of various kinds hosted by some very sharp people with truly interesting—and in some cases, somewhat complicated—trading methodologies. A number of the presenters had advanced degrees and managed money with the techniques they were showing us. Originally called System Writer, TradeStation started as a computer program for developing trading systems that could use a plethora of technical analysis tools. By 2004 it had evolved into a very sophisticated platform complete with automated trading: If you built a model with specific rules for buying and selling, you could put the system on automatic pilot.

On the last day of the seminar there was an elaborate lunch. Following our meal we were introduced to the guest speaker, Nelson Freeburg. I remember quite well his discussion of real-time models, and how so few of them actually continue to work as time passes. After investigating many models he had found only four true to their back-testing promises. He discussed the details of each, and when he got to number four he emphasized that he had saved the best for last. Then he proceeded to show the real-time results for the bond model presented in Marty Zweig's book *Winning with New IRAs*. I nearly choked on my carrot cake as I listened to him go over the details of the model that I had built for Marty's book in early 1986! I had long forgotten that model and had no inkling of its real-time performance. Ned was right: I did learn something!

I'll go over the model in detail, but in reality there is not a whole lot to go over. The late, great Marty Zweig, an accomplished investment advisor and market technician, was adamant that the model be as simple as possible. He wanted his readers to be able to calculate each indicator weekly in just a few minutes themselves. No laborious calculations, no hard-to-find data, no complicated concepts. As he pointed out in his book: "We tried to keep the model as simple as possible while adhering to two of my key general principles, which apply to the stock market as well—namely, staying in gear with the tape and in gear with the Fed."

Ned and I had our guidelines, but Marty had the final say. Since the book was about individual retirement accounts, it would have been nice to have developed the model with something tradable, like a bond mutual fund. But there was a dearth of historical mutual-fund data, so we instead used the Dow Jones 20 Bond Average, for which we had the weekly history going back to 1965. That index was composed of Baa-graded corporate bonds, and we had a facsimile for its yield. That let us back-test the model and then evaluate its predictive results against the index's actual total return. The very first version of the model I sent to Marty included moving-average and momentum calculations. "No," he said, "too complicated." (Computers weren't too common in the average home in 1986.) I made it still simpler. Here are the model's original four indicators:

1. The short-term slope of the Dow Jones 20 Bond Average: buy when the index rises from a bottom by 0.6 percent and sell when the index falls from a peak by 0.6 percent.
2. The longer term slope of the Dow Jones 20 Bond Average: buy when the index rises from a bottom by 1.8 percent and sell when it falls from a peak by 1.8 percent.
3. Changes in the discount rate: buy when the discount rate—the rate at which banks borrow from the Federal Reserve Bank—drops by at least one half of a percentage point and sell when the discount rate rises by at least a half point. This series ceased to be very relevant in 1989 when the central bank began influencing short-term rates via the Fed Funds rate—the rate at which banks borrow from one another. Now the indicator looks at half-point moves in the target rate that the Fed sets for Fed Funds.
4. The yield curve, based on the difference between the yields on AAA corporate bonds and 90-day commercial paper: buy when the spread crosses above 0.6 of a percentage point and sell when the spread falls below −0.2. Go neutral between −0.2 and 0.6.

In keeping with our KISS methodology, the model is a simple sum of the indicators' values. Thus its range is −4 to +4. Marty designed this model to give concrete buy and sell signals that were to be followed implicitly—no questions asked. He gave a detailed account of the model in Chapter 12 of *Winning with New IRAs*, complete with examples of how to trade with it and instructions on how to calculate each indicator. Figure 21.1 is a modernized version of the original chart of the model equity line as it appeared in the book. This was obviously a time in which managing risk was

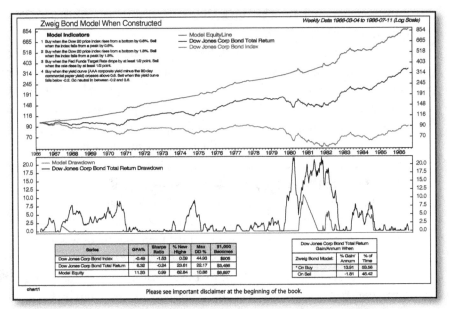

FIGURE 21.1 Zweig Bond Model When Constructed (1966–1986).

very important; in much of the 1966–1986 period interest rates climbed and bond prices fell. The model was long the benchmark only 54 percent of the time. Since this is a trading model, I have added the equity drawdown history in the bottom panel. (*Drawdown* is a Wall Street euphemism for a word investors despise: loss.) This reveals a nearly 11 percent drop on September 26, 1980.

The chart in Figure 21.2 shows how the model has done since Marty's book was sent to press in July 1986. During this period bond prices have gone nearly straight up. Timing a move like that is challenging and quite often disappointing. In this case, the

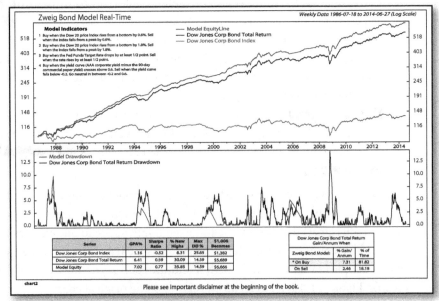

FIGURE 21.2 Zweig Bond Model Real-Time (1986–2014).

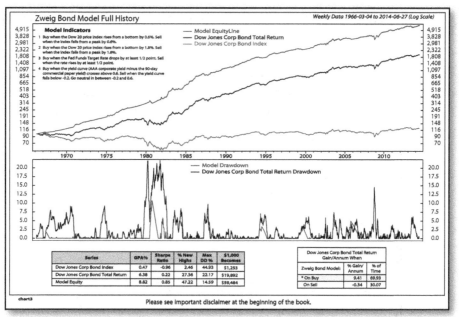

Chart details:

Zweig Bond Model Full History — Weekly Data 1966-03-04 to 2014-06-27 (Log Scale)

Model Indicators
1 Buy when the Dow 20 price index rises from a bottom by 0.6%. Sell when the index falls from a peak by 0.6%.
2 Buy when the Dow 20 price index rises from a bottom by 1.8%. Sell when the index falls from a peak by 1.8%.
3 Buy when the Fed Funds Target Rate drops by at least 1/2 point. Sell when the rate rises by at least 1/2 point.
4 Buy when the yield curve (AAA corporate yield minus the 90-day commercial paper yield) crosses above 0.6. Sell when the yield curve falls below -0.2. Go neutral in between -0.2 and 0.6.

— Model EquityLine
— Dow Jones Corp Bond Total Return
— Dow Jones Corp Bond Index

— Model Drawdown
— Dow Jones Corp Bond Total Return Drawdown

Series	GPA%	Sharpe Ratio	% New Highs	Max DD %	$1,000 Becomes
Dow Jones Corp Bond Index	0.47	-0.96	2.46	44.93	$1,253
Dow Jones Corp Bond Total Return	6.38	0.22	27.36	22.17	$19,892
Model Equity	8.82	0.85	47.22	14.59	$59,484

Dow Jones Corp Bond Total Return Gain/Annum When

Zweig Bond Model:	% Gain/ Annum	% of Time
* On Buy	9.41	69.93
On Sell	-0.34	30.07

chart3

Please see important disclaimer at the beginning of the book.

FIGURE 21.3 Zweig Bond Model Full History (1966–2014).

model has spent only about a quarter of the time in cash. The worst period was during the 2008 debacle, when both monetary indicators were bullish while both trend indicators went bearish, causing the prior buy signal to become locked in. This caused a drawdown of 14.6 percent. The same thing happened in 2013, although the drawdown was somewhat less painful at just above 6 percent. Still, as can be seen from the Sharpe ratios the model has handily beaten a buy-and-hold strategy, with less risk. (The Sharpe ratio measures risk-adjusted performance; the higher the number, the better.)

Figure 21.3 shows the model for the full date range (1966–2014).

■ A Slight Modification

Back in 2004, following the TradeStation seminar, I put revisiting the model on the back burner. When the decision was made to update *Being Right or Making Money*, we thought we would just reprise the bond model from the 2000 edition. But then we thought it might be fun to actually highlight a model that had come to life in the mid-1980s and had been quite successful.

Now that we have done that, let's look more deeply at the model. Two things jump out: (1) the losses show that the trend component doesn't get you out of the market when the Fed is easy and prices are falling, and (2) you couldn't really trade the Dow 20 when it existed, let alone now, when it doesn't.

To minimize potential losses, I added a simple trend indicator: a 50-day (10-week) moving average of the Dow 20's price with a cross of 1 percent (this is a favorite of ours for calculating diffusion indices). If the Dow 20's price crosses below its 50-day average by at least 1 percent, this indicator goes negative. Crossing above the 50-day by at least 1 percent sends the indicator positive. With this addition the model is now a five-indicator model, and as with the original model, the sum of all the indicators needs to be a −1 or a +1 to get a signal. Figures 21.4, 21.5, and 21.6 show the modified model for the time ranges shown in Figures 21.1, 21.2, and 21.3, respectively. Note the dramatic reduction in losses and the added amount of time spent long. Also, the equity line spends more time making new highs in all three periods shown.

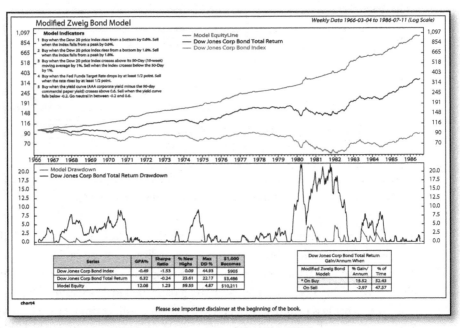

FIGURE 21.4   Modified Zweig Bond Model (1966–1986).

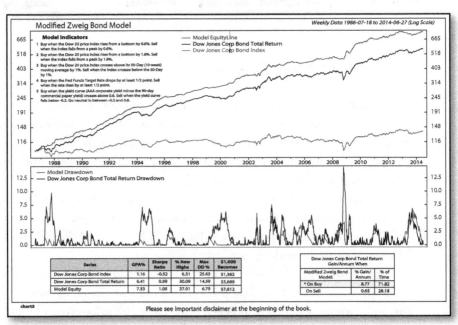

FIGURE 21.5   Modified Zweig Bond Model (1986–2014).

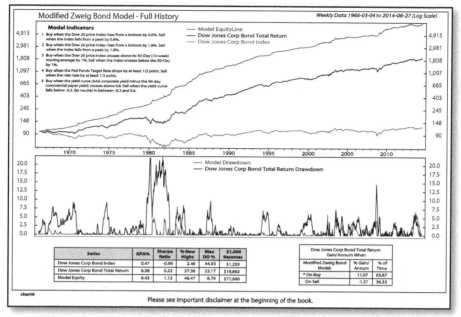

FIGURE 21.6 Modified Zweig Bond Model Full History (1966–2014).

Now let's apply this model to something that is actually tradable today. Staying with the spirit of the Dow 20 Index, I looked in our database for a corporate bond fund that might match it and have a significant history. A good match was the Fidelity Investment Grade Bond Fund (FBNDX), known as Fidelity Flexible Bond in the 1980s. The results using the modified Zweig Bond Model signals can be seen in the chart in Figure 21.7. At the outset they don't appear impressive. But remember that

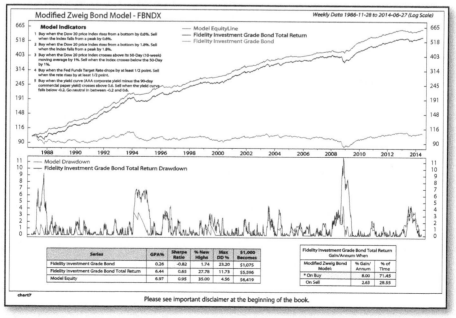

FIGURE 21.7 Modified Zweig Bond Model with FBNDX.

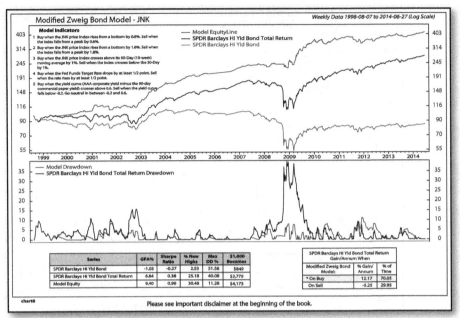

FIGURE 21.8 Modified Zweig Bond Model with JNK.

we have been dealing with a very strong bond market during the time frame covered (1986–2014). What is significant is that the model does work, as reflected by the higher Sharpe ratio, lower drawdowns, and increased time spent long.

For those of you who really like to trade: we've found over the years that a decent model built for one index can produce surprising results when applied to another that's highly correlated but more volatile. Figure 21.8 shows the same model shown in Figure 21.7 calculated on the price of the SPDR Barclays High Yield Bond ETF (JNK) instead, with the results based on its total return. As for trade frequency, the trades averaged about 0.7 per year.

■ Summary

A note for those of you who have Marty Zweig's *Winning with New IRAs* or plan to obtain a copy: in it, Marty did a great job explaining this model. His book includes numerous details, tables, and charts to accompany the dialog. However, he writes that a buy signal comes at +3 and a sell at −3. This reflects an error in communication between the two of us. In reality, all of the results summarized in Chapter 12 of his book are based on signals at −1 and +1. Since Marty's book was published, the Dow Jones 20 Bond Index has morphed into the Dow Jones Equal Weight U.S. Issued Corporate Bond Index, and it can be found in many places, including Google and Yahoo Finance.

In sum, the Zweig Bond Model shows that keeping it simple can pay off. Marty Zweig knew this when he approached us to build it back in 1985. The basic principles were true then and still true now: don't fight the tape, and don't fight the Fed. In the words of the inimitable Stan Lee: 'nuff said!

CHAPTER 22

Perspectives on Active and Passive Money Management

From Robert A. Weigand, *Applied Equity Analysis and Portfolio Management* (Hoboken, New Jersey: John Wiley & Sons, 2014), Chapter 1.

Learning Objective Statements

- Give an example of a Relative return and an Absolute return vehicle
- Explain the difference between Alpha and Beta
- List the four stages of the top-down fundamental analysis process
- Describe seven anomalies the Efficient Market Hypothesis does not explain
- Summarize the three explanations of how information becomes incorporated into securities prices

The learning objectives for this chapter are:

1. Display an understanding of the chapter terminology and describe the top-down fundamental analysis process.
2. Explain why stocks with superior fundamentals often have higher returns and lower risk over long horizons.
3. Summarize the results of studies that investigate the performance of professional investors and what motivates investors to trade more actively.
4. Identify the three major theories of the way information gets incorporated into stock prices, and summarize the major premises of each theory.
5. Summarize the perspectives of esteemed investors and authors provided in the chapter.
6. Interpret the insights into financial markets from Chapter 23 of John Maynard Keynes's *General Theory of Employment, Interest and Money*.
7. Discuss the importance of an investment policy statement.

Terminology: Investors, Investment Vehicles, Risk and Return

Equity investing can be divided into two main categories: passive and active. *Passive investors* buy and hold stocks for the long term. They construct portfolios or choose investment vehicles that minimize costs, including research costs, trading costs, administrative costs, performance fees, and taxes on realized gains. The most popular types of passive investment vehicles include "index" mutual funds and exchange-traded funds (ETFs), which are designed to imitate the performance of indexes like the S&P 500. *Active investors*, however, seek to outperform the indexes by identifying individual stocks to buy and sell. Because they trade more often, active investors turn their portfolios over more frequently than passive investors and usually incur higher costs.

Relative versus Absolute Return Investing

Active investing can be further divided into two main categories. *Relative return* vehicles seek to outperform a benchmark index (like the Standard & Poor's [S&P] 500), where "outperformance" is measured as a combination of either earning higher returns and/or achieving lower risk exposure. Most equity portfolios, including equity mutual funds and student investment funds, are relative return vehicles, where the fund's performance is evaluated relative to a widely followed benchmark. *Absolute return* vehicles seek to deliver returns that are less risky but are also usually lower than the returns of most index benchmarks. Many equity hedge funds are absolute return vehicles. Examples include long-short funds that make both positive bets (by owning stocks long) and negative bets (by selling stocks short).

You may notice that the terms active and passive are, to some degree, "loaded" words. In many cultures (especially the United States), being passive is usually considered less desirable than being active. Later in this chapter, you will learn that this is rarely the case in investing, however. The results of numerous research studies show that one of the main reasons passive, buy-and-hold investing is so prevalent is that the majority of active professional investors underperform their benchmarks.

Alpha and Beta: Excess Returns and Market Risk

Alpha refers to the *excess* returns earned by relative return investors, either above or below the market index to which their performance is benchmarked. When a portfolio outperforms its benchmark index, the percentage return by which the portfolio exceeds the index return will be termed positive alpha. If a portfolio underperforms its benchmark index, we'll say it earned a negative alpha.

Beta is a measure of risk that can apply to an individual stock or to a portfolio of stocks. The average market beta = 1.0. In the case of an individual stock, beta measures how much risk, or *volatility*, that stock is expected to contribute to the overall volatility of a diversified portfolio. High-beta stocks usually exhibit a more volatile reaction to market-wide or macroeconomic news, on both the upside and downside. Examples of high-beta stocks include *cyclical stocks* like Caterpillar and Ford. The stock prices of these companies are more volatile because businesses and consumers buy more tractors, cars, and trucks during strong economic times, and cut back on investments in capital assets and purchases of durable goods during weak economic times. Low-beta stocks tend to be less volatile, however, and therefore contribute less volatility to a diversified portfolio. Examples include consumer staples stocks like Nestlé and pharmaceutical stocks like Bristol-Myers. These companies produce items consumers tend to buy regardless of economic conditions.

When applied to a well-diversified equity portfolio, beta is a measure of the market risk, or volatility, of the portfolio. If a portfolio emphasizes high-beta stocks, its returns will tend to be more volatile, and vice-versa if it emphasizes low-beta stocks. Finance theory asserts that *risk and expected returns are positively related*, which implies that high-beta stock stocks should earn higher returns and low-beta stocks should earn lower returns over long holding periods. Thus, high-beta stock portfolios should outperform low-beta portfolios, as higher returns compensate investors for bearing greater risk. One of the principles of this book is that investors can construct winning portfolios by investing in *low*-beta stocks, which contradicts the basic wisdom of finance. After introducing a clearer picture of the job of the fundamental analyst in the following section, we will revisit this apparently contradictory assertion. Can investors really have it both ways—lower risk and *higher* returns?

■ The Top-Down Fundamental Analysis Process

Next we'll take an overview of the fundamental analysis process featured in this book. Our process is termed *top-down* because it begins with an analysis of the overall economy, with an emphasis on gauging the stage of the business cycle in which the economy is operating. As we'll see, this activity helps the analyst identify sectors of the stock market in which to deploy new capital, and sectors from which capital should be withdrawn and redeployed.

Analysts divide the stock market into 10 sectors. When an actively managed portfolio allocates funds by sector in a way that differs from their current market weights, we will say the portfolio manager is employing **sector overweights and underweights**. Once an analyst determines the sectors to over- and underweight relative to the market, he will next determine the stocks with the best prospects to overweight within each sector (and the stocks to sell or sell short, if the fund allows short selling). Figure 22.1 depicts the stages of the top-down fundamental analysis process.

The decision to buy a stock and hold it in a portfolio indicates confidence, or conviction, in the security. But it is unlikely that managers will have the same degree of conviction regarding each stock they own. Figure 22.2 shows the possible "weights" (the percentage of total portfolio wealth invested in each stock) in a 12-stock portfolio, ranked by analyst conviction. Notice how the highest-conviction stocks receive the highest weight and the lowest-conviction stocks receive the lowest weight.

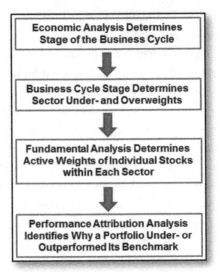

FIGURE 22.1 The Top-Down
Fundamental Analysis Process.

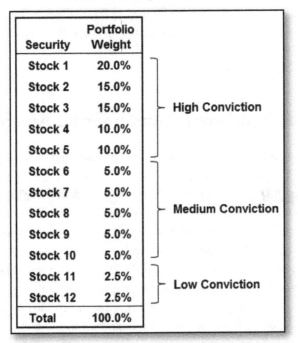

FIGURE 22.2 Analyst Conviction and Active
Portfolio Weights.

Active investors therefore allocate portfolio wealth among stocks differently than
these stocks' market-determined weights in the benchmark index. The active investor's weighting scheme will be called *active portfolio weights*.

Why Stocks with Solid Fundamentals Outperform over Long Horizons

Now that you understand the overall fundamental process, let's take a closer look at exactly how portfolios emphasizing stocks with solid fundamentals outperform over long

horizons. First, let's be more specific about what we mean by fundamentals. We're going to learn how to identify stocks whose prices are well supported by the basic building blocks, or fundamentals, that support intrinsic value: revenues, profits, free cash flows, and a commitment to return a large share of that free cash flow to investors, preferably in the form of cash dividends. These characteristics conform to another basic finance principle, which states that *an asset's **intrinsic value** equals today's value of the future free cash flows the asset is expected to generate over its lifetime.* This means that we'll learn to identify:

1. Stocks with steadily growing revenues, profits, free cash flows, and dividends.
2. Stocks that achieve this growth by making prudent capital investments.
3. Companies with strong competitive positions that allow them to defend and maintain their market presence, which supports further growth in their fundamentals.

Next, recall the idea of beta—the index of how volatile a stock is likely to be and how much volatility it will contribute to a diversified portfolio. Beginning students of finance often ask an obvious question about volatility that shows more savvy than finance theorists have been able to handle: "Don't we only want to avoid *downside* volatility?"

There is a lot of wisdom contained in that question, because it indirectly describes how stocks with superior fundamentals win. These types of stocks almost never surge ahead during the market's bull phase. But when markets correct or enter a bear phase—and they always do—stocks with superior fundamentals tend to decline in value much less than their high-beta counterparts. Moreover, after the market correction is over, these stocks usually resume following the market's next upward trend, albeit at a somewhat slower pace. We'll consider three examples to help you better understand these tendencies.

The second quarter of the year is an excellent period to study how the stock market works. Research shows that the stock market tends to earn much of its total annual return early in the calendar year (usually beginning in late December). After the first quarter, however, an old adage holds that investors can "sell in May and go away," as the market tends to trend sideways or correct after the early-year euphoria fades and investors become more discriminating about the specific stocks they want to own. Let's take a look at the returns of several stocks with solid fundamentals during the second quarter of 2012: Bristol-Myers and Johnson & Johnson.

Figure 22.3 shows how Bristol-Myers (BMY) follows the market through early April, but as investors become increasingly nervous about an impending correction, buyers gradually bid BMY's stock price up until it decouples from the market trend. This occurs because during market corrections, investors sell many of their risky, high-beta stock positions and invest the proceeds in stocks with superior fundamentals. The prices of these stocks are supported by their fundamentals, which makes them most attractive to investors during the market's darkest moods. And because these stocks have a predictable tendency to decline in value by much less than the market, investors' portfolios suffer far less damage (known as drawdowns) during corrections and bear markets. Warren Buffett best summed up this essential

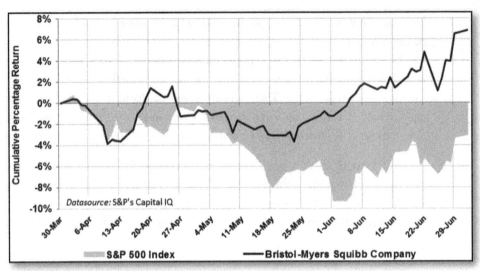

FIGURE 22.3 Bristol-Myers Rises During the Spring 2012 Market Correction.
Source: S&P's Capital IQ.

principle of investing when he said, "The best way to make a dollar is not to lose a dollar" (Lowe, 1997).

Figure 22.4 depicts a similar pattern for Johnson & Johnson (JNJ), which is one of the "most widely held stocks" among institutional investors. The graph reveals why so many institutions hold JNJ: because it's a great portfolio diversifier. Notice how the stock initially follows the market's downward move, but investors only allow it to fall so far before it offers compelling value in a declining market. Toward the end of the three-month market correction, JNJ has outperformed the market by almost 6 percent. And, in the world of investing, not losing 6 percent is just as good as gaining 6 percent. This is how stocks with solid fundamentals contribute to superior portfolio returns and lower volatility over long horizons.

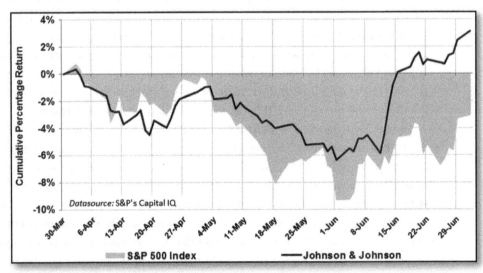

FIGURE 22.4 J&J Reaches a 3-Month High During the Spring 2012 Market Correction.
Source: S&P's Capital IQ.

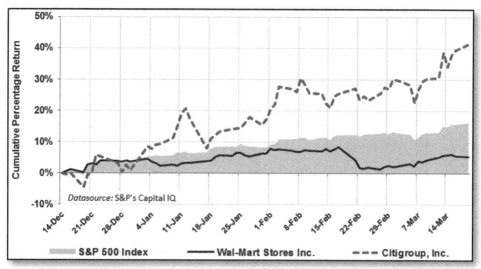

FIGURE 22.5 Citigroup Outperforms Wal-Mart in Early 2012.
Source: S&P's Capital IQ.

Let's consider one more example to fully make the point. Figure 22.5 depicts the cumulative returns to Wal-Mart, Citigroup, and the S&P 500 during the first quarter of 2012 (we begin in mid-December, which is when large turn-of-the-year moves in the stock market often begin). The stock market gained 16 percent through late March, propelled by speculative names like Citigroup. Years of blunders by this financial services giant directly contributed to the financial crisis of 2008, and it has subsequently suffered through a series of scandals and mismanagement—none of which prevented it from accepting government assistance that enabled it to continue operating without proper financial discipline. In late 2011 through early 2012, a bet on Citigroup was a purely speculative play.

Notice how a stock like Wal-Mart, which models up well on a fundamental basis, initially gets left behind in the market's turn-of-the-year frenzy. During the first quarter of 2012, Wal-Mart's stock earns less than half of the total market return, and far less than Citigroup. At this point you might be thinking "Why *wouldn't* an investor want to own Citigroup?"

Next we'll shift our attention to Figure 22.6, which shows the cumulative returns to Wal-Mart, Citigroup, and the S&P 500 during the second quarter, when the market corrected downward by approximately 10 percent. What a difference 90 days makes. Citigroup's stock declines by more than three times as much as the market because they were weighed down by poor fundamentals. Notice how midway through the market correction, investors began the same predictable rotation into safer stocks with strong fundamentals. Wal-Mart outperforms the S&P 500 by approximately 16 percent during this period, and it beats Citigroup by almost 40 percent!

Figure 22.7 completes the story. Despite Citigroup's strong showing in the first quarter, Wal-Mart handily outperforms Citigroup through spring, summer, and most of the fall, albeit in a sort of tortoise-versus-the-hare manner. Fundamental

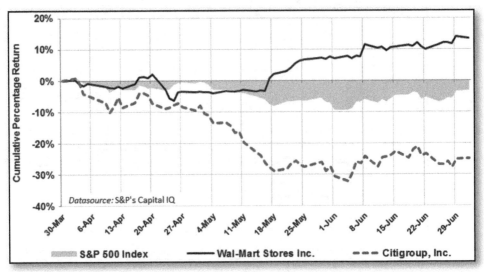

FIGURE 22.6   Wal-Mart Outperforms Citigroup During Spring 2012 Market Correction.
Source: S&P's Capital IQ.

investors might have felt a little nervous early in 2012 when Citigroup was bounding ahead, but in the slow and patient buy-and-hold race, the stock with the superior fundamentals eventually won out—as most often happens. Moreover, Wal-Mart out-performed with lower volatility, taking investors on less of a roller-coaster ride. Wal-Mart's beta versus the S&P 500 equals only 0.35, versus Citigroup's beta of approximately 2.0.

Now that we understand why fundamentally sound stocks outperform over long horizons, we're going to take a closer look at the long-term track record of profes-sional money managers.

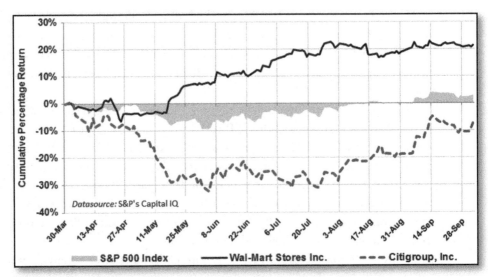

FIGURE 22.7   Citigroup Plays Catch-up for the Rest of the Year.
Source: S&P's Capital IQ.

■ The Record of Professional Money Managers

Earlier in this chapter, we reduced fundamental analysis to a multistep process that sounded as easy to implement as following a recipe. As we'll see, things are not quite that simple. In this section we'll review the record of professional money managers, and consider why they often achieve such disappointing results.

Most research into active money management concludes that the majority of managers underperform their benchmarks (they earn negative alphas). Let me assure you that this is not some abstract academic result, or a partisan misreading of the facts. It's probably one the best-kept secrets on Wall Street, however. The prevalenceof negative alphas among mutual funds (net of expenses and trading costs) is well documented by studies conducted by respected researchers, including Elton et al. (1993), Carhart (1997), and John Bogle (2002), the founder of Vanguard. More recently, Standard & Poor's Indices vs. Active Funds (SPIVA) 2009 scorecard reported that over the period 2004–2008, 63 percent of large-cap mutual funds, 74 percent of mid-cap funds, and 68 percent of small-cap funds underperformed their benchmarks. Among international mutual funds, the underperformance rates ranged between 60 and 90 percent. If those results aren't bad enough, Standard & Poor's reported that 84 percent of actively managed funds underperformed in 2011. And these findings are not confined to calendar-year periods. For example, Ludwig (2012) reports that almost 90 percent of professionally managed funds underperformed from June 2011 through June 2012. These findings are not unusual. It is extremely rare for active investment vehicles to outperform passive vehicles in the aggregate, and it has never occurred consistently over any extended period of time.

The performance of investment managers in the absolute return/hedge fund space is similarly disappointing. Malkiel and Saha (2005) conclude that hedge fund returns are lower than commonly supposed, and that hedge funds are significantly riskier than more conventional investments. Fung, Xu, and Yau (2004) also report negative average alphas for hedge funds, and Pojarliev and Levich (2008) find negative risk-adjusted alphas among a sample of funds that invest in international currencies. Writing about long-short funds for *Institutional Investor* magazine, O'Hara (2009) asks, "If managers can't beat the market, what purpose do they serve?" Statman (2010) provides one possible answer to O'Hara's question. His research suggests that investors use their relationships with money management firms to express their social class and lifestyles, implying that investors are willing to accept lower returns if they can place funds with prestigious firms and/or managers.

Mark Hulbert is well known for publishing the *Hulbert Financial Digest*, a newsletter that tracks the performance and sentiment of mutual fund managers. Hulbert's survey shows that investment manager sentiment is a contrarian indicator (meaning that investment managers are too pessimistic at market bottoms and too optimistic at market tops).

Hulbert is also a columnist for the *New York Times* and *Dow Jones Marketwatch*. In 2008 he reviewed a working paper by Barras, Scaillet, and Wermers (published in 2010) that concludes that even fewer managers beat the market than previously thought. After accounting for fees, the vast majority of active mutual funds had negative returns. But these authors also conclude that the proportion of zero-alpha mutual funds is *higher* than previously thought. They find that 75 percent of funds earn zero alphas, implying that the pros earn just enough to cover their fees and other costs. Less than 1 percent of funds delivered positive alpha in a way that is consistent with manager skill, however.

Why Do Active Managers Underperform?

The research reviewed in the previous section convincingly concludes that in the aggregate, active managers underperform their benchmarks, and they do so with surprising consistency. These results were not covered with the purpose of picking on the pros—just the opposite, as the key mission of this book is to teach you to conduct your own stock research effectively and professionally. It's necessary to confront the track record of the pros to illustrate the challenging and competitive landscape of professional money management, however. We need to understand why such a group of intelligent, competitive, well-trained individuals consistently post such disappointing results so that we don't make the same mistakes. We'll start by taking a closer look at step 3 of the top-down process: conducting fundamental analysis to determine which stocks to under- and overweight relative to their weights in the overall market.

After we determine the financial health and stability of a company, we will conduct a valuation analysis to determine if the company's stock is trading above or below what we'll call its ***intrinsic value***. As mentioned previously, a stock's intrinsic value equals today's value of all the free cash flows the company is expected to generate over its remaining lifetime. Estimating intrinsic value is as much a science as an art, as it involves forecasting the company's future revenues, expenses, and a variety of other income statement and balance sheet items.

This step of the fundamental analysis process involves a logical inconsistency, or paradox, that only the best analysts confront. The paradox occurs whenever an analyst concludes that a stock is under- or overvalued, because the analyst is implicitly asserting that the market is making a mistake in the way it's valuing the stock. Notice that market mistakes are a possibility that we must allow for if we're going to be active investors. If we believe the market price is correct 100 percent of the time, then only low-cost indexing makes sense. Why would anyone spend time and money researching companies and estimating the intrinsic value of stocks when all they have to do is check their market price?

So here's the paradox: if the analyst believes the market is mispricing a stock today, why shouldn't it be the case that this mispricing will continue to persist? For an analyst to rationally make the case, for example, that shares of ABC are worth $100, but are temporarily undervalued at $80, he should also be able to identify the upcoming information or change of perception that will convince other investors and traders to begin paying more for the stock. There must be an event that changes the market's mind about the value of ABC, or the analyst will simply own many shares of a stock whose price is stuck at $80.

Therefore, identifying a mispriced security (an irrational valuation by the overall market) is a necessary but insufficient step in the fundamental analysis process. The final step is to anticipate the *catalysts* that will help the rest of the market recognize the true value of the under- and overvalued securities identified by our fundamental process. There are many stocks that model up as undervalued—some based on their dividends alone. But concluding that a stock is undervalued is not the same as concluding that it's overdue for a significant price correction. Yet the investment theses of many professional analysts fail to include this important perspective.

Before an analyst can anticipate the forthcoming catalysts that will finally move a stock's price closer to his estimate of fair value, he needs a theory, or model, of how the market processes information under certain conditions. This model will inform his understanding of why the market may be mispricing a certain security, and also guide his thinking about how information regarding the company's true value will eventually become reflected in its stock price.

■ Market Efficiency, Behavioral Finance, and Adaptive Expectations

In this section we'll consider three competing explanations of the way investors process information and incorporate it into their trading decisions, and thus securities prices as well. The first explanation, the *efficient markets hypothesis* (EMH), is the oldest, known for emphasizing a high level of rationality in investor behavior and aggregate market outcomes. The second comes from the newer field of *behavioral finance*, which allows investor emotions to play a larger role in securities pricing. Behavioral finance recognizes that pricing errors can not only exist but sometimes persist for long periods. The third explanation, the *adaptive markets hypothesis* (AMH), is the newest of the three. The AMH views the interactions among investors, securities, markets, and institutions as a dynamically evolving ecosystem. Within the AMH framework, winners are determined by their ability to both compete and adapt to constantly changing circumstances.

Market Efficiency

We begin with a discussion of the concept of market efficiency, formally known as the efficient markets hypothesis, or EMH. No matter how much you may have heard this theory praised or ridiculed in previous coursework or via other exposure, it's important to understand what this theory says and its implications for active investors. Any time we're talking about "beating the market"—actively investing to earn risk-adjusted returns that are higher than the returns of a benchmark index—we're talking about market efficiency, because we're asserting that we possess tradable information that the market does not fully understand, or cannot accurately pass through to a security's price for some reason. Understanding market efficiency is a useful first step in understanding and exploiting deviations from efficiency. When information is not accurately reflected in a stock's price, there may be an opportunity to buy or sell the mispriced security and earn excess returns.

Based on the typical textbook treatment, one could get the idea that market efficiency is a theoretically abstract concept that has no application in the real world, yet nothing could be further from the truth. Securities traders and finance professionals of all types are concerned with the issue of market efficiency (as we'll see in the Morgan Stanley investment policy statement below). They just employ a perspective and use a vocabulary that's different than those of finance professors. This point is best illustrated by comparing an academic perspective on market efficiency with a practitioner perspective.

The academic perspective says: "A securities market is informationally efficient when news is rapidly and accurately reflected in the prices of financial securities." Although that's a perfectly accurate statement, representing the usual treatment of this topic in finance textbooks, thinking about market efficiency this way makes it sound dull, abstract, and uninteresting.

The practitioner perspective, however, asks the question: "Are there any trading strategies based on historical and/or publicly available information that outperform the market with reasonable consistency after adjusting for risk?" Although both definitions are concerned with whether all available information is accurately reflected in the price, approaching the topic from this perspective allows for the possibility that our understanding of market efficiency will make us better investors, which is our main goal.

Securities Prices in an Efficient Market   The prices of stocks and other securities in an efficient market will react rapidly and accurately to news, where news is defined as information that is (1) relevant to the value of the security and (2) unanticipated by the market (in other words, "new"). Thus, securities prices are thought to reflect all information that is relevant regarding stocks' valuation all the time. Markets are thought to be efficient due to the research conducted by rational, wealth-maximizing analysts and investors. The large potential profits from making the right call motivate analysts to work hard to identify new information, assess its relevance for securities prices, and immediately trade on the results of their analysis. It's the diligent efforts of investors that keep prices efficient.

The Three Levels of Market Efficiency   Market efficiency is often described as having three possible "levels," which define the type and amount of information assumed to be fully reflected in prices. This classification can be understood by inserting one of the three bullet-point phrases into the first and second blank spaces shown in the following sentence: "Securities markets are _____ efficient if gathering and analyzing all _____ information does *not* consistently produce excess returns."

- Weak form/historical

- Semistrong form/current and publicly available

- Strong form/private or inside

If you believe market prices fully reflect all historical information, but not necessarily current, publicly available information, then you are classifying the market as weak form efficient. In other words, all historical information is so well reflected in market prices that it's almost always impossible to trade on that information to earn excess returns. If, however, you believe market prices fully reflect both historical and current, publicly available information, then you are classifying the market as semistrong efficient. In this case, analyzing past *and* current information is not useful in consistently outperforming the market (although occasional outperformance by investors is not ruled out). There's not much point in talking about whether prices fully reflect private or inside information because it's impossible to investigate scientifically (questionnaires asking about illegal trading are never completed and returned for some strange reason). We will focus on the semistrong level of efficiency and assume that investors are proficient in both technical analysis (studying past price patterns by using charts) and fundamental analysis (studying all historical and current information, including financial statements, research conducted by other analysts, etc.).

The Behavior of Securities Prices in an Efficient Market   Let's say that news is released regarding a large, unexpected change in the profit outlook for a firm. In an efficient market we would expect to see the stock price react immediately upon release of that information. Since the market is so competitive, only the investors who receive the news first and immediately act on it will earn excess returns. Everyone else will be too late to use the news profitably, as the trades of the first investors cause the stock's price to quickly correct to fair value.

Figure 22.8 depicts an efficient market reaction to news. IBM announced its earnings for the third quarter of 2012 after the market closed on October 16. Analysts were expecting earnings of $25.4 billion, but IBM came in a little light at $24.7 billion. As shown in the graph, IBM's stock price reaction was swift. The stock declined 4.92 percent on October 17, and another 2.83 percent on October 18. Over those two days the S&P 500 rose 0.17 percent, so IBM's large price decline was clearly due to the company-specific news release and not broader information pertaining to the entire market.

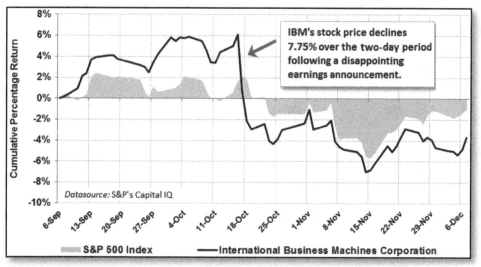

FIGURE 22.8   **IBM's Earnings Miss Analysts' Expectations in October 2012.**
Source: S&P's Capital IQ.

IBM's reaction is also considered efficient due to the way the stock price behaves *after* the announcement. Notice that after the two-day price adjustment, IBM's price begins following the market trend once again. There is no significant price "drift" in either a positive or negative direction. For the following two trading months, IBM loses another 1.5 percent and the market loses 2.9 percent. IBM's reaction to the earnings news therefore appears to be confined to the two-day period following the announcement, consistent with the predictions of the EMH.[1]

Now that we've considered an example of when the efficient markets theory works, let's consider a more subtle example that is representative of the type of criticism many have leveled at the EMH. This criticism concerns market partici-pants' ability and willingness to see all the way through the numbers reported by companies. Do analysts really think critically, or are they too eager to parrot back the information that's fed to them?

Do Analysts Dig Deep Enough?   Figure 22.9 shows Amazon's stock price reaction to its April 26, 2012, earnings announcement. The market was expecting Amazon to earn 7 cents a share, but the company reported 28 cents—*four times* the expected number. There was a large, positive stock price reaction of 17.97 percent over the following two trading days. Over those same days, the S&P 500 declined by 0.15 percent, so once again, the stock price reaction was almost certainly due to the re-lease of company-specific news rather than market-wide information.

Next we'll focus on Amazon's stock returns following the announcement. Through mid-June, the stock lost 6.58 percent. Is it possible that Amazon's price overreacted to the news, and the market "took back" some of those large gains from the April earnings announcement? In this case, probably not. Even though the downward postannouncement price drift is evident in the graph, the market de-clined by 5.27 percent over the same period. Amazon's stock returns following the

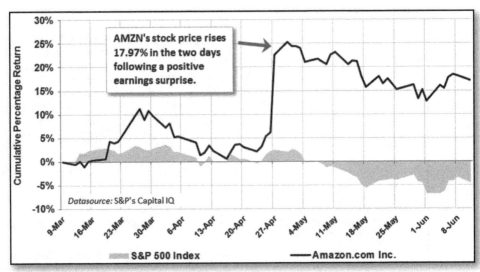

FIGURE 22.9   **Amazon's Earnings Beat Analysts' Expectations in April 2012.**
Source: S&P's Capital IQ.

announcement are therefore most likely due to the overall market trend, and not a reconsideration of Amazon's valuation based on their earnings.

Thus far, it looks like the market was efficient around Amazon's earnings announcement. There are actually several reasons to think that the market was not functioning with perfect accuracy and objectivity in this case, however. The first reason is that Amazon was on pace to report earnings per share of 7 cents in the weeks leading up to the earnings announcement, according to the "guidance" the company provided to analysts in the preannouncement period. It was only a last-minute decision to transfer profits from other entities in which Amazon has minority ownership onto their income statement that allowed Amazon to report earnings that were four times larger than analysts anticipated. Of course, there was nothing illegal about this move. It is allowed based on the "equity-method investment activity, net of tax" provision in U.S. generally accepted accounting principles (GAAP) rules. What's concerning about Amazon's decision to declare these profits is that the average value for that equity-method account was −$500,000 for the past eight quarters. Amazon's decision therefore looks a bit like opportunistic "earnings management," a practice used by many companies to make their profits look larger and more consistent than they would be without some manipulation.

The second, somewhat more disturbing criticism regarding the accuracy of the market's reaction was described by Peter Eavis, writing for the *New York Times'* DealBook blog on April 27, 2012. Mr. Eavis's article makes note of the following facts:

- Amazon's first-quarter earnings diverged significantly from the guidance provided by the company.

- Amazon offered no explanation for this large divergence.

- There were 17 analysts on the earnings call, yet none thought to ask why earnings were four times larger than the preannouncement number.

- Amazon's investor relations department did not respond to Mr. Eavis's subsequent e-mail inquiries and phone messages.

I find it odd that there were 17 analysts on the earnings announcement call, but none of them asked the simple question, "Why were your profits four times larger than expected?" That type of behavior is not consistent with analysts' digging deep to uncover the ultimate truth about a company. The criticism of the EMH in this case is that without access to all relevant information, including information that requires fervent due diligence by analysts, markets can't be efficient.

Taking a longer-term perspective on this issue, analysts have consistently ignored a variety of "inconvenient truths" about Amazon's profitability for quite some time. Figure 22.10 depicts Amazon's operating margin from the first quarter of 2010 through the third quarter of 2012. The graph shows that Amazon's operating margin has been in a steady downtrend for years. The company does not comment on this trend, and analysts don't ask. As shown in the graph, Amazon's operating margin turned *negative* in the third quarter of 2012. The only way to declare positive profits with negative margins is via accounting gimmicks, such as suddenly switching to the

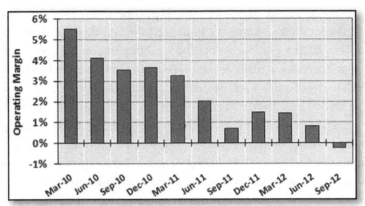

FIGURE 22.10 Amazon's Operating Margin 2010–2012.
Source: S&P's Capital IQ.

equity method for reporting subsidiary profits described above. As of early 2013, the market remained unconcerned, and Amazon's stock price continued achieving new record highs. The key question is whether Amazon's stock price objectively reflects all relevant information about the company.

Anomalies the EMH Cannot Explain   While the efficient markets hypothesis is a good starting point for understanding markets, researchers have documented numerous empirical facts about investing and markets that are inconsistent with the EMH. The existence of consistent patterns in securities prices and price volatility implies tradable opportunities based on past and current information that would not exist in a highly efficient market. A short list of these anomalies includes:

- *Correlations in security returns.* Individual security returns are negatively correlated on a daily basis, positively correlated over intermediate horizons, and negatively correlated over long horizons. Consistent correlation patterns would not exist in highly efficient markets.

- *Mean reversion or a reversal effect in securities prices.* Portfolios of stocks with the best records over the past two to three years subsequently underperform the market, and portfolios of stocks with the worst records over the past two to three years go on to outperform the market.

- *Underreaction to news.* There is significant short-term "drift" in prices following both good and bad news announcements (drift is the tendency for stock prices to keep moving in the same direction).

- *The size effect.* Small stocks outperform large stocks by more than would be expected based on their higher volatility. From 1931 to 1975, the 50 smallest stocks on the NYSE outperformed the 50 largest by 1 percent per month.

- *The price-to-earnings ratio (P/E) or value stock effect.* Studies show that the risk-adjusted returns of the lowest P/E stock portfolios are as much as 7 percent per year larger than the risk-adjusted returns of the highest P/E stock portfolios.

- *The January effect*. Stocks of small-cap companies experience unusually high returns in the first two weeks of January, then their returns revert to average for the rest of the year.

- *Patterns in volatility*. Returns are more volatile during bear markets, market volatility is greater at the open and the close than during the trading day, and overall market volatility is excessive relative to changes in the fundamentals affecting stocks' intrinsic values.

While the EMH remains the most studied theory of how information is reflected in securities prices and is a good entry point for understanding the extent to which prices accurately reflect relevant information, it is also clear that the EMH is subject to much criticism because it does not explain many outcomes observed in financial markets. Next, we'll consider an alternative explanation for investor behavior and the level of rationality reflected in securities prices, known as behavioral finance.

Behavioral Finance

The growing field of behavioral finance can trace its roots to a study by Amos Tversky and Daniel Kahneman, published in *Econometrica* in 1979. Their paper, "Prospect Theory: An Analysis of Decision Under Risk," is the most widely cited work in the history of this influential journal. Their original "prospect theory" has evolved into what we now call behavioral finance, a theory of information, securities prices, and investor behavior that competes with and frequently contradicts the highly rational premises and predictions of the efficient markets hypothesis.

Behavioral finance maintains that investors suffer from cognitive biases, or inefficiencies in the way they process information and draw conclusions. Some of the major biases include the use of **heuristics**, or mental shortcuts that make decision making easier. These mental "rules of thumb" can lead to biased reasoning and suboptimal investment decisions, however, especially when circumstances are changing (because the old mental shortcuts are no longer applicable). **Extrapolation errors**, which occur when investors assume that current and recent conditions will prevail well into the future, also cause them to ignore evidence of changing circumstances. Research by Barber and Odean (2001) shows that people tend to be **overconfident** regarding their abilities, which leads to mistakes such as too little diversification and too much trading. Barber and Odean find that men are more overconfident than women and thus trade more, despite the fact that the performance of their stock portfolios worsened as the tendency to trade increased.

Statman (2010), Nofsinger (2010), and others have identified additional cognitive biases that often derail investors' thinking. Some of the most popular biases include **hindsight error**, which tricks people into thinking they can foretell the future because they can easily observe the past. **Confirmation errors** occur when investors place too much weight on information that confirms their prior opinions (**cognitive consonance**), but underweight or completely disregard evidence that contradicts their prior opinions (**cognitive dissonance**). Whitney Tilson (2005), managing director of the T2 Partners Hedge Fund, cites additional biases that affect the behavior of value investors, including **misunderstanding randomness**, which involves seeing patterns where none exist, and **vividness bias**, which causes investors to overweight particularly memorable experiences, even though they may not be relevant given current circumstances.

A complete treatment of behavioral finance is beyond the scope of this book, but the point should be well made: recent research in this field leaves little doubt that individuals are not consistently rational and frequently make cognitive errors. Behavioral finance adds to our understanding of markets because it alerts us to the many intellectual errors that investors and traders are capable of committing, and allows that aggregate market outcomes can reflect these errors (such as systematic market mispricings, or **bubbles**). Next, we'll consider the latest theory of information and investor behavior, the adaptive markets hypothesis.

The Adaptive Markets Hypothesis

The adaptive markets hypothesis (AMH) views financial markets from a biological perspective. This theory of investor behavior asserts that the interactions among markets, institutions, securities, and investors result in an evolutionary-type process that unfolds according to the laws of "economic selection." The AMH allows for economic agents to adapt via their competitive interactions, but does not require that markets and institutions evolve toward optimal outcomes (see Farmer and Lo 1999; Farmer, 2002; and Lo, 2002, 2004, and 2005). This is the first major conflict between the AHM and the EMH, which maintains that market outcomes are always optimal.

The roots of the AMH can be found in E.O. Wilson's (1975) concept of sociobiology, which applied the principles of competition and natural selection to social interactions. Joseph Schumpeter's (1942) view of business cycles, which emphasized the need for "creative destruction" in capitalism that clears the way for "bursts of entrepreneurial activity," also provides a foundation for the adaptive markets theory.

According to Lo (2008), one of the major proponents of the adaptive markets view, the AMH is preferable as a theory of investor behavior because it allows for the cognitive biases identified by behavioral finance while also recognizing that the high level of competition prevailing in markets requires agents to continually adapt to change. The AMH can explain how market behaviors that appear anomalous under the EMH can emerge, persist for a while, and then disappear. This would include pricing bubbles that can plague markets for years, as well as shorter-term trading fads, such as the "dollar down, stocks up" trade that dominated the U.S. stock market in 2011, and the "risk-on, risk-off" trade, which seemed to be all markets were concerned with for much of 2012. These (and many other) trading opportunities often become popular overnight, dominate traders' thinking for months or years, and then vanish just as quickly as soon as traders adapt and invent new ways to stay ahead of the competition.

Researchers continue to make progress in understanding the connections between emotions, rationality and investor behavior. Some of this research appears to come full circle, such as Lo and Repin's (2002) study, which asserts that emotional responses are not always confusing or harmful, but can actually be important in help-ing investors understand financial risk in real time. These authors document that the ability to channel emotions in specific ways under certain market conditions can be a valuable tool for traders, which contradicts the EMH-based view that strong emo-tions confound the decision-making process because they interfere with rationality.

Summary of the Three Theories   In this section we considered three competing explanations of how information becomes incorporated into securities prices. The first, known as the efficient markets hypothesis, emphasizes a high degree of ratio-nality in the market pricing mechanism. The second, behavioral finance, expressly recognizes that investors commit numerous cognitive errors and that these mistakes can affect market prices. The third, the adaptive markets hypothesis, views markets as a complex evolutionary system in which investors are constantly evolving and adapting to both rational and irrational circumstances. Under the AMH, real-world investors aren't concerned with being rational or irrational—they are just trying to figure out if what worked yesterday will still work today. If not, they quickly move on and invent new methods for remaining competitive.

In the sections that follow, we will consider additional perspectives from well-known investors to further synthesize our understanding of these three theories into a practical investment framework. Renowned investors like John Bogle and Charles Ellis will caution us against careless attempts to beat the market; as we've already established, this can be much harder than it sounds. We'll also consider the results of recent research that examines why some investors trade excessively, and finish with a review of Chapter 23 of John Maynard Keynes's *General Theory of Employment, Interest and Money* (1936), a work that anticipated the efficient mar-kets versus behavioral finance debate decades before academics embraced it in earnest.

■ Additional Perspectives on Investing

This section of the chapter presents a variety of perspectives that will further inform our investment philosophy and guide our efforts to construct and manage a portfolio of stocks that outperforms its benchmark. This section reviews the main points of several articles representative of the approach and analytical methods.

John Bogle: An Index Fund Fundamentalist (2002)

John Bogle is the founder of Vanguard Investments and is widely credited as the cre-ator of the equity index fund. Bogle was invited to review and extend his work re-garding the superiority of indexing by the *Journal of Portfolio Management*, one of the leading investment journals. Bogle shows that for almost all types of equity port-folios (various combinations of large versus small and growth versus value stocks), passively managed index funds earn higher returns with lower risk versus actively managed funds. This finding holds for every category except small-capitalization growth stocks, implying that active managers were able to add value only for stocks that require the most research to fully understand. (Small-cap stocks are less widely followed by analysts, therefore, less information is available about these stocks; growth stocks have little or no previous track records, which means that most of their success or failure is dependent on future activities that are hard to predict.)

Bogle also refutes a view regarding market efficiency by Minor (2001). (If the founder of Vanguard thinks understanding the subtleties of market efficiency is important, then we probably should as well.) Minor makes a clever argument: If investors increasingly believe in market efficiency, they will engage in more indexing and less active investing. After a while, security prices will reflect greater mispricings from this lack of research, and active investors will once again have an advantage as the market becomes less efficient. Bogle disagrees, arguing that Minor does not take the higher costs of active investing into account. Bogle argues that even if active investors earn higher gross returns, after considering the fees they charge, their clients would still have been better off indexing. As reviewed earlier, subsequent research by Barras, Scaillet, and Wermers (2010) confirms that Bogle's view is correct.

Charles Ellis: "Levels of the Game" (2000)

Charles ("Charley") Ellis is a legendary investment manager and the author of 16 books at the latest count. In addition to managing a significant portion of the Yale Endowment for years, he sits on the board of Vanguard Investments, and serves as an associate editor of the two most influential investments journals, *The Journal of Portfolio Management* and *Financial Analysts Journal*. Like John Bogle, Ellis is a valuable source of well-intentioned advice regarding investments and financial markets.

In his 2000 article "Levels of the Game," Ellis cites Bogle's earlier research, which shows that over the most recent 10-year period (at the time the article was published), 89 percent of all actively managed U.S. mutual funds had underperformed their benchmarks. Ellis attributes this underperformance to the increasing competitiveness of the active money management industry, which is dominated by highly educated, motivated professionals—consistent with the view of efficient markets developed earlier in this chapter.

Ellis points out that over the past several decades, professionals have become the market. Well over 90 percent of all trading volume is now generated by the pros, with over 50 percent generated by the top 50 firms. This means that the pros are constantly buying and selling shares to and from each other. Thus, if a firm raises its rating on a stock from hold to buy and wants more shares, they're probably buying from another professional who wants to sell (as Meir Statman (2010) humorously phrases it, "the idiot on the other side of the trade"). Ellis also classifies investing activities into one of five "levels":

- *Level 1: Asset Mix.* Determining the optimal proportion of equities, bonds, currencies, commodities, real estate and cash to hold in a portfolio or fund.

- *Level 2: Equity Mix.* Establishing a "normal" policy of growth versus value stocks, large-cap versus small-cap, and domestic versus international stocks.

- *Level 3: Active versus Passive Management.* This level involves further implementation of the normal policy established in Levels 1 and 2, specifically addressing the proportion of an investor's assets that should be in active versus passive vehicles.

- *Level 4: Specific Manager Selection.* Deciding which investment firms will manage each component of the investor's portfolio.

- *Level 5: Active Portfolio Management.* Deciding when to change portfolio strategy, the selection of specific securities or assets, and how to execute transactions.

Ellis's experience has led him to believe that keeping investors focused on Levels 1 and 2 helps them avoid major mistakes and, most important, maximizes their wealth accumulations over long horizons. Notice that Ellis's advice regarding the need to diversify and hold positions for long periods is consistent with the efficient markets hypothesis, and how his recommendation that investors avoid complex, higher-level activities that result in more errors that lower their portfolio returns follows from behavioral finance.

Charles Ellis: "The Winner's Game" (2003)

One of the most valuable perspectives Ellis provides in his 2003 article "The Winner's Game" is to partition life's activities into one of two categories: winner's games and loser's games. In loser's games, outcomes are most often determined by participant mistakes—like amateur tennis. In winner's games, however, outcomes are usually determined by decisive winning moves, as is the case in most high-level professional sports. Ellis's point is that individuals are the amateurs in the game of investments, and should focus more on minimizing mistakes instead of attempting higher-level winning moves versus professional investors. Additionally, with so many well-trained investments professionals competing against each other, individuals should not be incurring the costs of competing with the pros. Ellis stresses that individuals need to remain aware that in most cases they are disadvantaged in terms of the information they possess, the trading strategies they're capable of executing (and the skill with which they can trade), and their total cost of trading.

Perhaps the most valuable perspective Ellis brings to the active investing debate is his belief that *active investing triggers a higher error rate*, and that this is the most plausible explanation regarding why actively managed equity funds underperform their benchmarks so consistently. His recommendation: "Most investors would benefit from giving more attention to their defenses, and to not losing." Ellis is also well versed in behavioral finance, as illustrated by the following advice regarding which mistakes to avoid:

1. We are confirmation-biased—we seek out and overweight the significance of data that support our initial impressions.
2. We allow ourselves to use an initial idea or fact as a reference point for future decisions even when we know it is "just a number" (the behavioral error known as "framing" or "anchoring").
3. We distort our perceptions of our decisions, almost always in our favor, so that we believe we are better than we really are at making decisions (cognitive consonance).
4. We have a tendency to be overconfident.

Ellis closes his article by pointing out that another common error he sees investors make is switching to a new money manager with a superior record just as that manager is about to begin underperforming. This is consistent with the previously reviewed research findings on mean reversion, which describes how portfolios that outperform their benchmarks for two- to three-year periods tend to underperform over the next two to three years (and vice versa).

Dorn, Dorn, and Sengmueller: "Why Do People Trade?" (2008)

This article by Dorn, Dorn, and Sengmueller (2008) is based on a previous paper entitled "Trading as Entertainment." The bottom line of the study is that investors who indicated on surveys that they "enjoy investing" and "enjoy risky propositions" traded twice as much as peer investors. The authors provide us with an important conclusion: "Entertainment appears to be a straightforward explanation for why . . . active traders trade much more than others, and why active traders underperform their peers after transactions costs." The Dorn et al. findings complement results from the behavioral finance literature and Ellis's advice: sticking to a simple game plan and avoiding cognitive errors should be an important part of an investor's strategy. These authors remind us to ask ourselves: "Am I trading for strategic or tactical reasons, or simply to entertain myself?"

John Maynard Keynes: Chapter 23 of the *General Theory*

Keynes' *General Theory of Employment, Interest and Money* is an inarguable classic in the economics literature. In Chapter 23 Keynes dispenses practical advice for investors, along with many keen observations about human nature. His genius—and elegant writing style—are on full display. Keynes's unique perspectives can be attributed to the many roles he undertook in his lifetime. He served as chancellor of the Exchequer in England (equivalent to secretary of the Treasury in the United States) during the Great Depression. Accordingly, much of his *General Theory* is concerned with understanding how free-market economies can jolt themselves out of depressionary cycles. In addition to being recognized as one of the most brilliant economists of his day, Keynes was also a currency speculator; much of his advice therefore stems from his practical experiences as an investor. He amassed a significant fortune through his trading activities, lost it all, and earned it back again. In the analysis of Keynes's Chapter 23 that follows, notice in particular how he anticipates both the efficient markets and behavioral finance theories, which would be further developed by economists and psychologists decades later.

Long-Term Expectations   Keynes begins with a thought experiment on how investors form their expectations regarding the future. Keynes writes that it would be foolish to put too much weight on matters that are highly uncertain (the future is, of course, inherently unknown). In particular, Keynes has noticed that humans have a habit of taking the current situation—whatever it is—and extrapolating it into the future, until they see definite evidence that they need to change that expectation (behavioral finance now refers to these tendencies as "extrapolation errors").

Keynes goes on to write that our long-term expectations should not depend only on the best forecast we can make, but also on the certainty with which we can make this forecast. Predictions regarding the future are usually made on an extremely precarious basis, but investors are overconfident regarding their ability to forecast (here he anticipates the overconfidence bias identified by the behaviorists).

Keynes then launches into a long meditation on the state of business and financial markets in the 1930s. He notes that, in earlier times, business ventures were started by people who focused less on precise calculations of profits and returns, and more on the adventure associated with the enterprise. These old-time entrepreneurs often earned lower returns than they had planned on—but, according to Keynes, earning high returns was not their primary focus; they were more concerned with building something.

Keynes is particularly concerned with how the stock market allows for such a profound disconnection between ownership and management—something that was relatively new in his day, but we take for granted in the twenty-first century. With this observation Keynes anticipates another field of finance and economics, known as agency theory, which has long recognized the "separation of ownership and control" as a key factor contributing to suboptimal corporate performance.

Long-Term Expectations and Stock Values

Keynes connects his ideas regarding how long-term expectations are formed and the way modern financial markets allow for investment valuation to be determined by those who are far removed from the operations of the businesses. Thus, he notes, stock values may often reflect irrelevant concerns and ideas, and not the close knowledge of the people actually running the companies. Keynes not only anticipates the efficient markets hypothesis with this statement but goes on to criticize the idea. He notes that the convention in the stock market is to assume that whatever value a stock is selling for is correct, and that the habit of continuously projecting the current state of affairs into the future is what led to both the 1920s stock market bubble and the prolonged bear market of the 1930s (extrapolation errors). Keynes asserts that in both cases prices remained on a trend determined by people who don't really know what's going on in the businesses they are valuing (a question of market efficiency). Additionally, note that Keynes is working on the problems of asset bubbles and market crashes over half a century before the dot-com, credit, and residential real estate bubbles wreaked havoc on modern markets.

Keynes Says Markets Can't Be Efficient

Keynes reinforces his point that market valuations cannot be correct most of the time because they result from a flawed expectations-forming process conducted by people who are far removed from the businesses they are valuing. Keynes says these conventions persist because people like the appearance of stability and continuity in their daily lives. This makes people feel that, at least in the short term, they are not exposed to excessive risk, because stock values must at least be close to their fair value (cognitive consonance). Of course, Keynes believes people are deluding themselves in this regard:

Due to the gradual increase in the proportion of equity owned by persons who neither manage nor have special knowledge of the enterprise, the element of real knowledge in the valuation of investments has declined. Day-to-day fluctuations in the profits of existing investments, which are obviously of an ephemeral nature, have an excessive—even absurd—influence on markets.

Groundless Expectations Are the Source of Excessive Volatility One of the criticisms of the EMH is that securities prices exhibit more volatility than would be justified based on changes in companies' fundamentals alone. Keynes asserts that investors' "groundless expectations" are actually the source of this excess market volatility:

> A conventional valuation that is established as the outcome of the mass psychology of a large number of ignorant individuals is liable to change violently as the result of a sudden fluctuation of opinion due to factors that do not really make much difference to future returns, since there will be no strong roots to hold it steady.

Keynes goes on to say that during abnormal times when things are changing fast, and investors are deprived of the comfort of believing in the "indefinite continuance of the existing state of affairs," markets will be subject to waves of optimistic and pessimistic sentiment that is irrational, but also somewhat legitimate, because no solid basis exists for reasonable calculations of any sort. Even though Keynes is describing his own mid-1930s period, his observations also apply to the behavior of global financial markets from 2008 to 2013, an era characterized by alternating periods of both unusually high and low volatility.

Investment Professionals and Market Efficiency Keynes goes on to write that there is one viewpoint in particular that deserves our attention. We might suppose that competition among expert professionals, who are supposed to have knowledge beyond that of the average private investor, would correct the pricing mistakes committed by ignorant individuals. Not exactly, Keynes says:

> The energies and skill of the professional investor are not concerned with making long-term forecasts of the probable return of an investment, but with foreseeing changes in valuation a short time ahead of the public. Professional investors are not concerned with what an investment is worth to a man who buys it "for keeps," but rather what the market will value it at, under the influence of mass psychology, three months or a year hence. Moreover, this behavior is not the result of a wrong-headed propensity...it is not sensible to pay $25 for an investment you believe is worth $30 if you also believe the market will value it at $20 in three months.

How the Pros Play the Game Keynes further writes that the professional investor is therefore forced to concern himself with the anticipation of impending changes—in the news or in the atmosphere—that most influence the mass psychology of the market. This is an inevitable result of investment markets organized with the goal of so-called "liquidity" (which Keynes calls a "fetish"). Keynes's point is that there is no such thing as liquidity for the entire investment community at the same time. When everyone wants to sell, there is no liquidity without dramatic price declines (a.k.a. panic). This, of course, describes the essence of our recent global financial crisis. From 2000 to 2007 there was a boom in the origination of mortgage loans to people who could not afford to make the payments. Many of these loans were created simply because they could be bundled into complex financial instruments and sold to the next greater fool. Everything worked fine until the day that *everyone* wanted to sell their securities, which caused the market—and the balance sheets of most large banks—to collapse.

Keynes goes on to say that the game of investing might be called "beat the gun." The investors he knows are more concerned with outwitting the crowd and passing the "bad, ever-depreciating half-crown to the other fellow." Keynes further notes that this game can be played by professional investors among themselves. No uninformed individuals are required, and it is not even necessary that any of the players believe in the long-term validity of the value of any of the securities they are trading.

Keynes's Famous Beauty Contest Analogy   This is probably Keynes's most memorable passage. He compares professional investing to newspaper competitions that were popular in his day in which readers voted for the prettiest faces from a hundred photographs. Depending on which face they voted for, readers' choices were placed into a jar, and a winning card was randomly selected from the jar containing the most votes. Keynes says that the stock market works just like this game. Intelligent investors don't simply pick the stocks they think are best, but the winning strategy instead involves anticipating which face will get the most votes. If your card is not in the right jar—determined by popular opinion—then you cannot win the contest:

> It is not a case of choosing those faces which, to the best of one's judgment, are really the prettiest, nor even those which average opinion genuinely thinks the prettiest. We have reached the third degree where we devote our intelligences to anticipating what average opinion expects the average opinion to be.

The Reduced Role of Fundamental Investors   Next, Keynes anticipates—and refutes—the type of objections that believers in market efficiency still raise today:

> If the reader is motivated to interject that there must surely be large profits to be gained in the long run by a skilled individual who remains undistracted by the prevailing pastime and continues to purchase investments on the best genuine long-term expectations he can frame, he must be answered, first of all, that there are such serious-minded individuals, and that it makes a vast difference to an investment market whether or not they predominate in their influence over the game-players.

But Keynes adds that there are several factors that jeopardize the predominance of such individuals in modern investment markets:

> Investment based on genuine long-term expectation is so difficult to-day that it is basically impractical. He who attempts it must surely lead more laborious days and run greater risks than he who tries to guess better than the crowd how the crowd will behave; and, given equal intelligence, he may make more disastrous mistakes.

This statement echoes Ellis's advice about the importance of avoiding mistakes.

Keynes's Warning for Long-Term Investors

> Notice that it is the long-term investor—he who most promotes the public interest—who will in practice come under the greatest criticism whenever investment funds are managed by committees or boards or banks. For it is the essence of his behavior that he should appear eccentric, unconventional and rash in the eyes of average opinion. If he is successful, that will only confirm his rashness; and if in the short run he is unsuccessful, which is very likely, he not receive much mercy.

Keynes has a little career advice for us as well: "Worldly wisdom teaches that it is better for one's reputation to fail conventionally than to succeed unconventionally." (I have found this to be an ironic truth in my own professional career path from time to time.)

Keynes on Bubbles

> Speculators may do little or no harm when they are only bubbles on a steady stream of long-term investors; but they can be seriously harmful when long-term investors become the bubble on a whirlpool of speculators. When the capital development of a country becomes a by-product of the activities of a casino, the job is likely to be ill-done.

And Keynes coins a term—bubble—that has remained in the investor's lexicon ever since.

Animal Spirits

> A large proportion of our positive activities depend on spontaneous optimism rather than on a mathematical expectation. Our decisions to do something positive are usually taken as a result of animal spirits—a spontaneous urge to action rather than inaction—and not as the outcome of a weighted average of quantitative benefits multiplied by quantitative probabilities. If the animal spirits are dimmed and the spontaneous optimism falters, leaving us to depend on nothing but a mathematical expectation, enterprise will fade and die.

Animal spirits is another Keynes term that investors and traders still use every day.

■ Professional Investment Policy Statements

We will wrap up this chapter by examining a professional investment policy statement (IPS) and synthesizing the viewpoints from this chapter into a sample IPS that summarizes the type of stocks we'll be looking for and the type of portfolio we'll construct using these stocks. An IPS makes clear statements about an investor's or fund's objectives, return expectations, risk tolerance, time horizon, and portfolio allocations. Highlights from the IPS from Morgan Stanley's Focus Growth Strategy team are presented below. You will notice similarities with items mentioned in this chapter (including market efficiency), as well as considerations such as favorable trends in return on invested capital, focusing on free cash flow instead of accounting earnings, taking a long-term perspective, and analyzing whether a company has a genuine competitive advantage that is sustainable.

Morgan Stanley Focus Growth Strategy Profile (2013, Edited)

Investment Philosophy[2]

- Permitted market capitalization: within the market capitalization of the benchmark index

- Sector concentrations result from security selection; no specified minimum or maximum exposure

- Security weight: 1 to 5 percent of the portfolio

- Typical number of holdings: 20–30 securities

- Invest in high-quality established and emerging companies

- The investment team seeks companies with:

  - Inherent sustainable competitive advantages

  - Favorable return on invested capital trends

  - Long-term capital appreciation rather than short-term events

- Stock selection is informed by rigorous fundamental analysis

- Guiding principles combined with intellectual and process flexibility are critical to strong decision-making in pursuit of attractive investments

When assessing businesses, the team seeks to capitalize on market inefficiencies by investing in companies that it believes are underappreciated due to one or more of the following reasons:

- *Relative lack of coverage.* Companies transitioning from one market capitalization category to another—as well as recapitalizations or spin-offs—tend to be underfollowed, creating potential investment opportunities for the team.

- *Conventional valuation bias:* There is a tendency to view companies with low price-to-earnings (P/E) ratios as more attractive than those with higher ratios. However, the team believes that earnings-related measures can be limiting, as they do not incorporate the return on invested capital (ROIC) or free-cash-flow generation profile of a company. In addition, corporate earnings can often make comparisons both within industries and across sectors less meaningful.

- *Coverage bias.* Experts typically use traditional valuation rules of thumb to assess companies in their coverage areas—rules that the team believes may be less appropriate in analyzing companies with new or unique business models that are generating substantially different economic value.

- *Short-term bias.* The team believes that it can exploit inefficiencies stemming from the fact that market participants increasingly focus on short-term considerations (such as quarterly earnings) in their analysis rather than on long-term value creation.

Investment Process   The team follows a disciplined investment process that entails the following steps:

- *Idea generation.* The team generates investment ideas through an ongoing set of activities conducted individually and collaboratively, including: (1) involvement in contact networks across industries and in the investment management business; (2) its reading network; (3) its focus on ROIC and free-cash-flow yield; (4) team discussions; (5) the identification of patterns; (6) conventional-valuation and coverage biases, among others; and (7) continual research on current company holdings.

- *Bottom-up analysis and valuation.* The team narrows its idea generation by seeking stocks that reside in the intersection between its views of a company's business quality, growth quality, and risk/reward characteristics (see diagram, Figure 22.11). Valuation focuses on free-cash-flow yield three to five years in the future.

- *Disruptive change research.* To complement its in-depth, bottom-up research, the team's disruptive change researcher investigates big ideas and emerging themes that typically may have far-reaching consequences, such as nanotech, infrastructure and the global water shortage.

- *Portfolio construction and implementation.* The team's portfolios are actively managed and built to maximize expected value. Company weightings are primarily determined by the quality of the idea and the team's conviction. Each member of the investment team helps drive stock-picking, with at least two of the three most senior members typically involved in final construction decisions. The team reviews factor analysis on a monthly basis in order to ensure that the portfolio's risk is more idiosyncratic than systematic. The team anticipates holding between 20 and 30 securities.

- *Culture.* The team's culture is shaped by four core values that are cultivated and reinforced in many ways: intellectual curiosity and flexibility, perspective, self-awareness, and partnership.

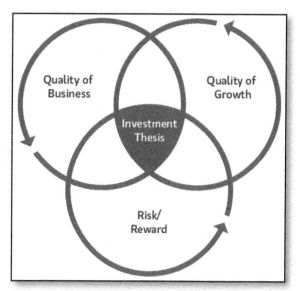

FIGURE 22.11 The Investment Thesis: Business Quality, Growth Quality, and Risk/Reward Trade-off.

Source: Morgan Stanley Investment Management (2013).

A Sample Investment Policy

After reading through the highlights of the Morgan Stanley IPS, you should be ready to draft one for your portfolio or student investment fund. Following is a draft of a basic IPS (adapted from Krinsky and Hall (2012) and Putnam Investments (2013)):

Description of the Client. The University Foundation (or other entity).

Purpose of the IPS. To establish a clear understanding between the investor and the adviser regarding the Student Investment Fund's (SIF) objectives for return, risk management, security suitability, and portfolio review.

Duties of the Parties. The adviser shall design and implement an appropriate portfolio, monitor the performance of the portfolio, periodically review the investment strategy and investment policy statement, and prepare and make available all related reports. The University Foundation will promptly notify the adviser of changes in risk tolerance or other issues pertaining to security suitability.

Objectives: Return. The SIF aims to outperform the S&P 500 on a risk-adjusted basis over the long term. We favor large-capitalization stocks with sustainable competitive advantages that earn a high return on invested capital and pay above-average dividends.

Objectives: Risk. The SIF targets a level of risk (defined as portfolio beta) equal to or less than the S&P 500.

Constraints: Sector Weightings. None. Sector concentrations result from a combination of macroeconomic analysis and favorable investment opportunities identified by stock-specific fundamental analysis; no specified minimum or maximum exposure to any particular sector.

Constraints: Liquidity. None. The SIF's goal is to be fully invested in equities at all times.

Constraints: Time Horizon. The SIF assumes an infinite time horizon. The investment thesis for all securities must specify if the security is a short-term (1–2 years) or long-term (3–5 years) component of the SIF portfolio. Short-term positions are limited to 50 percent of the portfolio's holdings.

Constraints: Taxes. The University Foundation is a tax-free not-for-profit.

Constraints: Legal and Regulatory. The SIF strives to maintain compliance with the Uniform Prudent Investor Act (UPIA) to the best of its ability, subject to the constraints it faces in terms of enrollment and the current class's ability to perform a comprehensive portfolio review.

Unique Circumstances. No leverage, short selling, derivative securities or non-equity securities. The SIF invests in equities and cash. Equities may be U.S. or international, provided the security trades on a major U.S. exchange (American depositary receipts, or ADRs, are acceptable securities for the SIF).

Asset Allocation Targets and Ranges. U.S./global equities approaching 100 percent, with a small cash balance until proceeds from security sales or dividends can be prudently reinvested.

Guidelines for Portfolio Adjustments and Rebalancing. The SIF's goal is to review the entire portfolio annually. A full allocation to a new position is approximately 5 percent of the total value of the portfolio. Positions approaching 10 percent of the total value of the portfolio must be reviewed for possible rebalancing in the current or next semester.

Sell Discipline. We will reduce or sell a position if valuation levels significantly exceed industry or sector averages, a previous investment thesis is invalidated by subsequent events, our confidence in management's integrity and ability to execute is compromised, or new ideas offer better risk/reward profiles than an existing holding. If a stock experiences a sudden decline and our research signals a deterioration of our original investment thesis, we will sell the position.

Schedule for Portfolio and IPS Review. Annually, or as permitted by course enrollment and the capacity of the current class to perform a complete portfolio review.

■ Summary

- Active equity investors seek to outperform a market index benchmark by identifying individual stocks to buy and sell.

- Passive investors buy and hold stock portfolios for the long term or choose other investment vehicles that minimize costs, including research costs, trading costs, administrative costs, performance fees, and taxes on realized gains.

- The fundamental analysis process featured in this book is termed *top-down* because it begins with an analysis of the overall economy. Gauging the stage of the business cycle in which the economy is operating helps an analyst identify sectors of the stock market to over- and underweight in pursuit of market-beating returns.

- Passive investors outperform active investors in the aggregate.

- Research suggests that two main factors contribute to the outperformance of passive investors: lower costs of trading and committing fewer cognitive errors.

- Active investors need a theory, or model, of how rapidly and accurately new information affects stock prices.

- The three main theories of information and prices are the efficient markets hypothesis, behavioral finance, and the adaptive markets hypothesis.

- An investment policy statement makes clear statements about an investor's or fund's objectives, return expectations, risk tolerance, time horizon, and portfolio allocations that inform the decisions of stock analysts and portfolio managers.

NOTES

1. If we were conducting a formal academic study, we would have also adjusted IBM's stock returns around the announcement for risk by taking IBM's risk (measured as beta) into account.
2. Excerpted with permission of Morgan Stanley Investment Management, © 2013.

■ References

Barber, Brad, and Terry Odean. 2001. "Boys Will Be Boys: Gender, Overconfidence, and Common Stock Investment." *Quarterly Journal of Economics* 116: 261–92.

Barras, Laurent, Olivier Scaillet, and Russ Wermers. 2010. "False Discoveries in Mutual Fund Performance: Measuring Luck in Estimated Alphas." *Journal of Finance* 65, February 179–216.

Bogle, John. 2002. "An Index Fund Fundamentalist Goes Back to the Drawing Board." *Journal of Portfolio Management*, Spring 31–38.

Carhart, M. 1997. "On Persistence in Mutual Fund Performance." *Journal of Finance* 52: 57–82.

Dorn, Anne, Daniel Dorn, and Paul Sengmueller. 2008. "Why Do People Trade?" *Journal of Applied Finance,* Fall/Winter: 37–50.

Eavis, Peter. April 27, 2012. "Analyzing the Unusual Items in Amazon's Earnings." Dealbook, *New York Times Online*, http://dealbook.nytimes.com/2012/04/27/analyzing-the-unusual-items-in-amazons-earnings/. Accessed January 28, 2013.

Ellis, Charles D. "Levels of the Game." *Journal of Portfolio Management,* Winter: 12–15.

Ellis, Charles D. "The Winner's Game." *Journal of Portfolio Management,* Spring: 27–24.

Elton, Edwin, Martin Gruber, Sanjiv Das, and Matthew Hlavka. 1993. "Efficiency with Costly Information: A Reinterpretation of Evidence from Managed Portfolios." *Review of Financial Studies* 6(1): 1–22.

Farmer, D. 2002. "Market Force, Ecology and Evolution." *Industrial and Corporate Change* 11: 895–953.

Farmer, Doyne, and Andrew Lo. 1999. "Frontiers of Finance: Evolution and Efficient Markets." *Proceedings of the National Academy of Sciences* 96: 9991–92.

Fung, H., X. Xu, and J. Yau. 2004. "Do Hedge Fund Managers Display Skill?" *Journal of Investing* 6 (4): 22–31.

Hulbert, Mark. 2008. "The Prescient Are Few." *New York Times*, July 13, www.nytimes.com/2008/07/13/business/13stra.html. Accessed March 2013.

Keynes, John Maynard. 2010. *The General Theory of Employment, Interest and Money*. Whitefish, MT: Kessinger Publishing, LLC (originally published in 1936).

Krinsky, Simon, and Kathryn Hall. 2012, March. "A Roadmap for the Roadmap: Creating an Investment Policy Statement for Endowments and Foundations." San Francisco, CA: Hall Capital Partners, LLC.

Lo, A. 2008. "Where Do Alphas Come From?" Working paper, MIT Sloan School of Management and AlphaSimplex Group (October).

Lo, A., and D. Repin. 2002. "The Psychophysiology of Real-Time Financial Risk Processing." *Journal of Cognitive Neuroscience* 14: 323–39.

Lo, Andrew. 2002. "Bubble, Rubble, Finance in Trouble?" *Journal of Psychology and Financial Markets* 3: 76–86.

Lo, Andrew. 2004. "The Adaptive Markets Hypothesis: Market Efficiency from an Evolutionary Perspective." *Journal of Portfolio Management* 30: 15–29.

Lo, Andrew. 2005. "Reconciling Efficient Markets with Behavioral Finance: The Adaptive Markets Hypothesis." *Journal of Investment Consulting* 7: 21–44.

Lowe, Janet. 1997. *Warren Buffett Speaks: Wit and Wisdom from the World's Greatest Investor*. New York: John Wiley & Sons.

Ludwig, Olly. 2012. "Passive Reigns as of First Half of 2012." Index Universe. Available online at www.indexuniverse.com/sections/features/14686-spiva-passive-reigns-as-of-first-half-2012.html. Accessed January 28, 2013.

Malkiel, Burton, and Atanu Saha. 2005. "Hedge Funds: Risk and Return." *Financial Analysts Journal* 61(6): 80–88.

Minor, Dylan. 2001. "Beware of Index Fund Fundamentalists." *Journal of Portfolio Management,* Summer: 45–50.

Morgan Stanley. 2013. *Focus Growth Strategy Profile*. New York: Morgan Stanley Investment Management.

Nofinsger, John. 2010. *The Psychology of Investing*. Upper Saddle River, NJ: Prentice Hall.

O'Hara, N. 2009. "They're Supposed to Be Better Than This." *Institutional Investor,* February 19. Available online at www.institutionalinvestor.com/Article/2113414/Theyre-Supposed-to-Be-Better-Than-This.html. Accessed January 28, 2013.

Pojarliev, M., and R. M. Levich. 2008. "Do Professional Currency Managers Beat the Benchmark?" *Financial Analysts Journal* 64(5): 18–32.

Putnam Investments. 2013. "Investment Policy Statement and Sample Checklist." Putnam Investments, available online at https://content.putnam.com/literature/pdf/ID093.pdf. Accessed January 28, 2013.

Schumpeter, J. 1975. *Capitalism, Socialism and Democracy.* New York: Harper (originally published in 1942).

Standard & Poor's. 2008. Standard & Poor's Indices Versus Active Funds (SPIVA) Scorecard, Mid-Year 2008, November 12, www.standardandpoors.com. Accessed March 2013.

Statman, Meir. 2010. *What Investors Really Want*. New York: McGraw-Hill.

Tilson, W. 2005, November. "Applying Behavioral Finance to Value Investing." Monograph. Denver, CO: T2 Partners LLC.

Wilson, E. 1975. *Sociobiology: The New Synthesis*. Cambridge, MA: Belknap Press of Harvard University Press.

MARKETS

Market participants are prone to the weaknesses commonly found in human psychology. The field of behavioral finance documents the tendency of investors to underappreciate or overreact to otherwise significant data. The CMT Level II text includes these chapters as a way of helping candidates understand what kind of influence the natural human biases of individual investors can have on the market.

■ What Candidates Need to Know

Candidates should be able to identify how various perception biases and cognitive errors, when evident among larger groups of market participants, can influence overall market trends.

CHAPTER 23

Prospect Theory

From Edwin T. Burton and Sunit N. Shah,
Behavioral Finance (Hoboken, New Jersey:
John Wiley & Sons, 2013), Chapter 9.

Learning Objective Statements

- Describe two insights from prospect theory
- Describe the single greatest limitation of prospect theory

Economists assume each individual has a function that maps from every possible relevant level of wealth to a number that represents his or her happiness, and that under uncertainty each individual acts to maximize the expected level of happiness. One objection to expected utility is known as the Allais Paradox.

A second problem with expected utility maximization lies in the assumption that individuals make decisions under uncertainty based solely on the eventual levels of his or her wealth. One simple way to see that this is unlikely to be a good approximation of human behavior is to realize that most individuals are unable to report their levels of wealth in a short amount of time within a reasonable degree of accuracy. Consumers could not be acting based on anticipated levels of wealth if they are not even aware of current wealth levels.

So if wealth isn't the issue, what is?

■ The Reference Point

Consider the following set of choices, taken from Kahneman:[1]

In addition to what you already own, you receive $1,000 for sure and either:

- Another $500 for sure, or
- A 50 percent chance of nothing and a 50 percent chance of $1,000.

Second, consider this alternative set of choices.

In addition to what you already own, you receive $2,000 for sure and either:

---

[1] Daniel Kahneman, *Thinking, Fast and Slow* (New York: Farrar, Straus and Giroux, 2011), 280.

- Lose $500 for sure, or
- Face a 50 percent chance of losing nothing and a 50 percent chance of losing $1,000.

A large majority of respondents picked the first option in the first choice set and the second option in the second choice set. Note, however, that the two choice sets represent exactly the same ending levels of wealth—what you own plus $1,500 versus what you own plus a 50 percent chance of $1,000 and a 50 percent chance of $2,000.

What is different in the two examples is the reference point. In the first example, individuals use an initial wealth of $1,000 as their beginning reference point. When considering their choices, they exhibit risk aversion, preferring the certain gain of $500 over a risky choice with an identical expected value.

In the second choice set, individuals consider $2,000 as their reference point and see a decision between a certain loss or a risky alternative with the identical expected value. In this case, the majority of individuals choose the latter option— the risky one—even though there is no risk premium to compensate them for the expected risk. In this second choice situation, individuals tend to be risk seekers, not risk averters, as in the first choice.

Economists generally would have ruled this possibility out entirely because agents would have been assumed to be risk averse in levels of wealth, and this risk aversion would apply regardless of the reference point. In contrast, what this example demonstrates is that individuals may be risk averse when considering gains but risk seeking when considering losses.

■ The S-Curve

Consider another choice between two lotteries:

- Get $900 for sure, or
- Have a 90 percent chance of getting $1,000.

Now consider this alternative set of choices:

- Lose $900 for sure, or
- Have a 90 percent chance of losing $1,000.[2]

In the first choice set, the expected value of each option is $900. Since the latter option carries more risk, a risk-averse individual would choose the first option, while a risk-loving individual would choose the second. In the latter choice set, both options have an expected value of −$900 (i.e., losing $900). The second option carries more risk, and hence would be chosen only by a risk-loving person, whereas a risk-averse individual would choose the first option.

In practice, most individuals choose the first option in the first choice set as expected. However, most choose the second option in the second choice set. In other

---

[2] Kahneman, 280.

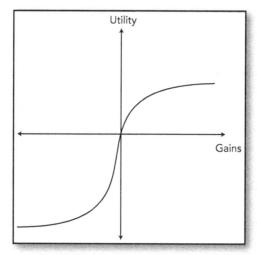

FIGURE 23.1   The S-Curve.

words, when facing potential losses, individuals become risk loving rather than risk averse. This occurrence is irrespective of their initial levels of wealth—all that matters is that they take their current levels of wealth as their reference points and face losses from there.

This behavior is not particular to this example; it is typical of the way people make choices when facing potential losses, which is fundamentally different than the way people make choices when facing potential gains. Figure 23.1 summarizes this phenomenon graphically.

For gains, an individual's utility function is concave,[3] representing his or her risk aversion. Conversely, for losses, the utility function is convex, representing risk-loving behavior.[4]

But there is more to the graph in Figure 23.1 than that observation.

■ Loss Aversion

The segment of the curve representing losses is steeper than that representing gains. This reflects the fact that for the representative individual, losses hurt much more than commensurate gains help.

As an example, consider choosing whether to take a gamble in which you have a 50 percent chance of getting $150 and a 50 percent chance of losing $100. Despite the positive expected value, most people find this lottery unappealing because the psychological cost of losing $100 is greater than the psychological gain of earning $150. This phenomenon is called *loss aversion*.[5] In the previous example,

---

[3] Concave means the second derivative is negative, as shown in the portion of the curve above the gains axis.

[4] Convex means the second derivative is positive, as depicted in the segment of the curve below gains axis.

[5] Kahneman, 283–284.

some may need a potential gain of $200 or so, or about twice as high as the loss, to accept the gamble. This loss aversion ratio has been estimated at between 1.5 and 2.5 in practice.

One might think that this loss-averse behavior could be explained by traditional wealth-based utility functions. However, in a now-famous theorem by Matthew Rabin,[6] such attempts yield ludicrous implications for human behavior in the face of other gambles. For example, Rabin shows that any individual with a concave utility function in wealth that rejects the gamble "50 percent chance of losing $100 and 50 percent chance of gaining $200" also rejects the gamble "50 percent chance of losing $200 and 50 percent chance of winning $20,000." In practice, many people might reject the former gamble, whereas very few would reject the latter.

Rabin showed that under traditional decision theory, an individual with initial wealth of $290,000 who would reject a 50/50[7] gamble of losing $100 or gaining $110 for any initial level of wealth under $300,000 must also reject a 50/50 gamble of losing $1,000 or gaining $718,190. Finally, one who would reject a 50/50 gamble of losing $100 or gaining $125 for any initial level of wealth must also reject a 50/50 gamble of losing $600 or gaining any positive amount of money, regardless of how large the potential gain is.[8]

It is not likely that these implications would hold up in practice. One could envision an individual rejecting a 50/50 gamble of winning $100 or losing $110, but it is hard to envision someone rejecting a 50/50 gamble of losing $600 or winning $10 million.

Loss aversion has an important implication for utility theory—specifically, that decisions in the face of uncertainty are *path dependent*. If an individual gains $500 and then loses $500, traditional wealth-based utility theory would predict that there was no change in the individual's happiness after both transactions took place. However, under prospect theory,[9] if there were enough time between the two transactions that the individual reset her reference point to the wealth level after the gain, she would feel an overall loss in happiness over the two transactions. Initially, she feels a benefit from the gain, but under loss aversion, the disutility she feels from the subsequent loss outweighs that benefit so that the net change is negative.

This feature of prospect theory has important consequences for utility theory. When looking at the decisions an individual makes over time, traditional wealth-based utility theory looks at the net change in wealth over the course of all decisions to assess the overall impact on utility. Under prospect theory, one must look at each

THEORY AND ANALYSIS

---

[6] Matthew Rabin, "Risk Aversion and Expected-Utility Theory: A Calibration Theorem," *Econometrica* 68, no. 5 (September 2000):1281–1292.

[7] 50/50 means there is a 50 percent chance of each alternative outcome occurring.

[8] Rabin, 1284–1285.

[9] Prospect theory was introduced by Daniel Kahneman and Amos Tversky in 1979. Prospect theory is an attempt to formalize a utility function approach that captures the concept of loss aversion. Daniel Kahneman and Amos Tversky, "Prospect Theory: An Analysis of Decision Under Risk," *Econometrica*, 47(1979): 263–291.

of the movements in wealth in turn because the path one takes to get from initial wealth to ending wealth impacts the overall change in happiness.

This path dependence complicates the task of examining human behavior when facing various choice decisions. An econometrician who wishes to model the behavior of agents under prospect theory needs to acquire a data set complete with every decision the agent makes over time as well as the outcome of each such decision. In the case of modeling stock-trading behavior, this data set would not only need the outcome of each trade executed, but also the paper gains or losses at each time when the trader checked his or her portfolio, and the econometrician would need to approximate the trader's thoughts on the distribution of possible returns at each time the portfolio is checked as well. This is a rather onerous task, unnecessary for applications that rely on traditional utility theory, which would require data only on trades that were executed or possibly even just on the beginning and ending portfolio contents and values. Acquiring end-of-period data is a significantly easier task than acquiring much of the data within periods and part of the reason why traditional utility theory has remained a much more attractive modeling technique for finance theory.

■ Prospect Theory in Practice

Prospect theory has been tested in a variety of experimental settings, even in contexts outside of finance. List[10] looked at the behavior of individuals in a well-functioning marketplace and found that newcomers to the marketplace behaved in better accordance with prospect theory than with traditional utility models. Bleichrodt and colleagues[11] examine the behavior of individuals when the payoffs are in states of health rather than in monetary amounts and also finds that prospect theory explained the agents' behavior better than traditional expected utility theory did. Similar implications have been found outside of the experimental setting.

The implications of prospect theory for finance are profound. If investors consider paper gains and losses each time they check their portfolios, then not only will loss aversion tend to drive their choices, but the frequency with which they check their portfolios will greatly affect the decisions they make as well. How frequently one checks one's portfolio will lead to different levels of utility and to different investment decisions. Such behavior could account for a significant premium in markets with more active investors despite any risk factors for which such a premium should be rewarded.

---

[10] John A. List, "Neoclassical Theory Versus Prospect Theory: Evidence from the Marketplace," *Econometrica* 72, no. 2 (2004): 615–625.

[11] H. Bleichrodt, J. M. Abellan, J. L. Pinto, and I. Mendez, "Resolving Inconsistencies in Utility Measurement under Risk: Tests of Generalizations of Expected Utility," *Management Science* 53(2007): 469–482.

■ Drawbacks of Prospect Theory

Despite the benefits of prospect theory in modeling how humans make decisions, the theory is not complete. There are many aspects of human behavior that are inconsistent with the implications of prospect theory. Consider the following prospects:

- A one in a thousand chance to win $1 million.
- A 90 percent chance to win $10 and a 10 percent chance to win nothing.
- A 90 percent chance to win $1 million and a 10 percent chance to win nothing.

The possibility of winning nothing exists in each choice, but it would be difficult to argue the impact of winning nothing would be the same in each case. In the first case, winning nothing is the expected outcome. In the second, it's not expected, but it would not be too harmful a result, since the individual only missed out on winning $10. However, in the last case, winning nothing would be devastating to most, since the alternative involved winning a large sum and the chances of its happening were so great the individual was probably already planning what he or she would do with the money.

In other words, prospect theory does not deal with the effect of disappointment. Winning nothing is not that disappointing when the alternative involves a modest sum, but it is extremely disappointing when one expects to win a much larger amount. Realizing you are not going to have a job on Monday is not that painful when you have been unemployed for a while, but it is much more painful when you lost your job on the previous Friday.[12]

To see a second drawback of prospect theory, consider the following gamble choice:

- A 90 percent chance to win $1 million and a 10 percent chance to win nothing, or
- Receiving $10 with certainty

versus this one:

- A 90 percent chance to win $1 million and a 10 percent chance to win nothing, or
- Receiving $100,000 with certainty,

and consider how one would feel after choosing the gamble and receiving nothing in each case. Most people would think receiving nothing would be much more painful in the latter case than in the former, but prospect theory is incapable of assigning a different value to receiving nothing in the two cases. That is, it cannot account for regret. Receiving nothing in the latter case is so painful because one is faced with the reality that he or she could have received a large sum; in the former case, the alternative was not much better than receiving nothing anyway. It is this regret that drives the increased negative value associated with receiving nothing in the second case versus the first.[13]

---

[12] Kahneman, 287.
[13] Ibid.

■ Conclusion

Traditional wealth-based utility theory falls short in a number of areas, such as the even more foundational assumption that individuals make decisions based on prospective levels of wealth. A more realistic assumption is that each person makes decisions based on gains and losses from a given starting point, and that after these gains and losses are realized, he or she resets the reference point to the current situation. That people make decisions based on the prospects available to them from a given starting point underlies the dynamics of prospect theory.

A more detailed analysis of how humans behave reveals that they also exhibit loss aversion—that is, they feel a larger pain from losses than they realize a benefit from commensurate gains. An implication of this is that utility outcomes are path dependent. Traditional utility theory implies that a trader that starts out with a wealth of $1,000, makes five trades, and ends with a wealth of $1,500 has a particular known level of happiness at the end. However, under prospect theory, one cannot know his or her ending utility without knowing the outcomes of each trade and hence the path that the portfolio value took along the way. This model of human behavior corresponds more closely to observation, but it also complicates the business of analyzing such behavior in practice.

Prospect theory formalizes the decision process in a way that corresponds more closely to how people behave than the utility approach of traditional economics. There are limitations, however, to the use of prospect theory. The biggest single limitation is its inability to provide insight into general asset pricing theory. Prospect theory has a distinctly dynamic flavor to it because of its implicit path dependence. No one has yet constructed a satisfactory asset pricing theory based on prospect theory utility functions. Other problems with prospect theory have been emphasized by Kahneman and referenced in this chapter. The failure to deal with the emotions of disappointment and regret are major limitations of prospect theory's descriptive power.

For whatever weaknesses there may be with prospect theory, it is unquestionably a step forward in our ability to generalize actual human decision-making and provides a convenient formalization of loss aversion as well.

CHAPTER 24

Perception Biases

From Edwin T. Burton and Sunit N. Shah,
Behavioral Finance (Hoboken, New Jersey:
John Wiley & Sons, 2013), Chapter 10.

Learning Objective Statement

- Explain problems that might inhibit investors afflicted with one or more of the following perception biases: Saliency, Framing, Anchoring, and Sunk-Cost bias

A perception bias arises when an individual has difficulty figuring out what the problem is that needs to be solved. Perception biases come in many forms. We look at several perception biases in this chapter, including saliency, framing, anchoring, and sunk-cost biases. All four of these biases have been extensively studied by Kahneman and Tversky and others and are well established. While the four perception biases that we discuss in this chapter do not exhaust the list of perception biases, these four appear to be the most important.

■ Saliency

When we have not encountered something recently, we have a tendency to ignore that thing even if it is important to an upcoming decision. No one seems interested in buying flood insurance unless there has been a recent flood. Airplane accident insurance is almost never purchased except in airports just prior to boarding a flight, though it is available to be purchased from the moment travel plans are made. When the economy has been strong and vigorous for a long time, fears of an economic slowdown recede almost to the point of being completely ignored.

Saliency works in two ways. If an event has not occurred recently, then that event tends to be perceived as having zero or negligible probability of occurring in the future. However, if the same event has occurred very recently, the perceived probability of a future occurrence becomes overstated. A dramatic example of saliency seems to take place when financial crises occur. During an economic boom, people forget that crashes can occur and underweight their likelihood of occurrence.

Gennaioli, Shleifer, and Vishny (GSV) have constructed a theory of financial intermediation[1] based upon the idea that the occurrence of "bad" economic states seems to be perceived as almost impossible when the economy is strong and the demand for credit is high. This theory then uses an overweight of the probability of the "bad" economic state once the crisis has passed. Shleifer's theory formalizes the idea that credit standards for commercial lending seem to decline dramatically during periods of economic prosperity and then during economic recovery credit standards are tightened up to extreme levels. The opposite pattern would be more favorable to the economy, but saliency drives policy makers and market participants to incorrectly perceive the true environment in which they are operating.

The authors state their formalization of saliency in their model in the following way:

> [W]e assume that both investors and financial intermediaries do not attend to certain improbable risks when trading new securities. This assumption captures what we take to be the central feature of the historical episodes we describe: the neglect of potentially huge defaults in the housing bubble and of the sensitivity of AAA-rated securities to these defaults, the neglect of the possibility of massive prepayments in the early 1990s, or the neglect of the possibility that a money market fund can break the buck.[2]

GSV describes this as "formalization of the notion that not all contingencies are represented in the decision maker's thought process."[3]

The authors find that their model fits the financial crisis well and that attempts to account for the crisis without incorporating this element of surprise into their model significantly hinder its accuracy. They also address other research efforts that attempt to model the financial crisis. Much of this research models the crisis as an extremely low probability event that agents do rationally incorporate into their decision making. GSV finds that these models do not fit the financial crisis as well as a model incorporating saliency. They conclude that the agents involved in the crisis used incorrect investment models that assigned a zero probability to a potential financial crisis. A correct model would assign a very low, yet nonzero, probability to the chances of a prospective financial collapse.

■ Framing

The correct answer to a question should not depend on how the question is phrased. Unless the alternative way of asking a question is truly different, the answer should be independent of phrasing, or *framing,* as it has come to be known in the behavioral finance literature. The simplest setting for framing is

---

[1] Nicola Gennaioli, Andrei Shleifer, and Robert Vishny, "Neglected Risks, Financial Innovation and Financial Fragility," *Journal of Financial Economics* 104(2012); 452–468.

[2] Ibid., 453.

[3] Ibid., 453.

the consideration of alternative policies that involve an unavoidable loss of life. Kahneman and Tversky pose the following example.[4]

Problem 1

Imagine that the country is preparing for the outbreak of an unusual disease, which is expected to kill 600 people. Which of the following programs would you favor?

Program A: Has the effect of saving 200 people.

Program B: Has a 1/3 chance of saving 600 people and a 2/3 chance that no one will be saved.

Most people will choose Program A when given the choice. This is the risk-averse choice since 200 people are saved for certain as compared to the risky option in which 200 people are saved on average but it is possible that no one is saved.

Now consider the same problem phrased slightly differently.

Problem 2

Program C: 400 people will die for certain.
Program D: 1/3 chance that no one will die and 2/3 chance that 600 people will die.

In Problem 2, most respondents, when offered the choice, will opt for Program D. Program D is riskier than Program C, so risk-preferring behavior characterizes those who choose Program D over Program C.

Note that Programs A and C are identical and that Programs B and D are identical. So why are over 70 percent of respondents choosing A over B and nearly 80 percent of respondents choosing D over C? The choices are inconsistent. Kahneman and Tversky use the expression *invariance* to capture the idea that the same answer should be given to questions that vary only in phrasing but are substantively identical. Here, there seems to be a clear violation of invariance. "The failure of invariance is both pervasive and robust. It is as common among sophisticated respondents as among naïve ones, and it is not eliminated even when the same respondents answer both questions within a few minutes."[5]

What seems to drive this particular example is the reference point. Problem 1 is written in the context of saving lives, while Problem 2 is written from the viewpoint of people dying. Respondents consider saving zero people the reference point in the former and zero people dying the reference point in the latter. The outcome choices are of course the same in both problems, just written from a different standpoint. But that different standpoint motivates people to make different decisions.

---

[4] Daniel Kahneman and Amos Tversky, "Choices, Values, and Frames," reprinted from *American Psychologist* 39, no. 2(1984). In Daniel Kahneman and Amos Tversky, *Choices, Values and Frames* (Cambridge, UK: Cambridge University Press, 2000). The example of Problems 1 and 2 are taken, in slightly altered form, from this publication.

[5] Kahneman and Tversky, 5.

In Problem 1, respondents think of each person they save as a gain, and therefore make the risk-averse choice—saving 200 people for sure is more palatable than taking the chance that everyone might die. In Problem 2, respondents think of each person that dies as a loss, so they make the risk-loving choice. Sending 400 people to their deaths seems rather Draconian when the other option presents a reasonable chance that all might live.

Kahneman and Tversky[6] also provide a simple choice among lotteries that verified the failure of invariance in settings that most directly apply to finance.

Problem 3

Program E: 25 percent chance to win $240 and 75 percent chance to lose $760.
Program F: 25 percent chance to win $250 and 75 percent chance to lose $750.

In Problem 3, virtually everyone will choose F over E since F dominates E.[7] The rational and proper choice is F. Now consider the following problem, Problem 4.

Problem 4

Imagine that you face the following pair of concurrent decisions. First, examine both decisions, then indicate the options you prefer.

Decision (i)—choose between:
A. A sure gain of $240.
B. 25 percent chance to gain $1,000 and 75 percent chance to gain nothing.

Decision (ii)—choose between:
C. A sure loss of $750.
D. 75 percent chance to lose $1,000 and 25 percent chance to lose nothing.

In Problem 4, 73 percent of respondents in Kahneman and Tversky's experiments chose A and D, while only 3 percent chose B and C. But B and C together equate to F from Problem 3, and A and D together are nothing more than E. Therefore, more than 70 percent of respondents are effectively choosing E over F. What is happening in this example is that identical options are presented to respondents and their choices will differ depending on the framing that surrounds the choices, even though the actual content of the choices presented is identical.

What framing is doing is exploiting our attitude toward bad events. In the first example, respondents do not wish to do harm. Therefore, when the choice is between saving people and rolling the dice, respondents want to save people. But when the identical choice set is presented and framed as if the respondent is choosing that 400 people will die with certainty, respondents go for the choice that

---

[6] Kahneman and Tversky, 6.
[7] Dominance is implied since the probabilities are identical but the payoffs are better in F than in E.

presents the possibility of saving everyone, even though all 600 might die. Perception is the key.

In the monetary lotteries of Problem 3, the choice of F is obvious for almost all respondents. In Problem 4, C is where the real difficulty lies for most respondents who fail to choose the dominant B-C combination. C is a sure loss of $750 against D, which provides a way of avoiding the loss. Similarly, A is attractive because you are certain to win and avoid the possible loss entailed in choice B. Framing is taking advantage of loss aversion in Problems 3 and 4. Most respondents choose A, expressing risk aversion, and D expressing risk seeking. Such choices are routine to loss aversion. What makes Problems 3 and 4 striking is that the choice combination in 4 seems unpalatable once it is reframed as Problem 3.

■ Anchoring

Anchoring is a perception bias that arises when you are attempting to make a guess at something about which you have limited information. An *anchor* biases your guess in the direction of the anchor. A famous example of anchoring comes from attempting to guess the number of jellybeans in a jar. Staring at the jar, it would be difficult to imagine how to even begin to guess the number of jellybeans that can be stored in a jar. But imagine that just before you attempted to guess the number of jellybeans in a jar someone says: "Wow, there are a 1,000 stars in the sky!" Would that influence your guess? Would your guess be closer to 1,000 after such a comment was made? Suppose the comment were made, instead: "Wow, there are 10,000 stars in the sky!" Would your guess be significantly larger than if the anchor was 1,000?

Experiments using a single jar of jellybeans have been conducted numerous times using separated classrooms of responders. Very different estimates arise from the respondents in each room, and the average estimate for each room is biased in the direction of the anchor that applied to that room.[8]

A similar bias can occur in the context of historical guesses. Suppose one plans to ask what century Galileo lived in, but just before posing the question about Galileo, one says: "Columbus discovered America in 1492." If one compares respondent guesses when 1492 is the anchor to a different anchor such as: "The Magna Carta was signed in 1215," the group that hears 1492 will place Galileo closer to the end of the fifteenth century than the latter group, who will place Galileo's life much closer to the beginning of the thirteenth century.[9]

Anchoring can be characterized as an example of lazy thinking, but there is a possible reason for such lazy thinking. Often, limited observations can provide a

---

[8] For similar examples, see Paul Slovic, Baruch Fischolff, and Sarah Lichtenstein, "Facts versus Fears: Understanding Perceived Risk," reprinted in Daniel Kahneman, Paul Slovic, and Amos Tversky, eds., *Judgment under Uncertainty: Heuristics and Biases* (Cambridge, UK: Cambridge University Press, 1982).
[9] Galileo was born in 1564 and died in 1642.

reasonable basis for an estimate. One of the more famous examples of this is the Secretary Problem. Generally, this describes any situation where:

- There are n objects (prizes) drawn in succession.
- If all are seen together, they can be ranked from best to worst unambiguously.
- The order in which they are actually seen is random.
- Immediately after seeing each object, you must reject or accept the object most recently seen, and the decision is irreversible.
- The only information you have on the objects is the value of each object you've seen so far.
- The objective is to maximize the probability with which you select the best object.

Consider a situation where there are 10 monetary prizes available and you get to observe each prize, one by one. As you select one of the prizes and learn how much money there is, you are given a choice: You may take the money and then the game ends, or you can reject it, in which case that prize is discarded and you move on to the next prize. Once you get to the last prize, you must, of course, accept it as there are no other remaining prizes left to examine.

In this 10-prize situation, what is your best strategy? Remember that the only information you have are the prize values you have seen. Any arbitrary amount of money can be contained in each of the 10 prizes. Clearly, you need to gain some information—the question is how much information should you gain before making a selection. After all, each prize that you discard means that you can no longer have that prize, which may have been the largest of all the prizes.

This is a classic optimization problem and the optimal strategy is to select the first three prizes, observe the dollar amounts of each prize, and then discard each of them regardless of their values. Then consider the fourth prize. If its value is greater than what was observed in the each of the first three prizes, accept that prize and the game is over. If not, reject it and continue until you do find a prize of an amount greater than any of the first three. There is the possibility that one of the first three is the largest prize, in which case you will end up gaining the last of the 10 prizes selected, regardless of its dollar value.

Note that in some sense you are anchoring your ultimate choice by examining the first three prizes. In this process, you have constructed a "rational" anchor. It just might be that experience with rationally selecting anchors in the manner of this 10-prize example provides the backdrop for the effectiveness of seemingly irrelevant anchors in the biasing of estimates. Irrelevant anchors are latched on to in the absence of any other information. This might be harmless if the irrelevant anchor itself is unbiased noise. But if the anchor is provided intentionally such as in a purchase-and-sale situation, the perception bias triggered by anchoring can lead to biased behavior that may be in the interest of the person providing the anchor.

■ Sunk-Cost Bias

Imagine that you paid $200 for a nonrefundable, nontransferable ticket to see a great country-and-western singer—your favorite—perform next Thursday. But when Thursday rolls around, you no longer want to go. You've decided you don't like that singer after all. You try to give away your ticket or sell it, to no avail. So do you go to the performance, even though you no longer think that you would enjoy it? Traditional economics says that a rational person will choose not to go to the performance. You might feel bad if you don't go to the performance because you will regret having wasted $200, but feelings of regret are not part of the makeup of the rational person typically assumed by economists. Utility is derived from consumption, not from wistful looks back about things you wish that you had done or not done. Feelings of regret play no role whatsoever in traditional economic analysis.

An economist normally argues that paying for something and then using it are two entirely separate decisions. The decision to pay for a ticket to attend a future event is based on expectations about the utility of that future event. Having paid for the ticket, once the future event arrives, you must make a new decision—should you attend or not? What you paid for the ticket earlier should be irrelevant, economists argue, to the decision to attend. The ticket is viewed as a *sunk cost* that is an entirely separate event from the attendance at the concert for which the ticket was purchased.

Classifying sunk costs as a perception bias is questionable. The sunk-costs bias involves something left out of the utility function, which most of us know probably does affect decisions—regret. People feel regret for things done and not done. But such things are in the past, and since they cannot be changed, they should not influence a current choice. Does having bought a ticket in the past make today's attendance at a concert more pleasurable? Not likely. But wasting the ticket one has paid for makes one regret a past decision. That regret can be avoided by going to the concert, even if you would rather not. If you had not bought a ticket and someone offered you a free one, you would likely say no. But, having paid, you wish to avoid the feeling of regret, and so you go. To an economist those two situations are identical and you should make the same decision in each.

A slight variation of the sunk-cost bias is the situation that arises if you lose your $200 ticket on the way to the concert and are faced with having to purchase or not purchase another ticket. Suppose in this case you really do want to attend the concert. If, along the way to the concert, you had lost $200, rather than the ticket that you purchased for $200, you might react differently about these two situations. Where money is lost, you might not associate the lost money with the concert and therefore you might be more likely to pay $200 for a ticket than if you had recently lost a ticket to the concert of exactly the same value. This example is usually classified as an example of mental accounting, but sunk costs are involved regardless of the classification.

Because sunk costs involve regret, the bias that results is similar to the bias an investor shows when reluctant to purchase a stock after missing the opportunity to buy the stock at a cheaper price. Investors who "go to cash" in the midst of a financial crisis are sometimes disappointed that, after they sell out, stocks rally to higher prices. Will they get back in? Often, the answer is no. The investor will wait and hope that stocks fall back to the levels at which they had made their earlier exit. What if that never happens? Then investors may wait until the regret they feel from not getting back in goes away. Once the feeling of regret is no longer present simply because of the passage of time, the investor might invest again, often at much higher prices.

■ Conclusion

Perception biases run counter to the normal utility maximization paradigm that permeates economic and finance theory. Emotions, to the extent they matter in traditional economics and finance, have their impact on the utility function, which is presumed to be a function only of expected consumption or expected net worth, where net worth is obviously a proxy for future consumption. But in real life, psychologists have found that emotions do play a role in how problems and the impact of choices are perceived. Those perceptions can be altered even when the plain substance of the problems or choices are unchanged. If a car is described as pink in color and later as rose in color, but the color has not changed, has the car changed? To the observer, it might be a different car, and that is the rub, if physically nothing has been altered.

Feelings of regret are real enough for most people and clearly affect choices that people make, but how can we take account of feelings of regret in economic or finance theory? If you choose X when Y was available, and Y turns out to be the better choice, do you feel a pang of regret? Where is that in the standard treatment of utility maximization? It is not easy to brush regret aside as of little importance when it influences investor behavior in important ways such as looking back and wishing it weren't so or worrying that if I do this, I might live to regret it. Major financial decisions seem potentially affected by feelings of regret. None of this bodes well for the efficient market hypothesis.

CHAPTER 25

Inertial Effects

From Edwin T. Burton and Sunit N. Shah, *Behavioral Finance* (Hoboken, New Jersey: John Wiley & Sons, 2013), Chapter 11.

Learning Objective Statement

- Explain problems that might inhibit investors afflicted with one or more of the following inertial effects: endowment effect, status quo effect, disposition effect

Imagine two identical people making a choice between two options, option A and option B. The only difference between the two people is that the first starts at A and is asked whether or not he or she would like to move to B, whereas the second starts at B and is offered the ability to move to A.

It might be surprising to find that the majority of the time, individuals in these situations tend to stay where they start, regardless of the context around the decision choice or with which option they began. Experiments show that individuals tend to stick with the status quo, and that tendency persists across a variety of scenarios and in a variety of contexts. In this chapter, we explore the research that investigates such phenomena as well as the consequences of the outcomes such behavior elicits.

■ Endowment Effect

In *The Winner's Curse,* Richard Thaler tells the story of a wine-loving economist.[1] As the story goes, this particular oenophile purchased several bottles of exquisite Bordeaux wine at auction years ago at extremely low prices, $10 per bottle. The wine has since appreciated significantly in value, and now routinely sells for $200 per bottle at auction.

The economist enjoys one bottle from his collection each year. One day, the economist finds himself conversing with a student who shares his affinity for wine. The

---

[1] Richard Thaler, *The Winner's Curse: Paradoxes and Anomalies of Economic Life* (New York: Free Press, 1992), 63.

student asks why the professor does not purchase more of his beloved wine at auction, and the professor replies that the prices have grown too high for his liking. The student then asks if he could possibly buy a bottle from the professor's inventory at the auction price of $200, to which the professor replies that he cannot sell any from his stash—the bottles are simply worth too much to him.

This example probably does not sound that surprising. However, the example flies directly in the face of traditional economic theory. In traditional economic theory, an individual must have a specific reservation price for a given good, such that he or she would be willing to sell some positive amount of the good for any price greater than the reservation price and buy some positive amount for any lesser price. If someone is not willing to sell a unit of a good for p_1 and is also not willing to buy one unit for p_2, with $p_2 < p_1$, according to traditional economic theory, that person would be acting irrationally.

One might argue that this is simply a question of sentimental value, but similar results have been observed in a number of experiments that eliminate such an effect. Kahneman, Knetsch, and Thaler[2] ran one experiment in which half the participants, chosen at random, were each endowed with a coffee mug (the "sellers") and the other half with nothing (the "buyers"). Each seller was asked to list his or her reservation price to sell the mug and each buyer to list his or her reservation price to buy the mug. Economic theory would predict the average selling price and buying price to be the same, but this was not the case—in fact, the average selling price was approximately twice as large as the average buying price.

In a further instantiation of the same experiment, a third group was included, called "choosers," who could receive either a mug or a sum of money. Individuals in this group were asked to list the amount of money that was as desirable as receiving the good. The reservation prices were as follows:

Buyers	$2.87
Choosers	$3.12
Sellers	$7.12

Sellers listed a reservation price approximately twice as high as both buyers and choosers. The contrast between sellers and choosers is striking, since both faced the choice of either having a mug or a commensurate amount of money—the only difference is whether they were given the mug at the outset or not. The results clearly show that the simple effect of owning the mug in the beginning nearly doubles the reservation price.

Jack Knetsch, one of the researchers from these experiments, performed a similar study[3] in which participants were chosen at random to receive either $4.50 or five ballpoint pens, and then were asked to accept or reject a series of offers that were

[2] Daniel Kahneman, Jack L. Knetsch, and Richard H. Thaler, "Experimental Tests of the Endowment Effect and the Coase Theorem," *Journal of Political Economy* 98, no. 6 (1990): 1325–1348.

[3] Jack L. Knetsch, "Preferences and Non-Reversibility of Indifference Curves," *Journal of Economic Behavior & Organization* 17, no. 1 (1992): 131–139.

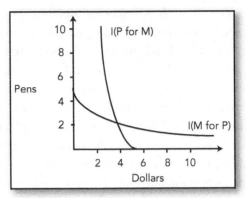

FIGURE 25.1 Crossing Indifference Curves.

designed to elicit their preferences for varying allotments of money and pens. From this data, Knetsch calculated indifference curves, or lines in two-dimensional space that represent allotments of the two goods (each corresponding to one of the two dimensions) such that the consumer is perfectly indifferent across those allotments.

Knetsch's results are displayed in Figure 25.1. The nearly vertical line represents the average indifference curve for those who were initially endowed with money. These individuals needed a lot of pens to compensate for the loss of a dollar. The nearly horizontal line represents the average indifference curve for those who started with pens—they required a lot of money to give up even a single pen.

The indifference curves on this graph violate one of the basic laws of traditional economics—namely, that indifference curves can never cross. Crossing indifference curves are ruled out by the definition of the indifference curve itself. An indifference curve is the collection of all bundles that a consumer prizes equally. If two separate indifference curves cross, the consumer must be indifferent between all bundles on each curve and the crossing point between the curves—but then it must be the case that he is indifferent between any bundle on either curve and any bundle on the other curve. This is a contradiction, since each curve was supposed to represent an exhaustive collection of bundles of indifference in the first place.

At the heart of the disruption lies the underlying assumption that an individual must be indifferent across the same exhaustive set of bundles regardless of his or her starting point. Traditional economic theory assumes the value an individual places on a bundle is unaffected by what he or she is endowed with to start; behavioral finance shows that, in practice, this need not be the case.

Consider two identical individuals with the indifference curves for salary and vacation days shown in Figure 25.2.[4] Both start at position A in the graph. Each receives an offer to get either an extra $10,000 in salary per year, ending in position B, or an extra 12 vacation days per year, ending in position C. As they are both indifferent between the two outcomes, they each flip a coin, and one takes the extra money while the other takes the extra vacation.

[4] Daniel Kahneman, *Thinking, Fast and Slow* (New York: Farrar, Straus and Giroux, 2011), 289–291.

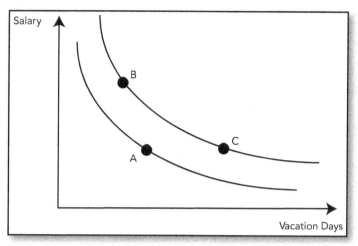

FIGURE 25.2

Some time passes and then their employers allow them to reconsider their decisions. Standard economic theory states that the starting point is irrelevant, and
that both individuals should still find the two options equivalent and hence still be
indifferent. However, from the point of view of the first individual, the choice is
between:

- Stay at Position B: Incur no gain or loss.
- Move to Position C: Receive an extra 12 vacation days but lose $10,000.

The second individual sees the choice as:

- Stay at Position C: Incur no gain or loss.
- Move to Position B: Receive an extra $10,000 but lose 12 vacation days.

It is not difficult to imagine that one might stay in his or her current position in
both situations; in fact, it would be surprising if this were not the case. However, traditional economic theory would say that anyone in this situation should be indifferent
between the choices regardless of the status quo.

Examples such as these show that indifference curves are not *reversible*—moving
to another point and then back does not necessarily represent a net zero change in
happiness. A movement from A to B along an indifference curve changes the indifference curve itself because the reference point changes.

Prospect theory provides an explanation for this irreversibility. Regardless of the
position each individual starts from, he faces a choice between a loss along one dimension plus a gain along the second and no movement at all. Since each was indifferent between the two points when starting at point A, the gain along one dimension is the same as the loss along the other. However, from prospect theory, a loss of a
given size looms larger than a commensurate gain, so from a utility perspective, each
individual sees the move as a net loss. Since the alternative involves no movement at

all and therefore no change in happiness, neither individual will move, and both will remain at their current allocation.

The magnitude of the discrepancy in the coffee mug experiment is consistent with the results of prospect theory research—the average seller's reservation price was approximately twice as large as the average buyer's, the same two-to-one ratio that individuals exhibit when asked a question like, "How high would x have to be in order for you to accept a gamble of the following form: 50 percent chance of losing $100 and 50 percent chance of gaining x?" fMRIs[5] taken during the mug transactions have indicated that selling goods that have another use activated areas of the brain normally associated with disgust and pain, as did buying mugs at prices perceived to be too high, whereas buying mugs at low prices activated pleasure centers instead.[6]

The endowment effect does a better job of predicting human behavior than traditional economic theory, but it is worth noting that there are circumstances in which people do not succumb to this effect. This was shown as early as 1976, in a famous study by Vernon Smith.[7] Smith dispersed tokens, which had no alternative use outside of the experiment, as well as differing redemption values for the tokens themselves, to the various participants at random. Hence, a token may have been worth $1 to one participant and $3 to another. The participants were then allowed to publicly announce offers to buy or sell tokens which could be accepted or rejected publicly by the other participants. The results went as predicted by economic theory—the tokens ended up in the hands of those with the highest redemption values for them[8] and the market prices ended up as predicted by economic theory as well.

Similar results occur in more commonplace scenarios, such as when one changes a large bill for smaller ones or buys a product from a retail merchant in exchange for cash. Kahneman provides an explanation for such results. In such transactions, as in the token experiment by Smith, the item at hand serves as a placeholder for the other item in the exchange that will be received at a future point in time. When a lamp merchant trades a lamp for $20, the merchant feels no endowment effect from the lamp itself; mentally, the lamp served simply as a placeholder for the $20 that would be received for it in the future. Similarly, in the token experiment, the participants saw the tokens solely as a means to a monetary end; that the tokens had no alternative use outside of the experiment is key to the results. Along a similar vein, many of the results of experiments where the endowment effect does occur disappear when the participants are simply instructed to "think like traders" as they are making their decisions. Ironically, traders often do not think like traders themselves, as will be seen later in this chapter in the discussion of the disposition effect.[9]

---

[5] fMRIs (functional magnetic resonance imaging) are brain-wave measures used in neuroeconomics.

[6] Kahneman, 296.

[7] Vernon Smith, "Experimental Economics: Induced Value Theory," *American Economic Review* 66, no. 2 (1976): 274–279.

[8] This is an example of the Coase Theorem, which states (in part) that, absent transaction costs and barriers to trade, resources will end up in the hands of those that place the highest value on them.

[9] Kahneman, 294.

■ Status Quo Effect

A similar result occurs when individuals are asked to choose among several options, with one option being the default, defined as the option implicitly chosen if no action is taken at all. In such situations, standard economic theory predicts that individuals should make the same choice regardless of which option is selected as the default. Experiments, however, show that individuals are influenced by which option is presented as the default one. The tendency to stick with the default option is known in the literature as the *status quo bias*.

Many experiments have demonstrated and explored this bias. Samuelson and Zeckhauser[10] asked a group of participants a series of questions phrased one of two ways, one providing a clear status quo default option and another providing no default option. For example, one question involved a decision about what to do with a significant sum of money that had been inherited. Two versions of the question appeared. Both listed investing in Company A as the first possibility. However, one version prefaced the explanation with the quote "A significant portion of this portfolio is invested in moderate-risk Company A." Samuelson and Zeckhauser found that a significantly higher percentage of individuals choose to invest in company A when it was listed as the status quo than would otherwise. Other research has consistently found the same effect.

Thaler and Sunstein have suggested that governments take advantage of such a phenomenon in the course of making policy decisions.[11] They argue for a school of thought they term *libertarian paternalism*. They define this as a central body giving several options to its constituents with the one that it deems the best for the greatest percentage of people as the default (this is the *paternalism* part), while still giving individuals the right to opt out of the default and into another choice if they deem it appropriate for themselves (the *libertarian* part). At the heart of this philosophy lies the idea that people will tend to stick with the defaults except when they find them significantly unpalatable and that then and only then will they make a change. The government is able to nudge individuals in one direction or another without giving them a hard shove.

This might seem surprising as a regulatory philosophy, but such a strategy has been observed in practice. One example comes from the state of Virginia's Retirement System, or VRS for short. In 1997, the VRS set up a new benefit program for employees covered under the state's public employee retirement system called the "cash match" benefit program. Under this program, the state matched dollar-for-dollar the contributions of its employees on a pretax basis. For example, if an employee's marginal tax rate is 30 percent, and she contributed $10 to her retirement fund, the state contributed another $10 on her behalf, so she essentially received a

---

[10] William Samuelson and Richard Zeckhauser, "Status Quo Bias in Decision Making," *Journal of Risk and Uncertainty* 1, no. 1 (1988): 7–59.

[11] Richard Thaler and Cass Sunstein, *Nudge: Improving Decisions About Health, Wealth and Happiness* (New York: Penguin, 2008).

$20 contribution for an out-of-pocket cost of $7—a pretty favorable exchange of money now for retirement assets later.

Shockingly, most employees did not take advantage of this deal; in fact, less than 20 percent of new employees joined the program. VRS chalked this up to the status quo effect—that is, not entering the program was the default option, and new employees were loath to change away from it unless they were sure it was better to do so.

So, the VRS Board changed the default option to the maximum cash match option. Sure enough, going forward, 91 percent of new employees took that option. When presented with the options with no action resulting in maximum cash match, only 9 percent of new employees ended up not in the program.

In the same way that it helped explain the endowment effect, prospect theory can help explain the status quo bias as well. Many individuals might consider the default option as their reference point, considering losses and gains from that point in making their decisions. If there is uncertainty around the various options, they might feel that switching could result in a potential gain but could also result in a potential loss from the reference point, and the potential for losses will weigh heavier than the potential benefit from gains due to loss aversion.

Sticking with the default option also helps avoid regret, which prospect theory itself cannot explain.[12] If actively choosing away from the default option terminates in a poor outcome for the individual, it would be hard to argue that they did not make a mistake and hence the feeling of regret would be hard to avoid. However, if they were simply passive and never committed to an option themselves one way or another, it is easier to think that the government or even fate made the choice for them and hence it was not their fault that things went awry. Consequently, these individuals may feel safer sticking with the default choice unless they are relatively certain that moving away from it is the best option.

■ Disposition Effect

Another effect, closely related to the endowment effect and status quo bias listed earlier as well as the sunk-cost bias, is the *disposition effect*. Consider the following example. You have paid $200 for a ticket to an event you no longer think you will enjoy and have been unable to sell the ticket thus far. Do you attend the event simply because you paid $200 for the right to go? Many people would do just that, even though traditional economic theory would frame this behavior as irrational. In that light, the $200 you paid has been sunk and cannot be recovered, so the only relevant question is whether the event is worth the transportation cost to go and the opportunity cost of the time spent there.

However, most individuals make decisions based on *mental accounting*. In a sense, one has a mental account set up related to this event, and thus far the event has cost

---

[12] A point that Kahneman sees as an important weakness of prospect theory. See Kahneman, 287–288.

$200 on one side of the balance sheet with the corresponding right to attend appearing on the other side. If one were to close the account without going to the event, he or she would be locking in a loss, which is an unpleasant feeling for most people. By attending, the individual could assign some sort of value to the other side of the balance sheet, which is a better feeling—even if the expected value of the event net of transportation and time costs is actually negative.[13]

A similar effect occurs prominently in investing behavior, with important consequences for financial markets. When liquidating investments in order to obtain cash for other uses, investors routinely liquidate stocks that hold paper gains before liquidating stocks that at current prices have lost them money. This is true regardless of the perceived future investment prospects of each stock.

As an example, consider two stocks into each of which an individual had initially invested $10,000, currently facing the following prospects:

- Stock 1 currently has a gain of −$2,000 (i.e., a loss), and going forward has a 50 percent chance of going down $1,000 and a 50 percent chance of going up $2,500.
- Stock 2 currently has a gain of $2,000, and going forward has a 40 percent chance of going down $1,000 and a 60 percent chance of going up $2,500.

The individual needs to close out one position to pay off other debts. Which is he or she more likely to choose? From an investment standpoint, the current gain or loss is irrelevant—the goal is to maximize the expected return from this point forward, and hence all that matters is the future probability of returns. However, in practice, many close out the winning stock so that they can close that mental account out as a gain, hoping the losing stock will come back up as well, which it has a 50 percent chance of doing, so that they can close that account out as a gain in the future.

This is true despite the tax benefits of closing out losing stocks.[14] The majority of the time, investors close out winners before closing out losers, in every month of the year except one, December, when the tax implications are more on the investors' minds due to saliency. Otherwise, investors are significantly more apt to sell winning stocks than losing ones, even if the winning stocks have better future potential.

Prospect theory provides a clear rationale behind this behavior. The idea of closing out an account and locking in a loss weighs heavily on an investor's mind—so heavy that it often feels better to close out a winner and lock in a gain, even despite the tax benefits, and even if the loser is likely to become an even bigger loser. Losses invoke such a negative emotion that this force outweighs the motivation to invest in such a way as to maximize the expected return.

---

[13] Kahneman, 243.

[14] In the United States, under certain conditions (e.g., the sale is not a wash sale, etc.), investors can write off losses from an investment sale on their tax returns, paying lower taxes overall.

■ Conclusion

Humans naturally have a tendency to stick with the conditions of their current situations, even in the light of strong motivations to do otherwise. When we are given items that have a potential use to us other than for trade, we place a significantly higher value on these items than we do if we are given currency and asked to buy those items instead. We also have a strong tendency to stick with the default option in a list of options, regardless of which option is labeled as such.

Prospect theory provides an explanation for these behaviors. When we are endowed with an item to start, we adjust our reference point to that particular endowment and feel that giving up the item we were endowed with would entail a loss for us. As prospect theory explains, it would take a higher-than-commensurate gain for us to feel compensated for such a loss due to loss aversion. Similarly, we tend not to move away from a default option, because we think of that option as our reference point, and hence moving away from it carries with it a risk of loss that we often do not feel comfortable bearing.

Prospect theory also provides an explanation for the so-called disposition effect, that investors are more likely to lock in a win by selling a winning stock than they are to sell a losing stock for cash, even if the prospects for the losing stock are less attractive. In our minds, we keep mental accounts of our paper positions; locking in a paper position as a loss carries with it such a negative feeling that it can outweigh the strong incentive we have to maximize our overall portfolio return.

STATISTICAL ANALYSIS AND SYSTEM DEVELOPMENT

Effective statistical analysis and system development require CMT candidates to understand both the mathematical tools they use for taking a close look at the market and the principles for understanding how to interpret what they observe. This section includes a fair amount of discussion on the scientific methods and study on the Efficient Markets Hypothesis (EMH) because candidates must understand the philosophical background for making systematic investment decisions.

This section devotes an entire chapter to a single case study. The chapter is meant to be an example of what can be learned from the effort of generating objective rules for a trading system.

■ What Candidates Need to Know

Candidates should be able to explain why using a system for trading or investing is likely to produce superior results. They should also be able to read a scatter chart generated from a regression analysis and determine what the data is telling them in relation to current market conditions.

CHAPTER 26

Correlation

From Markos Katsanos, *Intermarket Trading Strategies* (Hoboken, New Jersey: John Wiley & Sons, 2008), Chapter 2.

Study the past if you would divine the future.

—Confucius

Learning Objective Statements

- Identify three methods of calculating the correlation coefficient
- Recognize confirmation signals given from correlation data

■ 26.1 The Correlation Coefficient

26.1.1 Pearson's Correlation

The correlation coefficient measures the strength and direction of correlation or corelation between two variables.

There are several methods, depending on the nature of data being studied, for calculating the correlation coefficient, but the best known is Pearson's product-moment correlation coefficient, usually denoted by r, which is obtained by dividing the covariance of the two variables by the product of their standard deviations. The formula for calculating Pearson's r is:

$$r = \frac{\sigma_{XY}}{\sigma_X \sigma_Y} \qquad (26.1)$$

where σ_{XY} is the covariance of variables X and Y and σ_X, σ_y are their standard deviations. The covariance is the cross product of the deviations from the mean and is calculated by the following formula:

$$\sigma_{XY} = \frac{\sum (x - \overline{x})(y - \overline{y})}{n-1}. \qquad (26.2)$$

Unfortunately the size of the covariance depends on the values of measurement of each variable and is not normalized between −1.0 and +1.0 as is the correlation coefficient.

Substituting for the covariance in (26.1) we get:

$$r = \frac{\sum Z_x Z_y}{\sigma_x \sigma_y (n-1)} \qquad (26.3)$$

which is the average product of the z-scores, where $z_x = \sum (x_i \ \bar{x})$ and $z_y = \sum (y_i - \bar{y})$.

The correlation coefficient varies between −1 and 1. A value of +1 indicates a perfect linear relationshipwith positive slope between the two variables; a value of −1 indicates a perfect linear relationship with negative slope between the two variables and a correlation coefficient of 0means that there is no linear relationship between the variables. Values in between indicate the degree of correlation and their interpretation is subjective depending to some extent on the variables under consideration.

The interpretation is different for medical research, social, economic or financial time series data. In the case of financial time series the interpretation can again be different depending on whether we compare raw price data or percent changes (yields), as the direct calculation of the correlation based on absolute prices tends to overestimate the correlation coefficient as relations between financial price series are seldom linear. Correlations based on price percent changes, on the other hand, produce more realistic values for the correlation coefficient as they deviate less from linearity.

Therefore, although the correlation coefficient between two time series is unique, two different interpretations are included in Table 26.1, according to the method used for the calculation, in order to take into account the error resulting from the violation of the linearity assumption.

TABLE 26.1 Interpretation of Pearson's Correlation Coefficient. The second column applies to the correlation between raw price data and the last column to percent weekly changes or yields. The interpretation for negative values of Pearson's correlation is exactly the same.

Correlation Coefficient r	Interpretation	
Absolute Value	Price Comparison	Percent Changes
0.9 to 1	Extremely strong	Extremely strong
0.8 to 0.9	Very strong	Very strong
0.7 to 0.8	Strong	Very strong
0.6 to 0.7	Moderately strong	Strong
0.5 to 0.6	Moderate	Moderately strong
0.4 to 0.5	Meaningful	Moderate
0.3 to 0.4	Low	Meaningful
0.2 to 0.3	Very low	Low
0.1 to 0.2	Very slight	Very low
0 to 0.1	Non-existent	Non-existent

A more precise interpretation arising from the correlation coefficient is recommended by some statisticians and requires one further calculation. If the correlation coefficient is squared, the result, commonly known as r^2 or r square or coefficient of determination (see also Section 26.1.2), will indicate approximately the percent of the "dependent" variable that is associated with the "independent" variable or the proportion of the variance in one variable associated with the variance of the other variable. For example, if we calculated that the correlation between the S&P 500 and the 10-year Treasury yield (TNX) is 0.50 then this correlation squared is 0.25, which means that 25% of the variance of the two indices is common. In thus squaring correlations and transforming the result to percentage terms we are in a better position to evaluate a particular correlation.

There is also another factor we must consider when we try to interpret the correlation coefficient—the number of points we have used.

If we plotted only two points, then we would be bound to get a straight line between them. With three points there is still a chance that the points will lie close to a straight line, purely by chance. Clearly, a high correlation coefficient on only a few points is not very meaningful.

Traders often need to know if time series of commodity or stock prices are cyclic and, if they are, the extent of the cycle. The correlation coefficient can also be used in this case by testing for auto-correlation at different lags (testing whether values in a given series are related to other values in the same series). By doing many correlations with differing lags, the extent or duration of the cycle can be determined.

26.1.2 Coefficient of determination

The coefficient of determination r^2 is the square of Pearson's correlation coefficient. It represents the percent of the data that is the closest to the line of best fit. For example, if $r = 0.922$, then $r^2 = 0.850$, which means that 85% of the total variation in y can be explained by the linear relationship between x and y (as described by the regression equation). The other 15% of the total variation in y remains unexplained and stems from other exogenous factors. In regression, the coefficient of determination is useful in determining how well the regression line approximates the real data points but it can also be used (as explained above) to interpret the correlation coefficient.

26.1.3 Spearman's ρ

The best known non-parametric correlation coefficient is Spearman's rank correlation coefficient, named after Charles Spearman and often denoted by the Greek letter ρ (rho). Unlike Pearson's correlation coefficient, it does not require the assumption that the variables are normally distributed but, like Pearson's correlation, linearity is still an assumption.

The main advantage of using the Spearman coefficient is that it is not sensitive to outliers because it looks at ranks as opposed to actual values.

The formula for calculating Spearman's correlation, ρ is:

$$\rho = 1 - \frac{6 \sum d^2}{n(n^2 - 1)} \qquad (26.4)$$

where d is the difference between paired ranks on the same row.

Similar to Pearson's correlation coefficient, Spearman's ρ takes values between -1 and $+1$. In calculating Spearman's coefficient some information is lost because the prices are converted to ranks. Therefore, when two variables appear to be normally distributed it is better to use Pearson's correlation coefficient.

The concept of correlation will be discussed extensively in the rest of the book and should be fully understood by the readers, so I have included an example of calculating both Pearson's and Spearman's correlation coefficients in the Excel worksheets in Tables 26.2 and 26.3 respectively.

■ 26.2 Assumptions

26.2.1 Linearity

The formula used when calculating the correlation coefficient between two variables makes the implicit assumption that a linear relationship exists between them. When this assumption is not true, the calculated value can be misleading. In practice this assumption can virtually never be confirmed; fortunately, the correlation coefficient is not greatly affected by minor deviations from linearity. However, it is always prudent to look at a scatterplot of the variables of interest before making important conclusions regarding the relation between two variables.

To understand what a linear relationship is, consider the scatterplots in Figures 26.1, 26.2, and 26.3.

The first scatterplot in Figure 26.1, between the S&P 500 and the British FTSE 100, illustrates an approximate linear relationship, as the points fall generally along a straight line. Keep in mind that in the financial markets there is no such thing as a perfect linear relationship. In contrast, the plot in Figure 26.2 between the S&P 500 and the Nasdaq 100 exhibits a curvilinear relationship. In this case increasingly greater values of the Nasdaq 100 are associated with increasingly greater values of the S&P 500 up to a certain value (approximately 1200 on the Nasdaq scale).

A statistician, not knowing what each variable represents, would try to fit a cubic line of the form

$$SP = a + b.NDX + c.NDX^2 + d.NDX^3$$

and predict future values of the S&P 500 using the cubic equation above.

A chart of the two indices in Figure 26.4, however, reveals the true reason of discontinuity of the linear relationship: a decoupling of the two indices which

TABLE 26.2 — Example of Calculating Pearson's r in Excel. The Variables X and Y Are the Daily Percent Change in Gold and the Dollar Index Respectively from 8 December 2006 to 29 December 2006.

	A	B	C	D	E	F	G	H	I
	Date	X	Y	$X-\mu$	$(X-\mu)^2$	$Y-\mu$	$(Y-\mu)^2$	$(X-\mu)(Y-\mu)$	2
	12-8-06	−1.344	0.640	−1.386	1.921	0.570	0.325	−0.790	3
	12-11-06	0.929	−0.132	0.887	0.787	−0.202	0.041	−0.179	4
	12-12-06	−0.008	−0.289	−0.050	0.003	−0.359	0.129	0.018	5
	12-13-06	−0.325	0.470	−0.367	0.135	0.400	0.160	−0.147	6
	12-14-06	−0.430	0.444	−0.472	0.223	0.374	0.140	−0.176	7
	12-15-06	−1.664	0.406	−1.706	2.910	0.336	0.113	−0.573	8
	12-18-06	0.163	−0.036	0.121	0.015	−0.106	0.011	−0.013	9
	12-19-06	1.088	−0.667	1.046	1.094	−0.737	0.543	−0.771	10
	12-20-06	−0.402	0.096	−0.444	0.197	0.026	0.001	−0.011	11
	12-21-06	−0.250	0.072	−0.292	0.085	0.002	0.000	−0.001	12
	12-22-06	0.332	0.263	0.290	0.084	0.193	0.037	0.056	13
	12-26-06	0.613	0.298	0.571	0.326	0.228	0.052	0.130	14
	12-27-06	0.401	−0.107	0.359	0.129	−0.177	0.031	−0.064	15
	12-28-06	1.133	−0.179	1.091	1.190	−0.249	0.062	−0.272	16
	12-29-06	0.394	−0.227	0.352	0.124	−0.297	0.088	−0.105	17
Σ		0.630	1.052		9.223		1.733	−2.897	18
N		15	15						19
mean μ		0.042	0.070			Covariance σ_{xy} =		−0.207	20
σ		0.812	0.352			Pearson's Correlation **r**		−0.725	21

Excel Formula   19

ROW 17

COLUMN

			20		21
B	B17−B$20	COUNT(B3:B17)	B18/B19		SQRT(E18/(B19−1))
C	D17*D17	COUNT(C3:C17)	C18/C19		SQRT(G18/(C19−1))
D	C17−C$20				
E	F17*F17				
F	F17*F17				
G	D17*F17				
H	D17*F17	H18/(B19−1)			H19/B21/C21

567

CORRELATION

TABLE 26.3 Example of Calculating Spearman's ρ in Excel. The Variables X and Y Are the Daily Percent Change in Gold and the Dollar Index Respectively from 8 December 2006 to 29 December 2006.

A	B	C	D	E	F	I
Date	X	Y	Rank	Rank	d^2	2
12-8-06	−1.344	0.640	14	1	169	3
12-11-06	0.929	−0.132	3	11	64	4
12-12-06	−0.008	−0.289	9	14	25	5
12-13-06	−0.325	0.470	11	2	81	6
12-14-06	−0.430	0.444	13	3	100	7
12-15-06	−1.664	0.406	15	4	121	8
12-18-06	0.163	−0.036	8	9	1	9
12-19-06	1.088	−0.667	2	15	169	10
12-20-06	−0.402	0.096	12	7	25	11
12-21-06	−0.250	0.072	10	8	4	12
12-22-06	0.332	0.263	7	6	1	13
12-26-06	0.613	0.298	4	5	1	14
12-27-06	0.401	−0.107	5	10	25	15
12-28-06	1.133	−0.179	1	12	121	16
12-29-06	0.394	−0.227	6	13	49	17
Σ	0.630	1.052				18
N	15					19
		Spearman's Correlation ρ=			−0.707	20

Excel Formula

ROW	17	18	20
COLUMN			
B		SUM(B3:B17)	
C		SUM(C3:C17)	
D	RANK(B17,B$3:B$17)		
E	RANK(C17,C$3:C$17)		
F	(D17−E17)^2		1-6*F18/B19/(B19^2-1)
H	D17*F17	SUM(F3:F17)	

started in the middle of 1998, with the Nasdaq outperforming the S&P until the bubble peak of March 2000, and its subsequent devastating collapse which happened to coincide for values of the Nasdaq greater than 1200. This is the reason for the breakout of the linear relationship as depicted in Figure 26.2 by the vertical line AB.

The third scatterplot in Figure 26.3 plots the S&P 500 vs. Japan's Nikkei 225.

Pearson's coefficient of correlation is −0.445 and Spearman's ρ is −0.4, suggesting a negative correlation for the period from 1 January 1992 to 13 December 2006. Both values are, however, meaningless for making any useful predictions for the Nikkei based on the S&P 500 as their relationship is not linear.

A closer examination of the scatterplot, however, reveals that the scatter is clustered around three distinct areas, each having completely different slopes: Area A at the top left of the chart exhibits a distinct positive correlation with the S&P; area B in the center of the chart with a negative correlation; and area C at the bottom right with no correlation at all. The time period of the above different correlations can be identified more precisely by superimposing a chart of the Nikkei on the S&P (Figure 26.5). The period from 1992 to 2007 under study can be divided into six types.

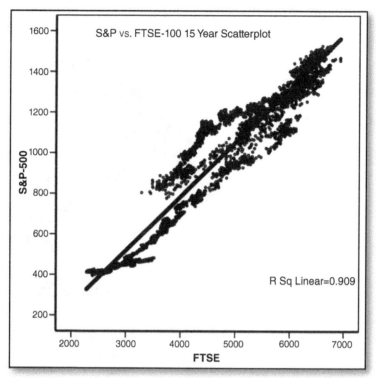

FIGURE 26.1 Scatterplot of the S&P 500 and the British FTSE 100, for the Last 15-Year Period. The relationship is approximately linear, as the points fall generally along a straight line.

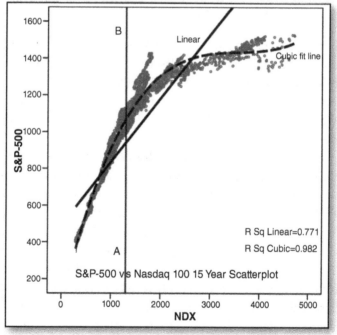

FIGURE 26.2 Scatterplot of the S&P 500 and the Nasdaq 100, for the Last 15-Year Period. The relationship is not linear, as the best fit line is curvilinear.

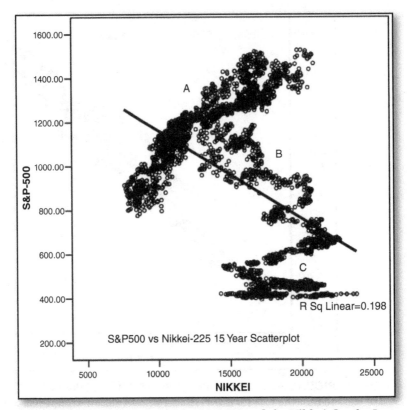

FIGURE 26.3 Scatterplot of the S&P 500 and the Nikkei, for the Last 15-Year Period. The relationship is not linear, as the points deviate significantly from the best fit line.

The first five from 1992 to 1999 (marked A, B, C, D and E) feature alternate positive and negative correlations and the last one (marked F in Figure 26.5) a distinct positive correlation for the period from 1999 to 2007. The positive correlation periods can be allocated to area A in Figure 26.3 and the negative correlated periods to area B.

Area C consists of smaller periods with zero or near zero correlation enclosed inside the longer periods.

In view of the above, it is evident that neither Pearson's nor Spearman's correlation coefficients are appropriate for analyzing nonlinear relationships. In these cases, mathematicians use the so-called coefficient of nonlinear correlation or Eta (denoted by the Greek letter η) which is computed by splitting one of the variables into groups of equal width according to their rank. Eta is then calculated by dividing the group by the total variance. Eta can be used to measure the degree of linearity of a relationship, as the extent to which Eta is greater than r is an estimate of the extent to which the data relationship is nonlinear. Unfortunately, Eta is not particularly useful for analyzing financial markets because, in the case of time series, the groups should be categorized according to time and not rank.

In cases of minor deviations from linearity (for example the relation between the FTSE and the S&P 500), transforming raw prices into percentage yields usually enhances the linear relationship between two variables, resulting in a more reliable correlation and regression analysis.

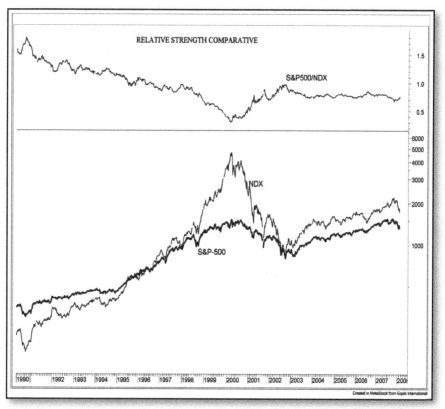

RELATIVE STRENGTH COMPARATIVE

S&P500/NDX

NDX

S&P-500

Created in MetaStock from Equis International

FIGURE 26.4 Weekly Chart of the S&P 500 (Thick Line) with the Nasdaq 100 Superimposed (Thin Black Line) from 1990 to 2007. The relative strength between the S&P 500 and the NDX is plotted in the top window.

Fortunately there are methods more appropriate for analyzing the nonlinear nature of the financial markets: artificial neural networks and kernel regression. Neural networks are nonparametric models which are inherently nonlinear in their computational elements and provide potentially the greatest opportunity for exploiting time series with low correlation dimension estimates by analyzing complex nonlinear relationships without making prior assumptions about the data distribution.

26.2.2 Normality

A correlation coefficient derived using Pearson's formula makes the implicit assumption that the two variables are jointly normally distributed. In the case of most financial series this assumption is not justified, and a nonparametric measure such as the Spearman rank correlation coefficient might be more appropriate.

Consider the histogram of 15-year S&P daily changes in Figure 26.6. Overlaying the normal (Gaussian) distribution we notice that these are not fully described by the Gaussian model. There are two problems with approximating S&P returns with the normal distribution model. The first is that the vast majority of the returns tend to be located near the center of the distribution and the second—and most important—is that the actual distribution has fatter and longer tails. This means that the probability

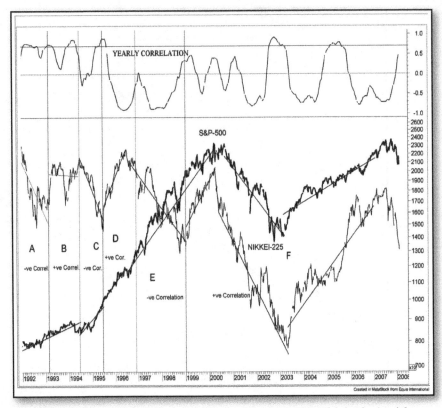

FIGURE 26.5 Weekly Composite Chart of the S&P 500 (Thick Line) with Japan's Nikkei Superimposed (Thin Black Line) from 1990 to 2007. The 52-Week Pearson's correlation strength between the S&P 500 and the Nikkei is plotted in the top window.

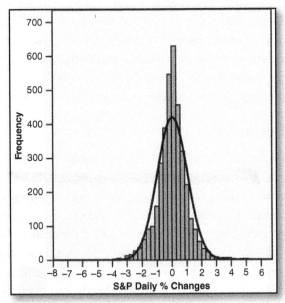

FIGURE 26.6 Distribution of S&P 500 Daily % Returns for the 15-Year Period from 1992–2006.

of a larger movement in the index is much higher than that predicted by the normal distribution. The Gaussian model predicted a virtually nil (0.000027) probability of a one day 4% decline in the index whereas such events occurred six times during the period from 1 January 1992 to 31 December 2006. This is more obvious in the normal plot in Figure 26.8 where it can be seen that for daily changes greater than 2% or less than −2% the distribution deviates significantly from normality. The volatility and hence the deviation from the normal curve has been exacerbated since the "uptick rule" (a regulation that prohibited short selling following downticks) was abolished by the SEC on 6 July 2007. The effect of the abolition of the uptick rule can be seen graphically in Figure 26.9 which has "fatter" tails (that is, higher frequency at extreme values) than the distribution in Figure 26.6. In addition, the standard deviation of daily changes, which was only 1.0 before the uptick was abolished, increased by more than 30% to 1.3 after the uptick rule was eliminated. It is not certain, however, that the increased volatility can be wholly contributed to the repeal of the uptick rule as it coincided with the sub prime mortgage financial upheaval and the collapse of Bear Stearns. At the time of writing, the situation with the financials has not yet normalized but it would be interesting to see the net effect of this rule on the distribution of daily changes of the S&P 500 as soon as enough data are available for such a study.

In any case, if we have to use statistical metrics that assume normality, it is preferable to use daily or weekly changes instead of raw index values. A comparison of the distribution of raw S&P values in Figure 26.7 with that of daily returns in Figure 26.6 will make this more obvious. In fact, Figure 26.7 bears no resemblance to a normal distribution at all.

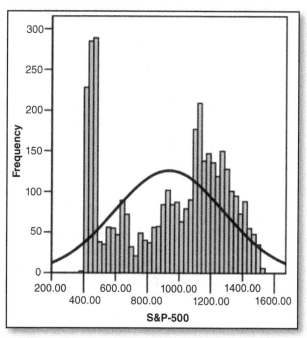

FIGURE 26.7 Distribution of S&P 500 Daily Prices for the 15-Year Period from 1992–2006.

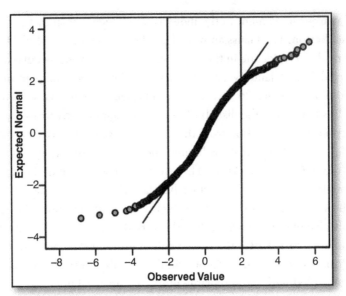

FIGURE 26.8 Normality Plot of the S&P 500 15-Year Daily % Returns.

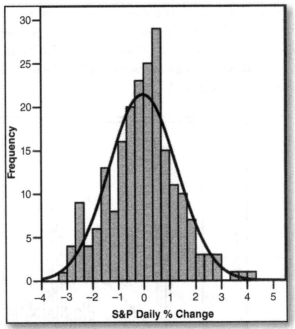

FIGURE 26.9 Distribution of S&P 500 Daily % Returns since the Elimination of the Uptick Rule (from 9 July 2007 Until 5 May 2008). Notice the unusually high frequency of more than −2.5% daily declines during the relatively short period of 210 trading days. the standard deviation also increased by more than 30% and the Kurtosis (which is the variance due to infrequent extreme deviations) increased by more than 700% from 0.43 to 3.77.

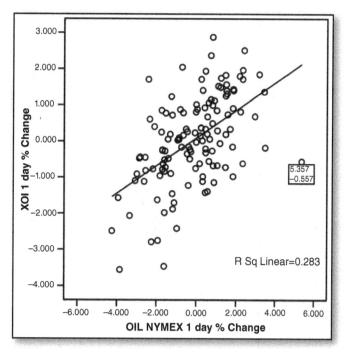

FIGURE 26.10 Six Month Scatterplot of the Amex Oil Index (XOI) vs. Nymex Oil Futures. By removing just one outlier (enclosed in the square on the far right of the graph), the correlation improved from 0.523 to 0.568.

■ 26.3 Outliers

Because of the way in which the regression line is determined (especially the fact that it is based on minimizing the sum of the *squares* of distances of data points from the line and not the sum of simple distances) outliers have a significant influence on the slope of the regression line and, consequently, on the value of the correlation coefficient. This is more of a problem when working with financial series with small samples (less than a year's data).

A single outlier is capable of changing the slope of the regression line considerably and, consequently, the value of the correlation, as demonstrated in the following example in Figure 26.10 of the six month scatterplot of the Amex oil index (XOI) vs. the Nymex oil futures daily changes. By removing just one outlier (on the far right of the graph), the correlation improved from 0.523 to 0.568 and the coefficient of determination (r^2) from 0.283 to 0.323.

■ 26.4 Homoscedasticity

In calculating Pearson's correlation coefficient or the regression coefficients, the variance is assumed to be the same at any point along the linear relationship. Otherwise the correlation coefficient is a misleading average of points of higher and lower correlation. A set of random variables having the same variance is called homoscedastic.

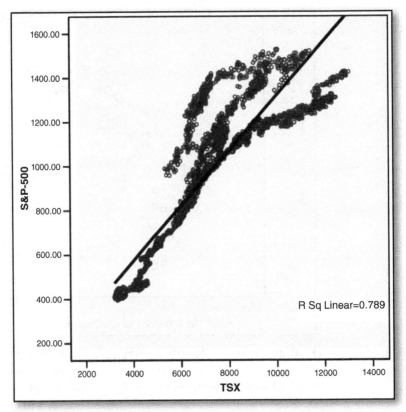

FIGURE 26.11 Fifteen Year Scatterplot of the S&P 500 vs. Canada's TSX Composite Index. The plot shows a violation of the assumption of homoscedasticity. For lower values on the TSX-Axis, the points are all very near the regression line, while for higher values the variability around the regression line increases dramatically.

Serious violations in homoscedasticity (assuming a distribution of data is homoscedastic when in actuality it is heteroscedastic) result in underemphasizing the Pearson coefficient. Heteroscedasticity does not invalidate the analysis and can be usually rectified by transforming the price data to yields or logarithms. An example of heteroscedasticity is depicted in Figure 26.11 of the scatterplot of the S&P vs. Canada's TSX index, where the variance is greater for larger values of the indices at the top right of the graph.

CHAPTER 27

Regression

From Markos Katsanos, *Intermarket Trading Strategies* (Hoboken, New Jersey: John Wiley & Sons, 2009), Chapter 3.

> *Man loves company, even if only that of a small burning candle.*
> —**Georg Christoph Lichtenberg**

Learning Objective Statements

- Recognize the meaning of values calculated by linear regression and multiple regression
- Explain why linearity is the most important assumption before using a regression model

Regression involves the use of the concept of correlation in predicting future values of one security (dependent variable), in terms of another (independent or predictor variable). For example, if there is high correlation between the S&P 500 and the Euro Stoxx 50 index we can use the linear regression equation to predict future values of the S&P by extending the least squares or linear regression line into the future (Figure 27.1).

The mere fact that we use our knowledge of the relationship between the two indices to predict values of the S&P 500 from the Euro Stoxx doesn't imply that changes in the Euro Stoxx cause changes in the S&P. These could be caused by a number of economic or geopolitical reasons which affect both indices.

■ 27.1 The Regression Equation

The general form of a simple linear regression is:

$$y = bx + a \tag{27.1}$$

where a (regression constant) is the intercept and b (regression coefficient) is the slope of the line, y is the dependent variable and x is the independent variable.

Estimates for the values of a and b can be derived by the method of ordinary least squares. The method is called "least squares" because estimates of a and b minimize the sum of squared error estimates for the given data set. The regression constant a and the coefficient b are calculated using the following formulae:

$$b = \frac{\Sigma(x_i - \overline{x})(y_i - \overline{y})}{\Sigma(x_i - \overline{x})^2} = \frac{n\Sigma(xy) - \Sigma x \Sigma y}{n\Sigma x^2 - (\Sigma x)^2} \qquad (27.2)$$

$$a = \frac{\Sigma y - b\Sigma x}{n} = \overline{y} - b\overline{x} \qquad (27.3)$$

where $\overline{x}$ is the mean of the x values, and $\overline{y}$ is the mean of the y values.

The formula for the regression coefficient b can be alternatively expressed in terms of Pearson's correlation coefficient r:

$$b = r\frac{s_y}{s_x} \qquad (27.4)$$

where s_x is the standard deviation of the predictor variable x and s_y is the standard deviation of the dependent variable y.

Table 27.1 shows an Excel sheet of one day changes between gold and the dollar index, illustrating the calculation of the regression coefficient and the constant.

Thus the regression equation to predict the dollar index in terms of gold is
Y (dollar) $= -0.314 * X$ (gold) $+ 0.083$

In the following example only 15 data sets were used but in practice more than two years' data need to be taken into account for a reliable prediction.

■ 27.2 Multiple Regression

The concept of linear regression with a single predictor variable can be extended for more than one variable combined into the following equation:

$$y = b_1 x_1 + b_1 x_1 + \ldots + b_k x_k + a \qquad (27.5)$$

In single regression we fitted a straight line to the scatterplot of points in a two dimensional graph. Extending this concept, the geometry of multiple regression (where two or more predictor variables are involved), would involve fitting a plane in multi-dimensional space.

However, since we live in a three-dimensional world, we cannot visualize the geometry when more than two independent variables are involved. We can extend, however, the same method only mathematically.

The practical problem in multiple linear regression is to select an effective set of predictor variables which will maximize the coefficient of determination, r squared, which is the proportion of variance in the dependent variable that can be explained by the variance of the predictor variables. Therefore, we want to include predictor variables that are highly correlated with the dependent variable but have low correlations among themselves.

TABLE 27.1 Example of calculating the regression coefficient *b* and the intercept *a* using Excel. The Greek letter μ depicts the mean for both the X and Y variables. The variables X and Y are the one day percentage change of gold (spot) and the dollar index respectively from 8 December 2006 to 29 December 2006.

	A	B	C	D	E	F	G	H	
	Date	X	Y	X − μ	(X − μ)²	Y − μ	(Y − μ)²	(X − μ)(Y − μ)	
3	12/8/06	−1.344	0.60	−1.386	1.921	0.570	0.325	−0.790	
4	12/11/06	0.929	−0.132	0.887	0.787	−0.202	0.041	−0.179	
5	12/12/06	−0.008	−0.289	−0.050	0.003	−0.359	0.129	0.018	
6	12/13/06	−0.325	0.470	−0.367	0.135	0.400	0.160	−0.147	
7	12/14/06	−0.430	0.444	−0.472	0.223	0.374	0.140	−0.176	
8	12/15/06	−1.664	0.406	−1.706	2.910	0.336	0.113	−0.573	
9	12/18/06	0.163	−0.036	0.121	0.015	−0.106	0.011	−0.013	
10	12/19/06	1.088	−0.667	1.046	1.094	−0.737	0.543	−0.771	
11	12/20/06	−0.402	0.096	−0.444	0.197	0.026	0.001	−0.011	
12	12/21/06	−0.250	0.072	−0.292	0.085	0.002	0.000	−0.001	
13	12/22/06	0.332	0.263	0.290	0.084	0.193	0.037	0.056	
14	12/26/06	0.613	0.298	0.571	0.326	0.228	0.052	0.130	
15	12/27/06	0.401	−0.107	0.359	0.129	−0.177	0.031	−0.064	
16	12/28/06	1.133	−0.179	1.091	1.190	−0.249	0.062	−0.272	
17	12/29/06	0.394	−0.227	0.352	0.124	−0.297	0.088	−0.105	
18	Σ	0.630	1.052		9.223		1.733	−2.897	
19	n	15	15					−0.207	Covariance σ_{xy} =
20	mean μ	0.042	0.070					−0.725	Pearson's Correlation **r** =
21	μ	0.812	0.352					−0.314	Regression Coef. *b* (formula 13.2)
22								−0.314	Regression Coef. *b* (formula 13.4)
23								0.083	Regression Constant *a* =
24								0.083	Regression Constant *a* =

Formula for Column H

Row	
21	H18/E18
22	H20*C21/B21
23	(C18-H21*B18)/B19
24	(C18-H21*B18)/B19

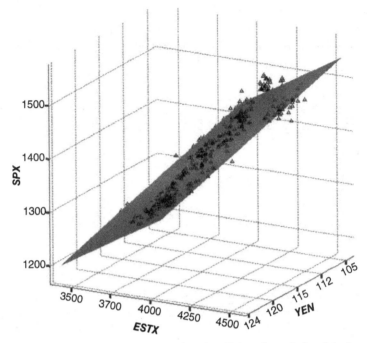

FIGURE 27.1 Three-dimensional scatterplot visualizing the relationship between the S&P 500 (on the Y-axis) vs. the Euro Stoxx 50 (on the X-axis) and the yen (on the Z-axis) for the 2-year period from 1 January 2006 to 31 December 2007. The more points fall inside the regression plane the better the predictive power of the regression model.

As a rule of thumb, intercorrelation among the independents above 0.80 signals a possible problem and may cause the system to become unstable. The statistically preferred method of assessing multicollinearity is to calculate the tolerance coefficient for each independent variable.

Tolerance is $1 - r^2$ (one minus the coefficient of determination) for the regression of each independent variable on all the other independents, ignoring the dependent. There will be as many tolerance coefficients as there are independents. The higher the intercorrelation of the independents, the more the tolerance will approach zero. As a rule of thumb, if tolerance is less than 0.20, a problem with multicollinearity is indicated.

High multicollinearity can be ignored when two or more independents are components of an index, and high intercorrelation among them is intentional and desirable. These are usually combined in an index prior to running regression, but when this is not practically possible they can be entered individually. For example, if data for an obscure index are not readily available some of the component stocks can be used instead of the index itself.

Perhaps this is better understood with an example. Let's say that we want to design an intermarket system to trade the S&P 500. The first step is to calculate the correlation between the S&P 500 with major international equity, commodity and financial indices.

Because of normality and linearity problems associated with raw index prices, these are converted to weekly percentage yields and the correlation matrix is calculated (depicted in Table 27.2). The next step is to add to the regression equation

581

TABLE 27.2 Correlation matrix of weekly % yields of major international indices, the CBOE volatility index (VIX,) the Utility Index (UTY) and the 10-year Treasury yield (TNX) with the S&P 500 for the 5-year period from 1 January 2001 to 31 December 2006.

	S&P 500	ESTX	DAX	CAC 40	FTSE	Nikkei	VIX	UTY	TNX
S&P 500	1	0.81	0.80	0.80	0.74	0.42	−0.72	0.60	0.39
ESTX	0.81	1	0.94	0.97	0.88	0.49	−0.57	0.43	0.45
DAX	0.80	0.94	1	0.92	0.82	0.51	−0.56	0.39	0.49
CAC 40	0.80	0.97	0.92	1	0.89	0.49	−0.56	0.43	0.46
FTSE	0.74	0.88	0.82	0.89	1	0.45	−0.54	0.40	0.42
Nikkei	0.42	0.49	0.51	0.49	0.45	1	−0.36	0.21	0.29
VIX	−0.72	−0.57	−0.56	−0.56	−0.54	−0.36	1	−0.43	−0.25
UTY	0.60	0.43	0.39	0.43	0.40	0.21	−0.43	1	0.04
TNX	0.39	0.45	0.49	0.46	0.42	0.29	−0.25	0.04	1

the predictor variables one at a time and calculate the coefficient of determination (r squared) and the tolerance for each variable. As you can see in Table 27.3, including more than three variables will only improve r squared marginally or not at all and the tolerance drops below 0.2 for a number of cross correlated variables. Thus the first step is to exclude the DAX, FTSE, and CAC 40 since they are highly correlated with the ESTX (Euro Stoxx). The Nikkei is then dropped from the analysis as it doesn't improve the r squared coefficient at all. The remaining variables are the ESTX, VIX, and UTY (model 3) and the regression equation becomes:

$$SP = 0.366 \,^* ESTX - 0.067 \,^* VIX + 0.206 \,^* UTY + 0.045 \qquad (27.6)$$

where SP, ESTX, VIX, TNX, and UTY are weekly percentage changes of the corresponding indices.

TABLE 27.3 The coefficient of determination (r^2), the r^2 change and the tolerance are depicted for each model. The first model includes only the Euro Stoxx, the second includes the Euro Stoxx and the VIX, and one more index is added for each subsequent model.

Model	r^2	r^2 change	Tolerance							
			ESTX	VIX	UTY	TNX	DAX	FTSE	CAC 40	Nikkei
1	0.65	0.65	1.00							
2	0.75	0.10	0.67	0.67						
3	**0.79**	**0.05**	**0.63**	**0.63**	**0.77**					
4	0.80	0.01	0.52	0.63	0.74	0.77				
5	0.81	0.01	0.12	0.62	0.74	0.74	0.12			
6	0.81	0.00	0.08	0.62	0.74	0.73	0.12	0.21		
7	0.81	0.00	0.05	0.62	0.73	0.73	0.11	0.19	0.05	
8	0.81	0.00	0.05	0.60	0.73	0.73	0.11	0.19	0.05	0.72

Substituting the values for ESTX, VIX, and UTY for 11/7/06 in (3.6):

$$SP = 0.366^* 1.7 - 0.067^* (-0.09) + 0.206^* (-1.6) + 0.045 = 0.343\% \text{vs} 0.36\%$$

the actual S&P 500 weekly change for the specific week.

27.3 Assumptions

The most important assumption is that of linearity. Checking that the linearity assumption is met is an essential task before using a regression model, as substantial violation of linearity means regression results may be more or less unusable.

Simple inspection of scatterplots is a common, if nonstatistical, method of determining if nonlinearity exists in a relationship. An alternative is to fit a preliminary linear regression and to use the appropriate diagnostic plots to detect departures from linearity. Transforming one of the variables (for example by taking differences or logs) can sometimes help linearize a nonlinear relationship between two financial series.

Normality is also a problem when considering raw stock or index prices but it is less of a problem when taking log differences or percentage yields. The problem of the longer tails can be partially overcome by removing some of the most extreme outliers.

Normality can be visually assessed by looking at a histogram of frequencies. Alternatively you can use a formal normality test such as the Shapiro-Wilks W test or the Kolmogorov-Smirnov D test.

27.4 Nonparametric Regression

Nonparametric regression relaxes the usual assumption of linearity and makes no assumptions about the population distribution.

A more accurate estimate of the prediction is usually obtained by using nonparametric regression in cases of severe violations of linearity at the expense of much greater computation and a more difficult-to-understand result.

Two common methods of nonparametric regression are kernel regression and smoothing splines. The smoothing splines method minimizes the sum of squared residuals, adding a term which penalizes the roughness of the fit. The kernel regression algorithm falls into a class of algorithms called "SVMs" or "Support Vector Machines." SVM-based techniques typically use a kernel function to find an optimal separating hyperplane so as to separate two classes of patterns with maximal margin. SVM models are closely related to neural network models.

In recent years, SVMs have received considerable attention because of their superior performance in forecasting high noise and nonstationary financial time series. A major advantage of SVMs over other nonparametric methods is that they can have good performance even in problems with a large number of inputs. However, unlike other nonparametric methods the major difficulty of the SVM approach lies in the selection of its kernel, as choosing different kernel functions will produce different SVMs.

CHAPTER 28

Regression Analysis

From Perry J. Kaufman, *Trading Systems and Methods, +Website*, 5th Edition (Hoboken, New Jersey: John Wiley & Sons, 2013), Chapter 6.

Learning Objective Statements

- Explain why an ARIMA model may be thought of as an adaptive process
- Explain how you would apply ARIMA trading strategies to a given chart scenario
- Show how you might use linear regression to compare relative strength of various markets

■ ARIMA

An *Autoregressive Integrated Moving Average (ARIMA)* model is created by a process of repeated regression analysis over a moving time window, resulting in a forecast value based on the new fit. An ARIMA process automatically applies the most important features of regression analysis in a preset order and continues to reanalyze results until an optimum set of parameters or coefficients is found. An ARIMA model does all of this as part of its special process. Because it is used to recalculate the *best fit* each time a new piece of data appears, it may be thought of as an *adaptive process*.

G. E. P. Box and G. M. Jenkins refined ARIMA at the University of Wisconsin,[1] and their procedures for solution have become the industry standard. This technique is often referred to as the *Box-Jenkins forecast*. The two important terms in ARIMA are *autoregression* and *moving average*. *Autoregression* refers to the use of the same data to self-predict, for example, using only gold prices to arrive at a gold price forecast.

---

[1] G.E.P. Box and G.M. Jenkins, *Time Series Analysis: Forecasting and Control,* 2nd ed. (San Francisco: Holden-Day, 1976).

Moving average refers to the normal concept of smoothing price fluctuations, using a rolling average of the past *n* days. This process uses an exponential smoothing technique, which is convenient for computation.

In the ARIMA process, the autocorrelation is used to determine to what extent past prices will forecast future prices. In a *first-order autocorrelation*, only the prices on the previous day are used to determine the forecast. This would be expressed as

$$P_t = a \times P_{t-1} + e$$

where P_t = the price being forecast (dependent variable)

P_{t-1} = the price being used to forecast (independent variable)

a = the coefficient (constant factor)

e = the forecast error

In a *second-order autoregression*, the previous two prices are used,

$$P_t = a_1 \times P_{t-1} + a_2 \times P_{t-2} + e$$

where the current forecast p_t is based on the two previous prices p_{t-1} and p_{t-2}; there are two unique coefficients and a forecast error. The moving average is used to correct for the forecast error, e. There is also the choice of a first- or second-order moving average process,

$$\text{First-order:} \quad E_t = e_t - be_{t-1}$$

$$\text{Second-order:} \quad E_t = e_t - b_1 e_{t-1} - b_2 e_{t-2}$$

where E_t = the approximated error term

e_t = today's forecast error

e_{t-1} and e_{t-2} = the two previous forecast errors

b_1 and b_2 = the two regression coefficients

Because the two constant coefficients, b_1 and b_2, can be considered percentages, the moving average process is similar to exponential smoothing.

The success of the ARIMA model is determined by two factors: high correlation in the autoregression and low variance in the final forecast errors. The determination of whether to use a first- or second-order autoregression is based on a comparison of the *correlation coefficients* of the two regressions. If there is little improvement using the second-order process, it is not used. The final forecast is constructed by adding the moving average term, which approximates the errors, back into the autoregressive process

$$P_t' = p_t + E_t + e'$$

where P_t' = the new forecast

e' = the new forecast error

The moving average process is again repeated for the new errors e', added back into the forecast to get a new value p'' and another error e''. When the variance of the errors becomes sufficiently small, the ARIMA process is complete.

The contribution of Box and Jenkins was to stress the simplicity of the solution. They determined that the autoregression and moving average steps could be limited to first- or second-order processes. To do this, it was first necessary to *detrend* the data, thereby making it *stationary*. Detrending can be accomplished most easily by *differencing* the data, creating a new series by subtracting each previous term p_{t-1} from the next p_t. Of course, the ARIMA program must remember all of these changes, or *transformations,* in order to restore the final forecast to the proper price notation by applying these operations in reverse. If a satisfactory solution is not found in the Box-Jenkins process, it is usually because the data are still not stationary and further differencing is necessary.

With the three features just discussed, the Box-Jenkins forecast is usually shown as *ARIMA (p, d, q),* where p is the number of autoregressive terms, d is the number of differences, and q is the number of moving average terms. The expression *ARIMA* $(0,1,1)$ is equivalent to simple exponential smoothing. In its normal form, the Box-Jenkins ARIMA process performs the following steps:

1. **Specification.** Preliminary steps for determining the order of the autoregression and moving average to be used:

   - *The variance must be stabilized.* In many price series, increased volatility is directly related to increased price. In stocks, the common assumption is that this relationship is *log-normal*, that increasing volatility takes the shape of a logarithmic curve. A simple test for variance stability, using the log function, is checked before more complex transformations are used.

   - *Prices are detrended.* This uses the technique of first differences; however, a second difference (or more) will be performed if it helps to remove further trending properties in the series (this is determined by later steps).

   - *Specify the order of the autoregressive and moving average components.* This fixes the number of prior terms to be used in these approximations (not necessarily the same number). In the Box-Jenkins approach, these numbers should be as small as possible; often one value is used for both. Large numbers require a rapidly expanding amount of calculation, even for a computer.

     The number of terms is a critical part of the ARIMA solution. The object of this last step is to find the fewest terms necessary to solve the problem. All ARIMA programs will print a *correlogram,* a display of the autocorrelation coefficients. The correlogram is used to find whether all the trends and well-defined periodic movements have been removed from the series by differencing. Figure 28.1 shows the output from ProStat for 15 lags using the first differences of 20 years of gold futures prices. If any of the correlations had been significant (for example, over 0.40), the data would be

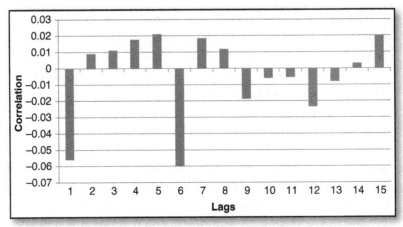

FIGURE 28.1   ARIMA Correlograms from Autocorrelations. Lags shown along the bottom give correlations at the left. None of them are significant (output from ProStat based on gold futures).

differenced again. The correlogram is one way of visualizing serial correlation, the dependence of current data on previous data. This same objective will be accomplished differently using a Monte Carlo process to estimate investment risk.

2. **Estimation: determining the coefficients.** The previous step was used to reduce the number of autoregressive and moving average terms necessary to the estimation process. The ARIMA method of solution is one of minimizing the errors in the forecast. In minimization, it will perform a linear or nonlinear regression on price (depending on the number of coefficients selected), determine the errors in the estimation, and then approximate those errors using a moving average. It will next look at the resulting new error series, attempt to estimate and correct the errors in that one, and repeat the process until it cannot improve results further.

To determine when an ARIMA process is completed, three tests are performed at the end of each estimation pass:

1. *Compare the change in the coefficient value.* If the last estimation has caused little or no change in the value of the coefficient(s), the model has successfully converged to a solution.
2. *Compare the sum of the squares of the error.* If the error value is small or if it stays relatively unchanged, the process is completed.
3. *Perform a set number of estimations.* Unless a maximum number of estimations is set, an ARIMA process might continue indefinitely. This safety check is necessary in the event the model is not converging to a solution.

Once completed, the errors can be examined using an O-statistic to check for any trend. If one exists, an additional moving average term may be used to eliminate it.

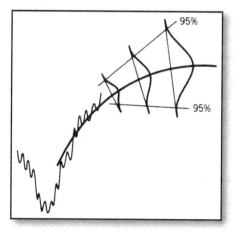

FIGURE 28.2   ARIMA Forecast Becomes Less Accurate as It Is Used Further Ahead.

Forecast Results

Once the coefficients have been determined, they are used to calculate the forecast value. These forecasts are most accurate for the next day and should be used with less confidence for subsequent days (see Figure 28.2).

What if the forecast does not work? First, the process should be checked to be certain that it was performed properly. Be sure that any data transformations were reversed. Pay particular attention to the removal of trends using the correlogram. Next, check the data used in the process. If the data sample is changing (which can be observed on a price chart), select either a shorter or longer period that contains more homogeneous data, that is, data similar to the current market period.

ARIMA Trading Strategies

In the article that originally piqued the interest of traders,[2] Anon uses a 5-day-ahead forecast. If the ARIMA process forecasts an uptrend and prices fall below the forecast value, the market can be bought with added confidence (expecting lower risk and more profit by buying at a price that is below estimated value). This technique of selecting better entry points may compensate for some of the inaccuracies latent in any forecasting method. The danger of this approach is that prices may continue to move counter to the forecast.

Following the Trend   Use the 1-day-ahead forecast to determine the trend position. Hold a long position if the forecast is for higher prices, and take a short position if the process is expecting lower prices.

---

[2] Louis J. Anon, "Catch Short-Term Profits with ARIMA," *Commodities Magazine* (December 1981).

Mean-Reverting Indicator Use the ARIMA confidence bands to determine overbought/oversold levels. Not only can a long position be entered when prices penetrate the *lowest* 95% confidence band, but they can be closed out when they return to the normal 50% level. Although mean reversion trades are tempting, they always carry more risk than trend trading. A conservative trader will enter the market only in the direction of the ARIMA trend forecast. As shown in Figure 28.2, if the trend is up, only the penetrations of a lower confidence band will be used to enter new long positions.

Use of Highs and Lows The implied highs and lows, as well as the independently forecasted highs and lows, can be the basis for other interesting strategies.[3] The following two are used with intraday prices.

1. Using confidence bands based on the closing prices, buy an intraday penetration of the expected high or sell short a penetration of the expected low, and liquidate the position on the close. Use a stop-loss. Take positions only in the direction of the ARIMA trend.
2. Using the separate ARIMA models based on the daily high and low prices, buy a penetration of the 50% level of the high and sell a penetration of the 50% level of the lows. Liquidate positions on the close. Use a stop-loss.

Slope The 1-day-ahead forecast suggested in "Following the Trend" a few paragraphs earlier is essentially a projection of the slope of the trendline. The purpose of directional analysis, whether regression or moving averages, is to uncover the true direction of prices by discarding the noise. Therefore, the slope of the trendline, or the direction of the regression forecast, is the logical answer.

The popular alternate for triggering a new directional signal is a price penetration of an envelope or band value. Using regression analysis, that band can be replaced by a confidence level. While it is true that the number of random, or false, penetrations declines as the confidence band gets farther away from the trendline, so does the total number of penetrations. At any band distance, there are still a large number of erroneous signals. The slope itself should be viewed as the best approximation of direction.

Kalman Filters

Kalman offers an alternative approach to ARIMA, allowing an underlying forecasting model (*message model*) to be combined with other timely information (*observation model*). The message model may be any trading strategy, moving average, or regression approach. The observation model may be the specialist's or floor broker's opening calls, market liquidity, or earlier trading activity in the same stock or index market on a foreign exchange—all of which have been determined to good candidate inputs for forecasting.

---

[3] John F. Kepka, "Trading with ARIMA Forecasts," *Technical Analysis of Stocks & Commodities* (August 1985).

Assume that the original forecast (message) model can be described as

$$M(p_t) = c_f P_{t-1} + me_t$$

and the observation model as

$$O(p_t) = c_o P_t + oe_t$$

where me and oe are the message and observation model errors, respectively.

The combined forecast would then use the observation model error to modify the result

$$p'_{t+1} = c_f p'_t + K_{t+1} oe_t$$

where K is the Kalman gain coefficient,[4] a factor that adjusts the error term.

■ Basic Trading Signals Using a Linear Regression Model

A linear regression, or straight-line fit, could be the basis for a simple trading strategy similar to a moving average. For example, an n-day linear regression, applied to the closing prices, can produce a 1-day-ahead forecast price, F_{t+1}, a projection of the slope. We can use this with the following rules for trading:

- *Buy* when tomorrow's closing price (C_{t+1}) moves above the forecasted value of tomorrow's close (F_{t+1}).

- *Sell short* when tomorrow's closing price (C_{t+1}) moves below the forecasted value of tomorrow's close (F_{t+1}).[5]

Adding Confidence Bands

Because the linear regression line passes through the center of price movement during a steady period of rising or falling prices, these rules would produce a lot of buy and sell signals. To reduce the frequency of signals and avoid changes of direction due to market noise, confidence bands are drawn on either side of the regression line. A 90% confidence band is simply 1.65 times the standard deviation of the residuals (R_t, the difference between the actual prices and the corresponding value on the regression line as of time t, the most recent price). A 95% confidence band uses a multiplier of 1.96; however, most people use 2.0 simply for convenience. The new trading rules using a 95% confidence band would then become

---

[4] For a more complete discussion, see Andrew D. Seidel and Philip D. Ginsberg, *Commodities Trading* (Englewood Cliffs, NJ: Prentice-Hall, 1983), or R. E. Kalman, "A New Approach to Linear Filtering and Prediction Problems," *Journal of Basic Engineering* (March 1960).

[5] These rules were used by Frank Hochheimer and Richard Vaughn in *Computerized Trading Techniques 1982* (New York: Merrill Lynch Commodities, 1982).

- *Buy* when tomorrow's closing price (C_{t+1}) moves above the forecasted value of tomorrow's close (F_{t+1}) + ($2.0 \times R_t$).

- *Sell short* when tomorrow's closing price (C_{t+1}) moves below the forecasted value of tomorrow's close (F_{t+1}) − ($2.0 \times R_t$).

An important difference between a model based on linear regression and one founded on a moving average is the lag. Both methods assume that prices will continue to move according to the pattern identified using the last price data available. If prices continue higher at the same rate, a moving average system will initially lag behind, then increase at the same rate. The lag creates a safety zone to absorb some minor changes in the direction of prices without indicating that the trend has changed.

A regression model, however, identifies a change of direction sooner by measuring tomorrow's actual price against the projected future price (a straight-line projection for a linear regression). Confidence bands around the straight-line projection will decide the size of the price move up or down needed to change the trend direction. Figure 28.3 shows the changing direction of a rolling linear regression at three points in time compared to a moving average. At the most recent period on the chart the reversal point for the trend direction is much closer using the confidence bands of the regression than the lagged moving average. This may not be the case during the intervals where price changes direction at the bottom of the chart. The Companion Website

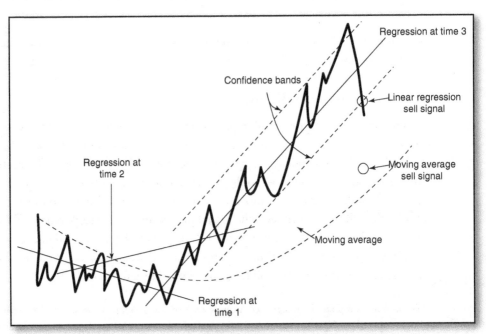

FIGURE 28.3 Linear Regression Model. Penetration of the confidence band turns the trend from up to down. When prices move steadily up, the regression model will signal a change of direction faster than a moving average.

has a spreadsheet, *Bund regression with bands*, that produces trading signals and performance using regression bands. It also compares the results with the slope method described in the next section.

In general, the use of regression lines works well for finding the price trend, although actual trading signals differ from moving average and breakout strategies. As with most trending systems, performance tends to improve as the calculation period increases, capturing the largest economic trends.

Using the Linear Regression Slope

The slope of the linear regression line, the angle at which it is rising or falling, is an effective way to simplify the usefulness of the regression process. The slope shows how quickly prices are expected to change over a unit of time. The unit of time is the same as the period of data used to find the regression values. When you use a longer calculation period, the slope of the regression line changes slowly; when you use only a few days in your calculation, the slope changes quickly. Using only the slope, you can trade with the following rules:

- *Buy* when the value of the slope is positive (rising).
- *Sell* when the value of the slope is negative (falling).

When using the slope, there is less need for a confidence band because the longer calculation periods smooth out erratic price movement. The scale of the slope is different from the prices; therefore it will be seen in a separate panel on a chart (the middle panel in Figure 28.4).

Adding Correlations

The slope is a practical substitution for the regression line and confidence bands, but it can also be misleading. It is possible to have the same slope value while prices are moving higher in both a smooth pattern or in a very noisy, erratic one. Using

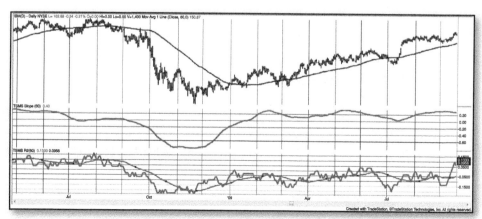

FIGURE 28.4   IBM Trend Using the Slope and R.

the correlation coefficient, R^2, will provide a measurement of the consistency of the price movement.[6]

Instead of R^2, which is always positive, R will be used. And, instead of using the usual price differences (or return differences), the actual prices will be used and correlated against a series of sequential numbers. This should give us a better value for whether the prices are trending. If R becomes negative then prices are trending down. This can be seen in the bottom panel of Figure 28.4. A 60-day moving average of prices is shown at the top, a corresponding 60-day slope is in the middle, and a 60-day R is at the bottom along with a 30-day (R-period/2) trend of R.

The trading rules for the slope are normally the same as those for a moving average: a long position is entered when the trendline or slope turns up and a short sale begins when the trendline turns down; however, the slope today can be less than yesterday but still positive, which means that the trend is still up. Then another rule would be to buy when the slope turns positive and sell short when it turns negative.

Figure 28.4 shows that using the moving average trend is good, but has the greatest lag. The slope is much faster but less stable. Adding R gives a different view of where the trends change and can complement either method.

Forecast Oscillator

Tushar Chande used the regression forecast and its residuals to create trend-following signals called the *Forecast Oscillator*.[7] Using a 5-day regression, find the residuals and calculate the percentage variation from the regression line. A buy signal occurs when the 3-day average of the residuals crosses above the regression line; a short sale is when the 3-day average of the residuals crosses below the regression line. If

$$\%F_t = 100 \times \frac{y_t - \hat{y}_t}{y_t}$$

and $\%F_t(3)$ is the 3-day moving average of $\%F$, then

> *buy* when $\%F_t(3)$ crosses above $\hat{y}_t$
> *sell short* when $\%F_t(3)$ crosses below $\hat{y}_t$

This makes the assumption that the residuals have a trending quality.

■ Measuring Market Strength

One of the natural applications of the linear regression is to measure and compare the strength of one market against another. For example, we might want to ask, "Which market is leading the other, Hewlett Packard or Dell? The slope of the linear

[6] See Rudy Tesco, "LRS + R-Squared = the 95% Solution," *Technical Analysis of Stocks & Commodities* (February 2003).

[7] Tushar S. Chande and Stanley Kroll, *The New Technical Trader* (New York: John Wiley & Sons, 1994).

regression, measured over the same calculation period, is the perfect tool for comparing, or *ranking*, a set of markets. Figure 28.5 shows the prices of four pharmaceutical companies, Amgen (AMGN), Johnson & Johnson (JNJ), Merck (MRK), and Pfizer (PFE). Which of them is the strongest during the last 60 days? No doubt it's PFE, the line at the bottom. But the weakest is not as clear.

In order to rank these correctly, it is best to index the stock prices, starting at 100 on the same date. For only stocks, indexing is not necessary, but if you are mixing stocks and futures, or just using futures, indexing will be needed to put the trading units into the same notation. Figure 28.6 shows the indexed stocks beginning at the value of 100.

Once indexed, apply a rolling linear regression slope to each market using the same calculation period, 60 days in this example. Figure 28.7 shows that that PFE was the

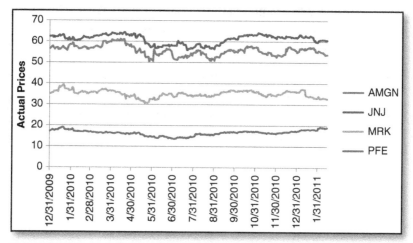

FIGURE 28.5 Prices of Four Pharmaceutical Companies, 2010 through January 2011.

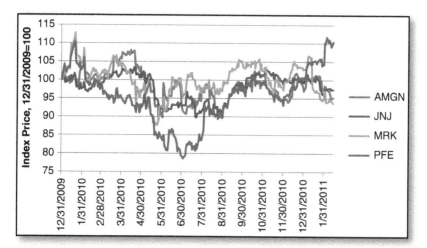

FIGURE 28.6 Indexed Stocks beginning at 100 Give a Better View of Relative Performance.

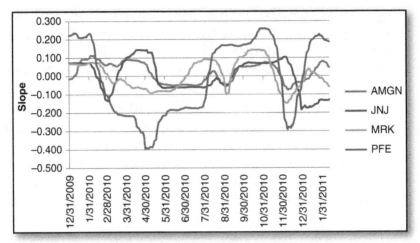

FIGURE 28.7 Rolling Linear Regression Slope, Using a 60-day Calculation Period, Shows That Each Market Changes from Stronger to Weaker over the 1-Year Period.

most volatile because the slope varied from much higher to much lower than the others, while each stock had its turn at being the strongest and weakest. At the right side of the chart, PFE finishes the strongest followed by AMGN, MRK, and JNJ.

CHAPTER 29

The Scientific Method and Technical Analysis

From David Aronson, *Evidence-Based Technical Analysis: Applying the Scientific Method and Statistical Inference to Trading Signals* (Hoboken, New Jersey: John Wiley & Sons, 2006), Chapter 3.

Learning Objective Statements

- Give an example of the applicability of the scientific method towards technical analysis research
- Explain the three forms of the EMH
- Explain the three consequences, articulated in this chapter, of adopting the scientific method in technical analysis

TA's central problem is erroneous knowledge. As it is traditionally practiced, much of TA is a body of dogma and myth, founded on faith and anecdote. This is a consequence of the informal, intuitive methods used by its practitioners to discover patterns with predictive power. As a discipline, TA suffers because it is practiced without discipline.

Adopting a rigorous scientific approach would solve this problem. The scientific method is not a cookbook procedure that automates knowledge discovery. Rather it is "a set of methods designed to describe and interpret observed or inferred phenomena, past or present aimed at building a testable body of knowledge open to rejection or confirmation. In other words, (it) is a specific way of analyzing information with the goal of testing claims."[1] This chapter summarizes its logical and philosophical foundations and discusses the implications of its adoption by TA practitioners.

■ The Most Important Knowledge of All: A Method to Get More

"Of all the kinds of knowledge that the West has given to the world, the most valuable is the scientific method, a set of procedures for acquiring new knowledge. It was invented by a series of European thinkers from about 1550 to 1700."[2] Compared to informal approaches it is unsurpassed in its ability to separate fact from falsehood. The dramatic increase in our understanding of and control over the natural world over the last 400 years attests to the power of the scientific method.

The method's rigor protects us from the frailties of mind, which often impair what we learn from experience using less formal methods. Although informal knowledge acquisition works well for many of the obvious truths of daily living, sometimes what seems obvious is not true. It was obvious to the ancients that the sun revolved around the earth. It took science to show this was false. Informal observation and intuitive inference are especially prone to failure when phenomena are complex or highly random. Financial market behavior displays both.

Historically, TA has not been practiced in a scientific manner, but this is now changing. In academia and the business world, a new breed of practitioners, known as quants, have been adopting a scientific approach. Indeed, some of the most successful hedge funds are using strategies that could be called scientific TA.

Unsurprisingly, many traditional TA practitioners have resisted this change. Vested interests and habitual ways of thinking are hard to abandon. No doubt there was opposition when folk medicine evolved into modern medicine, when alchemy progressed into chemistry, and when astrology advanced into the science of astronomy. Rancor between traditional and scientific practitioners is to be expected. However, if history is any guide, traditional TA will, in the end, be marginalized. Astrologers, alchemists, and witch doctors still practice, but they are no longer taken seriously.

■ The Legacy of Greek Science: A Mixed Blessing

The Greeks were the first to make an effort at being scientific, though their legacy proved to be a mixed blessing. On the positive side of the ledger was the invention of logic by Aristotle. The formal reasoning procedures he developed remain a pillar of today's scientific method.

On the negative side were his faulty theories of matter and motion. Instead of being generalized from prior observations and tested against freshly observed facts, as is the practice in modern science, his theories were deduced from metaphysical principles. When observations conflicted with theory, Aristotle and his disciples were prone to bending the facts rather than altering or abandoning the theory. Modern science does the opposite.

Aristotle ultimately realized that deductive logic was insufficient for learning about the world. He saw the need for an empirical approach based on inductive logic—observation followed by generalization. Its invention was his most significant contribution to science. However, he failed in the application of his own invention. At his institution of higher learning, the famed Lyceum in Athens, Aristotle and his students made meticulous observations on a wide range of natural phenomena. Unfortunately, the inferences they drew from these facts were biased by Aristotelian dogma and often based on inadequate evidence.[3] There was too much theorizing from too little evidence. When facts contradicted favored first principles, Aristotle would contort the facts to conserve the principle.

Ultimately the Aristotelian legacy would prove to be an obstruction to scientific progress. Because his authority was so great, his flawed theories were transmitted as unquestioned dogma through the next 2,000 years. This hindered the growth of scientific knowledge, or at least the sort of knowledge that we now characterize as scientific.[4] In a like manner, the teachings of TA's pioneers like Dow, Schabacker, Elliott, and Gann have been passed along unquestioned and untested. Just as there is no room for dogma in science, neither should there be in TA.

■ The Birth of the Scientific Revolution

"Science was the major discovery, or invention, of the seventeenth century. Men of that time learned—and it was a very revolutionary discovery—how to measure, explain, and manipulate natural phenomena in a way that we call scientific. Since the seventeenth century, science has progressed a great deal and has discovered many truths, and it has conferred many benefits that the seventeenth century did not know, but it has not found a new way to discover natural truths. For this reason, the seventeenth century is possibly the most important century in human history."[5]

The revolution began in Western Europe around 1500 in an atmosphere of intellectual stagnation. At that time, all knowledge was based on authoritarian pronouncements rather than observed facts. The doctrines of the Roman Church and the dogma of Greek science were taken as literal truths. On Earth, objects were assumed to be governed by Aristotelian physics. In the heavens, the laws invented by the Greek astronomer Ptolemy and later endorsed by the Church were thought to rule. The Ptolemaic system held that the earth was the center of the universe and that the sun, stars, and planets orbited about it. To the casual observer, the facts seemed to agree with the Church's orthodox theory.

Everyone was happy until people began to notice facts that conflicted with these accepted truths. Artillerymen observed that projectiles hurled by catapults and shot from cannons did not fly in conformity with Aristotle's theory of motion (Figure 29.1). The objects were repeatedly observed to follow arced paths—a

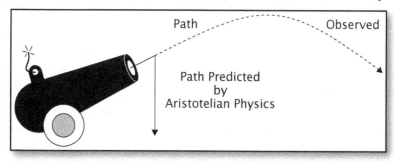

FIGURE 29.1 Prediction versus Observation.

distinct departure from the trajectory predicted by Greek theory, which would have had them fall directly to earth as soon as they left the apparatus. Either the theory was wrong or the soldiers were deceived by their senses. The notion of testing the validity of a theory by comparing its predictions with subsequent observations is fundamental to the modern scientific method. This was an early step in that direction.

Also, at that time, observations of the heavens began to collide with the Church's theory of an Earth-centered universe. Increasingly accurate astronomical measurements revealed that planets did not move as the theory said they should. For a time, bewildered astronomers were able to patch up the Church's theory to make it agree with observed planetary paths. As discordant observations occurred, new assumptions were added to the theory, in the form of smaller orbits revolving about a planet's principal orbit. These ad hoc fixes, called epicycles, permitted the theory to account for the troublesome observations. For example, epicycles were able to explain why planets were sometimes seen to move backwards (retrograde motion) rather than follow a continuous path across the sky. Over time, a succession of epicycle fixes transformed the fundamentally incorrect theory of an Earth-centered universe into an unwieldy monstrosity of complexity with epicycles upon smaller epicycles upon even smaller epicycles.

A landmark in scientific history took place when the telescope of Galileo Galilei (1564–1642) showed that four moons circled the planet Jupiter. This observation contradicted Church orthodoxy that all celestial objects must revolve around the Earth. Galileo's findings would have called for the rejection of deeply held beliefs and the destruction of the Church's view of reality. Religious authorities were not about to face these facts. Though Galileo had originally been given permission by the Church to publish his findings, it subsequently withdrew the permission and found him guilty ex post facto. As punishment, he was forced to give up astronomy and live out his days under house arrest.6

Eventually, the Church's theory of the heavens was replaced by the far simpler and more correct Copernican model. It placed the sun at the center of the universe and managed to explain astronomical observations with far fewer assumptions. Today we know that the sun is not the center of the universe, but at the time the Copernican model represented a true increase in man's knowledge of the heavens.

■ Faith in Objective Reality and Objective Observations

Science makes a fundamental assumption about the nature of reality; there is an objective reality that exists outside and independent of those who observe it, and this reality is the source of the observer's sensory impressions. This faith is the basis of science's emphasis on observation. It is properly characterized as a faith because there is no experiment or logic that can prove the existence of an objective reality. For example, I cannot prove that my perception of a red traffic signal is caused by a light that exists outside of myself rather than by something that arose entirely within my own mind.

One might ask why we should make a big deal about a fact that seems so obvious to common sense. Everyone can see there is a world out there. However, in the eyes of science this issue is a mountain and not a molehill, and it points to an important difference between knowing scientifically and knowing intuitively. Science does not accept something as true simply because it seems to be so. The history of science has shown repeatedly that the obvious is not necessarily true. Science assumes the truth of an independent objective reality, not because it is self-evident, but because it is consistent with a principle that shapes much of the scientific enterprise—*the principle of simplicity*.

The principle says simpler is better. Thus, when judging which of several theories is most likely to be true, when all theories are equally good at fitting a set of observed facts, the principle of simplicity urges us to accept the simplest theory. This is the theory that invokes the fewest and least complicated assumptions. The principle of simplicity, also known as Ockham's Razor, tells us to cut away a theory's excess complexity. The Copernican model of the universe was preferable to the Church's model because it replaced a complex arrangement of epicycles with one orbit for each planet. In a like manner, if a segment of market history can be explained either as a random walk, which assumes very little, or as an Elliott wave pattern that assumes waves embedded within waves, golden ratios, Fibonacci sequences, and a host of other complexities, the random walk is the preferred explanation. That is, unless the Elliott Wave Principle is able to make more accurate predictions than the random-walk theory.

Assuming the existence of an external reality simplifies matters greatly. To do otherwise would require a far more complex set of assumptions to explain why two people, observing the same phenomenon, will come away with generally the same impression. Explaining why I see other cars stopping when I see the traffic signal turning red is simple if I assume that there really is a traffic light out there. However, without that assumption, many more complicated assumptions would be required to explain why other motorists stop when I do.

As a consequence of its faith in an objective reality, science holds that objective and subjective perceptions are essentially different. My objective observation of a red traffic signal and my subjective experience of being annoyed because it will make me late for work are not the same. Objective observations can be shared with and confirmed by other observers. For this reason, objective observations lend themselves to the establishment of knowledge that can be shared with and confirmed by others. Subjective thoughts, interpretations, and feelings cannot, and this flaw alone is sufficient to disqualify subjective TA as legitimate knowledge.

■ The Nature of Scientific Knowledge

Albert Einstein once said; "One thing I have learned in a long life: that all our science, measured against reality is primitive and childlike—and yet it is the most precious thing we have."[7] Scientific knowledge is different than wisdom gained by other modes of inquiry such as common sense, faith, authority, and intuition. These differences, which account for science's higher reliability, are considered in this section.

Scientific Knowledge Is Objective

Science strives for maximum objectivity by confining itself exclusively to facts about the world out there, although it is understood that perfectly objective knowledge is never attainable. This eliminates from consideration subjective assessments that are inherently private and accessible by only one person. Inner thoughts and emotive states cannot be shared accurately with others, even when that is the intent of an artist, poet, writer, or composer. In *Naked Lunch*, William Burroughs attempts to convey his personal experience of heroin. However, I will never know his experience and may take away from those passages something quite different than Burroughs's experience or that of someone else reading it. Scientific knowledge is, therefore, public in the sense that it can be shared with and verified by as many people as possible. This promotes maximum possible agreement among independent observers.

Scientific knowledge is empirical or observation based. In this way it differs from mathematical and logical propositions that are derived from and consistent with a set of axioms but need not refer to the external world or be confirmed by observation. For example, the Pythagorean Theorem tells us that the squared length of the hypotenuse of a right triangle, c, is equal to the sum of the squares of the other two sides a and b or

$$c^2 = a^2 + b^2$$

However, this truth was not derived by studying thousands of examples of right triangles and generalizing from those many observations. Rather, it is derived from a set of accepted mathematical postulates.

Scientific Knowledge Is Quantitative

The notion that the world is best understood when described in quantitative terms originated with the Greek mathematician Pythagoras [569 B.C.–approx. 475 B.C.]. It was his contention that both the world and the mind are essentially mathematical. The importance science places on quantification cannot be overemphasized. "Wherever mankind has been able to measure things, which means transform or reduce them to numbers, it has indeed made great progress in understanding them and controlling them. Where human beings have failed to find a way to measure, they have been much less successful, which partly explains the failure of psychology, economics, and literary criticism to acquire the status of science."[8]

Observations must be reduced to numbers if they are to be analyzed in a rational and rigorous fashion. Quantification makes it possible to apply the powerful tool of statistical analysis. "Most scientists would say that if you cannot describe what you are doing in mathematical terms, you are not doing science."[9] Quantification is the best way to ensure the objectivity of knowledge and to maximize its ability to be shared with and tested by all qualified practitioners.

The Purpose of Science: Explanation and Prediction

The goal of science is the discovery of rules that predict new observations and theories that explain previous observations. Predictive rules, often referred to as scientific laws, are statements about recurring process, such as 'event A tends to predict event B,' but laws don't try to explain why this happens.

Explanatory theories go further than predictive rules by telling us why it is that B tends to follow A, rather than simply telling us that it does.

Scientific laws and theories differ with respect to their generality. The most prized are the most general—that is, they predict and/or explain the widest range of phenomena. A TA rule that is effective on all markets and all time scales would have higher scientific stature than one that works only on copper futures on hourly data.

Laws also differ with respect to their predictive power. Those that depict the most consistent relationships are the most valuable. All other things being equal, a TA rule that is successful 52 percent of the time is less valuable than one that works 70 percent of the time.

The most important type of scientific law is the functional relationship. It summarizes a set of observations in the form of an equation. The equation describes how a variable that we wish to predict (dependent variable) typically denoted by the letter Y, is a function of (i.e., dependent on) one or more other variables called predictors, usually designated by the letter X. This is illustrated as

$$Y = f(X_i)$$

Typically the values of the predictors are known, but the value of the dependent variable is not. In many applications, this is because the dependent variable Y refers to a future outcome, whereas the X variables refer to values that are currently known. Once a functional relationship has been derived, it is possible to predict values for the dependent variable by plugging in known values of the predictor variables.

Functional relationships can be derived in two ways. They can be deduced from explanatory theories or they can be estimated (induced) from historical data by function fitting (e.g., regression analysis). Currently, TA is primarily constrained to the latter because theories of TA are just now being formulated

■ The Role of Logic in Science

Scientific knowledge commands respect, in part because its conclusions are based on logic. By relying on logic and empirical evidence to justify its conclusions, science avoids two of the common fallacies that contaminate informal reasoning: *appeals to authority* and *appeals to tradition*. An appeal to authority offers as proof the statement of a purportedly knowledgeable person. An appeal to tradition offers a long-standing way of doing things as proof.

To its detriment, much of popular TA is justified on grounds of tradition or authority rather than formal logic and objective evidence. In many instances, current authorities merely quote prior authorities who, in turn, quote yet earlier experts and so on back to an original source whose knowledge was primarily intuitive. Thus the fallacies of authority and tradition are mutually reinforcing.

The First Rule of Logic: Consistency

Aristotle (384–322 B.C.) is credited with the invention of formal logic, which evolved from geometry. The Egyptians had been making accurate measurements of lines and angles and calculating areas for over two thousand years, but it was the "Greeks who extended these basic notions and transformed them into a compelling system of irrefutable conclusions derived from mathematical definitions (axioms)."[10]

Formal logic is the branch of mathematics concerned with the laws of correct reasoning that are used to formulate and evaluate the validity of arguments. In contrast to informal inference, if the rules of formal logic are followed, a true conclusion is guaranteed.

The most fundamental principle of formal logic is the rule of consistency. It is expressed in two laws: the *Law of the Excluded Middle* and the *Law of Noncontradiction*. "The law of the excluded middle requires that a thing must either possess or lack a given attribute. There is no middle alternative. Or said differently, the middle ground is excluded."[11] A statement is either true or false. It cannot be both. However, the law is only properly applied to situations that are binary and is easily misapplied to situations that are not truly two-state.

"Closely related to the law of the excluded middle is the law of noncontradiction. It tells us that a thing cannot both be and not be at the same time."[12] A statement cannot be true and not true at the same time. An argument that allows for its conclusion to be true and not true at the same time is said to be a self-contradictory.

As will be shown in subsequent sections, these laws of logic are used to great effect in science. Although observed evidence, such as the profitable back test of a TA rule, cannot logically prove that the rule has predictive power, that same evidence can be used to logically disprove (contradict) the assertion that the rule is devoid of predictive power. By the Law of Noncontradiction, this indirectly proves that the rule does possess predictive power. This method of proving empirical laws, called the method of indirect proof or proof by contradiction, is the logical basis of the scientific method.

Propositions and Arguments

Logical inference takes two distinct forms: deduction and induction. We will consider each separately and then see how they are used together in the logical framework of modern science, the hypothetico-deductive method. However, before considering these forms of inference some definitions are in order.

- *Proposition:* a declarative statement that is either true or false sometimes referred to as a claim. For example, the statement *The head-and-shoulder pattern has more predictive power than a random signal* is a proposition. A proposition differs from other kinds of statements that do not possess the attribute of truth of falsity such as exclamations, commands, and questions. Therefore, only propositions may be affirmed or denied.

- *Argument:* a group of propositions, one of which is referred to as the *conclusion*, which is claimed to follow logically from the other propositions, called *premises*. Thus, an argument asserts that its premises provide the evidence to establish the truth of its conclusion.

Deductive Logic

As mentioned earlier, the there are two forms of logic, deductive and inductive. This section considers deductive logic; the next considers inductive.

Categorical Syllogisms   A deductive argument is one whose premises are claimed to provide conclusive, irrefutable evidence for the truth of its conclusion. A common form of deductive argument is the categorical syllogism. It is comprised of two premises and a conclusion. It is so named because it deals with logical relations between categories. It begins with a premise that states a general truth about a category, for example *All humans are mortal*, and ends with a conclusion that states a truth about a specific instance, for example *Socrates is mortal*.

Premise 1: *All humans are mortal.*

Premise 2: *Socrates is a human.*

Therefore: *Socrates is mortal.*

Notice that the argument's first premise establishes a relationship between two categories, humans and mortals: *All humans are mortal*. The second premise makes a statement about a particular individual member of the first category: *Socrates is a human*. This forces the conclusions that this individual must also be a member of the second category: *Socrates is mortal*.

The general form of a categorical syllogism is as follows:

Premise 1: *All members of category A are members of category B.*

Premise 2: *X is a member of category A.*

Therefore: *X is a member of category B.*

Deductive logic has one especially attractive attribute—certainty. A conclusion arrived at by deduction is true with complete certainty, but this is so if and only if two conditions are met: the premises of the argument are *true* and the argument has *valid* form. If either condition is lacking, the conclusion is false with complete certainty. Therefore, a valid argument is defined as one whose conclusion must be true if its premises are true. Or, said differently, it is impossible for a valid argument to have true premises and a false conclusion.

In summary, conclusions arrived at by deduction are either true or false. If either valid form or true premises are lacking, then the conclusion is false. If both are present, the conclusion is true. There is no middle ground.

It is important to note that *truth* and *validity* are two distinct properties. Truth, and its opposite, falsity, are properties that pertain to an individual proposition. A proposition is true if it conforms to fact. Because premises and conclusions are both propositions, they are aptly characterized as either true or false. The premise *All pigs can fly* is false. The premise *Socrates is a man* is true as is the conclusion *Socrates is mortal*.

Validity is a property that pertains to the form of an argument. In other words validity refers to the logical relationships between the propositions comprising the argument. Validity or lack thereof describes the correctness of the logical inference linking the premises to the conclusion, but validity makes no reference to the factual truth of the argument's premises or conclusion. An argument is said to be valid if, when its premises are true, its conclusion must also be true.

However, an argument can be valid even if is composed of false propositions so long as the logical connections between the propositions are sound. The categorical syllogism that follows has valid form because its conclusion is logically compelled by its premises, yet its premises and conclusion are clearly untrue.

> *All humans are immortal.*
>
> *Socrates is a human.*
>
> *Therefore, Socrates is immortal.*

Because validity has nothing to do with matters of fact, validity can best be demonstrated with arguments or diagrams of arguments, called Euler circles, which make no factual references whatsoever. In a Euler diagram, the set of elements comprising a category is represented by a circle. To show that one category, such as sports cars, is a subset of the more general category—cars in general—the circle representing sports cars resides within the larger circle representing cars. See Figure 29.2.

Figure 29.3 makes clear why argument 1 is valid but argument 2 is not. Argument 1 is valid because its conclusion, *X is a B*, follows necessarily from (i.e., is compelled by) its premises. However, Argument 2 is not valid because it conclusion, *X is an A*, is not logically compelled by its premises. X may belong to category A but not necessarily. The Euler diagrams portray validity more forcefully than the argument itself because the argument alone requires some thinking.

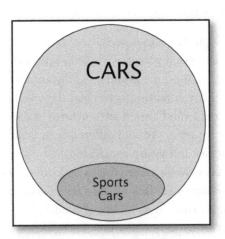

FIGURE 29.2 Euler Circles.

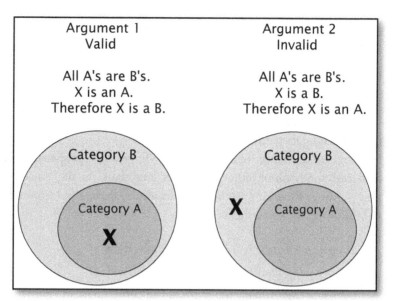

FIGURE 29.3   Valid and Invalid Categorical Syllogisms.

Argument 1

All A's are B's.

X is an A.

Therefore, X is a B.

Argument 2

All A's are B's.

X is a B.

Therefore, X is an A.

Conditional Syllogisms: The Logic of Scientific Arguments   Another form of deductive argument, and the one that is central to scientific reasoning, is the *conditional* syllogism. It is the logical basis for establishing the discovery of new knowledge.

Like the categorical syllogism, the conditional syllogism is also composed of three propositions: two premises and a conclusion. It is so named because its first premise is a conditional proposition.

A conditional proposition is a compound statement that combines two simple propositions using the words *If–then*. The proposition following *if* is referred to as the *antecedent* clause and the proposition following *then* is referred to as the *consequent* clause. The general form of a conditional proposition is

If (antecedent clause), *then* (consequent clause)

For example:

If it is a dog, then it has four legs.

In the example, *it is a dog* is the antecedent clause and *it has four legs* is the consequent clause. A second example that is closer to the purpose at hand would be

> *If the TA rule has predictive power, then its back tested rate of return will exceed zero.*

Our ultimate goal will be to establish the truth of the antecedent clause of these conditional propositions like the preceding example. As will become clear, the route to establishing its truth is an indirect one!

The second premise of a conditional syllogism is a proposition that either affirms or denies the truth of either the antecedent clause or the consequent clause of the first premise. Referring to the prior example, the second premise could be one of the following four statements:

> *It is a dog*: Affirms the truth of the antecedent.
>
> *It is not a dog*: Denies the truth of the antecedent.
>
> *It has four legs*: Affirms the truth of the consequent.
>
> *It does not have four legs*: Denies the truth of the consequent.

The conclusion of the conditional syllogism affirms or denies the truth of the remaining clause of the first premise. In other words, the conclusion references the clause that is not mentioned in the second premise. For example, if the second premise refers to the antecedent clause of the first premise, *It's a dog*, then the conclusion would refer to the consequent clause, *It has four legs*.

An example of a conditional syllogism is as follows:

> *If* it is a dog, *then it has four legs.*
>
> *It is a dog* (affirms the truth of the antecedent).
>
> *Therefore, it has four legs (affirms the truth of the consequent).*

When a conditional syllogism possesses valid form, its conclusion is logically compelled by the two premises. Moreover, if it has valid form and its premises are factually true, then the conclusion of the conditional syllogisms must also be true.

Valid Forms of the Conditional Syllogism   There are two valid forms of the conditional syllogism; *affirming the antecedent* and *denying the consequent*. In an argument that affirms the antecedent, the second premise affirms the truth of the antecedent clause of the first premise. In an argument that *denies the consequent*, the second premise asserts that the consequent clause of the first premise is not true. These two valid forms of argument are shown here. They assume all dogs possess four legs.

> Affirming the antecedent:
>
> Premise 1: *If it is a dog, then it has four legs.*
>
> Premise 2: *It is a dog.*
>
> Valid Conclusion: *Therefore, it has four legs.*

In this valid form, the second premise *affirms the antecedent* clause by stating *It is a dog*. These two premises deductively compel the conclusion *It has four legs*. The general form of a conditional syllogism in which the antecedent is affirmed is

Premise 1: *If A is true, then B is true.*

Premise 2: *A is true.*

Valid Conclusion: *Therefore, B is true.*

The other valid form of the conditional syllogism is *denial of the consequent*. In this form, the second premise asserts that the consequent clause of premise 1 is a falsehood. From this, one may conclude that the antecedent clause of premise 1 is also false. This is illustrated by the following example:

Premise 1: *If it is a dog, then it has four legs.*

Premise 2: *It does NOT have four legs.*

Valid Conclusion: *Therefore, it is not a dog.*

Denial of the consequent follows the general form:

Premise 1: *If A is true, then B is true.*

Premise 2: *B is not true.*

Valid Conclusion: *Therefore, A is not true.*

This is sometimes shortened to

If A, then B.

Not B.

Therefore, not A.

Notice that this form of argument uses evidence (creature does not have four legs) to prove that antecedent (*It is a dog*) is false. It is this form of reasoning that is used in science to prove that a hypothesis is false. The hypothesis plays the role of the antecedent. We hypothesize that the creature is a dog. The consequent clause predicts what will be observed if the hypothesis is true. That is, if the creature is truly a dog, then, when it is observed, it will be seen to possess four legs. In other words, the conditional proposition, *If A, then B*, predicts that B would be observed in an experiment if the hypothesis (A) were in fact true. The second premise states that when the observation was made, the observation contradicted the prediction, that is, B was not observed. Given this, we can validly deduce that the hypothesis A is false.

As will be shown in due course, if we can prove that hypothesis A is false, we can indirectly prove that some other hypothesis is true. That other hypothesis is the new knowledge that we wish to establish as true, for example that a new vaccine is more effective than a placebo or that some TA rule predicts more effectively than a randomly generated signal.

Invalid Form of the Conditional Syllogism

An important reason for using formal logic is the difficulty people often have when reasoning informally about conditional syllogisms. Psychological studies[13] have shown that people tend to commit two fallacies when reasoning about conditional propositions: the fallacy of *affirming the consequent*, and the fallacy of *denying the antecedent*. An example of the fallacy of affirming the consequent is

Premise 1: *If it is a dog, then it has four legs.*

Premise 2: *It has four legs.*

Invalid Conclusion: *Therefore, it is a dog.*

The fact that a creature has four legs certainly does not compel the conclusion that the creature is a dog. It may be a dog. The evidence is consistent with the fact that it is a dog. However, the evidence is also consistent with other conclusions. It could just as easily be a cow, a horse, or any other four-legged creature. The fallacy of affirming the consequent has the general form:

Premise 1: *If A is true, then B is true.*

Premise 2: *B is true.*

Invalid Conclusion: *Therefore, A is true.*

This fallacy is a very common error in poor scientific reasoning and one committed in many articles on TA. Consider the following syllogism, which commits the fallacy of affirming the consequent.

Premise 1: *If TA rule X has predictive power, then it should produce profits in a back test.*

Premise 2: *The back test was profitable.*

Invalid Conclusions: *Therefore, the TA rule has predictive power.*

Both of these premises may be true, but the conclusion is not necessarily true. With respect to the first premise, it is true that if the TA rule X does possess predictive power it should back test profitably. In other words, a profitable back test would be consistent with the supposition that the rule has predictive power. However, a profitable back test could also be consistent with the supposition that the rule was merely lucky. Similarly, just as evidence of four legs is consistent with a dog, it is also consistent with all other four-legged creatures.[14] The fallacy of affirming the consequent is the reason that empirical evidence cannot be used to prove that a hypothesis is true. As we shall see, one philosopher of science, Karl Popper, contended that the scientific method must, therefore, rest on denial (falsification) of the consequent, which, as pointed out earlier, is a valid form of inference.

The other fallacy associated with conditional syllogisms is the fallacy of denying the antecedent. It is illustrated here:

Premise 1: *If it is a dog, then it has four legs.*

Premise 2: *It is not a dog.*

Invalid Conclusion: *Therefore, it does not have four legs.*

The fact that a creature is not a dog does not preclude its having four legs. The general form of this fallacy is

Premise 1: *If A is true, then B is true.*

Premise 2: *A is not true.*

Invalid Conclusion: *Therefore, B is not true.*

In logical shorthand

If A, then B.

Not A.

Therefore, not B.

Invalid arguments can be hard to notice when they concern complex subjects. The best way to reveal them is to plug in commonplace items for A and B and see if the conclusion follows from the premises.

Figures 29.4 and 29.5 summarize the preceding discussion of the conditional syllogism.

As mentioned, the great strength of deductive reasoning is its ability to deliver conclusions that are true with certainty. However, deductive logic has a great weakness; it is unable to reveal new knowledge about the world. All that a deductive argument can do is to reveal truths that were already implicit in its premises. In other words, deductive reasoning can only tease out truths that were already present in the premises though they may not have been evident.

Valid	Invalid
Affirming the Antecedent If A, then B. A. Therefore, B.	**Denying the Antecedent** If A, then B. Not A. Therefore, Not B.
Denying the Consequent If A, then B. Not B. Therefore, Not A.	**Affirming the Consequent** If A, then B. B. Therefore, A.

FIGURE 29.4 Conditional Syllogisms: General Form.

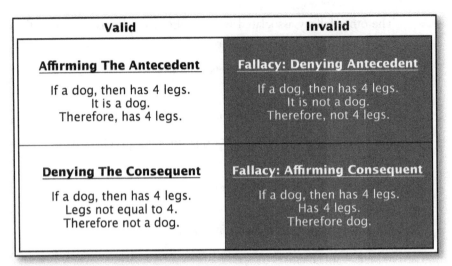

Valid	Invalid
Affirming The Antecedent If a dog, then has 4 legs. It is a dog. Therefore, has 4 legs.	**Fallacy: Denying Antecedent** If a dog, then has 4 legs. It is not a dog. Therefore, not 4 legs.
Denying The Consequent If a dog, then has 4 legs. Legs not equal to 4. Therefore not a dog.	**Fallacy: Affirming Consequent** If a dog, then has 4 legs. Has 4 legs. Therefore dog.

FIGURE 29.5 Conditional Syllogisms: Example.

This is not meant to minimize or trivialize deduction but to clarify its role. It may well be that a conclusion implied by the premises is far from obvious. Great mathematical discoveries are exactly that—the revealing of truths that had been implicit in the axioms of a mathematical system but that had not been understood prior to being proven. Such was the case with the much-publicized proof of Fermat's last theorem. It was first hinted at in the margin of a book in 1665 but not proven until 1994, by Andrew Wiles and Richard Taylor.

Inductive Logic

Induction is the logic of discovery. It aims to reveal new knowledge about the world by reaching beyond the knowledge contained in the premises of an inductive argument. However, this new knowledge comes with a price—uncertainty. Conclusions reached by induction are inherently uncertain. That is, they can only be true with some degree of probability. Thus, the notion of probability is intimately connected with induction.

Induction proceeds in a manner opposite to deduction. We saw that deduction progresses from a premise expressing a general truth that is held to apply to an unlimited number of instances, *All men are mortal* to a conclusion about a specific instance *Socrates is mortal*. In contrast, inductive reasoning moves or, better said, leaps from a premise based on a limited number of observed instances to a general conclusion about an unlimited number of similar but not-yet-observed instances. Thus, this form of inference is often referred to as inductive generalization. It is in leaping beyond what has been directly experienced by observation that induction incurs uncertainty—the possibility that its conclusion may be wrong.

Inductive generalization is illustrated by the following:

Premise: *Each of one thousand healthy dogs had four legs.*

General conclusions: *All healthy dogs will have four legs.*

The conclusion, in this example, is called a universal generalization, because it asserts that *all* members of the class dog have the attribute four legs. Universal generalizations have the form

All X's are Y's.

or

100 percent of X's have the attribute Y.

Generalizations need not be universal. Nonuniversal generalizations have the form

P percent of X's are Y's.

or

P percent of X's have attribute Y.

or

X's have attribute Y with probability P.

Again, we see that probability is inextricably tied to the concept of generalization. In fact, nonuniversal generalizations are also known as probabilistic generalizations. An example would be: *A higher percentage of bulldogs are prone to violence than poodles.* This statistically sound nonuniversal generalization[15] does not claim all bulldogs are prone to violent behavior, nor does it claim that even a majority are so inclined. However, it does say that, as a group, statistics show that bulldogs have a higher probability of being dangerous than poodles.

Aristotle's defeat as scientist was in part attributable to his failure to appreciate that nonuniversal generalizations convey useful knowledge. His fascination with the certainty of deductive proofs led him to restrict his search to universal generalizations. He was unable to see that many important regularities of the natural world are inherently probabilistic.

Induction by Enumeration

The most common form of inductive argument is based on enumeration. It proceeds from a premise that enumerates the evidence contained in a set of observations, and then draws a general conclusion that pertains to all similar observations outside the enumerated set.

Premise: *Over the past 20 years there have been 1,000 instances in which TA rule X gave a buy signal and in 700 of those instances the market moved higher over the next 10 days.*

Conclusion: In the future, when rule X gives a buy signal, there is a 0.7 probability that the market will be higher at the end of 10 days.

This conclusion or any conclusion reached by induction is inherently uncertain because it extends to observations that have not yet been made. However, some inductive arguments are stronger than others, and hence, arrive at conclusions that are more certain. The strength of an inductive argument and the certainty of its conclusion depend upon the quantity and quality of the evidence enumerated in its premise. The more numerous the instances cited and the higher their quality, the more likely the conclusion will generalize accurately to future observations.

Suppose that the conclusion about TA rule X had been based on only 10 instances with a 70 percent success rate instead of 1,000. In such a case, the conclusion would have been at least 10 times more uncertain.[16] This means we should be less surprised if the signal's future accuracy differs greatly from its historic success rate. In science, the evidence offered in support of a conclusion is typically evaluated with statistical methods. This allows one to make quantitative statements about the conclusion's uncertainty.

The strength of an inductive argument also depends upon the quality of the evidence. Evidence quality is an entire subject unto itself, but suffice it to say that some observational methods produce higher quality evidence than others. The gold standard in science is the controlled experiment, where all factors but the one under study are held constant. TA does not permit controlled experiments, but there are better and worse ways to make observations. One issue that is relevant to TA is the matter of systematic error or bias.

Also relevant to the strength of an inductive argument is the degree to which the evidence cited is representative of the kinds of observations that are likely to be encountered in the future. An inference about a rule that generates long/neutral (+1,0) signals that was back-tested only during rising markets is unlikely to be accurate about the rule's performance in a declining market environment. Even if the rule had no predictive power, its restriction to long or neutral positions makes it likely that it would have generated a profit because it was tested during a rising market period.

The most common fallacy of induction is the hasty generalization—an induction based on too little evidence or evidence of poor quality. Rule studies that cite a small number of successful signals as a basis for concluding that the rule has predictive power are likely to be hasty generalizations.

■ The Philosophy of Science

The philosophy of science seeks to understand how and why science works. It explains such things as: the nature of scientific propositions and how they differ from nonscientific and pseudoscientific propositions; the way scientific knowledge is produced; how science explains, predicts, and, through technology, harnesses nature; the means for determining the validity of scientific knowledge; the formulation and use of the scientific method; and the types of reasoning used to arrive at conclusions.[17]

That the scientific method is one of man's greatest inventions and is by far the most effective method for acquiring objective knowledge about the natural world is beyond question. "The part of the world known as the Industrial West could, in its entirety, be seen as a monument to the Scientific Revolution. . . ."[18] Humankind's ability to predict and control the natural world has improved more in the last 400 years, since the scientific revolution began, than it had in the prior 150,000 years that modern humans, *homo sapiens*, walked the face of the Earth.

Strange as it may seem, the invention of the scientific method and its first fruits came before it was understood why the method worked as well as it did. That insight came gradually, over the course of several centuries, as practicing scientists and their erstwhile critics, the philosophers of science, wrestled with perfecting the method and, in parallel, developed an understanding of how and why it worked.

The mere fact that the scientific method did work was not enough. It was seen as necessary to understand why. What philosophers found so vexing was the following apparent contradiction. On the one hand were the great victories of science, such as Newton's laws of motion and gravity and humanity's expanding technological control over nature. On the other was the fact that scientific knowledge was inherently uncertain, because conclusions arrived at by logical induction were inherently uncertain. How could so much useful knowledge result from such a flawed method of inference?

This section discusses the keys steps in the method's development and the milestones in our deepening understanding of how and why it works. The reader may wish to skip this historical development and go directly to the summary of the key aspects of the scientific method.

Bacon's Enthusiasm

Without invitation, philosophers poke their noses into all sorts of matters. It's their nature. They tell us how to act (ethics), how governments should rule (political philosophy), what is beautiful (aesthetics), and of greatest concern to us, what constitutes valid knowledge (epistemology) and how we should go about getting it (philosophy of science).

The scientific revolution was, in part, a revolt against Aristotelian science. The Greeks regarded the physical world as an unreliable source of truth. According to Plato, mentor of Aristotle, the world was merely a flawed copy of the truth and perfection that existed in the world of *Forms*, a metaphysical nonmaterial realm, where archetypes of the perfect dog, the perfect tree, and every other imaginable thing could be found.

When the revolt against this view of reality finally arrived, it was harsh and unremitting.[19] The new school of thought, empiricism, resoundingly rejected the Greek paradigm. It contended that, not only was the natural world worthy of study, but that careful observation could lay bare its truths. A pioneer of empiricism and perhaps the first philosopher of science was Francis Bacon (1561–1626). "Nature, for Bacon was an open book that could not possibly be misread by an unprejudiced mind."[20] In his famous work the *Novem Organum* (the new tool) Bacon extolled the power of observation and induction. He held science to be a completely objective rational practice that could conclusively confirm or falsify knowledge simply by observing without bias or prejudice and then generalizing from those observations. In many situations, this approach seemed to work.

However, empiricism was not the perfect tool Bacon and his disciples claimed, and philosophers made it their business to say why. First, they pointed out that empiricism, an observation-based enterprise, rested on a crucial assumption that could not be confirmed by observation, the assumption that nature was uniform over all time and space. That assumption was critical in justifying the empiricists' position that if a scientific law was observed to hold true here and now it would also hold true everywhere and forever. Because the uniformity of nature assumption could not be confirmed by observation, it had to be taken on faith. Second, science often deals with phenomena and concepts that defy direct observation: atomic structure, the force of gravity, and electric fields. Though their effects are observable, these constructs could not be arrived at exclusively by observation and induction. They are better understood as human inventions that explain and predict rather than observable physical realities.

Nevertheless, Bacon's contributions to the development of the scientific method were important. He promoted the idea of experiment and made room for doubt by taking special note of discordant observations. Both ideas eluded the Greeks.

Descartes's Doubt

If philosophers are good for anything it's raising doubt, and no one was better than Rene Descartes (1596–1650). Regarded as the father of modern philosophy and a key figure in the birth of science, Descartes shared Bacon's skepticism for the authoritarian knowledge of the Greeks and the dogma of the Roman Church. However, Descartes was just as skeptical of the claims made by the empiricists about the power of observation and inductive generalization. His famous expression, "I think, therefore I am," expressed the position that science must start by doubting everything except the existence of the person who experiences doubt. From that point of solidity, knowledge must be built purely by deductive reasoning without being contaminated by error-prone observations made with the imperfect five senses.

As a consequence of Descartes' anti-empirical stance and penchant for theorizing in a factual vacuum, his scientific findings were almost meaningless.[21] However, his contributions to science were lasting. Skepticism is central to the scientific attitude. In addition, Descartes' invention of analytic geometry paved the way for Newton's invention of the calculus which, in turn, allowed him to specify his famous equations of motion and gravity.

Hume's Critique of Induction

Another dose of doubt was administered by Scottish empiricist and philosopher David Hume (1711–1776). His seminal work, the *Treatise on Human Nature*, published in 1739, grappled with a central problem of epistemology: how to distinguish knowledge from lesser forms of knowing, such as opinions that happen to be true. Prior to Hume's publication, philosophers generally agreed that the distinction was related to the quality of the method used to acquire the knowledge. What justified calling one bit of wisdom knowledge but not another was the pedigree of the method of inquiry.[22]

Philosophers could not, however, agree on the best method of knowledge acquisition. Empiricists argued that objective observation followed by inductive generalization was the route to wisdom. Rationalists, on the other hand, contended that pure deductive reasoning from self-evident truths was the correct method.

Hume took issue with both schools of thought and ultimately even with himself. As an empiricist, Hume disparaged the rationalists' purely deductive approach because it was disconnected from observed facts. Also, in the spirit of empiricism, Hume said that it was wise to adjust the strength of one's beliefs in proportion to the evidence and that theories should be evaluated by the degree to which they matched observation. But then Hume went on to contradict himself by attacking the logical basis of empiricism. He denied the validity of inductive generalization and disparaged the ability of science to establish causal laws. His searing critique of induction has come to be known as Hume's problem.

Hume's attack on induction was on both psychological and logical grounds. First, he said the belief that induction could establish correlative or causal connections between events was a nothing more than a by-product of human psychology. Hume asserted that the perception of cause and effect was merely an artifact of the mind. The belief that A causes B or is even correlated to B, simply because A has always been followed by B was nothing more than a habit of mind, and a bad habit at that.

From a logical perspective, Hume claimed that induction was flawed because no amount of observed evidence, no matter how objectively collected, can compel a conclusion with the force of a valid deduction. Moreover, he said that there was no rule of induction that tells us when we have evidence of sufficient quantity or quality to justify the leap from a finite set of observations to a conclusion about an infinite number of similar but not yet observed instances. A rule of induction would, itself, have had to be the result of a prior valid induction made on the basis of an even earlier rule of induction, and so forth and so on, ad infinitum. In other words, an attempt to justify induction inevitably rests on an infinite regress—a logically impossible absurdity.

In light of Hume's attack, supporters of induction retreated to a narrower claim saying inductive generalizations were merely correct in a probabilistic sense. So as evidence accumulates in favor of a relationship between A and B, the probability that the relationship is authentic also increases. However, philosophers were quick to point out that a probabilistic justification of induction was also flawed. The probability that A predicts B is equal to the number of times that A was followed by B divided by the total number of instances of A regardless of whether it was followed by B.[23]

Because the future holds an infinite number of instances, the probability will always be zero, no matter how numerous the past observations (any number divided by an infinitely large number is still zero).

Thus, Hume and his allies created a paradox. On one hand were their seemingly valid concerns about the flaws of induction. On the other hand was the accumulation of stunning scientific discoveries. If science was based on such a flawed logic, how could it have managed to be so successful?

William Whewell: The Role of Hypothesis

It took philosophers and scientists two hundred years of watching the scientific method succeed to understand how it worked and why it had been so triumphant. By the middle of the nineteenth century, it was becoming clear that science employs a synergistic combination of inductive and deductive logic. In 1840, William Whewell (1794–1866) published *The History and Philosophy of Inductive Sciences*.

Whewell was the first to understand the crucial role of induction in the formulation of a hypothesis. Whewell called it a happy guess, He said that scientific discovery starts with a bold inductive leap to a new hypothesis, but it is followed by deduction. That is to say, after a hypothesis has been induced, a prediction is deduced from said hypothesis. This prediction takes the form of a conditional statement:

If the hypothesis is true, then specific future observations are predicted to occur.

When the observations are made, they will either be consistent with the prediction, thus confirming the hypothesis, or conflict with the prediction, thus contradicting the hypothesis.

What is a scientific hypothesis? It is a conjecture of a suspected pattern, for example:

X predicts Y.

or

X brings about Y.

This conjecture is spawned by a scientist's prior experience—noticing repeated pairings of X and Y. Once the XY hypothesis has been put forward, a testable prediction is deduced from it. This takes the form of a conditional proposition, which is composed of two clauses: an antecedent and a consequent. The hypothesis serves as the antecedent clause, and the prediction serves as the consequent clause. In situations where it is merely asserted that X is correlated (predicts) with Y the following conditional proposition would apply:

IF X predicts Y, then future instances of X will be followed by instances of Y.

In cases where the hypothesis asserts that X causes Y, the following conditional proposition would apply:

IF X causes Y, then if X is removed, Y should not occur.

The predictions embodied in the consequent clause of the conditional proposition are then compared with new observations. These must be observations whose outcome is not yet known. This is crucial! This does not necessarily mean that the observations concern some future event. It simply means that when the prediction is made, the outcome of the observations is not yet known. In historical sciences like geology, archeology, and so forth, the observations are about events that have already taken place. However, the outcomes have not yet been observed.

If it turns out that future observations of X are not followed by Y or if removal of X does prevent the occurrence of Y, then the hypothesis (antecedent) is proven to be false by the valid deductive form falsification of the consequent.

> *If X, then Y.*
>
> *Not Y.*
>
> Valid Deduction: *Therefore, not X.*

If, however, future instances of X are indeed followed by Y, or if the removal of X does cause the disappearance of Y, the hypothesis is not proven! Recall that affirming the consequent is not a valid deductive form.

> *If X, then Y.*
>
> *Y.*
>
> Invalid: *Therefore, X.*

That the prediction has been confirmed merely offers tentative confirmation of the hypothesis. The hypothesis survives for the moment, but more stringent tests of it are sure to follow.

Whewell agreed with Hume that inductive conjecture was a habit of human thought, but the habit that Hume so disparaged Whewell regarded as fruitful though mysterious. He was unable to explain the mental processes that gave rise to such creative thoughts though he believed inductive generalization was part of it. He called the ability to conjure a hypothesis an unteachable inventive talent but a crucial one, because, without a hypothesis, a set of observations remain nothing more than a disconnected collection of facts that could neither predict nor explain. However, with one came the breakthroughs of science.

Whewell's description of this crucial creative aspect of science reminds me of a conversation I had many years ago with Charles Strauss, a prolific composer of some of Broadway's most successful musicals. In my early twenties at the time, short on tact and long on audacity, I asked him to explain how he managed to be so productive. With more forbearance than I deserved, Charles described a daily discipline of religiously sitting at the piano from 8 until 11 each morning and from 2 until 5 each afternoon, whether he felt inspired or not. He told me he treated composing music like a job. During this time he would test tentative melodies—musical hypotheses. He modestly attributed his high productivity to 99 percent discipline and 1 percent creative talent. However, as I thought about this conversation years later, it seemed otherwise. With an almost infinite number of note combinations, his success at creating infectious tunes had to be a creative talent—some special ability to see which of those musical conjectures had the potential to be melodies and which did not. This was what Whewell called the happy guess—that unteachable talent of seeing a theme that meaningfully relates a disparate set of observations or notes that eludes the average person. A few folks have it. The vast majority do not.

Whewell's realization that proposing a hypothesis was an act of invention no less than the creation of the steam engine or the light bulb represented a profoundly important advance in thinking about science.[24] Induction could not produce truths on its own, but it was a necessary first step. This was a profound departure from the prior notion of science as a systematic objective investigation followed by inductive generalization. Whewell saw the scientist as a creator as much as an investigator.

Karl Popper: Falsification and Bringing Deduction Back into Science

In two landmark works, *The Logic of Scientific Discovery*[25] and *Conjectures and Refutations*,[26] Karl Popper (1902–1994) extended the insight of Whewell and redefined the logic of scientific discovery by clarifying the role of deduction. Popper's central contention was that a scientific inquiry was unable to prove hypotheses to be true. Rather, science was limited to identifying which hypotheses were false. This was accomplished by using observed evidence in combination with the valid deductive form of falsification of the consequent.

> **If** hypothesis H is true, **then** evidence E is predicted to occur under specified conditions (e.g., back test of a TA rule).
>
> *Evidence E did not occur under the specified conditions.*
>
> *Therefore, hypothesis H is false.*

In taking this stance, Popper challenged the prevailing view advocated by a school of philosophy called logical positivism. Just as Francis Bacon had revolted against the strictures of the Greek tradition, Popper was in revolt against the Vienna Circle, the home of logical positivism. Logical positivists believed that observations could be used to prove hypotheses to be true. Popper demurred, saying that observed evidence could only be used to prove a hypothesis false. Science was a baloney detector, not a truth detector.

Popper justified his method, called falsificationism, as follows. A given set of observations can be explained by or is consistent with numerous hypotheses. Therefore, the observed data, by itself, cannot help us decide which of these hypotheses is most likely correct.[27] Suppose the data is that one of my shoes is missing. One hypothesis that might explain this observation is that I'm a disorganized housekeeper who is always misplacing things. Another hypothesis, which is equally consistent with the observation of a missing shoe, would be that my house was burglarized by a one-legged thief who only had use for one shoe. In fact, an infinite number of hypotheses could be proposed that are consistent with (explain) the missing shoe.

We have already seen that data cannot be used logically to deduce the truth of a hypothesis. Attempts to do so commit the fallacy of affirming the consequent.[28] However, and this is the key to Popper's method of falsificationism, data can be used to validly deduce the falsehood of a hypothesis by denial of the consequent. In other words, disconfirming evidence can be used to reveal a false explanation. For example, finding the other shoe would be evidence that would falsify the one-legged thief hypothesis. The logical argument is as follows:

> Premise 1: *If a one-legged thief is responsible for my missing shoe, then I will not find the shoe in my home.*
>
> Premise 2: *Missing shoe is found (consequent denied).*
>
> Conclusion: *Therefore, the one-legged thief hypothesis is false.*

Popper's method of falsification runs against the grain of common sense, which is biased in favor of confirmatory evidence. Intuition often tells us to test the truth of a hypothesis by seeing if confirmatory evidence can be found. We do so under the mistaken impression that confirmatory evidence is sufficient to establish truth. However, using evidence in this way commits the fallacy of affirming the consequent. We are not wrong to suspect that confirmatory evidence should be found if the hypothesis is true, but we are wrong to think that confirmatory evidence is sufficient to establish its truth. Said differently, confirmatory evidence is a necessary condition of a proposition's truth but not a sufficient condition.[29] Popper's point was that the absence of necessary evidence is sufficient to establish the falsity of a hypothesis, but the presence of necessary evidence is not enough to establish its truth. Having four legs is a necessary condition of a creature being a dog, but the presence of four legs is not sufficient to establish that a creature is a dog. However, the observation that the creature does not have four legs is sufficient to falsify the contention it is a dog. Popper's logic of falsification can be seen as a protection against the confirmation bias that infects informal inference.

One final example may help clarify the power of falsifying evidence and the weakness of confirmatory evidence. It is the famous problem of the black swan posed by philosopher John Stuart Mill (1806–1873). Suppose we wish to ascertain the truth of the proposition: 'All swans are white.' Mill said, and Popper concurred, that no matter how many white swans have been observed—that is, no matter how voluminous the confirmatory evidence—the proposition's truth is never proven. A black swan may lurk just around the next corner. This is the limitation of induction that so upset Hume. However, by merely observing a single non-white swan, one may declare with certitude that the proposition is false. The conditional syllogism below shows that the falsity of the proposition *All swans are white* is based on the valid deductive form falsification of the consequent.

> Premise 1: *If it is true that all swans are white, then all future observations of swans will be white.*
>
> Premise 2: *A nonwhite swan is observed.*
>
> Valid Conclusion: *The proposition that all swans are white is false.*

The general form of argument used to test a hypothesis under Popper's method of falsification is:

Premise 1: *If the hypothesis is true, then future observations are predicted to have property X.*

Premise 2: *An observation occurs that lacks property X.*

Valid Conclusion: *Therefore, hypothesis is false.*

This is the logic used to test statistical hypotheses.

The Provisional and Cumulative Nature of Scientific Knowledge   One implication of Popper's method of falsification is that all existing scientific knowledge is provisional. Whatever theory is currently accepted as correct is always a target for empirical challenge and the possibility of its being replaced by a more correct theory always exits. Today Einstein's Theory of Relativity is taken as correct. Though its predictions have withstood countless tests, tomorrow a new test may show it to be false or incomplete. Thus, science is a never-ending cycle of conjecture, prediction, testing, falsification, and new conjecture. It is in this way that the body of scientific knowledge continually evolves toward an ever more accurate representation of objective reality.

In most instances when older theories are replaced, it is not because they are proven false so much as they are shown to be incomplete. When Newton's laws of motion were replaced by Einstein's theories, Newtonian physics was still mostly correct. Within the limited domain of everyday experience, where bodies travel at normal speeds (approximately less than 90 percent of the speed of light), Newton's laws still held true. However, Einstein's theory was correct in a wider domain, which not only included the motions of everyday objects, but also objects traveling up to and including the speed of light. In other words, Einstein's theory, which built upon Newton's, was more general and thus subsumed it.

The net result of building upon prior successful ideas (those whose predictions have been confirmed) and pruning away wrong ideas (those whose predictions have been falsified) is a body of knowledge that continually improves. This cannot be said of any other intellectual discipline, where new styles are introduced but where newer is not necessarily better. The fact that a scientist in any field of science knows more today than even the best one living just a generation ago is beyond debate. However, whether gangsta rap is better or worse than Mozart could be argued endlessly.

The Restriction of Science to Testable Statements   Another implication of Popper's method is that science must restrict itself to testable hypotheses—propositions that generate predictions about observations not yet made. To say that a hypothesis has been tested and has survived or has been tested and falsified means that predictions deduced from it have either been confirmed or contradicted by new observations. The comparison of predictions with new observations is the crucial mechanism that fosters the continual improvement of scientific knowledge. For this reason, propositions that do not generate testable predictions must be excluded from the domain of scientific discourse.

The term *prediction*, in the context of hypothesis testing, warrants some clarification, because TA is essentially an enterprise dedicated to prediction. When we speak of prediction as it pertains to testing a hypothesis, it does not necessarily mean foretelling the future though the predicted observations may indeed lie in the future. Rather, the term *prediction* refers to the fact that the observations' outcomes are not yet known.

Predictions made in historical sciences, such as geology, refer to events that have already taken place perhaps eons ago. For example, geology's dominant theory, plate tectonics, may predict that specific geologic formations that were created millions of years ago would be observed if an investigation of some specific location were to be carried out tomorrow. In finance, the efficient market's hypothesis predicts that if a TA rule were to be back tested, its profits, after adjustment for risk, would not exceed the risk adjusted return of the market index.

Once the prediction has been deduced from the hypothesis, the operations necessary to produce the new observations are carried out. They may involve a visit to the location of the predicted geologic formation or the back test of the TA rule. Then it becomes a matter of comparing prediction with observation. Measuring the degree of agreement between observation and prediction and making the decision about whether the hypothesis is left intact or falsified is what statistical analysis is all about.

What is important from the standpoint of science is that the hypothesis is able to make predictions about observations whose outcomes are not yet known. This is what allows a hypothesis to be tested. Observations whose outcomes are known cannot serve this purpose because it is always possible to fashion an explanation, after-the-fact that is consistent with said observations. Therefore, activities that are unable or unwilling to make testable predictions, thus opening them to the possibility of falsification, do not qualify as scientific.

The Demarcation Problem: Distinguishing Science from Pseudoscience An important consequence of Popper's method was that it solved a key problem in the philosophy of science—defining the boundary between science and nonscience. The domain of science is confined to propositions (conjectures, hypotheses, claims, theories, and so forth) that make predictions that are open to refutation with empirical evidence. Popper referred to such propositions as falsifiable and meaningful. Propositions that cannot be challenged in this manner are unfalsifiable or meaningless. In other words they do not say anything of substance, something that sets up a testable expectation.

Unfalsifiable propositions may appear to assert something, but, in fact, they do not. They cannot be challenged because they do not say, with any degree of specificity, what can be expected to happen. In effect, they are not informative. Hence, the falsifiability of a proposition is related to its information content. Falsifiable propositions are informative because they make specific predictions. They may prove to be wrong, but at least they say something of substance. A proposition that cannot generate falsifiable predictions essentially says any outcome can happen. For example, a weather forecast that says, *It will be cloudy or sunny, wet or dry, windy or calm, and cold or hot*, allows for all possible outcomes. It cannot be falsified. The only thing good that can be said about it is that its lack of information is completely obvious.

The problem is that pseudoscientists and pseudoforecasters are clever about the way they word their predictions so as to obscure their lack of information and non-falsifiability. Consider the astrologer's forecast "You will meet a tall dark stranger, and your life will be changed." This statement is impossible to refute no matter what the outcome. Should you ever go back for a refund, you will be given one of two answers: (1) be patient—you will meet the stranger soon, or (2) you already did meet a dark stranger and you life is indeed different, but you are oblivious to the change. These answers cannot be challenged because the prediction was vague. It neither stated when your life would change or in what measurable (verifiable) manner. This is a far cry from the prediction, "Before 7:00 p.m. next Wednesday you will see a man wearing one red shoe, walking east on 42nd Street whistling 'Satin Doll.'" By 7 p.m. next Wednesday, the evidence will be in and you will have had the opportunity to evaluate the prediction as true or false. Even if the prediction turns out to be false, it was at least falsifiable allowing you to decide if future visits to the astrologer are worthwhile.

The infomercial pitchmen that inhabit late-night television are masters of the meaningless claim. "Wearing our copper bracelet will improve your golf game." What does *improve* mean? How is it to be measured and when? As with the astrologer's forecast, the claim's vagueness makes it impossible to deduce a testable (falsifiable) prediction. However, it is quite easy to imagine after-the-fact anecdotal evidence that is seemingly confirmatory. "Holy cow, I feel so much more relaxed wearing my copper bracelet. I used get all tensed up before teeing off. Now my drives seem straighter. Last week I almost had a hole in one, and I don't curse nearly as much as I used to. My wife even says I look more handsome in my golf outfit, and I think my hair has stopped falling out." Although meaningless claims invite confirmatory anecdotes, they are protected from objective falsifying evidence. The claimant never gets nailed and the claim gains support from seemingly confirmational anecdotal reports.

In contrast, the statement, "Wearing a copper bracelet will increase the length of your drives by 25 yards," is informative and meaningful because it generates a testable prediction. You hit 100 golf balls not wearing the copper bracelet and determine their average distance. The next day, do the same thing while wearing a copper bracelet and get their average distance. Repeat this alternating series of experiments for 10 days. If the drives on copper-bracelet days are less than 25 yards better, evidence refuting the claim would be in hand.

Limitations of Popper's Method   As important as Popper's method of falsification is to modern science, it has been criticized on a number of grounds. Critics assert that Popper's contention that hypotheses can be definitively falsified overstates matters. Although the observation of a black swan can neatly and logically falsify the universal generalization that all swans are white, the hypotheses of real science are far more complex[30] and probabilistic (nonuniversal). They are complex in the sense that a newly proposed hypothesis rests on numerous auxiliary hypotheses that are assumed to be true. Thus, if a prediction deduced from the new hypothesis is later falsified, it is not clear whether the new hypothesis was in error or one of the many auxiliary hypotheses was incorrect. This proved to be the case when the solar system's eighth planet, Neptune, was discovered. The aberrant path of Uranus was not due to flaws in Newton's laws but in the auxiliary hypothesis that the solar system contained only seven planets. However, when the theory did fail early in the twentieth century, it was indeed because of imperfections in Newton's laws. Doing real science is tricky business. TA is a long way from facing these problems because we are still at the at the point of scratching the data for reliable predictive rules.

Moreover, because many of the hypotheses of science are probabilistic, as would be the case in TA, an observation that contradicts the hypothesis can never be taken as certain evidence of falsity. The aberrant observation may be a chance occurrence. It is here that statistical analysis enters the picture. The decision to reject a hypothesis on the basis of observed evidence runs a certain probability of being wrong. Statistics helps us quantify this probability.

Despite these and other limitations that go beyond our concerns here, Popper's contributions to the development of the scientific method have been enormous.

The Information Content of Scientific Hypotheses

To recap, a hypothesis is informative if it can make testable predictions. This opens it to the possibility of being found false. Thus, the falsifiability of a hypothesis and its information content are related.

Within the domain of scientifically meaningful hypotheses, there are degrees of information content and falsifiability. Some hypotheses are more information rich and hence more falsifiable than others.

When Popper referred to a *bold conjecture* he was speaking of a highly informative hypothesis from which many falsifiable predictions could be deduced. The scientist's job, therefore, is to continually attempt to refute an existing hypothesis and to replace it with an even more informative one. This spurs the improvement of scientific knowledge.

An information-rich hypothesis makes many precise (narrow ranged) predictions about a broad range of phenomena. Each prediction presents an opportunity to show the hypothesis is false. In other words, the more informative a hypothesis the more opportunities it presents for falsification. In contrast, low information, timid hypotheses make fewer or less-precise predictions. Consequently they are more difficult to falsify. For example, a TA rule that claims high profitability on any instrument in any time frame makes a bold and information-rich claim that that could be falsified by showing that it is unprofitable on one market in one time frame. In contrast, a method that only claims to be marginally profitable on S&P futures on the one-week bar time scale is timid, has low information content, and is hard to falsify. The only opportunity to refute it would be limited to back test of the S&P 500 on a weekly showing that was not at all profitable.

Some TA methods that are seemingly informative are not. Elliott Wave Principle is a case in point. On the surface, it bravely proclaims that all price movement in all markets over all time scales can be described by a single unifying principle. This proposition is seemingly confirmed by the ability of EWP practitioners to produce a wave count for any prior segment of price data. In fact, EWP is timid to the point of being meaningless because it makes no falsifiable predictions of future price motion.[31]

A second case in point, one more pleasing to the TA community, is the Efficient Markets Hypothesis (EMH). In this context, the term *efficiency* refers to the speed with which prices reflect all known and knowable information that is relevant to the future returns of an asset. In an efficient market, relevant information is presumed to be reflected in price almost instantaneously. EMH comes in three flavors. In descending order of boldness, information content, and falsifiability they are: EMH strong, EMH semistrong, and EMH weak.

EMH strong asserts that financial markets are efficient with respect to all information, even private inside information. This version predicts that all investment strategies, be they based on an inside tip from the president about an impending takeover, or based on public information of a fundamental or technical nature, will be useless in earning market-beating (excess) returns. This most audacious version of EMH is also seemingly the most informative and falsifiable because any evidence of abnormal profits from any investment strategy whatsoever, irrespective of the type of information or form of analysis used, would be sufficient to refute EMH strong. However, because information that is known privately can never be confirmed, this version is not testable in a practical sense.

The semistrong version of EMH makes a less informative and narrower claim, saying that the market is only efficient with respect to public information. This version of EMH can be falsified with any evidence of market-beating returns produced by an investing strategy based on either public fundamental data (P/E ratios, book values, and so forth) or technical data (relative strength rank, volume turnover ratios, and so forth). In effect, EMH semistrong denies the utility of fundamental and technical analysis.

Finally we have EMH weak, which makes the least bold and least informative claim. It asserts that the market is only efficient with respect to past price, volume, and other technical data. Because EMH weak only denies the utility of technical analysis, it presents the smallest and hardest-to-hit target by would-be falsifiers. Their only hope would be to present evidence that shows excess returns generated by an investment strategy based on TA.

Because EMH weak is the hardest version to falsify and is thus the least likely to be proven false, its falsification would also generate the most surprise. In other words, of all versions of EMH, falsification of EMH weak would generate the biggest increase in knowledge. This points out a general principle of science: the largest gains in knowledge occur when the most timid and hardest to falsify hypotheses are falsified. A test showing that inside information, like the tip from a corporate president, was able to generate excess returns (i.e., falsification of EMH strong) would not be surprising nor would we learn very much from it. Big deal, so inside information generates profits. What else is new? In contrast, the falsification of EMH weak would be a highly informative event for both TA practitioners and EMH supporters. Not only would it mean the final destruction of the EMH, an important principle of finance for over 40 years, but it would be an important confirmation of TA's validity. Both would represent large changes in the current state of knowledge.

Thus, it can be said that the gain in knowledge that occurs upon falsification of a hypothesis is inversely related to its information content. Likewise, it can be said that the knowledge gained by confirmation of a hypothesis (observations consistent with its predictions) is directly related to the information content of the hypothesis. The most informative hypotheses make the most audacious claims of new knowledge. They attempt to bring within the realm of understanding the broadest range of phenomena with the greatest degree of precision while at the same time involving the fewest assumptions. When such a hypothesis is falsified, we are not very surprised nor do we learn very much. Few would have expected the hypothesis to be confirmed, except perhaps for the bold scientist proposing it. For example, suppose a bold new theory of physics is put forward, one of whose predictions is that it is possible to build an antigravity device. If true, such a theory would represent a major increase in knowledge. However, if the device fails to work, no one would be surprised by the prediction's failure. However, it is exactly the opposite when a timid hypothesis is falsified. For example a timid hypothesis would be one that merely asserts that the currently accepted theories of physics are true and predicts that the antigravity device should fail. The falsification of this weak hypothesis via observations of the antigravity device working would result in a very significant gain in knowledge—the verification of new physics.

The most timid hypothesis that can be put forward is one that asserts that there have been no new discoveries. In other words, it says that all that is currently known is all that there is to know. This hypothesis denies the truth of any other hypothesis that asserts that something new has been discovered. The timid hypothesis that asserts that nothing new had been discovered has a special name in science. It is called the *null hypothesis* and it is the starting assumption in the investigation of any claim that a new discovery has been made. Whether that claim asserts that a new vaccine will cure a dreaded disease, that a new principle of physics tells us how to nullify gravity, or that a TA rule has predictive power, we always start by assuming that the null hypothesis is true. Then, if evidence can be produced that falsifies the null hypothesis, a most timid claim, it generates a big gain in knowledge.

Thus, science proceeds as follows. Every time a bold new hypothesis is put forward, it spawns an opposing claim, the null hypothesis. The null is as timid as the new hypothesis is bold. Jonas Salk's bold hypothesis that his vaccine would prevent polio better than a placebo spawned a competing claim, the null hypothesis. It made the timid prediction that the vaccine's ability to prevent infection would be no better than a placebo. This was a timid prediction because every prior attempt to develop a vaccine against polio had failed. These two competing claims left no middle ground. If one hypothesis could be falsified, by logic's Law of the Excluded Middle, we know that the other must be true. Salk's experimental evidence made it clear that the rate of infection among those receiving the real vaccine was significantly less than those receiving the placebo. In other words it was sufficient to falsify the null's prediction. This was a surprising result that represented a huge increase in medical knowledge!

How Scientists Should Respond to Falsification

How should a scientist respond when a hypothesis or theory that has survived many prior tests is ultimately falsified because recent observations conflict with predictions? The proper response is whatever leads to the biggest increase in knowledge. Because scientists are human beings, they sometimes fail to do what is scientifically correct.

There are two possible responses that increase knowledge. The first is to preserve the existing hypothesis by using it to predict new, previously unknown facts. If these new facts are confirmed and can explain why the observations that had been in conflict with the hypothesis are no longer in conflict, then the hypothesis deserves to be retained. The new facts represent an increase in what we know about the world. A second proper response is to throw out the old hypothesis and propose a new one that not only accounts for all observations that had been explained by the prior hypothesis but also explains the new discordant observations. This also represents an increase in knowledge in the form of a new hypothesis with greater explanatory or predictive power. However, in either case the correct response is to do whatever advances the frontier of knowledge the most.

Unfortunately the interests of science sometimes take a back seat to personal agendas. Human nature gets in the way of good science. Emotional, economic and professional ties to a prior hypothesis can motivate attempts to explain away the discordant evidence in a way that reduces the information content and falsifiability of their cherished hypothesis. This moves the frontier of knowledge backward. Fortunately science is a collective self-correcting enterprise. The community of scientists happily takes their fallen brothers to task when they stray from the path of righteousness in this way.

Some examples will clarify these abstract concepts. First, I present an example of a proper response to predictions being contradicted by new observations. In this case, new facts were predicted to rescue an established theory from falsification. This high road was taken by two astronomers during the nineteenth century, and it led to new knowledge in the form of a new planet being discovered. At that time, Newton's laws of motion and gravity were the accepted physics of planetary motion. They had been confirmed and reconfirmed by countless observations, but then, to the surprise of astronomers of that day, new and more powerful telescopes showed the planet Uranus was deviating from the orbit predicted by Newton's laws. A rigid and improper application of falsificationism would have called for an immediate rejection of Newtonian mechanics. However, all theories rest on a bed of auxiliary assumptions. A key assumption in this case was that the solar system contained only seven planets with Uranus being the seventh and furthest from the sun. This led astronomers Adams and Leverrier to boldly predict the existence of a yet undiscovered eighth planet (the new fact), lying beyond Uranus. If this were true, that new planet's gravitational effects could explain the aberrant motion of Uranus, which seemed to be in conflict with Newton's laws. In addition, if an eighth planet did exist, one of Newton's laws would predict the exact spot in the sky where the new planet would be observable. This was a bold, informative, and highly falsifiable prediction that put Newton's laws to a most stringent test. The astounding prediction made by Adams and Leverrier about where the new planet would appear in the sky was indeed confirmed in 1846 with the discovery of Neptune. They saved Newton's laws from falsification by demonstrating that the theory was not only able to explain the deviant behavior of Uranus but was also able to make a highly accurate prediction. This is the kosher way to retain a theory when it is confronted with dissonant observations.

In the end, however, Newton's laws proved to be provisionally true, as is ultimately the case for all laws and theories. Although Newton's laws had worked perfectly for more than 200 years, early in the twentieth century more precise astronomical observations were found to be truly inconsistent with the theory's predictions. The old theory had finally been falsified and it was time for a new one. In 1921, Albert Einstein responded properly by putting forward his new and more informative Theory of General Relativity. Today, almost one hundred years later, Einstein's theory has survived all attempts to falsify it.

Newton's theory qualified as scientific because it was open to empirical refutation. In fact, Newton's theory was not wrong so much as it was incomplete. Einstein's General Theory of Relativity not only accounted for all of the phenomena covered by the Newtonian model, but it accommodated the new observations that conflicted with Newton's more limited theory. This is how science progresses. Longevity and seniority mean nothing. Predictive accuracy and explanatory power are everything.

The case of Adams and Leverier make clear why claims must be open to empirical refutation. Falsifiability alone gives scientific knowledge a large advantage over conventional wisdom. The ability to jettison false or incomplete ideas and replace them with ever more informative ones produces a body of knowledge that is self-correcting and in a continual state of improvement. This in turn provides a stable base upon which new ideas can be erected that reach ever higher levels of understanding. Intellectual activities that have no procedure for eliminating erroneous knowledge inevitably get bogged down in nonsense. This is precisely the problem with the popular version of TA.

Now we will consider an example of an improper response to falsification. It occurs in the field of finance. The injection of science into finance is relatively recent. Perhaps this explains the defensive, unscientific response of those who support the efficient markets hypothesis. When observations collided with their favorite theory, they tried to save it from falsification by reducing its information content. As mentioned earlier, its least informative version, EMH weak, predicts that investment strategies based on TA[32] will not be able to earn risk adjusted returns that beat the market index. When EMH supporters were faced with studies showing that TA-based strategies were able to earn excess returns,[33] they responded by trying to immunize their theory from falsification. They did so by inventing new risk factors and claimed that the excess returns earned by TA were merely compensation for risks inherent in pursuing such a strategy. In other words, EMH defenders claimed that investors who followed the TA strategy were exposing themselves to a risk that was specific to that strategy. This allowed the EMH supporter to characterize the TA strategy's returns as non-market-beating. Recall EMH does not claim that earning returns higher than the market is impossible. It only says that higher returns entail the assumption of additional risk. If the returns earned by the TA strategy were indeed compensation for bearing higher risk, then EMH would remain intact despite the studies that show TA strategy earning a return higher than the market index.

There was one problem with the way EMH supporters did this. They cooked up the risk factor after the TA studies had been performed.[34] This is not kosher science. It would have been scientifically correct if EMH had defined the risk factor in advance of the study and predicted that a test of the TA method would generate what appeared to be market-beating returns. Had they done this, the status of EMH would have been enhanced with a successful prediction. Instead, EMH supporters took the low road to save their favored hypothesis by giving themselves the license to invent a new risk factor any time they needed to explain away findings that conflicted with their favored theory. In so doing, EMH supporters rendered their hypothesis unfalsifiable, thereby draining it of any information content.

The precedent for this knowledge-regressive method of immunizing the EMH hypothesis against falsification had already been established by earlier flawed defenses of EMH. These earlier, and similarly misguided, efforts to save EMH were in response to studies that had shown that public fundamental information, such as the price-to-book ratio and PE ratio, could be used to generate excess returns.[35] In response to this inconvenient evidence, EMH defenders claimed that low price-to-book ratios and low PE ratios were merely signals of stocks with abnormally high risk. In other words, the fact that a stock's price is low relative to its book value is an indication that the company is facing difficulties. Of course, this reasoning is circular. What is key here is the fact that EMH advocates had not defined low price-to-book or low PE as risk factors in advance of the studies showing that stocks with these traits were able to earn excess returns. Had EMH theorists done so, it they would have bolstered the information content of EMH with an additional dimension of risk. Instead, EMH theorists invented these risk factors after the fact, for the specific purpose of explaining away discordant observations that had already been made. Such explanations are termed ad-hoc hypotheses—explanations invented after the fact for the specific purpose of saving a theory or hypothesis from being falsified. Popper referred to this knowledge regressive, save-the-theory-at-any-cost behavior as falsification immunization.

Had Popper known of it, he would have chastised the die-hard supporters of EMH, but he would have probably applauded the efforts of those advocating behavioral finance. This relatively new field has proposed testable hypotheses that explain the profitability of strategies based on public technical and fundamental data as arising from the cognitive biases and illusions of investors. It is ironic that erroneous beliefs in the validity of subjective TA and the valid profitability of some forms of objective TA may both be the result of cognitive foibles.

The Scientific Attitude: Open yet Skeptical

Falsificationism makes a clear distinction between two phases of scientific discovery: proposal and refutation. These phases demand different mindsets—openness and skepticism. The coexistence of these opposite mindsets defines the scientific attitude.

An attitude of openness to new ideas is vital when hypotheses are being formulated. The willingness[36] to see things in a new way, to advance new explanations and take bold inductive leaps characterizes the proposal phase. Most practitioners of TA function well in this mode. New indicators, new systems, and new patterns get proposed all the time.

However, once a bold conjecture has been made, receptivity must morph into skepticism. Doubt about the new idea motivates a relentless search for its flaws. Thus, there is an ongoing tension in the scientist's mind between speculative curiosity and hard-nosed disbelief. However, the doubt is not an unremitting skepticism but one that yields to persuasive new evidence. This is the quasi-schizoid state that defines the scientific attitude.

Beyond the distrust of the new hypothesis, another form of skep-ticism thrives in the mind of a scientist: doubt about the mind itself. This springs from a profound awareness of the all-too-human tendency to generalize hastily and leap to unfounded conclusions. The procedures of science can be seen as safeguards against these tendencies.

629

■ The End Result: The Hypothetico-Deductive Method

Some would say there is no such thing as the scientific method.[37] "The scientific method, as far as it is a method is nothing more than doing one's damnedest with one's mind no holds barred."[38] At its essence it is intelligent problem solving.

The problem-solving method used in science today has come to be known as the hypothetico-deductive method. It is commonly described as having five stages: observation, hypothesis, prediction, verification, and conclusion. "In actual scientific work these stages are so intertwined that it would be hard to fit the history of any scientific investigation into this rigid scheme. Sometimes the different stages are merged or blurred, and frequently they do not occur in the sequence listed."[39] Rather, it is a useful way to think about the process.

The hypothetico-deductive method was initiated by Newton in the seventeenth century, but was not formally named until after Popper's contributions were introduced. It is the outgrowth of several hundred years of tussling between scientists and philosophers. The method integrates both inductive and deductive logic, paying heed to their individual limits while leveraging their respective powers.

The Five Stages

1. **Observation:** A possible pattern or relationship is noticed in a set of prior observations.

2. **Hypothesis:** Based on a mysterious mixture of insight, prior knowledge, and inductive generalization, it is hypothesized that the pattern is not an artifact of the particular set of observations but one that should be found in any similar set of observations. The hypothesis may merely assert that the pattern is real (scientific law) or it may go further and offer an explanation about why the pattern exists (scientific theory).

3. **Prediction:** A prediction is deduced from the hypothesis and embodied in a conditional proposition. The proposition's antecedent clause is the hypothesis and its consequent clause is the prediction. The prediction tells us what should be observed in a new set of observations if the hypothesis is indeed true. For example: **If** the hypothesis is true, **then** X should be observed if operation O is performed. The set of outcomes defined by X makes clear which future observations would confirm the prediction and, more importantly, which future observations would be in conflict with it.

4. **Verification:** New observations are made in accordance with the operations specified and compared to the predictions. In some sciences the operation is a controlled experiment. In other sciences it is an observational study.

5. **Conclusion:** An inference about the truth or falsity of the hypothesis is made based on the degree to which the observations conform to the prediction. This stage involves statistical inference methods such as confidence intervals and hypothesis tests.

An Example from TA

The following is an example of the hypothetico-deductive method as it would be applied to testing a new idea about technical analysis.

1. **Observation:** It is noticed that when a stock market index, such as the Dow Jones average or the S&P 500, rises above its 200-day moving average, it generally continues to appreciate over the next several months (probabilistic generalization).

2. **Hypothesis:** On the basis of this observation, inductive generalization, and prior findings of technical analysis, we propose the following hypothesis: Upward penetrations of the 200-day moving average by the DJIA will, on average, produce profitable long positions over the next three months. I'll refer to this hypothesis as 200-H.

3. **Prediction:** On the basis of the hypothesis, we predict that an observational investigation, or back test, will be profitable. The hypothesis and the prediction are turned into the following conditional statement: **If** 200-H is true, **then** the back test *will be profitable.* However this prediction creates a logical problem. Even if the back test is profitable it will not be helpful in proving the truth of 200-H because, as previously pointed out, while a profitable back test would be consistent with the truth of 200-H, it cannot prove that 200-H is true. An attempt to do so would commit the fallacy of affirming the consequent (see Argument

1 following). If, on the other hand, the back test turns out to be unprofitable, it would be valid to conclude 200-H is false by the valid logical form falsification of the consequent. See Argument 2 below.

Argument 1

Premise 1: *If 200-H is true, then a back test will be profitable.*

Premise 2: *The back test was profitable.*

Invalid Conclusion: Therefore, 200-H is true. (fallacy of affirming the consequent)

Argument 2

Premise 1: *If 200-H is true, then a back test will be profitable.*

Premise 2: *The back test was NOT profitable.*

Valid Conclusion: *Therefore, 200-H is false.*

However, our objective is to prove the truth of 200-H. To get around this logical problem, suppose we had formulated a null hypothesis at stage 2, specifically, *Upward penetrations of a 200-day moving average do not generate profits over the following three months.* Let's refer to this as Null-200. From this we can formulate the following conditional proposition: **If** *Null-200 is true,* **then** *a back-test will NOT be profitable.* If the back test does turn out to be profitable, we can validly argue that the null hypothesis has been falsified (falsifying the consequent). By the Law of the Excluded Middle, either 200-H is true or Null-200 is true. There is no middle ground; there is no other hypothesis possible. Thus by disproving the null we will have indirectly proven that 200-H is true. Thus we have the following conditional syllogism:

Premise 1: *If Null-200 is true, then the back test will be unprofitable.*

Premise 2: *The back test was NOT unprofitable (i.e., it was profitable).*

Valid Conclusion: Null-200 is false, therefore 200-H is true.

4. **Verification:** The proposed rule is back tested and its profitability is observed.

5. **Conclusion:** Determining the meaning of the results is a matter of statistical inference.

Rigorous and Critical Analysis of Observed Results

The fifth phase of the hypothetico-deductive method points to another important difference between science and nonscience. In science, observed evidence is not taken at face value. In other words, the obvious implication of the evidence may not be its true implication. The evidence must be subjected to rigorous analysis before a conclusion can be drawn from it. The evidence of choice in science is quantitative data, and the tool of choice for drawing conclusions is statistical inference.

An important scientific principle is the preference for simpler explanations (Ockham's Razor). As such, astounding hypotheses are given serious consideration only after more commonplace hypotheses have been rejected. Sightings of a UFO are not immediately interpreted as evidence of an alien visit. More mundane accounts such as ball lightning, weather balloons, or a new aircraft must first be discredited before an invasion from outer space is taken seriously.

Thus a scientific attitude toward an extraordinarily profitable rule back test would first consider and reject other explanations before entertaining the possibility that a significant TA rule has been discovered. The possible explanations of good performance unrelated to a rule's predictive power are good luck due to sampling error and systematic error due to data-mining bias.

■ Summary of Key Aspects of the Scientific Method

The following is a summary of the key points of the scientific method:

- No matter how voluminous the evidence, the scientific method can never conclusively prove a hypothesis to be true.

- Observed evidence used in combination with the deductive form falsification of the consequent can be used to disprove a hypothesis with a specified degree of probability.

- Science is restricted to testable hypotheses. Propositions that are not testable are not within the domain of scientific discourse and are considered to be meaningless.

- A hypothesis is testable if and only if predictions about yet-to-be-made observations can be deduced from the hypothesis.

- A hypothesis that can only explain past observations but that cannot make predictions about new observations is not scientific.

- A hypothesis is tested by comparing its predictions with new observations. If predictions and observations agree, the hypothesis is not proven, but merely receives tentative confirmation. If they don't agree, the hypothesis is taken to be false or incomplete.

- All currently accepted scientific knowledge is only provisionally true. Its truth is temporary until a test shows it to be false, at which point it is replaced or subsumed by a more complete theory.

- Scientific knowledge is cumulative and progressive. As older hypotheses are shown to be false, they are replaced by newer ones that more accurately portray objective reality. Science is the only method of inquiry or intellectual discipline which can claim that newer is better. Though knowledge, styles, and methods in other disciplines, such as music, art, philosophy, or literary criticism, may change over time, it cannot be claimed that new is necessarily better.

- Any set of past observations (data) can be explained by an infinite number of hypotheses. For example, Elliott Wave Theory, Gann Lines, classical chart patterns, and a roster of other interpretive methods can all explain past market behavior according to their own paradigm of analysis. Therefore, all these explanations are said to be empirically equal. The only way to decide which ones are better is by seeing how well they can predict observations whose outcomes are not yet known. Those methods that cannot generate testable (falsifiable) predictions about new observations can be eliminated immediately on the grounds that they are scientifically meaningless. Those methods that can generate predictions that are found to conflict with future observations can be eliminated on grounds that they have been falsified. Thus, only methods that can make testable predictions that display genuine predictive power deserve to be retained in the body of TA knowledge.

If TA Were to Adopt the Scientific Method

This section examines consequences of TA adopting the scientific method.

The Elimination of Subjective TA

The most important consequence of TA adopting the scientific method would be the elimination of subjective approaches. Because they are not testable, subjective methods are shielded from empirical challenge. This makes them worse than wrong. They are meaningless propositions devoid of information. Their elimination would make TA an entirely objective practice.

Subjective TA would be eliminated in one of two ways: by transformation into objective methods or abandonment. Perhaps Gann Lines, subjective divergences, trend channels, and a host of subjective patterns and concepts embody valid aspects of market behavior. In their present subjective form, however, we are denied this knowledge.

Transforming a subjective method into an objective version is not trivial. To illustrate a case where this has been done, I discuss an algorithm for the automated diction of head and shoulder patterns and test results in the section "Objectification of Subjective TA: An Example."

Elimination of Meaningless Forecasts

It is not practical to assume that all subjective practitioners will follow my call to objectify or close up shop. For those who continue to use subjective approaches, there is an important step that can be taken to make their output, if not their methodology, objective. Henceforth, they would issue only falsifiable forecasts. This would at least make the information they provide meaningful and informative. In this context, informative does not necessarily mean correct but rather that the forecasts have cognitive content that passes the discernable difference test discussed in the Introduction. In other words, the forecast would convey something of substance, the truth of which can be clearly determined by subsequent market action. In other words, the forecast will make explicit or clearly imply which outcomes would show it to be wrong. As stated previously, a forecast that does not make clear what future events constitute prediction errors in essence says that any outcome can happen.

At the present time, most subjective forecasts, often referred to as market calls, are meaningless. In all likelihood, this is not obvious to either consumers or the analysts issuing the forecasts. First, consider a forecast that is clearly meaningless: "My indicators are now predicting the market will either go up an infinite percentage, down 100 percent, or something in between." On its face, the statement is unfalsifiable because there is no outcome that could possibly conflict with the prediction. The only good thing about the forecast is that its lack of meaning and lack of falsifiability are transparent. A more typical market call goes something like this: "On the basis of my indicators [fill in one or more TA methods], I am bullish." This unfalsifiable statement is just as meaningless, but its lack of substance is not obvious. Though there is a prediction of a rise, the prediction leaves unclear when it might occur or under what circumstances the prediction would be wrong.

This bullish stance could have been made meaningful by clearly excluding certain outcomes. For example, *I expect the market to rise more than 10 percent from current levels before it declines by more than 5 percent from current levels.* Any instance of a decline of greater than 5 percent before a rise of 10 percent would be sufficient to classify the forecast as an error.

If you ever suspect that you are being fed a meaningless prediction, here are some good antidotes. Ask the following question: "How much adverse movement (opposite to the direction predicted) would have to occur for you to admit this forecast is mistaken?" Or "What outcomes are precluded by your prediction?" Or "When, and under what conditions, can the forecast be evaluated, such as the passage of time, change in price (adverse or favorable), or a specific indicator development?" Reader, I warn you not to do this if you are squeamish about watching people squirm.

Making subjective forecasts meaningful with an up-front statement of when and how the forecast will be evaluated would eliminate the market guru's after-the-fact wiggle room. Some ways of adding meaning to a subjective forecast include (1) defining a future point in time when the forecast will be evaluated, (2) defining the maximum degree of adverse movement that would be allowed without declaring the prediction wrong, and (3) predicting a specified magnitude of favorable movement prior to a specified magnitude of unfavorable movement (X percent favorable before Y percent unfavorable). Steps like these would allow a subjective practitioner to develop a track record of meaningful market calls. Meaningful track records can also result from specific transaction recommendations made in real time.

One limitation of this recommendation is that it would still leave unclear what the profitable track record represents. This is because subjective forecasts are derived in an undefined way, so even if a profitable track record of meaningful predictions is built up over time, it cannot be known that they were the result of a consistent analysis procedure that can be repeated in the future. In fact, it is likely that the method of analysis is not stable over time. Studies of expert subjective judgment indicate that experts do not combine information in a consistent manner from one judgment to the next. "Intuitive judgments suffer from serious random inconsistencies due to fatigue, boredom, and all the factors that make us human."[40] In other words, given the exact same pattern of market data at different times, it is quite possible that a subjective analyst would not give the same forecast.[41]

Paradigm Shift

Refashioning TA into an objective practice would be what Thomas Kuhn calls a paradigm shift. In his highly influential book, *The Structure of Scientific Revolutions*, Kuhn rejected Popper's notion that science evolves strictly by falsification and conjecture. Instead, Kuhn saw the evolution of a science as a sequence of paradigms, or world views. While a given paradigm is in place, practitioners indoctrinated in that point of view confine their activities to posing questions and hypotheses that are consistent with and answerable within that view.

A large number of TA analysts have been indoctrinated with the nonscientific, intuitive analysis paradigm developed by TA pioneers like Dow, Gann, Shabacker, Elliott, Edwards and Magee, and so forth. They established the subjective research tradition and postulated the background wisdom that is accepted as true and taught to aspiring practitioners. The certification exam given by the Market Technicians Association to aspiring Chartered Market Technicians (CMT) exemplifies this tradition.

The shift to an evidence-based objective approach would challenge much of this material as either meaningless or not sufficiently supported by statistical evidence. Many of the teachings will go the way of early Greek physics and astronomy. Some methods will survive objectification and statistical testing and will warrant a position in a legitimate body of TA knowledge.

Lest the reader think my position too harsh, I am not advocating that the falsifiability criterion be used to cut off all research in budding TA methods just as they are being formulated. Many of the brilliant theories of science began as halfbacked prescientific ideas on the wrong side of the falsifiability criterion. These ideas needed time to develop, and one day some turned into meaningful science. One example in TA is the new field of socionomics, an outgrowth of Elliott Wave Theory. At the current time, I regard this newly developing discipline as prescientific, though it may have the potential to become a science. According to a conversation I had with Professor John Nofsinger, who is working within the field of socionomics, at this time the discipline is not able to make testable predictions. This will require the quantification of social mood, the key determinant of market movement according to socionomics.

Nascent areas of research such as this and others should not be short-circuited simply because they are not at this time able to generate testable predictions. One day they may be able to do so.

■ Objectification of Subjective TA: An Example

One of the challenging aspects of moving TA to a science will be transforming subjective chart patterns into objectively defined testable patterns. This section presents an example of how two academic technicians, Keving Chang and Carol Osler (C&O) objectified the head-and-shoulders pattern).[42] Not all elements of their pattern are included here. Rather, I have included enough of their rules and the problems they faced and solved to illustrate the challenges of transforming a subjective method into an objective one. For further details please refer to their original articles.

Descriptions of the head-and-shoulders pattern can be found in many TA texts[43] and are typically accompanied by a diagram similar to the one in Figure 29.8. It represents the pattern as a sequence of noise-free price swings. When the pattern manifests in perfect textbook form, even a beginning student of TA can spot it.

The problem occurs when an actual chart pattern departs from this ideal. Even seasoned chartists can debate whether a given pattern qualifies as a legitimate head and shoulders, an unavoidable consequence of the lack of an objective pattern definition. Subjective pattern definitions generally describe how the head-and-shoulders pattern should look, but they do not provide clear rules for discriminating patterns that do qualify as head and shoulders from patterns that possess some head-and-shoulders-like features but do not qualify. In other words, the definitions lack clear rules for which patterns to exclude. This problem is conceptualized in Figure 29.6.

Without objective rules for deciding what does and what does not qualify as a legitimate head-and-shoulders pattern it is impossible to evaluate the pattern's profitability or predictive power. The solution to the problem is to define objective rules that discriminate valid head-and-shoulders patterns from those that are not.[44] This notion is illustrated in Figure 29.7. The challenge of turning a subjective pattern into an objective one can be thought of as the problem of defining the pattern as a clear subset in the super-set of all possible TA price patterns.

C&O defined the head-and-shoulders top pattern as composed of five pivot or price reversal points that, in turn, define the pattern's three peaks and two troughs.

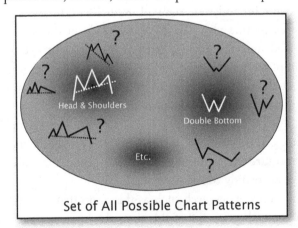

FIGURE 29.6 Subjective Patterns—No Definitive Exclusion Rules.

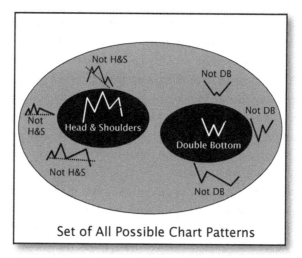

FIGURE 29.7 Objective Patterns—Definitive Exclusion Rules.

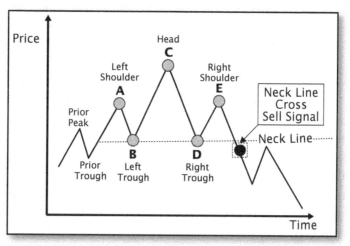

FIGURE 29.8 Head and Shoulders.

These pivots are denoted by letters A through E on Figure 29.8. All eight texts consulted by C&O were clear that the head, denoted by letter C, must be higher than the two surrounding peaks (shoulders) denoted by letters A and E. There has been some debate among chartists about several auxiliary features including the Adam's apple, the double chin, and the cowlick. However, the TA manuals consulted by C&O were inconsistent on these aspects and they were not included.

One challenge that faces the real-world chartist is the fact that actual price oscillations do not trace out clearly identifiable peaks and troughs. Rather, peaks and troughs occur at numerous oscillation scales from tiny waves lasting minutes to very large ones lasting years or decades. This property, called fractal scaling, imposes a burden on the subjective analyst trying to identify a head-and-shoulders pattern. The analyst must visually filter the price behavior to isolate peaks and troughs at one particular scale of interest. This is relatively easy in retrospect, but it is quite difficult as the pattern is actually unfolding in real time.

C&O addressed this problem by using a percentage filter, also known as an Alexander filter[45] or a zigzag indicator, which is discussed by Merrill in *Filtered Waves*.[46] It is an objective method for identifying peaks and troughs as prices evolve. Troughs are identified after prices have moved up from a recent price low by an amount greater than a specified threshold percentage and peaks are identified after prices have moved down from a recent price high by the threshold percentage. The problem is that the identification occurs with a time lag, the time it takes for prices to move the threshold amount. For example, if the threshold is set at 5 percent, then a peak is not detected until prices have fallen at least 5 percent from the most recent price maximum, and troughs are not detected until prices have risen at least 5 percent from the recent price minimum. The minimum required price movement causes a lag between the time the peak or trough actually occurred and the time at which it is detected by the zigzag filter.

Next, C&O addressed how to determine the correct threshold percentage to define the zigzag filter. Different filter thresholds would reveal head-and-shoulders patterns of different size (scale). For example, a 3 percent filter might reveal a head-and-shoulders pattern that a 10 percent filter would completely ignore. This makes it possible for multiple head-and-shoulders patterns of differing scale to exist simultaneously. C&O addressed this problem by subjecting each financial instrument (stock or currency) to 10 different zigzag filters employing a range of threshold values. This allowed them to identify head-and-shoulders patterns on a variety of scales.

This raised yet another problem. What should the 10 filter thresholds be? Clearly, a set of thresholds that would be good for one instrument may not be good for another because they are characterized by different levels of volatility. Realizing this, C&O take each instrument's recent volatility into account to arrive at the set of 10 filter thresholds used for that instrument. This insight allowed their head-and-shoulders algorithm to generalize across markets with different volatilities. C&O defined a market's volatility, V, as the standard deviation of daily percentage price changes over the most recent 100 trading days. The 10 thresholds were arrived at by multiplying V by 10 different coefficients; 1.5, 2.0, 2.5, 3.0, 3.5, 4.0, 4.5, 5.0, 5.5, 6.0. This resulted in 10 zigzag filters with varying sensitivity. The validity of the set of coefficients chosen by C&O were confirmed by visual inspection of price charts by TA practitioners who agreed that the 10 zigzag filters did a reasonable job of identifying head-and-shoulders patterns.

Next C&O addressed the problem of defining rules that qualify a candidate pattern as a valid head-and-shoulders. These rules were applied to the instrument once its price had been zigzag filtered and the peaks and troughs at a given scale had been identified.

First, the head and shoulders identified by C&O's algorithm had to satisfy the following basic rules:

1. The head of the pattern must be higher than both the left and right shoulders.
2. The instrument must be in an uptrend prior to the formation of the head-and-shoulders pattern. Thus, the pattern's left shoulder has to be above the prior peak (PP) and the pattern's left trough has to be above the prior trough (PT).

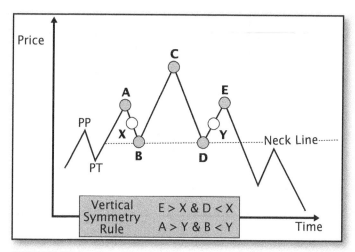

FIGURE 29.9 Good Vertical Symmetry.

Next C&O grappled with more subtle and complex issues to qualify a candidate pattern as a valid head-and-shoulders. They accomplished this with a set of innovative measurements that qualified the pattern in terms of its vertical and horizontal symmetry and the time it took for the pattern to complete. These rules allowed them to definitively label a candidate pattern as either head-and-shoulders or a non–head-and-shoulders.

Vertical Symmetry Rules

The vertical symmetry rules exclude patterns with necklines that are too steeply sloped. The pattern in Figure 29.9 has acceptable vertical symmetry.

The rules compare the price levels of the right and left shoulders (A and E) and the price levels of the right and left troughs (B and D) with a price level defined by the midpoint of segment AB, designated as point X, and the midpoint of segment DE designated as point Y. To qualify as a vertically symmetrical head-and-shoulders, the pattern must satisfy the following rules.

1. The price level of the left shoulder peak, point A, must exceed the price level of point Y.
2. The price level of the right shoulder peak, point E, must exceed the price level of point X.
3. The price level of the left trough, point B, must be less than the price level of point Y.
4. The price level of the right trough, point D, must be less than the price level of point X.

Figures 29.10 and 29.11 show two head-and-shoulders patterns that would be excluded because the vertical symmetry criteria have not been satisfied.

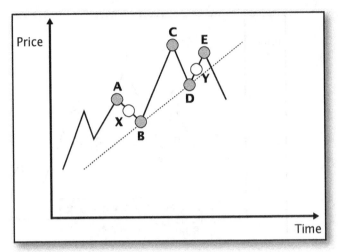

FIGURE 29.10 Poor Vertical Symmetry—Neckline Slope Too Steep.

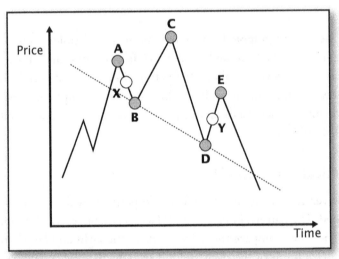

FIGURE 29.11 Poor Vertical Symmetry—Neckline Slope Too Steep.

Horizontal Symmetry Rule

Another feature used by C&O to distinguish head-and-shoulders patterns from non-head-and-shoulders patterns was horizontal symmetry. A pattern with good horizontal symmetry is one for which the head, at point C, is roughly equidistant from the peaks representing the pattern's two shoulders (points A and E). C&O's rule was that the distance from the head to one shoulder should not be greater than 2.5 times the distance of the head to the other shoulder. There is nothing magical about the value 2.5 other than it seemed reasonable. See Figure 29.12.

Figure 29.13 is an example of a pattern that fails the test for horizontal symmetry. Note the right shoulder is stretched too far to the right. A pattern with excessive leftward stretch would also be disqualified.

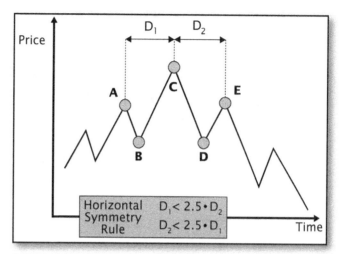

FIGURE 29.12 Good Horizontal Symmetry.

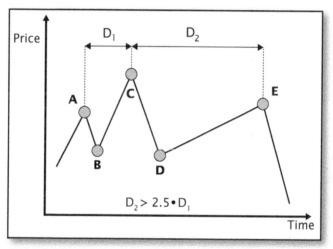

FIGURE 29.13 Poor Horizontal Symmetry.

Pattern Completion Rule: Maximum Time to Neckline Penetration

C&O also specified a rule that excludes patterns that take too long to penetrate the neckline once the right shoulder, point E, has been formed. As with other features, this criterion is defined in terms of the pattern's internal proportions rather than some fixed number of time units. This allows the rule to be applied to all patterns irrespective of their time frame or scale.

The maximum time allowed for the movement from the right shoulder, point E, until the penetration of the neckline is the temporal distance separating the two shoulders, points A and E. The pattern in Figure 29.14 meets the time to completion criterion because the temporal distance from the right shoulder until neckline penetration (D4) is less than the temporal separation of the shoulders (D3). The pattern in Figure 29.15 does not qualify because D4 exceeds D3.

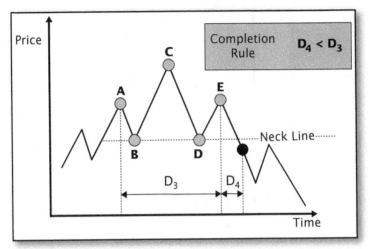

FIGURE 29.14 Pattern Completion Rule Satisfied.

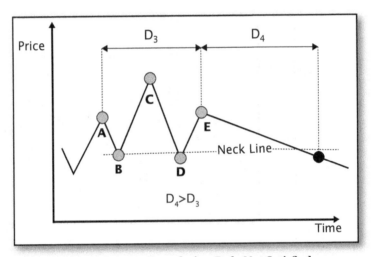

FIGURE 29.15 Pattern Completion Rule Not Satisfied.

Future Information Leakage: Look-Ahead Bias

In their simulation of head-and-shoulders patterns, C&O took precautions against the future information leakage or look-ahead bias problem. This problem afflicts back tests that assume the possession of knowledge that was not truly available when a trading decision was made. In the context of back testing, this can make results appear more profitable than would be possible in actual trading. An extreme example would be assuming access to the *Wall Street Journal* the day before its publication.

In the context of back testing the head-and-shoulders pattern, future information leakage can occur if the zigzag threshold percentage is larger than the percentage distance between the right shoulder peak and the neckline. It would not be legitimate to assume a short-sale signal due to a neckline penetration until the right shoulder (point E) has been detected. However, it is possible for prices to cross the neckline before the right shoulder is identified by the zigzag filter. To clarify, suppose the right shoulder, point E, lies only 4 percent above the neckline, but the threshold for the zigzag filter is 10 percent. It would not be legitimate to assume that a trader knew about the neckline penetration because a 10 percent decline from the right shoulder would have been required to identify the right shoulder of the head-and-shoulders pattern. In this example, assuming an entry price only 4 percent below the right shoulder would be more favorable than waiting for a price 10 percent below the right shoulder, the price movement required to have a fully formed head-and-shoulders pattern. To avoid this problem, C&O assumed an entry after the right shoulder had been objectively identified by the zigzag filter. Though this was a less favorable entry price in some instances, the back test was unencumbered by look-ahead bias. I mention this because it shows C&O's attention to detail.

C&O's pattern definition also deals with numerous other issues regarding entry and exit of positions, stop-loss levels, and so forth, but the point has been made that it is possible to transform subjective chart patterns into objective testable patterns. Readers may take exception to arbitrary aspects of C&O's pattern. All well and good if the reader has a better objective definition to offer.

As a final sanity check, C&O showed patterns that had been identified by their automated head-and-shoulders algorithm to a number of chartists. C&O claim that the chartists agreed that the patterns identified by the objective head-and-shoulders algorithm did indeed conform to subjective head-and-shoulders criteria.

Head-and-Shoulders Back Test Results

Does the head-and-shoulders pattern carry predictive information with respect to stocks or currencies? In a word, the pattern hailed as a cornerstone of charting is a bust. Tests by C&O show that it is worthless on stocks and only modestly profitable on currencies. The pattern was profitable in two out of six currencies tested, but the relatively complicated head-and-shoulders algorithm was far outperformed by a much simpler objective signal based on zigzag filters. Moreover, when C&O tested the occurrence of a head-and-shoulders in conjunction with the zigzag rule either as a confirming or disconfirming signal, the head-and-shoulders pattern added no value. In other words, zigzag signals did no better when the head-and-shoulders signal was in the same direction as the zigzag signal and the zigzag did no worse when the head-and-shoulders signal was in the opposite direction. The bottom line for currency traders: the value of head-and-shoulders is doubtful.[47]

The head-and-shoulders performed worse on stocks. C&O evaluated the head-and-shoulders on 100 randomly selected equities[48] over the period from July 1962 until December 1993. On average, each stock gave one head-and-shoulders signal per year, counting both long and short signals, giving a sample of over 3,100 signals. To test the pattern's profitability on actual stock prices, C&O established a benchmark based on the pattern's performance on pseudo-price histories. These simulated price histories were generated from actual historical price changes strung together in a random fashion. By using actual price changes, the pseudo-price histories had the same statistical characteristics as real stocks, but any predictability due to authentic temporal structure—the structure TA patterns are intended to exploit—was eliminated despite the fact that the pseudo-price histories were randomly generated, head-and-shoulders patterns that fit C&O's definition still emerged. This confirms the results of Harry Roberts referred to earlier.

If the head-and-shoulders patterns appearing in real stock data are useful, they should generate profits superior to those achieved by trading the patterns appearing in the fake stock price histories. C&O found that head-and-shoulders patterns in actual stock prices lost slightly more money than the signals on pseudo-price histories. According to the study "the results uniformly suggest that head-and-shoulders trading are not profitable." The signals lose on average about 0.25 percent over a 10-day holding period. This compares with an average loss of 0.03 percent for head-and-shoulders patterns in the pseudo-stock data. C&O referred to traders using the pattern as "noise traders," speculators who mistake a random signal for an informative one.

Confirming C&O's findings is the work of Lo et al.[49] Lo used an alternative method of objectifying the H&S pattern based on kernel regression, a sophisticated local[50] smoothing technique. Their study was unable to unseat the null hypothesis that the head-and-shoulders pattern is useless.[51]

Bulkowski[52] found the head-and-shoulders was profitable, but his research falls short. He does not provide an objective pattern definition that back-testable pattern or entry and exit rules. In other words, his study is subjective TA. In addition, his results fail to adjust for the trend of the general stock market over the time period in which he tested the patterns.

■ Subsets of TA

Given the preceding discussion, TA can be seen as comprised of four subsets: (1) subjective TA, (2) objective TA with unknown statistical significance, (3) objective TA that is not statistically significant, and (4) objective TA that is statistically significant.

The first subset, subjective TA, has already been defined as methods that cannot be reduced to a back-testable algorithm. Subsets two, three, and four refer to objective methods.

The second subset is comprised of objective methods of unknown value. Though these methods are objective and may have been back tested, their results have not been evaluated for statistical significance. This is not meant to suggest that applying statistical methods to back test results is simple, but rather that the decision to do so is.

The third subset, which I refer to as useless TA, consists of objective TA rules for which results have been comprehensively back tested and evaluated with statistical methods, but have been reveled to add no value either on a stand-alone basis or when used in combination with other methods. In all likelihood, the majority of objective TA methods will fall into this subset. This is to be expected because financial markets are extremely difficult to predict due to their inherent complexity and randomness. In fact, in all fields of science, most proposed ideas do not work. Important

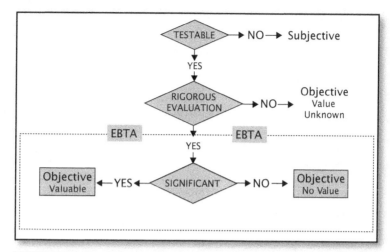

FIGURE 29.16 Subsets of Technical Analysis.

discoveries are rare. This is not obvious because the numerous failures are typically not reported in the lay press or even in scientific journals. What is most important is having a procedure in place for getting rid of methods that do not work.

The fourth subset, useful TA, consists of objective methods that produce statistically significant or, better yet, economically significant results. Though some rules will be useful on a stand-alone basis, the complexity and randomness of financial markets make it likely that most rules will add value when used in combination with other rules to form complex rules.

Evidence-based technical analysis (EBTA) refers to subsets (3) and (4)—objective TA that has been back tested and subjected to statistical analysis. Given the preceding discussion, the categorization of TA is illustrated in Figure 29.16.

■ Notes

1. M. Shermer, *Why People Believe Weird Things: Pseudoscience, Superstition, and Other Confusions of Our Time* (New York: W.H. Freeman, 1997).
2. C. Van Doren, *A History of Knowledge: Past, Present, and Future* (New York: Ballantine Books, 1991).
3. S. Richards, *Philosophy & Sociology of Science: An Introduction* (Oxford, UK: Basil Blackwell, 1983), 45.
4. Ibid.
5. Ibid., 189.
6. Ibid., 201.
7. As quoted by Shermer, *Why People Believe*.
8. Van Doren, *History of Knowledge*, 189.
9. Ibid.
10. Richards, *Philosophy & Sociology of Science*, 14.
11. D.J. Bennett, *Logic Made Easy: How to Know When Language Deceives You* (New York: W.W. Norton, 2004), 30.
12. Ibid., 31.
13. Ibid., 99 and 108; referring to P.C. Wason, "Self-Contradictions," in *Thinking: Readings in Cognitive Science* (Cambridge, UK: Cambridge University Press, 1977), 114–128; S.S. Epp, "A Cognitive

Approach to Teaching Logic," *DIMACS Symposium, Teaching Logic and Reasoning in an Illogical World*, Rutgers, The State University of New Jersey, July 25–26, 1996, available at www.cs.cornell.edu/Info/People/gries/symposium/symp.htm.

14. The fact that a given set of observations can be consistent with (explained by) more than one theory or hypothesis and perhaps an infinite number of alternative theories is a problem known in philosophical and scientific circles as the *underdetermination of theories problem*. Because a multitude of hypotheses can be consistent with the same set of observations, the hypotheses are said to be empirically identical. The implication is that observational data, on its own, cannot tell us which of them is correct.

15. F. Schauer, *Profiles, Probabilities and Stereotypes* (Cambridge, MA: Belknap Press of Harvard, 2003), 59. References to studies on dog breed behavior are found in footnote 7.

16. In this case the uncertainty would be 10 times greater with 10 observations than with 1,000 if price changes conform to the normal distribution, but may be far more uncertain if they do not.

17. http://en.wikipedia.org/wiki/Philosophy_of_science.

18. Shermer, *Why People Believe*, 24.

19. Richards, *Philosophy & Sociology of Science*, 45.

20. B.L. Silver, *The Ascent of Science* (New York: Oxford University Press, 1998), 15.

21. Ibid., 14.

22. R.S. Percival, *About Karl Popper*, adapted from his PhD thesis, available at www.eeng.dcu.ie/~tkpw/intro_popper/intro_popper.html.

23. This is the frequency definition of probability. There are others.

24. Richards, *Philosophy & Sociology of Science*, 52.

25. K.R. Popper, *The Logic of Scientific Discovery* (London: Hutchinson, 1977).

26. K.R. Popper, *Conjectures and Refutations* (London: Routledge & Kegan 1972).

27. This is known as the underdetermination of theories problem.

28. *If hypothesis is true, then X should be observed. X is observed* (affirms the consequent). Invalid conclusion: *The hypothesis is true* (fallacy of affirming the consequent).

29. A *necessary* condition is one that is required to produce an effect, but it alone is not enough to produce the effect. For example if X is a necessary condition of Y, it means that, if X is lacking, Y will not occur but the fact that X is present is not enough to insure Y. In shorthand: *If not X, then not Y*. A *sufficient* condition is more comprehensive in that its presence is enough (is sufficient) to produce the effect. Thus it means: *If W, then Y*.

30. Richards, *Philosophy & Sociology of Science*, 59.

31. My contention may be challenged in the near future by an objective version of EWT called EWAVES developed by Robert Prechter's firm, Elliott Wave International. Prechter claims it generates definitive signals for which financial performance can be measured.

32. Descriptions of EMH-weak vary. Some say only historical price data cannot be used to generated excess returns. Other versions say any stale market data, price, volume, or any other data series that TA practitioners study cannot be used to generated excess returns.

33. N. Jegadeesh and S. Titman, "Returns to Buying Winners and Selling Losers: Implications for Stock Market Efficiency," *Journal of Finance* 56 (1993), 699–720.

34. R.A. Haugen, *The Inefficient Stock Market: What Pays Off and Why* (Upper Saddle River, NJ: Prentice-Hall, 1999), 63.

35. F. Nicholson, "Price-Earnings Ratios in Relation to Investment Results," *Financial Analysts Journal* (January/February 1968), 105–109; J.D. McWilliams, "Prices and Price-Earnings Ratios," *Financial Analysts Journal* 22 (May/June, 1966), 136–142.

36. Because there are not infinite time and resources to test all ideas, receptivity is tempered with prior knowledge, experience, and intuition. Some new ideas merit more attention than others. However, being overly restrictive at this phase could have a big cost—missing a breakthrough. In this phase, if one is to err, it is better to err on the side of openness.

37. W.A. Wallis and H.V. Roberts, *Statistics: A New Approach* (New York: The Free Press of Glencoe, 1964), 5.

38. P.W. Bridgman, "The Prospect for Intelligence," *Yale Review* 34 (1945), 444–461, quoted in J.B. Conant, *On Understanding Science* (New Haven: Yale University Press, 1947), 115.

39. Wallis and Roberts, *Statistics*, 6.

40. J.E. Russo and P.J.H. Schoemaker, *Decision Traps: The Ten Barriers to Brilliant Decision-Making and How to Overcome Them* (New York: Doubleday, 1989), 135.

41. L.R. Goldberg, "Man versus Model of Man: A Rationale, Plus Some Evidence for a Method of Improving Clinical Inference," *Psychological Bulletin* 73 (1970), 422–432.

42. P.H.K. Chang and C.L. Osler, "Methodical Madness: Technical Analysis and the Irrationality of Exchange-Rate Forecasts," *Economic Journal*, 109, no. 458 (1999), 636–661; C.L. Osler, "Identifying Noise Traders: The Head-and-Shoulders Pattern in U.S. Equities," Publication of Federal Reserve Bank of New York, 1998.

43. R.D. Edwards, J. Magee, and W.H.C. Bassetti (Eds.), *Technical Analysis of Stock Trends*, 8th ed., (Boca Raton, FL: CRC Press, 2001); M.J. Pring, *Technical Analysis Explained*, 4th ed. (New York: McGraw-Hill, 2002); J.J. Murphy, *Technical Analysis of the Financial Markets: A Comprehensive Guide to Trading Methods and Applications* (New York: New York Institute of Finance, 1999).

44. It may be possible to define chart patterns using fuzzy logic where class membership is given a class membership function (0 to 1.0) rather than a yes or no. However, evaluating pattern effectiveness will still require a threshold on the class membership function to decide which patterns belong in a given class and which do not.

45. S.S. Alexander, "Price Movements in Speculative Markets: Trends or Random Walks," *Industrial Management Review* 2 (1961), 7–26; S.S. Alexander, "Price Movements in Speculative Markets: Trends or Random Walks No. 2," *Industrial Management Review* 5 (1964), 25–46.

46. A.A. Merrill, *Filtered Waves: Basic Theory* (Chappaqua, NY: Analysis Press, 1977).

47. P.H.K. Chang, and C.L. Osler, "Methodical Madness: Technical Analysis and the Irrationality of Exchange-Rate Forecasts," *Economic Journal* 109, no. 458 (1999), 636–661.

48. C.L. Osler, "Identifying Noise Traders: The Head-and-Shoulders Pattern in U.S. Equities," Publication of Federal Reserve Bank of New York, 1998.

49. A.W. Lo, H. Mamaysky, and W. Jiang, "Foundations of Technical Analysis: Computational Algorithms, Statistical Inference, and Empirical Implementation," *Journal of Finance* 55, 4 (August 2000), 1705–1765.

50. Kernel regression estimates the value of a smoothed curve by averaging nearby or local observations, where the weight of each observation is inversely related to its distance from the location for which a smoothed value is desired. Thus, nearby observations are given the greatest weight. The term *kernel* refers to the shape of the weighting function used. One common weight function is based on the shape of the normal probability distribution (Gaussian kernel).

51. The authors of the paper do not come out directly and say the patterns are not useful for forecasting trends, but the data they present indicates this as does the commentary on the paper provided by Narasimahan Jegadeesh (pp. 1765–1770). In Table 1 he shows that the post pattern returns (trends) are not significantly different than when the patterns are not present.

52. T.N. Bulkowski, *Encyclopedia of Chart Patterns* (New York: John Wiley & Sons, 2000), 262–304.

CHAPTER 30

Theories of Nonrandom Price Motion

From David Aronson, *Evidence-Based Technical Analysis: Applying the Scientific Method and Statistical Inference to Trading Signals* (Hoboken, New Jersey: John Wiley & Sons, 2006), Chapter 7.

Learning Objective Statements

- Describe the two paradoxes of the EMH
- Identify examples of studies that contradict semi-strong and weak forms of the EMH
- Explain insights from the BSV< DHS, and HS hypotheses that use Behavioral Finance to help address problems with the EMH
- Describe insights from theories that attempt to explain how markets may be predictable even if largely random at times

At the risk of stating the obvious, if market fluctuations were completely random, TA would be pointless. TA is a justifiable endeavor if and only if price movements are nonrandom to some degree some portion of the time. This chapter offers several theories explaining why episodes of nonrandom price movements ought to occur in financial market prices.

Although the occurrence of nonrandom price motion is necessary to justify TA, this alone is not sufficient to justify any specific TA method. Each method must demonstrate, by objective evidence, its ability to capture some part of the nonrandom price motion. Part Two will evaluate a large number of TA rules with respect to their ability to do just that.

◼ The Importance of Theory

Several new theories from the field of behavioral finance explain why price movements are nonrandom to some degree and therefore potentially predictable. Thus, these novel theories take a position that is contrary to the efficient markets hypothesis (EMH), a cornerstone of finance theory for over 40 years. EMH contends that price changes in financial markets are random and, therefore, unpredictable. Therefore, these new theories hold out hope for TA.

The reader may wonder why theoretical support for nonrandomness is even necessary. If a TA method has a profitable back test, isn't that all that should be needed? It could be asserted that a significantly profitable back test not only establishes that markets are nonrandom, it also establishes that the method is able to exploit some portion of the market's nonrandomness.

This view misses the importance of theoretical support. Even when all statistical precautions have been taken, a profitable back test that is not supported by sound theory is an isolated result and possibly still a lucky one. A successful back test always provokes the question: Will the rule continue to work in the future? Theory can be helpful here because a back test that is consistent with sound theory is less likely to be a statistical fluke. When a back test has theoretical foundation, it is no longer an isolated fact, but part of a larger cohesive picture in which theory explains fact and fact confirms theory.

For example, the profitability of technical trend-following systems in commodity futures can be explained as compensation (i.e., a risk premium) for providing a valuable service to commercial hedgers, that of risk transference. In other words, economic theory predicts that futures markets should manifest enough profitable trends to motivate trend followers to accept the price risks hedgers wish to shed.[1] This is discussed later in this chapter.

◼ Scientific Theories

In everyday speech, a theory is a speculative conjecture about why something is the way it is. A scientific theory is something different. First, it offers a succinct explanation for a broad range of prior observations. Second, and most importantly, it makes specific predictions that are later confirmed by new observations.

Kepler's laws of planetary motion[2] concisely explained a large number of prior astronomical observations and made specific predictions that were subsequently confirmed by additional observations. However, as good as Kepler's laws were, Newton's theory of gravitation was better because it was broader in scope. It not only explained why Kepler's laws worked but explained a far wider variety of phenomena. Theories of nonrandom price motion need not predict with the accuracy of physical theories. However, to be useful, they must not only succinctly describe a wide variety of previously observed market behavior, but must also make testable predictions confirmed by subsequent observations.

What Is Wrong with Popular TA Theory?

Many TA texts offer no explanation about why their proposed methods work. The statement of John Magee, author of one of TA's seminal works[3] is typical. He said, "We can never hope to know why the market behaves as it does, we can only aspire to understand how. History obviously has repetitive tendencies and that's good enough."

Some TA texts do offer explanations, but these are typically ad-hoc rationales that generate no testable predictions. According to author John Murphy, the cornerstone premise of TA is "anything that can possibly affect the price—fundamentally, politically, psychologically, or otherwise—is actually reflected in the price of that market."[4] One would be hard pressed to extract testable predictions from such a vague statement.

Actually, this statement, which purports to explain why TA works, contains a logical contradiction. For, if it were true that price did reflect (i.e., discount) all possible information, it would imply that price was devoid of any predictive information. To understand why, assume a hypothetical price pattern has just occurred in stock XYZ, which is currently at $50, and based on the pattern a move to $60 is implied. Then, by definition, when the pattern occurs its predictive implication has yet to be reflected in prices. However, if the premise that price reflects all information were true, the price would already be at the level predicted by the pattern, thus negating the pattern's forecasting ability.

This logical contradiction is even more apparent when it is pointed out that EMH, a school of thought that rejects the efficacy of TA, rests on the very same premise; "prices fully reflect all available information."[5] Technical analysis cannot be based on the same premise as its mortal enemy. This contradiction is an example of cloudy uncritical thinking that is all too common in the popular version of TA.

Fortunately for TA, its cornerstone premise that price reflects all information appears to be contradicted by fact. One example is the so-called underreaction effect, which has been postulated by behavioral finance. It says that, because prices sometimes fail to respond to new information as rapidly as EMH theorists contend, a systematic price movement, or trend, toward a price level that does reflect the new information occurs. The failure of prices to respond rapidly is caused by a several cognitive errors that afflict investors, such as the conservatism bias and the anchoring effect. These are discussed later in this chapter.

Another popular justification of TA is based on pop psychology. By pop psychology, I mean principles of human behavior that seem plausible but lack scientific support. According to noted economist and authority in the field of behavioral finance, Robert Shiller, "In considering lessons from psychology, it must be noted that the many popular accounts of the psychology of investing are simply not credible. Investors are said to be euphoric or frenzied during booms or panic-stricken during market crashes. In both booms and crashes, investors are descried as blindly following the herd like so many sheep, with no minds of their own."[6] The fact is, people are more rational than these pop-psychology theories suggest. "During the most significant financial events, most people are preoccupied with other personal matters, not with the financial markets at all. So it is hard to imagine that the market as a whole reflects the emotions described by these psychological theories."[7] We will need to look beyond the platitudes of popular texts for TA's justification. Fortunately, theories developed in the field of behavioral finance and elsewhere are beginning to offer the theoretical support TA needs.

■ The Enemy's Position: Efficient Markets and Random Walks

Before discussing theories that explain why nonrandom price movements should exist, we need to consider the enemy's position, the EMH. Recently, some have argued that EMH does not necessarily imply that prices follow unpredictable random walks,[8] and that efficient markets and price predictability can coexist. However, the pioneers of EMH asserted that random walks were a necessary consequence of efficient markets. This section states their case and examines its weaknesses.

What Is an Efficient Market?

An efficient market is a market that cannot be beaten. In such a market, no fundamental or technical analysis strategy, formula, or system can earn a risk-adjusted rate of return that beats the market defined by a benchmark index. If the market is indeed efficient, the risk-adjusted return earned by buying and holding the market index is the best one can hope for. This is so because prices in an efficient market properly reflect all known and knowable information. Therefore, the current price provides the best estimate of each security's value.

According to EMH, markets achieve a state of efficient pricing because of the vigorous efforts of numerous rational investors attempting to maximize their wealth. In their pursuit of true value, these investors are constantly updating their beliefs with the latest information in a probabilistically correct manner[9] so as to project each security's future cash flows. Although no single investor is all knowing, collectively they know as much as can possibly be known. This knowledge motivates investors to buy and sell in such a way that prices settle at the *equilibrium* or rational price level.

In such a world, prices change only when new information arrives. When it does, prices change almost instantly to a new rational price that properly reflects the news. Thus, prices do not gradually trend from one rational price level to the next, giving the trend analyst a chance to get on board. Not at all. In the world posited by EMH, prices trace a step function as they move almost instantly from one rational level to the next. If the news is favorable, prices rise, and if it's unfavorable, prices fall. Because it is not predictable whether the news will be favorable or unfavorable (it wouldn't be news if it was), price changes will be unpredictable as well. This is illustrated in Figure 30.1.

The Consequences of Market Efficiency: Good and Bad

Market efficiency has good and bad implications. They are good for the economy as a whole but bad—very bad—for TA. They are good for the economy because rational prices send vital signals of asset values that, in turn, encourage the efficient allocation of scarce resources, such as capital and labor. This fosters economic growth.[10]

However, prices in an efficient market are unpredictable rendering all forms of TA useless. According to Paul Samuelson, financial market prices follow a random walk

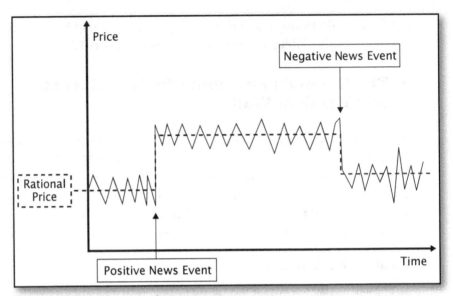

FIGURE 30.1 Efficient Market's Response to Positive and Negative News.

because of the actions of many intelligent/rational investors. In seeking to maximize wealth, they buy undervalued assets pushing their prices higher and sell overvalued assets pushing prices lower.[11] "Taken to its logical extreme, it means that a blindfolded monkey selecting stocks by throwing darts at a newspaper's financial pages could do just as well as one carefully selected by the experts."[12]

"EMH rules out the possibility of trading systems, based on available information, that have expected profits or returns in excess of equilibrium expected profit or return."[13] "In plain English, an average investor—whether an individual, pension fund, or a mutual fund—cannot hope to consistently beat the market, and the vast resources that such investors dedicate to analyzing, picking and trading securities are wasted."[14] Although, under EMH, it is still possible to generate positive returns from an investment strategy, when those returns are adjusted for risk, they will not be superior to the return of buying and holding the market index portfolio.

The efficient markets hypothesis also declares that when there is no news entering the market, prices tend to oscillate in a random and unbiased fashion above and below the rational price level. See Figure 30.2. Because this level is itself subject to uncertainty, no technical or fundamental indicator can reliably indicate when prices are above or below it. This means, for example, that in an efficient market stocks with a low price to book ratio, a well known fundamental indicator, are no more likely to appreciate than stocks with a high price to book ratio. This is a cold world for anyone looking for an edge.

False Notions of Market Efficiency

There are a number of commonly held but false notions about market efficiency. First is the idea that efficiency requires the market price to be equal to rational value at all times. In fact, market efficiency simply requires that price deviates from rational value in an unbiased fashion. Therefore, positive deviations from rational value are just as likely as negative deviations, and at any point in time there is a

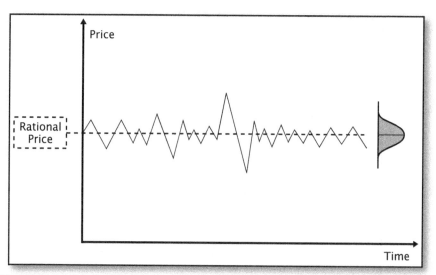

FIGURE 30.2 Efficient Market Hypothesis (Random and Unbiased Pricing Errors).

roughly equal chance that the asset's price will be above its rational value as below it. Moreover, these deviations are random. Thus the time series of pricing errors in an efficient market is a random variable whose probability distribution is centered at the rational price and is approximately symmetrical about it.

A second false notion about market efficiency is that it implies that no one can beat the market. Actually, in any given time period, about 50 percent of all investors will outperform the benchmark index, while the remaining 50 percent underperform. The notion that no single investor or money manager can beat the market over the long term is equally false. Given enough players, a small number are likely to have lengthy streaks of market beating returns even if their strategies are totally without merit. Nassim Taleb[15] shows that even if we assume money managers are no better than a blind monkey throwing darts[16] (probability of beating the market = 0.5) and the universe of managers is large enough, say 10,000, after five years there is likely to be about 312 firms who have beaten the market five years in a row. These lucky folks are the ones who will send salesmen calling. The other 9,682 are less likely to knock on your door.

The Evidence in Favor of EMH

As previously discussed, a scientific hypothesis plays a dual role: explanation and prediction. Its veracity is tested by comparing its predictions with new observations. Predictions are meaningful only if they are specific enough to offer the possibility of empirical falsification. If new observations do contradict a hypothesis's predictions, the hypothesis is either reformulated and tested anew or thrown out. However, what should be inferred when observations and predictions agree?

On this issue there is debate. Philosophers in the camp of David Hume contend that no amount of confirmatory evidence is ever sufficient to prove a theory, but in the practical world of science, confirmation does add strength to a hypothesis. If test after test yields observations that are consistent with its predictions, that means something to most scientists.

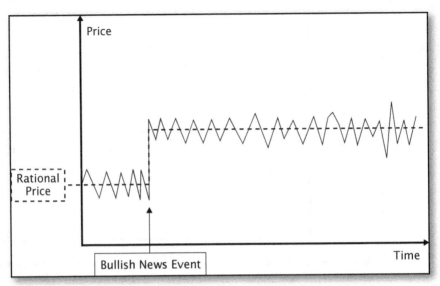

FIGURE 30.3 Efficient Market Response to Bullish News.

So EMH advocates have put forward a roster of supporting evidence. Their evidence comes in two flavors because EMH comes in two testable flavors: semistrong and weak.[17] The semistrong form asserts it is impossible to beat the market with public information. Because this includes all fundamental and technical data, the semistrong form predicts that neither fundamental nor technical analysis can beat the market. This informal prediction is not sufficiently specific to be testable, but it is in agreement with the observation that people have great difficulty profiting consistently from market fluctuations—and a lot try.

The semistrong form also makes several specific predictions that are testable. One is that a security's price will react quickly and accurately to any news that bears on its value. The proper response of an efficient market to news is illustrated in Figure 30.3.

This prediction implies prices should neither overreact nor underreact to news. This is testable in the following way. Imagine for a moment that prices did not behave efficiently and did systematically over- or underreact to new information. If this were the case, it would imply that price movements would be predictable. To see why, consider what would happen if a stock overreacted to news either by going up too much in response to good news or down too much in response to bad. Because EMH says prices must stay close to rational values, overshooting rational value would necessarily lead to a corrective movement back toward rational value. This correction would not be random meandering but rather a purposeful movement, as if the price were being magnetically drawn to the rational level. Such a movement would be, to some degree, predictable. Because EMH denies predictability, it must also deny the possibility of overreactions to news. A hypothetical overreaction to bullish news and a subsequent systematic movement back to rational levels is illustrated in Figure 30.4.

By the same logic, EMH must also deny the possibility of underreaction to news, where prices move less than the news justifies. In this case, a systematic price movement would also develop as prices continued to trend (drift) toward

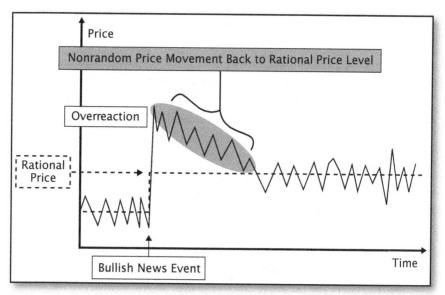

FIGURE 30.4 Overreaction to Bullish News (Implies Nonrandom Price Movements).

the new rational level implied by the news. Underreaction to bullish and bearish news events and the resultant nonrandom movement toward rational value are illustrated in Figure 30.5.

Evidence supporting EMH's prediction that overreactions and underreactions do not occur is presented in the event studies of Eugene Fama.[18] He examined all types of corporate news events such as earnings and dividend announcements, takeovers, mergers, and so forth and found that after an initial, almost instantaneous, nonexploitable price movement triggered by the news, there was no additional movement.

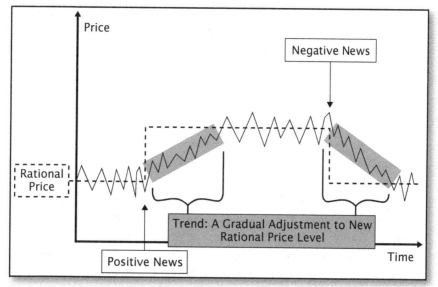

FIGURE 30.5 Underreaction to News Can Explain Nonrandom Trends.

These observations are consistent with EMH's prediction that the markets quickly and accurately discount news events.[19]

A second prediction of EMH is that prices should change only when news arrives. It follows then, that prices should not change dramatically in the absence of news or in response to noninformative events.[20] These two predictions suggest yet a third that is most crucial to TA. EMH implies that stale information, information already in the public domain, should have no predictive power and be of no value in making investment profits. Clearly, all information used by TA qualifies as stale. Thus, EMH predicts that all TA methods should fail. If this were to be confirmed, it's lights out for TA.

The prediction that all stale information strategies should have no predictive power seems cut and dried until one tries to test it. Recall, EMH says an investment strategy based on stale information should not be able to generate excess profits after risk adjustment. So the mere fact that a strategy based on stale information makes gains is not sufficient to rebut EMH. To contradict EMH, it must be demonstrated that the gains are excessive after adjusting for the strategy's risk.

The notion of judging investment strategies on the basis of risk-adjusted returns is entirely reasonable. For example, if a strategy makes 20 percent per year and the benchmark makes 10 percent, but the strategy exposes the investor to three times the risk, the strategy has not beaten the index after risk adjustment. The question is: How does one define and quantify risk?

Quantifying risk requires a risk model. The most well known is the capital asset pricing model[21] (CAPM), which explains systematic differences in the returns of securities in terms of a single risk factor, the security's relative volatility. This is to say, the risk of a stock is quantified by its volatility relative to the volatility of the market as a whole. Thus, if a stock is twice as volatile as the market index, its returns should be twice that of the market. Such a stock is said to earn excess returns when it earns more than twice the market return. This approach works well when measuring the risk of a single stock or a portfolio of long stock positions. However, CAPM cannot quantify the risk exposures of more complex strategies. In response to this limitation, capital market theorists have proposed other risk models. One of the best known is APT (arbitrage pricing theory), which attributes risk to several independent risk factors.[22]

However, EMH advocates have tacitly given themselves the liberty of cooking up new risk factors whenever they wish. This makes it nearly impossible to refute their claim that stale information strategies cannot beat the market. For, it is always possible to propose a new risk model that explains away a strategy's excess returns as compensation for risk. This is not a scientific sin if the risk factor(s) were identified before the stale information strategy earning excess returns was discovered. However, proposing a new risk factor(s) after a market-beating strategy has been discovered is nothing more than an ad hoc hypothesis. This is an explanation cooked up after the fact for the specific purpose of immunizing a theory, in this case EMH, from falsification. This practice is frowned upon in science for good reason. Also, the information content of a scientific theory is roughly equivalent to the opportunities it presents for falsification. The unbridled ability to explain away any and all dissonant evidence effectively drains the theory of its information content. Thus, the freedom to concoct new risk factors to explain each and every investment strategy that beats the market with stale information effectively reduces EMH to a meaningless theory.

The evidence confirming the weak form of EMH, which states that stale prices and indicators derived from them—such as price momentum—are without value, is based on auto-correlation studies. They measure the degree to which price changes are linearly correlated with prior changes, at various lag intervals.[23] These studies have confirmed that price changes (i.e., returns) are indeed linearly independent. This means that a linear function of current and past returns cannot be used to predict future returns.[24] Based on these findings, it was concluded by EMH advocates, that security returns are an unpredictable random walk.

However, autocorrelation studies are relatively weak tests in the sense that they can only detect linear dependencies. Searching for linear structure is merely one way to determine if a time series is behaving in a nonrandom fashion. Edgar Peters[25] and Andrew Lo and A. Craig MacKinlay[26] have shown that alternative data analysis methods indicate that financial market time series do not behave like random walks. For example, the test statistic used by Lo and McKinlay, called the variance ratio, can detect more complex (nonlinear) nonrandom behaviors that would be invisible autocorrelation studies.

■ Challenging EMH

A good theory is consistent in two ways. Its logic is internally consistent and it is consistent with observed evidence. Thus a theory can be challenged either by showing that it contradicts itself or that it is contradicted by evidence.

A theory is self-contradicting if it implies or predicts something that would contradict the theory. An example was given earlier in this chapter: I showed that a cornerstone premise of popular TA, which asserts that price perfectly reflects all information, contradicts another of its central premises, that price contains predictive information.

The Smart versus Dumb Paradox

One implication of market efficiency is that knowledgeable investors should not be able to earn higher returns than investors who are less knowledgeable. This follows from the premise that market efficiency means that whatever information is known or knowable has already been reflected in security prices. In an efficient market, there is no competitive advantage to being smart or disadvantage to being dumb.

However, this implication conflicts with another of EMH's assumptions—that the arbitrage activities of rational investors are able to drive prices toward rational levels. (See the heading titled "The Assumptions of EMH" later in this chapter.) Arbitrage can only act as an enforcer of rational prices if arbitrageurs have more trading capital and, thus, greater price-moving power than irrational, dumb investors. Having more trading capital implies that smart arbitrageurs must have earned higher returns in the past than less well informed (dumb) investors. Either market prices are set by the smartest, richest participants or they are not. EMH implies both. Paradoxical, isn't it!

The Cost of Information Paradox

Another logical inconsistency of EMH has to do with the cost of information. It is reasonable to assume that it costs time, money, and intelligence to gather information and process it into useful investing strategies. At the same time EMH contends that such information cannot earn incremental returns for investors who incur these costs. Remember, EMH contends that information is instantly reflected in prices. This implies that no matter how wide or deep the research effort, whatever is discovered will be of no value.

However, if EMH is correct that there is no payoff for information gathering and processing, then investors would lack the motivation to incur the costs of doing so. With no one to dig out the information and act on it, it would not get reflected in price. In other words, if it is costly to make markets informationally efficient, investors would be motivated to do it only if they were compensated with excess risk-adjusted returns. Thus the contradiction—EMH requires that information seekers be compensated for their efforts and simultaneously denies that they will be.

This paradox is argued persuasively by Grossman and Stiglitz in their article "On the Impossibility of Informationally Efficient Markets."[27] They contend that inefficiencies are necessary to motivate rational investors to engage in information gathering and processing. The returns they earn from the market's pricing errors are compensation for their efforts, which, in turn, have the effect of moving prices toward rational levels. The gains of these rational investors are financed by the losses of noise traders and liquidity traders. Noise traders are investors who buy and sell based on signals that they think are informative but that are not. Rational investors also earn profits from the losses of investors who trade to increase their cash reserves (liquidity traders). One way for the rational investor to gain would be if there were a delay between the time information is discovered and the time it is reflected in prices, but EMH denies the possibility of gradual price adjustments. This is yet another logical inconsistency of EMH.

A similar logic applies to the costs of acting on information (e.g., commissions, slippage, bid-asked spreads). Unless investors were compensated for incurring trading costs there would be no point to their trading activities, which are required by EMH to move the price to its rational level. The bottom line is that any factor that limits trading—costs to trade, costs to generate information, the rule that impairs short-selling, and so forth—limits the ability of the market to attain efficiency. It simply does not hold logically that there would be no compensation to those engaged in trading.

The Assumptions of EMH

To appreciate the arguments made by EMH's critics, it is necessary to understand that EMH rests on three progressively weaker assumptions: (1) investors are rational, (2) investors' pricing errors are random, and (3) there are always rational arbitrage investors to catch any pricing errors. Let's examine each of these in a bit more detail.

First is EMH's contention that investors are, by and large, rational. To recap, rational investors, in aggregate, are purported to value securities correctly. This means prices will reflect, as accurately as possible, the present discounted value of a security's future cash flows and risk characteristics. As rational investors learn new information, they respond quickly, bidding up prices when news is good and letting the price fall when news is bad. As a consequence, security prices adjust, almost instantly, to new information.[28]

Even if this assumption were incorrect, EMH advocates still insist that prices adjust quickly to rational levels anyway because of their second assumption: The valuation mistakes of individual investors are uncorrelated. This means that if one investor erroneously values a security too high, that error will be offset by another investor's error of valuing it too low. Taken in aggregate, these valuation errors are self-canceling and have an average value of zero. That is to say pricing errors are unbiased. This is presumed to be true because the error-prone investors are likely to be using different, though useless, investment strategies. Therefore, their actions should be uncorrelated. To put it bluntly, as one foolish investor gets an uninformative signal to buy, another investment fool is equally likely to get an uninformative signal to sell. In effect they wind up trading with each other, leaving prices very close to rational levels.

Moreover, even if this second assumption fails to keep prices at rational levels, EMH invokes yet a third assumption. That is, if the valuation mistakes of irrational investors turn out to be biased (i.e., have an average value that is greater than or less than zero), arbitrage investors will come to the rescue. They will notice that prices have systematically diverged from rational values. The arbitrageurs will buy when prices are too low or sell when they are too high, thus forcing prices back to where they should be.

In the EMH world, arbitrage is as close as it gets to a free lunch. An arbitrage transaction incurs no risk, requires no capital, and earns a guaranteed return. As envisioned by efficient market advocates, an arbitrage trade goes something like this: Consider two financial assets, stocks X and Y, which sell at equal prices and which are equally risky. However, they have different expected future returns. Obviously, one of the two assets is improperly priced. If asset X has a higher future return, then to take advantage of the mispricing, arbitrageurs would buy asset X while short-selling Y. With the activities of like-minded arbitrageurs, the price of each stock will converge to its proper fundamental value.[29] Market efficiency attained in this manner assumes there are always arbitrageurs ready, willing, and able to jump on these opportunities. The better ones become very wealthy, thereby enhancing their ability to drive prices to proper levels, while the irrational investors eventually go broke losing their ability to push prices away from equilibrium levels. The uninformed, irrational investors are driven out of the market the way a weak species is driven from an ecosystem, while the rational, well-informed arbitrageurs thrive.

Flaws in EMH Assumptions

This section considers each of the assumptions of EMH and how they miss the mark.

Investors Are Rational Investors do not appear to be as rational as EMH assumes. Many investors react to irrelevant information, what noted economist Fischer Black calls "noise signals."[30] Though they think they are acting intelligently, these investors can expect to earn the same return as an investor who buys and sells based on a coin flip. Investors who follow the advice of financial gurus who base their advice on noise signals are noise traders by proxy.

In fact, investors are guilty of numerous departures from rationality. For example, they fail to diversify, they trade too actively, they increase their tax liabilities by selling appreciated stocks but hold onto losing positions, and they trade mutual funds with high fees. Moreover, their failures are recurring. "Investors' deviations from the maxims of economic rationality turn out to be highly pervasive and systematic."[31] These departures from rationality can be classified into three areas: inaccurate risk assessments, poor probability judgments, and irrational decision framing. I discuss each of these in turn.

Investors typically do not assess risks in conformity with the normative ideal put forward by Neumann and Morgenstern, known as "expected utility theory." In a perfectly rational world, an individual faced with choosing among several options selects the one with the highest expected value. The expected value of a particular choice is equal to a sum of products, where each product is the probability of each possible outcome multiplied by the value or utility of that outcome to the decision maker. The problem is people do not actually behave this way. Research has shown that investors make numerous systematic errors when assessing risks and making choices.

These mistakes have been incorporated into a framework called Prospect Theory, which was proposed by Kahneman and Tversky (1979).[32] It explains how people actually make decisions under conditions of uncertainty. For example, it explains that investors hold onto losing stocks but sell profitable positions to avoid the psychic pain of realizing a loss. It also explains why investors overvalue low-probability long-shot speculations.

The second way investors depart from the rational ideal of EMH is in their judgments of probability. EMH assumes that, as investors receive new information, they update their probability assessments in accordance with Bayes' theorem, a formula for combining probabilities in a theoretically correct way. However, to their detriment, investors do not behave this way. One common error is the crime of small numbers—drawing grand conclusions from small samples of data. This explains why investors will rashly conclude that a corporation with a short string of successful quarterly earnings reports is likely to continue to grow rapidly. Their overreaction to this small sample of positive earnings changes causes the stock to become overpriced.

Lastly, investors' decisions can be strongly impacted by how choices are described (framed). By incorrectly framing a decision situation, investors tend to misperceive the true expected value of a choice. For example, when choices are framed in terms of potential gains, investors tend to choose the option most likely to earn a gain, even if it is insignificant in size. However, when the same choices are framed in terms of potential losses, investors will assume the risk of a very significant loss just to avoid the certainty of a small loss. This error, called the "disposition effect," is thought to explain why investors sell winners quickly, so as to be sure to earn a gain, even if it's small, but hold on to losers even if it means there is a chance the loss will turn into a much larger one.

Investor Errors Are Uncorrelated The assumption that investors' errors are uncorrelated is contradicted by psychological research which shows people do not deviate from rationality randomly in situations characterized by uncertainty. In reality, most people tend to make similar mistakes in such situations and hence their deviations from rationality are correlated. Many investors will be tempted to buy the same stock because the stock appeals to a common heuristic rule of judgment that makes it look like a candidate for further appreciation. For example, a company that has three positive earning quarters can be perceived by many investors to be a growth stock that warrants a high price-to-earnings ratio or P/E. This problem is made worse by social interactions, or herding, between investors. "They follow each other's mistakes listening to rumors and imitating the actions of their fellow traders."[33]

Money managers, who should know better, make these mistakes as well. They are guilty of creating portfolios that are excessively close to the benchmarks against which they are measured, all in an effort to reduce the chance they will underperform. Professional money managers also engage in imitative behavior and move herd-like into the same stocks, for fear of falling behind the pack. They dress up their portfolios by adding stocks that have done well and eliminate those that have not, so year-end portfolio reports show the fund invested in the highest performing stocks.

Arbitrage Forces Prices to Rational Levels This assumption fails because the power of arbitrage activities to push prices toward rational levels is limited. First, no one rings a bell when securities become mispriced. The rational price is the discounted value of a stream of future cash flows, which is, by definition, uncertain. Investors try to estimate future earnings, but their forecasts are prone to significant error.

Second, arbitrageurs do not have unlimited tolerance for adverse price movement—for example, when an underpriced stock that has been purchased continues to go lower, or an overpriced security that has been sold short continues to soar. The actions of noise traders can easily push prices further away from rational levels before they return to them. Therefore, even if an arbitrageur spots a truly mispriced security, the pricing error may grow larger before it is finally eradicated. Should this adverse price movement become too large, the arbitrageur may have to close the position with a loss. If this happens often enough, the noise traders can drive rational investors out of business. This is referred to as noise trader risk[34] and it limits the motivation and commitments of arbitrage traders. Behavioral finance expert Andre Shleifer says even an arbitrage trade that looks nearly perfect from the outside is in reality quite risky so the number of investors who go after it will be limited. The bottom line is arbitrage activities cannot always enforce rational pricing.

Noise trader risk was a factor in the blow-up of the Long Term Capital Management (LTCM) hedge fund in the fall of 1998. The fund's crash nearly took the entire financial market with it. Ultimately, the mispricings that LTCM had identified were corrected, but because they had overleveraged their positions, the fund lacked the staying power to hold its positions through a short-term period of even greater mispricing.

Improper use of leverage is yet another factor that can impair the role arbitrage plays in driving markets to efficiency. Thus, even if arbitrageurs can accurately identify over- and under-priced securities, if they use too much leverage they can get wiped out. There is an optimal leverage for favorable bets (i.e., speculations with a positive expectancy).[35] If this level is exceeded, the probability of ruin rises despite the positive expectation.

I show this to my students during a class I call Casino Night. We play a game in which everyone starts off with an imaginary $100. I have a friend come in to act as coin flipper. Before each flip, the students determine what fraction of their capital to bet on the next coin toss. If a head results, the payoff is twice the amount of the bet. If a tail results, only the amount of the bet is lost. We play the game for 75 flips. This game has a very favorable expectation.[36] However, even in a game with such a favorable expectancy, many students wind up losing money because they bet too aggressively (i.e., the fraction of capital wagered on a bet is too large). A formula worked out by Kelly, an electrical engineer at Bell Labs in the 1950s, now known as the Kelly Criterion, specifies the optimal fraction to bet on each coin flip so as to maximize the growth rate of the bettor's capital. The optimal fraction depends on the probability of a win and the ratio of the average win to average loss. In this particular game, the optimal fraction to wager on each bet is 0.25. If this level is exceeded, the bettor faces greater risk without the benefit of a faster growth of capital. If one were to employ a bet fraction of 0.58 it is likely all funds would be lost, despite the favorable expectation. This is what happens to an arbitrageur with good information who uses too much leverage.

Another constraint on an arbitrage's ability to enforce efficient pricing is the lack of perfect substitute securities. An ideal (riskless) arbitrage transaction involves the simultaneous purchase and sale of a pair of securities with identical future cash flows and identical risk characteristics. An arbitrage transaction based on securities that do not conform to this ideal necessarily involves risk. And it is risk that limits the degree to which arbitrage activity can force prices to efficient levels. When a broad class of assets, such as all stocks, become overpriced, as they did in the spring of 2000, there is no substitute security to use as the long-side hedge to a short sale of the entire stock market. Even in the case where the securities in an arbitrage transaction are close substitutes, there can be substantial risks. Each stock has its own specific or idiosyncratic risks, and this makes arbitrageurs wary. For example, if GM were undervalued and it were purchased against an offsetting short sale in Ford, there would be the risk that some bullish event unique to Ford or a bearish event unique to GM would create a loss for the arbitrage trader.

There are still other constraints that prevent arbitrage from playing the price-policing role envisioned by EMH. Arbitrageurs do not have unlimited funds to correct pricing errors nor do they have total freedom to pursue any and all opportunities. Most arbitrage investors manage money for other investors in the form of hedge funds. The management contracts under which the fund managers operate typically constrain their actions to some degree. Without a completely free hand and unlimited funds, some mispricings will remain unarbitraged.

As a result of these limits, the EMH assumption that all arbitrage opportunities will be eradicated appears to be an oversimplification.

Empirical Challenges to EMH

The EMH is not only riddled with logical inconsistencies, its predictions are contradicted by a growing body of empirical evidence. This section summarizes these findings.

Excessive Price Volatility   If security prices were as tightly connected to fundamental values as EMH asserts, then the magnitude of price changes should be similar to the magnitude of changes in the underlying fundamentals. However, studies show prices are far more volatile than fundamentals. For example, when fundamental value is defined as the net present value of future dividends,[37] changes in fundamental value are unable to explain the high volatility of prices. The technology stock bubble that ruptured in the spring of 2000 and the bubble in Japanese stock prices in the late 1980s are examples of price movements that cannot be explained by changes in fundamental value.

EMH also predicts that large price changes should occur only when significant new information enters the market. The evidence does not agree. For example, the stock market crash of October 1987 was not accompanied by news that would have justified a price drop that exceeded 20 percent. A 1991 study by Cutler cited by Shleifer[38] examined the 50 largest one-day price movements since the end of World War II. Many of these price events were not associated with significant news announcements. In a similar study, Roll[39] showed that fluctuations in the price of frozen orange juice futures often occurred without any developments in the weather, the major fundamental influence on that market. Roll also showed that individual stock movements are often not associated with corporate news events.

Evidence of Price Predictability with Stale Information   The evidence most damning to EMH are studies showing that price movements can be predicted to a meaningful degree with publicly known (stale) information. In other words, strategies based on stale information can generate risk-adjusted returns that beat the market. If it were true that prices quickly incorporate all known information, as EMH asserts, this should not be possible.

How Cross-Sectional Predictability Studies Are Performed   The April 2001 issue of *Journal of Finance* notes that many predictability studies show that publicly available information is not fully reflected in stock prices and that numerous strategies based on this information are profitable.[40] These studies measure the degree to which indicators based on public information are able to forecast the relative performance of stocks.[41] Indicators tested included a stock's price-to-earnings ratio, its price-to-book-value ratio, its recent relative price performance, and so forth.

Predictability studies employ a cross-sectional design. That is to say, they examine a large cross section of stocks at a given point in time, for example, all stocks in the S&P 500 Index as of December 31, 1999. For that date, the stocks are ranked on the basis of an indicator[42] that is being examined for its predictive power, such as a stock's rate of return over the past six months (price momentum). With this done, the stocks are arranged into a number of portfolios on the basis of rank, with each portfolio containing an equal number of stocks. Ten portfolios is a common number. Thus portfolio 1 would contain the top 10 percent of all stocks ranked by their prior six-month rate of return. That is to say, the portfolio is composed of those stocks whose prior six-month rate of return was in greater than the ninetieth percentile. A second portfolio is formed containing stocks ranked from the eightieth percentile to the eighty-ninth percentile, and so on until a final portfolio is formed from the 10 percent of stocks with the worst prior six-month performance.

To determine if six-month momentum has predictive power, the future performance of the top decile portfolio (1) is compared to the future performance of the bottom decile portfolio (10). The forward prediction horizon is typically one time period. Therefore, using monthly data, it would be one month.[43] Typically these studies quantify the indicator's predictive power as the return earned by a long portfolio versus a short portfolio. In other words, a long position is assumed to be taken in all portfolio 1 stocks and a short position in all portfolio 10 stocks. For example, if in a given time period, the long portfolio earned 7 percent while the short portfolio lost 4 percent (e.g., the stocks sold short went up 4 percent), the long-versus-short strategy would have earned 3 percent. Although in this example the indicator used to rank stocks was the six-month price momentum, any item of information that was known at the time the portfolios are constructed could be used. I illustrate this concept in Figure 30.6, where the indicator used is each stock's P/E ratio.

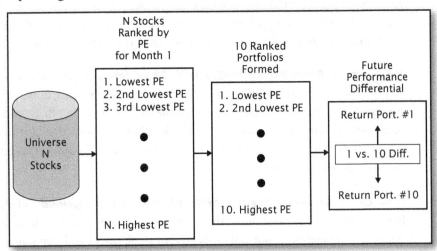

FIGURE 30.6 Cross-Sectional Study to Determine the Predictive Power of P/E Ratio.

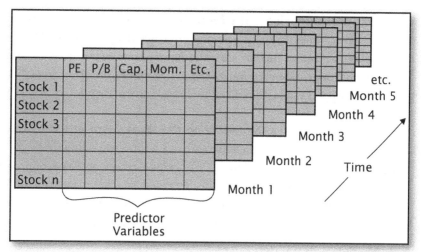

FIGURE 30.7   Cross-Sectional Time Series Study.

I just described how a cross-sectional study is carried out for a single month (December 1999). However, cross-sectional studies are carried out over many months (cross-sectional time series). Thus, the predictive power of an indicator is measured as the average return on portfolio 1 minus the average return on portfolio 10 over an extended period of time. Such studies often examine a number of candidate predictor variables. This idea is illustrated in Figure 30.7.

Predictability Studies Contradicting Semistrong EMH   The semistrong form of EMH is the boldest testable version of EMH.[44] It asserts that no information in the public domain, fundamental or technical, can be used to generate risk-adjusted returns in excess of the market index. The bottom line of numerous well-conducted cross-sectional time series studies is this: Price movements are predictable to some degree with stale public information, and excess risk-adjusted returns are possible. Here, I summarize some of these key findings:

- **Small capitalization effect:** A stock's total market capitalization, defined as the number of shares outstanding multiplied by its price per share, is predictive of future returns.[45] Stocks in a portfolio composed of the lowest decile portfolio of market capitalization earned about 9 percent per year more than stocks in the highest decile portfolio.[46] This effect is most pronounced in the month of January. Recent studies show this indicator's predictive power has disappeared since the mid to late 1980s.

- **Price-to-earnings ratio effect:** Stocks with low P/E ratios outperform stocks with high P/E ratios.[47]

- **Price-to-book-value effect:** Stocks with low price to book value ratios outperform stocks with high price to book value ratios.[48] The cheapest stocks, in terms of price to book, outperformed the most expensive stocks by almost 20 percent per year.

- **Earnings surprise with technical confirmation:** Stocks reporting unexpected earnings or giving earnings guidance that is confirmed by strong price and volume action on the day after the news is announced earn an annualized return spread (longs – shorts) over the next month of over 30 percent.[49] This strategy is a marriage of fundamental and technical information.

Predictability Studies Contradicting the Weak Form of EMH The weak form of EMH is the least bold version of the theory. It claims that only a subset of public information, past prices, and price returns[50] is unhelpful in earning excess returns. The following studies show that stale prices and other data used in technical indicators are indeed useful. This is very good news for TA and very bad news for EMH. The narrowest, most timid, and most difficult to falsify version of EMH has been contradicted with evidence.

- **Momentum persistence:** Jegadeesh and Titman (1993)[51] showed that price momentum measured over the past six to twelve months persists. In other words, the stocks that have been strongest over the past 6 months, 7 months, 8 months, and so on, up to 12 months, tend to outperform over the following 6 to 12 months. Their study simulated a strategy of holding long positions in stocks with the highest returns over the prior 6 months (top decile) and holding short positions in stocks with the worst performance (lowest decile). The portfolio of long and short positions was then held for 6 months. This strategy earned an annualized return of 10 percent. In light of this evidence, even one of the high priests of EMH, Eugene Fama, had to admit that past stock returns can predict future stock returns.[52] Score a big one for TA!

- **Momentum reversal:** Although stocks with strong trends over the past 6 to 12 months tend to maintain those trends over the following 6 to 12 months, something different is observed when momentum is measured over longer time spans. Strong trends measured over the prior three to five years display a tendency to reverse. De Bondt and Thaler tested a strategy of buying stocks with the most negative five-year trends (losers) and selling short stocks with the most positive five-year trends (winners). The long-versus-short portfolio averaged an 8 percent annualized return over the next three years,[53] and most importantly, this return difference was not attributable to risk. The prior losers (future winners) were not more risky than the prior winners (future losers).[54] This contradicts a central proposition of EMH that higher returns can only be earned by assuming higher risks. Additionally, it bolsters the notion that a very simplistic form of TA is useful.

- **Nonreversing momentum:** When a stock's momentum is measured by its proximity to its 52-week high, rather than its prior rate of return, profits are greater and momentum does not reverse.[55] The author of this study speculates that investors become mentally anchored to prior 52-week price highs. Anchoring is known to prevent people from making appropriate adjustments to new information. The author of this study, Michael Cooper, conjectured that this prevents stocks near their 52-week highs from responding to new fundamental developments as rapidly as they should. Retarded news response engenders systemic price trends (momentum) that correct the mispricing.

- **Momentum confirmed by trading volume:** Further support for the validity of TA comes from studies showing that, when trading volume is used conjointly with price momentum, even higher returns can be earned. That is to say, a synergism can be attained by combining price and volume indicators. The return of the combination is 2 to 7 percent higher than the return can be earned using price momentum alone.[56] Stocks with high volume and positive price momentum do better going forward than stocks with positive price momentum alone. Moreover, stocks with high volume and negative price momentum do worse going forward than stocks that merely have negative price momentum. Said differently, the discrimination power of price momentum is greater for high-volume stocks.

EMH Digs for a Defense

When an established theory is contradicted with empirical evidence, its supporters do not simply roll over and say never mind. The cognitive mechanisms of belief persistence don't work that way for trained scientists any more than they do for common folk. Cynical observers of science say adherents to a theory that has been falsified never really change their minds. They have far too much invested in its survival to do that. With time, they just fade away.

With EMH having served, and served well, for 40+ years, as the foundation of finance, its backers were just not about to go away with heads hanging low. Two of its standard bearers (read pall bearers), Eugene Fama and Kenneth French, said gains earned by stale-information strategies such as price-to-book value and market capitalization were nothing more than fair compensation for risk. Recall that EMH does not deny the possibility that stale public information can earn profits. It merely says that when those gains are adjusted for risk, they will not be better than investing in an index fund.

So long as the term *risk* is left undefined, EMH defenders are free to conjure up new forms of risk after the fact. As Elliott wavers have proven, after-the-fact fiddling allows any prior observations to be explained or explained away. And that, it seems to me, is what Fama and French did.[57] They invented a new, ad hoc risk model using three risk factors to replace the old standby, the capital asset pricing model,[58] which uses only one risk factor, a stock's volatility relative to the market index. Quite conveniently, the two new risk factors that Fama and French decided to add were the price-to-book ratio and market capitalization. By citing these as proxies for risk, Fama and French neatly explained away their predictive power. "According to the new risk model, stocks of smaller firms (low-market cap) or firms with low market-to-book ratios are fundamentally riskier companies and thus must offer higher average returns to compensate the investors willing to own them. Conversely, large capitalization stocks because they are safer, and high price-to-book ratio stocks, which are in effect growth stocks with more certain future prospects, earn lower average returns because they expose their owners to lower risk."[59]

This was nothing more than an ad hoc after-the-fact explanation conjured up to save a dying theory. Had Fama and French predicted that price-to-book and market capitalization were valid risk factors before these variables were discovered to earn excess returns, that would have been a much different story. It would have shown that EMH was a powerful theory whose deductive consequences were confirmed by subsequent observations. However, Fama and French did not do this. They invented the new risk factors after price-to-book and market cap had been shown to produce excess returns.

As pointed out earlier, Fama and French justified their new risk model by suggesting that low market-cap and low price relative to book are signals of corporations at higher risk of failure. If this were true, it would imply (predict) that value strategies (buying low price-to-book stocks) and small cap strategies would earn subpar returns in bad economic times, when distressed companies are most likely to suffer.

Empirical evidence contradicts this prediction. A 1994 study found no evidence that value strategies do worse when the economy suffers.[60] Also, the disappearance of the excess return to small-cap stocks in the last 15 years presents a problem. If cap size were indeed a legitimate risk factor, the returns to strategies based on it should continue to earn a risk premium. Finally, neither the Fama-French risk model, nor any other EMH model, is able to explain the predictive power of price momentum indicators or the conjoint effect of price momentum and trading volume.

■ Behavioral Finance: A Theory of Nonrandom Price Motion

New theory is needed when existing theory confronts dissonant evidence. EMH has now been bombarded with a lot of evidence that contradicts its predictions. It is time for a new theory.

The relatively new field of behavioral finance has come forward with several variations of a new theory of financial market behavior that explains phenomena that EMH cannot. These theories are scientifically meaningful in that they do not simply explain (fit) what has occurred, but they make testable predictions that have been confirmed by subsequent observational studies.

Behavioral finance incorporates elements of cognitive psychology, economics, and sociology to explain why investors depart from full rationality and therefore why markets depart from full efficiency. By considering the impact of emotions, cognitive errors, irrational preferences, and the dynamics of group behavior, behavioral finance offers succinct explanations of excess market volatility as well as the excess returns earned by stale information strategies.

Behavioral finance does not assume that all investors are irrational. Rather, it views the market as a mixture of decision makers who vary in their degree of rationality. When irrational investors (noise traders) trade with rational investors (arbitrageurs), markets can depart from efficient pricing. In fact, market efficiency is a rather special condition that is less probable than other more plausible market conditions, where prices are likely to diverge from rational levels and thus likely to experience systematic predictable movements toward those levels.[61] This explains why systematic strategies based on stale information can profit.

This is all quite ironic with respect to TA. Cognitive errors can explain how people form erroneous beliefs in the validity of subjective TA in the absences of sound supportive evidence or even in the face of contradictory evidence. At the same time, however, cognitive errors may also explain the existence of market inefficiencies that spawn the systematic price movements that allow objective TA methods to work. That which explains the foolishness of subjective TA practitioners also explains the reasonableness of some objective TA methods.

Foundations of Behavioral Finance

Behavioral finance rests on two foundational pillars: The limited ability of arbitrage to correct pricing errors, and the limits of human rationality.[62] When both notions are combined, behavioral finance is able to predict specific departures from market efficiency that produce systematic price movements. For example, under certain circumstances, trends are predicted to persist, whereas, under other circumstances, trends are predicted to reverse. We will consider each of these pillars.

Limits of Arbitrage   To recap briefly, arbitrage is not the perfect enforcer of efficient pricing that EMH assumes. The lack of perfect security substitutes turns arbitrage from a risk-free, no-investment-required transaction into one that requires capital and incurs risk. Even where there are very good substitute securities, there is a risk that prices will diverge further from rational values before returning to them. Moreover, the investors who supply trading capital to arbitrageurs don't have unlimited patience, or unlimited capital. Consequently, they do not grant unlimited latitude to arbitrageurs in terms of the types of opportunities that can be considered for exploitation.

These constraints explain why security prices do not always react properly to new information. Sometimes, prices underreact, and sometimes, they overreact. Add to this the impact of noise traders, who act on uninformative signals,[63] and it becomes clear how security prices can systematically depart from rational levels for extended periods of time.

Limits of Human Rationality   The constraints on arbitrage predict that inefficiencies will occur, but they alone do not predict under what conditions the inefficiencies will manifest. For example, arbitrage constraints do not tell us under which circumstances markets are more likely to underreact to new information than overreact. That is where the second pillar of behavioral finance, the limits of human rationality, comes in.

Cognitive psychology has revealed that, under conditions of uncertainty, human judgment tends to err in predictable (systematic) ways. By taking into account the systematic errors of human judgment, behavioral finance can predict the type of departure from market efficiencies that are most likely to occur in a given set of circumstances.

Of the two pillars of behavioral finance, more is understood about the limits of arbitrage than about investor irrationality. This is because arbitrageurs are expected to be rational, and economic theory has a firmer grasp on the behavior of rational actors than irrational ones. For example, it is not yet clear which specific cognitive biases and systematic judgment errors are most important in finance, but a picture is gradually emerging. This section describes the current state of behavioral finance's understanding of irrational investor behavior and the systematic price movements that arise as a result of them.

In contrast to traditional finance theory, behavioral finance asserts investors make biased judgments and choices. In effect, market prices systematically deviate from rational values because investors systematically deviate from full rationality. However, these mistakes are not a sign of ignorance, but rather a consequence of the generally effective ways human intelligence has developed to cope with complexity and uncertainty.

Behavioral finance and EMH are similar in that they both contend that the market eventually does get it right—that is, prices ultimately converge toward rational valuations. They merely differ about the character of these departures and their duration. EMH says prices depart from rational levels randomly and briefly. Behavioral finance says some departures are systematic and last long enough to be exploited by certain investment strategies.

Psychological Factors

Cognitive errors impact subjective technicians and result in erroneous beliefs. In the context of behavioral finance, we will consider how cognitive errors impact investors and result in systematic price movements. The cognitive errors discussed in the sections that follow are not completely distinct, nor do they operate independently. However, they are presented separately for the purpose of clarity.

Conservatism Bias, Confirmation Bias, and Belief Inertia The conservatism bias[64] is the tendency to give too little weight to new information. Consequently, people fail to modify their prior beliefs as much as the new information would warrant. Prior beliefs tend to be conserved. Because of this, investors tend to underreact to new information that is relevant to security values and so security prices fail to respond adequately. Over time, however, prices do systematically catch up with value. This gradual, purposeful adjustment appears on a chart as a price trend. This is illustrated in Figure 30.5.

This conservatism bias is encouraged by the confirmation bias, which causes people to accept evidence that is consistent with a prior belief and reject or give too little credence to evidence that contradicts it. Thus, when investors hold an existing view about a security and new information arrives that confirms that belief, they will tend to give it more weight than it deserves and overreact to it. Conversely, when new information arrives that contradicts the prior belief, they tend to treat it skeptically and underreact.

The confirmation bias also causes investors' beliefs, whatever they may be, to become more extreme over time. The reason is as follows: Over time, news items arrive as a random mixture of confirmatory and contradictory information. However, the confirmation bias causes them to be treated differently. Confirmatory information is given credence, thus strengthening the prior belief, while contradictory information will tend not to be believed and thus have a negligible impact on the investors' prior belief. Consequently, over time it is likely that prior beliefs strengthen.

However, prior beliefs can be subject to a radical and irrational weakening if several bits of contradictory information arrive in a streak. Even though streaks are common in a random sequence, investors may commit the crime of small numbers and attribute too much significance when several pieces of information that contradict the prior beliefs arrive sequentially. In other words, the random streak may be erroneously interpreted as an authentic trend. These ideas are illustrated in Figure 30.8.

Too Much Anchoring and Too Little Adjustment In uncertain situations, people rely on heuristics to simplify and speed complex cognitive tasks like estimating probabilities. One heuristic, not discussed thus far, is called anchoring. It is relied upon to estimate quantities. The rule is applied as follows: An initial estimate of the quantity is made, based on preliminary information called the anchor. Then upward or downward adjustments are made to the initial estimate based on additional information. The anchoring rule seems to make sense.

However, in practice, people commonly make two mistakes when applying this heuristic. First, initial estimates can be strongly influenced by a completely irrelevant anchor. This occurs even when the anchor's irrelevance is completely obvious. Second, even in cases where the initial estimate is based on relevant anchoring information, there is a tendency for subsequent adjustments up or down to be too small (the conservatism bias). In other words, the additional information is given too little weight relative to the initial estimate.

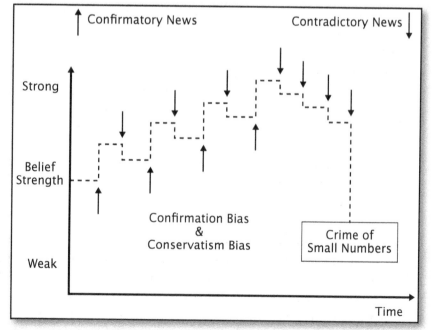

FIGURE 30.8 Revising Beliefs.

The tendency to seize on an irrelevant anchor was demonstrated in a study in which people were asked to estimate the length of the Mississippi River (actual length = 2,348 miles). Subjects were first asked if the length was greater than or less than some arbitrary length. This number assumed the role of anchor in the subject's minds. When the question posed was: Is the length greater or less than 800 miles? Most people correctly said the Mississippi was longer than 800 miles. Subjects were then asked to give an estimate of its actual length. Other subjects were given the number 5,000 miles in the greater than or less than part of the question. Again, most people correctly said the river's length was less than 5,000 miles, but their estimates of the river's actual length were, on average, greater than the estimates given by subjects who were asked to make a comparison with 800 miles. This revealed that the subjects seized on the number of miles given in the question as an anchor, and then made inadequate adjustments from there. If the figure 800 or 5,000 were not truly influencing the estimate, the estimates of length would have been about the same, irrespective of whether the question involved a comparison with 800 miles or 5,000 miles.[65] The anchor had a strong influence.

Another experiment showed that people will anchor on a number even when it is obviously irrelevant.[66] Subjects were asked about facts that are typically not part of common knowledge—for example, "What is the percentage of African nations in the United Nations?" The answers to each question involved a percentage (0 to 100). Before each question, a wheel of fortune with 100 numbered slots was spun in front of the subjects. The study showed that the subjects' answers were strongly affected by the wheel's obviously random result. For example, if the wheel landed on the number 10, the median estimate was 25 percent, but when the wheel stopped on 65 the median estimate was 45 percent.

The anchoring heuristic is thought to be related to investor underreaction. Underreactions to bullish news cause asset prices to remain too cheap, whereas underreactions to bearish news leave prices too dear. Over time, the market's temporary state of inefficiency is resolved as prices drift (trend) to the rational level. Thus, anchoring can help explain the occurrence of price trends.

Anchoring may explain the profitability of a momentum strategy alluded to earlier.[67] It is based on a simple technical indicator, a stock's proximity to its 52-week high. Because this information is available in newspapers and on various web sites, investors may fixate (anchor) on it. In other words, investors may fixate or anchor on the 52-week high price if a stock is currently trading near that level. In effect, the stock gets stuck near its 52-week high. Thus the price fails to respond properly to new bullish information, and it becomes temporarily underpriced. Ultimately the pricing error is corrected as the stock responds with a systematic movement higher.

Anchoring to Stories Investors not only become anchored to numbers; they can get stuck on intuitively compelling[68] stories, too. The effect is the same; prices do not respond efficiently to new information and thus depart from rational valuations.

Stories are compelling because "much of human thinking that results in action is not quantitative, but instead takes the form of storytelling and justification."[69] Investors rely more on causal narratives than on weighing and combining evidence to estimate probabilities and make decisions. People seem to need simple rationales to justify their actions.[70] The most compelling rationales are plausible, easily understood, easily retold, cause and effect chains filled with concrete and colorful details. These are the tales that captivate investors and incite buying and selling. These are the stories that get stuck in investors' minds.

Optimism and Overconfidence To recap, people are generally too confident about the quality and precision of their knowledge. Thus, investors tend to be overconfident about their private interpretations of public information and overly optimistic about the profits they will achieve. The combined effect of overconfidence and overoptimism leads investors to overreact to their private information, and in turn pushes security prices too far. Overextended price movements lead to price reversals and systematic movements back toward rational levels.

The Crime of Small Numbers (Sample Size Neglect) The crime of small numbers is the failure to consider the number of observations comprising a sample being used to form a conclusion. Thus, it is fallacious to judge whether a datum was produced by a random or nonrandom process or to estimate a population parameter on the basis of a small sample. For example, if a sequence of 10 coin flips produces 7 heads, it would be invalid to conclude the coin has a 0.7 probability of producing heads. The true head rate for a coin can be reliably inferred from only a large number of flips.

Investors who neglect sample size are easily deceived when trying to decide if a time series is random or not. For example, by generalizing too hastily from too little evidence, investors may incorrectly conclude that a few quarters of positive earnings growth indicate that the company has established a valid growth trend. We have already seen that a small cluster of positive quarters can easily occur in a random-earnings stream. Thus, the crime of small numbers helps explain why investors may overreact to a short sequence of good earnings reports.

The crime of small numbers can cause two different judgment errors: the gambler's fallacy and the clustering illusion. Which of these two errors results depends on the observer's prior belief about the process being watched. Suppose an investor is watching a sequence of price changes that are truly independent of each other (a random walk).

If the investor holds a prior belief that the process is random, the error will most likely be the gambler's fallacy. Recall that on the basis of common sense we expect random processes to display more flip-flops and fewer streaks (trends) than actually do occur. As a result, a streak of positive price changes will lead naive observers to falsely conclude that a trend reversal (a negative price change) is due. Thus, after five heads, the observer erroneously concludes a tail is more likely than 50/50, its true likelihood. In reality, a random-walk sequence has no memory. Thus, the occurrence of a positive streak does not alter the probability of the next outcome in any way. The false expectation of a reversal is called the "gambler's fallacy" because the statistically naive tend to make this mistake when watching a roulette wheel; a sequence of black outcomes is thought to increase the chance of a red. Wrong!

The other fallacy stemming from sample-size neglect is the clustering illusion. It occurs when an observer has no prior belief about whether the process generating the data is random or nonrandom The clustering illusion is the misperception of order (nonrandomness) in data that is actually a random walk. Again, imagine someone observing the outcomes of a process that is truly a random walk trying to determine if the process is random or nonrandom (orderly, systematic).[71] Recall that small samples of random walks often appear more trended (clustered) than common sense would lead us to expect (the hot hand in basketball). As a result of the clustering illusion, a sequence of positive price or earnings changes is wrongly interpreted as a legitimate trend, when it is nothing more than an ordinary streak in a random walk.

Social Factors: Imitative Behavior, Herding, and Information Cascades[72]

We have just seen how investor behavior viewed at the level of the individual investor can explain several types of systematic price movement. This section examines investor behavior at the group level to explain systematic price movements. In contrast to conventional TA theories of investor psychology, we will see that some group behaviors are quite rational.

When faced with uncertain choices, people often to look to the behavior of others for cues and imitate their actions. This is what is meant by herd behavior. I should clarify that herd behavior is not defined by similarity of action. Similar actions by many individuals can also occur when individuals have made similar choices but those choices have been arrived at independently. Herd behavior refers specifically to similarity of action arising from imitation. As I will point out, the choice to imitate can be entirely rational.

There is a major difference between similar behaviors arising from herding and similar behaviors arising from many individual decision makers making the same choice independently. Herd behavior stops the diffusion of information throughout a group, but independent decision making does not. When information diffusion is impeded, it becomes more likely that investors will make the same mistakes and prices will systematically diverge from rational levels.

To see why herd behavior impedes the spread of information, consider the opposite case, where individuals evaluate information independently and make autonomous choices. Suppose a large number of investors are independently evaluating a stock. Some may mistakenly value it too high, while others mistakenly value it too low. Because the mistakes are made independently, they will tend to be offsetting, making the average valuation error close to zero. Here, each investor has made an individual appraisal and in effect acted on a unique signal. This makes it far more likely that all the available information about the stock will have been considered and built into the price of the stock. Even if no single investor was in full possession of all the facts, the group, taken as a whole, is likely to be nearly fully informed.

In contrast, when investors elect to imitate the behavior of others rather than deciding independently, all the relevant information about the stock is less likely to be fully diffused throughout the entire group, making it more likely that the stock's price will not reflect all relevant information. However, an individual investor electing to imitate may be making a perfectly rational choice. Not everyone has the time or expertise to evaluate a stock, so it can make sense to copy an investor with a good track record, such as Warren Buffett. Once Buffett does his analysis and makes his buy or sell decision known, investors may cease their own efforts to gather information and evaluate the stock. This makes it more likely that, if some factor has escaped Buffett's notice, it will remain unnoticed by the community of investors. So here is a case where individuals take actions that are fully rational on an individual basis but harmful to them as a group.

Why Do We Imitate? At one time it was thought that imitative behavior was a consequence of social pressure to conform. Early experimental evidence seemed to confirm this.[73] In one study, an authentic subject was asked to estimate the length of line segments in the presence of fake subjects who also gave estimates. The fakes, who were actually part of the experiment, intentionally gave wrong answers. Even though the correct answer was obvious, the authentic subjects often went along with the group rather than give the obviously correct answer. However, a later experiment,[74] in which the authentic subject was isolated from the group of confederates, showed the subject still imitated the group's obviously wrong answer. This finding implied that social pressure does not explain imitative behavior. A better explanation emerged. The subjects seemed to be relying on a social heuristic: When one's own judgment is contradicted by the majority, follow the majority. In other words, people operate with an implicit rule: The majority is unlikely to be wrong.

"This behavior is a matter of rational calculation: in everyday living we have learned that when a large group of people is unanimous in its judgment on a question of simple fact, the members of the group are almost certainly right."[75] Similarly, most of us operate with the principle that, when an expert tells us something that contradicts our common sense, we tend to heed the expert. So it is entirely rational under conditions of uncertainty to look to the advice of experts or the actions of the majority.

Information Cascades and Herd Behavior The uncertainties of investing make it likely that investors would rely on an imitation heuristic rather than independent decision making. This has important implications for the emergence of systematic price behavior because imitation gives rise to "information cascades."[76] An information cascade is a chain of imitative behavior that was initiated by the action of one or just a few individuals. In some instances that initiating action may have been a random choice.

The emergence of an information cascade can be illustrated with a hypothetical example. Suppose two new restaurants open for business on the same day, right next door to each other. The first hungry customer to arrive must choose one, and has little information on which to base a decision. That customer's choice is, therefore, a random decision. However, when the second customer arrives, there is an additional piece of information: one of the restaurants has a patron. This may trigger the second customer to go into the same place. Because the first customer's selection was a guess, we know that the second customer's choice was based on an uninformative signal.

When the third customer arrives and sees one restaurant empty and the other with two customers, the chance is increased that the third customer will also make an imitative choice. In the end, a cascade of dependent choices, triggered by the first customer's random choice, may ultimately cause one establishment to thrive and the other to fail, and it is entirely possible that the failing establishment offered better food.

Thus, an initial random event sets the course of history down one particular path (restaurant 1 succeeds) rather than another path (restaurant 2 succeeds). As time goes on, the likelihood that one restaurant will thrive increases while the likelihood that the second establishment will fail increases. In the same way, an initial random price movement can trigger successive rounds of imitative investor behavior, resulting in a long-duration large amplitude price swing.

Now consider what would have happened if many customers had made independent restaurant choices, allowing both establishments to be sampled by many customers. By combining their findings, they would have discovered which was the better of the two restaurants. However, in an information cascade, imitative behavior prevents the accumulation and sharing of many independent appraisals. Thus, information cascades block the diffusion of information and rational choice.

The information cascade model reveals the flaw in the common sense notion that financial market prices are determined by a process like voting, in which many individuals make their own assessment.[77] In an information cascade, investors make the rational choice of copying the actions of others, rather than expending the considerable effort required to arrive at an independent choice. Voters do one thing, and investors sometimes do something entirely different.

The Diffusion of Information Among Investors We have seen that information cascades can explain why the rational behavior of individual investors can impede the diffusion of information. This is important for TA because the rate at which information spreads among investors can explain the occurrence of systematic price movements. EMH assumes almost instantaneous information diffusion and, consequently, almost instantaneous price adjustments. Such price adjustments are too quick to be exploited by TA methods. However, information that diffuses slowly allows for gradual, systematic price movements that can be exploited by TA methods.

Despite the prevalence of advanced communications technology, the preferred method of exchanging investment information is still a good story told person to person. This predilection, a result of several million years of evolution, has been confirmed by the studies of behavioral-economist Robert Shiller. He has shown that the word-of-mouth effect is strong even among people who read a lot. A story about a hot new issue has greater impact in conversation than a statistic about the high failure rate of new companies.

The way stories spread among investors has been studied with mathematical models similar to those used by epidemiologists to study the spread of disease within a population. Unfortunately, these models have not been as accurate in the investor domain as they have been in the realm of biology. This is explained by the fact that the mutation rate of circulating ideas is far higher than the mutation rate of organisms. However, the models have been enlightening in another way; they explain how stories spread so rapidly.

One reason a "new" story can spread so rapidly is that it is not really new. Investors' minds are already infested with many familiar story scripts, and it does not matter that the panoply of stories residing in investors' minds contradict each other. For example, investors can be comfortable with the notion that the stock market cannot be predicted and at the same time hold the opposing notion that it can. No doubt, most investors have been exposed to experts who have espoused both points of view. Our minds are able to accommodate a wide variety of contradictory ideas because the scripts lie there inert with no demand that we choose one side or the other.

Nevertheless, this state of affairs can change rapidly. Even a slight random perturbation in the news or the market's behavior can cause an idea that had been hibernating in investors' minds to spring to life and consume their attention.

Shifts in Investor Attention Where investors are focusing their attention at any given moment can shift dramatically due to minor changes in the news. "The human brain is structured to have essentially a single focus of attention at a time and to move rapidly from one focus to another."[78] The brain had to evolve a capacity to selectively attend to only a tiny trickle of the torrent of information that pours in from the world. This filtering process is both a mark of human intelligence and a source of judgment error. Numerous instances of expert error are attributable to missing important details. However, before outcomes are known, we never know which details deserve our attention.

Among the automatic unconscious rules used by the brain to filter relevant from irrelevant information is the rule to look to other people for cues. In other words, we presume that what grabs the attention of others must be worthy of our attention as well. According to economist Robert Shiller, "the phenomenon of social attention is one of the great creations of behavioral evolution and is critical for the functioning of human society."[79] Although communal attention has great social value, because it promotes collaborative action, it has a downside. It can lead an entire group to hold an incorrect view and take similar mistaken actions.

In the opposite situation, where individuals form their own views independently, errors of attention would be random and self-canceling. Although this mode of thought makes it harder to organize joint efforts around common views and goals, it is less likely to overlook important details. Dramatic market movements can easily grab the attention of the community of investors and encourage them to act in ways that amplify the movement, even if there is no fundamental reason for it.

Robert Shiller has studied the way dramatic price movements capture investor attention and trigger herd behavior. Even institutional investors, who would be expected to select stocks in systematic ways based on statistically valid characteristics, are prone to buying a stock simply because it has experienced a rapid price increase.[80] This mechanism can explain how a market boom can be triggered just by a vivid initial price movement that calls attention to the stock market. Moreover, Shiller's studies show that investors are often not even aware that it was a dramatic price movement that motivated them to act.

The Role of Feedback in Systematic Price Movements Social interaction among investors creates feedback. Feedback refers to the channeling of a system's output back into the system as input. See Figure 30.9, where two systems are compared—one with no feedback and one with feedback.

There are two types of feedback, positive and negative. One way to think of the difference is as follows. In the case of negative feedback, the system output is multiplied by a negative number and the result is feedback in. In the case of positive feedback the multiplier is a positive number. This is illustrated in Figure 30.10.

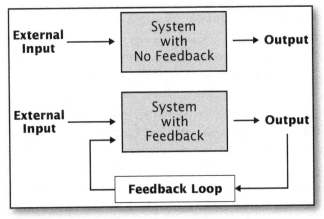

FIGURE 30.9   Feedback: Output Becomes Input.

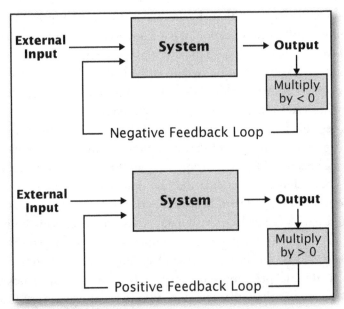

FIGURE 30.10   Positive and Negative Feedback Loops.

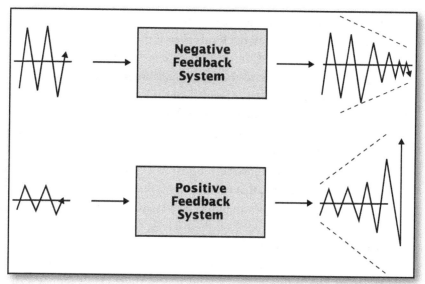

FIGURE 30.11 Positive and Negative Feedback Loops: Dampening versus Amplifying.

Negative feedback has the effect of dampening system behavior, driving the output back toward a level of equilibrium. Positive feedback has the opposite effect, amplifying a system's behavior, thus driving its output further from equilibrium. This is illustrated in Figure 30.11.

An example of a negative feedback system is a household heating & air conditioning system. When the temperature falls below a desired or equilibrium level, the thermostat turns on the furnace, returning the system's output, the household temperature, back to the desired level. Temperature above the desired level turns on the A/C, bringing the temperature back down. This is all accomplished by feeding the system's output back into the system as an input. This allows the system to self-regulate its way toward equilibrium.

Positive feedback is illustrated by the growing screech in a public-address system when the speakers are placed too close to the microphone. The normal hum coming out of the speakers (output) gets fed back into the audio system via the microphone, where it is amplified by the system. With each cycle, the sound comes out louder, developing into a loud screech. Positive feedback is also known as the snowball effect or vicious cycle.

Financial markets, like other self-organizing self-regulated systems, rely on a healthy balance between negative and positive feedback.[81] Arbitrage provides negative feedback. Prices that are too high or too low trigger arbitrage trading that pushes prices back toward rational levels. Positive feedback occurs when investor decisions are dominated by imitative behavior rather than independent choice. In this regime, investors will hop aboard an initial price movement, buying after first signs of strength or selling after first signs of weakness, thus amplifying an initial small price movement into a large-scale trend. A TA approach, known as trend following, depends on large-scale price moves for its profitability and thus is most effective during times when positive feedback dominates.

Positive feedback can cause a vicious cycle of price increases or decreases, which take prices far beyond rational levels even if the initial price move that triggered the whole affair was justified. In other words, price trends can go far above or below rational levels simply due to the amplifying effect of positive feedback.

Positive feedback can also result from the way people adapt their expectations to recent changes. Although it generally makes sense to alter expectations when conditions change, people do it imperfectly. At times, they adjust insufficiently (the conservatism bias), whereas at other times they are overly sensitive to change and alter their expectations more than is justified. Investors are especially likely to over-react to new information that is prominent. Either a single large price change or a sequence of similar changes can induce investors to alter their expectations too much. These price changes can feed on themselves, thus generating price momentum that may lead to a bubble or crash.

A judgment error that sometimes contributes to positive feedback is mental accounting. This is the irrational tendency to think about money as if it belonged in separate accounts, which should be treated differently. Gains from prior speculative ventures may be assigned to the hot-action account, whereas money accumulating in the home-equity account is treated with greater conservatism. Rationally, all of an investor's money, regardless of how it was made or in which asset it is invested, should be treated in the same way. A dollar is a dollar. However, speculative gains from a recent market rise are often, irrationally, earmarked for further speculation, thus adding fuel to a rising market.

At some point, the increasing expectations that fuel a bubble run out. Common sense would suggest, and some analysts insist, that a price bubble necessarily ends in market crashes (i.e., a negative bubble). At times they do, but other bubble termination patterns are possible. Computer simulations of systems that incorporate feedback loops show that bubbles not only develop in a jagged fashion with many intervening pauses, but they can also deflate in a similar manner. If the late 1990s was a price bubble, it seems to be ending with many intervening pauses.

Self-Organizing Ponzi Schemes

The feedback theory of price bubbles is appealing because of its plausibility and the numerous historical examples that seem to confirm its validity. However, it is hard to prove that a simple feedback mechanism involving heightened investor focus, imitative behavior, and exaggerated investor confidence is truly operational in financial markets.

Nevertheless, Yale economist Robert Shiller believes actual cases of pyramid frauds known as Ponzi schemes offer evidence that confirms the feedback theory. The scheme, named after the infamous Charles Ponzi, who invented the idea in the 1920s, involves promising investors a high rate of return from some sort of business venture or investment. However, the investors' money is never put to work in the way promised. Instead, the commitments of new investors are used to pay off earlier investors. This serves two purposes: it makes the venture look legitimate and it encourages the first investors to spread the story of their success. As the tale gains popularity, new investors are motivated to make investments. Their funds are, in turn, used to pay off a prior round of investors, who now go out and tell their story. This cycle of using Peter's investment to pay off Paul to prove the success of the enterprise continues and grows. The number of people influenced by the scam follows a curve similar to the diffusion of an infection throughout a population. Ultimately, a saturation level is reached. The supply of noninfected speculators gets exhausted, and so there are no new investments with which to pay off the last round of investors. At this point, the scheme crashes.

Recently a housewife from a small town in Alaska collected an estimated $10 to $15 million over a six-year period by promising a 50 percent return. Her business was purportedly based on unused frequent flyer miles accumulated by large companies. In fact, this was very similar to Ponzi's original scheme, which was based on international postage coupons.

Ponzi scams evolve in a typical pattern. Initially, investors are skeptical and invest only small amounts, but once early investors reap profits and tell their success story, later-stage investors gain confidence and the flow of capital into the scheme gains momentum. Frequently there are rational skeptics issuing warnings, but the greedy pay no heed. Well-founded cynical arguments cannot compete with vivid accounts of fat profits. The moths dive into the flame.

Shiller contends that speculative bubbles are naturally occurring Ponzi schemes that emerge spontaneously in financial markets, without requiring the machinations of a fraudulent promoter.[82] Such self-organizing phenomena are common in complex systems. There is no need for false stories because there is always some buzz about the stock market anyway. A trend of rising prices acts as a call to action much like the gains of early investors in a Ponzi scheme. The message is then amplified by Wall Street's salesmen, and they need not tell lies. They simply pitch the upside potential while downplaying the risk side of the story. The parallels between Ponzi schemes and speculative bubbles are so clear in Shiller's opinion that the burden of proof is on those who deny the similarity.

Competing Hypotheses of Behavioral Finance

A mathematical model quantifies a scientific hypothesis about some aspect of the world, This allows quantitative predictions to be made that can be tested against future observations. Of course, those proposing the model hope its predictions will coincide with said observations. Nevertheless, if they should clash, a true scientist stands ready to formulate a new model that both explains the discordant observations and makes additional predictions that can be tested against further observations. This cycle of refinement never ceases because knowledge is never complete.

Pseudoscientific stories resemble legitimate scientific hypotheses, but only superficially. A scientific hypothesis is compact, yet it accounts for a wide range of observations. Pseudoscientific stories tend to be complicated. Scientific hypotheses make precise predictions that can be checked against future observation. Pseudoscientific accounts make vague predictions that are consistent with prior observations but never make predictions specific enough to permit clear refutation. Thus, pseudoscientific accounts survive in the minds of the gullible, no matter how far off the mark they may be.

On this basis, behavioral finance qualifies as science, albeit a young one. Although as yet, there is no agreement on a single theory, there has been substantial progress. Within the last decade behavioral-finance practitioners have proposed several hypotheses to explain investor behavior and key features of market dynamics. These are important to TA because they provide a rationale for the occurrence of systematic price movements, the "without-which-not" of TA.

The behavioral-finance hypotheses have been formulated as mathematical models, thus allowing them to generate testable predictions of how markets would behave if the hypothesis were correct. This opens the hypotheses to refutation if markets do not manifest the predicted behaviors. For example, if a model predicts the occurrence of trend reversals similar to those actually observed in market data, the hypothesis gains some confirmation. However, if the model's predicted scenarios are contradicted by actual market behavior, then the hypothesis would be refuted. This makes the hypotheses of behavioral finance scientifically meaningful.

Recall that the random-walk model of EMH predicts that systematic price motion should not be observed in market behavior. In contrast, the behavioral-finance hypotheses described later predict the occurrence of systematic price motion and offer an explanation about why they should occur. Even though none of the hypotheses provides a comprehensive theory of market behavior, they have a common a message of importance to TA: There is good reason to believe financial markets are not entirely random walks.

Biased Interpretation of Public Information: The Barberis, Shleifer, and Vishny (BSV) Hypothesis Empirical studies show that investors display two distinct errors in response to news releases. Sometimes they underreact, and consequently prices change less than the new fundamentals say they should. At other times, investors overreact, causing prices to change more than is justified by the news. Ultimately, however, these pricing errors are rectified by systematic price movements toward price levels that accurately reflect the new information.

The puzzle is: Why do investors sometimes overreact while at other times they underreact? A hypothesis proposed by Barberis, Shleifer, and Vishny[83] (BSV) offers an explanation. First, BSV asserts that two distinct cognitive errors are involved: conservatism bias and sample-size neglect. Second, they assert that the particular error that is operative at a given point in time depends on circumstances.

To briefly recap: The conservatism bias describes the tendency to alter a prior belief less than new information would warrant. Existing opinions are sticky. Sample-size neglect, also known as the crime of small numbers, is the tendency to draw too grand a conclusion from a small sample of observations. Thus, the conservatism bias is the opposite of the crime of small numbers. In the former, new evidence is given too little weight; in the latter, it is given too much.

The conservatism bias is at work when investors underreact to news, leaving prices too low after good news or too high after bad news. However, as investors gradually realize the new information's true significance, prices make a gradual systematic march to a level that properly reflects the news. Thus, some price trends can be explained by investor underreaction.

The crime of small numbers explains investor overreaction. For example, if investors observe a small number of positive earnings changes, they may conclude, too hastily, that a valid growth pattern has been established. This stimulates overly aggressive buying that pushes prices higher than warranted. Investors can overreact in the same way to a few negative observations and push the price too low.

The mathematical model put forward by BSV makes the following simplifying assumptions: (1) the market has a single stock, (2) its earnings stream follows a random walk, but (3) investors do not realize this,[84] so (4) investors labor under the false impression that the stock's earnings stream shifts back and forth between two distinct regimes, a growth trend phase and a mean-reverting (oscillating) phase, but they do not consider the possibility that the earning may follow a random walk, (6) therefore, investors believe their job is to figure out which of these two regimes is operative at any given point in time.

Let's see how BSV's mythical investor might react to the releases of new earnings information. At any given time, the investors hold a belief that the earnings are in either one of two nonrandom regimes: a growth trend or mean reverting process. The possibility of a random walk is not considered. Recall that a random walk displays less mean reversion than a true mean-reverting process and also displays streaks that are shorter in duration than those found in a truly trending process. As we pick up the story, an investor holds some prior belief about the earnings regime and hears news about earnings. Suppose the news announcement contradicts the investor's belief. For example, if the investor had believed the stock's earnings had been in a growth trend, and a negative earnings report came out, the investor would be surprised. Similarly, if the investor had been under the belief that earnings were in a mean-reverting regime, a streak of similar changes would also be surprising. According to the BSV hypothesis, both kinds of surprises would trigger an underreaction by the investor due to the conservatism bias. In other words, regardless of whether the investor's prior belief was in a mean-reverting regime or in a growth regime, news contradicting the belief would be given too little weight causing prices to underreact to the new information. However, if news that is at odds with a prior belief continues to occur, the investor will become convinced that the regime has switched, either from mean reverting to growth or from growth to mean reverting. In this case, the BSV hypothesis predicts that investors will switch from the mistake of being too stuck with their prior beliefs and underreacting (the conservatism bias) to the mistake of committing the crime of small numbers and overreacting. Thus, the BSV model accounts for both kinds of investor error as well as the systematic price movement that corrects both forms of errors.

I illustrate the type of behavior predicted by BSV in Figure 30.12. Here I posit the case where investors initially believe that earnings are in a mean-reverting regime. Thus, they expect positive earnings reports to be followed by a negative report. For this reason, they underreact to the first two positive earnings reports. However, after the third positive report, not at all unusual in a random process

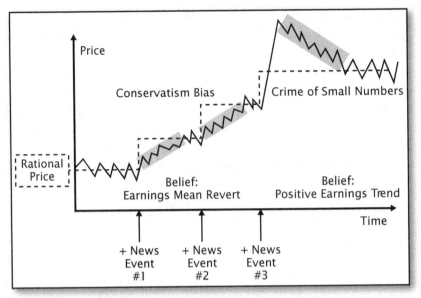

FIGURE 30.12 BSV: Underreaction Followed by Overreaction.

(three heads in a row), they abandon their earlier belief and adopt the idea that earnings have entered a growth regime and have established an uptrend. Consequently they now expect that future reports will also be positive. This causes investors to overreact, pushing the stock above a rational level. The systematic price movements resulting from both types of investor error are highlighted in grey.

Thus BSV's model also shows how a feedback loop emerges from the crime of small numbers. When investors see earnings move in the same direction several times in succession, they switch from doubting the trend to assuming it is real.[85] However, the conservatism bias initially impedes the adoption of the new belief. The interaction between the crime of small numbers and the conservatism bias determines the speed at which speculative feedback develops.[86] Simulations of the BSV model show several kinds of actual market behavior such as price trends following surprising earnings, price momentum, long-term reversals, and the forecasting power of fundamental ratios such as price-to-book. Thus, the BSV model explains how investors' biased interpretations of public information can predict the occurrence of phenomena that are observed in actual market data. This suggests that the model does capture some of the dynamics of real financial markets.

Biased Interpretation of Private Information: The Daniel, Hirshleifer, and Subrahmanyam (DHS) Hypothesis An alternative hypothesis proposed by Daniel, Hirshleifer, and Subrahmanyam (1998, 2001)[87] (DHS) suggests a different explanation for systematic price movements such as trend reversals and trend persistence (momentum). In contrast to BSV, the DHS hypothesis is founded upon investors' biased interpretations of private research. In addition, DHS emphasizes somewhat different cognitive errors: the endowment bias, the confirmation bias, and the self-attribution bias.

Private research refers to an investor's independently derived interpretations of public information (i.e., proprietary research). The hypothesis put forward by DHS predicts that investors will be overly confident about the quality of their private research and hence will have a tendency to overreact to it. This prediction is based on the endowment bias—the predisposition to place too high a value on what we own or create. This overreaction pushes prices beyond rational levels, which ultimately leads to a price reversal back toward rational prices. So in DHS's view of the world, price reversals are an effect of overconfidence in privately derived signals.

DHS also explains price momentum (nonrandom price trends) as the result of two other cognitive biases: confirmation bias and self-attribution bias. They assert price momentum develops because news releases and price movements impact investors in a biased manner. Because of the confirmation bias, news or price movements that confirm an investor's prior beliefs, (i.e., those founded on their private signals and research), will be given excessive weight. News events and/or price movements that are confirmatory have the effect of increasing the investors' confidence that their private research was indeed accurate. This induces them to take additional action (buying or selling), which amplifies the momentum of the current price trend. The self-attribution bias also causes investors to view confirmatory news or price movement as a sign that their private research is good. Recall that self-attribution causes people to take credit for outcomes, even if they occur because of good luck, but to deny responsibility for bad outcomes by attributing them to bad luck. Thus, both the confirmation bias and self-attribution bias induce investors to overreact to confirmatory evidence, thereby amplifying the market's positive feedback.

Conversely, if public information or price behavior contradicts the investor's private research, it will be given too little weight (confirmation bias) and investors will attribute it to bad luck rather than to poor private research (self-attribution bias). Therefore, regardless of whether the news or the price movement confirms or contradicts the investor's private information, the DHS model predicts that investors' confidence in their private research will increase. "This unequal treatment of new information means initial overconfidence is on average followed by even greater overconfidence, thus generating price momentum."[88] However, after a sequence of contradictory public news signals, the investors' confidence in their private information will be shattered (crime of small numbers), and price trends will reverse.

Both DHS and BSV predict that investors are sometimes excessively optimistic and sometimes excessively pessimistic. In addition, these beliefs are predicted to be subject to reversal when a streak of disconfirming information arrives. If DHS and BSV are valid, then the profits earned by strategies that exploit trend reversals should be concentrated at the times of information releases. This predicted consequence, which opens both hypotheses to refutation, has been confirmed.[89] Indeed, a large fraction of the excess returns earned by buying value stocks (low price to book, low P/E, and so forth) and buying the weakest stocks of the past three to five years do occur near the times of earnings information releases.

News Traders and Momentum Traders: The HS Hypothesis As just described, certain instances of price momentum can be explained by prices catching up with fundamentals due to an initial underreaction to news. Other trends can be explained by positive feedback, in which a price increase stimulates additional buying and price weakness stimulates additional selling.[90] Thus, some investors look for signals in recent price changes rather than news.

From the perspective of TA, trends spawned by positive feedback can be viewed as a cascade of progressively less sensitive trend-following signals being triggered. An initial price movement (news inspired or random) triggers the most sensitive trend signals (e.g., a very short-term moving average crossover signal). Transactions triggered by that signal push prices enough to trigger a somewhat less sensitive trend signal (e.g., medium-term moving average), which in turn triggers even less sensitive signals and so on. Whatever the mechanism, investor actions become correlated, forming a herd effect.

The hypothesis proposed by Hong and Stein[91] (HS) explains three market phenomena: momentum, underreaction, and overreaction. To do so, they postulate two classes of investors, news watchers (fundamentalists) and momentum traders (technicians). The HS hypothesis asserts that an interaction between these two classes of investors creates positive feedback and, therefore, price momentum. The HS assumption that there is more than one class of investors is grounded in the notion that investors, by dint of their intellectual limits, must confine their attention to a restricted portion of the available information. News watchers confine their attention to fundamental developments. On the basis of this information, they derive private estimates of future returns. In contrast, momentum traders confine their attention to past price changes and derive their private forecast of future trends.

Hong and Stein posit that news watchers pay little or no attention to price changes. As a result, their private assessments of the news fail to spread quickly throughout the community of news watchers. To understand how an exclusive focus on the fundamental news impedes the diffusion of information, consider what would happen if the news watchers also paid attention to price action. Watching price movements would allow them to infer, to some degree, the private information of other news watchers. For example, rising prices might imply that other news watchers were interpreting the news as favorable, whereas falling prices might imply the opposite. As we have seen, any investor behavior that slows the process by which prices incorporate new information can cause price trends. That is, instead of prices instantaneously adjusting to new information, they move gradually to a higher or lower level justified by new information. For momentum (trend-following) strategies to work, prices must change in a gradual enough fashion to allow signals based on an initial price change to predict additional price change. Thus, the failure of news traders to extract information from price action slows the rate at which prices adjust to new information, thus resulting in price trends.

Now consider the effect on market dynamics caused by momentum traders (trend-followers). The HS hypothesis claims that momentum traders only pay attention to signals from price behavior. Trend following assumes that newly emerging price trends are an indication that important new fundamental information is starting to diffuse throughout the market. Momentum traders make the bet that the diffusion is incomplete and that the price trend will continue after the initial momentum signal. Actions taken by subsequent waves of trend followers keep prices moving, thus generating positive price feedback. Ultimately, as more trend followers join the party, prices may carry further than fundamentals justify. The overshooting occurs because momentum traders are unable to judge the extent to which the news has been diffused and understood by all investors. When the news is fully diffused and all investors have acted on it, no further price movement is fundamentally justified. Thus, HS assert that the overshooting of rational price levels, resulting from the positive feedback of momentum traders, sets up the conditions for a trend reversal back toward rational levels based on fundamentals.

The Bottom Line   Behavioral finance has offered a number of testable hypotheses that attempt to explain systematic price motion. It is not yet clear which, if any, of these are correct. No doubt new hypotheses will be offered. So long as they generate testable (falsifiable) predictions, they should be entertained. What is of importance to TA is that these theories suggest that systematic price movements should occur in financial market prices.

■ Nonrandom Price Motion in the Context of Efficient Markets

The preceding section explained how systematic price movement can arise in markets that are not fully efficient. However, even if markets are fully efficient, the case for TA is not lost. A case can be made for the existence of systematic price motion in markets that are fully efficient. This section presents this case.

How Systematic Price Motion and Market Efficiency Can Coexist

Some economists contend that systematic price movements are possible even if markets are fully efficient.[92] In other words, the existence of nonrandom price behavior and the possibility of price prediction does not necessarily imply that financial markets are inefficient.[93]

Other economists state the case more strongly, asserting that some degree of predictability is not only possible but necessary for markets to function properly. In their book *A Non-Random Walk Down Wall Street*, Andrew Lo and Craig MacKinlay say, "predictability is the oil that lubricates the gears of capitalism."[94] A similar position is taken by Grossman and Stiglitz.[95] They contend that efficient markets must offer profit opportunities to motivate investors to engage in the costly activities of information processing and trading. For it is these very activities that drive prices toward rational valuations.

In fact, there is only one special condition under which market efficiency necessarily implies that price movement must be random and, therefore, unpredictable.

This occurs when all investors have the same attitude toward risk, a condition that is simply not plausible. Is there any type of risk about which all people have the same attitude? To see how far-fetched this assumption is, imagine for a moment a world in which all people have the same attitude toward risk. There would be either too many test pilots and high steel workers or not enough of them. Either everyone would be into skydiving and alligator wrestling, or no one would.

It is far more realistic to assume a world of investors with highly diverse attitudes toward risk. In such a world, some investors would be more adverse to risk than others, and they would be willing to pay other investors to accept the burden of additional risk. Also, there would likely be risk-tolerant investors looking to profit from the opportunity to assume additional risk. All that would be needed in such a world is a mechanism by which risk can be transferred from the risk adverse to the risk tolerant and for compensation to be paid to those willing to accept said risk.

Let's step away from markets for a moment to consider one mechanism by which the risk adverse can compensate the risk inclined—the insurance premium. Home-owners dread the possibility of a fire, so they enter into a transaction with a fire insurance company. The homeowner transfers the financial risk of a fire to the insurance company and, in exchange, the insurance company earns a premium. This is a profitable business if the insurance company can predict the likelihood of a house burning down (over a large number of homes—Law of Large Numbers) and charge a premium that compensates it for that risk plus a bit more for profit. The bottom line: The insurance company provides a risk acceptance service and is compensated for doing so.

Participants in financial markets have exposures to various risks and vary in their tolerance for them. These ingredients motivate transactions that transfer risk from one party to another. In this situation, the investors willing to bear greater risks can reasonably demand compensation in the form of a higher return than that offered by riskless investments, just as test pilots and high steel workers can demand a premium salary for the additional risks they bear. In financial market terms, compensation for accepting increased risk is called a risk premium or economic rent.

Financial markets offer several kinds of risk premiums:

- **The equity market risk premium:** Investors provide working capital for new business formation and are compensated by receiving a return that is above the risk-free rate for incurring the risk of business failure, economic downturns, and such.

- **Commodity and currency hedge risk transfer premium:** Speculators assume long and short positions in futures to give commercial hedgers (users and producers of the commodity) the ability to shed the risk of price change. Compensation is in the form of profitable trends that can be captured with relatively simple trend-following strategies.

- **Liquidity premium:** Investors assume positions in less liquid securities and in securities being aggressively sold by investors with acute short-term needs for cash. Compensation is in the form of higher returns for holding illiquid securities or in the form of short-term gains for buying stocks that have recently been very weak (i.e., engaging in countertrend strategies).

- **Information or price discovery premium for promoting market efficiency:** This premium compensates investors for making buy-and-sell decisions that move prices toward rational levels. Because these decisions are often based on complex models developed by sophisticated research, this premium might also be called a complexity premium.[96] For example, a strategy that sells overvalued stocks and buys undervalued stocks helps move prices back to rational values (price discovery).

The good news about returns that come in the form of a risk premium is that they are more likely to endure into the future. Of course, it is every analyst's dream to discover true market inefficiencies because the returns earned from them do not entail additional risk.[97] However, inefficiencies are ephemeral. Sooner or later they tend to be discovered and wiped out by other diligent researchers. However, returns that are justified as a risk premium are more likely to endure as they represent payment for service.

How do risk premiums explain the existence of systematic price movements? Such price movements can provide a mechanism for risk-accepting investors to be compensated. The investor who is willing to provide liquidity to a stockholder with a strong desire to sell winds up buying stocks that have a systematic tendency to rise over the near term. These stocks can be identified with countertrend strategies.[98]

Therefore, in the context of efficient markets, the profits-earned by TA strategies may be understood as risk premiums; compensation for the beneficial effect the strategy confers on other investors or the market as a whole. In other words, TA signals may generate profits because they identify opportunities to assume risks that other investors wish to shed.

I should point out that the mere fact that an investor is willing to bear a risk does not guarantee that a return will be earned. The risk taker must be clever about it. Just as a careless high steel worker or test pilot may not live long enough to collect a wage that includes the hazardous-duty premium, a careless seeker of risk premiums may not stay in the game long enough to collect, either.

Hedge Risk Premium and the Gains to Trend-Following Commodity Futures

This section describes how the profits to trend followers in the commodities markets may be explained as a risk transfer premium. The commodities futures markets perform an economic function that is fundamentally different from the stock and bond markets. The stock and bond markets provide companies with a mechanism to obtain equity and debt financing[99] and provide investors with a way to invest their capital. Because stocks and corporate bond investments expose investors to risks that exceed the risk-free rate (government treasury bills), investors are compensated with a risk premium—the equity risk premium and the corporate-bond risk premium.

The economic function of the futures markets has nothing to do with raising capital and everything to do with price risk. Price changes, especially large ones, are a source of risk and uncertainty to businesses that produce or use commodities. The futures markets provide a means by which these businesses, called commercial hedgers, can transfer price risk to investors (speculators).

At first blush, it may seem puzzling that commercial hedgers would even need investors to assume their price risk. Because some hedgers need to sell, like the farmer who grows wheat, and some need to buy, like the bread company that uses wheat, why don't hedgers simply contract with each other? They do, but often there is an imbalance in their hedging needs. Sometimes wheat farmers have more wheat to sell than bakery companies and other commercial users of wheat need to buy. At other times, the situation is the opposite. Thus there is often a gap between the farmers' supply and the bakers' demand. This creates the need for a third group of market participants who are willing to buy or sell. That is, they are willing to fill the supply-demand gap that develops between commercial producers and commercial users.

The existence of a supply-demand gap is a predicable consequence of the law of supply and demand; as the price of wheat rises, supply goes up while demand goes down. As the price falls, supply goes down while demand goes up. Data from the Commodity Futures Trading Commission (CFTC), which tracks the buying and selling of commercial hedgers, confirms this is exactly what occurs in the futures markets. During rising price trends, commercial hedge selling exceeds hedge buying (i.e., hedgers are net sellers). During falling trends, commercial hedge buying exceeds commercial hedge selling (hedgers are net buyers).

In the futures markets, the amount sold and the amount bought must be equal just as in real estate transactions the number of homes sold must equal the number of homes bought. It cannot be otherwise. Given that a rising trend motivates more commercial hedge selling than hedge buying, there is a need for additional buyers during rising markets to accommodate the excess hedge selling. During falling trends, excessive commercial hedge buying creates the need for additional sellers.

Enter the price trend speculator who is willing to buy during uptrends to meet the unfilled needs of commercial hedge sellers and willing to sell short during falling price trends, to meet the unmet needs of the commercial hedge buyers. In other words the futures markets need speculators to be trend followers. And it is the invisible hand of the marketplace that creates the trends to compensate them for filling this need.

However, trend followers are exposed to significant risks. For example, most trend-following systems generate unprofitable signals 50 to 65 percent of the time. These occur when markets are trendless, which is the case a majority of the time. During these times, the trend followers experience the dreaded equity drawdown. During drawdowns it is not unusual for successful trend followers to lose up to 30 percent of their trading capital. Thus they need a strong motive to tolerate drawdown risk. That motive is the opportunity, though not the guarantee, to profit from price trends when they do occur. In other words, large-scale trends provide a profit opportunity to trend followers who are adequately capitalized and who manage leverage correctly.

The Mt. Lucas Management Index of Trend Following Returns

The risk premium earned by commodity trend followers has been quantified with the creation of a benchmark index called the Mt. Lucas Management Index (MLM). It is a historical record of the returns that can be earned by an extremely simplistic trend-following formula. In other words, it assumes no specialized knowledge of a complex forecasting model. If it did it could not legitimately be called a benchmark index, whose function is to estimate the returns that can be earned by investing in an asset class with no special skill.

The risk-adjusted returns earned by the MLM index suggest that commodity futures markets contain systematic price movements that can be exploited with relatively simple TA methods. The MLM index monthly returns, which have been computed back to the 1960s, are derived by applying a 12-month moving-average crossover strategy to 25 commodities markets.[100] At the end of each month, the price of the nearby futures contract for each of the markets is compared to its 12-month moving average. If the price is greater than the moving average, a long position is held in that market for the next month. If the price is below the average, a short position is held.

The annualized return[101] and risk, as measured by the standard deviation in annual returns, of the MLM index is compared with returns and risks of several other asset-class benchmarks in Figure 30.13.

The risk-adjusted excess return or Sharpe ratio for the MLM index, and the other asset classes are shown Figure 30.14. The trend follower earns a risk premium that is somewhat better than the other asset-class benchmarks.[102] The MLM index provides some evidence that the futures markets offer compensation in the form of systematic price movements.

If a risk-transfer premium is a valid explanation of trend-follower returns, then trend following in stocks should not be as rewarding as it is in the commodity futures markets. A trend follower in stocks is not providing a risk-transfer service. There are data suggesting that trend following in stocks is indeed a less rewarding enterprise.[103] Lars Kestner compared the performance of trend-following systems for a portfolio of futures and a portfolio of stocks. The futures considered were 29

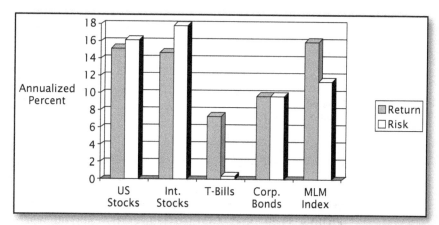

FIGURE 30.13 **Returns and Standard Deviations for Five Benchmarks.**

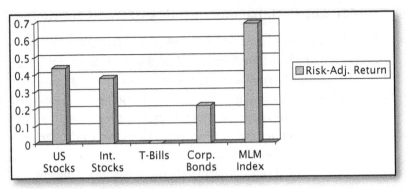

FIGURE 30.14 Risk-Adjusted Excess Returns.

commodities in 8 different sectors.[104] The stocks were represented by 31 large-cap stocks in 9 different industry sectors,[105] and 3 stock indices. Risk-adjusted performance (Sharpe ratio) was computed for 5 different trend-following systems,[106] over the period January 1, 1990 through December 31, 2001. The Sharpe ratio averaged over the five trend-following systems in futures was .604 versus .046 in stocks. These results support the notion that futures trend followers are earning a risk premium that is not available to trend followers in stocks. See Figure 30.15.

Liquidity Premium and the Gains to Counter Trend Trading in Stocks

The stock market offers risk-taking stock traders a different form of compensation. They can earn a premium for providing liquidity to highly motivated sellers. In other words, there are systematic price movements in stocks that can be exploited with countertrend strategies that buy stocks that have been very weak over the recent past.

Owners of stock with an urgent need to liquidate their holdings need buyers. This suggests that the market should offer compensation to traders who are willing to meet unmet needs for liquidity. Evidence presented by Michael Cooper shows that buyers of oversold stocks can earn above-average short-term returns.[107] His study shows that stocks that have displayed negative price momentum on declining

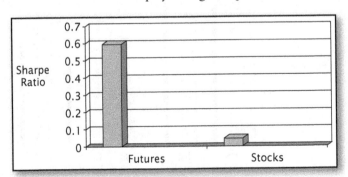

FIGURE 30.15 Risk-Adjusted Returns to Trend-Following Futures Versus Stocks.

trading volume earn excess returns. In other words, the pattern identifies stocks with distressed sellers in search of buyers. The excess returns appear to be a liquidity premium. Cooper's study showed that stocks that have declined sharply over the prior two weeks on declining volume display a systematic tendency to rise over the following week. The declining volume aspect of this pattern is plausible because it can be interpreted to mean that there are insufficient buyers to meet the acute needs of the sellers. To guard against the possibility of data mining, Cooper used a walk-forward out-of-sample simulation to form portfolios of long and short positions over the period 1978 to 1993. The long/short portfolios, created from 300 large capitalization stocks, earned an annualized return of 44.95 percent versus a benchmark buy-and-hold return of 17.91 percent. Again, we see evidence of systematic price movements that can be explained as a risk premium, in this case a liquidity premium, which can be exploited with TA.

In the context of efficient equity and futures markets, signals given by TA methods can be viewed as identifying opportunities to fill a market need. In effect, they are want ads, "risk adopter for hire by hedgers," or "desperately seeking liquidity provider—will pay." TA traders profiting from these signals are not getting a free lunch. They are simply reading the market's Help Wanted advertisements.

■ Conclusion

In this chapter, I have made a case for the existence of nonrandom price movements in financial markets. Without them, there can be no justification for technical analysis. With them, TA has an opportunity to capture some portion of that nonrandom behavior. Ultimately, it is up to each method of TA to prove that it can.

■ Notes

1. C.R. Lightner, "A Rationale for Managed Futures," *Technical Analysis of Stocks & Commodities* (March 1999).
2. Kepler actually proposed three distinct laws.
3. R.D. Edwards and J. Magee, *Technical Analysis of Stock Trends*, 4th ed. (Springfield, MA: John Magee, 1958).
4. J.J. Murphy, *Technical Analysis of the Futures Markets: A Comprehensive Guide to Trading Methods and Applications* (New York: New York Institute of Finance, 1999), 2.
5. E. Fama, "Efficient Capital Markets: A Review of Theory and Empirical Work" *Journal of Finance* 25 (1970), 383–417.
6. R.J. Shiller, *Irrational Exuberance* (Princeton, NJ: Princeton University Press, 2000), 135.
7. Ibid.
8. In this chapter in section "Nonrandom Price Motion in the Context of Efficient Markets," I state the case of those who say EMH allows for price predictability, namely, that random walks are not a necessary implication of EMH.
9. Updating a belief in a probabilistically correct way implies that new information impacts a prior belief in accord with Bayes' theorem, whereby the prior belief is altered in accord with the predictive value of the new information.

10. Correct prices induce the proper allocation of resources among different possible uses. For example, if the price of corn is too high, more of it than necessary will be produced, flooding the economy with more corn than is needed at the expense of something else such as wheat. Net result: too many boxes of Corn Flakes and too few boxes of Wheaties to meet consumer demand.

11. P. Samuelson, "Proof That Properly Anticipated Prices Fluctuate Randomly," *Industrial Management Review* 6 (1965), 41–49.

12. B.G. Malkiel, *A Random Walk Down Wall Street* (New York: W.W. Norton & Company, 2003).

13. E. Fama, "Efficient Capital Markets: A Review of Theory and Empirical Work," Journal of Finance 25 (1970), 383–417, as cited by A. Shleifer in *Inefficient Markets: An Introduction to Behavioral Finance* (Oxford, UK: Oxford University Press, 2000), 1.

14. A. Shleifer, *Inefficient Markets: An Introduction to Behavioral Finance* (Oxford, UK: Oxford University Press, 2000), 1.

15. N.N. Taleb, *Fooled by Randomness: The Hidden Role of Chance in the Markets and in Life* (New York: Texere, 2001).

16. A money manager with no skill whatsoever has a 0.5 probability of beating the market in any given time period (e.g., 1 year). In this experiment, Taleb assumed a universe of money managers with a 0.50 probability of beating the market in a given year.

17. Actually there are three forms of EMH—strong, semistrong, and weak. The strong form contends that no information, including inside information, can be used to beat the market on a risk-adjusted basis. This form is impossible to test because it cannot be reliably ascertained who knew what and when they knew it. The testimony of those who trade on inside information is notoriously untrustworthy.

18. E. Fama, L. Fisher, M. Jensen, and R. Roll, "The Adjustment of Stock Prices to New Information," *International Economic Review* 10 (1969), 1–21.

19. These results conflict with later studies in behavioral finance that found markets did not properly discount surprising earnings announcements. My interpretation is that Fama's studies did not consider the degree to which earnings announcements differed from prior Street expectations. Later studies done by V. Bernard showed that stock prices do experience trends after earnings announcements, if the degree of surprise in the announcement is large. V. Bernard, "Stock Price Reactions to Earnings Announcements," *Advances in Behavioral Finance*, R. Thaler (Ed.) (New York: Russell Sage Foundation, 1992; V. Bernard and J.K. Thomas, "Post-Earnings Announcement Drift: Delayed Price Response or Risk Premium?," *Journal of Accounting Research, Supplement* 27 (1989), 1–36; V. Bernard and J.K. Thomas, "Evidence That Stock Prices Do Not Fully Reflect the Implications of Current Earnings for Future Earnings," *Journal of Accounting and Economics* 13 (1990), 305–341.

20. A noninformative event is one that carries no implications for the future cash flows of the asset or the future returns of the security.

21. The capital asset pricing model was proposed by William F. Sharpe in "Capital Asset Prices: A Theory of Market Equilibrium under Conditions of Risk," *Journal of Finance* 19 (1964), 425–442.

22. APT was first proposed by S. Ross, "The Arbitrage Theory of Capital Asset Pricing," *Journal of Economic Theory* (December 1976). APT says a linear model relates a stock's returns to a number of factors, and this relationship is the result of arbitrageurs hunting for riskless, zero-investment opportunities. APT specifies factors, including the rate of inflation, the spread between low and high quality bonds, the slope of the yield curve, and so on.

23. In other words, the current price change is correlated with the prior change (i.e., a lag interval of 1), then with the change prior to that (lag interval = 2), and so forth. A correlation coefficient is computed for each of these lags. Typically, in a random data series, the correlations drop off very quickly as a function of the lag interval. However, if the time series of price changes is non-random in a linear fashion, some of the autocorrelation coefficients will differ significantly from the pattern of autocorrelations of a random sequence.

24. E. Fama, "The Behavior of Stock Market Prices," *Journal of Business* 38 (1965), 34–106.

25. E.E. Peters, *Chaos and Order in the Capital Markets: A New View of Cycles, Prices and Market Volatility* (New York: John Wiley & Sons, 1991); E.E. Peters, *Fractal Market Analysis: Applying Chaos Theory to Investment and Economics* (New York: John Wiley & Sons, 1994).

26. A.W. Lo and A.C. MacKinlay, *A Non-Random Walk Down Wall Street* (Princeton, NJ: Princeton University Press, 1999).

27. S.J. Grossman and J.E. Stiglitz, "On the Impossibility of Informationally Efficient Markets," *American Economic Review* 70, no 3 (1980), 393–408.

28. Shleifer, *Inefficient Markets*, 2.

29. V. Singal, *Beyond the Random Walk: A Guide to Stock Market Anomalies and Low Risk Investing* (New York: Oxford University Press, 2004), 5.

30. F. Black, "Noise," *Journal of Finance* 41 (1986), 529–543.

31. Shleifer, *Inefficient Markets*, 10.

32. D. Kahneman and A. Tversky, "Prospect Theory: An Analysis of Decision Making under Risk," *Econometrica* 47 (1979), 263–291.

33. R. Shiller, "Stock Prices and Social Dynamics," *Brookings Papers on Economic Activity* 2, (1984), 457–498.

34. Cited by Shleifer, *Inefficient Markets*; J.B. De Long, A. Shleifer, L. Summers, and R. Waldmann, "Noise Trader Risk in Financial Markets," *Journal of Political Economy* 98 (1990), 703–738.

35. R. Merton and P. Samuelson, "Fallacy of the Log-Normal Approximation to Optimal Portfolio Decision-Making over Many Periods," *Journal of Financial Economics* 1 (1974), 67–94.

36. The expectation of a game is (probability of a win × amount won) − (probability of a loss × amount lost). Thus, per dollar bet, the expectation is +50 cents. In investment-strategy terms, this would be called a profit factor of 2.0. Very few investment strategies have such a favorable edge.

37. R. Shiller, "Do Stock Prices Move Too Much to Be Justified by Subsequent Changes in Dividends?," *American Economic Review* 71 (1981), 421–436.

38. Cited by Shleifer, *Inefficient Markets*, 20; D. Cutler, J. Poterba, and L. Summers, "Speculative Dynamics," *Review of Economic Studies* 58 (1991), 529–546.

39. Cited by Shleifer, *Inefficient Markets*; R. Roll, "Orange Juice and Weather," *American Economic Review* 74 (1984), 861–880; R. Roll, "R-squared," *Journal of Finance* 43, (1988), 541–566.

40. Singal, *Beyond the Random Walk*, ix.

41. *Relative performance* refers to the stock's performance relative to the performance of the average stock, or a benchmark. Relative performance is also known as excess return.

42. Stocks can also be ranked on the basis of a prediction model that employs a multitude of indicators, typically referred to as factors.

43. When multiperiod horizons are used, the number of independent observations are also reduced, so a one-month horizon, based on monthly data, is often used.

44. The strong form of EMH is broader yet in claiming that not even inside information is useful in generating superior returns, but this version is not testable.

45. R. Banz, "The Relation between Market Return and Market Value for Common Stocks," *Journal of Financial Economics* 9 (1981), 3–18.

46. E. Fama and K. French, "The Cross-Section of Expected Stock Returns," *Journal of Finance* 47 (1992), 427–465.

47. Cited by Shiller, *Irrational Exuberance*; S. Basu, "The Investment Performance of Common Stocks Relative to Their Price-Earnings Ratios: A Test of the Efficient Markets," *Journal of Finance* 32, no. 3 (1977), 663–682.

48. Cited by Shiller, Irrational Exuberance; E. Fama and K. French, "The Cross Section of Expected Stock Returns," Journal of Finance 47 (1992), 427–466.

49. Singal, *Beyond the Random Walk*.

50. Although the weak form of EMH typically only talks about past prices and past price changes, I believe advocates of this position would also claim that any other data relied upon by TA would be useless for predicting future returns.

51. N. Jegadeesh, and S. Titman, "Returns to Buying Winners and Selling Losers: Implications for Market Efficiency," *Journal of Finance* 48 (1993), 65–91.

52. E. Fama, "Efficient Capital Markets: II," *Journal of Finance* 46 (1991), 1575–1617.

53. W. De Bondt and R. H. Thaler, "Does the Stock Market Overreact?," *Journal of Finance* 40, no. 3 (1985), 793–805.

54. In this case, risk is as defined by CAPM, volatility relative to the market.

55. T.J. George and C.-Y. Hwang, "The 52-Week High and Momentum Investing," *Journal of Finance* 59, no. 5 (October 2004), 2145.

56. C.M.C. Lee and B. Swaminathan, "Price Momentum and Trading Volume," *Journal of Finance* 55, no. 5 (October 2000), 2017–2067; S. E. Stickel and R.E. Verecchia, "Evidence That Trading Volume Sustains Stock Price Changes," *Financial Analysts Journal* 50, no. 6 (November–December 1994), 57–67. It should be noted that when the forward-looking horizon is 3 to 12 months, high volume increases the price momentum's effect. However, when the return is looked at 3 years out, high-momentum stocks with low volume are more persistent on the upside, whereas negative-momentum stocks with high volume persist on the downside.

57. E. Fama and K. French, "1996 Common Risk Factors in the Returns on Bonds and Stocks," *Journal of Financial Economics* 33 (1993), 3–56; E. Fama and K. French, "Multifactor Explanations of Asset Pricing Anomalies," *Journal of Finance* 51 (1996), 55–84.

58. W. Sharpe, "Capital Asset Prices: A Theory of Market Equilibrium under Conditions of Risk," *Journal of Finance* 19 (1964), 435–442; also see J. Lintner, "The Valuation of Risk Assets and the Selection of Risky Investments in Stock Portfolios and Capital Budgets," *Review of Economics and Statistics* 47 (1965), 13–37.

59. Shleifer, *Inefficient Markets*, 19.

60. J. Lakonishok, A. Shleifer, and R. Vishny, "Contrarian Investment, Extrapolation, and Risk," *Journal of Finance* 49 (1994), 1541–1578.

61. Shleifer, *Inefficient Markets*, 24.

62. Ibid.

63. Ibid.

64. W. Edwards, "Conservatism in Human Information Processing," in *Formal Representation of Human Judgment*, B. Kleinmutz (Ed.) (New York: John Wiley & Sons, 1968), 17–52.

65. D.G. Myers, *Intuition, Its Powers and Perils* (New Haven: Yale University Press, 2004), 157.

66. A. Tversky and D. Kahneman, *Judgment under Uncertainty Heuristics and Biases, in Judgment under Uncertainty: Heuristics and Biases*, D. Kahneman, P. Slovic, and A. Tversky (Eds.) (New York: Cambridge University Press, 1982), 14.

67. George and Hwang, "52-Week High."

68. Shiller, *Irrational Exuberance*, 138.

69. Ibid., 139.

70. E. Shafir, I. Simonson, and A. Tversky, "Reason–Based Choice," *Cognition* 49 (1993), 11–36.

71. Systematic process can exhibit real trends, which are streaks that are longer in duration than those found in random walks, or they can exhibit true meanreversion behavior, which means that streaks will be shorter in duration (i.e., more frequent flip-flops between positive and negative outcomes) than is true for random walks. In both truly trended processes and true mean-reverting process, prior observations contain useful predictive information. In true random- walk processes, prior observations contain no predictive information.

72. Shiller, *Irrational Exuberance*, 148–169.

73. A. Asch, *Social Psychology* (Englewood Cliffs, NJ: Prentice-Hall, 1952), 450–501.

74. M. Deutsch and H.B. Gerard, "A Study of Normative and Informational Social Influence upon Individual Judgment," *Journal of Abnormal and Social Psychology* 51 (1955), 629–636.

75. Shiller, *Irrational Exuberance*, 148–169.

76. R.J. Shiller cites D.D. Bikhchandani, D. Hirshleifer, and I. Welch, "A Theory of Fashion, Social Custom and Cultural Change," *Journal of Political Economy* 81 (1992), 637–654; A.V. Nanerjee, "A Simple Model of Herd Behavior," *Quarterly Journal of Economics* 107, no. 3 (1993), 797–817.

77. Shiller, *Irrational Exuberance*, 152.

78. Ibid., 164.

79. Ibid., 165.

80. Ibid., 166.

81. See Carl Anderson, "Notes on Feedback and Self-Organization," at www.duke.edu/~carl/pattern/characteristic_student_notes.htm.

82. Shiller, *Irrational Exuberance*, 67.

83. N. Barberis, A. Shleifer, and R. Vishny, "A Model of Investor Sentiment," *Journal of Financial Economics* 49 (1998), 307–343.

84. This assumption is consistent with studies showing that people have difficulty distinguishing random series from series that display systematic behavior such as mean-reversion or trending behavior. This failure accounts for sports fans' misperception of the hot hand and chartists' inability to distinguish real from random charts.

85. Shiller, *Irrational Exuberance*, 144.

86. R.J. Shiller cites Barberis, Shleifer, and Vishny, "Model of Investor Sentiment," and N. Barberis, M. Huang, and T. Santos, "Prospect Theory and Asset Prices," *Quarterly Journal of Economics* 116, no. 1 (February 2001), 1–53; K. Daniel, D. Hirshleifer, and A. Subrahmanyam, "Investor Psychology and Security Market Over and Underreaction," *Journal of Finance* 53, no. 6 (1998), 1839–1886; H. Hong and J. Stein, "A Unified Theory of Underreaction, Momentum Trading, and Overreaction in Asset Markets," *Journal of Finance* 54, no. 6 (December 1999), 2143–2184.

87. Daniel, Hirshleifer, and Subrahmanyam, "Investor Psychology"; and K. Daniel, D. Hirshleifer, and A. Subrahmanyam, "Overconfidence, Arbitrage and Equilibrium Asset Pricing," *Journal of Finance* 56 (2001), 921–965.

88. N. Barberis, "A Survey of Behavioral Finance," in *Handbook of the Economics of Finance*, Volume 1B, G.M. Constantinides, M. Harris, and R. Stulz (Eds.) (New York: Elsevier Science, B.V., 2003).

89. N. Chopra and R. Lakonishok, "Measuring Abnormal Performance: Do Stocks Overreact?," *Journal of Financial Economics* 31 (1992), 235–268; R. La Porta, R. Lakonishok, A. Shleifer, and R. Vishny, "Good News for Value Stocks: Further Evidence on Market Efficiency," *Journal of Finance* 49 (1997), 1541–1578.

90. J.B. De Long, A. Shleifer, L. Summers, and R. Waldmann, "Positive Feedback Investment Strategies and Destabilizing Rational Speculation," *Journal of Finance* 45, no. 2 (1990), 379–395; N. Barberis and A. Shleifer, "Style Investing," *Journal of Financial Economics* 68 (2003), 161–199.

91. Hong and Stein, "Unified Theory."

92. S.F. LeRoy, "Risk Aversion and the Martingale Property of Stock Returns," *International Economic Review* 14 (1973), 436–446; R.E. Lucas, "Asset Prices in an Exchange Economy," *Econometrica* 46 (1978), 1429–1446.

93. A.W. Lo and A.C. MacKinlay, *A Non-Random Walk Down Wall Street* (Princeton, NJ: Princeton University Press, 1999), 5.

94. Ibid.

95. S. Grossman, "On the Efficiency of Competitive Stock Markets Where Traders Have Diverse Information," *Journal of Finance* 31 (1976), 573–585; S. Grossman and J. Stiglitz, "On the Impossibility of Informationally Efficient Markets," *American Economic Review* 70 (1980), 393–408.

96. L. Jaeger, *Managing Risk in Alternative Investment Strategies: Successful Investing in Hedge Funds and Managed Futures* (London: Financial Times–Prentice Hall, 2002), 27.

97. Gains from a true inefficiency are not a free lunch, because it is costly to identify them, but they need not entail the risk of additional volatility in returns. Thus true inefficiencies can generate investment performance with a high relative Sharpe ratio.

98. H.D. Platt, *Counterintuitive Investing: Profiting from Bad News on Wall Street* (Mason, OH: Thomson Higher Education, 2005).

99. Equity and bond markets provide a quick way for owners of equities to sell their position to other investors. The liquidity of stocks and bonds thus makes them attractive to the initial investors, thereby making it easier for companies to raise debt and equity financing.

100. Grains (corn, soybeans, soybean meal, soybean oil, and wheat); financials (5-year T-notes, 10-year T-notes, long-term treasury bonds); currencies (Australian, British, Canadian, German, Swiss, and Japanese); energy (heating oil, natural gas, crude oil, and unleaded gas); cattle; metals (gold, copper, and silver); and soft/tropical (coffee, cotton, and sugar).

101. G.R. Jensen, R.R. Johnson, and J.M. Mercer, "Tactical Asset Allocation and Commodity Futures," *Journal of Portfolio Management* 28, no. 4 (Summer 2002).

102. An asset-class benchmark measures the returns earned and risks incurred by investing in a specific asset class, with no management skill.

103. Lars Kestner, *Quantitative Trading Strategies: Harnessing the Power of Quantitative Techniques to Create a Winning Trading Program* (New York: McGraw-Hill, 2003), 129–180.

104. The eight market sectors tested were foreign exchange, interest rates, stock index, metals, energy, grains, meats, and softs.

105. The nine industry sectors were energy, basic materials, consumer discretionary, consumer staples, health care, financials and information technology, telecom. The three stock indexes were S&P 500, NASDAQ 100, and Russell 2000.

106. The five trend-following systems were channel breakout, dual moving-average crossover, two version of momentum, and MACD versus its signal line. For more description see Kestner's *Quantitative Trading Strategies*.

107. M. Cooper, "Filter Rules Based on Price and Volume in Individual Security Overreaction," *Review of Financial Studies* 12, no. 4 (Special 1999), 901–935.

CHAPTER 31

Case Study of Rule Data Mining for the S&P 500

From David Aronson, *Evidence-Based Technical Analysis: Applying the Scientific Method and Statistical Inference to Trading Signals* (Hoboken, New Jersey: John Wiley & Sons, 2006), Chapter 8.

Learning Objective Statement

- Explain the usefulness of the following indicators as described in this chapter: channel breakout operator, moving average operator, channel-normalization operator

This chapter describes a case study in rule data mining. The study evaluates the statistical significance of 6,402 individual TA rules back tested on the S&P 500 Index over the period from November 1, 1980 through July 1, 2005.

■ Data Mining Bias and Rule Evaluation

The primary purpose of the case study is to illustrate the application of statistical methods that take into account the effects of data-mining bias. To recap, data mining is a process in which the profitability of many rules is compared so that one or more superior rules can be selected. This selection process causes an upward bias in the performance of the selected rule(s). In other words, the observed performance of the best rule(s) in the back test overstates its (their) expected performance in the future. This bias complicates the evaluation of statistical significance and may lead a data miner to select a rule with no predictive power (i.e., its past performance was pure luck). This is the fool's gold of the objective technician.

This problem can be minimized by using specialized statistical-inference tests. The case study illustrates the application of two such methods: an enhanced version of White's

Note: This chapter is intended to be a demonstration of proper research and evaluation technique with regards to using technical analysis in system development.

reality check and Masters's Monte-Carlo permutation method. Both take advantage of a recent improvement,[1] which reduces the probability that a good rule will be overlooked (Type II error). That is to say, the improvement increases the power of the tests.

A secondary purpose of the case study was the possible discovery of one or more rules that generate statistically significant profits. However, when the case study's rules were proposed, it was unknown if any would be found to be statistically significant.

■ Avoidance of Data Snooping Bias

In addition to data mining bias, rule studies can also suffer from an even more serious problem, the *data-snooping bias*. *Data snooping* refers to using the results of prior rule studies reported by other researchers. Because these studies typically do not disclose the amount of data mining that led to the discovery of whatever it was that was discovered, there is no way to take its effects into account and hence no way to properly evaluate the statistical significance of the results. Depending on which method is being used—White's Reality Check or the Monte Carlo permutation method—information about each rule tested must be available to construct the appropriate sampling distribution.

For example, suppose the case study in this book had included a rule developed by Dr. Martin Zweig known as the *double 9:1 upside/downside volume* rule. This rule signals long positions when the daily ratio of upside to downside volume on the NYSE exceeds a threshold value of 9 on two instances within a three-month time window. Note, this rule has three free parameters: the threshold value on the ratio (9), the number of instances on which the ratio exceeds the threshold (2), and the maximum time separation between the threshold violations (3 months). According to tests of this rule conducted by students in my technical analysis class, the signal does have predictive power over the following 3, 6, 9, and 12 months. In other words, the rule is statistically significant, but only under the assumption that Zweig did not engage in data mining to discover the parameter values he recommends: 9, 2, and 3. Zweig has not reported if he tested other versions of the rule using different parameter combinations or, if he did, how many combinations were tried to find the specific set that defines his rule. If Zweig's rule were to be included in the case study and it was selected as the best rule, it would be impossible to take into account the true amount of data mining that led to its discovery.

In an effort to avoid data-snooping bias, the case study did not explicitly include any rules discussed by other researchers. Even though it is possible, perhaps even likely, that some of the study's rules were similar to those tested in prior rule studies, these similarities were by accident, not by design. This precaution mitigated the data-snooping bias but could not eliminate it entirely because, in proposing the 6,402 rules tested, I could not help but be affected by rule studies I have previously read.

■ Analyzed Data Series

Although all rules were tested for their profitability on the S&P 500 Index, the vast majority of rules utilized data series other than the S&P 500 to generate buy-and-sell signals. These other data series included: other market indices (e.g., transportation stocks), market breadth (e.g., upside and downside volume), indicators that combine price and volume (e.g., on-balance volume), prices of debt instruments (e.g., BAA bonds), and interest-rate spreads (duration spread between 10-year treasury notes and 90-day treasury bills). This approach is in the spirit of intermarket analysis as discussed by Murphy.[2] All series and rules are detailed below.

■ Technical Analysis Themes

The 6,402 rules tested were derived from three broad themes of TA: (1) trends, (2) extremes and transitions, and (3) divergences. Trend rules generate long and short market positions based on the current trend of the data series analyzed by the rule. Extreme and transition rules generate long and short positions when the analyzed series reaches an extreme high or low value or as it makes a transition between extreme values. Divergence rules generate signals when the S&P 500 Index trends in one direction while a companion data series trends in the other. The specific data transformations and signal logic for each rule are described later in this chapter.

The rules employ several common analysis methods including moving averages, channel breakouts, and stochastics, which I refer to as channel normalization.

■ Performance Statistic: Average Return

The performance statistic used to evaluate each rule was its average return over the period (1980 to 2005) when back tested on detrended S&P 500 data. Detrending involves subtracting the S&P 500's average daily price change over the back-test period from each day's actual price change. This results in a new data series for which the average daily change is equal to zero.

Detrending eliminates any benefit or detriment that would accrue to a rule's performance as a result of either a long or short position bias. A binary rule can be position biased if one of its conditions (long or short) is restrictive relative to the other condition (long or short). For example, if the long-position condition is more difficult to satisfy than the short-position condition, the rule will have a short-position bias and tend to spend a majority of its time in short positions. If such a rule were to be applied to market data with a positive trend (average daily price change > 0), its average return would be penalized. This reduction in the rule's performance would have nothing to do with its predictive power and thus cloud its evaluation.

■ No Complex Rules Were Evaluated

To keep the scope of the case study manageable, it was restricted to tests of individual rules. Complex rules, which are derived by combining two or more individual rules with mathematical and/or logical operators, were not considered. The combining method can be as simple an unweighted average or as complex as an arbitrarily nonlinear function derived with sophisticated data-modeling software.

Limiting the case study to individual rules was detrimental for two reasons. First, few practitioners rely on a single rule to make decisions. Second, complex rules exploit informational synergies between individual rules. It is not surprising, therefore, that complex rules have demonstrated higher levels of performance. At least one study[3] has shown that complex rules can produce good performance, even when the simple rules combined to form the complex rule are individually unprofitable. Combining rules intuitively is extremely difficult, but there are now effective automated methods[4] for synthesizing complex rules.

■ The Case Study Defined in Statistical Terms

The following section defines the case study in terms of the key elements of a statistical study: the population at issue, the parameter of interest, sample data used, the statistic of interest, the null and alternative hypotheses considered, and the designated significance level.

The Population

The population at issue is the set of daily returns that would be earned by a rule if its signals were to be applied to the S&P 500 over all possible realizations of the *immediate practical future*.[5] This is an abstract population, in the sense that its observations have not yet occurred and it is infinite in size.

Population Parameter

The population parameter is the rule's expected average annualized return in the immediate practical future.

The Sample

The sample consists of the daily returns earned by a rule applied to detrended S&P 500 Index prices over the back-test period from November 1, 1980 until July 1, 2005.

Sample Statistic (Test Statistic)

The sample statistic is the average annualized return earned by a rule when applied to the detrended S&P 500 price data from November 1, 1980 until July 1, 2005.

The Null Hypothesis (H_0)

The null hypothesis states that all 6,402 rules tested are without predictive power. This implies that any observed profits in a back test were due to chance (sampling variability).

In reality, there are two version of the null hypothesis in the case study. This stems from the fact that two different methods were used to assess statistical significance: White's reality check and Masters's Monte Carlo permutation method. Although both methods assert that all rules considered were devoid of predictive power, they implement this assumption differently. The null hypothesis tested by White's reality check is that all rules tested have expected returns equal to zero (or less). The null tested by Masters's Monte Carlo permutation is that all rules generated their long and short positions in a random fashion. In other words, long and short were randomly permuted with the market's one-day-forward price change.

The Alternative Hypothesis

This study's alternative hypothesis asserts that a rule's back-tested profitability stems from genuine predictive power. Again, the two methods assert this in slightly different ways. In the case of White's reality check, the alternative hypothesis says that there is at least one rule within the tested universe that has an expected return greater than zero. It should be noted that White's reality check does not assert that the rule with the highest observed performance is necessarily that best rule (i.e., the rule with the highest expected return). However, under fairly reasonable conditions, they are one and the same.[6] The alternative hypothesis declared by Masters's method is that a rule's back-tested profitability is the result of an informative pairing of its long and short positions with the market's one-day-forward price change. In other words, the rule has predictive power.

The Statistical Significance Level

A 5 percent level of significance was chosen as a threshold for rejection of the null hypothesis. This means there was a 0.05 probability of rejecting the H_0 hypothesis when the H_0 was, in fact, true.

Practical Significance

The practical significance of a result is different from its statistical significance. The latter is the probability that a rule that has no predictive power (i.e., H_0 is true) would earn a return as high as or higher than the return produced by the rule in a back test by luck. In contrast, practical significance relates to the economic value of the observed rule return. When sample sizes are large, as they are in the case study (i.e., over 6,000 days), the H_0 can be rejected even if a rule's return is positive by a very minor amount. In other words, a rule can be statistically significant even though its practical value is negligible. Practical significance depends upon a trader's objectives. One trader may be satisfied with a rule for which expected return is 5 percent whereas another may reject any rule for which expected return is less than 20 percent.

■ Rules: Transforming Data Series into Market Positions

A rule is an input/output process. That is to say, it transforms input(s), consisting of one or more time series, into an output, a new time series consisting of +1's and −1's that indicate long and short positions in the market being traded (i.e., S&P 500). This transformation is defined by the one or more mathematical,[7] logical,[8] or time series[9] operators that are applied to the input time series. In other words, a rule is defined by a set of operations. See Figure 31.1.

Some rules utilize inputs that are raw time series. That is to say, the one or more time series used as inputs to the rule are not transformed in any way prior to the rule's position logic being applied, for example the S&P 500 closing price. This is illustrated in Figure 31.2.

Other rules utilize input series that have been derived from one or more raw market series by applying various transformations to the market data. These preprocessed inputs are referred to as constructed data series or *indicators*. An example of an indicator is the *negative volume index*. It is derived from transformations of two raw data series; S&P 500 closing price and total NYSE daily volume. This is illustrated in Figure 31.3. The transformations used in the creation of the negative volume index and other indicators used in the case study are described in the following section.

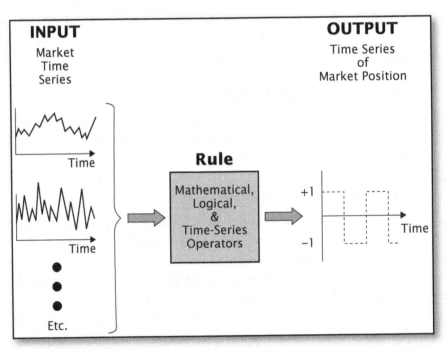

FIGURE 31.1 TA Rule Transforms Input into Output.

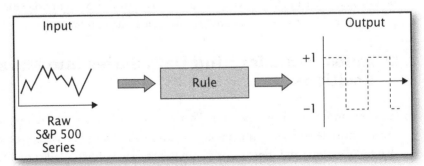

FIGURE 31.2 Raw Market Time Series as Rule Input.

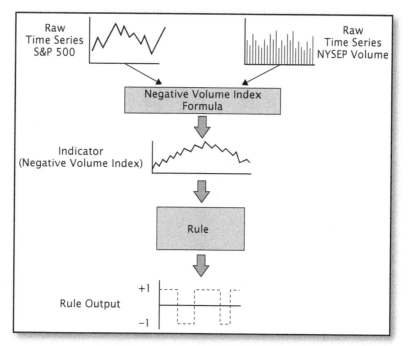

FIGURE 31.3 Transformed Market Time Series as Rule Input.

▆ Time-Series Operators

This section describes the time-series operators used in the case study to transform raw data series into indicators. Time-series operators are mathematical functions that transform a time series into a new time series. The case study utilized several common time-series operators: channel breakout, moving average, and channel normalization. The channel breakout operator is used to identify trends in a time series for rules that are based on trends. The moving-average operator, which can also identify trends, is used in the case study for smoothing. The channel-normalization operator, or stochastics, is used to eliminate the trend of a time series (i.e., detrending).

Channel Breakout Operator (CBO)

"The purpose of all trend identification methods is to see past the underlying noise in a time series, those erratic moves that seem to be meaningless, and find the current direction of the series."[10] One such method is the *n*-period channel-breakout operator.[11] Here, *n* refers to the number of time periods (days, weeks, and such) into the past that are examined to define the upper and lower channel boundaries that enclose the time series. The lower boundary is defined by the minimum value of the time series over the past *n*-periods, not including the current period. The upper boundary is defined by the time series' maximum value over the past *n*-periods, not including the current period. Despite its extreme simplicity, the channel-breakout operator has proven to be as effective as more complex trend-following methods.[12]

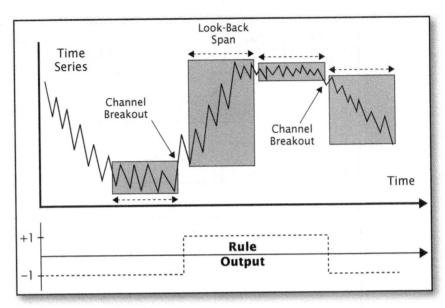

FIGURE 31.4 Channel-Breakout Operator.

As conventionally interpreted, the channel breakout operator signals long positions if the analyzed series exceeds its maximum value established over the past n-periods. Conversely, short positions are signaled when the time series falls below its n-period minimum. This is illustrated in Figure 31.4. In practice, the channel is redrawn as each new data point becomes available, but in Figure 31.4 only several channels are shown to illustrate its function. Although the channel has a constant look-back span with respect to the time axis, its vertical width with respect to the axis that represents the value of the time series adjusts dynamically to the range of the series over the past n-periods. This feature may explain the effectiveness of the method. This is to say, the channel breakout's dynamic range may reduce the likelihood of false signals caused by an increase in the series' volatility rather than an actual change in its trend.

The n-period breakout operator has a single free parameter, its look-back span, the number of time periods into the past used to establish the channel's boundaries. In general, the larger the look-back span, the wider the channel, and hence, the less sensitive the indicator. Thus, larger values of n are used to identify larger trends. The case study tested 11 different look-back spans for which lengths were separated by a factor of approximately 1.5. The specific spans used were: 3, 5, 8, 12, 18, 27, 41, 61, 91, 137, and 205 days.

Moving-Average Operator (MA)

The moving average is one of the most widely used times-series operators in TA. It clarifies trends by filtering out high frequency (short-period) fluctuations while passing through low frequency (long-period) components. Thus, the moving-average operator is said to function as a low-pass filter. This is illustrated

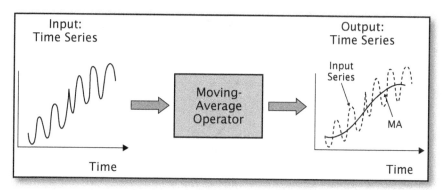

FIGURE 31.5   Moving-Average Operator: Low-Pass Filter.

in Figure 31.5, where the moving average has been centered[13] (lagged by 0.5 × period −1). Note that the output of the moving-average operator is essentially the trend of the original time series with the high frequency oscillations about the trend removed.

The smoothing effect is accomplished by averaging the values of the time series within a moving data window called the *look-back span*. This eliminates or reduces the magnitude of fluctuations with durations that are equal to or less than the duration of the look-back span. Thus, a 10-day moving average will reduce the amplitude of fluctuations for which peak-to-peak or trough-to-trough duration is less than 10 days, and it will completely eliminate a fluctuation with a duration that is exactly equal to 10 days.

The benefit of smoothing comes at a cost—lag. In other words, fluctuations in the raw price that manifest in the smoothed version experience some delay. Thus, a trough in the raw price does not produce a trough in the moving average until some later date. The amount of lag depends upon the length of the look-back span. A longer look-back span produces more smoothing while producing more lag.

The lag induced by a *simple moving average*, which gives equal weight to all elements in the window, is equal to one-half of the look-back span minus one. Thus, the output of an 11-day simple moving average has a lag of $(11 − 1)/2$ or 5 days. This means that trend reversals in the input time series, which are of sufficient duration to manifest in the moving average, will not show up until 5 days later.

There are many types of moving averages, from the simple moving average that gives equal weight to each element in the data window, to sophisticated smoothing methods that use complex data-weighting functions. The benefit conferred by a complex weighting is improved filter performance—less lag for a given degree of smoothing. The field of digital signal processing is concerned with, among other things, the design of weighting functions that maximize filter performance. Digital filters that are relevant to TA are discussed in two books by Ehlers.[14]

The calculation for a simple moving average is given by the following formula.[15]

Moving Average Operator

$$MA_t = \frac{P_t + P_{t-1} + P_{t-2} \ldots + P_{t-n+1}}{n}$$

$$= \frac{\sum_{i=1}^{n} P_{t-i+1}}{n}$$

Where:
P_t = Price at time t
MA_t = Moving average at time t
n = Number of days used to compute moving average

The lag of a simple moving average can be reduced while maintaining the same degree of smoothing by using a linearly weighted moving average. As pointed out by Ehlers[16] the lag of a linearly weighted moving average with a look-back span of n days is $(n-1)/3$ compared with $(n-1)/2$ for a simple moving average. Thus, a linearly weighted moving average with a span of 10 days will have a lag of 3 days whereas a simple moving average with the same span will have a lag of 4.5 days. The linear-weighting scheme applies a weight of n to the most recent data point, where n is the number of days in the moving average look-back span, and then the weight is decreased by one for each prior day. The sum of the weights becomes the divisor. This is illustrated in the following equation:

Linear Weighted Moving Average

$$WMA_t = \frac{\overbrace{(n) \times P_t + (n-1) \times P_{t-1} + \ldots + (n-(t-n+1)) \times P_{t-n+1}}^{\text{Weights}}}{\underbrace{n + n-1 + \ldots + n-(t-n-1)}_{\text{Sum of Weights}}}$$

Where:
P_t = Price at time t
WMA_t = Weighted moving average at time t
n = Number of days used to compute moving average

The case study used a four-day linearly weighted moving average to smooth indicators used in rules that signal when the indicator crosses above or below a critical threshold. Smoothing mitigates the problem of excessive signals that an unsmoothed version of the indicator wiggling back and forth across the threshold would produce. The calculation of a four-day linearly weighted moving average is illustrated in the following equation:

Four Day Linear Weighted Moving Average

$$
WMA_t = \frac{\overbrace{(4) \times P_{t0} + (3) \times P_{t-1} + (2) \times P_{t-2} + (1) \times P_{t-3}}^{\text{Weights}}}{\underbrace{10}_{\text{Sum of Weights}}}
$$

Where:
P_t = Price at time t
WMA_t = Weighted moving average at time t
n = Number of days used to compute moving average

Channel-Normalization Operator (Stochastics): CN

The channel-normalization operator (CN) removes the trend in a time series, thus clarifying short-term fluctuations around the trend. Channel normalization detrends the time series by measuring its current position within a moving channel. The channel is defined by the maximum and minimum values of the time series over a specified look-back span. In this way it is similar to the channel breakout operator discussed earlier.

The channel normalized version of a time series is scaled to the range 0 to 100. When the raw time series is at its maximum value within the look-back span, CN assumes the value of 100. When the series is at the minimum value within the look-back span the CN is equal to zero. A value of 50 indicates the series is currently midway between its maximum and minimum values.

The calculation of CN is illustrated in the following equation:

Channel Normalization Operator

$$
CN_t = \left(\frac{S_t - S_{min-n}}{S_{max-n} - S_{min-n}} \right) 100
$$

Where:

CN_t = n day channel normalized value on day t
S_t = Value of time series at time t
S_{min-n} = Minimum value of time series, last n days
S_{max-n} = Maximum value of time series, last n days
n = Channel look-back span in days

An example of the calculation is illustrated in Figure 31.6.

In terms of its filtering properties, the CN operator functions as a high-pass filter. In contrast to the moving average, a low-pass filter, CN expresses the short-period (high-frequency) oscillations in its output while filtering out the long-period fluctuations or trend. This is illustrated in Figure 31.7. Note that the input series has a distinct upward trend, but the output series has no trend.

The CN operator has been known in TA at least as far back as 1965 when Heiby[17] used it to formulate divergence rules. He measured divergences by comparing the channel normalized value of the S&P 500 with the channel normalized value of a market breadth indicator. According to Heiby, a divergence occurred when one series was in the upper quartile of its 50-day range (CN > 74) while the other series was in the lower quartile of its range (CN <26). Sometime in the early 1970s, a virtually identical

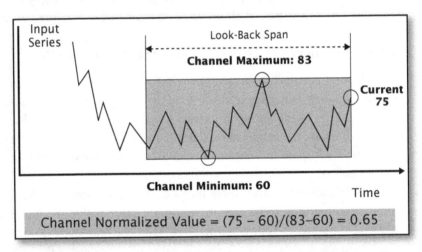

FIGURE 31.6 Channel Normalization.

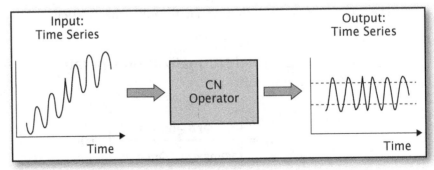

FIGURE 31.7 Channel Normalization Operator: A High-Pass Filter.

operator was described by George Lane,[18] who dubbed it *stochastic*. Unfortunately, the name is a misnomer. In reality, *stochastic* is a mathematical term that refers to the evolution of a random variable through time. There is nothing random about the CN operator, which is a completely deterministic data transformation. This text uses the term channel normalization (CN) rather than Lane's term, because it accurately describes what the operator does. Most TA writings continue use the term *stochastics*. The case study utilizes the CN operator for two types of rules: (1) extremes and transitions and (2) divergences. They are discussed in following sections.

Indicator Scripting

As discussed earlier, the time series that are used as inputs to the rules may either be in raw form, just as they comes from the market, or in the form of indicators—times series that have been created by applying one or more mathematical, logical, or time-series operators to one or more raw time series. The specification of an indicator may require the application of several operators. For example, the raw time series might first be smoothed with a moving average and then channel normalization is applied to the smoothed version. When the creation of an indicator involves multiple steps, it is convenient to express it in terms of an *indicator scripting language* (ISL). An ISL expression succinctly depicts the set of transformations used to create the indicator from raw time series.

My first exposure to an ISL was *Gener*, which was developed in 1983 for Raden Research Group by friend and colleague Professor John Wolberg. Today, ISLs are common. All rule back-testing platforms,[19] such as TradeStation, Wealth-Lab, Neuro-Shell, Financial Data Calculator, and so forth have an ISL. Though each ISL has features unique to it, they share similar syntaxes. The most basic ISL statement is a time-series operator followed by a set of parentheses that contain the arguments of the operator. The arguments are the items that must be defined for the operator to do its thing. Operators differ in terms of the number of arguments required. For example, the moving-average operator requires two arguments: a data series to which the operator will be applied and the number of periods in the look-back span. Thus a moving-average indicator would be specified by a statement such as this:

Moving Average Indicator = MA (input series, N)

Where:
MA is the moving average operator
N is the number of days in the moving average.

The general form of an indicator expression in scripting language is:

Indicator = Operator (Argument$_1$, Argument$_2$, . . . , Argument$_i$)

Where:
i is the number of arguments required by the operator.

```
┌─────────────────────────────────────────────────────┐
│         Channel-Breakout Operator (CBO)               │
│                                                       │
│            Number of Arguments = 2:                   │
│                                                       │
│         Indicator = CBO (Time Series, n)              │
│─────────────────────────────────────────────────────│
│                                                       │
│  Moving-Average Operator (MA) or Linear Weighted MA (LMA) │
│                                                       │
│            Number of Arguments = 2:                   │
│                                                       │
│       Indicator = MA or LMA (Time Series, n)          │
│─────────────────────────────────────────────────────│
│                                                       │
│        Channel-Normalization Operator (CN)            │
│                                                       │
│            Number of Arguments = 2:                   │
│                                                       │
│          Indicator = CN (Time Series, n)              │
└─────────────────────────────────────────────────────┘
```

FIGURE 31.8 Indicator Scripting Language for Three TA Operators.

Figure 31.8 shows the ISL syntax for the operators defined thus far: channel breakout, moving average, and channel normalization.

A key benefit of ISL is the ability to define complex indicators by nesting operators. In nesting, the output of one operator becomes an argument for a second operator and so on. For example, if one wanted to define an indicator that is the 60-day channel normalization of another time series that is a 10-day moving average of the Dow Jones Transportation Index, the expression for the indicator in ISL would look something like this:

$$\text{Indicator} = \text{CN } [\text{MA(DJTA, 10), 60}]$$

■ Input Series to Rules: Raw Time Series and Indicators

This section describes the 24 raw time series used in the case study as well as the 39 time series that were ultimately used as rule inputs. Ten of the 39 inputs were in the form of raw unprocessed time series: S&P 500 closing price, Dow Jones Transportations Index closing price, NASDAQ Composite Index closing price, and so forth. The additional rule 29 inputs were indicators derived from one or more raw time series.

Raw Time Series

The 24 raw time series used in the case study came from two sources: Ultra Financial Systems[20] and Market Timing Reports.[21] They are shown in Table 31.1.

TABLE 31.1   Raw Time Series

Number	Raw Data Series	Abbreviation	Source
1	S&P 500 Daily Close	SPX	Ultra 8
2	S&P 500 Open	SPO	Ultra 8
3	DJIA High	DJH	Ultra 8
4	DJIA Low	DJL	Ultra 8
5	DJIA Close	DJC	Ultra 8
6	S&P Industrials	SPIA	Market Timing Reports
7	Dow Jones Transports	DJTA	Market Timing Reports
8	Dow Jones Utilities	DJUA	Market Timing Reports
9	NYSE Financial Index	NYFA	Market Timing Reports
10	Dow Jones 20 Bonds	DJB	Ultra 8
11	NASDAQ Composite Close	OTC	Ultra 8
12	Value Line Geometric Close	VL	Ultra 8
13	NYSE Advancing Issues	ADV	Ultra 8
14	NYSE Declining Issues	DEC	Ultra 8
15	NYSE Unchanged Issues	UNC	Ultra 8
16	NYSE New 52-Week Highs	NH	Ultra 8
17	NYSE New 52-Week Lows	NL	Ultra 8
18	NYSE Total Volume	TVOL	Ultra 8
19	NYSE Upside Volume	UVOL	Ultra 8
20	NYSE Downside Volume	DVOL	Ultra 8
21	3-Month T-Bill Yields	T3M	Market Timing Reports
22	10-Year T-Bond Yields	T10Y	Market Timing Reports
23	AAA Bond Yields	AAA	Market Timing Reports
24	BAA Bond Yields	BAA	Market Timing Reports

Indicators

Twenty-nine of the 39 rule inputs were indicators derived by transforming one or more raw time series with various mathematical, logical, and time-series operators. This section describes the transformations used to produce these indicators.

The indicators are presented in four categories: (1) price and volume functions, (2) market-breadth indicators, (3) prices-of-debt instruments, and (4) interest-rate-spread indicators.

Price and Volume Functions   Fifteen (15) indicators were functions that combine price and volume information. A number of studies have shown that trading volume contains useful information both on its own and when used in conjunction with price.[22] Technical analysis practitioners have suggested a number of price and volume functions: on-balance volume, accumulation distribution volume, money flow, negative volume, and positive volume. Each of these functions is described below.

The price-volume functions were used to create two types of indicators: (1) cumulative sums and (2) moving averages. An indicator defined as a cumulative sum is the algebraic sum of all prior daily values of the price-volume function. The daily value of a price-volume function can either be a positive or negative quantity. Thus, an indicator defined as the cumulative sum of the on-balance volume, at a given point in time, is equal to the sum of all prior values of the daily on-balance-volume quantity. An indicator defined as a cumulative sum will display long-term trends similar to those observed in the levels of asset prices and interest rates. In other words, these indicators are nonstationary time series.

In contrast, a moving average of a price-volume function will be a stationary time series. In other words, it will not display trends. This is explained by the fact that a moving average only considers the observations within the look-back span. Since price and volume functions can assume both positive or negative values, a moving average will tend to remain within a relatively confined range near zero. See Figure 31.9.

Cumulative On-Balance Volume Perhaps the first invented price & volume function was the cumulative on-balance-volume indicator, which is attributed to Joseph Granville and Woods and Vignolia.[23] It is a cumulative sum of signed (+ or −) total market volume. The algebraic sign of the volume for any given day is determined by the sign of the change in a market index for the current day, week, or whatever time interval is being used. The case study used daily market changes in the

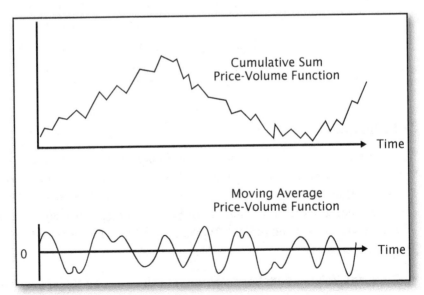

FIGURE 31.9 Cumulative Sum Versus Moving Average of Price-Volume Functions.

S&P 500 to determine the appropriate sign for the volume. If the price of the index rose on a given day, that day's entire NYSE volume was assigned a positive value and the number of shares traded was added to the prior cumulative sum. On days when the price declined, the NYSE volume was assigned a negative value and added to the prior cumulative sum (i.e., subtracted).

The computation for the cumulative on-balance volume is shown in the following equation:[24]

Cumulative On-Balance Volume (COBV)

$$COBV_t = COBV_{t-1} + (f_t V_t)$$

$$f_t = 1.0 \qquad \text{if } Pc_t > Pc_{t-1}$$
$$f_t = -1.0 \qquad \text{if } Pc_t < Pc_{t-1}$$
$$f_t = 0 \qquad \text{if } Pc_t = Pc_{t-1}$$

Where:
$OBV_t = (f_t Vt) =$ On-Balance Volume for day t
$COBV_t =$ Cumulative On-Balance Volume for day t
$V_t =$ NYSE volume for day t
$Pc_t =$ Closing price S&P 500 for day t

Moving Averages of On-Balance Volume   In addition to the cumulative on-balance volume, two moving averages of daily on-balance volume were considered: for 10 and 30 days (OBV10, OBV30). In ISL they would be:

$$OBV10 = MA(OBV, 10)$$
$$OBV30 = MA(OBV, 30)$$

where OBV represents the on-balance volume for a given day.

Cumulative Accumulation-Distribution Volume (CADV)   Another price-volume function, *accumulation distribution volume*, is attributed to Marc Chaiken.[25] However, there are several similar functions including: *Intra-day Intensity* developed by David Bostian and *Variable Accumulation Distribution* developed by Larry Williams. These transformations attempt to overcome a perceived limitation in on-balance volume, which treats the entire day's volume as positive (negative) even if the market index had a miniscule positive (negative) price change. It was felt that minor price changes should not be treated the same as large price changes. The proposed modifications to on-balance volume sought to ameliorate on-balance volume's all-or-none approach.

Chaiken proposed that a day's price activity could be more accurately characterized by quantifying the position of the closing price within the high-low range. Specifically, his calculation takes the difference between the closing price and the midpoint of the daily range and divides the difference by the size of the range. The assumption is that, when the market closes above the midpoint of its daily range, bullish or accumulation activity dominated the day's trading activity (accumulation) and should predict higher prices. Conversely when the market closes below the midpoint of its daily range, the day is said to be dominated by bearish or distribution activity and should predict lower prices. Only if the index closed at the low of the day or the high of the day is the entire day's volume assigned a negative (distribution) or positive (accumulation) value. More typically, the close is somewhere within the day's range resulting in some fraction of the volume being assigned to accumulation (positive volume) or to distribution (negative volume). The range factor, which is defined below, quantifies the position of the closing price within the day's range. The range factor is multiplied by the daily volume, and this figure is accumulated to produce the cumulative sum. The calculation is shown in the following equation.[26]

Cumulative Accumulation/Distribution Volume

$$CADV_t = CADV_{t-1} + (V_t \times Rf_t)$$

$$\text{Range Factor } (Rf_t) = \frac{(Pc_t - Pl_t) - (Ph_t - Pc_t)}{(Ph_t - Pl_t)}$$

Where:
$ADV_t = V_t \times Rf_t$ = Accumulation/Distribution Volume for day t
$CADV_t$ = Cumulative Accumulation/Distribution Volume for day t
V_t = NYSE volume for day t
Rf_t = Range factor for day t
Pc_t = Closing price Dow Jones Industrials for day t
Pl_t = Low price Dow Jones Industrials for day t
Ph_t = High price Dow Jones Industrials for day t

The case study used data for Dow Jones Industrials for the calculation of the accumulation-distribution function rather than the S&P 500 because daily high and low prices were not available for it. I assumed that the closing position of the Dow Industrials within its range would be similar to the closing position of the S&P 500 within its range.

Moving Averages of Accumulation Distribution Volume   Moving averages of daily accumulation/distribution values were constructed for 10- and 30-day periods. In ISL they are:

$$ADV10 = MA(ADV, 10)$$
$$ADV30 = MA(ADV, 30)$$

Cumulative Money Flow (CMF)   Cumulative money flow (CMF) is similar to CADV with the exception that the product of volume and range factor is further multiplied by the price level in dollars of the S&P 500 Index. This is intended to measure the monetary value of the volume. The price level used is an average of the daily high, low, and closing prices. The computation is shown in the following equation:[27]

Cumulative Money Flow

$$CMF_t = CMF_{t-1} + (V_t \times Ap_t \times Rf_t)$$

$$\text{Range Factor } (Rf_t) = \frac{(Pc_t - Pl_t) - (Ph_t - Pc_t)}{(Ph_t - Pl_t)}$$

Where:
$MF_t = (V_t \times Ap_t \times Rf_t) = $ Money Flow for day t
$CMF_t = $ Cumulative Money Flow for day t
$Ap_t = $ Average price S&P 500 for day t: (Hi + Lo + Close)/3
$V_t = $ NYSE volume for day t
$Rf_t = $ Range Factor for day t
$Pc_t = $ Closing price Dow Jones Industrials for day t
$Pl_t = $ Low price Dow Jones Industrials for day t
$Ph_t = $ High price Dow Jones Industrials for day t

Moving Averages of Money Flow   Moving averages of money flow were constructed for 10- and 30-day periods. In ISL they are:

$$MF10 = MA(MF, 10)$$
$$MF30 = MA(MF, 30)$$

Cumulative Negative Volume Index (CNV)   Cumulative negative volume is an accumulation of price changes on days of lower trading volume. In other words, it is a continuous algebraic sum of daily percentage changes in a stock market index on days when volume is less than the prior day. When volume is equal to or greater than a prior day, the CNV remains unchanged.

The inventor of CNV is unclear. Several sources attribute it to Norman Fosback[28] but several sources, including Fosback, attribute the idea to Paul Dysart.[29] However, it seems clear that it was Fosback who developed objective signal rules for CNV and evaluated their predictive power.[30]

The notion of negative volume is based on the conjecture that "trading by unsophisticated investors occurs predominately on days of exuberantly rising volume, whereas informed buying and selling (i.e., smart-money activity) usually occurs during quieter periods of declining volume. Therefore, the direction that the market assumes on days of negative volume purportedly reflects accumulation (buying) or distribution (selling) of stock by those who are in the know."[31]

The computation of the index is as shown in the following equation:

Cumulative Negative Volume Index (CNV)

$$CNV_t = CNV_{t-1} + f_t$$

$$f_t = [(Pc_t/Pc_{t-1})-1] \times 100 \quad \text{if } V_t < V_{t-1}$$

$$f_t = 0 \quad \text{if } V_t > \text{ or } = V_{t-1}$$

Where:
$NV_t = f_t$ = Negative Volume Index for day t
CNV_t = Cumulative Negative Volume Index for day t
V_t = NYSE volume for day t
Pc_t = Closing price S&P 500 for day t

Moving Averages of Negative Volume Index   Moving averages of the daily value of negative volume index (i.e., index's percentage change on lower volume days) were constructed for 10- and 30-day periods. In ISL:

$$NV10=MA(NV,10)$$
$$NV30=MA(NV,30)$$

Cumulative Positive Volume Index (CPV)   Cumulative positive volume (CPV) is the opposite of CNV. It is an algebraic accumulation of market index changes for days when volume is greater than the prior day. Positive volume index is variously attributed to Fosback[32] and to Dysart. The calculation is presented in the equation that follows. It seems as if Dysart proposed the positive volume index and suggested ways of interpreting it in a subjective manner, whereas Fosback defined objective rules and formally tested them:

Cumulative Positive Volume Index (CPV)

$$CPV_t = CPV_{t-1} + f_t$$

$$f_t = [(Pc_t/Pc_{t-1})-1] \times 100 \quad \text{if } V_t > V_{t-1}$$

$$f_t = 0 \quad\qquad\qquad\qquad \text{if } V_t < \text{ or } = V_{t-1}$$

Where:
$PV_t = f_t$ = Positive Volume Index for day t
CPV_t = Cumulative Positive Volume Index for day t
V_t = NYSE volume for day t
Pc_t = Closing price S&P 500 for day t

Moving Averages of Positive Volume Moving averages of daily values of the positive volume index were constructed for 10- and 30-day periods (PV10 and PV30). In ISL:

$$PV10=MA(PV,10)$$
$$PV30=MA(PV,30)$$

Market Breadth Indicators *Market breadth* refers to the spread or difference between the number of stocks advancing and the number declining on a given day, week, or other defined time interval. Breadth has been measured in a variety of ways, and they are reviewed in a scholarly study by Harlow.[33] For purposes of the case study, breadth is defined as the daily advance-decline ratio; that is, it is the difference between a day's advancing and declining issues divided by the total number of issues traded. The data is based on all issues traded on the NYSE rather than an alternative version that is restricted to NYSE common stocks. The series restricted to common stocks, which some have claimed is superior because it excludes closed-end stock and bond funds and preferred stocks, was not available in computer-readable form for the time period required.

The case study's breadth indicators are of two forms: cumulative sums of daily figures and moving averages of daily figures. For reasons previously explained, the breadth indicators that are cumulative sums display long-term trends, whereas moving-average breadth indicators tend to have reasonably stable mean values and fluctuation ranges.

Cumulative Advance-Decline Ratio (CADR)   The cumulative advance decline ratio or CADR is a cumulative sum of the daily advance-decline ratio:

$$CADR_t = CADR_{t-1} + ADR_t$$

$$ADR_t = \frac{adv_t - dec_t}{adv_t + dec_t + unch_t}$$

Where:
$CADR_t$ = Cumulative Advance/Decline Ratio for day t
ADR_t = Advance/Decline Ratio for day t
adv_t = NYSE advancing issues for day t
dec_t = NYSE declining issues for day t
$unch_t$ = NYSE unchanged issues for day t

Moving Averages of Advance-Decline Ratio   Moving averages of daily advance-decline ratio (ADR) were constructed for 10- and 30-day periods (ADR10 and ADR30). In ISL they are:

$$ADR10 = MA(ADR,10)$$
$$ADR30 = MA(ADR,30)$$

Cumulative Net Volume Ratio (CNVR)   Another measure of market breadth is the net volume ratio. It is based on the difference between daily upside and downside volume. Upside (downside) volume is the total number of shares traded in stocks that closed up (down) for the day. The innovation of calculating and analyzing upside and downside volume separately is attributed to Lyman M. Lowry in 1938.[34] The daily net volume ratio, a quantity that can assume either positive or negative values, is the difference between upside and downside volume divided by total trading volume. The case study used statistics released daily by the New York Stock Exchange. The cumulative net volume ratio (CNVR) is the cumulative sum of daily ratios:

Cumulative Net Volume Ratio (CNVR)

$$CNVR_t = CNVR_{t-1} + NVR_t$$

$$NVR_t = \frac{upvol_t - dnvol_t}{upvol_t + dnvol_t + unchvol_t}$$

Where:
$CNVR_t$ = Cumulative Net Volume Ratio for day t
NVR_t = Net Volume Ratio for day t
$upvol_t$ = NYSE advancing volume for day t
$dnvol_t$ = NYSE declining volume for day t
$unchvol_t$ = NYSE unchanged volume for day t

Moving Averages of Net Volume Ratio   Moving averages of the daily net volume ratio were constructed for 10- and 30-day periods (NVR10 and NVR30). In ISL:

$$NVR10 = MA(NVR, 10)$$
$$NVR30 = MA(NVR, 30)$$

Cumulative New Highs-Lows Ratio (CHLR)   A third measure of breadth, the cumulative new highs and new lows ratio (CHLR), takes a longer-term view. In contrast to CADR and CNVR, which are based on daily price changes and daily volumes, CHLR is based on a stock's current price relative to its maximum and minimum price over the preceding year. Specifically, CHLR is the cumulative sum of the daily new highs-new lows ratio (HLR), a quantity that can assume positive or negative values. The high-low ratio is defined as the difference between the number of stocks making new 52-week highs on the day and the number of stocks making new 52-week lows on the same day divided by the total number of issues traded that day. This figure is accumulated algebraically to obtain CHLR.

There is nothing particularly significant about using a look-back interval of 52 weeks. It is simply the mostly widely available statistic for new high and new low data. Prior to 1978, the number of issues making highs and lows was not based on a consistent 52-week look-back span. From the middle of March in any given year, the data were based only on the current calendar year. Prior to the middle of March, the figures were based on the current and prior years. Thus, over the course of a given year, the look-back span used to determine if a stock was making a new low or a new high varied from 2.5 months in mid-March to as long as 14.5 months just before mid-March. Most of the data used in this study was post-1978.

Despite the distortions created by the variable look-back span, rule tests based on pre-1978 high-low data suggested that the indicator's information content was robust to this distortion. For example, Fosback developed and tested an indicator called the high-low logic index over the period 1944 to 1980. His results showed that indicator demonstrated predictive power over the entire period even though the bulk of the data was infected with the variable look-back span distortion.[35] The formula for constructing the CHLR series is shown here:[36]

Cumulative New Highs New Lows (CHLR)

$$CHLR_t = CHLR_{t-1} + HLR_t$$

$$HLR_t = \frac{nuhi_t - nulo_t}{adv_t + dec_t + unch_t}$$

Where:
$CNHL_t$ = Cumulative New Highs New Lows on day t
HLR_t = New Highs New Lows on day t
$nuhi_t$ = NYSE new 52-week highs day t
$nulo_t$ = NYSE new 52-week lows day t
adv_t = NYSE advancing issues for day t
dec_t = NYSE declining issues for day t
$unch_t$ = NYSE unchanged issues for day t

Moving Averages of New Highs/New Lows Ratio (HLR1 and HLR30)

Moving averages of the daily high/low ratio were constructed for 10- and 30-day periods (HLR10 and HLR30). In ISL they are:

$$HLR10 = MA(HLR, 10)$$
$$HLR30 = MA(HLR, 30)$$

Prices-of-Debt Instruments from Interest Rates Typically, interest rates and stock price levels move inversely. However, by taking the reciprocal (1/interest rate) interest rates can be transformed into price-like time series that are, in general, positively correlated with stock prices. This reciprocal series can be multiplied by a scaling factor such as 100. Thus, a rate of 6.05 percent would be equivalent to a price of 15.38 (1/6.05 × 100).

This transformation was used in the case study and was performed on four interest rate series: three-month treasury bills, 10-year treasury bonds, Moody's AAA corporate bonds, and Moody's BAA corporate bonds.

Interest Rate Spreads An interest-rate spread is the difference between two comparable interest rates. Two types of interest-rate spreads were constructed for the case study; the *duration* spread and the *quality* spread. The duration spread, also known as the *slope of the yield curve*, is the difference between yields on debt instruments having the same credit quality but having different durations (i.e., time to maturity). The duration spread used in the case study was defined as the yield on the 10-year treasury note minus the yield on the three-month treasury bills (10-year yield minus 3-month yield). The spread was defined in this way rather than 3-month minus 10-year so that an upward trend in the spread would presumably have bullish implications for the stock market (S&P 500).[37]

A quality spread measures the difference in yield between instruments with similar durations but with different credit qualities (default risk). The quality spread for the case study was based on two of Moody's[38] long-term corporate bond series: AAA,[39] which are the highest rated corporate debt, and BAA,[40] a lower rated grade of corporate debt. The quality spread is defined here as AAA yield −BAA yield. When rates on lower quality debt (higher default risk such as BAA rated bonds) are falling faster than rates on higher quality debt such as AAA rated bonds, it is interpreted as indication that investors are more willing to assume additional risk to earn the higher yields on lower quality debt. In other words, a rising trend in the quality spread is a signal that investors are willing to take higher risks to earn higher returns. By this reasoning, the quality spread should trend in the same direction as stocks.

■ Table of 40 Input Series Used in Case Study

Table 31.2 lists all of the data series used as rule inputs in the case study.

Number	Description	Abbreviation	Form
	TABLE 31.2 Input Series Used in the Case Study		
1	S&P 500 Close	SPX	Raw
2	S&P 500 Open	SPO	Raw
3	S&P Industrials Close	SPIA	Raw
4	Dow Jones Transportation Index	DJTA	Raw
5	Dow Jones Utility Index	DJUA	Raw
6	NYSE Financial Index	NYFA	Raw
7	NASDAQ Composite	OTC	Raw
8	Value Line Geometric Close	VL	Raw
9	Cumulative On-Balance Volume	COBV	Indicator
10	On-Balance Volume 10-Day MA	OBV10	Indicator
11	On-Balance Volume 30-Day MA	OBV30	Indicator
12	Cumulative Accum. Distr. Volume	CADV	Indicator
13	Accum. Distr. Volume 10-Day MA	ADV10	Indicator
14	Accum. Distr. Volume 30-Day MA	ADV30	Indicator
15	Cumulative Money Flow	CMF	Indicator
16	Money Flow 10-Day MA	MF10	Indicator
17	Money Flow 30-Day MA	MF30	Indicator
18	Cumulative Negative Volume Index	CNV	Indicator
19	Negative Volume Index 10-Day MA	NV10	Indicator
20	Negative Volume Index 30-Day MA	NV30	Indicator
21	Cumulative Positive Volume Index	CPV	Indicator
22	Positive Volume Index 10-Day MA	PV10	Indicator
23	Positive Volume Index 30-Day MA	PV30	Indicator
24	Cum. Advance Decline Ratio	CADR	Indicator
25	Advance Decline Ratio 10-Day MA	ADR10	Indicator
26	Advance Decline Ratio 30-Day MA	ADR30	Indicator
27	Cum. Up Down Volume Ratio	CUDR	Indicator
28	Up Down Volume Ratio 10-Day MA	UDR10	Indicator
29	Up Down Volume Ratio 30-Day MA	UDR30	Indicator
30	Cum. New Highs/New Lows Ratio	CHLR	Indicator
31	New Highs/New Lows Ratio 10-Day MA	HLR10	Indicator
32	New Highs/New Lows Ratio 30-Day MA	HLR30	Indicator
33	NYSE Volume	TVOL	Raw
34	Dow Jones 20 Bond Index	DJB	Raw
35	Price 3-Month T-Bill	PT3M	Indicator
36	Price 10-Year Treasury Bond	PT10Y	Indicator
37	Price AAA Corporate Bonds	PAAA	Indicator
38	Price BAA Corporate Bonds	PBAA	Indicator
39	Duration Spread (10 Year −3 Month)	DURSPD	Indicator
40	Quality Spread (BAA–AAA)	QUALSPD	Indicator

■ The Rules

The rules tested in the case study can be grouped into three categories, each representing a different theme of technical analysis: (1) trends, (2) extremes and transitions, and (3) divergence. The following sections describe the rules in each category.

Trend Rules

The first category of rules is based on trends. A foundational principle of TA is that prices and yields move in trends that can be identified in a sufficiently timely manner to generate profits. Practitioners have developed a variety of objective indicators to define the direction of the current trend and signal trend reversals. Among the most widely used are moving averages, moving-average bands, channel breakout, and Alexander filters also known as zigzag filters. These are described in Kaufman[41] and there is no need to cover them all here.

The trend rules in the case study used the channel breakout operator or CBO to define trends in the input time series. Thus, the CBO operator transformed the input time series into a binary valued time series consisting of $+1$ and -1. When the trend of the input series was in an uptrend, as determined by the CBO, the rule's output was $+1$. Conversely, when the analyzed series was determined to be in a downtrend, the output was -1.

The identification of trend reversals in the input series by CBO is subject to lag. All trend indicators necessarily incur lag—a delay between the time the input series experiences a trend reversal and the time the operator is able to detect it. Lag can be reduced by making the indicator more sensitive. For example, in the case of CBO, lag can be reduced by decreasing the number of periods in the look-back span. However, this fix creates a different problem—an increased number of false signals. In other words, there is a tradeoff between a trend-following indicator's lag and its accuracy. Therefore, all trend indicators attempt to strike a reasonable balance between signal accuracy and signal timeliness. Finding the optimum is a challenge in the design of any signaling system, be it a household smoke detector or a TA trend rule. In the end, optimal is whatever maximizes the indicator's performance, such as average return, risk-adjusted rate of return, and so forth. Since the behavior of financial market time series changes over time, the optimal look-back span for the CBO operator would change as well. Adaptive versions of CBO were not used in the case study.

Of the 40 input series depicted in Table 31.2, 39 were used as inputs for the trend rules. The open price of the S&P 500, input series 2 in Table 31.2, was excluded on grounds of being redundant of the S&P 500 close.

Each trend rule was defined by two parameters or arguments: the CBO look-back span and a time series chosen from the set of 39 candidates shown in Table 31.2. A set of 11 values were tested as look-back spans. They were 3, 5, 8, 12, 18, 27, 41, 61, 91, 137, and 205 days. The values were chosen to be separated by a multiplier of approximately 1.5. For example, the look-back span of 205 days is approximately 1.5 times 137 days. This resulted in a total of 858 trend rules, 429 (39×11) based on a traditional TA interpretation, and an additional 429 inverse-trend rules.

A traditional version of a trend rule produced an output value of $+1$ (long position in the S&P 500) when the input time series was determined to be in an upward trend by CBO operator, and an output value of -1 (short position in the S&P 500) when the time series was in downtrend according to CBO operator. Inverse trend rules simply produced the opposite signals (e.g., short S&P 500 when the analyzed series was determined to be in an uptrend).

The following shorthand naming convention will be used for the traditional and inverse trend rules. A naming convention was necessitated by the large number of rules. The syntax of the naming convention is as follows (note this syntax is different from the syntax used for indicator scripting):

Rule (TT or TI) – Input Series Number – Look-back Span
Where TT stands for a traditional trend rule
and
TI stands for an inverse trend rule

For example, the rule named TT-15-137, is a traditional trend rule applied to input series 15 (Cumulative Money Flow) using a look-back span of 137 says. A rule named TI-40-41 is an inverse trend rule applied to input series 40 (the quality spread BAA−AAA) using a look-back span of 41 days.

Extreme Values and Transitions

The second category of rules considered in the case study is "Extreme Values and Transitions" or *E* rules. This category is based on the notion that a time series conveys information when it assumes an extreme high or low value or as it makes the transition between extremes. High and low extremes can be defined in terms of fixed value thresholds if the time series has a relatively stable mean and fluctuation range (i.e., is stationary). All input series used for E rules were made stationary by applying the CN operator.

Thirty-nine of the 40 input series were used for the E-type rules. The open price of the S&P 500 was excluded on grounds of redundancy. The input series used for E rules were first smoothed with a four-day linearly weighted moving average (LMA) before applying the CN operator. The smoothing was done to reduce the number of signals that would have resulted from an unsmoothed version of the input series wiggling above and below the signal threshold. Though smoothing may have been inappropriate for series that were already smoothed, for example the 30-day moving average of negative volume, all series were treated with the LMA on grounds of consistency.

In ISL, the expression for the input time series used for E rules is given by the expression:

=CN (LMA (Input Series, 4), *N*-days)

Where:

CN is the channel normalization operator
LMA is a linearly weighted moving-average operator

This sequence of transformations is illustrated in Figure 31.10.

E-rule signals were generated when the channel normalized smoothed series crossed a threshold. Given that there are two thresholds, an upper and lower, and

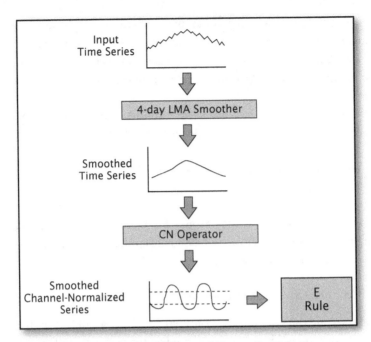

FIGURE 31.10 Smoothed Channel Normalized Series.

given that there are two directions in which a crossing can occur (up or down) there are four possible threshold-crossing events:

1. Lower threshold is crossed in the downward direction.
2. Lower threshold is crossed in the upward direction.
3. Upper threshold is crossed in the upward direction.
4. Upper threshold is crossed in the downward direction.

These events are illustrated in Figure 31.11.

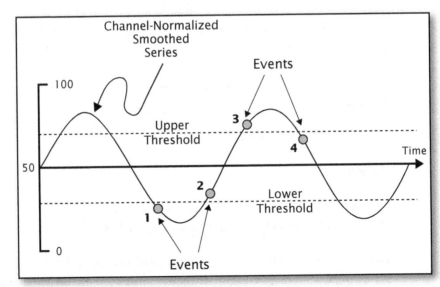

FIGURE 31.11 Threshold Crossing Events.

Each E rule was defined in terms of two threshold-crossing events: one specifying the long entry/short exit and the other specifying the short entry/long exit. This scheme yields 12 possible E-rule types. They are listed in Table 31.3. Because they cover all possibilities, there would be no point in including inverse versions. Note that type 7 is an inversion of Type 1, Type 8 is an inversion of Type 2, and so on.

The 12 E-rule types are illustrated in Figures 31.12 to 31.23.

TABLE 31.3	The 12 E-Rule Types Defined in Terms of Threshold Crossing Events	
E-Rule Types	**Long Entry/Short Exit**	**Short Entry/Long Exit**
1	Event 1	Event 2
2	Event 1	Event 3
3	Event 1	Event 4
4	Event 2	Event 3
5	Event 2	Event 4
6	Event 3	Event 4
7	Event 2	Event 1
8	Event 3	Event 1
9	Event 4	Event 1
10	Event 3	Event 2
11	Event 4	Event 2
12	Event 4	Event 3

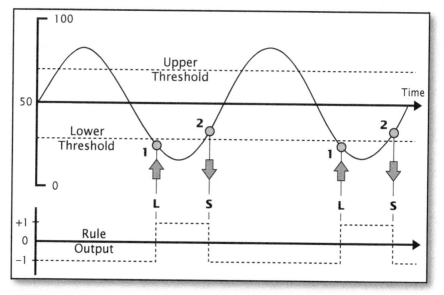

FIGURE 31.12 Extreme Value and Transition Rule: Type 1.

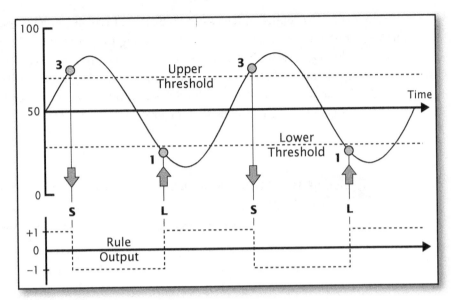

FIGURE 31.13 Extreme Value and Transition Rule: Type 2.

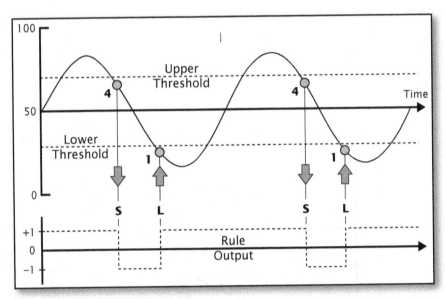

FIGURE 31.14 Extreme Value and Transition Rule: Type 3.

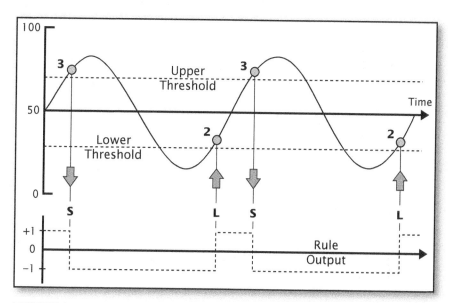

FIGURE 31.15 Extreme Value and Transition Rule: Type 4.

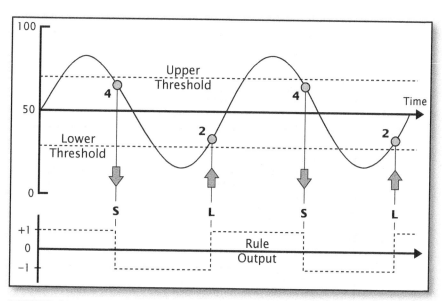

FIGURE 31.16 Extreme Value and Transition Rule: Type 5.

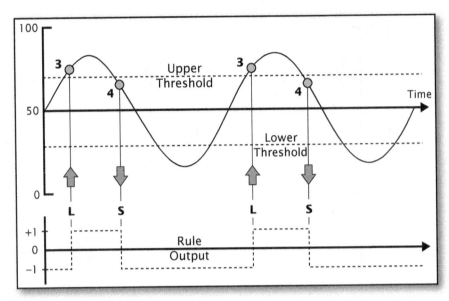

FIGURE 31.17 Extreme Value and Transition Rule: Type 6.

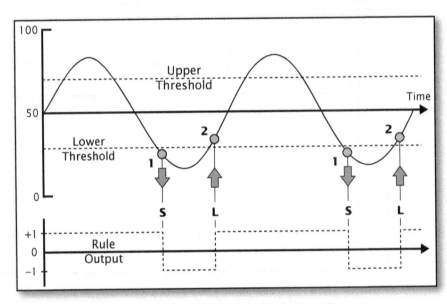

FIGURE 31.18 Extreme Value and Transition Rule: Type 7.

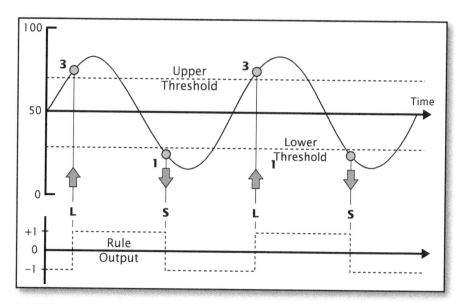

FIGURE 31.19 Extreme Value and Transition Rule: Type 8.

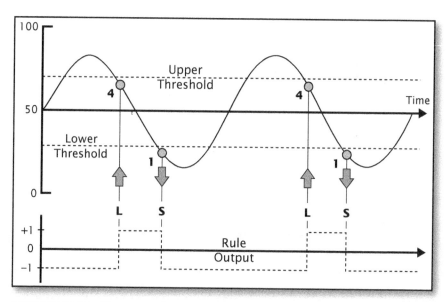

FIGURE 31.20 Extreme Value and Transition Rule: Type 9.

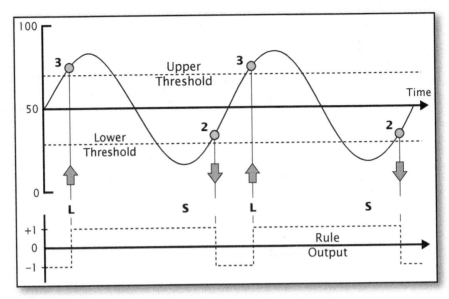

FIGURE 31.21 Extreme Value and Transition Rule: Type 10.

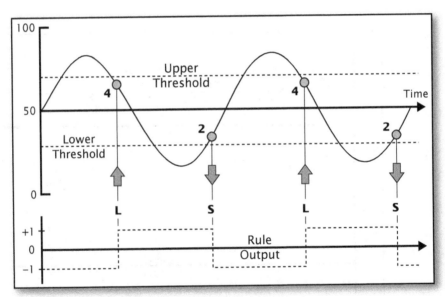

FIGURE 31.22 Extreme Value and Transition Rule: Type 11.

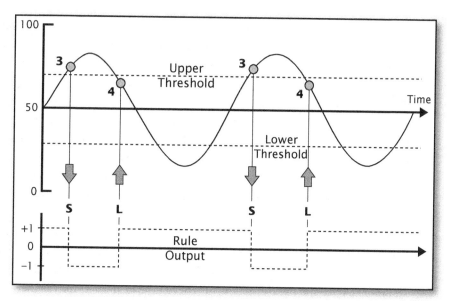

FIGURE 31.23 Extreme Value and Transition Rule: Type 12.

Parameter Sets and Total Number of E Rules An E rule is defined by four parameters: type (1 through 12), input series, displacement of the thresholds form 50, and look-back span for the channel normalization. Because both the upper and lower thresholds are displaced equally from the midvalue of 50, it is possible to specify them with a single number, their displacement from 50. For example, a threshold-displacement 10 places the upper threshold at 60 (50 + 10) and the lower threshold at 40 (50 − 10). Two different values for the threshold displacement parameter were tested: 10 and 20. The displacement value of 20 gave the upper threshold as 70 and the lower threshold as 30. Three different values were considered for the channel normalization look-back span: 15, 30, and 60. All parameter values were chosen without optimization on the basis of intuition.

Given 12 possible rule types, 39 possible candidate input series, 2 possible threshold displacements, and 3 possible channel normalization look-back spans, there were 2,808 E-type rules ($12 \times 39 \times 2 \times 3$).

Naming Convention for Extreme Value and Transition Rules The following naming convention will be used to report results for E rules:

(E)-(type)-(Input Series)-(Threshold Displacement)-(Channel Normalization Look-Back Span)

For example, E-4-30-20-60 would be: E rule, type 4, input series 30 (cumulative new highs/new lows ratio), a threshold displacement of 20 (upper = 70, lower = 30), and a channel normalization look-back span of 60 days.

Divergence Rules

Divergence analysis is a foundational concept of TA that concerns the relationship between a pair of time series. It is premised on the notion that, under normal circumstances, certain pairs of market time series tend to move up and down together, and when they fail to do so it conveys information. A divergence is said to occur when one member of the pair departs from their shared trend. Typically, a divergence manifests itself as follows: both series have been trending in the same direction, but then one series reverses its prior trend while its companion continues its prior trend. This event, according to divergence analysis, is a potential signal that the prior shared trend has weakened and may be about to reverse. This is illustrated in Figure 31.24. Hussman contends that divergence signals are most informative when numerous time series are analyzed and a significant number begin to diverge.[42]

The Dow theory is based on divergence analysis. It asserts that when an index of industrial stocks and an index of transportation stocks are trending in the same direction, the trend they share is healthy and likely to persist. However, if one series begins to diverge, it is taken as preliminary evidence that the trend is weakening and may reverse. Another application of divergence analysis considers the price of an instrument as one time series and its rate of change or momentum as the second series. Price/momentum divergence analysis is discussed by Pring.[43]

A divergence leads to one of two outcomes: either the series, for which the trend had remained undisturbed, will experience a reversal to join its diverging companion or the diverging series will end its errant ways and rejoin its companion. A completed signal of reversal is not presumed until both series have convincingly reversed and are again moving in the same direction. Thus, the fundamental idea behind divergence analysis is coherence, that is, the state of affairs when two waveforms are in phase with each other (see Figure 31.25). When two series are coherent, their common trend is considered strong and expected to continue. However, when their trends become incoherent, or out of phase, the future of the once shared trend is in question. Therefore, candidates for divergence analysis are pairs of time series that are generally coherent,

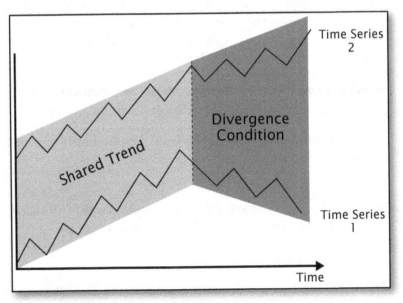

FIGURE 31.24 Divergence Analysis.

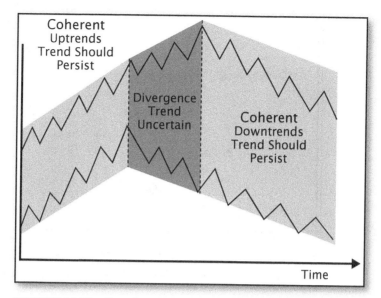

FIGURE 31.25 Trend Coherence and Divergence.

but when they do diverge, one particular member of the pair tends to have leading information about the other. In other words, there is a rather stable lead–lag relationship.

Subjective Divergence Analysis Subjective divergence analysis typically involves comparing the peaks and troughs of the two time series under consideration. A negative or bearish divergence is said to occur if one series continues to register peaks at successively higher levels while the other series begins forming peaks at lower levels. The failure by the second series to form peaks at successively higher levels is also termed a bearish nonconfirmation. This is illustrated in Figure 31.26.

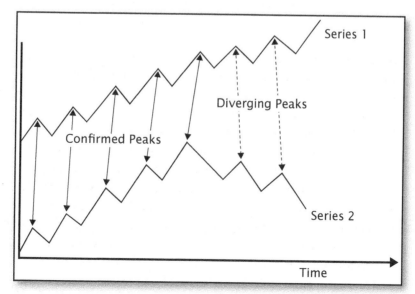

FIGURE 31.26 Negative Divergence (peaks compared).

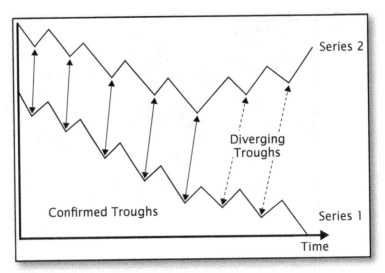

FIGURE 31.27 Positive (bullish) Divergence: Troughs Compared.

A *positive* or *bullish divergence* is said to occur when one series continues to register successively lower troughs in an established downtrend while the second series begins to form troughs at higher levels. This is also termed a *bullish nonconfirmation*. See Figure 31.27.

The problem with subjective divergence analysis, or any subjective method for that matter, is that it the procedure is neither repeatable nor testable. One issue requiring the analyst's subjective judgment is the timing of peaks and troughs. Because the two time series may not peak and trough at precisely the same time, it may be unclear which peaks and troughs should be compared. Another issue is related to duration: How long must the divergence be in existence before deciding that one has occurred? Still a third unresolved issue is how much upward (downward) movement in a series is required to establish that a new trough (peak) has formed.

An Objective Measure of Divergence These problems can be addressed with objective divergence analysis. A method that objectifies peak and trough comparisons is discussed by Kaufman[44] and he provides computer code. Kaufman also discusses a second method that uses linear regression to estimate the slopes in the two time series being compared. A divergence is defined as the differences in their slopes. Both methods look interesting but no performance statistics are offered.

The divergence rules considered in this case study were inspired by the objective divergence method discussed by Heiby[45] in his book, *Stock Market Profits through Dynamic Synthesis*. The two series being examined by Heiby were first detrended with channel normalization. He defined a divergence to be in effect if one series had a channel-normalized value of 75 or greater while the other series had a value of 25 or less. Thus, divergence was quantified in terms of the difference in channel-normalized values.

This suggested an initial formulation for a divergence indicator that is defined in the equation that follows. Note that one series is always the S&P 500, the target market of the case study. The companion series, for example the Dow Jones Transports, is the series with which the S&P 500 is compared. The case study compared the S&P 500 to all the time series in Table 31.2, except the S&P 500 open price, which was excluded on grounds of redundancy with the S&P 500 close.

Divergence Indicator
(Initial Formulation)

$$= CN \text{ (Companion Series, } n) - CN \text{ (S&P 500, } n)$$

Where:
CN = Channel normalization operator
n = Look-back span of the channel normalization

Because the channel normalized value of each series can vary between 0 and 100, this divergence indicator has a potential range of -100 to $+100$. For example, if the companion series is at the bottom of its channel range ($CN = 0$) and the S&P 500 is at the top of its range ($CN = 100$), the divergence indicator would have a value of -100. It should be noted that this quantification of divergence is merely one approach among several possibilities that may prove superior.

Limitations of the Proposed Divergence Indicator The proposed divergence indicator measures the degree to which two times series have similar positions within their respective channels. In general, this will give a reasonable quantification of the degree to which the series are in phase with one another. For example, when the indicator registers a value of zero, it indicates that there is no divergence; both series have the same channel normalized values and can be presumed to be trending together. However, there can be cases for which a value of zero does not indicate that the two series are in phase. For example, if two time series are negatively correlated, that is to say, they tend to move inversely with respect to each other within their channels, the divergence indicator will assume a value of zero as the series-normalized values cross paths. In this instance, a value of zero would be an erroneous indication that the two series are trending together. This is illustrated in Figure 31.28 and is clearly a limitation of the proposed divergence indicator.

This problem could have been avoided with a more complex formulation of divergence indicator based on cointegration,[46] a concept developed in the field of econometrics. Cointegration was proposed in 1987 by Engle and Granger.[47] This more sophisticated and potentially more accurate way of measuring divergences uses regression analysis to determine if a linear relationship exists between two time series. Because this method can easily accommodate the case in which the pair of series are strongly negatively correlated (180 degrees out of phase), it solves the problem discussed earlier that can occur with a divergence indicator based on channel normalization. An additional advantage of cointegration analysis is that it first applies a

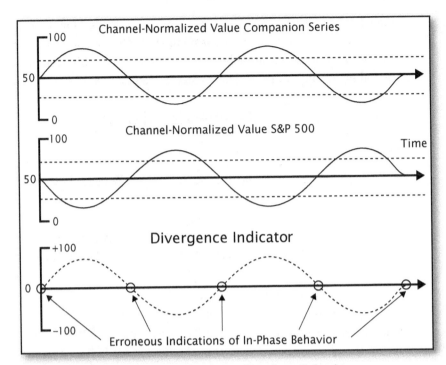

FIGURE 31.28 Erroneous Indications of In-phase Behavior.

statistical test[48] to determine if the two series have related trends (i.e., that they are cointegrated). If the test shows that they are cointegrated, a stationary divergence indicator[49] naturally falls out of the analysis. In cointegration terminology, this indicator is referred to as the *error-correction model*. It measures the degree to which one series has diverged from the typical linear relationship between the two series.

In most applications of cointegration, the error-correction model is used to predict the behavior of the spread between the cointegrated time series. In these applications, the divergence is predicted to revert back to the normal state of a shared trend when the error-correction model becomes extremely positive or negative. In other words, when the error, which is a departure from the normal linear relationship between the two series, becomes extreme, it is predicted to correct back to its normal value of zero.

A typical application of this analysis is *pairs trading*. For example, if it has been determined that Ford and GM stocks are cointegrated time series and Ford has gotten high relative to GM, a short position would be taken in Ford against a long position in GM. Thus, no matter how the divergence is corrected (Ford falls, GM rises, or some combination) the pairs trade will generate a profit.

Fosback[50] made an innovative use of cointegration analysis to develop a stock market predictor. His innovation was to use the measurement derived from the error correction model as an indicator to predict the movement of a third variable, the S&P 500, rather than predict the behavior of the spread between the cointegrated variables. The indicator, called the *Fosback Index*, exploits the fact that interest rates and mutual fund cash levels are cointegrated time series. Fosback's work is particularly noteworthy because it preceded the Engle and Granger publication on cointegration by over a decade. The Fosback Index signals when the mutual fund cash level diverges significantly from a level predicted by its linear relationship with short-term interest rates. The premise is that when mutual fund managers are excessively pessimistic about stock market prospects, they hold cash reserves that are substantially higher than the that predicted by interest rates. Excessive optimism is the opposite situation. Fosback found that both excessive pessimism and excessive optimism, measured in this fashion, correlated with future returns on the stock market. In effect, the Fosback Index removes the influence of short-term interest rates from mutual fund cash levels, thus providing a purer measure of fund manager sentiment than that provided by the raw cash level, which is contaminated by interest rates.

In the interests of simplicity, the cointegration technique was not used for the divergence indicators in the case study. It was assumed that if a companion series was not related to the S&P 500, it would be revealed by the poor financial performance of the divergence rule. However, I[51] believe that the cointegration methodology warrants further investigation in development of indicators.

Need for Double Channel Normalization A second problem with the initially proposed version of the divergence indicator was more serious and had to be remedied. The divergence rules in the case study involved pairing the S&P 500 with 38 other time series. Given that these series had varying degrees of co-movement with the S&P 500, the fluctuation range of the divergence indicator would vary considerably from one pair to the next. This would make it impractical to use the same threshold for all pairings. This problem is illustrated in Figure 31.29. Note that the high threshold displacement that would be suitable

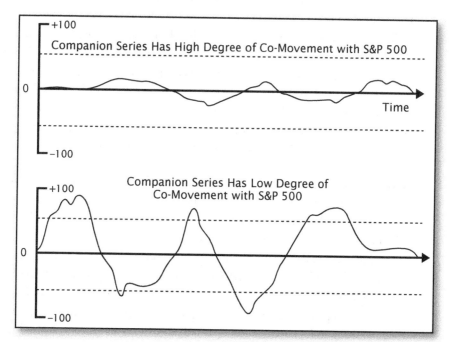

FIGURE 31.29 Divergence Indicator: Inconsistent Volatility.

for a companion series with a low degree of co-movement with the S&P 500 would never produce a signal for a companion series with a high degree of co-movement to the S&P 500. For this reason, the initial formulation of the divergence indicator was deemed impractical.

This problem was addressed with a modified formulation of the divergence indicator illustrated in the equation that follows. It employs the channel normalization operator twice. That is to say, the indicator is a channel-normalized version of the initial divergence indicator.

Divergence Indicator
(Double Channel Normalization)

$$= CN \{CN \text{ (Series 1, } n) - CN \text{ (S\&P 500, } n), 10n\}$$

Where:
CN = Channel normalization operator
Series 1 = Companion series
n = Look-back span of the first channel normalization

The second layer of channel normalization takes into account the fluctuation range of the initial formulation of the divergence indicator. This solves the problem of inconsistent fluctuation ranges across the 38 pairs of time series. As a result, the modified version of the divergence indicator will have roughly the same fluctuation range irrespective of the particular pair of time series being used, making it practical to use uniform thresholds.

The look-back span for the second level of channel normalization was set at 10 times the look-back interval used for first level. Thus, if the channel normalization used a look-back span of 60 days, the second layer of channel normalization used a look-back span of 600 days. It was assumed that a 10-fold look-back span would be sufficient to establish the fluctuation range of the basic divergence indicator. Note that a modified divergence indicator has a potential fluctuation range of 0 to 100, similar to any channel-normalized variable. See Figure 31.30.

Divergence Rule Types Upper and lower threshold were applied to the modified divergence indicator to generate signals. A positive or bullish divergence was in effect when the divergence indicator was above its upper threshold. This occurred when the companion series was moving up more or moving down less than the S&P 500. This was evidenced by the companion series having a higher relative position within its channel than the S&P 500. Conversely, a negative or bearish divergence existed when the divergence indicator was below the lower threshold. This occurred when the companion series was moving down more or moving up less than the S&P 500, resulting in its having a lower relative position within its channel than the S&P 500. This is illustrated in Figure 31.30.

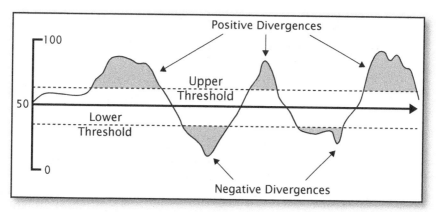

FIGURE 31.30 Modified Divergence Indicator.

The question was how to create signaling rules from the modified divergence indicator. Two rules seemed obvious: a bullish divergence rule, which would call for long positions in the S&P 500 when the divergence indicator was above the upper threshold, and a bearish divergence rule, which would call for short positions in the S&P 500 when the divergence indicator was below its lower threshold.

Both rules assumed that the companion series had leading information about the S&P 500. If the companion series was stronger than the S&P 500 (positive divergence), then a long position would be justified, whereas if the companion series was weak (negative divergence) a short position would be justified. However, this assumption may be incorrect. It may be the case that negative divergences are predictive of higher prices for the S&P 500, whereas positive divergences are predictive of lower prices. In other words, perhaps it is the S&P 500 that has the leading information. This suggests that inverse versions of each rule should be tried. In the end, it was determined that there are 12 possible divergence rule types, and all were tested.

These 12 rule types are exactly the same set used for the extreme value and transition rules. This makes sense because the modified divergence indicator is similar to the indicator used for the E rules because it has a fluctuation range of 0 to 100 and has two thresholds.

The 12 divergence rule types, presented in Table 31.4, include the basic bullish divergence (type 6), the bearish divergence (type 7) and their inversions (types 12 and 1). The 12 types are not illustrated because the illustrations would be redundant of those presented in the section on Extreme and Transition Rules.

Parameter Combinations and Naming Convention for Divergence Rules Each divergence rule is defined by four parameters: type, companion series, threshold displacement, and channel normalization look-back span. There are 12 types of the divergence rules (see Table 31.4), 38 companion data series, 2 threshold displacement values—10 and 20, and 3 look-back spans—15, 30, and 60 days. This gives a total of 2,736 divergence rules (12 × 38 × 2 × 3).

TABLE 31.4 **Divergence Rules and Associated Threshold Events**

Divergence Rule Types	Long Entry/Short Exit	Short Entry/Long Exit
1	Down Cross Lower Threshold Down Cross	Upper Cross Lower Threshold Upper Cross
2	Lower Threshold Down Cross	Upper Threshold Down Cross
3	Lower Threshold Up Cross	Upper Threshold Up Cross
4	Lower Threshold Up Cross	Upper Threshold Down Cross
5	Lower Threshold Up Cross	Upper Threshold Down Cross
6	Upper Threshold Up Cross	Upper Threshold Down Cross
7	Lower Threshold Up Cross	Lower Threshold Down Cross
8	Upper Threshold Down Cross	Lower Threshold Down Cross
9	Upper Threshold Up Cross	Lower Threshold Up Cross
10	Upper Threshold Down Cross	Lower Threshold Up Cross
11	Upper Threshold Down Cross	Lower Threshold Up Cross
12	Upper Threshold	Upper Threshold

The naming convention used for reporting results of divergence or D rules is as follows: (D)-type-companion series-threshold displacement-channel normalization look back span. Thus, a rule is named

$$D\text{-}3\text{-}23\text{-}10\text{-}30$$

Divergence rule, type 3, companion series 23 (positive volume index 30-day moving average), threshold displacement = 10 (upper threshold = 60, lower threshold = 40), 30-day channel normalization look-back span.

This completes the description of the rules tested in the case study.

■ Notes

1. J.P. Romano and M. Wolf, "Stepwise Multiple Testing as Formalized Data Snooping," *Econometrica* 73, no. 4 (July 2005), 1237–1282.

2. J.J. Murphy, *Intermarket Technical Analysis: Trading Strategies for the Global Stock, Bond, Commodity and Currency Markets* (New York: John Wiley & Sons, 1991). I was first exposed to the idea of using

relationships between markets for indicator development in 1979 by Michael Hammond and Norman Craig of Advance Market Technologies (AMTEC), Ogden, Utah. AMTEC was one of the first firms to apply artificial-intelligence methods to market prediction. AMTEC's modeling approach was based on the work of Roger Baron on adaptive learning networks, now known as polynomial networks, at Adaptronics Inc, in the 1970s. I routinely used intermarket indicators in work for clients of Raden Research Group, including Cyber-Tech Partners (1983), Tudor Investment Corporation (1987), and Manufacturer's Hanover Trust (1988).

3. P-H Hsu and C-M Kuan, "Reexamining the Profitability of Technical Analysis with Data Snooping Checks," *Journal of Financial Economics* 3, no. 4 (2005), 606–628.

4. Many of the automated methods are described in T. Hastie, R. Tibshirani, and J. Friedman, *The Elements of Statistical Learning: Data Mining, Inference and Prediction* (New York: Springer, 2001).

5. A segment of the future over which the rule's profitability persists that is long enough to compensate the effort required to discover the rule but not of unlimited duration.

6. H. White, "A Reality Check for Data Snooping," *Econometrica* 68, no. 5 (September 2000). Note that White uses the term data *snooping* to mean "datamining bias," as used in this book.

7. Mathematical operators include add, subtract, multiply, divide, powers, roots, and so forth.

8. Logical operators include *and; or; greater-than; less-than; if, then; else*, and so forth.

9. Time-series operators include moving average, moving channel normalization (stochastics), break-out channels, moving slopes, and such (described later).

10. P.K. Kaufman, 249.

11. Ibid., 200.

12. Ibid., 202. Kaufman notes that a study done in 1970 by Dunn & Hargitt Financial Services showed that a channel breakout using a four-week span, known as Donchian's four-week rule, was the best of several popular systems when tested on 16 years of data on seven commodities markets. Kaufman also compares the performance of channel breakout rules to four other trendfollowing methods (exponential smoothing, linear regression slope, swingbreakout, and point-and-figure) to Eurodollars for the 10-year period 1985 through 1994. The channel breakout method had the highest risk-adjusted performance over the 10-year period.

13. A simple moving average is centered by plotting the moving-average value in the center of the moving-data window. If N is the number of periods used to compute the moving average, the average is plotted to correspond with a value that is lagged by $(n-1)/2$ data points.

14. J.F. Ehlers, *Rocket Science for Traders: Digital Signal Processing Applications* (New York: John Wiley & Sons, 2001); J.F. Ehlers, *Cybernetic Analysis for Stocks and Futures: Cutting-Edge DSP Technology to Improve Your Trading* (New York: John Wiley & Sons, 2004).

15. Kaufman, 256.

16. Ehlers, *Rocket Science for Traders*, 27.

17. W.A. Heiby, *Stock Market Profits through Dynamic Synthesis* (Chicago: Institute of Dynamic Synthesis, 1965).

18. Although almost all sources attribute the development of this time series operator to Dr. George Lane in 1972, no source mentions the use of the same idea by Heiby at an earlier time. On this basis, I have attributed the development to Heiby. It is possible that Heiby based his work on yet an earlier author.

19. For information about various back-testing software platforms see: for TradeStation www.TradeStationWorld.com; for MetaStock www.equis.com; for AIQ Expert Design Studio www.aiqsystems.com; for Wealth-Lab www.wealth-lab.com; for eSignal www.esignal.com; for Neuroshell Trader www.neuroshell.com; for AmiBroker www.amibroker.com; for Neoticker, www.tickquest.com; for Trading$olutions www.tradingsolutions.com; for Financial Data Calculator www.mathinvestdecisions.com.

20. Ultra Financial Systems, PO Box 3938, Breckenridge, CO 90424; phone 970- 453-4956; web site www.ultrafs.com.

21. Market Timing Reports, PO Box 225, Tucson, AZ 85072; phone 520-795-9552; web site www. mktimingrpt.com.

22. Studies showing that trading volume contains useful information include the following: L. Blume and M. Easley O'Hara, "Market Statistics and Technical Analysis: The Role of Volume," *Journal of Finance* 49, issue 1 (March 1994), 153–181; M. Cooper, "Filter Rules Based on Price and Volume in Individual Security Overreaction," *Review of Financial Studies* 12 (1999), 901–935; C.M.C. Lee and B. Swaminathan, "Price Momentum and Trading Volume," *Journal of Finance* 55, no. 5 (October 2000), 2017–2069; S.E. Stickel and R.E. Verecchia, "Evidence That Trading Volume Sustains Stock Price Changes," *Financial Analysts Journal* 50 (November–December 1994), 57–67.

23. J.E. Granville, *Granville's New Strategy of Daily Stock Market Timing for Maximum Profit* (Englewood Cliffs, NJ: Prentice-Hall, 1976). The attribution to Woods and Vignolia can be found in the body of knowledge section on the web site of the Market Technicians Association.

24. This formulation of OBV is as presented in *Technical Indicators Reference* Manual for AIQ Trading Export Pro, a software product of AIQ Systems, PO Box 7530, Incline Village, NV 89452.

25. The MTA Body of Knowledge on Technical Indicators attributes the accumulation distribution indicator to Marc Chaiken, as does R.W. Colby, *The Encyclopedia of Technical Market Indicators*, 2nd ed. (New York: McGraw-Hill, 2003). No specific publication is referenced. The accumulation distribution indicator proposed by Chaiken is similar to an indicator developed by Larry Williams, *The Secrets of Selecting Stocks for Immediate and Substantial Gains* (Carmel Valley, CA: Conceptual Management, 1971), later republished by Windsor Books in 1986. Williams's indicator compares the open price to the close as the numerator of the range factor. Chaiken compares the close price to the midprice of the daily range.

26. As presented in *Technical Indicators Reference Manual for AIQ Trading Export Pro*, a software product of AIQ Systems, PO Box 7530, Incline Village, NV 89452.

27. Ibid.

28. Attribution of NVI to Norman Fosback can be found in the MTA web site Body of Knowledge and in S.B. Achelis, *Technical Analysis from A to Z* (New York: McGraw-Hill, 2001), 214.

29. Paul Dysart is credited with the creation of both positive- and negativevolume indexes by C.V. Harlow, *An Analysis of the Predictive Value of Stock Market "Breadth" Measurements* (Larchmont, NY: Investors Intelligence, 1968).

30. According to Fosback's study, the NVI identified the bullish phase of the primary trend with a probability of 0.96 over the time period 1941 to 1975. This compares to a base rate bull-trend probability of 0.70 over that time period.

31. N.G. Fosback, *Stock Market Logic: A Sophisticated Approach to Profits on Wall Street* (Dearborn, MI: Dearborn Financial Publishing, 1993), 120.

32. Ibid.

33. Harlow, *Analysis of the Predictive Value*.

34. R.W. Colby, *The Encyclopedia of Technical Market Indicators*, 2nd ed. (New York: McGraw-Hill, 2003).

35. Fosback, *Stock Market Logic*, 76–80.

36. This formulation of CNHL is as presented in *Technical Indicators Reference Manual* for AIQ Trading Export Pro, a software product of AIQ Systems.

37. C.R. Nelson, *The Investor's Guide to Economic Indicators* (New York: John Wiley & Sons, 1987), 129. The author points out that a positive spread (i.e., long-term rates higher than short-term rates) is often a bullish indicator for future changes in stock prices, especially for stock indexes that are not inflation adjusted.

38. Moody's Investors Service is a widely utilized source for credit ratings, research, and risk analysis for corporate debt instruments. Information can be found at www.moodys.com.

39. Aaa is the designated definition for the highest quality of corporate bond. Securities carrying this rating are judged to have the smallest degree of investment risk. The principal is secure and interest payments are protected by a robust margin. Although there is always a chance that

various protective elements can change, these changes are easy to visualize. The Aaa rating means that it is highly unlikely for any drastic changes to occur that would erode the fundamentally strong positions on these securities. Definition provided: www.econoday.com/clientdemos/demoweekly/2004/Resource_Center/about bondmkt/morefixed.html.

40. Baa bonds are considered medium-grade obligations. They are neither highly protected nor poorly secured. Interest payments and security on the principal appear adequate for the present, but there may be certain protective elements lacking. These securities have the possibility of being unreliable over any great length of time. These bonds lack outstanding investment characteristics, making them attractive to speculators at the same time. www.econoday. com/clientdemos/demoweekly/2004/Resource_Center/aboutbondmkt/m orefixed.html.

41. For a full discussion of alternative trend analysis methods and rules derived from them see Kaufman, Chapters 5 through 8.

42. J. Hussman, "Time-Variation in Market Efficiency: A Mixture-of-Distributions Approach," available at www.hussman.net/pdf/mixdist.pdf.

43. M.J. Pring, *Technical Analysis Explained*, 4th ed. (New York: McGraw-Hill, 2002).

44. Kaufman, 394–401.

45. Heiby, *Stock Market Profits*.

46. C. Alexander, *Market Models: A Guide to Financial Data Analysis* (New York: John Wiley & Sons, 2001), Chapter 12.

47. R.F. Engle and C.W.J. Granger, "Co-integration and Error-Correction: Representation, Estimation and Testing," *Econometrica* 55 (1987), 251–276.

48. Alexander, *Market Models*, 324–328, 353–361. One type of test used to establish the fact that a time series is stationary, called the unit-root test, is described.

49. The indicator is a time series of the errors (residuals) of the linear relationship between the two series.

50. Fosback, *Stock Market Logic*.

51. In 1983 the author, in association with Raden Research Group, developed a time series operator called *YY* that was similar in concept to cointegration analysis with the exception that *YY* values were normalized by the standard error of the regression and no explicit test was made for residual stationarity. *YY*'s development was inspired by an article by Arthur Merrill, "DFE: Deviation from Expected (Relative Strength Corrected for Beta)," *Market Technician Journal* (August 1982), 21–28. The *YY*-based indicators were used as candidate inputs for a variety of predictive modeling projects. One example was a sentiment indicator based on advisory sentiment on Tbonds. The predictive power of the raw consensus information was improved by a *YY* transformation that used past market changes as the regressor variable.

System Design and Testing

From Charles D. Kirkpatrick II and Julie R. Dahlquist, *Technical Analysis: The Complete Resource for Financial Market Technicians*, 3rd Edition (Old Tappan, New Jersey: Pearson Education, Inc., 2016), Chapter 32.

Learning Objective Statements

- Explain the importance of using a system for trading or investing
- Compare and analyze differences between a discretionary and nondiscretionary system
- Describe the mind-set and discipline required to develop and trade with a system
- Explain the basic procedures for designing a system
- Describe the role that risk management plays in system design
- Identify and evaluate various ways to test a system
- Compare and analyze standard measures of system profitability and risk

We have covered most of the methods used by technical analysts to analyze the trading markets. We now enter into the field of how to utilize this knowledge to produce profits and reduce risk. Any constant and consistent management of assets requires money management, and some type of system. Haphazardly investing or trading on intuition, rumor, or untested theories is a road to disaster. It is why most amateur traders and investors lose money.

A fundamental investor may use price-to-earnings, debt ratios, and so forth, whereas a technical investor will likely use relative strength, price trend, or volatility, and both investors will believe they are doing the correct analysis. They are not. In both cases, the methods may be correct, but making money requires a tested system. There are many myths in investing, and most investors succumb to them without further analysis. To trade or invest successfully, we need to know not only how profitable a method has been, but also what the risks of capital loss were. Not having an understanding of tested methods is flying blind in the financial markets. How do we test these methods? We create a system. The system must include not only the method for profit but also the means of controlling risk of loss. Both aspects of investing are extremely important. Some would argue that controlling loss is even more important than the profit method, that by buying and selling at the flip of a coin, one could make a decent return just by controlling risk of loss.

Let us begin this chapter by looking a little more closely at what a system is. Then we focus on what risk is and how to control losses. Once we have these foundations, we can focus on the mechanics of developing a system and testing investment strategies.

■ Why Are Systems Necessary?

No stock market goes up forever. Indeed, most world stock markets have declined to zero at one time or another. The buy-and-hold strategy so popular in the United States today is based on a statistical anomaly. It is a strategy based on a survival bias in the U.S. and the U.K. markets, the only countries in history, so far, whose markets have not completely disappeared at some time (Burnham, 2005). This has caused a misleading assumption that U.S. stocks and stocks in general will necessarily continue to rise. "It would be naïve to expect the future of U.S. stocks to be as bright as the past" (Burnham, 2005, p. 175).

We certainly know that individual stocks can go to zero. How about buggy whips in 1910, or canals in 1830, or bowling in 1950, or junk bonds and REITs in 1980, or more recently the autos and the banks? Thus, a long-term plan that excludes a means of controlling risk is eventually doomed.

On the other hand, most technical and fundamental methods, by themselves, are not profitable over time either. Some of the exceptions have been covered earlier in this book, but these methods primarily depend upon the market circumstances at the time, on the method used, and on controlling risk. Traders' and investors' greatest misconception is that the market has order and that by finding and acting on that order, profits will be consistent and large. It presumes that a magic formula exists somewhere that can predict markets. This belief is not true. In looking at the previous studies in this book, there is no magic order to the markets beyond the fact that they sometimes trend and, more often, remain in trading ranges. The money made is based on the use of well-controlled entries and exits, especially those that limit the amount of loss that can occur and that will react to changing conditions in the market. A system will aid the investor or trader in timing these market entries and exits.

Discretionary Versus Nondiscretionary Systems

Systems are the next step in the development of an investment plan after understanding the methods of either technical or fundamental investing. Systems can be discretionary, nondiscretionary, or a combination of both. In discretionary systems, entries and exits are determined by intuition; in other words, the trader or investor exercises some discretion in making trades. Nondiscretionary systems are those in which entries and exits are determined mechanically by a computer.

Think for a minute of the stereotypical discretionary trader. Imagine the ultimate discretionary trader behaving like the man in the antacid advertisement with two or three phones yelling, "Buy" in one, "Sell" in another, with computer screens showing prices and charts of securities all over the world, with ringing phones, with news broadcasts from financial TV stations, and with a large contact list of people in different specialties. This type of trader is generally looking for the home run. It is a great image, one that has in it a bit of the swashbuckler, the gunslinger, and so on. In fact, many truly exceptional traders are like this. They have the gifted intuition to be able to do this consistently and profitably.

Most people, however, do not have the time, the knowledge, the contacts, the equipment, the quickness of thought, or the stomach to do this. In fact, most people who attempt to trade like this either burn out or go broke. They have no way of evaluating what they are doing except from the equity in their account at the end of the day. It is as if the excitement is more important than making profits.

The nondiscretionary trader, on the other hand, is usually calm, calculating, and likely bored. The majority of successful traders and investors use nondiscretionary systems (Etzkorn interview of Babcock, 1996). Some have been engineers; others have that type of mind, familiar with statistics and systems. They have studied the markets, the methods of profit-making—both fundamental and technical—and have tested the techniques using modern statistical methods. They understand that nothing is perfect and that markets change character over time. However, by testing their methods and strategies, they have derived a mechanical system that minimizes risk of loss and maximizes return.

Rules are the structure of a system. An example of a rule would be "buy when one moving average A crosses above another moving average B." Variables are the numerical inputs required in the rules (length of moving average A and length of moving average B). Parameters are the actual values used in the variables (two days and seven days). A system will include all these factors; their usefulness is determined by testing different rules, variables, and parameters over varied markets and market conditions.

A purely nondiscretionary system is one that runs by itself on market data that is continually fed into it. If our rule is to buy when the two-day moving average crosses above the seven-day moving average, for example, a buy order automatically is placed when this occurs. Once the trader has determined the rule to follow, the system is on autopilot and the trader does not make decisions.

A trader or investor can also choose to use a partial discretionary system. The partial discretionary system is one that generates signals that then are acted upon by the investor based on personal confidence in them and experience with them. By having some discretion, however, the system cannot be tested accurately because emotion can enter into the trading decisions and cause unquantifiable errors.

Is it always better to choose a nondiscretionary, mechanical system over a discretionary one? Let us look at some of the advantages and disadvantages of this approach.

Benefits of a Nondiscretionary, Mechanical System A nondiscretionary, mechanical system provides a mathematical edge as determined by testing and adjusting. This is the principle behind the casino and an insurance business, both of which profit from many small profitable trades and occasional losses.

Using a nondiscretionary system avoids emotion. This is an advantage because traders often lose money due to emotional decisions. The nondiscretionary system also reduces other trading pitfalls—overtrading, premature action, no action, and constant decision making. Trading with a properly designed mechanical system also prevents large losses and risk of ruin, which most traders have never quantified or understood. In fact, risk control can be one of the most important advantages of a mechanical system.

Trading with a nondiscretionary system also provides certainty, develops confidence, and produces less stress. Anxiety comes from uncertainty and ambiguity. Although a nondiscretionary system cannot predict the future, it can structure how to react to possible outcomes. It gives a list of responses to events beyond one's control.

Pitfalls to a Nondiscretionary, Mechanical System Although there are many benefits to a nondiscretionary, mechanical system, pitfalls also exist. For one, extrapolating will not have the same results as tests; history does not repeat itself precisely. The more a system is optimized or curve-fitted, the less reliable it will be in the future. In fact, in their book *The Ultimate Trading Guide*, Hill, Pruitt, and Hill (2000) suggest that you should generally expect half the profits and twice the drawdowns as shown in tests of past data. Having been tested, the system designer expects results that are often unrealistic. The designer must be careful not to lose confidence when unrealistic expectations are not achieved.

Nondiscretionary systems often will make profits in clumps, especially if it is a trend-following system. The trader then loses small amounts waiting for the next clump and protecting from large losses. In other words, great creativity may have gone into inventing the system, but its operation is boring. In addition, some system designs allow large drawdowns but still eventually produce profits. The emotional problem for the user is the wait for the drawdown to be recovered and meanwhile the possible loss of confidence in the system. A loss of confidence results in fiddling with the rules or giving up just as the system is about to kick in.

Although a good system adjusts to a changing market, it does require periodic updates. This can often be a source of confusion for the designer. Is it time to update an underperforming system because of a changing marketplace? Alternatively, is the lackluster performance period a time for the trader to sit by patiently waiting for the system to kick in? The answers to these questions are not always obvious.

Remember that the system falls apart if it is not followed precisely. This is what the testing was for, and violations of the rules established from the testing negate the value of the system. This requires considerable discipline.

Using a nondiscretionary, mechanical system is not easy—otherwise, everyone would do it. There is a lot of work in coming up with a system, testing it, adjusting it, and trying it correctly and convincingly. The tendency for many people is to "wing it" and see if it works. That method leaves the trader nowhere.

■ A Complete Trading System

The following is from The Original Turtle Trading Rules by Turtle member Curtis Faith (bigpicture.typepad.com/comments/files/turtlerules.pdf):

Decisions required for successful trading:

■ Markets—What to buy or sell

■ Position Sizing—How much to buy or sell

■ Entries—When to buy or sell

■ Stops—When to get out of a losing position

■ Exits—When to get out of a winning position

■ Tactics—How to buy or sell

■ How Do I Design a System?

Now you are convinced that you need to design a system for trading. However, how do you do that? Let us look at some of the requirements and steps involved in creating an effective system.

Requirements for Designing a System

What is needed to design a successful system? Before even considering the components of a system, we must begin with something even more basic—designing a workable, profitable system begins with some basic personal attitudes. Some of the characteristics of the necessary mind-set include the following:

■ Understand what a discretionary or nondiscretionary system will do—be realistically knowledgeable, and lean toward a nondiscretionary, mechanical system that can be quantified precisely and for which rules are explicit and constant.

■ Do not have an opinion of the market. Profits are made from reacting to the market, not by anticipating it. Without a known structure, the markets cannot be predicted. A mechanical system will react, not predict.

- Realize that losses will occur—keep them small and infrequent.

- Realize that profits will not necessarily occur constantly or consistently.

- Realize that your emotions will tug at your mind and encourage changing or fiddling with the system. Such emotions must be controlled.

- Be organized—winging it will not work.

- Develop a plan consistent with one's time available and investment horizon—daily, weekly, monthly, and yearly.

- Test, test, and test again, without curve-fitting. Most systems fail because they have not been tested or have been overfitted.

- Follow the final tested plan without exception—discipline, discipline, discipline. No one is smarter than the computer, regardless of how painful losses may be and how wide spreads between price and stops may affect one's staying power.

Initial Decisions

Once you are committed to the mind-set and discipline of creating a system, you must make certain decisions about the characteristics of your system. The actual fundamental or technical method used as the basis for the system is relatively unimportant. What is important is that whatever is used can be defined precisely. Most fundamental and technical methods, by themselves, have a sketchy record of performance. Performance in the system will depend more on filters, adjustments, and the entry and exit strategies than the method itself. This does not mean that any old method will work. Pick a model (entry and exit method that has some statistical probability of success) that is familiar, sensible, comfortable, and has a decent record. Be sure it is based on facts, not opinion, and then concentrate on the process of developing a system.

Most systems designers argue that the simpler the system, the better. A system can become bogged down with large numbers of conditions and statistically will lose degrees of freedom, requiring more data and more signals to establish its significance. The market has **entropy**, an inherent disorder that changes periodically in unexpected ways. A system with few variables will reflect the patterns in the market with a certain accuracy. As more variables are added to the system, entropy causes the nonpattern variables to increasingly influence the results, causing the system to eventually decrease profitability because it can account only for the patterns but not the internal market changes. Indeed, when testing a system, the added variables should be tested for their effect on the system results, and if the performance declines, those variables should be eliminated even if they appear logical. Some designers such as Richard Dennis argue against simplicity (Collins, 2005), but they have enormous computer power and knowledge behind them. Hill and others argue that even with modern technology and mathematics, the success of systems now is no greater than the classic systems designed with a hand or crank calculator.

First, you must decide what kind of input and tested model is to be used to generate signals. Some investors depend on fundamental information; most traders depend on technical methods. Others use a combination. The important aspect is to have a clear understanding of the system's premises and to know that the rules will be easily quantifiable and precise. Specificity is much easier to use and to test than generality. You must also understand the logic of the system and be sure that it suits your style of trading or investing.

Second, you must decide on which markets to focus. Is the market suitable for the intended system? Are there opportunities for diversification between markets or instruments? How much volatility and liquidity is required, and what specific instruments will be traded?

Third, you must establish the time horizon for the system. For example, most trend-following systems work better over longer periods, but most pattern systems work in hours and days. Does the system intend to scalp trades, swing trade, or long-term invest? In addition, what is the psychologically best-suited time not only for system logic but also for ease of use? Do you have time to spend all day with the system, or can you monitor the system only daily, weekly, or monthly?

Fourth, you must have a risk control plan; otherwise, you will not know what to do when markets change. Understand that losses are inevitable, but be sure to keep them under control. Admitting losses separates the professional from the amateur. Rationalizing or excusing losses never helps. The market is never wrong—get out, the quicker the better. To do this, devise a stop-loss strategy— "no clinging to the mast of the sinking ship." This strategy should include protective and trailing stops, price targets, and adjustments for volatility, type of market, and any other state that the market might be in. Another option is to have a filter that shuts down the system when the market enters a trading range or has other characteristics that detract from the model's performance. Otherwise, the account may suffer a larger loss. Emotions and judgment become adversely affected, causing missed opportunities, selling profitable positions to get even, and other mistakes. Stop-losses free up nonproductive capital and cause less stress once accepted. In addition to risk control, you must decide whether you should use leverage or pyramiding.

Fifth, establish a time routine, which should include when to update the system and necessary charts, plan new trades, and update exit points for existing trades. As part of your system administration, maintain a trader's notebook, a trader's diary, and a daily equity chart. Maintain a daily trading sheet (similar to an accounting ledger) and a position sheet.

Types of Technical Systems

Technical analysts use a number of types of technical trading systems. Although there are numerous systems, they can be divided into four main categories: trend following, pattern recognition, range trading, and exogenous signals systems.

Trend Following From our knowledge of technical systems, we understand that markets trend at times and trade in a range at other times. The most profitable background is a trending background because the moves are larger and generate fewer transaction costs. While periodically trend trading becomes difficult and many traders begin to believe it is dead, it is not. As Bill Eckhardt, partner of Richard Dennis and originator of the Turtles, has been quoted, "I have lived through the death of trend-following a half dozen times, and, like Mark Twain's death, it was highly exaggerated." (Collins, 2005). Most large-scale mechanical system hedge funds and commodity trading advisors use trend-following systems. Rather than attempting to catch the peaks and valleys, the trend-following system acts in the direction of the trend as soon after it has begun as can be reliably detected. Contrary to the buy low and sell high philosophy, the trend-following system will buy high and sell higher. Schwager believes that slower, longer trend systems work better because the gains are larger, although less frequent, and the whipsaws are minimal. Most trend-following systems add a trend indicator such as the ADX to their set of rules to be sure that a trend is in existence. As we know from earlier studies on trends, the performance of a trend-following system can suffer during a trading range market.

Moving Average Systems The classic trend-following system is composed of two moving averages that generate signals when they cross over each other. In his book *The Definitive Guide to Futures Trading*, Larry Williams discusses how, as early as the 1940s, Donchian demonstrated the validity of this method and showed that it was more successful than the older system of using price versus a single moving average.

If two moving averages are better than one, would three be even better? No, studies have shown that adding more moving averages weakens performance because of the increased number of rules required. Although practitioners frequently report success using moving averages, we must mention that academic studies have shown that moving average crossover systems, even with simple filters, are generally unprofitable. However, academics have not used any kind of risk control in their experiments. Without the use of these important risk-control strategies, the academic studies are not a true measure of the profitability of using a moving average crossover system.

Breakout Systems A variation of the trend-following system is the breakout system. These systems generate buy and sell signals when price moves out of a channel or band. The most popular of these systems is based on a variation of the Donchian channel breakout system or some kind of volatility breakout system using Bollinger Bands or other measures of range volatility. The breakout system can be long term and use weekly figures, or short term, such as the open range breakout systems used intraday.

Problems with Trend-Following Systems Given their profitability, the moving average and breakout strategies are popular. Because many of these trend-following systems are being traded, many others will receive the same signal at roughly the same time and price you will. Liquidity can become strained, and slippage costs from wider spreads and incomplete fills will increase the transaction costs over what may have been anticipated. The solution to this problem is to devise an original system or to spread out or scale entry orders.

Another problem with trend-following systems is that whipsaws are common, especially during a trading range market, as the system attempts to identify the trend. In fact, trend-following systems often produce less than 50% wins because of the many whipsaws during ranging markets. This problem can be reduced with the use of confirmations, such as special price requirements (penetration requirement, time delay, and so on), once a signal has been given, or through filters and diversification into uncorrelated markets.

Inevitably, to avoid whipsaws, a trend-following system will be late in the trend and will thus miss profit potential at both ends of the trend. Unfortunately, this is the cost of a trend-following system. If an attempt is made to clip more profit at each end of the trend, the number of losses will increase from the ranging nature of the trend at its terminal points. On the exit side of a trend, specific trailing stops or such can be used to receive better prices, but again there is the risk of missing another leg in the trend by exiting prematurely.

Losses occur primarily in the trading range preceding the establishment of a trend, as the system tries to identify the next trend as closely as possible. One strategy to combat this is to use a countertrend system at the same time, even if it is not as profitable as the trend-following system. The gains from the countertrend system will offset some of the losses of the trend-following system, and the overall performance results will improve over the trend-following system alone.

Moving-average and breakout systems are usually limited to a one-directional signal only. Part of the advantage in following a trend is to pyramid in the direction of the trend as evidence of its viability becomes stronger. To accomplish this in a trend-following system, other indicators must be used, thus increasing the complexity and decreasing the adaptability of the system.

The greatest fault with trend-following systems is the large percentage of consecutive small losses that produce significant drawdowns. For example, let us say that the system suffers ten small losses in a row while in a trading range. The drawdown to the equity of the account accumulates during this period from the peak of the equity to the subsequent cumulative loss. A series of losses that cause a large drawdown affect not only the pocketbook but also the confidence in the system and often lead to further complications. One strategy to lessen a sequence of losses is the strategy mentioned previously of using a countertrend system. Another is to initiate only small positions on a signal until the trend is well established. Yet another is to run another trend-following system parallel that has a longer or shorter period.

Because a trend-following system often is characterized by clumps of large profits from the trend and many small losses from the trading range, extreme volatility occurs in equity. We will look at this later when we study equity curve smoothness, but the most-often-used countermeasure is to diversify into other markets or systems.

As with most mechanical systems, a trend-following system can work well during testing and then bomb in practice. In most cases, this is due to improper testing and adjusting. Some-times the improper testing is due to unrealistic assumption about transactions costs. Unrealistic assumptions including spreads during fast markets, limit days in the futures market, and other possible anomalies may have given false results during the testing stage of the system under consideration. Remember that the popularity of trend-following systems can affect slippage; this fact often is erroneously ignored in the testing phase.

Occasionally, substantial parameter shifts will occur that the adaptive system will not be able to recognize and accommodate. Again, by diversifying by using more than one system or using market character adjustments to volatility, such problems can be reduced.

Pattern Recognition Systems "Every ship at the bottom of the sea had plenty of charts" is attributed to noted systems trader Jon Najarian (Patel, 1997). Using patterns requires considerable testing and overcoming the problem of defining patterns. Larger patterns do not succumb to easy computer recognition because of their variable nature. System traders such as Larry Williams, Larry Connor, and Linda Raschke use short-term patterns, some of which we discussed in "Short-Term Patterns," and limit their exposure with specific position stops and price or time targets. Generally, such systems are partially discretionary because they require some interpretation during the trade entry.

Reversion to the Mean Reversion to the mean systems are based on the buy-low-sell-high philosophy within a trading range and are also called **trading range** systems. This type of system requires a certain amount of volatility between the peaks and valleys of ranges; otherwise, transaction costs, missing limits, and being stopped out on false moves chew up any potential profits. Generally, these systems are discretionary. They profit from **fading** small counter-trend moves or moves within a flat trend and using oscillators such as the stochastic, relative strength index (RSI), the Moving-Average Convergence/Divergence (MACD), or cycles. The largest potential problem in trading with one of these systems is the possibility of a trend developing that creates the risk of unlimited losses. Protective stops are a necessity.

Generally, this type of system does not perform well. A number of publicly available tests—for example, of buying and selling within Bollinger Bands—have been conducted, and invariably the best performance comes from buying and selling on breakouts from the bands rather than trading within them. The major use of countertrend systems is to run coincident with trend-following systems to dampen the series of losses in the trend-following system during a trading range.

Exogenous Signal Systems Some systems generate signals from outside the market being traded. Intermarket systems, such as gold prices for the bond market, would be an example of an exogenous signal system. Other examples are sentiment such as the VIX for S&P futures, volume, or open interest warnings of activity that trigger price systems or act as confirmation of price systems, or fundamental signals such as monetary policy or consumer prices.

Which System Is Best? Which type of system is the best? John R. Hill and George Pruitt, whose business is to test all manner of trading systems (www .futurestruth.com), maintain that the best and most reliable systems are trend-following systems. Within trend-following systems, the breakout systems have the best characteristics—specifically the Bollinger Band breakout systems, and the Donchian, or channel, breakout systems. Closely behind are the moving-average cross-over systems.

■ How Do I Test a System?

Testing a hypothetical system is absolutely necessary, and the testing process can be tedious because so many ideas of how to trade turn out to be unsuccessful. This is the most difficult aspect of designing a system, and unfortunately, because it is so time-consuming and discouraging, many analysts take short-cuts, such as not performing out-of-sample tests, and end up with a system that eventually blows up on them. The process begins with being sure the data being used in the testing is clean and the same as the data that will be used later when the system goes live. The next is to establish the rules for the model being chosen as the basis for the system and **optimize** the variables chosen. These rules include entry and exit signals atfirst and will have other filters added later depending on the results of the first series of tests. If a **walk-forward** program is not available, a large portion of the data, called **out-of-sample data**, must be kept aside to use later when testing the system for **robustness**. Once a viable system has been adequately optimized, the resulting parameters are then tested against the out-of-sample data to see if the system works with unknown data and was not the result of **curve-fitting** or **data mining**. This is the disheartening part of system design because invariably the out-of-sample test will fail, and the development must return to the beginning. It is at this point that most amateurs give up.

Clean Data

Not surprisingly, for an accurate evaluation of any system, the data must be impeccable. Without the correct data, the system tests are useless. Data should always be the same as what will be used when the system is running in real time. Not only the data but also the data vendor should be the same source as what will be used in practice. Different vendors receive different data feeds. This is especially a problem in short-term systems, where the sequence of trades is important for execution and for pattern analysis.

The amount of data required depends on the period of the system. A general rule of thumb is that the data must be sufficient to provide at least 30 to 50 trades (entry and exit) and cover periods where the market traveled up, down, and sideways. This will ensure that the test has enough history behind it and enough exposure to different market circumstances.

The real-time trader has enough difficulty with "dirty" data on a live feed, and this becomes just as crucial when testing back data. Cleanliness of data is a necessary requirement. Any anomalies or mispriced quotes will have an effect on the system test and will skew the results in an unrealistic manner. Cleaning of data is not an easy task and often must be relegated to the professional data providers.

Special Data Problems for Futures Systems

Although stock data has a few historical adjustments such as dividend payments, splits, offerings, and so on, the futures market has another more serious problem: which contract to test. Most futures contracts have a limited life span that is short enough not to be useful in testing most systems. The difficulty comes from the difference in price between the price at expiration and the price of the nearest contract on that date into which the position would be rolled. Those prices are rarely the same and are difficult to splice into something realistic that can be used for longer-term price analysis. To test a daily system, for example, two years or more of daily data is required at the very least, but no contract exists that runs back for two years. Of course, testing can be done on nearest contract series, but it is limited to the contract length. This is satisfactory if the system trades minute by minute but not for daily signals in a longer-term system.

To rectify this problem, two principal methods of splicing contract prices of different expirations together in a continuous stream have been used. These methods are known as perpetual contracts and continuous contracts. Neither is perfect, but these methods are the ones most commonly used in longer-term price studies.

Perpetual contracts, also called **constant forward contracts**, are interpolations of the prices of the nearest two contracts. Each is weighted based on the proximity to expiration of the nearest contract to the forward date—say, a constant 90 days. As an example, assume that today is early December, only a few days from expiration of the December contract of a commodity future and a little over three months from the expiration of the March contract, the next nearest. The 90-day perpetual would be calculated by proportioning each contract's current price by the distance each is in time from the date 90 days from now. This weighting in early December favors the March contract price, and each day as we approach the December expiration, the December contract receives less weight until expiration when the perpetual is just the March contract price. The following day, however, the March contract price begins to lose weighting as the June contract price begins to increase its weighting. This process gives a smooth but somewhat unrealistic contract price; it eliminates the problem of huge price gaps at rollover points, but you cannot literally trade a constant forward series. As Schwager points out, "the price pattern of a constant-forward series can easily deviate substantially from the pattern exhibited by the actual traded contracts—a highly undesirable feature" (1996, p. 664).

The continuous, or spread-adjusted, contract is more realistic, but it suffers from the fact that at no time is the price of the continuous contract identical to the actual price because it has been adjusted at each expiration or each rollover date. The continuous contract begins at some time in the past with prices of a nearby contract. A rollover date is determined based on the trader's usual rollover date—say, ten days before expiration. Finally, a cumulative adjustment factor is determined. As time goes on and different contracts roll over to the next contract, this spread between contracts is accumulated and the continuous contract price adjusted accordingly. With this method, the continuous prices are exactly what would have been the cost to the trader had the system signals been followed when they occurred. There is no distortion of prices. Price trends and formations occur just as they would have at the time. The only difference is that the actual prices are not those in the continuous contract. Percentage changes, for example, are not accurate. Nevertheless, the method demonstrates exactly what would have happened to a system during the period of the continuous contract, which is precisely what the systems designer wants to know.

As Schwager points out, "a linked futures price series can only accurately reflect either price *levels*, as does the nearest futures, or price *moves* as does continuous futures, but not both…" (1996, p. 669). Students interested in trading futures can refer to the book *Schwager on Futures: Technical Analysis*, to learn more about these techniques.

Testing Methods and Tools

Fortunately, the wheel need not be reinvented when it comes to testing software. Many trading software products include a testing section. Some are reliable; however, some are not. Before purchasing any such software, you should understand the testing methods and resulting reports of the software. Almost all such programs leave out crucial analysis data and may often define terms and formulas differently from others. For example, the term *drawdown* has different meanings, depending on intraday data, closing data, trade close data, and so forth. You must understand the meaning of all terms in any software program to correctly interpret tests performed by it. With this in mind, the systems analyst must establish exactly what information is desired, what evaluation criteria would be useful, and how the results should be presented.

Test Parameter Ranges

The initial test of a system is run to see if the system has any value and, if so, where the problem areas might lie. When the testing program is run, the parameters selected initially should be tested to see if they fall in a range or are independent spikes that might or might not occur in the future. A parameter range, called the **parameter set**, which gives roughly the same results, bolsters confidence in the appropriateness of the parameter value. If, when the parameter value is changed slightly, the performance results deteriorate rapidly, the parameter will not likely work in the future. It is just an aberration. When the results remain the same or similar, the parameter set is said to be stable—obviously a desirable characteristic.

BOX 32.1 DESIGNING A SYSTEM: "HAL" (NAME OF THE COMPUTER IN *2001: A SPACE ODYSSEY*)

Let us look at a simple case study of how to develop a trading system. Suppose we decide that we will trade International Business Machines (IBM), traditionally a less volatile blue chip. We also decide that we will start with an oscillator called the **Commodity Channel Index (CCI)**. The CCI is an oscillator similar to the Stochastic only it includes a volatility component and thus makes it a more realistic indicator of overbought or oversold. The signals will come from the CCI crossing levels determined by the optimization.

Looking at the monthly chart of IBM (see Figure 32.1) from 2005 through mid-2015, we see several periods of upward and downward trends and trading ranges. This is an ideal history to analyze and test because it includes the three possible trends in any market: up, down, and sideways. It also covers a period of more than nine years, roughly 2250 days, enough to give us plenty of signals.

Normally the CCI is contained with +300 and −300 but is not explicitly bounded. The only variables are the length of the moving averages used in its construction and the level of the two signal lines.

The account will assume a capitalization of $30,000, and commissions and slippage will be 10 cents per share for each entry and exit or 20 cents per share total. The entries will be limited to 100 shares per trade and only one 100-share position allowed. The reason for this model in our exercise is that we know it has worked well over the past two years, and we want to see if changing the parameters can improve its performance.

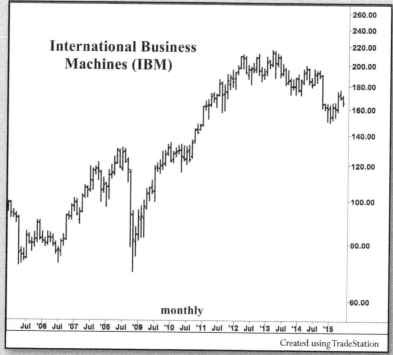

FIGURE 32.1 International Business Machines Corporation common stock price (monthly: January 2005–June 2015)

The equity curve for this system with the default length parameter of 14 and signal levels as +100 and –100 is shown in Figure 32.2. An equity curve is a chart of the equity in the account (vertical axis) versus time measured either by trade number or by time (horizontal axis). In Figure 32.2, time is along the horizontal axis. Looking at the chart, we can see that the system had a mixed performance and could easily be discarded as just another oscillator. However, if we change the parameters through optimization and walk-forward testing, perhaps we can find a more reliable formula that worked in the past for the entire period and will have a good chance of working in the future.

The tabulated data in Table 32.1 is from this one run using the standard Bollinger Band parameters.

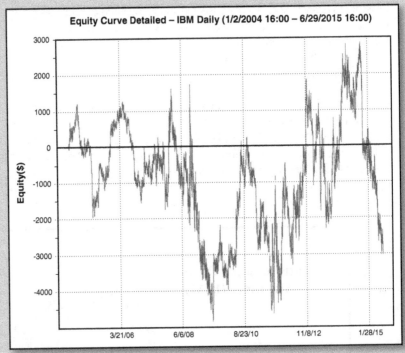

FIGURE 32.2 Equity curve for trading IBM using a Bollinger Band reversion to the mean model (IBM weekly: January 2, 2004–June 29, 2015)

TABLE 32.1 HAL Initial Test Statistics

Trades	All	Long	Short
Net profit	($2,153)	$2,991	$(5,144)
Gross profit	$32,773	$17,229	$15,544
Gross loss	($34,926)	($14,238)	($20,688)
Profit factor	0.94	1.21	0.75
Number of trades	139	69	70
Percent profitable	57.55	65.22	50.00
Average trade net profit	($15.49)	43.35	($73.49)
Largest winner as a % of gross profit	5.92%	6.32%	12.47%
Largest loser as a % of gross loss	7.76%	19.04%	9.60%

Trades	All	Long	Short
Maximum consecutive losing trades	4	3	5
Average days in winning position	14.41	15.2	13.5
Average days in losing position	29.51	26.13	31.83
Buy-and-hold return	80.7%		
Return on account	(40.41 %)		
Monthly average return	($31.63)		
Standard deviation of monthly return	$887.80		
Sharpe ratio	(0.01)		
System MAR (intraday)	(negative)	0.666	(negative)
Trade MAR	(negative)	0.883	(negative)

Source: TradeStation

Let's look at some of these statistics and learn what they tell us about the HAL system so far:

- **Net profit** is the difference between gross profit and gross loss. It is negative for this system as a whole but positive for long positions. This problem can be attacked in one of two ways: using different parameters for selling short or just using it for long signals. If we use long signals only, we already have a viable system that has worked in the past but not very well. We decide we will adjust both long and short signals with an optimization and walk-forward test.
- **Gross profit and gross loss** are the totals under each category for each trade. Gross profit is the total profit from profitable trades; gross loss is the total from all losing trades.
- The **profit factor** is the absolute value of the ratio of gross profit to gross loss. It shows the profitability of the system. In this case, for every dollar of loss, 0.94 dollars of profit are generated; in other words, it is a losing system. The long side only was favorable at 1.29. The better systems are above 2.00.
- Looking at the **number of trades,** this system generated 139 trades: 69 long trades and 70 short trades. This is a large enough number of trades for reliable statistics. Generally, at least 30–50 trades are required to test a system.
- **Percent profitable** is the percent of all trades that were profitable. In our example, 57.55% of the trades were profitable, yet the system lost money. This suggests that there is something wrong with the losing trades; although fewer in number, they are losing more than the winners.
- **Average trade net profit** is the average profit received per trade. This is negative and suggests that the system is vulnerable to transaction costs.
- The **largest winner or loser versus gross profit or gross loss** figure gives a hint as to whether the gain or loss was accounted for by only one trade. In this case, the largest winning trade accounted for 5.92% of the total gross profit. This is a reasonable size when considering that the total number of trades was greater than 139.

- The **maximum consecutive losing trades** is important because a long string of consecutive losses invariably causes a large drawdown and, thus, a high potential risk for the system. In this case, the number of successive losses is four trades in a row. It suggests that two whipsaws took place during the test period. Whipsaws can be controlled with stops.

- Considering the **average weeks in winning and losing positions,** there is not much question that the HAL has a problem with losing trades. There should be considerably less time in losing trades. The rule of thumb is that one-quarter of the time can be spent on losing trades versus winning trades, but with a long holding period, the system isn't kicking the losers out soon enough.

- **Buy-and-hold return (80.7%)** is the return gained if the investor bought the IBM on the first day and held it for the entire time period through all its gyrations. This is the number to beat.

- **Return on account (–40.41%)** is the total return on the minimum account size as determined by the maximum drawdown. It should be compared to the buy-and-hold return to see if the system outperforms a do-nothing approach. In this case, the system failed to exceed the do-nothing approach. Of course, such comparisons are not as easy as they look because the concept of risk has not been introduced to either method. The buy-and-hold method has infinite risk because the drawdown can be 100%. The risk of the system has been limited to a much smaller percentage, but we are still observing losses.

- **Average monthly return and standard deviation** of the monthly return are used to determine the volatility of returns. The average monthly return for this system is –$31.63, but it is highly volatile with a standard deviation of $887.80. Ideally, a system should have a standard deviation less than five times the monthly return. In this case, it is 31.5 times, far above the limit, and likely due to the large number of losses.

- The **Sharpe ratio** is a common measure of the return versus risk of a portfolio or system. As we saw in "Selection of Markets and Issues: Trading and Investing," it is a ratio of return—in this case, adjusted for the risk-free return of T-bills, to the standard deviation of return, a proxy for risk. As we stated earlier, however, risk is not just volatility, but is also the risk of capital loss. The Sharpe ratio fails to account for drawdown and fails to account for skewed deviations of return. An investment that deviates more to the upside, for example, will not be fairly represented by the Sharpe ratio, which assumes a normal distribution. These problems are why system designers shy away from the Sharpe ratio and have designed other ratios of return to risk that are more realistic. In this system, the Sharpe ratio is close to zero, suggesting that the return does not exceed the risk-free return of T-bills.

- **System MAR** is the ratio of annual percentage net gain for the system to the maximum percentage drawdown (MDD). The maximum percentage draw-down is the maximum percent that the equity curve corrected from a peak. The ratio measures the greatest decline that occurred during the system run and thus the potential loss in the future for the system. A ratio of greater than 1.0 is preferred.

Naturally, one wants a system that has no drawdown, but barring that, one wants a system that has profits considerably higher than any drawdown potential. A large drawdown lowers trust in the system and may cause a premature close of the system before it has a chance to perform. The HAL has a negative gain versus a maximum drawdown. The favored standard is anything above 1.00. The ratio is, thus, a gauge for comparing systems.

> ■ **Trade MAR** is the ratio of the net annual gain percentage to the largest trade drawdown in a trade, sometimes called the **Maximum Adverse Excursion.** Where maximum system drawdown may include many trades, the individual trade risk is also needed to gauge the systems performance and isolate where losses are occurring.

HAL may have promise if we can fix the problem with lengthy losing trades and the short selling losses. The long only section is satisfactory and will improve with improvement in the losses, but the entire system is bogged down by poor performance in the short side. This is not surprising in a market that has a generally upward trend, but it still is disappointing. We look next at ways to improve this system with optimized parameters and changes in the model logic.

■ Optimization

Once you determine that the parameters in your system are valid, you may optimize the system. **Optimizing** is simply changing the parameters of a system to achieve the best results. The most important benefit of optimization is that the designer may find parameters that do not work under any circumstances. If parameters do not work with the past data, it is highly likely they will not work in the future. Thus, optimizing can eliminate useless rules and parameters.

Optimizing is also useful in determining whether certain types of stops are useful. Often the designer finds that there is a limit—for example, to a protective stop—beyond which the stop does not add to the system performance. Often, the distance of trailing stops is too close to the last price, causing premature exits. These determinations can be analyzed more closely with optimization.

Although it can be beneficial, optimization does come with major hazards. With modern computers and sophisticated software, we can take any series of prices and find the best parameters for any predefined system. The problem is that by doing such an optimization, we are just fitting the data to a curve of results and have no idea whether the parameters we have derived will perform in the future. Because the future is what we are attempting to control, most optimization is useless and even dangerous because it gives us a false sense of confidence.

The principal concern with optimization is the tendency to **curve-fit**. Curve-fitting occurs when the optimization program finds the absolute best set of parameters. What the program is really doing is fitting the parameters to the data that is being tested. Thus, it is forming a mathematical model of that data and fitting parameters to that particular time in history. The only way that the parameters will work in the future is if the future exactly duplicates the history that was optimized. Of course, we know this will never happen and, thus, the parameters determined by optimization likely will be useless in the future. Any system could be made to look profitable if optimized; this is a problem that buyers of systems must face when considering purchasing an existing system for investing or trading. The trick is to optimize over a certain period and then test the parameters derived through optimization on a period in which no optimization has been conducted. This is called **out-of-sample (OOS) testing**. Invariably we will find that the results in the optimization will overstate the results in the out-of-sample period and, thus, the optimized parameters should never be used to evaluate the system's usefulness. Optimization should be kept simple. Fine-tuning the system just increases the level of false confidence that eventually will be dashed in real time when the system fails.

There is, thus, some controversy about the use of optimization in arriving at workable mechanical systems. The basic principles of realistic optimization are to keep it simple, test out-of-sample data against in-sample optimization results, preferably use baskets of securities, determine parameter sets instead of single parameters, understand that the best results are high profits with minimal risk, and avoid expecting to find the Holy Grail. Next, we discuss some optimization methods and some tests for statistical significance to perform after the most realistic parameter sets have been determined.

Before optimizing, the analyst must decide what the optimization is looking for in the data. Is it looking for net profit, maximum drawdown, Sharpe ratio, percentage of winning trades, or any other **objective function**? This objective function is an important aspect of the investigation for the best system. What is best? Many analysts use as their objective function a ratio of net profit to maximum drawdown, called the **MAR ratio**, to account not only for profits but also for risk of loss. Others use a **regression line** fit to the resulting profits. A tight fit suggests less volatility and thus less drawdown. A variation is called the **perfect profit correlation**. It assumes that the perfect system would buy every trough and sell every peak and thus generate a certain "perfect" profit. The tested system results are then compared to the perfect system to see how well it correlated.

Methods of Optimizing

As a general rule, an optimization should be done over a considerable period of price data and include those periods when the prices are in trends and in trading ranges. We do not know ahead of time whether the future will be similar, but we do know that there will be trends and trading ranges. Any system must be able to deal with both of these situations and have developed adjustable parameter sets or rules that will account for them. Parameters determined in this manner should be suitable for future conditions.

Whole Sample One method of optimizing is to take the entire price sample and run an optimization of the parameters. This is usually frowned upon because it is the closest to curve-fitting. To avoid curve-fitting, optimization should optimize only a portion of the data, called **in-sample (IS)** data, and test the resulting parameters on another portion of the data, called **out-of-sample (OOS)** data, to see if positive results continue in data not seen before by the optimization process. The selection of data can be a basket of stocks or futures rather than a single market average or issue and should have sufficient data to produce over 30 trades. The diversification of securities reduces the likelihood that any results are solely the result of peculiarities in a particular security, and the large number of signals increases the statistical significance of the results. After determining the optimal parameter sets—those that are consistent and give decent results (but not necessarily the best results)—the next step is to divide the optimization period into segments and run a test on each using the derived parameter sets. The results from these different periods then can be analyzed for consistency to see if the system generated similar results under all conditions. Things to look for are the amount of drawdowns, the number of signals, the number of consecutive losses, the net profit as a percentage of maximum drawdown, and so on. The actual amount of net profit is less important for each stage than are the determinants of risk and the consistency of results (Ruggiero, 2005). If the results are not consistent, the system has a major problem and should be optimized using other means or discarded.

Out-of-Sample Optimization (OOS) This is a method most often used in **neural network** and **regression** studies. We do not cover these particular methods because they are more useful with other data series. They can be used in market analysis, and some people, such as Lou Mendleson (www.profittaker.com), claim to have successfully been able to correlate different markets using neural network patterns. However, for purposes of this study of optimization, we ignore neural networks, multiple regressions, and others such as expert systems and artificial intelligence. Instead, we focus on the most common and productive methods—those used by the majority of systems designers.

One variation of OOS that is commonly used is to take the entire price data series to be optimized and divide it into sections, one of 70%–80% being the IS data and the remaining 20% to 30% being the OOS data. The out-of-sample data can include the first small portion of the total period and the last, or just the last, most recent data. As with all other test methods, the sample must include bull, bear, and consolidation periods. The total amount of data necessary is large in all optimization processes to account for periods of upward, downward, and sideways trends. All must be included so that the system can learn to adjust to any future change in direction or habit.

This method optimizes the in-sample data and then tests it on the out-of-sample data. The out-of-sample results are theoretically what the system should expect in real time. Invariably, the out-of-sample performance will be considerably less than the performance generated in the optimization. If the out-of-sample results are unsatisfactory, the method can be repeated with different parameters, but the more that the out-of-sample results are used as the determinant of parameter sets, the more that the objectivity of the optimization is compromised and the closer to curve-fitting the process becomes. Eventually, if continued in this manner, the out-of-sample data becomes the same as the sample data, and the optimization is just curve-fitting. One other method of reducing the effect of curve-fitting is to use more than one market as the out-of-sample test. It is difficult to have the same parameter set in different markets and at the same time curve-fit. This appears counterintuitive because most analysts would think that each market is different, has its own personality, and requires different parameters. Indeed, when looking at publicly available systems for sale, one method of eliminating a system from consideration is if it has different parameters for different markets. This usually indicates that the results are from curve-fitting, not real-time performance. A reliable system should work in most markets.

Walk Forward Optimization Walk forward optimization is also an OOS method that uses roughly the same price data series as the one described previously. Although there are many variations of this method, the most common procedure is to optimize a small portion of the data and then test it on a small period of subsequent data—for example, daily data over a year is optimized and then tested on the following six months' data. The resulting parameters of this test are recorded, and another year's data is optimized—this time, the in-sample data used includes the earlier OOS data plus six months of the earlier IS data. Again, the results are recorded, and the window is moved forward another six months until the test reaches the most recent data. Each optimization, thus, has an out-of-sample test. The results from all the recordings are then analyzed for consistency, profit, and risk. If some parameter set during the walk forward process suddenly changes, the system is unlikely to work in the future. The final decision about parameter sets is determined from the list of test results.

Optimization and Screening for Parameters We look next at all the different summaries and ratios that a system designer considers in measuring **robustness** (the ability of the system to adjust to changing circumstances), but first we must mention those that are used to screen out the better systems during optimization.

When optimization is conducted on a price series, the results will show a number of different parameter sets and a number of results from each parameter set. We can look at the net profit, the maximum drawdown, and any of the other statistics shown in Box 32.1. Many analysts screen for net profit, return on account, or profit factor as a beginning. They look at the average net profit per trade to see if the system generates trades that will not be adversely affected by transaction costs. Most important, they look at the net profit as a percentage of the maximum drawdown. The means of profiting from a system—any system of investing—are determined by the amount of risk involved. Remember the law of percentages. Risk of capital loss is the most important determinant in profiting. The net profit percentage of maximum drawdown describes quickly the bottom-line performance of the system. Unfortunately, the optimizing software of some commercial systems fails to include this factor, and it must be calculated from other reported statistics.

Measuring System Results for Robustness

When analyzing a system, we look at the system components, the profit, the risk, and the smoothness of the equity curve. We want to know how robust our results are. Robustness simply means how strong and healthy our results are; it refers to how well our results will hold up to changing market conditions. It is important that our system continues to perform well when the market changes because, although markets trend and patterns tend to repeat, the future market conditions will not exactly match the past market conditions that were the basis for our system design.

Components The most important aspect of the optimization and testing process is to be sure that all calculations are correct. This sounds simple, but it is surprising how often this is overlooked and computer program errors have led to improper calculations. The next aspect is to be sure that the number of trades is large enough to make the results significant. The rule of thumb is between 30 and 50 trades in the OOS data, with 50 or more being the ideal. We have mentioned previously that the comparisons between in-sample and out-of-sample results should differ in performance but should not materially differ in average duration of trades, maximum consecutive winners and losers, the worst losing trade, and the average losing trade. We should also be aware of the average trade result in dollars and the parameter stability. We could apply a student t test to the parameters and their results to see if their differences are statistically significant, and we should test for brittleness, the phenomenon when one or more of the rules are never triggered. Once we are satisfied that the preceding inspection shows no material problems, we can look at the performance statistics more closely.

Profit Measures Remember that the point of practicing technical analysis is to make money—or profit. On the surface, it seems as if this is a simple concept: if I end up with more money than I began with, then the system is profitable. Actually, measuring and comparing the profitability of various potential systems is not quite so straightforward. There are several ways in which analysts will measure the profitability of systems. The major ways are as follows:

- Total profit to total loss, called the **profit factor**, is the most commonly used statistic to initially screen for systems from optimization. It must be above 1.0, or the system is losing, and preferably above 2.0. Although a high number suggests greater profits, we must be wary of overly high numbers; generally, a profit factor greater than ten is a warning that the system has been curve-fitted. As a measure of general performance, the profit factor only includes profits and losses, not drawdowns. It, therefore, does not represent statistics on risk.

- **Outlier-adjusted profit** to loss is a profit factor that has been adjusted for the largest profit. Sometimes a system will generate a large profit or loss that is an anomaly. If the profit factor is reduced by this anomaly and ends up below 1.0, the system is a bust because it depended solely on the one large profit. The largest winning trade should not exceed 40% to 50% of total profit.

- **Percentage winning trades** is a number we use on the makeup of risk of ruin. Obviously, the more winning trades there are, the less chance of a run of losses against a position. In trend-following systems, this percentage is often only 30% to 50%. Most systems should look for a winning trade percentage greater than 60%. Any percentage greater than 70% is suspect.

- **Annualized rate of return** is used for relating the results of a system against a market benchmark.

- The **payoff ratio** is a calculation that is also used in the risk of ruin estimate. It is a ratio of the average winning trade to average losing trade. For trend-following systems, it should be greater than 2.0.

- The **length of the average winning trade** to average losing trade should be greater than 1. Otherwise, the system is holding losers too long and not maximizing the use of capital. Greater than 5 is preferable for trend-following systems.

- The **efficiency factor** is the net profit divided by the gross profit (Sepiashvili, 2005). It is a combination of win/loss ratio and wins probability. Successful systems usually are in the range of 38% to 69%—the higher the better. This factor is mostly influenced by the win percentage. It suggests that reducing the number of losing trades is more effective for overall performance than reducing the size of the losses, as through stop-loss orders.

For a system to be robust, we should not see a sudden dip in profit measures when parameters are changed slightly. Stability of results is more important than total profits.

Risk Measures   What happens if you find a system that has extraordinarily high profit measures? Chances are you have a system with a lot of risk. Remember, high profits are good, but we must balance them against any increased risk. Some of the major ways that analysts will measure the risk within their system are as follows:

- The **maximum cumulative drawdown** of losing trades can also be thought of as the largest single trade paper loss in a system. The maximum loss from an equity peak is the **maximum drawdown (MDD)**. The rule of thumb is that a maximum drawdown of two times that found in optimizing should be expected and used in anticipated risk calculations.

- The **MAR ratio** is the net profit percent as a ratio to maximum drawdown percent. It is also called the **Recovery Ratio**, and it is one of the best methods of initially screening results from optimization. In any system, the ratio should be above 1.0.

- **Maximum consecutive losses** often affect the maximum drawdown. When this number is large, it suggests multiple losses in the future. It is imperative to find out what occurred in the price history to produce this number if it is large.

- **Large losses** due to price shocks show how the system reacts to price shocks.

- The **longest flat time** demonstrates when money is not in use. It is favorable in that it frees capital for other purposes.

- The **time to recovery** from large drawdowns is a measure of how long it takes to recuperate losses. Ideally, this time should be short and losses recuperated quickly.

- **Maximum favorable and adverse excursions** from list of trades informs the system's designer of how much dispersion exists in trades. It can be used to measure the smoothness of the equity curve but also give hints as to where and how often losing trades occur. Its primary use is to give hints as to where trailing stops should be placed to take advantage of favorable excursions and reduce adverse excursions.

- The popular **Sharpe ratio,** the ratio of excess return (portfolio return minus the T-bill rate of return) divided by the standard deviation of the excess return. The excess rate of return has severe problems when applied to trading systems. First, it does not include the actual annual return but only the average monthly return. Thus, irregularities in the return are not recognized. Second, it does not distinguish between upside and downside fluctuations. As a result, it penalizes upside fluctuations as much as downside fluctuations. Finally, it does not distinguish between intermittent and consecutive losses. A system with a dangerous tendency toward high drawdowns from consecutive losses would not be awarded as high a risk profile as others with intermittent losses of little consequence.

Individual analysts will choose, and even create, the measure of risk that is most important to their trading objectives. Some of the other measures of risk mentioned in the literature are as follows:

- **Return Retracement ratio**—This is the average annualized compounded return divided by MR (maximum of either decline from prior equity peak [that is, worst loss from buying at peak] or worst loss at low point from any time prior).

- **Sterling ratio** (over three years)—This is the arithmetic average of annual net profit divided by average annual maximum drawdown; it is similar to the gain-to-pain ratio.

- **Maximum loss**—This is the worst possible loss from the highest point; using this measure by itself is not recommended because it represents a singular event.

- **Sortino ratio**—This is similar to the Sharpe ratio, but it considers only downside volatility. It is calculated as the ratio of the monthly expected return minus the risk-free rate to the standard deviation of negative returns. It is more realistic than the Sharpe ratio.

Smoothness and the Equity Curve Some analysts prefer to analyze risk in a graphic, visual manner. Two graphs commonly are used as a visual analysis of a system's performance: the **equity curve** and the **underwater curve**.

An equity curve chart is shown in Figure 32.2. It shows the level of equity profit in an account over time. Ideally, the line of the equity profits should be straight and run from a low level at the lower-left corner to a high level at the upper-right corner. Dips in the line are losses either taken or created by drawdowns.

The common measure of smoothness is the standard error of equity values about the linear regression trend drawn through those equity values. Smoothness of a system is affected by changes in the entry parameters or adjustments, such as filters. Because the majority of price action has occurred by the exit, the exit parameters and stops have little effect on smoothness.

The second type of graph used to look at system performance is the underwater curve chart. An example of this type of chart is shown in Figure 32.3. This displays the drawdown from each successively higher peak in equity. It is calculated in percentages and gives a representation not only of how much drawdown occurred, but also of how much time passed until equity recovered from that drawdown. As Figure 32.3 shows, the maximum percentage drawdown in the initial HAL system was a little over 90% of the original capital of $30,000. This chart helps us see that a major problem with the system is not only the size of the drawdowns but also the time it takes for the system to recover. In Box 32.2, we outline a method for improving the system.

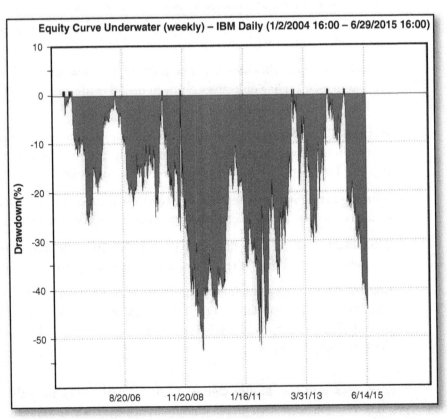

FIGURE 32.3   Weekly underwater curve for HAL in Box 32.1

BOX 32.2 UPGRADE IN THE HAL

Now it is time to upgrade our system based on the results of our initial testing. We first optimize the parameters of the given variables to see if there is a possibility of an improved system just by changing the parameters. This is the first step, and it showed that with curve-fitting, the net profit of over $35,000 was possible versus the loss incurred without adjustments. The second step is that we run a walk-forward test of the results and arrive at a system that we can expect to work in the near future. This is the one we report on here.

The changes made to HAL are threefold. First, we include a filter that will prevent the system from trading when the market is dull. We do this using a requirement that the ADX be higher than its predecessor some unknown number of days prior.

We use the ADX because it is a measure of trend and we don't want to play if there is no trend. There are other configurations of the ADX as a filter, but this is the one that worked best with HAL. Second, we add a percentage protective stop to lower the number of losses that accumulated time and loss while waiting for a buy signal. Third, we run optimizations on the parameters of ADX length, ADX lookback, CCI length, and upper and lower signal levels. The optimal results, using the perfect profit correlation as the objective function, were then run through a walk-forward optimizer to see which combination of parameters has the most likely chance of profiting in the next year.

TABLE 32.2	Tabulated Data for the Final Optimized System for HAL		
Trades	**All**	**Long**	**Short**
Net profit	$31,437	$20,294	$11,143
Gross profit	$40,879	$23,179	$17,700
Gross loss	($9,442)	($2,885)	($6,557)
Profit factor	4.33	8.03	2.70
Number of trades	68	32	36
Percent profitable	64.71%	78.13%	52.78
Average trade net profit	$462.31	$634.19	$609.53
Largest winner as a % of gross profit	8.03%	14.17%	16.77%
Largest loser as a % of gross loss	10.19%	31.85%	14.67%
Maximum consecutive losing trades	3	2	5
Average weeks in winning position	45.59	50.44	39.21
Average weeks in losing position	26.54	53.86	15.29
Buy-and-hold return	85.66%		
Return on account	1057.42%		
Monthly average return	$475.07		
Standard deviation of monthly return	$906.07		
Sharpe ratio	0.23		
System MAR (intraday)	5.09	3.68	2.75
Trade MAR (intraday)	10.57	22.08	2.94

Source: TradeStation

Look at how the system improves with the additions. Figure 32.4 shows the new equity curve for the system. Notice how smooth the curve is now. Net profit has increased from $2,000 to $31,000. The number of trades has decreased because of the ADX filter; the eliminated trades were obviously losers because the percentage of winners increased. The profit per trade is now high enough to withstand any extra trading costs, and the profit factor is now above the 2.00 standard threshold for a favorable system. The higher monthly return versus the standard deviation is well below the 5.00 normal ratio and explains why the equity curve is so smooth.

Do not use this system as it stands in any stock. It is presented only as an example of the process of looking for parameters, variables, and rules in a system development.

However, we hope that you can see the process of developing a reliable and profitable system and some of the types of adjustments that can be applied to systems— especially the use of stops—to improve performance and reduce risk. System development is a difficult and time-consuming task.

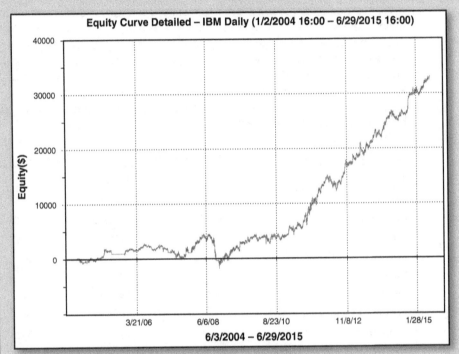

FIGURE 32.4   Equity curve of final optimized HAL

BOX 32.3   WHAT IS A GOOD TRADING SYSTEM?

In his book *Beyond Technical Analysis*, Tushar Chande discusses the characteristics of a good trading system. Chande's Cardinal Rules for a good trading system are the following:

- **Positive expectation**—Greater than 13% annually.
- **Small number of robust trading rules**—Less than ten each is best for entry and exit rules.
- **Able to trade multiple markets**—Can use baskets for determining parameters, but rules should work across similar markets, different stocks, different commodities futures, and so on.
- **Incorporates good risk control**—Minimum risk as defined by drawdown should not be more than 20% and should not last more than nine months.
- **Fully mechanical**—No second-guessing during operation of the system.

■ Conclusion

Throughout this book, we have looked at a number of technical indicators to guide our buying and selling of securities in reaction to particular market conditions. In this chapter, we turned our attention to mechanizing these reactions. A model is simply a plan or set of rules of when to buy and sell securities. A system uses the model as its base and lets us determine *a priori* how we will react to particular market situations. Having a system in place helps us follow a well-thought-out plan and prevents us from haphazardly trading based on emotion.

Of course, our basic objective in creating a system is to make a profit. Although this sounds like a straightforward goal, the goal of making a profit is not as simplistic as it sounds. Of course, we test our system to see how well it performs. But—and this is an important but—just because a system performs well using past, historical data in a trial situation does not guarantee that we will have the same stellar results in future, real-time trading. The most basic reason for this performance differential is that the market never repeats itself exactly; the system is operating in a different market environment than the one in which it was tested. There are also some system design and testing issues of concern. The system designer must be careful about data choice and not to overfit the data in the sample period. As we have seen in this chapter, even a system that has a high net profit in a test period is not necessarily a system that will perform well in the future. The system designer must consider a host of statistics about the system performance to determine whether the system is suitable for future trading. By following the guidelines laid out in this chapter, you should be ready to design systems and test them to determine their appropriateness for your trading situation.

■ References

Burnham, Terry. *Mean Markets and Lizard Brains*. New York, NY: John Wiley & Sons, Inc., 2005.

Chande, Tushar. *Beyond Technical Analysis*. New York, NY: John Wiley & Sons, Inc., 2001.

Collins, Art. "The Legend and the Lore of Richard Dennis." *Technical Analysis of Stocks & Commodities* 23, no. 4 (April 2005): 46-53.

Etzkorn, Mark. "Bruce Babcock: Market Realities." *Futures Magazine* (December 1996): 36–42.

Faith, Curtis. Way of the Turtle: The Secret Methods that Turned Ordinary People into Legendary Traders. New York, NY: McGraw-Hill, 2007.

Hill, John R., George Pruitt and Lundy Hill. *The Ultimate Trading Guide*. New York, NY: John Wiley & Sons, Inc., 2000.

Patel, Alpesh. *The Mind of the Trader*. London, UK: Financial Times/Pitman, 1997.

Ruggiero, Murray A., Jr. "Walking Before You Run with System Optimization." *Futures Magazine*. February 2005.

Ruggiero, Murray A., Jr. "Out of Sample, Out of Mind." *Futures Magazine*. April 2005.

Schwager, Jack D. *Schwager on Futures: Technical Analysis*. New York, NY: John Wiley & Sons, Inc., 1996.

Schwager, Jack D. *Technical Analysis*. New York, NY: John Wiley & Sons, Inc., 1996.

Sepiashvili, David, PhD. "How to Best Evaluate System Performance." *Futures Magazine*. March 2005.

Williams, Larry. *The Definitive Guide to Futures Trading*. Brightwaters, NY: Windsor Books, 1988.